SOCIETY, INSTITUTIONS, AND INDIVIDUALS

AN INTRODUCTION TO THE SOCIOLOGICAL IMAGINATION

SECOND EDITION

EDITED BY **DAVID G. EMBRICK** *University of Connecticut*

AND **BHOOMI K. THAKORE** *Elmhurst College*

Bassim Hamadeh, CEO and Publisher
Carrie Montoya, Manager, Author Care and Revisions
Kaela Martin, Project Editor
Alia Bales, Associate Production Editor
Jess Estrella, Senior Graphic Designer
Natalie Lakosil, Licensing Manager
Natalie Piccotti, Senior Marketing Manager
Kassie Graves, Director of Acquisitions and Sales
Jamie Giganti, Senior Managing Editor

Copyright © 2018 by Cognella, Inc. All rights reserved. No part of this publication may be reprinted, reproduced, transmitted, or utilized in any form or by any electronic, mechanical, or other means, now known or hereafter invented, including photocopying, microfilming, and recording, or in any information retrieval system without the written permission of Cognella, Inc. For inquiries regarding permissions, translations, foreign rights, audio rights, and any other forms of reproduction, please contact the Cognella Licensing Department at rights@cognella.com.

Trademark Notice: Product or corporate names may be trademarks or registered trademarks, and are used only for identification and explanation without intent to infringe.

Cover image copyright © Depositphotos/yienkeat.
Copyright © Depositphotos/Rawpixel.

Printed in the United States of America.

ISBN: 978-1-5165-2230-9 (pbk) / 978-1-5165-2231-6 (br)

DEDICATION

This book is dedicated to all the students who like to peek behind closed doors.

CONTENTS

DEDICATION III

ACKNOWLEDGMENTS IX

INTRODUCTION 1

Introduction to Societies, Insitutions, and Individuals 3
David G. Embrick

WHAT IS SOCIOLOGY? 9

Sociology as an Individual Pastime 11
Peter L. Berger

The Promise 19
C. Wright Mills

HOW DO SOCIOLOGISTS SEE THE WORLD? 31

Bourgeois and Proletarians 33
Karl Marx

The Protestant Ethic and the Spirit of Capitalism 41
Stephen Kalberg

The Social Construction of Race 47
Steven M. Buechler

HOW DO WE KNOW WHAT WE KNOW? 59

The Study of the Negro Problems 61
W.E.B. Du Bois

The Academy for Future Science Faculty 69
Bhoomi K. Thakore, Michelle E. Naffziger-Hirsch, Jennfer L. Richardson, Simon N. Williams, and Richard McGee, Jr.

IT'S A CULTURE THING ... YOU WOULDN'T UNDERSTAND! 85

From Culture to Hegemoy 87
Dick Hebdige

Subcultures, Cultures, and Class 95
John Clarke, Stuart Hall, Tony Jefferson, and Brian Roberts

The Knowing Consumer 105
Mark Patterson

PERSISTENT SOCIAL INEQUALITIES 117

CLASS 119

Class, Status, Party 121
Max Weber

Stupidity "Deconstructed" 131
Joanna Kadi

RACE 141

Racial Formation 143
Michael Omi and Howard Winant

Inequality Hidden in Plain View 159
Kasey Henricks

Whiteness as Contingent Hierarchies 171
Steve Garner

GENDER 185

Women's Perspective as a Radical Critique of Sociology 187
Dorothy E. Smith

Black Sexual Thought 197
Patricia Hill Collins

The Facebook Revolution 213
Margaret Cooper and Kristina Dzara

INTERSECTIONS OF CLASS, RACE, AND GENDER 223

When You Get Laid Off, It's Like You Lose a Part of Yourself 225
Lillian Rubin

Making Sense of Race, Class, and Gender 237
Celine-Marie Pascale

Moving Past Race and Gender 245
bell hooks

SOCIAL INEQUALITIES WITHIN INSTITUTIONS 249

POWER AND POLITICS 251

The Power Elite 253
C. Wright Mills

Political Power and Power Over the Media 263
Gadi Wolfsfeld

MEDIA 273

The Media and Class Warfare 275
Norman Solomon

South Asians in U.S. Television and Film 277
Bhoomi K. Thakore

EDUCATION 287

Schooling in Capitalist America 289
Samuel Bowles and Herbert Gintis

Education and Social Inequality 301
Judson G. Everitt

PRISON INDUSTRIAL COMPLEX 311

Disproportionate Minority Contact 313
Paul Ketchum, B. Mitchell Peck, and Patrick Polasek

Pathways to Downward Mobility 323
Rogelio Saenz, Karen M. Douglas, David G. Embrick, and Gideon Sjoberg

THE SOCIOLOGY OF DEVELOPMENT AND GLOBALIZATION 351

The Modern World-System 353
Immanuel Wallerstein

Slamming the Door on History 359
Naomi Klein

SO WHAT DO WE DO NOW? 373

Engaging Social Change by Embracing Diversity 375
Rashawn Ray

Resisting Homelessness 381
J. Talmadge Wright

Learning to Listen 399
Richard S. Orton

ACKNOWLEDGMENTS

In version 2.0, it remains the case that one has more projects and deadlines than time. This was certainly true in the case of the first editor and this project would have not seen the 2.0 light of day were it not for the generosity of the second editor who stepped in to lend a hand, or both hands as is the reality of the workload she put in to this project. We give thanks to the Cognella folks who were with the original edition of this book, and leave the comments below as such:

In fact, my plate was often overfilled and were it not for the kindness and often gentle nudging of the folks at Cognella, this project might have never gotten off of the ground. And so, I owe my biggest thanks to the Cognella editorial team for sticking with me to the bitter end. I give a very special thanks to Jamie Giganti for her steadfast loyalty, guidance, patience, and most importantly her professionalism throughout this long journey. Of all the editors I have had the pleasure of working with, Jamie is certainly one of the best.

That said, we need to give new thanks to the following Cognella folks for their part in the creation of this new edition—Carrie Montoya, Kaela Martin, Dani Skeen, and Alia Bales. Their assistance, patience, and constant reminders and "check-ins" made this current edition possible. We appreciate all that you do for us!

We created this text for several reasons. First, we wanted a reader that would allow us to teach the kind of course that we wanted to teach—one with a heavy emphasis on globalization and institutional inequalities. Second, we wanted a reader that included full-length research articles as opposed to snippets of articles that are typically found in many intro readers. Finally, we wanted students to be exposed to both classical sociological works as well as the freshest contemporary research on issues ranging from media to education to the prison industrial complex. In the latter, such a book would not be possible without the contributions of great colleagues and friends. And so we give great thanks to Judson Everitt, Kasey Henricks, Paul R. Ketchum, B. Mitch Peck, and Patrick Polasek for their chapters. Finally, we acknowledge the students of our introduction to sociology courses for the inspiration, laughter, and thoughts they bring us semester after semester. If we do our jobs right, we will have learned as much, if not more, than we hope our students learn from us.

INTRODUCTION

INTRODUCTION TO SOCIETIES, INSTITUTIONS, AND INDIVIDUALS

An Introduction to the Sociological Imagination

BY DAVID G. EMBRICK

Imagine yourself walking along a somewhat narrow downtown sidewalk late one afternoon. Shops line the main avenue on both sides and the road seems much smaller than it really is with all the cars parked along the sides. Mixed in with high-end boutiques are independent coffee shops and bookstores, several local cafés, and an independent pet supply store. You notice a few empty store-fronts. One has a bright white and black out-of-business sign posted on the door. Another is visibly empty. With the exception of a small flower shop at the end of your block, every corner seems to be occupied by a Starbucks or Panera Bread.

You decide to stop at one of the few benches along the path and as you survey the immediate area, you notice there are a lot of people on the street, more than you were aware of just a few minutes ago. They pass one another, barely acknowledging each other in their hurry to move along. Some folks move much quicker than others; they scurry along the path, perhaps late to wherever they feel they need to be. Other folks meander through the crowd effortlessly. They move in and out of the large swaths of people in front of them. Fewer individuals are less than quick in their pace. They take their time, traversing the path in front of them in a slow, yet steady pace. Their downward cast eyes speak volumes, yet seem lost in thought. Still others have expressions of confusion on their faces. They pause often and look around. Some people make frequent glances at their cellphones and other people make use of a map. You notice that a lot of people own cellphones.

As you peer ahead, you make a few more interesting observations. About a block ahead of you is a dark-skinned, somewhat rugged-looking man in his late fifties or maybe early sixties. He sits on the sidewalk with his back to one of the storefront walls, his legs crossed underneath him. His clothes are slightly worn and he looks slightly gaunt. He looks eagerly at the faces of all the people who pass him on the street. They do not look back. People pass the homeless man without the slightest gesture of acknowledgement that he is even there. As you approach this man you notice that he is holding a tattered Dixie cup from which he jingles its contents, presumably a few coins but you are unable to be sure. Around his immediate area are few possessions: an old rucksack, a few newspapers, and what appears to be a half-filled, rough-looking black trash bag. The newspapers vary in age and appearance but one is recent and you can just make out the headline on the front page, "'Pro-White Rally' Rally Ends with 3 Dead." You notice an empty beer container lying on its side against the wall a few feet from the man.

One block further ahead and across the street is an apartment complex for retired senior citizens. On previous visits to this location, the two brown wooden benches in front of the complex have been filled with residents of the building. They whittle away the day, often making friendly conversation with one another or with random folks who take the time to do more than make a friendly gesture of hello. They seem content for the most part people watching. Today, however, the benches are empty. Directly in front of the benches, parked on the street near the front entrance of the building is an ambulance. It stands silent on the side of the road, yet its lights flash loudly, a symbol of the grim realities of both life and death.

You move away from the bench and proceed along your journey. If you had time to think about the images you just witnessed, what do you think would have come to mind? Would you have asked yourself how we can live in a world so full of life and yet still be lonely? Would you have given a second thought about the homeless man on the block ahead of you? Do you wonder if you would also pass him by without so much as a glance, as countless people have done before you? Or would you give him a nod of acknowledgment, or even a friendly verbal hello? Would you spend more than a few seconds thinking about the downtown senior citizen complex, the folks who live there, or even the ambulance parked out front? Did you notice the overabundance of chain coffee shops? Do you wonder why some of the stores are closed down, or how they ended up that way?

It is often too easy to ignore what is going on around us or to be able to reduce certain situations to simple explanations of individual responsibility, natural inclinations, or just common sense. Yet, the way that people act, react, think, socialize, or behave is anything but simple. Often, humans are influenced or cause others to be influenced by social forces. It is these social forces that shape our lives.

What Is Sociology?

When you think about sociology, what comes to mind? Do you think about individuals? Or do you think about small groups of people, and large crowds? How about specific events or phenomena such as the recent fad of flash mobbing? Maybe you are slightly confused as to what exactly sociology is or what it is that sociologists do. If the latter is true, then you are not alone. Many folks have only a superficial understanding of what sociology is. The truth of the matter is that sociology is very important, important for allowing us to understand how the world works and important for helping us to understand everyday life. In general, sociology can be understood as the study of people in society. But within that larger umbrella, there is so much more to it. Sociology is about understanding why and how individuals interact and communicate within any given society. It is about examining the larger social structures that affect our lives and the lives of other people. It is also about understanding how societies are connected globally. More specifically, sociology can be defined as "the science of patterns of human social behavior." In order to understand how sociologists see the world, one must possess "the sociological imagination" and not be afraid to "peek behind closed doors."

How Do Sociologists See the World?

Making Use of the Sociological Imagination

According to American sociologist C. Wright Mills, it is the responsibility of sociologists to investigate and elaborate on the connections of the social environments of individuals and historical and social forces that shape their lives. In his groundbreaking 1959 book, *The Sociological Imagination*, Mills argued that in order to understand individuals in society, one must also understand the social context in which that individual is located. Thus, social outcomes are shaped by social context, social actions, and individuals. In order to understand the experience of a given person or group of people, one must know the social and historical context in which they lived. Sociological imagination then is a way "to describe the ability to see the link (relationship) between incidents in the lives of individuals and large social forces." It is the ability to get the "big picture." More aptly put, the sociological imagination enables us to grasp history and biography and the relations between the two in society.

Why is it important to develop a sociological imagination? Because without it, it is hard to pay attention to how larger social forces affect our lives and the lives of other people. Consider the homeless man mentioned previously. Other than the physical description of the man, what do you really know about him? What do you know about his life story? What do you think other people who pass by him daily know about him? One could imagine that at least some of the folks who pass this man on their way to destination A or B might feel like this man is a drain on society. They might wish that he would just "pull himself up by his bootstraps" and work hard instead of begging for a handout. Perhaps you also have had these thoughts. There is no shame in admitting that at some point in time, we have all taken an individual approach to understanding what we see in society. Yet, using our sociological imagination—and being able to identify larger social forces and connect them to our biographies or the biographies of others—allows us to ask questions that would help us to better understand the plight of this particular homeless man. How did he become homeless in the first place? What was his story before he became homeless? Did he get laid off because the company he was working for downsized? Did he have a family and, if so, where are they now? What are some of the constraints that make it hard for this person to resume his life such as it was before he became homeless? How does race (being dark-skinned) and gender (being a man) play into how other people see and treat this particular person? How might they see this person if he were a light-skinned woman? Would things be different and how so?

C. Wright Mills further elaborated on how we might better understand the sociological imagination through his distinction of personal troubles and public issues. For Mills, "troubles" have to do with personal character and is limited to an individual's area of social life in which s/he is directly and personally aware. In contrast, "issues" have to do with areas of life that transcend an individual's life. It concerns matters that are larger than an individual's area of social life. Thus, according to Mills, "troubles" is a private matter while "issues" is a public matter. Going back to the scenario of the homeless man, we can use our sociological imagination to ask different questions based on our understanding of issues and troubles. We might also propose different solutions based on our findings. If, for example, this man were the only homeless person in a city of 100,000, this would constitute a personal trouble. Such a trouble might be solved by looking at the character or skill sets of this person. However, if the homeless population is 10,000 in a city of 100,000, we would note that this is much beyond the range of an individual person and therefore, it would constitute an issue. The solutions for this issue would need to be larger in scope than that of an individual. Thus, we might want to know what is going on that we have so many homeless folks in a particular city.

Understanding the difference between troubles and issues is one of the best tools a sociologist possesses. It is all too easy to confuse the two and in many instances, the differences are intentionally presented in a way to be confusing. Mills noted that often governments will present public issues as personal troubles so as to obfuscate political realities. One example of how this might work is in politicians pushing for personal responsibility when it comes to unemployment or homelessness (e.g., individuals need to work harder) rather than discussing how high unemployment rates or homelessness could partially or fully be a result of structural or political arrangements.

"Peeking Behind Closed Doors": What Does It Mean to Be a Sociologist?

American sociologist Peter Ludwig Berger offers perhaps one of the best descriptions of what it means to be a sociologist. According to Berger, sociology is "devoted to discovering the general in the specific." Berger noted that sociologists are best equipped to expose truths and to learn the "bigger picture" about how the world works or about people who live in the world. Thus, sociology is about perspective—how we envision society, the world, or everyday occurrences in our lives. Unlike most folks who go through life with very limited ideas about how the world operates, the job of the sociologist is to not be content with common sense and simple explanations that are presented to us. Sociologists should never take the easy route to discover. Indeed, according to Berger:

- "People who like to avoid shocking discoveries, who prefer to believe that society is just what they were taught in Sunday school ... who feel no temptation before closed doors ... who are only interested in human beings if they can change or convert them... should stay away from sociology."

- "Sociology will be satisfying, in the long run, only to those who can think of nothing more entrancing than to watch men [sic] and to understand things human."

Sociology, in a sense, is about developing new perspectives about the world in which we live. It is about questioning and exposing social problems and concepts that have been pushed aside as supposedly "common sense" or "static" and examining them with a "deeper" lens.

Is Sociology a Science?

Contrary to popular opinion that sociology is either a pseudo-science or not a "real science," the truth of the matter is that sociology is very much a science. As previously mentioned, sociology can be defined as "the science of patterns of human social behavior." This definition can be broken down as follows:

- Science
- Behavior
- Social Behavior

Science

Science is "a way to explain **HOW** things work." Thus, sociology, by virtue of this definition, is a science; instead of looking at atoms, molecules, etc., sociologists look at individuals as the unit of analysis. Science is "a process of 5 sub-processes," otherwise known as the "scientific method." These 5 sub-processes include:

1. Collection of RELEVANT data, usually empirical (through the senses) in nature.
2. Develop a hypothesis consistent with observations.
3. Use the hypothesis to make predictions.
4. Test predictions using experiments or further observations; modify hypothesis if needed.
5. Repeat 3 & 4. Framework or theory (an abstract statement that explains why and how certain things happen or are as they are) is drawn.

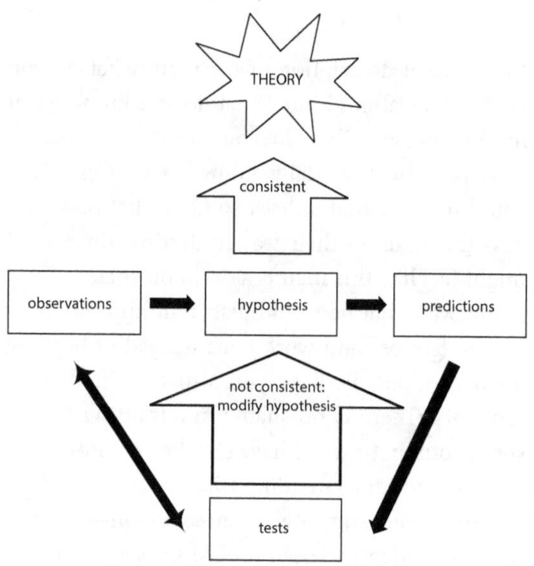

Behavior

Behavior can be defined as any change in the energy of a living organism (including feelings, cognition, perceptions and evaluations, or physiological responses such as blushing, etc.). Behavior is informed by the response of the system to these stimuli. In sociology, behavior can be considered to be the most basic human action. Individual behavior can also be differentiated from collective behavior and crowds. Collective behavior refers to social processes that emerge in "spontaneous" ways. Collective behavior involves short or limited social interactions, has no clear social boundaries, and generates weak or unconventional norms. Examples of collective behavior would include panics, riots, rumors, or even trends. Crowds are a gathering of people with an intent or purpose. Examples of crowds include gatherings at concerts, plays, sporting events, or other performances. All of these aspects inform sociological understanding.

Social Behavior

Social behavior is actions and responses that stimulate individuals from one to another. The question then would be: can one individual be "social?" The answer to that question is yes. Human beings are reflexive beings. That is, humans are able to respond to themselves. Hence, social behavior can be defined as any stimulus that responds to—past, present, or future; real or imagined—itself or any other organism.

Sociology then, is the science of patterns of human social behavior. More specifically, sociology is the use of the scientific method to understand and interpret repetitious commonality of human social behavior.

Getting the Most Out of This Book

This book was created with the intent of providing students an introduction to sociology, first and foremost. However, unlike most textbooks that read more like dictionaries or encyclopedias, or have become too commercialized and overrun with pictures, the intent with this anthology is to provide students with full and complete research articles of important sociological topics of the 21st century. For any sociology course, the content will vary depending on both the course and the expertise of the instructor who teaches it. While all sociology instructors will make sure to teach the basics in an introductory course in sociology, instructors may also choose to spend more time teaching specific subfields based on their interests or expertise in those subfields. And thus it is no different with this book. While the primary purpose of this book is to provide students with resources to help them explore the field of sociology, there is an emphasis in the areas of social inequalities and globalization. Students will be exposed to issues of race, class, gender, immigration, and other sociological examinations of power and privilege as it relates to education, the prison industrial complex, media, and other social institutions in society. It is the wish of the editor that after reading through this book, students will be able to make better sense of the world in which they live and be more open to peeking behind closed doors and seeing the big picture.

References

Berger, Peter L. 1963. *Invitation to Sociology: A Humanistic Perspective*. New York: Anchor.

Mills, C. Wright. 1959. *The Sociological Imagination*. London: Oxford University Press.

WHAT IS SOCIOLOGY?

Sociology as an Individual Pastime

The Promise

SOCIOLOGY AS AN INDIVIDUAL PASTIME

BY PETER L. BERGER

There are very few jokes about sociologists. This is frustrating for the sociologists, especially if they compare themselves with their more favoured second cousins, the psychologists, who have pretty much taken over that sector of American humour that used to be occupied by clergymen. A psychologist, introduced as such at a party, at once finds himself the object of considerable attention and uncomfortable mirth. A sociologist in the same circumstance is likely to meet with no more of a reaction than if he had been announced as an insurance salesman. He will have to win his attention the hard way, just like everyone else. This is annoying and unfair, but it may also be instructive. The dearth of jokes about sociologists indicates, of course, that they are not as much part of the popular imagination as psychologists have become. But it probably also indicates that there is a certain ambiguity in the images that people do have of them. It may thus be a good starting point for our considerations to take a closer look at some of these images.

If one asks undergraduates why they are taking sociology as a main subject, one often gets the reply, 'because I like to work with people'. If one then goes on to ask such students about their occupational future, as they envisage it, one often hears that they intend to go into social work. Of this more in a moment. Other answers are more vague and general, but all indicate that the student in question would rather deal with people than with things. Occupations mentioned in this connexion include personnel work, human relations in industry, public relations, advertising, community planning or religious work of the unordained variety. The common assumption is that in all these lines of endeavour one might 'do something for people', 'help people', 'do work that is useful for the community'. The image of the sociologist involved here could be described as a secularized version of the liberal Protestant ministry, with the YMCA secretary perhaps furnishing the connecting link between sacred and profane benevolence. Sociology is seen as an up-to-date variation on the classic American theme of 'uplift'. The sociologist is understood as one professionally concerned with edifying activities on behalf of individuals and of the community at large.

One of these days a great American novel will have to be written on the savage disappointment this sort of motivation is bound to suffer in most of the occupations just mentioned. There is moving pathos in the fate of these likers of people who go into personnel work and come up for the first time against the human realities of a strike that they must fight on one side of the savagely drawn battle lines, or who go into public relations and discover just what it is that they are expected to put over in what experts in the field have called 'the engineering of consent', or who go into community agencies to begin a brutal education in the politics of real estate speculation. But our concern here is not with the despoiling of innocence. It is rather with a particular image of the sociologist, an image that is inaccurate and misleading.

It is, of course, true that some Boy Scout types have become sociologists. It is also true that a benevolent

Peter L. Berger, "Selection from: Sociology as an Individual Pastime," *Invitation to Sociology: A Humanistic Perspective*, pp. 11-13, 15-19, 22, 27-36. Copyright © 1963 by Penguin Random House. Reprinted with permission.

interest in people could be the biographical starting point for sociological studies. But it is important to point out that a malevolent and misanthropic outlook could serve just as well. Sociological insights are valuable to anyone concerned with action in society. But this action need not be particularly humanitarian. Some American sociologists today are employed by governmental agencies seeking to plan more livable communities for the nation. Other American sociologists are employed by governmental agencies concerned with wiping communities of hostile nations off the map, if and when the necessity should arise. Whatever the moral implications of these respective activities may be, there is no reason why interesting sociological studies could not be carried on in both. Similarly, criminology, as a special field within sociology, has uncovered valuable information about processes of crime in modern society. This information is equally valuable for those seeking to fight crime as it would be for those interested in promoting it. The fact that more criminologists have been employed by the police than by gangsters can be ascribed to the ethical bias of the criminologists themselves, the public relations of the police and perhaps the lack of scientific sophistication of the gangsters. It has nothing to do with the character of the information itself. In sum, 'working with people' can mean getting them out of slums or getting them into jail, selling them propaganda or robbing them of their money (be it legally or illegally), making them produce better automobiles or making them better bomber pilots. As an image of the sociologist, then, the phrase leaves something to be desired, even though it may serve to describe at least the initial impulse as a result of which some people turn to the study of sociology.

Social work, whatever its theoretical rationalization, is a certain *practice* in society. Sociology is not a practice, but an *attempt to understand.* Certainly this understanding may have use for the practitioner. For that matter, we would contend that a more profound grasp of sociology would be of great use to the social worker and that such grasp would obviate the necessity of his descending into the mythological depths of the 'subconscious' to explain matters that are typically quite conscious, much more simple and, indeed, *social* in nature. But there is nothing inherent in the sociological enterprise of trying to understand society that necessarily leads to this practice, or to any other. Sociological understanding can be recommended to social workers, but also to salesmen, nurses, evangelists and politicians—in fact, to anyone whose goals involve the manipulation of men, for whatever purpose and with whatever moral justification.

This conception of the sociological enterprise is implied in the classic statement by Max Weber, one of the most important figures in the development of the field, to the effect that sociology is 'value-free'. Since it will be necessary to return to this a number of times later, it may be well to explicate it a little further at this point. Certainly the statement does *not* mean that the sociologist has or should have no values. In any case, it is just about impossible for a human being to exist without any values at all, though, of course, there can be tremendous variation in the values one may hold. The sociologist will normally have many values as a citizen, a private person, a member of a religious group or as an adherent of some other association of people. But within the limits of his activities as a sociologist there is one fundamental value only—that of scientific integrity. Even there, of course, the sociologist, being human, will have to reckon with his convictions, emotions and prejudices. But it is part of his intellectual training that he tries to understand and control these as *bias* that ought to be eliminated, as far as possible, from his work. It goes without saying that this is not always easy to do, but it is not impossible. The sociologist tries to see what is there. He may have hopes or fears concerning what he may find. But he will try to see regardless of his hopes or fears. It is thus an act of pure perception, as pure as humanly limited means allow, toward which sociology strives.

We would stress strongly that saying this does *not* imply that the sociologist has no responsibility to ask about the goals of his employers or the use to which they will put his work. But this asking is not sociological asking. It is asking the same questions that any man ought to ask himself about his actions in society. Again, in the same way, biological knowledge can be employed to heal or to kill. This does not mean that the biologist is free of responsibility as to which use he serves. But when he asks himself about this responsibility, he is not asking a biological question.

Another image of the sociologist, related to the two already discussed, is that of social reformer.

It is gratifying from certain value positions (including some of this writer's) that sociological insights have served in a number of instances to improve the lot of groups of human beings by uncovering morally shocking conditions or by clearing away collective illusions or by showing that socially desired results could be obtained in more humane fashion. One might point, for example, to some applications of sociological knowledge in the penological practice of Western countries. Or one might cite the use made of sociological studies in the Supreme Court decision of 1954 on racial segregation in the public schools. Or one could look at the applications of other sociological studies to the humane planning of urban redevelopment. Certainly the sociologist who is morally and politically sensitive will derive gratification from such instances. But, once more, it will be well to keep in mind that what is at issue here is not sociological understanding as such but certain applications of this understanding. It is not difficult to see how the same understanding could be applied with opposite intentions. Thus the sociological understanding of the dynamics of racial prejudice can be applied effectively by those promoting intragroup hatred as well as by those wanting to spread tolerance. And the sociological understanding of the nature of human solidarity can be employed in the service of both totalitarian and democratic régimes. It is sobering to realize that the same processes that generate consensus can be manipulated by a social group worker in a summer camp in the Adirondacks and by a Communist brainwasher in a prisoner camp in China. One may readily grant that the sociologist can sometimes be called upon to give advice when it comes to changing certain social conditions deemed undesirable. But the image of the sociologist as social reformer suffers from the same confusion as the image of him as social worker.

If these images of the sociologist all have an element of 'cultural lag' about them, we can now turn to some other images that are of more recent date and refer themselves to more recent developments in the discipline. One such image is that of the sociologist as a gatherer of statistics about human behaviour. The sociologist is here seen essentially as an aide-de-camp to an IBM machine. He goes out with a questionnaire, interviews people selected at random, then goes home, enters his tabulations on to innumerable punch cards, which are then fed into a machine. In all of this, of course, he is supported by a large staff and a very large budget. Included in this image is the implication that the results of all this effort are picayune, a pedantic restatement of what everybody knows anyway. As one observer remarked pithily, a sociologist is a fellow who spends $100,000 to find his way to a house of ill repute.

This image of the sociologist has been strengthened in the public mind by the activities of many agencies that might well be called para-sociological, mainly agencies concerned with public opinion and market trends. The pollster has become a well-known figure in American life, importuning people about their views from foreign policy to toilet paper. Since the methods used in the pollster business bear close resemblance to sociological research, the growth of this image of the sociologist is understandable. The Kinsey studies of American sexual behaviour have probably greatly augmented the impact of this image. The fundamental sociological question, whether concerned with premarital petting or with Republican votes or with the incidence of gang knifings, is always presumed to be 'how often?' or 'how many?' Incidentally the very few jokes current about sociologists usually relate to this statistical image (which jokes had better be left to the imagination of the reader).

Statistical data by themselves do not make sociology. They become sociology only when they are sociologically interpreted, put within a theoretical frame of reference that is sociological. Simple counting, or even correlating different items that one counts, is not sociology. There is almost no sociology in the Kinsey reports. This does not mean that the data in these studies are not true or that they cannot be relevant to sociological understanding. They are, taken by themselves, raw materials that can be used in sociological interpretation. The interpretation, however, must be broader than the data themselves. So the sociologist cannot arrest himself at the frequency tables of premarital petting or extramarital pederasty. These enumerations are meaningful to him only in terms of their much broader implications for an understanding of institutions and values in our society. To arrive at such understanding the sociologist will often have to apply statistical techniques, especially when he is dealing with the mass phenomena of modern social life. But sociology consists of statistics as little as philology consists of conjugating irregular verbs or chemistry of making nasty smells in test tubes.

How then are we to conceive of the sociologist? In discussing the various images of him that abound in the popular mind we have already brought out certain elements that would have to go into our conception. We can now put them together. In doing so, we shall construct what sociologists themselves call an 'ideal type'. This means that what we delineate will not be found in reality in its pure form. Instead, one will find approximations to it and deviations from it, in varying degrees. Nor is it to be understood as an empirical average. We would not even claim that all individuals who now call themselves sociologists will recognize themselves without reservations in our conception, nor would we dispute the right of those who do not so recognize themselves to use the appellation. Our business is not excommunication. We would, however, contend that our 'ideal type' corresponds to the self-conception of most sociologists in the mainstream of the discipline, both historically (at least in this century) and today.

The sociologist, then, is someone concerned with understanding society in a disciplined way. The nature of this discipline is scientific. This means that what the sociologist finds and says about the social phenomena he studies occurs within a certain rather strictly defined frame of reference. One of the main characteristics of this scientific frame of reference is that operations are bound by certain rules of evidence. As a scientist, the sociologist tries to be objective, to control his personal preferences and prejudices, to perceive clearly rather than to judge normatively. This restraint, of course, does not embrace the totality of the sociologist's existence as a human being, but is limited to his operations *qua* sociologist. Nor does the sociologist claim that his frame of reference is the only one within which society can be looked at. For that matter, very few scientists in any field would claim today that one should look at the world only scientifically. The botanist looking at a daffodil has no reason to dispute the right of the poet to look at the same object in a very different manner. There are many ways of playing. The point is not that one denies other people's games but that one is clear about the rules of one's own. The game of the sociologist, then, uses scientific rules. As a result, the sociologist must be clear in his own mind as to the meaning of these rules. That is, he must concern himself with methodological questions. Methodology does not constitute his goal. The latter, let us recall once more, is the attempt to understand society. Methodology helps in reaching this goal. In order to understand society, or that segment of it that he is studying at the moment, the sociologist will use a variety of means. Among these are statistical techniques. Statistics can be very useful in answering certain sociological questions. But statistics does not constitute sociology. As a scientist, the sociologist will have to be concerned with the exact significance of the terms he is using. That is, he will have to be careful about terminology. This does not have to mean that he must invent a new language of his own, but it does mean that he cannot naïvely use the language of everyday discourse. Finally, the interest of the sociologist is primarily theoretical. That is, he is interested in understanding for its own sake. He may be aware of or even concerned with the practical applicability and consequences of his findings, but at that point he leaves the sociological frame of reference as such and moves into realms of values, beliefs and ideas that he shares with other men who are not sociologists.

We daresay that this conception of the sociologist would meet with very wide consensus within the discipline today. But we would like to go a little bit farther here and ask a somewhat more personal (and therefore, no doubt, more controversial) question. We would like to ask not only what it is that the sociologist is doing but also what it is that drives him to it. Or, to use the phrase Max Weber used in a similar connexion, we want to inquire a little into the nature of the sociologist's demon. In doing so, we shall evoke an image that is not so much ideal-typical in the above sense but more confessional in the sense of personal commitment. Again, we are not interested in excommunicating anyone. The game of sociology goes on in a spacious playground. We are just describing a little more closely those we would like to tempt to join our game.

We would say then that the sociologist (that is, the one we would really like to invite to our game) is a person intensively, endlessly, shamelessly interested in the doings of men. His natural habitat is all the human gathering places of the world, wherever men come together. The sociologist may be interested in many other things. But his consuming interest remains in the world of men, their institutions, their history, their passions. And since he is interested in men, nothing that men do can be altogether tedious for him. He will naturally be interested in the events that engage men's ultimate beliefs, their moments of tragedy and grandeur and ecstasy. But he will also be fascinated by the commonplace, the everyday. He will know reverence, but this reverence will not prevent him from wanting to see and to understand. He may sometimes feel revulsion or contempt. But this also will not deter him from wanting to have his questions answered. The sociologist, in his quest for understanding, moves through the world of men without respect for the usual lines of demarcation. Nobility and degradation, power and obscurity, intelligence and folly—these are equally *interesting* to him, however unequal they may be in his personal values or tastes. Thus his questions may lead him to all possible levels of society, the best and the least known places, the most respected and the most despised. And, if he is a good sociologist, he will find himself in all these places because his own questions have so taken possession of him that he has little choice but to seek for answers.

It would be possible to say the same things in a lower key. We could say that the sociologist, but for the grace of his academic title, is the man who must listen to gossip despite himself, who is tempted to look through keyholes, to read other people's mail, to open closed cabinets. Before some otherwise unoccupied psychologist sets out now to construct an aptitude test for sociologists on the basis of sublimated voyeurism, let us quickly say that we are speaking merely by way of analogy. Perhaps some little boys consumed with curiosity to watch their maiden aunts in the bathroom later become inveterate sociologists. This is quite uninteresting. What interests us is the curiosity that grips any sociologist in front of a closed door behind which there are human voices. If he is a good sociologist, he will want to open that door, to understand these voices. Behind each closed door he will anticipate some new facet of human life not yet perceived and understood.

The sociologist will occupy himself with matters that others regard as too sacred or as too distasteful for dispassionate investigation. He will find rewarding the company of priests or of prostitutes, depending not on his personal preferences but on the questions he happens to be asking at the moment. He will also concern himself with matters that others may find much too boring. He will be interested in the human interaction that goes with warfare or with great intellectual discoveries, but also in the relations between people employed in a restaurant or between a group of little girls playing with their dolls. His main focus of attention is not the ultimate significance of what men do, but the action in itself, as another example of the infinite richness of human conduct. So much for the image of our playmate.

In these journeys through the world of men the sociologist will inevitably encounter other professional Peeping Toms. Sometimes these will resent his presence, feeling that he is poaching on their preserves. In some places the sociologist will meet up with the economist, in others with the political scientist, in yet others with the psychologist or the ethnologist. Yet chances are that the questions that have brought him to these same places are different from the ones that propelled his fellow-trespassers. The sociologist's questions always remain essentially the same: 'What are people doing with each other here?' 'What are their relationships to each other?' 'How are those relationships organized in institutions?' 'What are the collective ideas that move men and institutions?' In trying to answer these questions in specific instances, the sociologist will, of course, have to deal with economic or political matters, but he will do so in a way rather different from that of the economist or the political scientist. The scene that he contemplates is the same human scene that these other scientists concern themselves with. But the sociologist's angle of vision is different. When this is understood, it becomes clear that it makes little sense to try to stake out a special enclave within which the sociologist will carry on business in his own right. Like Wesley, the sociologist will have to confess that his parish is the world. But unlike some latter-day Wesleyans he will gladly share this parish with others. There is, however, one traveller whose path the sociologist will cross more often than anyone else's on his journeys. This is the historian. Indeed, as soon as the sociologist turns from the present to the past, his preoccupations are very hard indeed to distinguish from those of the historian. However, we shall leave this relationship to a later part of our considerations. Suffice it to say here that the sociological journey will be much impoverished unless it is punctuated frequently by conversation with that other particular traveller.

Any intellectual activity derives excitement from the moment it becomes a trail of discovery. In some fields of learning this is the discovery of worlds previously unthought and unthinkable. This is the excitement of the astronomer or of the nuclear physicist on the antipodal boundaries of the realities that man is capable of conceiving. But it can also be the excitement of bacteriology or geology. In a different way it can be the excitement of the linguist discovering new realms of human expression or of the anthropologist exploring human customs in faraway countries. In such discovery, when undertaken with passion, a widening of awareness, sometimes a veritable transformation of consciousness, occurs. The universe turns out to be much more wonder-full than one had ever dreamed. The excitement of sociology is usually of a different sort. Sometimes, it is true, the sociologist penetrates into worlds that had previously been quite unknown to him—for instance, the world of crime, or the world of some bizarre religious sect, or the world fashioned by the exclusive concerns of some group such as medical specialists or military leaders or advertising executives. However, much of the time the sociologist moves in sectors of experience that are familiar to him and to most people in his society. He investigates communities, institutions and activities that one can read about every day in the newspapers. Yet there is another excitement of discovery beckoning in his investigations. It is not the excitement or coming upon the totally unfamiliar, but rather the excitement of finding the familiar becoming transformed in its meaning. The fascination of sociology lies in the fact that its perspective makes us see in a new light the very world in which we have lived all our lives. This also constitutes a transformation of consciousness. Moreover, this transformation is more relevant existentially than that of many other intellectual disciplines, because it is more difficult to segregate in some special compartment of the mind. The astronomer does not live in the remote galaxies, and the nuclear physicist can, outside his laboratory, eat and laugh and marry and vote without thinking about the insides of the atom. The geologist looks at rocks only at appropriate times, and the linguist speaks English with his wife. The sociologist lives in society, on the job and off it. His own life, inevitably, is part of his subject matter. Men being what they are, sociologists too manage to segregate their professional insights from their everyday affairs. But it is a rather difficult feat to perform in good faith.

The sociologist moves in the common world of men, close to what most of them would call real. The categories he employs in his analyses are only refinements of the categories by which other men live—power, class, status, race, ethnicity. As a result, there is a deceptive simplicity and obviousness about some sociological investigations. One reads them, nods at the familiar scene, remarks that one has heard all this before and don't people have better things to do than to waste their time on truisms—until one is suddenly brought up against an insight that radically questions everything one had previously assumed about this familiar scene. This is the point at which one begins to sense the excitement of sociology.

Let us take a specific example. Imagine a sociology class in a Southern college where almost all the students are white Southerners. Imagine a lecture on the subject of the racial system of the South. The lecturer is talking here of matters that have been familiar to his students from the time of their infancy. Indeed, it may be that they are much more familiar with the minutiae of this system than he is. They are quite bored as a result. It seems to them that he is only using more pretentious words to describe what they already know. Thus he may use the term 'caste', one commonly used now by American sociologists to describe the Southern racial system. But in explaining the terra he shifts to traditional Hindu society, to make it clearer. He then goes on to analyse the magical beliefs inherent in caste taboos, the social dynamics of commensalism and connubium, the economic interests concealed within the system, the way in which religious beliefs relate to the taboos, the effects of the caste system upon the industrial development of the society and vice versa—all in India. But suddenly India is not very far away at all. The lecture then goes back to its Southern theme. The familiar now seems not quite so familiar any more. Questions are raised that are new, perhaps raised angrily, but raised all the same. And at least some of the students have begun to understand that there are functions involved in this business of race that they have not read about in the newspapers (at least not those in their hometowns) and that their parents have not told them—partly, at least, because neither the newspapers nor the parents knew about them.

It can be said that the first wisdom of sociology is this—things are not what they seem. This too is a deceptively simple statement. It ceases to be simple after a while. Social reality turns out to have many layers of meaning. The discovery of each new layer changes the perception of the whole.

Anthropologists use the term 'culture shock' to describe the impact of a totally new culture upon a newcomer. In an extreme instance such shock will be experienced by the Western explorer who is told, halfway through dinner, that he is eating the nice old lady he had been chatting with the previous day—a shock with predictable physiological if not moral consequences. Most explorers no longer encounter cannibalism in their travels today. However, the first encounters with polygamy or with puberty rites or even with the way some nations drive their automobiles can be quite a shock to an American visitor. With the shock may go not only disapproval or disgust but a sense of excitement that things can *really* be that different from what they are at home. To some extent, at least, this is the excitement of any first travel abroad. The experience of sociological discovery could be described as 'culture shock' minus geographical displacement. In other words, the sociologist travels at home—with shocking results. He is unlikely to find that he is eating a nice old lady for dinner. But the discovery, for instance, that his own church has considerable money invested in the missile industry or that a few blocks from his home there are people who engage in cultic orgies may not be drastically different in emotional impact. Yet we would not want to imply that sociological discoveries are always or even usually outrageous to moral sentiment. Not at all. What they have in common with exploration in distant lands, however, is the sudden illumination of new and unsuspected facets of human existence in society. This is the excitement and, as we shall try to show later, the humanistic justification of sociology.

People who like to avoid shocking discoveries, who prefer to believe that society is just what they were taught in Sunday School, who like the safety of the rules and the maxims of what Alfred Schuetz has called the 'world-taken-for-granted', should stay away from sociology. People who feel no temptation before closed doors, who have no curiosity about human beings, who are content to admire scenery without wondering about the people who live in those houses on the other side of that river, should probably also stay away from sociology. They will find it unpleasant or, at any rate, unrewarding. People who are interested in human beings only if they can change, convert or reform them should also be warned, for they will find sociology much less useful than they hoped. And people whose interest is mainly in their own conceptual constructions will do just as well to turn to the study of little white mice. Sociology will be satisfying, in the long run, only to those who can think of nothing more entrancing than to watch men and to understand things human.

It may now be clear that we have, albeit deliberately, understated the case in the title of this chapter. To be sure, sociology is an individual pastime in the sense that it interests some men and bores others. Some like to observe human beings, others to experiment with mice. The world is big enough to hold all kinds and there is no logical priority for one interest as against another. But the word 'pastime' is weak in describing what we mean. Sociology is more like a passion. The sociological perspective is more like a demon that possesses one, that drives one compellingly, again and again, to the questions that are its own. An introduction to sociology is, therefore, an invitation to a very special kind of passion. No passion is without its dangers. The sociologist who sells his wares should make sure that he clearly pronounces a *caveat emptor* quite early in the transaction.

THE PROMISE

BY C. WRIGHT MILLS

Nowadays men often feel that their private lives are a series of traps. They sense that within their everyday worlds, they cannot overcome their troubles, and in this feeling, they are often quite correct: What ordinary men are directly aware of and what they try to do are bounded by the private orbits in which they live; their visions and their powers are limited to the close-up scenes of job, family, neighborhood; in other milieux, they move vicariously and remain spectators. And the more aware they become, however vaguely, of ambitions and of threats which transcend their immediate locales, the more trapped they seem to feel.

Underlying this sense of being trapped are seemingly impersonal changes in the very structure of continent-wide societies. The facts of contemporary history are also facts about the success and the failure of individual men and women. When a society is industrialized, a peasant becomes a worker; a feudal lord is liquidated or becomes a businessman. When classes rise or fall, a man is employed or unemployed; when the rate of investment goes up or down, a man takes new heart or goes broke. When wars happen, an insurance salesman becomes a rocket launcher; a store clerk, a radar man; a wife lives alone; a child grows up without a father. Neither the life of an individual nor the history of a society can be understood without understanding both.

Yet men do not usually define the troubles they endure in terms of historical change and institutional contradiction. The well-being they enjoy, they do not usually impute to the big ups and downs of the societies in which they live. Seldom aware of the intricate connection between the patterns of their own lives and the course of world history, ordinary men do not usually know what this connection means for the kinds of men they are becoming and for the kinds of history-making in which they might take part. They do not possess the quality of mind essential to grasp the interplay of man and society, of biography and history, of self and world. They cannot cope with their personal troubles in such ways as to control the structural transformations that usually lie behind them.

Surely it is no wonder. In what period have so many men been so totally exposed at so fast a pace to such earthquakes of change? That Americans have not known such catastrophic changes as have the men and women of other societies is due to historical facts that are now quickly becoming 'merely history'. The history that now affects every man is world history. Within this scene and this period, in the course of a single generation, one sixth of mankind is transformed from all that is feudal and backward into all that is modern, advanced, and fearful. Political colonies are freed; new and less visible forms of imperialism installed. Revolutions occur; men feel the intimate grip of new kinds of authority. Totalitarian societies rise, and are smashed to bits—or succeed fabulously. After two centuries of ascendancy, capitalism is shown up as only one way to make society into an industrial apparatus. After two centuries of hope, even formal democracy is restricted to a quite small portion of mankind. Everywhere in the underdeveloped world, ancient

C. Wright Mills, "The Promise," *The Sociological Imagination*, pp. 3-24. Copyright © 1959, 2000 by Oxford University Press. Reprinted with permission.

ways of life are broken up and vague expectations become urgent demands. Everywhere in the overdeveloped world, the means of authority and of violence become total in scope and bureaucratic in form. Humanity itself now lies before us, the super-nation at either pole concentrating its most coordinated and massive efforts upon the preparation of World War Three.

The very shaping of history now outpaces the ability of men to orient themselves in accordance with cherished values. And which values? Even when they do not panic, men often sense that older ways of feeling and thinking have collapsed and that newer beginnings are ambiguous to the point of moral stasis. Is it any wonder that ordinary men feel they cannot cope with the larger worlds with which they are so suddenly confronted? That they cannot understand the meaning of their epoch for their own lives? That—in defense of selfhood—they become morally insensible, trying to remain altogether private men? Is it any wonder that they come to be possessed by a sense of the trap?

It is not only information that they need—in this Age of Fact, information often dominates their attention and overwhelms their capacities to assimilate it. It is not only the skills of reason that they need—although their struggles to acquire these often exhaust their limited moral energy.

What they need, and what they feel they need, is a quality of mind that will help them to use information and to develop reason in order to achieve lucid summations of what is going on in the world and of what may be happening within themselves. It is this quality, I am going to contend, that journalists and scholars, artists and publics, scientists and editors are coming to expect of what may be called the sociological imagination.

1

The sociological imagination enables its possessor to understand the larger historical scene in terms of its meaning for the inner life and the external career of a variety of a variety of individuals. It enables him to take into account how individuals, in the welter of their daily experience, often become falsely conscious of their social positions. Within that welter, the framework of modern society is sought, and within that framework the psychologies of a variety of men and women are formulated. By such means the personal uneasiness of individuals is focused upon explicit troubles and the indifference of publics is transformed into involvement with public issues.

The first fruit of this imagination—and the first lesson of the social science that embodies it—is the idea that the individual can understand his own experience and gauge his own fate only by locating himself within his period, that he can know his own chances in life only by becoming aware of those of all individuals in his circumstances. In many ways it is a terrible lesson; in many ways a magnificent one. We do not know the limits of man's capacities for supreme effort or willing degradation, for agony or glee, for pleasurable brutality or the sweetness of reason. But in our time we have come to know that the limits of 'human nature' are frighteningly broad. We have come to know that every individual lives, from one generation to the next, in some society; that he lives out a biography, and that he lives it out within some historical sequence. By the fact of his living he contributes, however minutely, to the shaping of this society and to the course of its history, even as he is made by society and by its historical push and shove.

The sociological imagination enables us to grasp history and biography and the relations between the two within society. That is its task and its promise. To recognize this task and this promise is the mark of the classic social analyst. It is characteristic of Herbert Spencer—turgid, polysyllabic, comprehensive; of E. A. Ross—graceful, muckraking, upright; of Auguste Comte and Emile Durkheim; of the intricate and subtle Karl Mannheim. It is the quality of all that is intellectually excellent in Karl Marx; it is the clue to Thorstein Veblen's brilliant and ironic insight, to Joseph Schumpeter's many-sided constructions of reality; it is the basis of the psychological sweep of W. E. H. Lecky no less than of the profundity and clarity of Max Weber. And it is the signal of what is best in contemporary studies of man and society.

No social study that does not come back to the problems of biography, of history and of their intersections within a society has completed its intellectual journey. Whatever the specific problems of the classic social analysts, however limited or however broad the features of social reality they have examined, those who have been imaginatively aware of the promise of their work have consistently asked three sorts of questions:

1. What is the structure of this particular society as a whole? What are its essential components, and how are they related to one another? How does it differ from other varieties of social order? Within it, what is the meaning of any particular feature for its continuance and for its change?
2. Where does this society stand in human history? What are the mechanics by which it is changing? What is its place within and its meaning for the development of humanity as a whole? How does any particular feature we are examining affect, and how is it affected by, the historical period in which it moves? And this period—what are its essential features? How does it differ from other periods? What are its characteristic ways of history-making?
3. What varieties of men and women now prevail in this society and in this period? And what varieties are coming to prevail? In what ways are they selected and formed, liberated and repressed, made sensitive and blunted? What kinds of 'human nature' are revealed in the conduct and character we observe in this society in this period? And what is the meaning for 'human nature' of each and every feature of the society we are examining?

Whether the point of interest is a great power state or a minor literary mood, a family, a prison, a creed—these are the kinds of questions the best social analysts have asked. They are the intellectual pivots of classic studies of man in society—and they are the questions inevitably raised by any mind possessing the sociological imagination. For that imagination is the capacity to shift from one perspective to another—from the political to the psychological; from examination of a single family to comparative assessment of the national budgets of the world; from the theological school to the military establishment; from considerations of an oil industry to studies of contemporary poetry. It is the capacity to range from the most impersonal and remote transformations to the most intimate features of the human self—and to see the relations between the two. Back of its use there is always the urge to know the social and historical meaning of the individual in the society and in the period in which he has his quality and his being.

That, in brief, is why it is by means of the sociological imagination that men now hope to grasp what is going on in the world, and to understand what is happening in themselves as minute points of the intersections of biography and history within society. In large part, contemporary man's self-conscious view of himself as at least an outsider, if not a permanent stranger, rests upon an absorbed realization of social relativity and of the transformative power of history. The sociological imagination is the most fruitful form of this self-consciousness. By its use men whose mentalities have swept only a series of limited orbits often come to feel as if suddenly awakened in a house with which they had only supposed themselves to be familiar. Correctly or incorrectly, they often come to feel that they can now provide themselves with adequate summations, cohesive assessments, comprehensive orientations. Older decisions that once appeared sound now seem to them products of a mind unaccountably dense. Their capacity for astonishment is made lively again. They acquire a new way of thinking, they experience a transvaluation of values: in a word, by their reflection and by their sensibility, they realize the cultural meaning of the social sciences.

2

Perhaps the most fruitful distinction with which the sociological imagination works is between 'the personal troubles of milieu' and 'the public issues of social structure'. This distinction is an essential tool of the sociological imagination and a feature of all classic work in social science.

Troubles occur within the character of the individual and within the range of his immediate relations with others; they have to do with his self and with those limited areas of social life of which he is directly and personally aware. Accordingly, the statement and the resolution of troubles properly lie within the individual as a biographical entity and within the scope of his immediate milieu—the social setting that is directly open to his personal experience and to some extent his willful activity. A trouble is a private matter: values cherished by an individual are felt by him to be threatened.

Issues have to do with matters that transcend these local environments of the individual and the range of his inner life. They have to do with the organization of many such milieux into the institutions of an historical society as a whole, with the ways in which various milieux overlap and interpenetrate to form the larger structure of social and historical life. An issue is a public matter: some value cherished by publics is felt to be threatened. Often there is a debate about what that value really is and about what it is that really threatens it. This debate is often without focus if only because it is the very nature of an issue, unlike even widespread trouble, that it cannot very well be defined in terms of the immediate and everyday environments of ordinary men. An issue, in fact, often involves a crisis in institutional arrangements, and often too it involves what Marxists call 'contradictions' or 'antagonisms.'

In these terms, consider unemployment. When, in a city of 100,000, only one man is unemployed, that is his personal trouble, and for its relief we properly look to the character of the man, his skills, and his immediate opportunities. But when in a nation of 50 million employees, 15 million men are unemployed, that is an issue, and we may not hope to find its solution within the range of opportunities open to any one individual. The very structure of opportunities has collapsed. Both the correct statement of the problem and the range of possible solutions require us to consider the economic and political institutions of the society, and not merely the personal situation and character of a scatter of individuals.

Consider war. The personal problem of war, when it occurs, may be how to survive it or how to die in it with honor; how to make money out of it; how to climb into the higher safety of the military apparatus; or how to contribute to the war's termination. In short, according to one's values, to find a set of milieux and within it to survive the war or make one's death in it meaningful. But the structural issues of war have to do with its causes; with what types of men it throws up into command; with its effects upon economic and political, family and religious institutions, with the unorganized irresponsibility of a world of nation-states.

Consider marriage. Inside a marriage a man and a woman may experience personal troubles, but when the divorce rate during the first four years of marriage is 250 out of every 1,000 attempts, this is an indication of a structural issue having to do with the institutions of marriage and the family and other institutions that bear upon them.

Or consider the metropolis—the horrible, beautiful, ugly, magnificent sprawl of the great city. For many upper-class people, the personal solution to 'the problem of the city' is to have an apartment with private garage under it in the heart of the city, and forty miles out, a house by Henry Hill, garden by Garrett Eckbo, on a hundred acres of private land. In these two controlled environments—with a small staff at each end and a private helicopter connection—most people could solve many of the problems of personal milieux caused by the facts of the city. But all this, however splendid, does not solve the public issues that the structural fact of the city poses. What should be done with this wonderful monstrosity? Break it all up into scattered units, combining residence and work? Refurbish it as it stands? Or, after evacuation, dynamite it and build new cities according to new plans in new places? What should those plans be? And who is to decide and to accomplish whatever choice is made? These are structural issues; to confront them and to solve them requires us to consider political and economic issues that affect innumerable milieux.

In so far as an economy is so arranged that slumps occur, the problem of unemployment becomes incapable of personal solution. In so far as war is inherent in the nation-state system and in the uneven industrialization of the world, the ordinary individual in his restricted milieu will be powerless—with or without psychiatric aid—to solve the troubles this system or lack of system imposes upon him. In so far as the family as an institution turns women into darling little slaves and men into their chief providers and unweaned dependents, the problem of a satisfactory marriage remains incapable of purely private solution. In so far as the overdeveloped megalopolis and the overdeveloped automobile are built-in features of the overdeveloped society, the issues of urban living will not be solved by personal ingenuity and private wealth.

What we experience in various and specific milieux, I have noted, is often caused by structural changes. Accordingly, to understand the changes of many personal milieux we are required to look beyond them. And the number and variety of such structural changes increase as the institutions within which we live become more embracing and more intricately connected with one another. To be aware of the idea of social structure and to use it with sensibility is to be capable of tracing such linkages among a great variety of milieux. To be able to do that is to possess the sociological imagination.

3

What are the major issues for publics and the key troubles of private individuals in our time? To formulate issues and troubles, we must ask what values are cherished yet threatened, and what values are cherished and supported, by the characterizing trends of our period. In the case both of threat and of support we must ask what salient contradictions of structure may be involved.

When people cherish some set of values and do not feel any threat to them, they experience *well-being*. When they cherish values but *do* feel them to be threatened, they experience a crisis—either as a personal trouble or as a public issue. And if all their values seem involved, they feel the total threat of panic.

But suppose people are neither aware of any cherished values nor experience any threat? That is the experience of *indifference*, which, if it seems to involve all their values, becomes apathy. Suppose, finally, they are unaware of any cherished values, but still are very much aware of a threat? That is the experience of *uneasiness*, of anxiety, which, if it is total enough, becomes a deadly unspecified malaise.

Ours is a time of uneasiness and indifference—not yet formulated in such ways as to permit the work of reason and the play of sensibility. Instead of troubles—defined in terms of values and threats—there is often the misery of vague uneasiness; instead of explicit issues there is often merely the beat feeling that all is somehow not right. Neither the values threatened nor whatever threatens them has been stated; in short, they have not been carried to the point of decision. Much less have they been formulated as problems of social science.

In the 'thirties there was little doubt—except among certain deluded business circles that there was an economic issue which was also a pack of personal troubles. In these arguments about 'the crisis of capitalism,' the formulations of Marx and the many unacknowledged re-formulations of his work probably set the leading terms of the issue, and some men came to understand their personal troubles in these terms. The values threatened were plain to see and cherished by all; the structural contradictions that threatened them also seemed plain. Both were widely and deeply experienced. It was a political age.

But the values threatened in the era after World War Two are often neither widely acknowledged as values nor widely felt to be threatened. Much private uneasiness goes unformulated; much public malaise and many decisions of enormous structural relevance never become public issues. For those who accept such inherited values as reason and freedom, it is the uneasiness itself that is the trouble; it is the indifference itself that is the issue. And it is this condition, of uneasiness and indifference, that is the signal feature of our period.

All this is so striking that it is often interpreted by observers as a shift in the very kinds of problems that need now to be formulated. We are frequently told that the problems of our decade, or even the crises of our period, have shifted from the external realm of economics and now have to do with the quality of individual life—in fact with the question of whether there is soon going to be anything that can properly be called individual life. Not child labor but comic books, not poverty but mass leisure, are at the center of concern. Many great public issues as well as many private troubles are described in terms of 'the psychiatric'—often, it seems, in a pathetic attempt to avoid the large issues and problems of modern society. Often this statement seems to rest upon a provincial narrowing of interest to the Western societies, or even to the United States—thus ignoring two-thirds of mankind; often, too, it arbitrarily divorces the individual life from the larger institutions within which that life is enacted, and which on occasion bear upon it more grievously than do the intimate environments of childhood.

Problems of leisure, for example, cannot even be stated without considering problems of work. Family troubles over comic books cannot be formulated as problems without considering the plight of the contemporary family in its new relations with the newer institutions of the social structure. Neither leisure nor its debilitating uses can be understood as problems without recognition of the extent to which malaise and indifference now form the social and personal climate of contemporary American society. In this climate, no problems of 'the private life' can be stated and solved without recognition of the crisis of ambition that is part of the very career of men at work in the incorporated economy.

It is true, as psychoanalysts continually point out, that people do often have 'the increasing sense of being moved by obscure forces within themselves which they are unable to define.' But it is not true, as Ernest Jones asserted, that 'man's chief enemy and danger is his own unruly nature and the dark forces pent up within him.' On the contrary: 'Man's chief danger' today lies in the unruly forces of contemporary society itself, with its alienating methods of production, its enveloping of political domination, its international anarchy—in a word, its pervasive transformations of the very 'nature' of man and the conditions and aims of his life.

It is now the social scientist's foremost political and intellectual task—for here the two coincide—to make clear the elements of contemporary uneasiness and indifference. It is the central demand made upon him by other cultural workmen—by physical scientists and artists, by the intellectual community in general. It is because of this task and these demands, I believe, that the social sciences are becoming the common denominator of our cultural period, and the sociological imagination our most needed quality of mind.

4

In every intellectual age some one style of reflection tends to become a common denominator of cultural life. Nowadays, it is true, many intellectual fads are widely taken up before they are dropped for new ones in the course of a year or two. Such enthusiasms may add spice to cultural play, but leave little or no intellectual trace. That is not true of such ways of thinking as 'Newtonian physics' or 'Darwinian biology.' Each of these intellectual universes became an influence that reached far beyond any special sphere of idea and imagery. In terms of them, or in terms derived from them, unknown scholars as well as fashionable commentators came to re-focus their observations and re-formulate their concerns.

During the modern era, physical and biological science has been the major common denominator of serious reflection and popular metaphysics in Western societies. 'The technique of the laboratory' has been the accepted mode of procedure and the source of intellectual security. That is one meaning of the idea of an intellectual common denominator: men can state their strongest convictions in its terms; other terms and other styles of reflection seem mere vehicles of escape and obscurity.

That a common denominator prevails does not of course mean that no other styles of thought or modes of sensibility exist. But it does mean that more general intellectual interests tend to slide into this area, to be formulated there most sharply, and when so formulated, to be thought somehow to have reached, if not a solution, at least a profitable way of being carried along.

The sociological imagination is becoming, I believe, the major common denominator of our cultural life and its signal feature. This quality of mind is found in the social and psychological sciences, but it goes far beyond these studies as we now know them. Its acquisition by individuals and by the cultural community at large is slow and often fumbling; many social scientists are themselves quite unaware of it. They do not seem to know that the use of this imagination is central to the best work that they might do, that by failing to develop and to use it they are failing to meet the cultural expectations that are coming to be demanded of them and that the classic traditions of their several disciplines make available to them.

Yet in factual and moral concerns, in literary work and in political analysis, the qualities of this imagination are regularly demanded. In a great variety of expressions, they have become central features of intellectual endeavor and cultural sensibility. Leading critics exemplify these qualities as do serious journalists—in fact the work of both is often judged in these terms. Popular categories of criticism—high, middle, and low-brow, for example—are now at least as much sociological as aesthetic. Novelists—whose serious work embodies the most widespread definitions of human reality—frequently possess this imagination, and do much to meet the demand for it. By means of it, orientation to the present as history is sought. As images of 'human nature' become more problematic, an increasing need is felt to pay closer yet more imaginative attention to the social routines and catastrophes which reveal (and which shape) man's nature in this time of civil unrest and ideological conflict. Although fashion is often revealed by attempts to use it, the sociological imagination is not merely a fashion. It is a quality of mind that seems most dramatically to promise an understanding of the intimate realities of ourselves in connection with larger social realities. It is not merely one quality of mind among the contemporary range of cultural sensibilities—it is *the* quality whose wider and more adroit use offers the promise that all such sensibilities—and in fact, human reason itself—will come to play a greater role in human affairs.

The cultural meaning of physical science—the major older common denominator—is becoming doubtful. As an intellectual style, physical science is coming to be thought by many as somehow inadequate. The adequacy of scientific styles of thought and feeling, imagination and sensibility, has of course from their beginnings been subject to religious doubt and theological controversy, but our scientific grandfathers and fathers beat down such religious doubts. The current doubts are secular, humanistic—and often quite confused. Recent developments in physical science—with its technological climax in the H-bomb and the means of carrying it about the earth—have not been experienced as a solution to any problems widely known and deeply pondered by larger intellectual communities and cultural publics. These developments have been correctly seen as a result of highly specialized inquiry, and improperly felt to be wonderfully mysterious. They have raised more problems—both intellectual and moral—than they have solved, and the problems they have raised lie almost entirely in the area of social not physical affairs. The obvious conquest of nature, the overcoming of scarcity, is felt by men of the overdeveloped societies to be virtually complete. And now in these societies, science—the chief instrument of this conquest—is felt to be footloose, aimless, and in need of re-appraisal.

The modern esteem for science has long been merely assumed, but now the technological ethos and the kind of engineering imagination associated with science are more likely to be frightening and ambiguous than hopeful and progressive. Of course this is not all there is to 'science,' but it is feared that this could become all that there is to it. The felt need to reappraise physical science reflects the need for a new common denominator. It is the human meaning and the social role of science, its military and commercial issue, its political significance that are undergoing confused re-appraisal. Scientific developments of weaponry may lead to the 'necessity' for world political rearrangements—but such 'necessity' is not felt to be solvable by physical science itself.

Much that has passed for 'science' is now felt to be dubious philosophy; much that is held to be 'real science' is often felt to provide only confused fragments of the realities among which men live. Men of science, it is widely felt, no longer try to picture reality as a whole or to present a true outline of human destiny. Moreover, 'science' seems to many less a creative ethos and a manner of orientation than a set of Science Machines, operated by technicians and controlled by economic and military men who neither embody nor understand science as ethos and orientation. In the meantime, philosophers who speak in the name of science often transform it into 'scientism,' making out its experience to be identical with human experience, and claiming that only by its method can the problems of life be solved. With all this, many cultural workmen have come to feel that 'science' is a false and pretentious Messiah, or at the very least a highly ambiguous element in modern civilization.

But there are, in C. P. Snow's phrase, 'two cultures': the scientific and the humanistic. Whether as history or drama, as biography, poetry or fiction, the essence of the humanistic culture has been literature. Yet it is now frequently suggested that serious literature has in many ways become a minor art. If this is so, it is not merely because of the development of mass publics and mass media of communication, and all that these mean for serious literary production. It is also owing to the very quality of the history of our times and the kinds of need men of sensibility feel to grasp that quality.

What fiction, what journalism, what artistic endeavor can compete with the historical reality and political facts of our time? What dramatic vision of hell can compete with the events of twentieth-century war? What moral denunciations can measure up to the moral insensibility of men in the agonies of primary accumulation? It is social and historical reality that men want to know, and often they do not find contemporary literature an adequate means for knowing it. They yearn for facts, they search for their meanings, they want 'a big picture' in which they can believe and within which they can come to understand themselves. They want orienting values too, and suitable ways of feeling and styles of emotion and vocabularies of motive. And they do not readily find these in the literature of today. It does not matter whether or not these qualities are to be found there; what matters is that men do not often find them there.

In the past, literary men as critics and historians made notes on England and on journeys to America. They tried to characterize societies as wholes, and to discern their moral meanings. Were Tocqueville or Taine alive today, would they not be sociologists? Asking this question about Taine, a reviewer in *The Times* (London) suggests:

> Taine always saw man primarily as a social animal and society as a collection of groups: he could observe minutely, was a tireless field worker and possessed a quality ... particularly valuable for perceiving relationships between social phenomena—the quality of springliness. He was too interested in the present to be a good historian, too much of a theorist to try his hand as a novelist, and he thought of literature too much as documents in the culture of an age or country to achieve first-class status as a critic ... His work on English literature is less about English literature than a commentary on the morality of English society and a vehicle for his positivism. He is a social theorist before all else.[1]

That he remained a 'literary man' rather than a 'social scientist' testifies perhaps to the domination of much nineteenth-century social science by the zealous search for 'laws' presumably comparable to those imagined to be found by natural scientists. In the absence of an adequate social science, critics and novelists, dramatists and poets have been the major, and often the only, formulators of private troubles and even of public issues. Art does express such feelings and often focuses them—at its best with dramatic sharpness—but still not with the intellectual clarity required for their understanding or relief today. Art does not and cannot formulate these feelings as problems containing the troubles and issues men must now confront if they are to overcome their uneasiness and indifference and the intractable miseries to which these lead. The artist, indeed, does not often try to do this. Moreover, the serious artist is himself in much trouble, and could well do with some intellectual and cultural aid from a social science made sprightly by the sociological imagination.

5

It is my aim in this book to define the meaning of the social sciences for the cultural tasks of our time. I want to specify the kinds of effort that lie behind the development of the sociological imagination; to indicate its implications for political as well as for cultural life; and perhaps to suggest something of what is required to possess it. In these ways, I want to make clear the nature and the uses of the social sciences today, and to give a limited account of their contemporary condition in the United States.[2]

---

1 Times Literary Supplement, 15 November 1957.

2 I feel the need to say that I much prefer the phrase, 'the social studies' to 'the social sciences'—not because I do not like physical scientists (on the contrary, I do, very much), but because the word 'science' has acquired great prestige and rather imprecise meaning. I do not feel any need to kidnap the prestige or to make the meaning even less precise by using it as a philosophical metaphor. Yet I suspect that if I wrote about 'the social studies,' readers would think only of high school civics, which of all fields of human learning is the one with which I most wish to avoid association. 'The Behavioral Sciences' is simply impossible; it was thought up, I suppose, as a propaganda device to get money for social research from Foundations and Congressmen who confuse 'social science' with 'socialism.' The best term would include history (and psychology, do far as it is concerned with human beings and should be as non-controversial as possible, for we should argue *with* terms, not

At any given moment, of course, 'social science' consists of what duly recognized social scientists are doing—but all of them are by no means doing the same thing, in fact not even the same sort of thing. Social science is also what social scientists of the past have done—but different students choose to construct and to recall different traditions in their discipline. When I speak of 'the promise of social science,' I hope it is clear that I mean the promise as I see it.

Just now, among social scientists, there is widespread uneasiness, both intellectual and moral, about the direction their chosen studies seem to be taking. This uneasiness, as well as the unfortunate tendencies that contribute to it, are, I suppose, part of a general malaise of contemporary intellectual life. Yet perhaps the uneasiness is more acute among social scientists, if only because of the larger promise that has guided much earlier work in their fields, the nature of the subjects with which they deal, and the urgent need for significant work today.

Not everyone shares this uneasiness, but the fact that many do not is itself a cause for further uneasiness among those who are alert to the promise and honest enough to admit the pretentious mediocrity of much current effort. It is, quite frankly, my hope to increase this uneasiness, to define some of its sources, to help transform it into a specific urge to realize the promise of social science, to clear the ground for new beginnings: in short, to indicate some of the tasks at hand and the means available for doing the work that must now be done.

Of late the conception of social science I hold has not been ascendant. My conception stands opposed to social science as a set of bureaucratic techniques which inhibit social inquiry by 'methodological' pretensions, which congest such work by obscurantist conceptions, or which trivialize it by concern with minor problems unconnected with publicly relevant issues. These inhibitions, obscurities, and trivialities have created a crisis in the social studies today without suggesting, in the least, a way out of that crisis.

Some social scientists stress the need for 'research teams of technicians,' others for the primacy of the individual scholar. Some expend great energy upon refinements of methods and techniques of investigation; others think the scholarly ways of the intellectual craftsmen are being abandoned and ought now to be rehabilitated. Some go about their work in accordance with a rigid set of mechanical procedures; others seek to develop, to invite, and to use the sociological imagination. Some—being addicts of the high formalism of 'theory'—associate and disassociate concepts in what seems to others a curious manner; these others urge the elaboration of terms only when it is clear that it enlarges the scope of sensibility and furthers the reach of reasoning. Some narrowly study only small-scale milieux, in the hope of 'building up' to conceptions of larger structures; others examine social structures in which they try 'to locate' many smaller milieux. Some, neglecting comparative studies altogether, study only one small community in one society at a time; others in a fully comparative way work directly on the national social structures of the world. Some confine their exact research to very short-run sequences of human affairs; others are concerned with issues which are only apparent in long historical perspective. Some specialize their work according to academic departments;

---

fight *over* them. Perhaps 'the human discipline' would do. But never mind. With the hope of not being too widely misunderstood, I bow to convention and use the more standard 'social sciences.'

One other point: I hope my colleagues will accept the term 'sociological imagination.' Political scientists who have read my manuscript suggest 'the political imagination'; anthropologists, 'the anthropological imagination'—and so on. The term matters less than the idea, which I hope will become clear in the course of this book. By use of it, I do not of course want to suggest merely the academic discipline of 'sociology.' Much of what the phrase means to me is not at all expressed by sociologists. In England, for example, sociology as an academic discipline is somewhat marginal, yet in much English journalism, fiction, and above all history, the sociological imagination is very well developed indeed. The case is similar for France: both the confusion and the audacity of French reflection since World War Two rest upon its feeling for the sociological features of man's fate in our time, yet these trends are carried by men of letters rather than by professional sociologists. Nevertheless, I use 'sociological imagination' because: (1) every cobbler thinks leather is the only thing, for better and for worse, I am a sociologist; (2) I do believe that historically the quality of mind has been more frequently and more vividly displayed by classic sociologists than by other social scientists; (3) since I am going to examine critically a number of curious sociological schools, I need a counter term on which to stand.

others, drawing upon all departments, specialize according to topic or problem, regardless of where these lie academically. Some confront the variety of history, biography, society; others do not.

Such contrasts, and many others of similar kind, are not necessarily true alternatives, although in the heat of statesman-like controversy or the lazy safety of specialization they are often taken to be. At this point I merely state them in inchoate form; I shall return to them toward the end of this book. I am hopeful of course that all my own biases will show, for I think judgments should be explicit. But I am also trying, regardless of my own judgments, to state the cultural and political meanings of social science. My biases are of course no more or no less biases than those I am going to examine. Let those who do not care for mine use their rejections of them to make their own as explicit and as acknowledged as I am going to try to make mine! Then the moral problems of social study—the problem of social science as a public issue—will be recognized, and discussion will become possible. Then there will be greater self-awareness all around—which is of course a pre-condition for objectivity in the enterprise of social science as a whole.

In brief, I believe that what may be called classic social analysis is a definable and usable set of traditions; that its essential feature is the concern with historical social structures; and that its problems are of direct relevance to urgent public issues and insistent human troubles. I also believe that there are now great obstacles in the way of this tradition's continuing—both within the social sciences and in their academic and political settings—but that nevertheless the qualities of mind that constitute it are becoming a common denominator of our general cultural life and that, however vaguely and in however a confusing variety of disguises, they are coming to be felt as a need.

Many practitioners of social science, especially in America, seem to me curiously reluctant to take up the challenge that now confronts them. Many in fact abdicate the intellectual and the political tasks of social analysis; others no doubt are simply not up to the role for which they are nevertheless being cast. At times they seem almost deliberately to have brought forth old ruses and developed new timidities. Yet despite this reluctance, intellectual as well as public attention is now so obviously upon the social worlds which they presumably study that it must be agreed that they are uniquely confronted with an opportunity. In this opportunity there is revealed the intellectual promise of the social sciences, the cultural uses of the sociological imagination, and the political meaning of studies of man and society.

6

Embarrassingly enough for an avowed sociologist, all the unfortunate tendencies (except possibly one) that I shall consider in the following chapters fall into what is generally thought to be 'the field of sociology,' although the cultural and political abdication implicit in them no doubt characterize much of the daily work in other social sciences. Whatever may be true in such disciplines as political science and economics, history and anthropology, it is evident that in the United States today what is known as sociology has become the center of reflection about social science. It has become the center for interest in methods; and in it one also finds the most extreme interest in 'general theory.' A truly remarkable variety of intellectual work has entered into the development of the sociological tradition. To interpret this variety as A Tradition is in itself audacious. Yet perhaps it will be generally agreed that what is now recognized as sociological work has tended to move in one or more of three general directions, each of which is subject to distortion, to being run into the ground.

Tendency I: Toward a theory of history. For example, in the hands of Comte, as in those of Marx, Spencer, and Weber, sociology is an encyclopedic endeavor, concerned with the whole of man's social life. It is at once historical and systematic—historical, because it deals with and uses the materials of the past; systematic, because it does so in order to discern 'the stages' of the course of history and the regularities of social life.

The theory of man's history can all too readily become distorted into a trans-historical strait-jacket into which the materials of human history are forced and out of which issue prophetic views (usually gloomy ones) of the future. The works of Arnold Toynbee and of Oswald Spengler are well-known examples.

Tendency II: Toward a systematic theory of 'the nature of man and society.' For example, in the works of the formalists, notably Simmel and Von Wiese, sociology comes to deal in conceptions intended to be of use in classifying all social relations and providing insight into their supposedly invariant features. It is, in short, concerned with a rather static and abstract view of the components of social structure on a quite high level of generality.

Perhaps in reaction to the distortion of Tendency I, history can be altogether abandoned: the systematic theory of the nature of man and of society all too readily becomes an elaborate and arid formalism in which the splitting of Concepts and their endless rearrangement becomes the central endeavor. Among what I shall call Grand Theorists, conceptions have indeed become Concepts. The work of Talcott Parsons is the leading contemporary example in American sociology.

Tendency III: Toward empirical studies of contemporary social facts and problems. Although Comte and Spencer were mainstays of American social science until 1914 or thereabout, and German theoretical influence was heavy, the empirical survey became central in the United States at an early time. In part this resulted from the prior academic establishment of economics and political science. Given this, in so far as sociology is defined as a study of some special area of society, it readily becomes a sort of odd job man among the social sciences, consisting of miscellaneous studies of academic leftovers. There are studies of cities and families, racial and ethnic relations, and of course 'small groups.' As we shall see, the resulting miscellany was transformed into a style of thought, which I shall examine under the term 'liberal practicality.'

Studies of contemporary fact can easily become a series of rather unrelated and often insignificant facts of milieu. Many course offerings in American sociology illustrate this; perhaps textbooks in the field of social disorganization reveal it best. On the other hand, sociologists have tended to become specialists in the technique of research into almost anything; among them methods have become Methodology. Much of the work—and more of the ethos—of George Lundberg, Samuel Stouffer, Stuart Dodd, Paul F. Lazarsfeld are present-day examples. These tendencies—to scatter one's attention and to cultivate method for its own sake—are fit companions, although they do not necessarily occur together.

The peculiarities of sociology may be understood as distortions of one or more of its traditional tendencies. But its promises may also be understood in terms of these tendencies. In the United States today there has come about a sort of Hellenistic amalgamation, embodying various elements and aims from the sociologies of the several Western societies. The danger is that amidst such sociological abundance, other social scientists will become so impatient, and sociologists be in such a hurry for 'research,' that they will lose hold of a truly valuable legacy. But there is also an opportunity in our condition: the sociological tradition contains the best statements of the full promise of the social sciences as a whole, as well as some partial fulfillments of it. The nuance and suggestion that students of sociology can find in their traditions are not to be briefly summarized, but any social scientist who takes them in hand will be richly rewarded. His mastery of them may readily be turned into new orientations for his own work in social science.

Bourgeois and Proletarians

The Protestant Ethic and the Spirit of Capitalism

The Social Construction of Race

HOW DO SOCIOLOGISTS SEE THE WORLD?

Sociological Theories

BOURGEOIS AND PROLETARIANS

Part One of the Manifesto of the Communist Party

BY KARL. MARX

I. Bourgeois and Proletarians

The history of all hitherto existing society is the history of class struggles.

Freeman and slave, patrician and plebeian, lord and serf, guild-master and journeyman, in a word, oppressor and oppressed, stood in constant opposition to one another, carried on an uninterrupted, now hidden, now open fight, a fight that each time ended, either in a revolutionary re-constitution of society at large, or in the common ruin of the contending classes.

In the earlier epochs of history, we find almost everywhere a complicated arrangement of society into various orders, a manifold gradation of social rank. In ancient Rome we have patricians, knights, plebeians, slaves; in the Middle Ages, feudal lords, vassals, guild-masters, journeymen, apprentices, serfs; in almost all of these classes, again, subordinate gradations.

The modern bourgeois society that has sprouted from the ruins of feudal society has not done away with clash antagonisms. It has but established new classes, new conditions of oppression, new forms of struggle in place of the old ones.

Our epoch, the epoch of the bourgeoisie, possesses, however, this distinctive feature: it has simplified the clash antagonisms: Society as a whole is more and more splitting up into two great hostile camps, into two great classes directly facing each other: Bourgeoisie and Proletariat.

From the serfs of the Middle Ages sprang the chartered burghers of the earliest towns. From these burgesses the first elements of the bourgeoisie were developed.

The discovery of America, the rounding of the Cape, opened up fresh ground for the rising bourgeoisie. The East-Indian and Chinese markets, the colonization of America, trade with the colonies, the increase in the means of exchange and in commodities generally, gave to commerce, to navigation, to industry, an impulse never before known, and thereby, to the revolutionary element in the tottering feudal society, a rapid development.

The feudal system of industry, under which industrial production was monopolized by closed guilds, now no longer sufficed for the growing wants of the new markets. The manufacturing system took its place. The guild-masters were pushed on one side by the manufacturing middle class; division of labor between the different corporate guilds vanished in the face of division of labor in each single workshop.

Meantime the markets kept ever growing, the demand ever rising. Even manufacture no longer sufficed. Thereupon, steam and machinery revolutionized industrial production. The place of manufacture was taken by the giant, Modern Industry, the place of the industrial middle class, by industrial millionaires, the leaders of whole industrial armies, the modern bourgeois.

Modern industry has established the world-market, for which the discovery of America paved the way. This market has given an immense development to commerce, to navigation, to communication by land. This

Karl Marx, "Bourgeois and Proletarians: Part One of the Manifesto of the Communist Party." Copyright in the Public Domain.

development has, in its turn, reacted on the extension of industry; and in proportion as industry, commerce, navigation, railways extended, in the same proportion the bourgeoisie developed, increased its capital, and pushed into the background every class handed down from the Middle Ages.

We see, therefore, how the modern bourgeoisie is itself the product of a long course of development, of a series of revolutions in the modes of production and of exchange.

Each step in the development of the bourgeoisie was accompanied by a corresponding political advance of that class. An oppressed class under the sway of the feudal nobility, an armed and self-governing association in the mediaeval commune; here independent urban republic (as in Italy and Germany), there taxable "third estate" of the monarchy (as in France), afterwards, in the period of manufacture proper, serving either the semi-feudal or the absolute monarchy as a counterpoise against the nobility, and, in fact, corner-stone of the great monarchies in general, the bourgeoisie has at last, since the establishment of Modern Industry and of the world-market, conquered for itself, in the modern representative State, exclusive political sway. The executive of the modern State is but a committee for managing the common affairs of the whole bourgeoisie.

The bourgeoisie, historically, has played a most revolutionary part.

The bourgeoisie, wherever it has got the upper hand, has put an end to all feudal, patriarchal, idyllic relations. It has pitilessly torn asunder the motley feudal ties that bound man to his "natural superiors," and has left remaining no other nexus between man and man than naked self-interest, than callous "cash payment." It has drowned the most heavenly ecstasies of religious fervour, of chivalrous enthusiasm, of philistine sentimentalism, in the icy water of egotistical calculation. It has resolved personal worth into exchange value, and in place of the numberless indefeasible chartered freedoms, has set up that single, unconscionable freedom—Free Trade. In one word, for exploitation, veiled by religious and political illusions, it has substituted naked, shameless, direct, brutal exploitation.

The bourgeoisie has stripped of its halo every occupation hitherto honoured and looked up to with reverent awe. It has converted the physician, the lawyer, the priest, the poet, the man of science, into its paid wage-laborers.

The bourgeoisie has torn away from the family its sentimental veil, and has reduced the family relation to a mere money relation.

The bourgeoisie has disclosed how it came to pass that the brutal display of vigour in the Middle Ages, which Reactionists so much admire, found its fitting complement in the most slothful indolence. It has been the first to show what man's activity can bring about. It has accomplished wonders far surpassing Egyptian pyramids, Roman aqueducts, and Gothic cathedrals; it has conducted expeditions that put in the shade all former Exoduses of nations and crusades.

The bourgeoisie cannot exist without constantly revolutionizing the instruments of production, and thereby the relations of production, and with them the whole relations of society. Conservation of the old modes of production in unaltered form, was, on the contrary, the first condition of existence for all earlier industrial classes. Constant revolutionizing of production, uninterrupted disturbance of all social conditions, everlasting uncertainty and agitation distinguish the bourgeois epoch from all earlier ones. All fixed, fast-frozen relations, with their train of ancient and venerable prejudices and opinions, are swept away, all new-formed ones become antiquated before they can ossify. All that is solid melts into air, all that is holy is profaned, and man is at last compelled to face with sober senses, his real conditions of life, and his relations with his kind.

The need of a constantly expanding market for its products chases the bourgeoisie over the whole surface of the globe. It must nestle everywhere, settle everywhere, establish connexions everywhere.

The bourgeoisie has through its exploitation of the world-market given a cosmopolitan character to production and consumption in every country. To the great chagrin of Reactionists, it has drawn from under the feet of industry the national ground on which it stood. All old-established national industries have been destroyed or are daily being destroyed. They are dislodged by new industries, whose introduction becomes a life and death question for all civilized nations, by industries that no longer work up indigenous raw material, but raw material drawn from the remotest zones; industries whose products are consumed, not only at home, but in every quarter of the globe. In place of the old wants, satisfied by the productions of the country, we find new wants, requiring for their satisfaction the products of distant lands and climes. In place of the old local and national seclusion and self-sufficiency, we have intercourse in every direction, universal interdependence of nations. And as in material, so also in intellectual production. The intellectual creations of individual nations become common property. National one-sidedness and narrow-mindedness become more and more impossible, and from the numerous national and local literatures, there arises a world literature.

The bourgeoisie, by the rapid improvement of all instruments of production, by the immensely facilitated means of communication, draws all, even the most barbarian, nations into civilization. The cheap prices of its commodities are the heavy artillery with which it batters down all Chinese walls, with which it forces the barbarians' intensely obstinate hatred of foreigners to capitulate. It compels all nations, on pain of extinction, to adopt the bourgeois mode of production; it compels them to introduce what it calls civilization into their midst, *i.e.*, to become bourgeois themselves. In one word, it creates a world after its own image.

The bourgeoisie has subjected the country to the rule of the towns. It has created enormous cities, has greatly increased the urban population as compared with the rural, and has thus rescued a considerable part of the population from the idiocy of rural life, just as it has made the country dependent on the towns, so it has made barbarian and semi-barbarian countries dependent on the civilized ones, nations and peasants on nations of bourgeois, the East on the West.

The bourgeoisie keeps more and more doing away with the scattered state of the population, of the means of production, and of property. It has agglomerated population, centralized means of production, and has concentrated property in a few hands. The necessary consequence of this was political centralization. Independent, or but loosely connected provinces, with separate interests, laws, governments and systems of taxation, became lumped together into one nation, with one government, one code of laws, one national class-interest, one frontier and one customs-tariff. The bourgeoisie, during its rule of scarce one hundred years, has created more massive and more colossal productive forces than have all preceding generations together. Subjection of Nature's forces to man, machinery, application of chemistry to industry and agriculture, steam-navigation, railways, electric telegraphs, clearing of whole continents for cultivation, canalization of rivers, whole populations conjured out of the ground—what earlier century had even a presentiment that such productive forces slumbered in the lap of social labor?

We see then: the means of production and of exchange, on whose foundation the bourgeoisie built itself up, were generated in feudal society. At a certain stage in the development of these means of production and of exchange, the conditions under which feudal society produced and exchanged, the feudal organization of agriculture and manufacturing industry, in one word, the feudal relations of property became no longer compatible with the already developed productive forces; they became so many fetters. They had to be burst asunder; they were burst asunder.

Into their place stepped free competition, accompanied by a social and political constitution adapted to it, and by the economical and political sway of the bourgeois class.

A similar movement is going on before our own eyes. Modern bourgeois society with its relations of production, of exchange and of property, a society that has conjured up such gigantic means of production and of exchange, is like the sorcerer, who is no longer able to control the powers of the nether world whom he has called up by his spells. For many a decade past the history of industry and commerce is but the history of the revolt of modern productive forces against modern conditions of production, against the property relations that are the conditions for the existence of the bourgeoisie and of its rule. It is enough to mention the commercial crises that by their periodical return put on its trial, each time more threateningly, the existence of the entire bourgeois society. In these crises a great part not only of the existing products, but also of the previously created productive forces, are periodically destroyed. In these crises there breaks out an epidemic that, in all earlier epochs, would have seemed an absurdity—the epidemic of overproduction. Society suddenly finds itself put back into a state of momentary barbarism; it appears as if a famine, a universal war of devastation had cut off the supply of every means of subsistence; industry and commerce seem to be destroyed; and why? Because there is too much civilization, too much means of subsistence, too much industry, too much commerce. The productive forces at the disposal of society no longer tend to further the development of the conditions of bourgeois property; on the contrary, they have become too powerful for these conditions, by which they are fettered, and so soon as they overcome these fetters, they bring disorder into the whole of bourgeois society, endanger the existence of bourgeois property. The conditions of bourgeois society are too narrow to comprise the wealth created by them. And how does the bourgeoisie get over these crises? On the one hand by enforced destruction of a mass of productive forces; on the other, by the conquest of new markets, and by the more thorough exploitation of the old ones. That is to say, by paving the way for more extensive and more destructive crises, and by diminishing the means whereby crises are prevented.

The weapons with which the bourgeoisie felled feudalism to the ground are now turned against the bourgeoisie itself.

But not only has the bourgeoisie forged the weapons that bring death to itself; it has also called into existence the men who are to wield these weapons—the modern working class—the proletarians.

In proportion as the bourgeoisie, *i.e.,* capital, is developed, in the same proportion is the proletariat, the modern working class, developed—a class of laborers, who live only so long as they find work, and who find work only so long as their labor increases capital. These laborers, who must sell themselves piece-meal, are a commodity, like every other article of commerce, and are consequently exposed to all the vicissitudes of competition, to all the fluctuations of the market.

Owing to the extensive use of machinery and to division of labor, the work of the proletarians has lost all individual character, and consequently, all charm for the workman. He becomes an appendage of the machine, and it is only the most simple, most monotonous, and most easily acquired knack, that is required of him. Hence, the cost of production of a workman is restricted, almost entirely, to the means of subsistence that he requires for his maintenance, and for the propagation of his race. But the price of a commodity, and therefore also of labor, is equal to its cost of production. In proportion, therefore, as the repulsiveness of the work increases, the wage decreases. Nay more, in proportion as the use of machinery and division of labor increases, in the same proportion the burden of toil also increases, whether by prolongation of the working hours, by increase of the work exacted in a given time or by increased speed of the machinery, etc.

Modern industry has converted the little workshop of the patriarchal master into the great factory of the industrial capitalist. Masses of laborers, crowded into the factory, are organized like soldiers. As privates of the industrial army they are placed under the command of a perfect hierarchy of officers and sergeants. Not only are they slaves of the bourgeois class, and of the bourgeois State; they are daily and hourly enslaved by the machine, by the over-looker, and, above all, by the individual bourgeois manufacturer himself. The more openly this despotism proclaims gain to be its end and aim, the more petty, the more hateful and the more embittering it is.

The less the skill and exertion of strength implied in manual labor, in other words, the more modern industry becomes developed, the more is the labor of men superseded by that of women. Differences of age and sex have no longer any distinctive social validity for the working class. All are instruments of labor, more or less expensive to use, according to their age and sex.

No sooner is the exploitation of the laborer by the manufacturer, so far, at an end, that he receives his wages in cash, than he is set upon by the other portions of the bourgeoisie, the landlord, the shopkeeper, the pawnbroker, etc.

The lower strata of the middle class—the small tradespeople, shopkeepers, and retired tradesmen generally, the handicraftsmen and peasants—all these sink gradually into the proletariat, partly because their diminutive capital does not suffice for the scale on which Modern Industry is carried on, and is swamped in the competition with the large capitalists, partly because their specialized skill is rendered worthless by new methods of production. Thus the proletariat is recruited from all classes of the population.

The proletariat goes through various stages of development. With its birth begins its struggle with the bourgeoisie. At first the contest is carried on by individual laborers, then by the workpeople of a factory, then by the operatives of one trade, in one locality, against the individual bourgeois who directly exploits them. They direct their attacks not against the bourgeois conditions of production, but against the instruments of production themselves;

they destroy imported wares that compete with their labor, they smash to pieces machinery, they set factories ablaze, they seek to restore by force the vanished status of the workman of the Middle Ages.

At this stage the laborers still form an incoherent mass scattered over the whole country, and broken up by their mutual competition. If anywhere they unite to form more compact bodies, this is not yet the consequence of their own active union, but of the union of the bourgeoisie, which class, in order to attain its own political ends, is compelled to set the whole proletariat in motion, and is moreover yet, for a time, able to do so. At this stage, therefore, the proletarians do not fight their enemies, but the enemies of their enemies, the remnants of absolute monarchy, the landowners, the non-industrial bourgeois, the petty bourgeoisie. Thus the whole historical movement is concentrated in the hands of the bourgeoisie; every victory so obtained is a victory for the bourgeoisie.

But with the development of industry the proletariat not only increases in number; it becomes concentrated in greater masses, its strength grows, and it feels that strength more. The various interests and conditions of life within the ranks of the proletariat are more and more equalized, in proportion as machinery obliterates all distinctions of labor, and nearly everywhere reduces wages to the same low level. The growing competition among the bourgeois, and the resulting commercial crises, make the wages of the workers ever more fluctuating. The unceasing improvement of machinery, ever more rapidly developing, makes their livelihood more and more precarious; the collisions between individual workmen and individual bourgeois take more and more the character of collisions between two classes. Thereupon the workers begin to form combinations (Trades Unions) against the bourgeois; they club together in order to keep up the rate of wages; they found permanent associations in order to make provision beforehand for these occasional revolts. Here and there the contest breaks out into riots.

Now and then the workers are victorious, but only for a time. The real fruit of their battles lies, not in the immediate result, but in the ever-expanding union of the workers. This union is helped on by the improved means of communication that are created by modern industry and that place the workers of different localities in contact with one another. It was just this contact that was needed to centralise the numerous local struggles, all of the same character, into one national struggle between classes. But every class struggle is a political struggle. And that union, to attain which the burghers of the Middle Ages, with their miserable highways, required centuries, the modern proletarians, thanks to railways, achieve in a few years.

This organization of the proletarians into a class, and consequently into a political party, is continually being upset again by the competition between the workers themselves. But it ever rises up again, stronger, firmer, mightier. It compels legislative recognition of particular interests of the workers, by taking advantage of the divisions among the bourgeoisie itself. Thus the ten-hours' bill in England was carried.

Altogether collisions between the classes of the old society further, in many ways, the course of development of the proletariat. The bourgeoisie finds itself involved in a constant battle. At first with the aristocracy; later on, with those portions of the bourgeoisie itself, whose interests have become antagonistic to the progress of industry; at all times, with the bourgeoisie of foreign countries. In all these battles it sees itself compelled to appeal to the proletariat, to ask for its help, and thus, to drag it into the political arena. The bourgeoisie itself, therefore, supplies the proletariat with its own elements of political and general education, in other words, it furnishes the proletariat with weapons for fighting the bourgeoisie.

Further, as we have already seen, entire sections of the ruling classes are, by the advance of industry, precipitated into the proletariat, or are at least threatened in their conditions of existence. These also supply the proletariat with fresh elements of enlightenment and progress.

Finally, in times when the class struggle nears the decisive hour, the process of dissolution going on within the ruling class, in fact within the whole range of society, assumes such a violent, glaring character, that a small section of the ruling class cuts itself adrift, and joins the revolutionary class, the class that holds the future in its hands. Just as, therefore, at an earlier period, a section of the nobility went over to the bourgeoisie, so now a portion of the bourgeoisie goes over to the proletariat, and in particular, a portion of the bourgeois ideologists, who have raised themselves to the level of comprehending theoretically the historical movement as a whole.

Of all the classes that stand face to face with the bourgeoisie today, the proletariat alone is a really revolutionary class. The other classes decay and finally disappear in the face of Modern Industry; the proletariat is its special and essential product.

The lower middle class, the small manufacturer, the shopkeeper, the artisan, the peasant, all these fight against the bourgeoisie, to save from extinction their existence as fractions of the middle class. They are therefore not revolutionary, but conservative. Nay more, they are reactionary, for they try to roll back the wheel of history. If by chance they are revolutionary, they are so only in view of their impending transfer into the proletariat, they thus defend not their present, but their future interests, they desert their own standpoint to place themselves at that of the proletariat.

The "dangerous class," the social scum, that passively rotting mass thrown off by the lowest layers of old society, may, here and there, be swept into the movement by a proletarian revolution; its conditions of life, however, prepare it far more for the part of a bribed tool of reactionary intrigue.

In the conditions of the proletariat, those of old society at large are already virtually swamped. The proletarian is without property; his relation to his wife and children has no longer anything in common with the bourgeois family-relations; modern industrial labor, modern subjection to capital, the same in England as in France, in America as in Germany, has stripped him of every trace of national character. Law, morality, religion, are to him so many bourgeois prejudices, behind which lurk in ambush just as many bourgeois interests.

All the preceding classes that got the upper hand, sought to fortify their already acquired status by subjecting society at large to their conditions of appropriation. The proletarians cannot become masters of the productive forces of society, except by abolishing their own previous mode of appropriation, and thereby also every other previous mode of appropriation. They have nothing of their own to secure and to fortify; their mission is to destroy all previous securities for, and insurances of, individual property.

All previous historical movements were movements of minorities, or in the interests of minorities. The proletarian movement is the self-conscious, independent movement of the immense majority, in the interests of the immense majority. The proletariat, the lowest stratum of our present society, cannot stir, cannot raise itself up, without the whole superincumbent strata of official society being sprung into the air.

Though not in substance, yet in form, the struggle of the proletariat with the bourgeoisie is at first a national struggle. The proletariat of each country must, of course, first of all settle matters with its own bourgeoisie.

In depicting the most general phases of the development of the proletariat, we traced the more or less veiled civil war, raging within existing society, up to the point where that war breaks out into open revolution, and where the violent overthrow of the bourgeoisie lays the foundation for the sway of the proletariat.

Hitherto, every form of society has been based, as we have already seen, on the antagonism of oppressing and oppressed classes. But in order to oppress a class, certain conditions must be assured to it under which it can, at least, continue its slavish existence. The serf, in the period of serfdom, raised himself to membership in the commune, just as the petty bourgeois, under the yoke of feudal absolutism, managed to develop into a bourgeois. The modern laborer, on the contrary, instead of rising with the progress of industry, sinks deeper and deeper below the conditions of existence of his own class. He becomes a pauper, and pauperism develops more rapidly than population and wealth. And here it becomes evident, that the bourgeoisie is unfit any longer to be the ruling class in society, and to impose its conditions of existence upon society as an over-riding law. It is unfit to rule because it is incompetent to assure an existence to its slave within his slavery, because it cannot help letting him sink into such a state, that it has to feed him, instead of being fed by him. Society can no longer live under this bourgeoisie, in other words, its existence is no longer compatible with society.

The essential condition for the existence, and for the sway of the bourgeois class, is the formation and augmentation of capital; the condition for capital is wage-labor. Wage-labor rests exclusively on competition between the laborers. The advance of industry, whose involuntary promoter is the bourgeoisie, replaces the isolation of the laborers, due to competition, by their revolutionary combination, due to association. The development of Modern Industry, therefore, cuts from under its feet the very foundation on which the bourgeoisie produces and appropriates products. What the bourgeoisie, therefore, produces, above all, is its own grave-diggers. Its fall and the victory of the proletariat are equally inevitable.

Discussion Questions

1. What is the critical difference between "bourgeoisie" and "proletarians"?
2. What factors increased the political power of the bourgeoisie?
3. Explain the revolutionary effect of the rise of the bourgeoisie on the nation-state.
4. Explain this statement: "The bourgeoisie itself … furnishes the proletariat with weapons for fighting the bourgeoisie."
5. To what extent does Marx's analysis reflect today's world? What's the same, and what's different?

THE PROTESTANT ETHIC AND THE SPIRIT OF CAPITALISM

A Brief Summary

BY STEPHEN KALBERG

Published originally as two long articles in 1904 and 1905 in the *Archiv für Sozialwissenschaft und Sozialpolitik,* Max Weber's classic, *The Protestant Ethic and the Spirit of Capitalism* (*PE*; 2011b), is one of the most enduring and widely read volumes in modern social science. A brief review of its major points will assist understanding of Weber's analysis of the American political culture.[1]

PE investigated whether the "Protestant ethic" found among seventeenth-century Puritans (Calvinists, Methodists, Baptists, Mennonites, and Quakers) "*co*-participated" in giving birth to a driving force Weber saw as contributing to the rise of the industrial West: a secular "spirit of capitalism." Adherents of this "modern economic ethic" viewed work as a systematic endeavor, he argued, namely, as a *calling* (*Beruf*). Characteristic was a rigorous—"an ascetic"— organization of occupational life according to a set of values, a methodical and dutiful striving for profit and wealth, and a systematic reinvestment of money rather than its enjoyment. The deeply rooted religious world of the sixteenth and seventeenth centuries must be briefly noted if Weber's argument is to be understood.

The "Spiritual Foundation"

The doctrine of Predestination anchors his argument in *PE*. According to John Calvin (1509–1564), a Swiss theologian, an omniscient and omnipotent God of the Old Testament has determined that only a chosen few will be reborn into heaven. Good works or ethical behavior can never influence His decisions, nor can mere mortals understand His motives. Unbearable anxiety and fatalism for the faithful were the consequence of this doctrine, Weber noted. However, revisions were undertaken in the later sixteenth and early seventeenth centuries by "Puritan divines," a group of ministers, theologians, and lay believers in England led by Richard Baxter (1615–1691). Herein lies the source of the Protestant ethic, Weber maintains. His analysis at this point can be seen to divide into two stages.

First, following Calvin, the Puritans saw their task in this short life in unequivocal terms: to construct on earth a Kingdom that would extoll His glory and majesty—that is, a Kingdom of wealth and abundance. Hence, work, as a means of constructing this Kingdom, was awarded with a "psychological premium," "commanded to all," and elevated by the sincere devout to the forefront of life. In addition, labor must involve a systematic element, the divines held; it must be performed *in a calling.* Moreover, by taming base wants and desires, systematic labor assists concentration on God and His plan. It also dispels the overwhelming doubt, anxiety, and sense of moral unworthiness caused by the doctrine of Predestination. In this manner this *ascetic Protestantism* bestowed clear premiums on constant labor and the search for riches. Both activities now lost their exclusively utilitarian meaning and became providential.

Although influential, this sanctification failed to fully overcome the long-standing ethos rooted in medieval Catholicism. According to this "traditional economic ethic," labor was understood as a necessary evil, and profit was seldom earned honestly. If a banishment of this frame of mind (*Gesinnung*) were to occur, work and wealth had to acquire an even more comprehensive sanctification, *PE* held. After all, this ethic had been uprooted only rarely. Entrepreneurial astuteness and "business savvy," all intelligent modes of making one's way in the world (*Lebensklugheit*), and even charismatic adventure capitalists had failed to bring about its weakening (2011c, pp. 79, 83–84). Furthermore, the all-important "certainty of salvation" *(certitudo salutis)* question to anxious believers—"am I among the saved?"—had not yet been answered adequately. In this regard, the second stage of Weber's analysis proves crucial.

Despite the Predestination decree, Baxter and other Puritan divines concluded that *signs* from God of the believer's salvation status could be discovered. Above all, the Deity's favor seemed apparent if the devout demonstrated a capacity, as required by their vocational calling, either to labor systematically or to remain focused on the onerous task of acquiring wealth. Indeed, the faithful convinced themselves that their strength and discipline to do so, as well as their deep devotion and righteous conduct, came from God: His energy was "operating within." Furthermore, surely in His cosmos, nothing occurred by chance: those believers who, by dint of methodical work, managed to acquire great wealth, understood their good fortune as a consequence of God's hand—and the devout could convince themselves that He would assist *only* the predestined. Systematic work, as well as the acquisition of profit and great wealth, became "evidence" of one's favorable salvation status.

Now awarded psychological premiums in an even more intense manner, constant labor and the possession of riches became viewed by the faithful as testifying to their salvation. They offered literal proof (*Bewährung*) to believers of redemption. As anxiety declined, the bleak Puritan became transformed into a disciplined "tool" of God's will, proudly engaged in the large task of building His glorious Kingdom on earth.

According to Weber, this *methodical-rational* organization of life and *inner-worldly asceticism*—a "Protestant ethic"—distinguished the "Puritan style of life." The devout now focused their energies and conduct in a comprehensive manner on God's will, restricted consumption, reinvested profits, banished the traditional economic ethic, and placed work at the center of life. Extreme loyalty to His grand design marked the faithful, as did cognizance that riches emanated from the hand of this omnipotent Deity and thus belonged exclusively to Him and His Kingdom. Wealth *must* be, on His behalf and for His community, invested instead of enjoyed.

Simultaneously, the image of those engaged in business and oriented to profit changed. Rather than viewed as calculating, greedy, and self-interested, as had been the case since antiquity, capitalists were now perceived as honest employers of good character sincerely engaged in a noble project given by God. The halo of religion—a "spiritual foundation"—surrounded their activities, and hence the understanding of the production and exchange of goods as involving exclusively utilitarian calculations and clever business procedures must be abandoned, Weber contends. Specialists in vocations—a new "human being" (*Menschentyp*) engaged in a calling—now embarked upon the stage of Western history.

He insists that the Puritan anchoring of methodical orientations toward work, wealth, and profit in the major question for believers— "am I among the saved?"—proved significant. The concerted bestowing of religion-based psychological rewards on vocational labor was alone endowed with the capacity to uproot the traditional economic ethic. The tenacity and "lasting resilience" (2011c, p. 91) of this *coherent group* of persons—Puritan employers and workers—must be acknowledged, he argues. The "internally binding" set of religious values that motivated work "from within," and the search for material success, introduced the life "organized around ethical principles." This forceful patterning of action confronted directly the traditional economic ethic. To Weber, the manifold ethical dimension that penetrated the Puritan's economic activity constituted a "revolutionary" force against this ethic (2011c, pp. 89, 134–135). It also called forth a spirit of capitalism.

From the Protestant Ethic to

Carried by churches and sects, the Protestant ethic spread throughout many New England, Dutch, and English communities in the seventeenth century. Disciplined, hard labor in a calling marked a person as among the chosen, as did the wealth that followed from a steadfast adherence to Puritan values. This ethos was cultivated in entire regions in Benjamin Franklin's era one century later. However, its religion-based, ethical component had become weaker with this expansion and became transformed—namely, into an "ethos with a utilitarian accent" (2011c, pp. 79, 173, 176–178).

Weber refers to this ethos as the spirit of capitalism: a configuration of values that implied the individual's duty to view work as an end in itself, to labor systematically in a calling, to increase capital, to earn money perpetually (while avoiding enjoyment of it), and to comprehend material wealth as a manifestation of "competence and proficiency in a vocational calling" (2011c, p. 81). Adherents to this mode of organizing life, rather than perceived by others as among the saved, were believed to be community-oriented citizens of good moral character. Immediately recognizable, their stalwart demeanor no longer served to testify to firm belief and membership among the elect; it indicated instead respectability, dignity, honesty, and self-confidence.[2]

Franklin represented this "spirit" in *PE*. Business astuteness, utilitarian calculations, and greed fail to account for the *origin* of his disciplined life, Weber contends; legacies of ascetic Protestantism contributed substantially. Indeed, such an interpretation is confirmed by the presence of an ethical element in Franklin's manner of organizing and directing his life, Weber holds (2011c, pp. 79–81). A conundrum, however, here appears. How had the ethical dimension in the Protestant ethic, now shorn of its foundational salvation quest and "in but not of" the world components, survived into Franklin's era?

Long before the religious roots of ethical action had become weakened, the Puritans' ethical values had expanded beyond their original social carriers—ascetic Protestant churches and sects—to another carrier organization: Protestant families. For this reason, these values remained central in childhood socialization *even* as Colonial America experienced a gradual loosening of the all-encompassing influence of these congregations. Parents taught children to set goals and organize their lives methodically, to be self-reliant and shape their own destinies as individuals, to behave in accord with ethical standards, and to work diligently. They encouraged their offspring to pursue careers in business and see virtue in capitalism's open markets, to seek material success, to become upwardly mobile, to live modestly and frugally, to reinvest their wealth, to look toward the future and the "opportunities" it offers, and to budget their time wisely—just as Franklin had admonished in his writings (2011c, pp. 77–78). Families also stressed ascetic personal habits, hard competition, and the importance of honesty and fair play in business transactions. Through intimate, personal relationships,[3] children were socialized to conduct themselves in a restrained, dispassionate manner—and to do so by reference to a configuration of ethical values.

In this way, action oriented toward values originally carried by ascetic Protestant sects and churches endured long after the weakening of these religious organizations. An orientation toward ethical action became cultivated also in community organizations, including schools. Protestantism's "sect spirit," now routinized into maxims, community norms, a particular demeanor, and familiar customs and traditions, continued to influence new generations; they remained integral in Franklin's America (see 2011a, pp. 227–232; see Nelson 1973, pp. 98–99, 106–108). Yet the ancestry of this spirit of capitalism was not "this-worldly" but "other-worldly," Weber contends. The Protestant ethic constituted its predecessor: "The Puritan's sincerity of belief must have been the most powerful lever conceivable working to expand the life outlook that we are here designating as the spirit of capitalism" (2011c, p. 170):

> Our analysis should have demonstrated that one of the constitutive components of the modern capitalist spirit and, moreover, generally of modern civilization, was the rational organization of life on the basis of the *idea of the calling*. It was born out of the spirit of *Christian asceticism*. (2011c, p. 176; emphasis in original):

Having illustrated "the way in which 'ideas' become generally effective in history" (2011c, p. 107), *PE* now reaches its conclusion. Weber has traced the lineage of the spirit of capitalism and discovered significant nonutilitarian, nonpolitical, and noneconomic roots. A Protestant ethic had, *PE* affirms, "*co*-participated" in the formation of the spirit of capitalism (2011c, p. 108).[4] The realm of values and ideas had played a prominent causal role.

The "Mechanical" Foundations

PE's last pages leap across the centuries in order briefly to survey a new theme: the "cosmos" of modern capitalism. In broad strokes and unforgettable passages, Weber briefly explores the fate today of "this-worldly" directed action and the life organized methodically by reference to a constellation of ethical values. The question of how we *can* live under modern capitalism preoccupied him for his entire life.

Firmly entrenched after the massive industrialization of the nineteenth century, "victorious capitalism" now sustains itself on the basis of *means-end rational* action alone, Weber argues. In this urban and bureaucratic milieu, neither Franklin's spirit nor the Protestant ethic's asceticism endows methodical work with subjective meaning. Sheer utilitarian calculations move to the forefront as these value configurations, so significant at the birth of modern capitalism, collapse and fade (2011c, pp. 175–176). Today, modern capitalism unfolds on the basis of an inescapable network of pragmatic necessities.

Whether employees or entrepreneurs, people born into this "powerful cosmos" are coerced to adapt to its market-based, functional exchanges in order to survive. The motivation to work in this "steel-hard casing" (*stahlhartes Gehäuse*) involves a mixture of constraint and means-end rational action. A "mechanical foundation" anchors our era. Modern capitalism—this "grinding mechanism"—will "[determine the style of life of all born into it] … with overwhelming force, and perhaps it will continue to do so until the last ton of fossil fuel has burnt to ashes" (2011c, p. 177).[5]

This acknowledgment of his brief commentary upon capitalist societies today reveals Weber's analysis in *PE* as characterized by four discrete stages (see the chart on page 45).

In sum, a dynamic tapestry characterizes the *PE* analysis. Despite regular indictments, the Weber thesis survives to this day and must be confronted by scholars seeking to understand the rise of modern capitalism in the West. By calling attention to the important historical roles played by both a Protestant ethic and a spirit of capitalism, *PE* questions all those theories that explain the rise of the modern world exclusively by reference to utilitarian activity (for example, rational choice theory) or structural transformations (whether of Marxian or Durkheimian lineage). The varying subjective meaning of persons in demarcated groups proved central to Weber, as did the otherworldly, value-oriented ancestry of the modern world. The Puritan's asceticism originated from his life "*in* but not *of*" the world.

PE must be comprehended as the father of all schools of sociological thought that, in seeking to explain long-range social change, explicitly attend to cultural forces. It must be further understood as declaring emphatically that the past is interwoven with, and influences, the present. Finally, in an age of universalizing globalization, *PE* conveys the causal significance of the indigenous cultural makeup inevitably manifest when a nation embarks upon economic modernization. Weber admonished social scientists generally to take account of religion-based, background contexts for social change.

Notes

1. This overview offers a succinct summary of "the Weber thesis." It provides the background context to Chapters 1 and 2. For a more detailed discussion, see Kalberg 2011a; 2011c, pp. 321–330.
2. The origins of the American emphasis on honesty and candor toward all as a central aspect of "good character," to be manifested both in personal conduct and even in the political realm (as an ideal for political activists), must be sought here. For the Puritan, righteous conduct that testified to one's elect status emanated ultimately from God's strength within the believer—and He could not be other than

candid. For the same reason, persons speaking to Puritans would not dare speak dishonestly.

3. Weber argues that the teaching of *ethical* values, if it is to occur, necessarily involves a strong personal bond. See, for example, 1927, pp. 357–358; 1946c, p. 331; 1968, pp. 346, 600, 1186–1187; 2005, pp. 251–254.
4. That Weber acknowledges the existence of other origins of this spirit is apparent. See 2011c, pp. 108, 399–400, note 142.
5. This theme has been visited at various points throughout this volume.

The Protestant Ethic and the Spirtt of Capitalism: Stages of Webers's Analysis

	Period	Organization	Type of Action	Devout
I. **Calvin**: Fatalism follows from Predesitnation Doctrine	16th. C.	small sects	value-rational	yes
II. **Baxter**: The Prostestant Ethic:	16th-17th C	churches and sects	value-rational (methodical worldy activity)	yes
elective ↕ affinity				
III. **Franklin**: The spirit of capitalism	18th. C.	communities	value-rational (methodical worldly activity)	no
IV. The "specialist": Modern campitalism as a "cosmos"	20th C.	industrial society	means-end rational	no

THE SOCIAL CONSTRUCTION OF RACE

BY STEVEN M. BUECHLER

The analysis of social class has been part of sociology from the beginning. Race is different. Although scholars like W. E. B. Du Bois (1903) had crucial insights into race relations more than a hundred years ago, sociology was slow to see race as an important subject in its own right.

This gradually changed after Gunnar Myrdal's *An American Dilemma* (1944) placed racial prejudice at the forefront of public consciousness. Along with other work, it helped establish race and ethnic relations as a major subfield within sociology. Group dynamics, racial conflict, prejudice, and discrimination attracted increasing sociological attention.

What really invigorated the study of race were not academic developments but social conflict. As the civil rights movement overturned the most explicit forms of racial segregation and discrimination in the 1950s and 1960s, race became even more central in public awareness and academic study. As the movement evolved from liberal integration to black power to cultural nationalism, different understandings of race emerged. These movement-inspired analyses revealed how race was embedded in social structure.

Current sociological understandings of race thus have a dual legacy. The slowly developing academic study of race has been infused with critical insights from race-based social movements. Much the same can be said for the impact of the feminist movement in jump-starting sociology's understanding of gender issues.

What is Race?

Few things seem more obvious than someone's race. As we interact with others, we unthinkingly place them within familiar racial categories. On rare occasions, someone doesn't easily fit the categories. We might regard them as odd or unusual, but we rarely use such cases to question the categories themselves.

When we "see" race like this, we are also likely to assume race is rooted in biology. The physical differences between races (skin color, facial features, eye shape, hair texture) seem so self-evident as to be beyond question. Everyday consciousness assumes these features reflect well-established biological, physiological, and genetic differences that distinguish races. Well-meaning people might struggle to avoid prejudices and stereotypes, but they are likely to see race as a biologically self-evident reality.

This is a good time to recall Peter Berger's (1963) sociological insight that things are not always what they seem. Beneath the seemingly self-evident biology of race, there are complex social, political, and cultural forces that sustain that appearance. Put differently, race is not biologically determined but rather socially constructed. This implies two seemingly contradictory things. First, racial categories are arbitrary. They have little scientific or biological foundation. They are not "real." Second, these categories nevertheless *become real* through social definitions. As W. I. Thomas noted long ago, if a situation is defined as real, it will be real in its consequences. When the definition is embedded in

Steven M. Bucheler, "The Social Construction of Race," *Critical Sociology*. Copyright © 2014 by Taylor & Francis Group. Reprinted with permission.

centuries of institutions and interactions, then race becomes as real as any social phenomenon can be. Race is an illusory biological fiction but a powerful social fact.

There are several reasons to question the biological basis of race. Human beings share almost 99 percent of our genetic composition with higher primates. Put differently, homo sapiens are only 1 to 2 percent genetically different from chimpanzees. If the genetic margin separating two species is so small, the likelihood that there will be consistent genetic differences *within* the category of homo sapiens that sort humans into genetically distinct races is highly implausible.

A second reason to doubt the biological basis of race involves the logic of categories and classification. Such logic makes sense when things fall into mutually exclusive categories based on many relevant traits. It makes less sense if there is a lot of overlap between things in supposedly separate categories. The logic is weakest when there is more individual variation within categories than the average variation between categories. And yet it is this weakest version that applies to race. On any number of physical traits, individual variations within races far exceed average differences between them. When categories persist in such situations, it is because they are based on social definitions rather than on logically compelling reasons or scientifically verifiable data.

A third reason to doubt the biological basis of race involves the history of racial typologies. Systems of racial classification have been proposed for centuries, with none of the logical consistency, cumulative advances, or increasing specificity that define scientific progress. Throughout this history, there has been major disagreement over things as basic as how many races exist. After centuries of work, the only real lesson here is that the very idea of distinguishing races in biological terms is not scientifically feasible.

A fourth reason to question the biological basis of race involves social and legal definitions. When Southern legislators defined people as "Negro" if one thirty-second of their ancestry was African, this was a social definition and not a biological fact. When Native American tribes use similar measures to determine who is a legitimate tribal member, this is also a social definition and not a biological fact. Because racial definitions vary by place, you can change your race by flying to Brazil where an unusually complex set of racial distinctions will define your race differently from the place you just left (Henslin 2005, 327). Racial definitions also change over time; consider "how the Irish became white" (Ignatiev 1995) in nineteenth-century US history.

One final example: People sometimes defend a biological conception of race based on medical conditions. In the United States, sickle-cell anemia is considered a "black disease." In reality, a predisposition to sickle-cell anemia derives from geography and evolution and not race. In places where malaria was a big threat to human health, a few people had a natural immunity. Through natural selection, they reproduced in greater numbers. However, the same factors creating the immunity also made them susceptible to sickle-cell anemia. Thus, some but not all Africans are susceptible, and some non-Africans from Mediterranean regions and South Asia are susceptible. It is difficult to see how this qualifies as a "racial" disease (Adelman 2003).

It is not physical but social facts that make races "real." This social construction of race is a historical process. People have always noted human differences, but a new discourse of race emerged during European exploration, conquest, and colonization typically dated from the "discovery" of the "New World" in 1492. Thus, Columbus's diaries refer to the "savages" he encountered. With each subsequent encounter between European colonizers and indigenous groups, the discourse of race grew to describe these "others" in racial terms (Winant 2004).

This discourse rested on two premises. The first was that races were biological realities. The second was that races existed in a hierarchy of superiority and inferiority. In these hierarchies, whites, Europeans, or some subgroup of Europeans were inevitably located at the top of the hierarchy. Despite many variations, some races (the people doing the classifying) were always superior to others (the people being classified). The very concept of race is *racist*, because beliefs about superiority and inferiority have always been part of the concept.

The reasons are not a big mystery. European colonization was often brutal and inhumane. It contradicted many social norms, religious principles, and moral imperatives of the colonizers. It required some type of legitimation of the contradiction between humane values and inhumane behavior. Thus the invention of race/racism

Colonialism only poses a moral dilemma if people are seen as equals. The social construction of race/racism defines the colonized group as inferior or subhuman. The more their humanity is denied, the more brutality becomes acceptable. Consider that few people have qualms about the slaughter and consumption of animals because they are seen as a different species. It hardly occurs to us that this requires a justification. Some versions of racism also suggest that "others" are a different species, so the moral code of the dominant group does not apply. The same logic operates in warfare; it is easier to kill people who are seen as less than human. It is no accident that the most extreme versions of racial thinking culminate in genocide, where others are not only seen as subhuman but as a threat that must be eliminated.

The social construction of race links biology, inferiority, and racism in fateful ways. Like race, racism has many variations. It can provide justifications for enslavement and genocide. It can seek to convert others who have not yet had the benefits of "civilization." It can portray "others" as innocent children requiring protection and guidance. In every version, however, a presumption of racial inferiority is central.

The social construction of race and racism was vital in legitimizing European colonization and conquest. The United States followed suit in the exploitation of African slaves, the conquest of Native peoples, and racist relations with Latino/a and Asian populations. The timing and groups were different, but the history of US race relations mirrors the European model quite closely.

Although race is a biological fiction, there is a social logic to why this fiction arose and how it shapes contemporary society. The challenge of seeing race as a social construction is to balance the seeming contradiction that something arbitrary has been socially constructed into something as "real" as any social fact can be.

Race vs. Ethnicity

The social construction of race also becomes evident by contrasting "races" and "ethnic groups." Common sense equates race with biology and ethnicity with culture. Although the link between race and biology is problematic, the equation of ethnicity and culture is sound.

Ethnic groups are distinguished by cultural differences in language, customs, norms, values, and religious beliefs. Although their members might be geographically dispersed, ethnic groups often trace their roots to a distinctive place. Although it is culturally learned, ethnicity "feels" natural to people. Ethnocentrism is a common expression of the "naturalness" or superiority of one's group and way of doing things.

As socially constructed categories, "races" lump together many ethnic groups in the same racial category. Each of the major races typically recognized in the United States (African Americans, European Americans, Latino/a Americans, Native Americans, and Asian Americans) includes multiple ethnicities. The most obvious expression of racism is the blatant division between the dominant racial group of European Americans and all other subordinate racial groups.

A subtler expression of racism is that ethnic variations within the dominant racial group are often recognized, whereas variations within subordinate racial groups are not. Thus, in both popular consciousness and much sociological work, ethnicity really means cultural variations among European Americans (Polish, Swedish, Italian, German, etc.) whereas race lumps others into broad racial categories (blacks, Hispanics, Native Americans, etc.). This practice obscures the fact that "white" is also a socially constructed race and that other races have internal ethnic differences.

A long history of unequal treatment has made these arbitrary distinctions into powerful realities. Consider the following contrasts. Members of white ethnic groups typically entered the United States voluntarily, could sometimes conceal their ethnicity, were seen as variations on a common theme of being white, were eventually pressured to assimilate, and had at least some opportunities for integration and upward mobility. Members of racial minorities, by contrast, became part of the United States involuntarily, could rarely conceal their race, were seen as fundamentally different, were subject to strict segregation, and had few opportunities for integration and upward mobility until quite recently. Such differences suggest different models of ethnic and race relations.

For white ethnic groups, the main story is assimilation. However, the melting pot image of assimilation is misleading by implying that all groups change equally as they are "melted" into something new. In reality, there has always been a hierarchy among white ethnic groups. WASPs, or white Anglo-Saxon Protestants, have been at the top, followed by other Northern Europeans, and then Central and Southern Europeans. Assimilation has not meant blending but rather change by subordinate white ethnic groups. Consider that the United States did not create a new language through assimilation. Assimilating groups gave up native languages and adopted English. Assimilation involved a trade-off in which subordinate white ethnic groups sacrificed ethnic distinctiveness in exchange for admission into mainstream society.

Assimilation involves several stages that begin with cultural assimilation (Gordon 1964). This occurs when a newly arriving white ethnic group learns and adopts the culture of the dominant group. This is the only stage the subordinate group can control. Indeed, they might initially resist this stage, in which case assimilation will not occur. If and when they do initiate the process, control passes to the dominant group.

This is evident in the second stage of structural assimilation. This means acceptance of the subordinate group by the dominant group. Such acceptance initially occurs in secondary groups like the workplace and other public settings. It then involves accepting people as neighbors or in churches and voluntary organizations. It culminates with acceptance into primary groups like friendship networks. At each stage, the subordinate group can initiate contact, but the dominant group retains the power to accept or reject it.

Assimilation then proceeds through other stages that reflect still greater acceptance. Marital assimilation occurs when members of different groups intermarry with increasing frequency and decreasing disapproval. Identificational assimilation occurs when members of the assimilating group switch identities from their original ethnicity to their new nation. This could take generations. Immigrants might retain their Italian identity, while the next generation identifies as Italian American, and subsequent generations identify as American.

Subsequent stages include attitudinal assimilation, indicated by a reduction in prejudicial attitudes about the subordinate group. This often corresponds with behavioral assimilation, evidenced by a reduction in discrimination against members of the group. The process culminates with civic assimilation, signified by the elimination of ethnic conflict.

Although the story of assimilation seems to offer a happy ending, it is shaped by unequal power throughout. The dominant group provides the standard for what assimilation means (becoming like them), and it controls the pace. They retain their dominance because their culture becomes normative for all. The subordinate group pays the cost by relinquishing their ethnic heritage. When the costs seem worth the benefits, groups seek assimilation. Although abstract models oversimplify complex histories, this model accurately describes the assimilation of a number of white ethnic groups in the United States.

Given their different treatment, it is not surprising that the assimilationist model doesn't fit racial groups in the United States. Some insist that with enough time, racial minorities will also assimilate, but this is a dubious claim. The histories of these groups are different, the scope of discrimination is wider, and resistance to assimilation has been substantial. Moreover, the persistence of distinctive racial cultures suggests that many people in these groups would not seek assimilation even if it were possible.

Such differences drew many scholars to the model of internal colonialism to analyze racial dynamics (Omi and Winant 1994, 44–46). This model rests on an analogy between race relations within a single country and colonial relations between countries. In the analogy, the white power structure in a single country is like the colonial power, and racial minorities in that country are like colonies.

Several parallels lend credence to the analogy. Both relationships begin with forced contact, because colonial powers and white power structures use coercion to establish the relationship in the first place. Coercion might be resisted, but the power imbalance has allowed colonial powers and white power structures to retain dominance for centuries.

A second parallel involves cultural domination. The beliefs and practices of the colonized group or the racial minority are denigrated as primitive or uncivilized. Sometimes there are efforts to convert the subordinate group to the culture of the dominant group, but in all cases the dominant group attempts to undermine the culture of the subordinate group.

Political control is a third parallel. In the colonial situation, extensive staffs of governors and administrators were sent to the colony to run its political affairs on behalf of the colonizing power. With internal colonialism, the dominant group uses both formal and informal political mechanisms to ensure a similar degree of control by the white power structure. The underrepresentation of racial minorities in positions of political power is the tip of the iceberg of political control by the dominant group.

Perhaps the most important parallel involves economic exploitation. This is the driving motive of colonial relations, whether the resources involve cheap labor, raw materials, or commodity markets. With internal colonialism, the role of racial minorities as a secondary labor force with lower pay, fewer benefits, and higher unemployment is merely one indicator of the economic exploitation that is central to this relationship.

Both traditional and internal colonialism create institutional discrimination, as social organizations and practices are built on discriminatory principles. This creates racial inequalities and racially coded practices not just in the economy and polity, but also in housing, education, health care, and criminal justice.

A final parallel is racist legitimation. Systematic beliefs about the inferiority of the subordinate group accompany both forms of colonialism. These beliefs seek to legitimate unequal treatment. At their most powerful, such racist legitimations make colonial domination seem logical, natural, and even beneficial for subordinate groups.

No analogy is perfect, but the history of US race relations more closely approximates internal colonialism than assimilationist integration. What the colonial model underscores is that race relations are rooted in conflicting interests between dominant and subordinate groups. Dominant groups who benefit have a vested interest in maintaining such relations; subordinate groups who pay the price of these relations can be expected to change them if possible.

The question of group interests requires a closer look. The dominant group is really a white power structure of elites who make economic, political, and cultural decisions with far-reaching consequences. This group most clearly benefits from exploitative race relations. The subordinate group refers to racial minorities disproportionately located toward the bottom of class and other hierarchies of inequality. This group most clearly pays the price of racial oppression.

What is less clear are the interests of "ordinary whites." They belong to the dominant racial group but are not in positions of institutional power and do not receive the same material benefits from institutional racism that dominant whites do. This status inconsistency between race and class could lead this group to define its interests in rather different ways.

On one hand, ordinary whites may primarily identify with their race. This links them to dominant whites of the same race but of a different class and distances them from racial minorities with whom they might share similar class positions. Historically, this identification allowed even poor whites to claim status on the basis of race; no matter how economically deprived they were, they were still white in a society where that meant a great deal. Ordinary whites can thus derive a social-psychological benefit from their racial identity regardless of material circumstances. But the benefits are more than psychological. Ordinary whites might also derive material benefits from discrimination against minorities if it expands their opportunities at the expense of minorities. By this logic, ordinary whites might see their interests in alignment with powerful whites despite their class differences.

On the other hand, ordinary whites might primarily identify with their class position, which would distance them from powerful whites and align them more closely with racial minorities. This suggests a class alliance across racial lines in which the material similarities of working-class whites and minorities trump racial differences. Such an alliance could challenge racial discrimination, and there is a logic for doing so. Where racial discrimination is high, it allows employers to use a divide-and-conquer strategy that ultimately undermines living standards for both whites and racial minorities (Reich 1981). Racial discrimination thus hurts minorities directly and ordinary whites indirectly. In this scenario, the collective self-interest of ordinary whites is to align with racial minorities and oppose racial discrimination.

The colonial model remains an imperfect analogy, but it frames important questions about the future of race relations. Even without clear answers, it sensitizes us to how group interests shape the social construction of race.

Forms of Discrimination

The colonial model offers a big picture of race relations that rests on many small episodes of discrimination. It is these practices, enacted on a daily basis, that sustain the social construction of race.

Discrimination ranges across many institutions and social arenas. It obviously includes the economy, employment, and political representation. It also includes differences in health, mortality, and life expectancy as a result of differential access to physical and mental health services. It includes deeply rooted patterns of residential segregation that create other problems like unequal access to education. It includes very different probabilities of becoming caught up in the criminal justice system. The effects of discrimination are cumulative, as initial disadvantages become larger inequities over time. Acts of discrimination are the building blocks of racial inequality.

The traditional view of discrimination is that prejudicial attitudes cause discriminatory behavior (Feagin and Feagin 1978). The term *prejudice* means to "prejudge" people on the basis of their group identity. Such judgments often involve negative stereotypes about an entire category of people that are attributed to all its members.

The discrimination that results from prejudice can be explicit, as when people engage in name-calling, racist behavior, or hate crimes. But it can also be subtle or covert. If someone is advertising a job or an apartment and the "wrong" applicant appears, that applicant might be told that the job has been filled or the apartment rented. When the "right" applicant comes along, the apartment or job suddenly becomes available again. In this case, intentional harm is done to someone who might not be aware that they have been the victim of discrimination. Explicit discrimination grabs headlines, but subtle, covert forms are more common and often go undetected. Indeed, it is impossible to know the full extent of discrimination, because much of it is hidden in this fashion. The common thread is a prejudicial attitude. In the traditional model, discrimination occurs when "evil motives" are translated into action.

This model implies that reducing prejudice reduces discrimination. This was part of the logic behind social policies and court decisions favoring integration. It was thought that, with more social contact between groups, people would rethink their prejudices and treat others as individuals and not stereotypes. If prejudice melted away, discrimination would, too. Although the logic seems plausible, there's a problem. By many measures, prejudice in the United States has declined, but racial discrimination has not shown a corresponding reduction.

This prompted a closer look at the traditional view. It became clear that prejudice alone might not lead to discrimination. Prejudiced people need the power to act on prejudice if it is to become discrimination. It also became more evident that discrimination can occur without prejudice. Thus, an employer might have no prejudice against certain people but still refuse to hire them out of a belief that it would drive customers away.

More generally, discrimination limits opportunities for "others" and increases them for discriminators. In such cases, discrimination simply flows from group interest without prejudice. Such discrimination without an "evil motive" can also be an unintentional by-product of institutional policies. As the limits of the traditional model became more evident, sociologists developed another way of thinking about what causes discrimination.

The result was the institutional model in which organizational practices replace prejudice as the major cause of discrimination (Feagin and Feagin 1978). The idea is that social institutions routinely discriminate against many people. In contrast to the traditional model, the institutional model sees discrimination as a normal, routine, chronic outcome rather than a sporadic one. It recognizes that most discrimination is subtle or covert, although overt institutional discrimination still happens, too. It sees discrimination as something that affects thousands if not millions of people, because it is embedded in major social institutions like the criminal justice system or the labor market. Finally, institutional discrimination can be either intentional or unintentional.

Intentional institutional discrimination occurs when there is a conscious goal of unequal treatment. It might be rooted in prejudice, racism, group interest, or some other motive. As with the traditional model, there is an "evil motive" behind such action. Unlike the traditional model, it is not individuals but large organizations that enact these behaviors. In systems of apartheid or legalized segregation, discriminatory purposes are officially proclaimed.

When segregation becomes illegal, intentions to discriminate might no longer be publicly stated but can continue to shape institutional functioning. The redlining of certain neighborhoods as poor credit risks is one example. The use of racial profiling in police practices is another example. The purging of voter registration lists is a third example of intentional, institutional discrimination (Moore 2001). While rarer hate crimes grab headlines, more routine institutional discrimination affects many more people on a daily basis.

Institutional discrimination can also be unintentional. This is indicated by effects rather than motives. Here, we must work backward from discriminatory outcomes to identify the practice or policy that produced them. An example is "side-effect" discrimination that occurs as an unintended by-product of some other practice. Imagine a university that uses an entrance exam to screen applicants. Assume the exam contains no subtle racial biases. Nonetheless, if applicants have been unequally prepared by previous schooling to perform well on this exam, it will produce discriminatory outcomes despite the best of intentions.

A related example is "past-in-present" discrimination where a current practice unwittingly perpetuates prior discrimination. Consider a layoff policy based on seniority. This is not discriminatory in itself. But to whatever extent racial minorities or women have shorter or more episodic work histories as a result of past discrimination, implementing layoffs by seniority will benefit white males and harm minorities and women despite good intentions.

Unintentional discrimination harms many but remains elusive, because it cannot be traced back to a specific person or group with evil motives. In a final twist, it is also possible for "sophisticated racists" who *do* have evil motives to use practices that do not *appear* to intentionally discriminate, knowing that such practices are difficult to identify (Feagin and Feagin 1978).

According to the traditional model, reducing discrimination requires reducing prejudice. According to the institutional model, reducing discrimination requires changing institutions. Whereas the traditional model is "optimistic" that increased social contact will reduce prejudice and discrimination, the institutional model is "pessimistic" that institutions will not simply evolve into less discriminatory behavior. Indeed, the institutional model suggests that if nothing is done, discrimination will continue indefinitely, because institutions are self-perpetuating and because some groups benefit from discriminatory practices.

This is the logic behind affirmative action. It assumes that discrimination will continue unless affirmative action is taken to change the practices that produce it. As a policy, most affirmative action programs involve voluntary efforts to increase the diversity of a pool of qualified applicants. Such policies target informal practices whereby people tend to recruit, hire, or admit people like themselves. By creating policies that require looking beyond familiar social circles when recruiting applicants, affirmative action programs have made modest contributions to reducing discriminatory outcomes.

The persistence of racial inequality in the United States has also prompted a rethinking of the traditional focus on individual prejudice. New research has led one analyst to conclude that in the post–civil rights era, we have entered a time of "racism without racists" (Bonilla-Silva 2003). This argument downplays prejudicial attitudes by suggesting that racism rests on a material foundation of group interests and white privilege. Racism persists because whites derive substantial material benefits from it. Thus, even when whites do not have stereotypical views of minorities, they often perpetuate racism in ways that obscure its victims and beneficiaries.

Where traditional prejudice often assumed biological differences, "color-blind racism" is a more complex racial ideology emphasizing cultural differences. Four distinct frames express color-blind racism (Bonilla-Silva 2003). "Abstract liberalism" uses familiar political discourse about individual rights and equal opportunity to subtly deny structural barriers and implicitly blame victims. "Naturalism" suggests that segregation reflects freely chosen preferences of people to associate with others like them. "Cultural racism" identifies supposedly defective values, beliefs, and practices within minority cultures that are responsible for their lack of progress. Finally, "minimizing racism" acknowledges lingering problems of discrimination while emphasizing how much progress has been made. The implication is that such problems no longer require systemic solutions.

None of these frames sound overtly racist. Indeed, they sound quite reasonable by comparison. They still function, however, as an ideology legitimizing racial inequality. Color-blind racism denies or minimizes institutional barriers and uses the rhetoric of individual opportunity and cultural differences to blame minorities and excuse whites for racial inequality. The emergence of "racism without racists" illustrates how racial meanings and definitions change over time. To analyze such changes, we need to revisit the idea that race is socially constructed.

Racial Formation

The theory of racial formation sees the social construction of race as a contested process of ongoing conflict (Omi and Winant 1994; Winant 1994, 2004). "[R]ace can be defined as *a concept that signifies and symbolizes socio-political conflicts and interests in reference to different types of human bodies*" (Winant 2004, 155; italics in original). The theory of racial formation also insists on the "reality" of race despite its origins as a social construction.

The challenge is to understand the simultaneous "arbitrariness" and "reality" of race. It arises once race is decoupled from biology. This has often led social scientists to reduce race to some other kind of group and transpose their experiences onto races. This problematic response implies that if race is not about biology, then it is not about anything real. The theory of racial formation maintains that race is not about biology, but it is still about something very real. That reality, moreover, needs to be understood on its own terms and not reduced to something else.

One way mainstream perspectives have denied the reality of race is by equating it with ethnicity and using the ethnicity paradigm to analyze race relations. This inevitably turns the discussion back to assimilation. Despite the different histories of racial minorities and white ethnics in the United States, some maintain that racial minorities will eventually undergo the same assimilation as white ethnic groups in earlier decades and centuries. Rather than analyzing race on its own terms, this substitutes the history of ethnic assimilation as a goal for race relations.

This reduction of race to ethnicity is problematic, because it denies the unique features of racial formation (Omi and Winant 1994). It falsely transposes white experience onto nonwhites. It denies ethnic variations within racial groups by equating broad racial categories ("African American") with specific white ethnicities ("Italian"). The ethnicity paradigm also advocates individualistic solutions like upward mobility. The reduction of race to ethnicity thus obscures the distinctiveness of racial oppression and proposes unachievable or undesirable solutions to racial conflict.

An alternative is the class paradigm. This approach reduces race to class or sees the real meaning of race through a class lens. The class paradigm underscores how members of racial minorities are disproportionately located in the working class or lower socioeconomic levels. The logic is that their fates are determined more by their class position than by their racial identity. Moreover, race has been used to reinforce class exploitation when employers designate racial minorities as a secondary labor force, divide workers along racial lines, and play one group off the other to the detriment of both. In this paradigm, race is important for its role in a more fundamental set of class dynamics.

Although it illuminates intersections of race and class, this paradigm is not sufficient for understanding racial formation on its own terms. It simply assumes class is fundamental and race is secondary. Moreover, the equation of racial minorities with only one class oversimplifies race and implies that middle- or upper-class minorities face no racial barriers. "It would be more accurate to say that race and class are competing modalities by which social actors may be organized" (Omi and Winant 1994, 32). If so, the class model with its reduction of race to class is insufficient.

A third alternative is the nation paradigm or the internal colonialism model discussed earlier. As we saw, this model emphasizes differences between the assimilationist history of white ethnic groups and the quasi-colonial status of racial minorities. The metaphor of colonial relations has much to tell us about the history of race relations within the United States. As a viable model of contemporary racial formation, however, it has serious limitations.

In a postcolonial world of global mobility, equating races with geographically bounded nations is an increasingly implausible way to think about race relations. There is substantially more interracial contact in contemporary, racially diverse societies than in classic colonial relations. The nation paradigm also obscures increasingly important class differences among minorities by reducing them to a homogeneous, cultural nationality. Although more instructive than the ethnicity and class paradigms, this one also falls short as a way to understand racial formation.

The problem is that each paradigm—ethnicity, class, and nation—reduces race to something else. Each fails to see race on its own terms. The solution is to move beyond these paradigms to a model that sees race as an independently constructed social reality.

This means seeing racial formation as a process in which social, economic, and political forces determine the meaning of racial categories in a given historical context. To emphasize the importance of process, the term racialization is coined (Omi and Winant 1994) to refer to the extension of racial meanings to relationships that were previously not classified in such terms.

Consider slavery. Although US planters used African Americans as slave labor for centuries, the practice did not originate for racial reasons. It derived from the economic realities of plantation agriculture. In order to be profitable, such agriculture requires the cheapest possible labor. Planters first used white indentured servants from Europe and then captured Native Americans (Geschwender 1978). Neither group worked out well in the long run. Importing African slave labor gradually emerged as a later alternative in the search for cheap labor. Once the practice was institutionalized, slavery was racialized through racist beliefs and legitimations to justify the use of black slave labor by white, "God-fearing" Christians. Slavery became racialized over time. In other words, "we know that racism did not create slavery, but that slavery created racism" (Winant 2004, 84).

Institutions, practices, and beliefs become "raced" when they are shaped and understood through racial categories. Consider how many urban social problems have become "raced," as popular consciousness and media representations link race with poverty, welfare, gangs, drugs, and crime. These issues involve many more whites than nonwhites, but their racialized nature becomes a self-fulfilling prophecy. Thus, people act on racialized beliefs about crime and who commits it, leading to highly disproportionate numbers of racial minorities being suspected, arrested, convicted, and incarcerated for "raced" definitions of crime. The differential penalties for crack cocaine used by minorities and powder cocaine favored by whites is one of the more blatant examples of such racialization.

The most important raced institution is the state. In a racially divided society, the state raciaizes many social dynamics. "For most of U.S. history, the state's main objective in its racial policy was repression and exclusion" (Omi and Winant 1994, 81). It commenced with the Naturalization Act of 1790 that limited citizenship to free, white immigrants. The pattern continued throughout the nineteenth century as racialized policies of repression and exclusion regulated race relations. A more recent example of state power is the creation of the category "Hispanic" in 1980, racializing a new group of people and embedding the category in state policies, practices, and institutions. States and racial formation are thus closely intertwined.

Racial formation is not just about top-down power. When a collective identity is constructed and used to dominate people, that same identity will eventually become a rallying point for resistance. Whether the identity involves race, ethnicity, gender, nationality, or sexuality, domination provokes resistance. Thus, racial formation is a contested process. People fight back, and even powerful elites cannot completely control racial formation for long. It is more accurate to see racial formation—and the social construction of race more generally—as an ongoing struggle over what race means. Authorities use race to subordinate groups, and racially defined groups use it to resist subordination.

The contested quality of racial formation is evident in recent racial politics. On the eve of the civil rights movement of the 1950s and 1960s, racial formation took the form of domination. White power was the norm, backed up by coercion, segregation, exclusion, and violence. In this period, racial formation was a top-down affair, because of the overwhelming power of whites. Collective resistance appeared futile.

Social changes nevertheless created opportunities to contest racial formation. The disruptions of World War II, the partial integration of the armed forces, the mechanization of Southern agriculture, and migration from the rural South to the urban North all undermined racial domination. When the civil rights movement appeared in the 1950s, it echoed the ethnicity paradigm with themes of individualism, opportunity, and integration. That such a modest agenda provoked such a ferocious backlash is revealing. Simply asking for what whites took for granted amounted to an almost revolutionary challenge to racial domination.

The movement soon transcended the ethnicity paradigm, in part because of the resistance it encountered to its integrationist goals. But the shift was also sparked by "the rearticulation of black collective subjectivity" (Omi and Winant 1994, 98). In other words, black activists made the redefinition of racial identity a central goal. The movement made racial formation a two-way street by challenging static notions of race and racial hierarchy. In effect, activists reclaimed the meaning of race from a white power structure and made it their own.

These events transformed the civil rights movement. Activists adopted multiple racial paradigms and diverse political strategies. "Entrists" argued that strategic participation in elections and mainstream institutions could transform the state. Socialists tried to build class alliances across racial lines and link struggles against racism and capitalism. Nationalists encouraged a separatist response of institution building and cultural pride within minority communities. None met with complete success. The entrist, socialist, and nationalist strategies had the same shortcomings as the ethnicity, class, and nation paradigms on which they were based. Each reduced race to something else and missed the complexity of racial formation. This activism nevertheless shattered older understandings of race and put racial formation center stage (Omi and Winant 1994).

As the movement became more complex, so did the response of the raced state. In some instances, it brutally repressed militant leaders and groups that challenged its authority. More broadly, the state shifted from racial domination to racial hegemony. This meant incorporating oppositional challenges in ways that defused their transformative potential. "Under hegemonic conditions, opposition and difference are not repressed, excluded, or silenced (at least not primarily). Rather, they are inserted, often after suitable modification, within a 'modern' (or perhaps 'postmodern') social order" (Winant 1994, 29). Although hegemony might be less violent than outright domination, it amounts to a more complex system of racial control.

Racial hegemony has sparked competing racial projects on both sides. On the reactionary side, the far right still equates race with biology and advocates violence to prevent all forms of "race mixing." The new right translates old-fashioned racism into code words that are not explicitly racist but nonetheless trigger racist attitudes and actions among those who know the code. The neoconservative right uses egalitarian language to advocate individualism and reject group-oriented solutions hey use the rhetoric of a color-blind society while ignoring the historical legacy of being a color-conscious society. This is the most sophisticated defense of the white power structure. It uses familiar, liberal ideas to argue for illiberal ends. It exemplifies "racism without racists" advocating "color-blind racism" (Bonilla-Silva 2003).

On the progressive side, pragmatic liberalism appeals to group identities to mobilize political support for racially progressive policies, including affirmative action. It advocates pluralism and tolerance and attempts a difficult balancing act between advancing minority rights and maintaining social peace. Finally, radical democrats seek full acceptance of racial difference and identities in the name of autonomy. They seek democratization of the state and redistributive policies to foster racial equality (Winant 1994).

Racial formation is thus a dynamic, contested set of social and political meanings. The current diversity of racial politics—consisting of at least five distinct and competing racial projects—testifies to the fluidity of racial formation and the social construction of race.

The Construction of Whiteness

It is intriguing that whites attribute "race" to "people of color" but don't see "white" as a "color."

It's as if race applies to people who differ from the norm but not the group that is the norm. Given this, it is important to turn the microscope back on the dominant group and its construction of whiteness.

Like other socially constructed racial categories, whiteness emerged historically. Consider how "the Irish became white" over decades of conflict and eventual assimilation in the United States. More pointedly, this is the story of "how the Catholic Irish, an oppressed race in Ireland, became part of an oppressing race in America" (Ignatiev 1995, 1). When Irish immigrants first arrived in the United States, they were perceived as an inferior race by Anglo-Saxon powers on both sides of the Atlantic. However, rather than joining with other subordinate races, the Irish distanced themselves from minorities and aligned with whites. They pursued the classic assimilationist trade-off: "In becoming white the Irish ceased to be Green" (Ignatiev 1995, 3). This suggests that assimilation means moving toward the dominant group and away from minorities, because the dominant group is defined precisely by its distance from racial minorities. Until a group made both moves, assimilation was unlikely.

The Irish example fits a broader template of how whiteness was created through an amalgamation of initially diverse ethnicities. This history falls into three periods (Jacobson 1998, 13–14). From the founding of the country into the mid-nineteenth century, citizenship was confined to "free white" immigrants, implicitly meaning Anglo-Saxon and sometimes other Northern European peoples. From the mid-nineteenth century to the early twentieth century, immigration from Southern, Central, and Eastern Europe challenged the equation of whiteness and Northern European descent. During this period, a complex racial politics initially defined. these immigrants as inferior races at the same time that they sought a broadening of the definition of "white" to include them. It has only been since the 1920s that ethnic differences were downplayed and a more generic white identity was forged. This period "redrew the dominant racial configuration along the strict, binary line of white and black, creating Caucasians where before had been so many Celts, Hebrews, Teutons, Mediterraneans, and Slavs" (Jacobson 1998, 14).

By the mid-twentieth century, whiteness became the dominant racial norm. This proved short-lived, as "it is no longer possible to assume a 'normalized' whiteness, whose invisibility and relatively monolithic character signify immunity from political or cultural challenge" (Winant 2004, 50). As race-based social movements recast their own racial subjectivity, white identity also became more self-conscious.

As white dominance was challenged, it triggered "grievances of the privileged." Some whites claimed they were under attack "simply for their race." Others decried a world in which minorities seemed to get advantages withheld from whites through "reverse discrimination." Still other whites lamented the lack of a distinct and vivid white culture they could identify with just as other races identified with theirs. Such defensive responses imply that although whites are still dominant, such dominance can no longer be taken for granted.

These responses also belie the ongoing privileges of the dominant group. White privilege means that despite recent challenges to the racial order, it continues to be organized in ways that benefit the dominant group. Such privilege is often invisible to those who benefit, while being highly visible to those who pay the price.

This is nicely captured in Peggy McIntosh's (2005) efforts to teach about male privilege in women's studies courses. Her female students quickly grasped the concept and readily supplied examples. Her male students conceded that women faced certain disadvantages but denied their male privilege. To understand this denial, McIntosh examined her own dual status as a white woman. As a woman, she could readily see male privilege. As a white, she had difficulty seeing her racial privilege, just as men had difficulty seeing male privilege. The broader pattern is that privileged groups rarely recognize their own privileges and perceive any challenge to them as victimization. Such complaints are not simply disingenuous; they reflect a real inability to see how whiteness and maleness continue conferring privileges even in a social order undergoing challenge and reformulation.

These privileges come in two categories. "Unearned advantages" are "positive" privileges that should not be abolished but made available to all. The privilege of not being a crime suspect simply on the basis of one's race is an unearned advantage for whites that should ideally be an unearned entitlement for all. "Conferred dominance" involves "negative" privileges that need to be abolished to create racial equality. Discrimination that benefits dominant groups at the expense of subordinate ones fits this type; it should be abolished in any society seeking racial equality (McIntosh 2005).

These are now the goals of a "new abolitionist racial project." Proponents of this movement identify white privilege as the lynchpin of white supremacy and see rejection of privilege by whites as essential to creating a just racial order. Advocates put a positive spin on the epithet "race traitor" by countering that "treason to whiteness is loyalty to humanity" (Winant 2004, 63). As this racial project unfolds alongside others described earlier, it is difficult to deny that we are in a period of highly contested racial formation.

Understanding race requires looking beyond taken-for-granted appearances. It also requires a multilayered analysis of domination. Critical sociology is tailor-made for both tasks. It illuminates both the social construction of race and the challenges seeking to deconstruct racial hierarchies in the name of a more egalitarian society.

The Study of the Negro Problems

The Academy for Future Science Faculty

HOW DO WE KNOW WHAT WE KNOW?

THE STUDY OF THE NEGRO PROBLEMS

BY W.E.B. DUBOIS

The present period in the development of sociological study is a trying one; it is the period of observation, research and comparison—work always wearisome, often aimless, without well-settled principles and guiding lines, and subject ever to the pertinent criticism: What, after all, has been accomplished? To this the one positive answer which years of research and speculation have been able to return is that the phenomena of society are worth the most careful and systematic study, and whether or not this study may eventually lead to a systematic body of knowledge deserving the name of science, it cannot in any case fail to give the world a mass of truth worth the knowing.

Being then in a period of observation and comparison, we must confess to ourselves that the sociologists of few nations have so good an opportunity for observing the growth and evolution of society as those of the United States. The rapid rise of a young country, the vast social changes, the wonderful economic development, the bold political experiments, and the contact of varying moral standards—all these make for American students crucial tests of social action, microcosmic reproductions of long centuries of world history, and rapid—even violent—repetitions of great social problems. Here is a field for the sociologist—a field rich, but little worked, and full of great possibilities. European scholars envy our opportunities and it must be said to our credit that great interest in the observation of social phenomena has been aroused in the last decade—an interest of which much is ephemeral and superficial, but which opens the way for broad scholarship and scientific effort.

In one field, however,—and a field perhaps larger than any other single domain of social phenomena, there does not seem to have been awakened as yet a fitting realization of the opportunities for scientific inquiry. This is the group of social phenomena arising from the presence in this land of eight million persons of African descent.

It is my purpose in this paper to discuss certain considerations concerning the study of the social problems affecting American Negroes; first, as to the historical development of these problems; then as to the necessity for their careful systematic study at the present time; thirdly, as to the results of scientific study of the Negro up to this time; fourthly, as to the scope and method which future scientific inquiry should take, and, lastly, regarding the agencies by which this work can best be carried out.

I. DEVELOPMENT OF THE NEGRO PROBLEMS.

A social problem is the failure of an organized social group to realize its group ideals, through the inability to adapt a certain desired line of action to given conditions of life. . If, for instance, a government founded on universal manhood suffrage has a portion of its population so ignorant as to be unable to vote intelligently, such ignorance becomes a menacing social problem.

W. E. B. DuBois, "The Study of the Negro Problems," *W. E. B. DuBois on Sociology and the Black Community*. Copyright © 1978 by University of Chicago Press. Reprinted with permission.

The impossibility of economic and social development in a community where a large per cent of the population refuse to abide by the social rules of order, makes a problem of crime and lawlessness. Prostitution becomes a social problem when the demands of luxurious home life conflict with marriage customs.

Thus a social problem is ever a relation between conditions and action, and as conditions and actions vary and change from group to group from time to time and from place to place, so social problems change, develop and grow. Consequently, though we ordinarily speak of the Negro problem as though it were one unchanged question, students must recognize the obvious facts that this problem, like others, has had a long historical development, has changed with the growth and evolution of the nation; moreover, that it is not one problem, but rather a plexus of social problems, some new, some old, some simple, some complex; and these problems have their one bond of unity in the act that they group themselves about those Africans whom two centuries, of slave-trading brought into the land.

2. THE PRESENT NEGRO PROBLEMS.

Such are some of the changes of condition and social movement which have, since 1619, altered and broadened the social problems grouped about the American Negro. In this development of successive questions about one centre, there is nothing peculiar to American history. Given any fixed condition or fact—a river Nile, a range of Alps, an alien race, or a national idea—and problems of society will at every stage of advance group themselves about it. All social growth means a succession of social problems—they constitute growth, they denote that laborious and often baffling adjustment of action and condition which is the essence of progress, and while a particular fact or circumstance may serve in one country as a rallying point of many intricate questions of adjustment, the absence of that particular fact would not mean the absence of all social problems. Questions of labor, caste, ignorance and race were bound to arise in America; they were simply complicated here and intensified there by the presence of the Negro.

Turning now from this brief summary of the varied phases of these questions, let us inquire somewhat more carefully into the form under which the Negro problems present themselves today after 275 years of evolution. Their existence is plainly manifested by the fact that a definitely segregated mass of eight millions of Americans do not wholly share the national life of the people; are not an integral part of the social body. The points at which they fail to be incorporated into this group life constitute the particular Negro problems, which can be divided into two distinct but correlated parts, depending on two facts:

First—Negroes do not share the full national life because as a mass they have not reached a sufficiently high grade of culture.

Secondly—They do not share the full national life because there has always existed in America a conviction—varying in intensity, but always widespread—that people of Negro blood should not be admitted into the group life of the nation no matter what their condition might be.

Considering the problems arising from the backward development of Negroes, we may say that the mass of this race does not reach the social standards of the nation with respect to

a. Economic condition.
b. Mental training.
c. Social efficiency.

Even if special legislation and organized relief intervene, freedmen always start life under an economic disadvantage which generations, perhaps centuries, cannot overcome. Again, of all the important constituent parts of our nation, the Negro is by far the most ignorant; nearly half of the race are absolutely illiterate, only a minority of the other half have thorough common school training, and but a remnant are liberally educated. The great deficiency of the Negro, however, is his small knowledge of the art of organized social life—that last expression of human culture. His development in group life was abruptly broken off by the slave ship, directed into abnormal channels and dwarfed by the Black Codes, and suddenly wrenched anew by the Emancipation Proclamation. He finds himself, therefore, peculiarly weak in that nice adaptation of individual life to the life of the group which is the essence of civilization. This is shown in the grosser forms of sexual immorality, disease and crime, and also in the difficulty of race organization for common ends in economic or in intellectual lines.

For these reasons the Negro would fall behind any average modern nation, and he is unusually handicapped in the midst of a nation which excels in its extraordinary economic development, its average of popular intelligence and in the boldness of its experiments in organized social life.

These problems of poverty, ignorance and social degradation differ from similar problems the world over in one important particular, and that is the fact that they are complicated by a peculiar environment. This constitutes the second class of Negro problems, and they rest, as has been said, on the widespread conviction among Americans that no persons of Negro descent should become constituent members of the social body. This feeling gives rise to economic problems, to educational problems, and nice questions of social morality; it makes it more difficult for black men to earn a living or spend their earnings as they will; it gives them poorer school facilities and restricted contact with cultured classes; and it becomes, throughout the land, a cause and excuse for discontent, lawlessness, laziness and injustice.

3. THE NECESSITY OF CAREFULLY STUDYING THESE PROBLEMS.

Such, barely stated, are the elements of the present Negro problems. It is to little purpose however to name the elements of a problem unless we can also say accurately to what extent each element enters into the final result: whether, for instance, the present difficulties arise more largely from ignorance than from prejudice, or vice versa. This we. do not know, and here it is that every intelligent discussion of the American Negro comes to a standstill. Nearly a hundred years ago Thomas Jefferson complained that the nation had never studied the real condition of the slaves and that, therefore, all general conclusions about them were extremely hazardous. We of another age can scarcely say that we have made material progress in this study. Yet these problems, so vast and intricate, demanding trained research and expert analysis, touching questions that affect the very foundation of the republic and of human progress, increasing and multiplying year by year, would seem to urge the nation with increasing force to measure and trace and understand thoroughly the underlying elements of this example of human evolution.

Now first we should study the Negro problems in order to distinguish between the different and distinct problems affecting this race. Nothing makes intelligent discussion of the Negro's position so fruitless as the repeated failure to discriminate between the different questions that concern him. If a Negro discusses the question, he is apt to discuss simply the problem of race prejudice; if a Southern white man writes on the subject he is apt to discuss problems of ignorance, crime and social degradation; and yet each calls the problem he discusses the Negro problem, leaving in the dark background the really crucial question as to the relative importance of the many problems involved. Before we can begin to study the Negro intelligently, we must realize definitely that not only is he affected by all the varying social forces that act on any nation at his stage of advancement, but that in addition to these there is reacting upon him the mighty power of a peculiar and unusual social environment which affects to some extent every other social force.

In the second place we should seek to know and measure carefully all the forces and conditions that go to make up these different problems, to trace the historical development of these conditions, and discover as far as possible the probable trend of further development. Without doubt this would be difficult work, and it can with much truth be objected that we cannot ascertain, by the methods of sociological research known to us, all such facts thoroughly and accurately. To this objection it is only necessary to answer that however difficult it may be to know all about the Negro, it is certain that we can know vastly more than we do, and that we can have our knowledge in more systematic and intelligible form. As things are, our opinions upon the Negro are more matters of faith than of knowledge. Every schoolboy is ready to discuss the matter, and there are few men that have not settled convictions. Such a situation is dangerous. Whenever any nation allows impulse, whim or hasty conjecture to usurp the place of conscious, normative, intelligent action, it is in grave danger. The sole aim of any society is to settle its problems in accordance with its highest ideals, and the only rational method of accomplishing this is to study those problems in the light of the best scientific research.

Finally, the American Negro deserves study for the great end of advancing the cause of science in general. No such opportunity to watch and measure the history and development of a great race of men ever presented itself to the scholars of a modern nation. If they miss this opportunity—if they do the work in a slip-shod, unsystematic manner—if they dally with the truth to humor the whims of the day, they do far more than hurt the good name of the American people; they hurt the cause of scientific truth the world over, they voluntarily decrease human knowledge of a universe of which we are ignorant enough, and they degrade the high end of truth-seeking in a day when they need more and more to dwell upon its sanctity.

4. The Work Already Accomplished.

It may be said that it is not altogether correct to assert that few attempts have been made to study these problems or to put the nation in possession of a body of truth in accordance with which it might act intelligently. It is far from my purpose to disparage in any way the work already done by students of these questions; much valuable effort has without doubt been put upon the field, and yet a careful survey of the field seems but to emphasize the fact that the work done bears but small proportion to the work still to be done.

Moreover the studies made hitherto can as a whole be justly criticised in three particulars: (1) They have not been based on a thorough knowledge of details; (2) they have been unsystematical; (3) they have been uncritical.

In few subjects have historians been more content to go on indefinitely repeating current traditions and uninvestigated facts. We are still gravely told that the slave trade ceased in 1808, that the docility of Africans made slave insurrections almost unknown, and that the Negro never developed in this country a self-conscious group life before 1860. In the hasty endeavor to cover a broad subject when the details were unknown, much superficial work has been current, like that, for instance, of a newspaper reporter who spent "the odd intervals of leisure in active newspaper work" for "nearly eighteen months," in the District of Columbia, and forthwith published a study of 80,000 Negroes, with observations on their institutions and development.

Again, the work done has been lamentably unsystematic and fragmentary. Scientific work must be subdivided, but conclusions which affect the whole subject must be based on a study of the whole. One cannot study the Negro in freedom and come to general conclusions about his destiny without knowing his history in slavery. A vast set of problems having a common centre must, too, be studied according to some general plan, if the work of different students is to be compared or to go toward building a unified body of knowledge. A plan once begun must be carried out, and not like that of our erratic census reports, after allowing us to follow the size of farms in the South for three decades, suddenly leave us wondering as to the relation of farms and farm families. Students of black codes should not stop suddenly with 1863, and travelers and observers whose testimony would be of great value if arranged with some system and reasonably limited in time and space, must not ramble on without definite plan or purpose and render their whole work of doubtful value.

Most unfortunate of all, however, is the fact that so much of the work done on the Negro question is notoriously uncritical; uncritical from lack of discrimination in the selection and weighing of evidence; uncritical in choosing the proper point of view from which to study these problems, and, finally, uncritical from the distinct bias in the minds of so many writers. To illustrate, the layman who does not pretend to first hand knowledge of the subject and who would learn of students is today woefully puzzled by absolutely contradictory evidence. One student declares that Negroes are advancing in knowledge and ability; that they are working, establishing homes, and going into business, and that the problem will soon be one of the past. Another student of equal learning declares that the Negro is degenerating—sinking into crime and social immorality, receiving little help from education, still in the main a menial servant, and destined in a short time to settle the problem by dying entirely out. Such and many other contradictory conclusions arise from the uncritical use of material. A visitor to a great Negro school in the South catches the inspiration of youth, studies the work of graduates, and imbibes the hopes of teachers and immediately infers from the situation of a few hundred the general condition of a population numbering twice that of Holland. A college graduate sees the slums of a Southern city, looks at the plantation field hands, and has some experience with Negro servants, and from the laziness, crime and disease which he finds, draws conclusions as to eight millions of people, stretched from Maine to Texas and from Florida to Washington. We continually judge the whole from the part we are familiar with; we continually assume the material we have at hand to be typical; we reverently receive a column of figures without asking who collected them, how they were arranged, how far they are valid and what chances of error they contain; we receive the testimony of men without asking whether they were trained or ignorant, careful or careless, truthful or given to exaggeration, and, above all, whether they are giving facts or opinions. It is so easy for a man who has already formed his conclusions to receive any and all testimony in their favor without carefully weighing and testing it, that we sometimes find in serious scientific studies very curious proof of broad conclusions. To cite an extreme case, in a recently published study of the Negro, a. part of the argument as to the physical condition of all these millions, is made to rest on the measurement of fifteen black boys in a New York reformatory.

The widespread habit of studying the Negro from one point of view only, that of his influence on the white inhabitants, is also responsible for much uncritical work. The slaves are generally treated as one inert changeless mass, and most studies of slavery apparently have no conception of a social evolution and development among them. The slave code of a state is given, the progress of anti-slavery sentiment, the economic results of the system and the general influence of man on master are studied, but of the slave himself, of his group life and social institutions, of remaining traces of his African tribal life, of his amusements, his conversion to Christianity, his acquiring of the English tongue—in fine, of his whole reaction against his environment, of all this we hear little or nothing, and would apparently be expected to believe that the Negro arose from the dead in 1863. Yet all the testimony of law and custom, of tradition and present social condition, shows us that the Negro at the time of emancipation had passed through a social evolution which far separated him from his savage ancestors.

The most baneful cause of uncritical study of the Negro is the manifest and far-reaching bias of writers. Americans are born in many cases with deep, fierce convictions on the Negro question, and in other cases imbibe them from their environment. When such men come to write on the subject, without technical training, without breadth of view, and in some cases without a deep sense of the sanctity of scientific truth, their testimony, however interesting—as opinion, must of necessity be worthless as science. Thus too often the testimony of Negroes and their friends has to be thrown out of court on account of the manifest prejudice of the writers; on the other hand, the testimony of many other writers in the North and especially in the South has to be received with reserve on account of too evident bias.

Such facts make the path of students and foreign observers peculiarly thorny. The foreigner's views, if he be not exceptionally astute, will depend largely on his letters of introduction; the home student's views, on his birthplace and parentage. All students are apt to fail to recognize the magnitude and importance of these problems, and to succumb to the vulgar temptation of basing on any little contribution they make to the study of these problems, general conclusions as to the origin and destiny of the Negro people in time and eternity. Thus we possess endless final judgments as to the American Negro emanating from men of influence and learning, in the very face of the fact known to every accurate student, that there exists today no sufficient material of proven reliability, upon which any scientist can base definite and final conclusions as to the present condition and tendencies of the eight million American Negroes; and that any person or publication purporting to give such conclusions simply makes statements which go beyond the reasonably proven evidence.

5. A Program of Future Study

If we admit the deep importance of the Negro problems, the necessity of studying them, and certain shortcomings in work done up to this time, it would seem to be the clear duty of the American people, in the interests of scientific knowledge and social reform, to begin a broad and systematic study of the history and condition of the American Negroes. The scope and method of this study, however, needs to be generally agreed upon beforehand in its main outlines, not to hinder the freedom of individual students, but to systematize and unify effort so as to cover the wide field of investigation.

The scope of any social study is first of all limited by the general attitude of public opinion toward truth and truth- seeking. If in regard to any social problem there is for any reason a persistent refusal on the part of the people to allow the truth to be known, then manifestly that problem cannot be studied. Undoubtedly much of the unsatisfactory work already done with regard to the Negro is due to this cause; the intense feeling that preceded and followed the war made a calm balanced research next to impossible. Even today there are certain phases of this question which we cannot hope to be allowed to study dispassionately and thoroughly, and these phases, too, are naturally those uppermost in the public mind. For instance, it is extremely doubtful if any satisfactory study of Negro crime and lynching can be made for a generation or more, in the present condition of the public mind, which renders it almost impossible to get at the facts and real conditions. On the other hand, public opinion has in the last decade become sufficiently liberal to open a broad field of investigation to students, and here lies the chance for effective work.

The right to enter this field undisturbed and untrammeled will depend largely on the attitude of science itself. Students must be careful to insist that science as such—be it physics, chemistry, psychology, or sociology—has but one simple aim: the discovery of truth. Its results lie open for the use of all men—merchants, physicians, men of letters, and philanthropists, but the aim of science itself is simple truth. Any attempt to give it a double aim, to make social reform the immediate instead of the mediate object of a search for truth, will inevitably tend to defeat both objects. The frequent alliance of sociological research with various panaceas and particular schemes of reform, has resulted in closely connecting social investigation with a good deal of groundless assumption and humbug in the popular mind. There will be at first some difficulty in bringing the Southern people, both black and white, to conceive of an earnest, careful study of the Negro problem which has not back of it some scheme of race amalgamation, political jobbery, or deportation to Africa. The new study of the American Negro must avoid such misapprehensions from the outset, by insisting that historical and statistical research has but one object, the ascertainment of the facts as to the social forces and conditions of one-eighth of the inhabitants of the land. Only by such rigid adherence to the true object of the scholar, can statesmen and philanthropists of all shades of belief be put into possession of a reliable body of truth which may guide their efforts to the best and largest success.

In the next place, a study of the Negro, like the study of any subject, must start out with certain generally admitted postulates. We must admit, for instance, that the field of study is large and varying, and that what is true of the Negro in Massachusetts is not necessarily true of the Negro in Louisiana; that what was true of the Negro in 1850 was not necessarily true in 1750; and that there are many distinct social problems affecting the Negro. Finally, if we would rally to this common ground of scientific inquiry all partisans and advocates, we must explicitly admit what all implicitly postulate—namely, that the Negro is a member of the human race, and as one who, in the light of history and experience, is capable to a degree of improvement and culture, is entitled to have his Interests considered according to his numbers in all conclusions as to the common weal.

With these preliminary considerations we may say that the study of the Negro falls naturally into two categories, which though difficult to separate in practice, must for the sake of logical clearness, be kept distinct. They are *(a)* the study of the Negro as a social group, *(b)* the study of his peculiar social environment.

The study of the Negro as a social group may be, for convenience, divided into four not exactly logical but seemingly most practicable divisions, viz:

1. Historical study,
2. Statistical investigation.
3. Anthropological measurement.
4. Sociological interpretation.

The material at hand for historical research is rich and abundant; there are the colonial statutes and records, the partially accessible archives of Great Britain, France and Spain, the collections of historical societies, the vast number of executive and congressional reports and documents, the state statutes, reports and publications, the reports of institutions and societies, the personal narratives and opinions of various observers and the periodical press covering nearly three centuries. From these sources can be gathered much new information upon the economic and social development of the Negro, upon the rise and decline of the slave-trade, the character, distribution and state of culture of the Africans, the evolution of the slave codes as expressing the life of the South, the rise of such peculiar expressions of Negro social history, as the Negro church, the economics of plantation life, the possession of private property by slaves, and the history of the oft-forgotten class of free Negroes. Such historical research must be sub-divided in space and limited in time by the nature of the subject, the history of the different colonies and groups being followed and compared, the different periods of development receiving special study, and the whole subject being reviewed from different aspects.

The collection of statistics should be carried on with increased care and thoroughness. It is no credit to a great modern nation that so much well-grounded doubt can be thrown on our present knowledge of the simple matters of number, age, sex and conjugal condition in regard to our Negro population. General statistical investigations should avoid seeking to tabulate more intricate social conditions than the ones indicated. The concrete social status of the Negro can only be ascertained by intensive studies carried on in definitely limited localities, by competent investigators, in accordance with one general plan. Statistical study by groups is apt to be more accurately done and more easily accomplished, and able to secure more competent and responsible agents than any general census. General averages in so complicated a subject are apt to be dangerously misleading. This study should seek to ascertain by the most approved methods of social measurement the size and condition of families, the occupations and wages, the illiteracy of adults and education of children, the standard of living, the character of the dwellings, the property owned and rents paid, and the character of the organized group life. Such investigations should be extended until they cover the typical group life of Negroes in all sections of the land and should be so repeated from time to time in the same localities and with the same methods, as to be a measure of social development.

The third division of study is anthropological measurement, and it includes a scientific study of the Negro body. The most obvious peculiarity of the Negro—a peculiarity which is a large element in many of the problems affecting him—is his physical unlikeness to the people with whom he has been brought into contact. This difference is so striking that it has become the basis of a mass of theory, assumption and suggestion which is deep-rooted and yet rests on the flimsiest basis of scientific fact. That there are differences between the white and black races is certain, but just what those differences are is known to none with an approach to accuracy. Yet here in America is the most remarkable opportunity ever offered of studying these differences, of noting influences of climate and physical environment, and particularly of studying the effect of amalgamating two of the most diverse races in the world—another subject which rests under a cloud of ignorance.

The fourth division of this investigation is sociological interpretation; it should include the arrangement and interpretation of historical and statistical matter in the light of the experience of other nations and other ages; it should aim to study those finer manifestations of social life which history can but mention and which statistics can not count, such as the expression of Negro life as found in their hundred newspapers, their considerable literature, their music and folklore and their germ of esthetic life—in fine, in all the movements and customs among them that manifest the existence of a distinct social mind.

The second category of studies of the Negro has to do with his peculiar social environment. It will be difficult, as has been intimated, to separate a study of the group from a study of the environment, and yet the group action and the reaction of the surroundings must be kept clearly distinct if we expect to comprehend the Negro problems. The study of the environment may be carried on at the same time with a study of the group, only the two sets of forces must receive distinct measurement.

In such a field of inquiry it will be found difficult to do more than subdivide inquiry in time and space. The attempt should be made to isolate and study the tangible phenomena of Negro prejudice in all possible cases; its effect on the Negro's physical development, on his mental acquisitiveness, on his moral and social condition, as manifested in economic life, in legal sanctions and in crime and lawlessness. So, too, the influence of that same prejudice on American life and character would explain the otherwise inexplicable changes through which Negro prejudice has passed.

The plan of study thus sketched is, without doubt, long, difficult and costly, and yet is not more than commensurable with the size and importance of the subject with which it is to deal. It will take years and decades to carry out such a plan, with the barest measure of success, and yet there can be no doubt but that this plan or something similar to it, points to the quickest path toward the ultimate solution of the present difficulties.

THE ACADEMY FOR FUTURE SCIENCE FACULTY

Randomized Controlled Trial of Theory-Driven Coaching to Shape Development and Diversity of Early-Career Scientists

BY BHOOMI K. THAKORE, MICHELLE E. NAFFZIGER-HIRSCH, JENNIFER L. RICHARDSON, SIMON N. WILLIAMS, AND RICHARD MCGEE, JR.

Abstract

Background

Approaches to training biomedical scientists have created a talented research community. However, they have failed to create a professional workforce that includes many racial and ethnic minorities and women in proportion to their representation in the population or in PhD training. This is particularly true at the faculty level. Explanations for the absence of diversity in faculty ranks can be found in social science theories that reveal processes by which individuals develop identities, experiences, and skills required to be seen as legitimate within the profession.

Methods/Design

Using the social science theories of Communities of Practice, Social Cognitive Career Theory, identity formation, and cultural capital, we have developed and are testing a novel coaching-based model to address some of the limitations of previous diversity approaches. This coaching intervention (*The Academy for Future Science Faculty)* includes annual in-person meetings of students and trained faculty Career Coaches, along with ongoing virtual coaching, group meetings and communication. The model is being tested as a randomized controlled trial with two cohorts of biomedical PhD students from across the U.S., one recruited at the start of their PhDs and one nearing completion. Stratification into the experimental and control groups, and to coaching groups within the experimental arms, achieved equal numbers of students by race, ethnicity and gender to the extent possible. A fundamental design element of the *Academy* is to teach and make visible the social science principles which highly influence scientific advancement, as well as acknowledging the extra challenges faced by underrepresented groups working to be seen as legitimate within the scientific communities.

Discussion

The strategy being tested is based upon a novel application of the well-established principles of deploying highly skilled coaches, selected and trained for their ability to develop talents of others. This coaching model is intended to be a complement, rather than a substitute, for traditional mentoring in biomedical research training, and is being tested as such.

Keywords

Biomedical sciences, Biomedical diversity, Graduate students, Intervention, Randomized control trial, Coaching model

Copyright © Bhoomi K Thakore, Michelle E Naffziger-Hirsch, Jennifer L Richardson, Simon N Williams and Richard McGee, Jr (CC by 4.0) at https://bmcmededuc.biomedcentral.com/articles/10.1186/1472-6920-14-160.

Background

From any perspective other than diversity, the United States has been very successful at developing a talented and creative community of biomedical scientists. However, previous approaches to training have failed to produce satisfactory improvement in the participation of women and individuals from underrepresented minority groups (URMs)a, especially beyond the early stages of training. Over the past several decades, the fraction of URMs in faculty and leadership positions has changed little [1, 2]. According to the 2010 Census, URMs make up approximately 30% of the U.S. population. However, individuals from these groups only make up approximately 9% of Science, Technology, Engineering and Math (STEM) PhD recipients [3]; National Academy of Sciences, National Academy of Engineering, Institute of Medicine, [4]. Furthermore, only 4% of faculty in basic science departments of U.S. medical schools and biological science departments at the top 50 colleges and universities are URM faculty – a number that has changed little in several decades [1]. This lack of improvement, despite vast infusions of money and the time and energy of many dedicated people, suggests that these efforts are either trying to fix the wrong problem or using the wrong methods to address the problems [3, 4, 5, 6]. This lack of diversity in the faculty ranks is the central problem our study is attempting to change. However, we are starting from the time of PhD as the vision and trajectories toward an academic career are critically set during early research training.

Most of the efforts to increase diversity have focused on getting a more diverse pool of young scientists up to the starting line of the PhD (e.g. [7]). These approaches are pursued with the assumption that standard training practices will propel more of them to higher levels of success. However, these standard practices often overlook the very strong social and psychological processes that mediate not only development but perceptions of ability and talent.

Young scientists acquire their research skills under the influences of a sequential series of research mentors through their PhD and postdoctoral training. There is nothing more central to the training of young scientists than a mentor's guidance. Done right, mentors with adequate skills and time to mentor can have positive impacts on students' scientific development. At its best, traditional mentoring has the ability to both pass on informal knowledge and allow individuals to "find" other young scientists with mutual interests and develop supportive networks [3, 8].

However, the amount and quality of learning and career advice passed on from mentor to mentee can vary widely. Indeed, one of the major limitations of classical mentoring is that it is pedagogically idiosyncratic. Research groups, usually led by a Principal Investigator (PI)/Mentor, in many ways emulate Darwinian natural selection and "survival of the fittest". The unspoken assumption is that everyone has the same opportunity to develop within the community and therefore the best will "naturally" rise to the top. In theory, mentors provide the informal and formal guidance needed so that those who are the most skilled and independent will thrive. This reliance on informal mentoring is in sharp contrast to many other approaches to development of talent, such as in athletics or the arts. In those fields, rising talent is developed through the guidance of highly skilled professional coaches, leaving less to the often unpredictable elements of mentoring.

A number of programs have focused on improving the quality of mentoring through systematic mentor training [9, 10, 11, 12]. Although the findings of these training programs are encouraging, we argue that mentoring as a construct is limited for four main reasons. First, mentors face many competing, sometimes incompatible, demands to both produce research for grant renewals and to enable students and postdocs to practice developing novel ideas. Second, good mentoring requires dedicated time, but time has become less available as PIs have to write more grants, lead research teams of increasing size and complexity, and focus on their own survival to support their research groups. Third, PIs constantly face the challenge of assessing the capabilities of different members of their lab group and making judgments of whom to promote to subsequent career stages. These assessments are often subject to unconscious or conscious biases about individual capabilities based on prior educational path and social assumptions based on gender, race, and ethnicity. Fourth, in the informal teaching and learning environment of research groups, a new member who comes from a background that is different from most group members will have a more difficult time figuring out how to excel within the group. As discussed later, we argue that a coaching model can serve to substantially offset these limitations of the traditional mentoring model.

A rare opportunity arose to develop and test our coaching intervention through the American Recovery and Reinvestment Act (ARRA) of 2009. Through an NIH Director's ARRA Funded Pathfinder Award to Promote Diversity in the Scientific Workforce, we created, "*The Academy for Future Science Faculty*" (referred to henceforth as the *Academy*). The *Academy* recruited established senior life scientists with demonstrated expertise in mentoring young scientists, and provided them with additional training to serve as Coaches in the *Academy*. We recruited two cohorts of PhD students: one just before they started the PhD (*Academy I*) and one near the end of the PhD (*Academy II*). These students were provided with an extensive and unique in-person and virtual coached experience over 2–3 years.

Methods

Coaching design and training informed by social science theories

The complexity of the social and cultural factors that impact all young scientists can be understood through the application of social science theories. As will become clear, the social science theories help to explain the lack of improvement in diversity and serve to substantiate the need for a new supplementary coaching model. Our prior research has utilized these social science theories in understanding how students explore and define their science career goals and science identity [13]. We build on these theories by applying them directly to the design of our *Academy* intervention, specifically through the choice and design of the activities and the training of Coaches.

Communities of Practice

Communities of Practice (CoP) theory derives from the work of Lave and Wenger [14] (see also [15, 16, 17]) and helps explain how individuals with common interests and goals work together toward those goals. CoP theory also identifies the processes by which new individuals enter groups and gradually acquire the informal knowledge and practices of the group. According to Wenger [15], the ideal trajectory leads from newcomer to fully accepted and valued member. However, other trajectories can lead to marginalization for individuals who seemingly "do not belong" based on perceptions of lesser competence with the core skills of the group.

PhD programs also function as critical CoPs for incoming students. In U.S. biomedical PhD programs, before students enter their dissertation lab, the program itself strongly informs students' experiences and helps shape their professional trajectory. But even in program CoPs, URM students can face greater barriers establishing their legitimacy and face greater risks of marginalization [18, 19]. Currently, there are a few examples of success in mitigating these issues. The Minority Access to Research Careers (MARC) and the Research Initiative in Scientific Enhancement (RISE) programs (two of the student development programs of the National Institute of General Medical Sciences (NIGMS)) are the entry point for many URM students into the biomedical research training community. These programs help ease entry into research lab CoPs and provide invaluable educational and social capital through program activities. They then serve to broker the transition of students from the undergraduate university community into the PhD training community. The Louis Stokes Alliance for Minority Participation (LSAMP), supported by NSF, plays a similar role in other STEM fields. In many ways, the Program Directors, key faculty, and other program leaders of undergraduate programs like MARC, RISE and LSAMP play the role of coaches and complement what students may or may not get from faculty research mentors.

The movement of a student from an untested newcomer to an accepted member of the lab community can greatly affect that student's professional future. Yet, it is at this very stage that differences between URM and non-URM members of the group can produce marginalization. More often than not, these non-URM students and faculty mentors are not even aware of this marginalization or are unable to articulate why they are reacting differently, since those reactions stem from unconscious assumptions and biases. With the *Academy*, we argue for the importance and relevance of targeted lectures, workshops and well-established coaching groups to facilitate increased awareness of these issues. Students have opportunities to talk about these CoP challenges and barriers with their coaches and coaching group peers, which in turn creates a supplemental CoP for students to rely on during their graduate school years and beyond.

Social Cognitive Career Theory

While CoP describes the process by which individuals become part of work groups allowing entry into the community, it does not address the many other variables related to the skill development required of biomedical scientists and the factors mediating career decisions. Any intervention designed to promote success in a particular career must also take into account the developmental processes individuals must undergo to decide to pursue and to be prepared for that career. Several well formulated theories of student development and career evolution describe the process by which students at the individual level transition into becoming scientists and employ their skills in different settings. One of these, Social Cognitive Career Theory (SCCT) has been found by others studying the early scientific development to be particularly useful in understanding their decisions (e.g. [20, 21]).

SCCT was established by Brown and Lent [22] and based on the work of Bandura [23] with the primary variables of self-efficacy, outcome expectations, personal goals, and contextual supports/barriers. We are using all of these variables to study the evolution of career interests among young URM and other scientists, but these principles can and are being consciously applied to the new experimental intervention for the development of scientific talent. For example, teaching critical skills such as grant writing can promote self-efficacy as a future PI, and a positive view of the outcome expectation as a future faculty member can be promoted by providing positive role models and tools for dealing with perceived un-achievability of academic careers.

(Science) Identity Formation

In our research, the conceptualization of "identity" as it pertains to scientific career development fits well with the reality that identities themselves are not static but constantly being constructed and reconstructed. Further, the various ways in which racial and gender identities can potentially shape individuals' experiences in new CoPs are important to examine. For our purposes, we are particularly interested in how an "identity-as-scientist" [24] makes an important contribution to persistence within science. Most prior studies and conceptualizations of science identity have focused on undergraduate students, but the continual refinement of identity during graduate training also impacts science career progression.

Studies have shown the critical importance of identity-as-scientist in decisions of individuals to pursue research careers. For example, Chemers et al. [20] and Estrada-Hollenbeck et al. [21] have shown how identity-as-scientist, along with self-efficacy, can predict commitment and persistence toward a science career. Through the *Academy*, we are also interested in learning how racial and gender identities impact individuals' identities-as-scientists. Another component of our coaching model is therefore its emphasis on *consciously* and *strategically* developing a student's "identity as a scientist" within a group setting. Coaches also engage students in open and safe discussions about the roles that different identities can play for 'atypical' newcomers in new communities of practice.

Cultural Capital

Cultural capital includes any type of useful cultural resource such as knowledge, skills, or behaviors that reside within the individual, or in the form of objects or institutions to which the individual has access. One way scholars have understood social promotion is by examining how cultural capital is valued by different groups [25, 26], and how powerful or dominant groups set standards of evaluation based on these values [27]. In general, this theory has been applied extensively in studies of educational inequalities (e.g. [28, 29]). Variances in access to the forms of cultural capital valued and rewarded by dominant groups can help account for unequal educational achievement performance in children who originate from different social and class backgrounds [26].

Cultural capital has also been used to understand promotion and fit within the field of science [25, 30]. Ovink and Veazey [30] discussed how minority science intervention programs must address not only academics, but also aspects related to the socialization of minority students into the scientific community. The authors argue that such interventions constitute concerted and formal efforts toward expanding the scientific *habitus* b which serves to redress minority students' relative lack of cultural and social capital. Cultural capital in the science field refers to such abilities and resources as networking, bridging cultural expectations between science and the home, interacting with professors, what to say and do during interviews, and how to interact with lab colleagues [30]. Thus, the coaching model attempts to *systematically* create an environment in which cultural capital can be transmitted from experienced Coaches to students, students can exchange cultural capital with each other, and provide both guidance and practice and deploying cultural capital within their PhD training environments.

The Coaching Model

An alternative construct to mentoring seldom considered in biomedical research training is based on the type of *coaching* most often seen in the development of talented athletes and artists. As a construct, coaches are highly skilled at teaching, motivating, and developing talents of others (e.g. [31, 32]). Career Coaches (to distinguish them from research mentors—hereafter referred to as Coaches) will have the necessary skills for developing the talents of others, but are at an advantage because they do not face the conflicts of interest and time constraints that traditional research mentors often do.

The *Academy* Coaches are not attempting to replace the expertise of research mentors. Rather, they provide complementary focus and expertise to develop student talents. From both their prior experiences and the new theoretical knowledge gained from our trainings, *Academy* Coaches are especially skilled in helping students acknowledge and address some of the extra barriers URM scientists face with each new CoP they enter. From the perspective of the young scientists in this study, these Coaches work to buffer many of the inherent limitations of classical mentoring that we believe play a pivotal role in their professional success and advancement.

Unlike mentoring, coaching as we deploy it emphasizes equally the value and utility of group activities in addition to one-to-one coaching. As such, it seeks to encourage students to learn from one another. Exercises designed to guide professional development, like self-assessment exercises and Individual Development Plans (IDPs), are completed after in-depth and critical discussion in a group setting. Furthermore, *Academy* Coaches are stakeholders in the success of the program, as they all contribute to the development of the coaching curriculum and annual meeting planning. Coaches form a unique coach CoP among themselves to learn from each other and experiment with new approaches to coaching, thus continually improving their coaching expertise.

Design

Coach Selection

To be an effective Coach, we argue that one must have demonstrated expertise and interest in mentoring, and an intimate knowledge of the requirements and expectations of the discipline or field—in this case, the biomedical research community. Thus, *Academy* Coaches were recruited from among leaders of research training and diversity efforts around the U.S. who had already demonstrated great skills as mentors plus a desire to further develop their skills in guiding others, particularly in diversity goals. In the fall of 2010, announcements advertising the *Academy* were distributed through the Graduate Research Education and Training (GREAT) group of the Association of American Medical Colleges (AAMC) (leaders of PhD and postdoctoral training at U.S. medical schools), and to NIGMS and NSF-funded program directors (e.g. MARC, RISE, Initiative for Maximizing Student Development (IMSD), and Post-baccalaureate Research Education Programs

(PREP), LSAMP) to solicit applications for Coaches.

In total, 11 Coaches were selected for *Academy I* (with one serving as an alternate, in case a coach was unable to fulfill their duties for the span of the intervention), and six coaches were selected for *Academy II*(including the one coach originally designated as an *Academy I* alternate). The 16 Coaches come from a range of life science disciplines and a wide range of backgrounds. Demographics of *Academy I* and *Academy II* Coaches are included in Table 3.2.1. What all have in common is their previously established record of commitment to diversity through their roles in various diversity efforts.

Coach Label	Race/Gender	Academic rank (at recruitment)	Administrative position(s) (at recruitment)	Institution
Academy 1				
A	White/Male	Professor	Associate Dean	Public Medical School
B	Hispanic/Female	Professor	Program Director	Public Medical School
C	White/Male	Associate Professor	Assistant Dean	Private Medical School
D	Hispanic/Female	Professor	Dean	Private Medical School
E	White/Male	Professor	Director/Senior Associate Dean	Public Medical School
F	White/Female	Professor	Associate Dean/Director	Private Medical School
G	White/Female	Assistant Professor	Associate Dean	Private Medical School
H	Asian/Female	Assistant Professor	Director/Assistant Dean	Private Medical School
I	White/Female	Professor	Associate Dean (Emeritus)	Private Medical School
J	Asian/Male	Professor	Dean/Director	Public Medical School
Academy II				
K	Black/Female	Professor	Director	Public Medical School
L	Black/Male	Associate Professor	Assistant Vice-President/ Director	Private Comprehensive University
M	Asian/Male	Professor	Co-Director/Associate Director	Private Medical School
N	White/Female	Professor	Associate Vice Chancellor/ Executive Director	Public Medical School
O	White/Male	Professor	Director	Public Medical School
P	Hispanic/Female	Assistant Professor	--	Private Medical School

Table 3.2.1: Demographics of *The Academy for Future Science Faculty Career* Coaches

Coaches training

The training of the Coaches for *Academy I* took place over a day and a half in February, 2011. The primary elements of this training included:

1. Coaches getting to know each other well—some already knew each other quite well but others did not so it was important to start establishing a Coaches Community
2. An introduction to the four social science theories and models—through lecture and practice looking at research training situations through this theory 'lenses'
3. Discussing and interpreting the similarities and differences between mentoring which the Coaches were doing extensively and the *Academy* model of coaching
4. Discussing the topics and design elements to include in the first *Academy* meeting to draw on the collective expertise of these very experienced and committed professionals
5. Important confidentially and privacy issued associated with the *Academy* experiment being conducted as an IRB approved randomized controlled trial

The training for the Coaches for *Academy II* took place in February of 2012. It was similar to the training of *Academy I* Coaches but also included more discussion of experiences from *Academy I* to date. It also had to focus on the needs of students nearing the end of their PhDs rather than just starting them as with *Academy I*. The six *Academy II* Coaches were a more diverse group of individuals than those for *Academy I* from the perspective of race, career stage, and institution type.

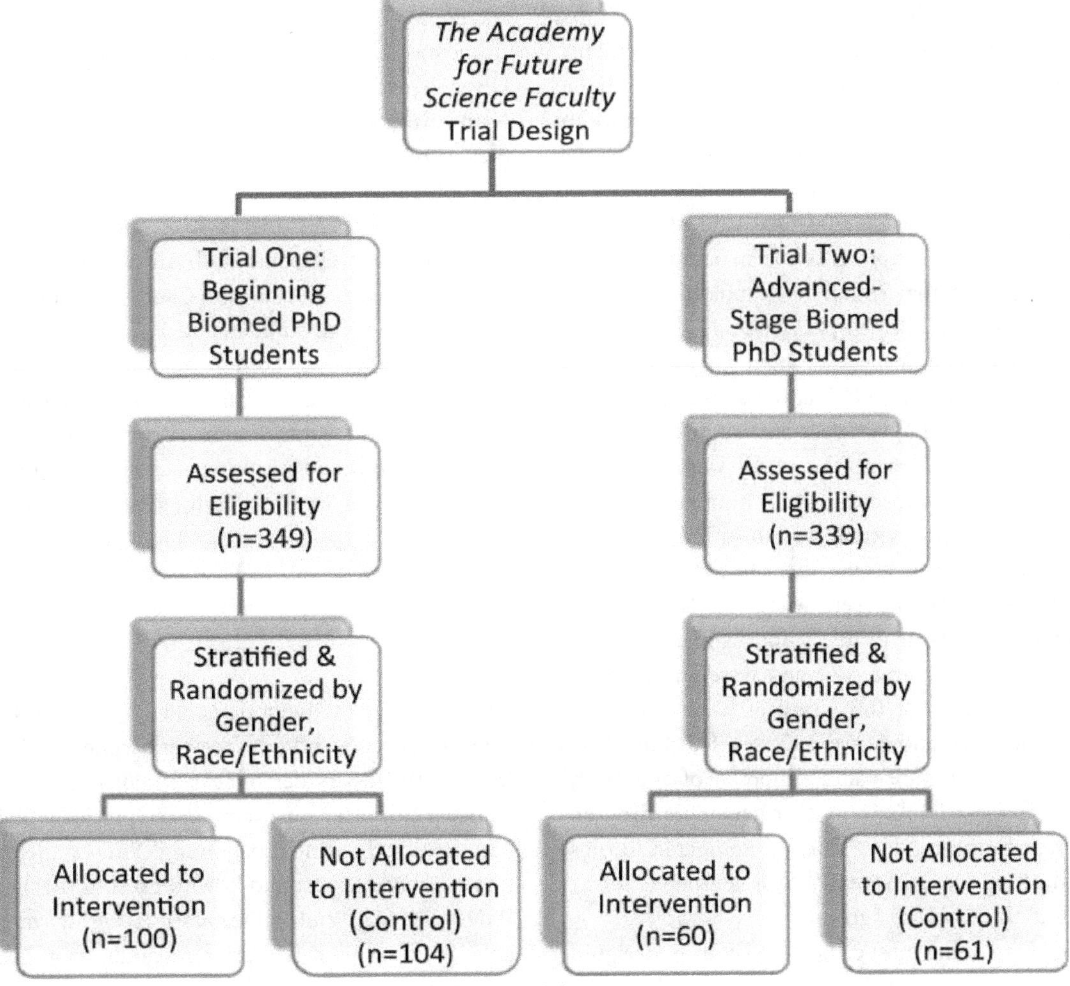

Figure 3.2.1: The Academy for Future Science Faculty trial design.

Student Recruitment

On April 10, 2011, an email describing the *Academy* was sent to biomedical graduate school leaders who were members of the GREAT group, graduate directors at other non-medical major research training universities, and leaders of undergraduate diversity STEM programs throughout the U.S. This date was chosen because it was just before the April 15 common deadline for students to make the final decision of where to pursue their PhDs among the offers of acceptance they had received. Those receiving the emails were asked to forward it to incoming PhD students, or undergraduates they had advised who were starting the PhD in fall 2011. It was advertised as multi-year professional development program particularly designed for those with a strong interest in a future academic career. It was made clear from the start that it was a randomized controlled trial of the program; applicants would not be reviewed, ranked or chosen based on credentials or prior experience. Three hundred and fifty students applied for the *Academy*, representing a wide variety of PhD programs in the U.S. From this applicant pool, 100 students were selected to participate in the *Academy*, and 104 students were selected as study controls who received no intervention. The 204 total students recruited for *Academy I* represents the maximum number of students that could be supported under our funding. Eligibility to participate in the *Academy* required: 1) an expressed interest in an academic career in science; 2) U.S. citizenship or permanent residency; and 3) first year PhD student status.

In April, 2012, a similar email was sent to the leaders of biomedical PhD training programs describing the second round of the *Academy II*, but this time asking them to forward it to all PhD students who were within 12–18 months of completing their degrees. Approximately 340 applications were received and were stratified and randomized. For this study, 60 were chosen for *Academy II*, and 61 were chosen for controls (to account for anticipated dropouts of the study) (Figure 3.2.1). As we anticipated more drop-offs from beginning PhD students compared to those finishing the PhD, the *Academy II* group is smaller than the *Academy I* group.

One of the most critical decisions in designing the *Academy* was whether to include students of all races/ethnicities, or to focus just on URM students. On one hand, it could be argued that an *Academy* for only URM students would concentrate efforts on students who might need these resources most, rather than non-URM students who are more likely to have the resources they need to succeed in the biomedical sciences. However, diversity efforts targeting URM students alone can create a significant stigmatizing effect on those who participate (e.g. [33]). There is also great value in exposing non-URM students to some of the issues and barriers faced by their URM peers as they are discussed in the *Academy* meetings and in the individual coaching groups. Our model also provides opportunities for non-URM students to share inside knowledge that they have gained with their URM peers who may have not yet acquired that knowledge. Finally, the inclusion of both URM and non-URM students was essential in order to determine if the *Academy* differentially could impact URM students vs. all biomedical science PhD students. Therefore, an equal number of men and women were chosen, and equal numbers by race and ethnicity. Thus, for *Academy I*, there are 24 each of Caucasian, Asian, Hispanic and African American students. Only 4 Native American students applied to *Academy I*, so they were all assigned to the *Academy* rather than controls as it would not be a meaningful comparison between just 2 students. In *Academy II*, there are 15 each of Hispanic and African American students, 14 each of Asian and Caucasian students, 1 Native American student, and 1 Pacific Islander student. Students in both Academies were then assigned to Coaching Groups of 10 students and 1 Coach. These groups were also randomly assigned but stratified such that each group had the maximum diversity possible by gender, race and ethnicity.

Study design

The *Academy* activities are designed to consciously promote success and advancement while keeping in mind the theory-derived extra challenges URM students can face. For example, the precision and accuracy with which beginning PhD students know what to expect and how to excel in the first PhD year (e.g. cultural capital) is highly variable. Students with less prior research, from less research-intensive universities, and from lower SES backgrounds often can face greater challenges.

URM students often face additional identity concerns around fitting in, belonging, finding others like themselves, and the heightened sense of everyone watching their performance. Activities at the *Academy* meetings were designed to bring everyone up to a high understanding of what to expect, acknowledge concerns about fitting in, and assist students to develop strategies for success.

A major focus for both Coaches and the research/program design team was to begin building a CoP among the larger group and individual coaching groups, so they could draw on the collective group expertise and knowledge. Reinforcing the idea that going into research is something that can be consciously and strategically planned and structured, we emphasized that becoming successful as scientists is a learned skill. Through the modeling of a creative and safe environment, another objective and focus of the *Academy* meetings was to encourage students to discuss issues of identity and diversity in science. Students explored their important primary identities, acquired insights into the importance and realities of developing and maintaining identities beyond the scientific identity of a graduate student, and were able to find others within the *Academy* community with whom they shared similar interests and identities. Further, by making the implicit process of what students could expect from mentors and PIs more explicit, students gained useful cultural capital in the form of insider knowledge about how biomedical science graduate programs function and operate.

One truly unique aspect of the *Academies* was the introduction of the three social science theories through short (15–30 minutes) lectures and discussions of each, showing how the theories translated to practices within the research community. By learning about the underlying, often invisible, social processes within research groups, students (and Coaches) could become more adept at navigating the process of scientific development, ideally preparing them to better fit in within the graduate program and research group CoPs. The *Academy* was therefore developed as a means to create a community of both students who have an expressed desire for a future academic career and successful scientists/professionals with a deep understanding of what is required to achieve and excel in such a career. The *Academy* was designed to encourage a supportive and cohesive community, both within the coaching groups and through the *Academy* as a whole.

Academy meetings

During the time of the *Academy* funded by the ARRA grant (September, 2010-August, 2013) the *Academy I* meetings consist of a 72 hour in-person meeting in July, 2011 in the Chicago area. Subsequent meetings of both groups lasted 48 hours were held over 3 days. For the meetings in 2012 and 2013, the meeting design included 1 day of overlap between *Academy I* and *II* to allow programming of value to both at the same time plus interactions between the early stage and later stage students. About half of the time at each meeting was devoted for full-group activities and half to Coaching Group time. During these meetings, students were provided with guidance relevant to their upcoming year and stage in graduate school. Every year, students were reminded of the social science theories to help them understand some of the invisible social processes that can affect scientific development. Coaches also reinforced the theories with their groups. The actual topics covered during each meeting were chosen to cover the most critical information and perspectives for the upcoming year, plus longer vision information. For example, in the first *Academy I* meeting, much time was spent on what to expect in the first year of the PhD and how to excel, but a detailed introduction to the road to an academic position was provided. The purpose was to not only facilitate success in the first year but provide a concrete vision of how on achieves an academic career. Equally important in the research design is the introduction of Coaches which is why equal time was spent in full-groups and coaching groups. Time was also scheduled at each meeting for one-to-one meetings between each student and his or her Coach.

One very unique and novel aspect of the *Academy* meetings was the design and testing of ways to open up meaningful conversations among students and Coaches around issues of privilege, race, bias, and the real-life issues about being 'different'. This was done subtly during the first 2011 meeting as it was unclear what kind of community would be created when everyone came together. The larger *Academy* community and the Coaching Groups bonded even faster and more strongly than we expected which made it possible to experiment with providing more explicit presentations to create conversations in 2012 and 2013. Those conversations were initiated in 2012 by bringing in an expert in critical race theories and the ongoing influences of racism in America to address the groups and start the conversations. In 2013, a different speaker was brought in to address the psychological and physiological stresses associated with isolation and being 'the only one,' and strategies to deal with those stressors. In both cases, the very open, honest, and deep conversations started by these presentations continued on in subsequent Coaching Group discussions and throughout the remainder of each meeting.

Activities of coaching and coaching groups between Academy in-person meetings

A core element of the *Academy* trial is the ongoing coaching and relationships between the yearly meetings. The need for and value of a Coach is ongoing, although by no means continuous. The *Academy* experiment is providing a variety of tools and approaches to keeping students and Coaches connected throughout the year. This part of the *Academy* is also experimental as Coaches and students are provided with several options to use as they prefer. The initial design called for Coaching Groups to have monthly or bi-monthly virtual meetings (video and audio) using a product called Adobe Connect. Over time, some groups have migrated to other virtual meeting platforms, some have stopped meeting formally, and others have adopted alternative ways of keeping in touch. Coaches check in with their students on a regular basis via email or phone as well, and students often contact each other independently. Thus, by not rigidly scripting group behavior, each group has been allowed to organically evolve and we are able to gather data on many different variations. A few webinars around specific topics were also delivered to determine how many individuals would find that mode of information delivery of interests.

The initial funding for the *Academy* trial ran out in August, 2013, but a second grant was obtained from NIH to continue some aspects of the study. The new grant enables support of the Coaches and their groups in their virtual meetings, our delivery of new material and experimenting with other ways to provide content, but does not have sufficient funding to enable the annual meeting. However, based on feedback from the last full meetings in 2013, there was a very strong desire to keep meeting in some way. As a result, we have found alternative funding to enable individual Coaching groups to meet, and a majority of them are making plans to do so in the summer of 2014. The new grant also supports the continuation of logistical support for the Coaching Groups, and full collection of data to study how they function, and the comparison between the *Academy* students and the Control. The Coaches, on their own from day one, made it clear to their students that they would be available to them for as long as they desired irrespective of external funding for the *Academy* study.

Analyses

The primary intention of our intervention is to continue supporting interactions between Coaches and their groups, and follow students longitudinally to see if the *Academy* makes a tangible difference in long-term career choices. The hypothesis is that experimental students will have a higher likelihood of pursuing an academic career after the PhD, and that the proportion of URM and non-URM students will be more equal than the past extremely low rate for URM students. These dynamics will be measured through annual interviews with students and quantitative responses on their perceptions of the achievability, desirability, and their commitment to an academic career throughout graduate school and subsequent career steps. These career steps, such as arranging post-doctoral positions that will likely lead to a successful academic career, will provide interim measures.

Data collection

Both experimental and control students participate in yearly telephone interviews. Interview question topics include experiences in graduate school, experiences with mentors and PIs, issues of work/life balance and identity, and future career plans. *Academy* experimental students also respond to specific questions regarding their Coaches and the intervention programming. In the past, these interviews took place just before the annual *Academy* meetings or during the summer for Controls. This timing of interviews prior to the individual Coaching group meetings will continue. Prior to their yearly interview, students will complete a pre-interview online survey in which they provide details about fellowships and grants, changes in skill sets, perceptions on the achievability and desirability of an academic career, and current commitment to an academic career. Both *Academy I* and *Academy II* students are asked to discuss their academic experiences over the past year, and to reflect on what will be important for them in the near future. However, *Academy I* students are asked questions related to their early experiences in graduate school, while *Academy II* students are asked questions related to their experiences finishing graduate school and moving on to the next stage of their careers. To compare professional accomplishments as objective measures of possible differences between *Academy* and control students, we intend to obtain a full curriculum vitae from each student about 6 months after graduation.

During *Academy* meetings, daily online surveys obtained evaluative and feedback information about the meeting activities as well as information on impact in real time. Additionally, a virtually complete audio record of all meeting activities was obtained. This included audio recordings throughout the Coaching Group meetings; each Coach was provided with a small digital recorder that was on during all of their discussion. Individual meetings between Coaches and students were NOT recorded, however, to provide a deeper level of privacy to promote open conversations even about delicate topics. *Academy* students also answer interview and survey questions specific to the *Academy* intervention including daily evaluations of the *Academy* meetings in 2011 (*Academy I* only), 2012, and 2013.

Finally, each of the Coaching Groups was assigned one of our PhD level social scientist Research Associates who observed and took field notes during their meetings. Given that we only had 3 Research Associates and 10 or 6 Coaching Groups, they were unable to be with their groups continuously but rather periodically throughout the meetings.

Data collected from and about Coaches

As noted above, the goal of this experiment is to study and learn from the Coaches as much as the students. The intent is to take what we learn about various approaches to coaching and synthesize it into a Coaching Institute to train future Coaches. To that end, Coaches completed daily evaluations and were debriefed as a group at the end of each day during *Academy* meetings, Research Associates compiled field notes on the approaches used by their Coaches, and individual interviews were conducted with Coaches after the *Academy* meetings and semi-annually between meetings. Annual student pre-interview surveys and interviews also asked questions about the students' interactions with and perceptions of their Coach and Coaching Group.

Quantitative methods and analysis

We collected quantitative data in the forms of yearly pre-interview surveys and yearly evaluations for the *Academy* in-person meetings. Quantitative data will be analyzed using SPSS version 21 [34]. We will utilize a variety of analyses of variances to determine difference between our sample populations of interest (e.g. control vs. experimental, men vs. women, URM vs. non-URM).

Qualitative methods and analysis

We collected a variety of qualitative data, including yearly interviews with students and Coaches, and qualitative information from the pre-interview surveys and self-assessments. At the meetings, Research Associates also observed the interactions among Coaches and their coaching group students, and track this information using ethnographic methods such as audio recording and participant observation notes. Qualitative data will be analyzed in NVivo qualitative software [35], and using an interpretation of Grounded Theory as discussed by Coffey and Atkinson [36] see also: [37, 38, 39]. Here, Grounded Theory can be seen as being built on abductive, rather than inductive, inference. Interesting themes within the data will be related to broader concepts—including those derived from the broad "stock of knowledge of comparable phenomena" ([36]: 156) of the researchers (including knowledge and experience of cultural capital, identity, social cognitive career theory and communities of practice). However, in keeping with Grounded Theory being an "open-minded intellectual approach", the analysis will allow for the generation of new (middle-range) theories or "configurations of ideas" ([36]: 156).

Ethical approval

All research related to the *Academy* was reviewed and accepted by Northwestern University's Institutional Review Board, Project STU00035424.

Discussion

The primary aim of this study is to determine the extent to which this theory-derived coaching intervention can address some of the inherent challenges and limitations of traditional research mentoring with respect to progression toward academic careers. Equally important, the trial is designed to study how different successful scientists approach the role of Career Coach, with the ultimate goal of creating a model depicting the critical elements of successful career coaching within the biomedical sciences. Creating the coaching intervention based on social science theories that explain differential acceptance and success within a professional discipline is a truly unique effort to translate theories into practice. The collection and analysis of extensive qualitative and quantitative data throughout the trial will provide an unusually deep and rich data source to understand how it impacts students and coaches.

Academy coaching groups were intentionally designed so that no one student is the majority or minority in terms of their race/ethnicity or gender. Additionally, students within coaching groups represent a wide variety of departments, universities, and biomedical subfields. This strategic design has the potential to create a truly objective group in which students can feel free to share their challenges and questions. One potential challenge that students might face with Coaches is the inability to get direct guidance on research, since the Coach's science expertise may not be in the same area. However, this is not the primary goal of the *Academy*. While students potentially have many resources they can tap into through their department and university, the role of the Coach is to provide the kind of advice and information that is likely unspoken or not readily available. Coaches are also trained to help students determine how to access resources at their home universities.

Future research will use quantitative and qualitative data to examine longitudinal findings among our experimental and control students. In addition to measuring changes in attitudes regarding the achievability, desirability, confidence, and commitment to an academic career, we will examine students' endeavors as scientists and the extent to which the social science theories inform and are evident and/or in the background in their everyday experiences. Current funding ensures that students and coaches will be followed for at least three more years, which will put *Academy I* students past graduation into next career steps, and *Academy II* students well into one or two next career steps. Further, we will be able to determine if *Academy* coaching and programming impacts the decisions among young life scientists to enter academia, and provided them with the tools needed to succeed.

Endnotes

a. In our research, we define underrepresented minority groups as those that have been underrepresented in the biomedical sciences–specifically African-Americans, Hispanics, and Native Americans. Asian-American students were considered non-URMs, along with white students, because they are numerically well-represented in science vis-à-vis African-American, Hispanic and Native American students.
b. Citing Bourdieu, the authors define habitus as "a system of class specific dispositions that shape an individual's actions so as to reproduce and perpetuate existing systems of hierarchy" (p. 373).

Abbreviations

URM: Underrepresented minorities
ARRA: American Recovery and Reinvestment Act
NIH: National Institute of Health
SCCT: Social Cognitive Career Theory
CoP: Community of Practice
IDP: Individual Development Plan
GREAT: Graduate Research Education and Training
AAMC: Association of American Medical Colleges
NIGMS: National Institute of General Medical Sciences
NSF: National Science Foundation
MARC: Minority Access to Research Careers
RISE: Research Initiative in Scientific Enhancement
IMSD: Initiative for Maximizing Student Development
PREP: Post-baccalaureate Research Education Programs
LSAMP: Louis Stokes Alliance for Minority Participation.

Declarations

Acknowledgements

This research was initiated with support from an NIH Director's Pathfinder Award to Promote Diversity in the Scientific Workforce "Translating Theory to Practice to Diversify the Biomedical Research Community" DP4 GM096807 (ARRA) and is being continued with support from R01 GM107701. This study also benefited from research supported by R01 GM085385, R01 GM085385-02S1 (ARRA) and R01 NR011987. The authors would like to thank our colleagues and other members of The Scientific Careers Research and Development Group for invaluable discussions throughout the course of this project: Jill Keller, PhD; Patricia Campbell, PhD; Lynn Gazley, MPH PhD; Toni Gutierrez, PhD; Ebony O. McGee, PhD; Robin Remich, MAT MEd; Christine Wood, PhD; Steven P. Lee, PhD, Letitia Onyango, BA; Adriana Brodyn, MA MA; Bruce Moses, MA; Nicole Langford, BA; Veronica Y. Womack, PhD.

Competing Interests

The authors state that there are no competing interests.

Authors' Contributions

RM serves as the Primary Investigator on all grants. All authors contributed to the design, implementation, and data collection of this project. All authors contributed to the writing of this paper. All authors read and approved the final manuscript.

References

1. National Science Foundation: Survey of Earned Doctorates. 2012, Available at http://www.nsf.gov/statistics/srvydoctorates/
2. Turner CST, Gonzales JC, Wood JL: Faculty of color in academe: what 20 years of literature tells us. J Divers High Educ. 2008, 1: 139-168./
3. McGee R, Saran S, Krulwick TA: Diversity in the biomedical research workforce: developing talent. Mt Sinai J Med. 2012, 79: 397-411. 10.1002/msj.21310./
4. Committee on Underrepresented Groups and the Expansion of the Science and Engineering Workforce Pipeline; Committee on Science, Engineering, and Public Policy; Policy and Global Affairs; National Academy of Sciences, National Academy of Engineering; Institute of Medicine: Expanding Underrepresented Minority Participation: America's Science and Technology Talent at the Crossroads. 2011, Washington, DC: National Academies Press/
5. Ginther DK, Schaffer WT, Schnell J, Masimore B, Liu F, Haak LL, Kington R: Race, ethnicity, and NIH research awards. Science. 2011, 2011: 1015-1019.View Article/
6. Committee for the Assessment of NIH Minority Research Training Programs, National Research Council: Assessment of NIH Minority Research and Training Programs:

Phase 3. 2005, Washington, DC: National Academies Press/

7. Goins G, Chen M, White C, Clemence D, Redd T, Kelkar V: An initiative to broaden diversity in undergraduate biomathematics training. CBE Life Sci Educ. 2010, 9: 241-247. 10.1187/cbe.10-03-0043./
8. De Welde K, Laursen SL: The 'Ideal Type' advisor: how advisors help STEM graduate students find their 'Scientific Feet'. Open Ed J. 2008, 1: 49-61. 10.2174/1874920800801010049./
9. Abedin Z, Biskup E, Silet K, Garbutt JM, Kroenke K, Mitchell D, Feldman R, McGee R, Fleming M, Pincus HA: Deriving competencies for mentors of clinical and translational scholars. Clin Transl Sci. 2012, 5: 273-280. 10.1111/j.1752-8062.2011.00366.x./
10. Entering Mentoring: A seminar to Train a New Generation of Scientists. Edited by: Handelsman J, Pfund C, Lauffner SM, Pribbenow CM. 2005, Madison: University of Wisconsin Press
11. Pfund C, House S, Spencer K, Asquith P, Carney P, Masters KS, McGee R, Shanedling J, Vecchiarelli S, Fleming R: A research mentor training curriculum for clinical and translational researchers. Clin Transl Sci. 2013, 6: 26-33. 10.1111/cts.12009.
12. Pfund C, House SC, Asquith P, Fleming MR, Buhr KA, Burnham EL, Eichenberger Gilmore JM, Huskins WC, McGee R, Schurr K, Shapiro ED, Spencer KC, Sorkness CA: Training mentors of clinical and translational research scholars: a randomized controlled trial. Acad Med. 2014, 89: 774-782. 10.1097/ACM.0000000000000218.
13. Gazley JL, Remich R, Naffziger-Hirsch ME, Keller J, Campbell PB, McGee R: Beyond preparation: Identity, cultural capital, and readiness for graduate school in the biomedical sciences. J Res Sci Teach. 2014, doi:10.1002/tea.21164
14. Lave J, Wenger E: Situated Learning: Legitimate Peripheral Participation. 1991, New York: Cambridge University Press
15. Wenger E: Communities of Practice: Learning, Meaning and Identity. 1998, Cambridge: Cambridge University Press
16. Wenger E: Communities of practice and social learning systems. Org. 2000, 7: 225-246.
17. Wenger E, White N, Smith J: Learning in Communities. Changing Cultures in Higher Education: Moving Ahead to Future Learning. Edited by: Ehlers UD, Schneckenberg D. 2010, Berlin: Springer Verlag
18. Gibbs KD, Griffin KA: What do I want to be with my PhD? The roles of personal values and structural dynamics in shaping the career interests of recent biomedical science PhD graduates. CBE Life Sci Educ. 2013, 12: 711-723.
19. McGee EO, Martin DB: "You would not believe what I have to go through to prove my intellectual value!": Stereotype management among academically successful Black mathematics and engineering students. Am Educ Res J. 2011, 48: 1347-1389. 10.3102/0002831211423972.
20. Chemers MM, Zurbriggen EL, Syed M, Goza BK, Bearman S: The role of efficacy and identity in science career commitment among underrepresented minority students. J Soc Issues. 2011, 67: 469-491. 10.1111/j.1540-4560.2011.01710.x.
21. Estrada-Hollenbeck M, Woodcock A, Hernandez PR, Schultz PW: Toward a model of social influence that explains minority student integration into the scientific community. J Educ Psychol. 2011, 103: 206-222.
22. Brown S, Lent R: A social cognitive framework for career choice counseling. Career Dev Quart. 1996, 44: 355-367.
23. Bandura A: Organizational application of social cognitive theory. Aus J Manage. 1998, 13 (2): 275-302.
24. Hunter AB, Laursen SL, Seymour E: Becoming a scientist: the role of undergraduate research in students' cognitive, personal, and professional development. Sci Educ. 2007, 91: 36-74. 10.1002/sce.20173.
25. Bourdieu P: Distinction: A Social Critique of the Judgement of Taste. 1984, Cambridge: Harvard University Press
26. Bourdieu P: The Forms of Capital. Handbook of Theory and Research for the Sociology of Education. Edited by: Richardson J. 1986, New York: Greenwood
27. Lareau A, Horvat EM: Moments of social inclusion and exclusion: race, class, and cultural capital in family-school relationships. Sociol Educ. 1999, 72: 37-53. 10.2307/2673185.
28. Dimaggio P: Cultural capital and school success: the impact of status culture participation on the grades of United States high school

students. Am Sociol Rev. 1982, 47: 189-201. 10.2307/2094962.
29. Warikoo N, Carter PL: Cultural explanations for racial and ethnic stratification in academic achievement: a call for a new and improved theory. Rev Educ Res. 2009, 79: 366-394. 10.3102/0034654308326162.
30. Ovink S, Veazey B: More than "Getting Us Through": a case study in cultural capital enrichment of underrepresented minority undergraduates. Res High Educ. 2010, 52: 370-394.
31. Bloom GA, Durand-Bush N, Schinke RJ, Salmela JH: The importance of mentoring in the development of coaches and athletes. Int J Sports Psychol. 1998, 29: 267-281.
32. Gould D, Dieffenback K, Moffett A: Psychological characteristics and their development in Olympic champions. J App Sport Psychol. 2002, 14 (3): 172-204. 10.1080/10413200290103482.
33. Hurtado S, Cabrera NL, Lin MH, Arellano L, Espinosa LL: Diversifying science: underrepresented student experiences in structured research programs. Res High Educ. 2009, 50: 189-214. 10.1007/s11162-008-9114-7.
34. SPSS: Statistical Analysis, Version 21.0. 2012, Armonk, NY: IBM Corp
35. NVivo qualitative data analysis software: 2012, Doncaster, Victoria, Australia: QSR International Pty Ltd. Version 10
36. Coffey A, Atkinson P: Making Sense of Qualitative Data: Complementary Research Strategies. 1996, London: Sage
37. Age LJ: Grounded theory methodology: positivism, hermeneutics, and pragmatism. Qual Report. 2011, 16 (6): 1599-1615.
38. Chamberlain-Salaun J, Mills J, Usher K: Linking symbolic interactionism and grounded theory methods in a research design: from Corbin and Strauss' assumptions to action. Sage Open. 2013, 3: Accessed 23 May 2014. http://sgo.sagepub.com/content/3/3/2158244013505757
39. Corbin J, Strauss A: Basics of Qualitative Research: Techniques and Procedures for Developing Grounded Theory. 2008, Los Angeles, CA: Sage

Pre-publication history

1. The pre-publication history for this paper can be accessed here: http://www.biomedcentral.com/1472-6920/14/160/prepub

Copyright

© Thakore et al.; licensee BioMed Central Ltd. 2014 This article is published under license to BioMed Central Ltd. This is an Open Access article distributed under the terms of the Creative Commons Attribution License (http://creativecommons.org/licenses/by/4.0), which permits unrestricted use, distribution, and reproduction in any medium, provided the original work is properly credited. The Creative Commons Public Domain Dedication waiver (http://creativecommons.org/publicdomain/zero/1.0/) applies to the data made available in this article, unless otherwise stated.

From Culture to Hegemony

Subcultures, Cultures and Class

The Knowing Consumer

IT'S A CULTURE THING ...YOU WOULDN'T UNDERSTAND!

Culture & Socialization

FROM CULTURE TO HEGEMONY

BY DICK HEBDIGE

Culture

> Culture: cultivation, tending, in Christian authors, worship; the action or practice of cultivating the soil; tillage, husbandry; the cultivation or rearing of certain animals (e.g. fish); the artificial development of microscopic organisms, organisms so produced; the cultivating or development (of the mind, faculties, manners), improvement or refinement by education and training; the condition of being trained or refined; the intellectual side of civilization; the prosecution or special attention or study of any subject or pursuit. (*Oxford English Dictionary*)

Culture is a notoriously ambiguous concept as the above definition demonstrates. Refracted through centuries of usage, the word has acquired a number of quite different, often contradictory, meanings. Even as a scientific term, it refers both to a process (artificial development of microscopic organisms) and a product (organisms so produced). More specifically, since the end of the eighteenth century, it has been used by English intellectuals and literary figures to focus critical attention on a whole range of controversial issues. The 'quality of life', the effects in human terms of mechanization, the division of labour and the creation of a mass society have all been discussed within the larger confines of what Raymond Williams has called the 'Culture and Society' debate (Williams, 1961). It was through this tradition of dissent and criticism that the dream of the 'organic society'—of society as an integrated, meaningful whole—was largely kept alive. The dream had two basic trajectories. One led back to the past and to the feudal ideal of a hierarchically ordered community. Here, culture assumed an almost sacred function. Its 'harmonious perfection' (Arnold, 1868) was posited against the Wasteland of contemporary life.

The other trajectory, less heavily supported, led towards the future, to a socialist Utopia where the distinction between labour and leisure was to be annulled. Two basic definitions of culture emerged from this tradition, though these were by no means necessarily congruent with the two trajectories outlined above. The first—the one which is probably most familiar to the reader—was essentially classical and conservative. It represented culture as a standard of aesthetic excellence: 'the best that has been thought and said in the world' (Arnold, 1868), and it derived from an appreciation of 'classic' aesthetic form (opera, ballet, drama, literature, art). The second, traced back by Williams to Herder and the eighteenth century (Williams, 1976), was rooted in anthropology. Here the term 'culture' referred to a

Dick Hebdige, "From Culture to Hegemony," *Subculture: The Meaning of Style*. Copyright © 1981 by Taylor & Francis Group. Reprinted with permission.

> ... particular way of life which expresses certain meanings and values not only in art and learning, but also in institutions and ordinary behaviour. The analysis of culture, from such a definition, is the clarification of the meanings and values implicit and explicit in a particular way of life, a particular culture. (Williams, 1965)

This definition obviously had a much broader range. It encompassed, in T. S. Eliot's words,

> ...all the characteristic activities and interests of a people. Derby Day, Henley Regatta, Cowes, the 12th of August, a cup final, the dog races, the pin table, the dartboard, Wensleydale cheese, boiled cabbage cut into sections, beetroot in vinegar, 19th Century Gothic churches, the music of Elgar .... (Eliot, 1948)

As Williams noted, such a definition could only be supported if a new theoretical initiative was taken. The theory of culture now involved the 'study of relationships between elements in a whole way of life' (Williams, 1965). The emphasis shifted from immutable to historical criteria, from fixity to transformation:

> ... an emphasis [which] from studying particular meanings and values seeks not so much to compare these, as a way of establishing a scale, but by studying their modes of change to discover certain general causes or 'trends' by which social and cultural developments as a whole can be better understood. (Williams, 1965)

Williams was, then, proposing an altogether broader formulation of the relationships between culture and society, one which through the analysis of 'particular meanings and values' sought to uncover the concealed fundamentals of history; the 'general causes' and broad social 'trends' which lie behind the manifest appearances of an 'everyday life'.

In the early years, when it was being established in the Universities, Cultural Studies sat rather uncomfortably on the fence between these two conflicting definitions—culture as a standard of excellence, culture as a 'whole way of life'—unable to determine which represented the most fruitful line of enquiry. Richard Hoggart and Raymond Williams portrayed working-class culture sympathetically in wistful accounts of pre-scholarship boyhoods (Leeds for Hoggart (1958), a Welsh mining village for Williams (1960)) but their work displayed a strong bias towards literature and literacy[1] and an equally strong moral tone. Hoggart deplored the way in which the traditional working-class community—a community of tried and tested values despite the dour landscape in which it had been set—was being undermined and replaced by a 'Candy Floss World' of thrills and cheap fiction which was somehow bland *and* sleazy. Williams tentatively endorsed the new mass communications but was concerned to establish aesthetic and moral criteria for distinguishing the worthwhile products from the 'trash'; the jazz—'a real musical form'—and the football—'a wonderful game'—from the 'rape novel, the Sunday strip paper and the latest Tin Pan drool' (Williams, 1965). In 1966 Hoggart laid down the basic premises upon which Cultural Studies were based:

> First, without appreciating good literature, no one will really understand the nature of society, second, literary critical analysis can be applied to certain social phenomena other than 'academically respectable' literature (for example, the popular arts, mass communications) so as to illuminate their meanings for individuals and their societies. (Hoggart, 1966)

The implicit assumption that it still required a literary sensibility to 'read' society with the requisite subtlety, and that the two ideas of culture could be ultimately reconciled was also, paradoxically, to inform the early work of the French writer, Roland Barthes, though here it found validation in a method—semiotics—a way of reading signs (Hawkes, 1977).

Barthes: Myths and signs

Using models derived from the work of the Swiss linguist Ferdinand de Saussure[2] Barthes sought to expose the *arbitrary* nature of cultural phenomena, to uncover the latent meanings of an everyday life which, to all intents and purposes, was 'perfectly natural'. Unlike Hoggart, Barthes was not concerned with distinguishing the good from the bad in modem mass culture, but rather with showing how *all* the apparently spontaneous forms and rituals of contemporary bourgeois societies are subject to a systematic distortion, liable at any moment to be dehistoricized, 'naturalized', converted into myth:

> The whole of France is steeped in this anonymous ideology: our press, our films, our theatre, our pulp literature, our rituals, our Justice, our diplomacy, our conversations, our remarks about the weather, a murder trial, a touching wedding, the cooking we dream of, the garments we wear, everything in everyday life is dependent on the representation which the bourgeoisie *has and makes us have* of the relations between men and the world. (Barthes, 1972)

Like Eliot, Barthes' notion of culture extends beyond the library, the opera-house and the theatre to encompass the whole of everyday life. But this everyday life is for Barthes overlaid with a significance which is at once more insidious and more systematically organized. Starting from the premise that 'myth is a type of speech', Barthes set out in *Mythologies* to examine the normally hidden set of rules, codes and conventions through which meanings particular to specific social groups (i.e. those in power) are rendered universal and 'given' for the whole of society. He found in phenomena as disparate as a wrestling match, a writer on holiday, a tourist-guide book, the same artificial nature, the same ideological core. Each had been exposed to the same prevailing rhetoric (the rhetoric of common sense) and turned into myth, into a mere element in a 'second-order semiological system' (Barthes, 1972). (Barthes uses the example of a photograph in *Paris-Match* of a Negro soldier saluting the French flag, which has a first and second order connotation: (1) a gesture of loyalty, but also (2) 'France is a great empire, and all her sons, without colour discrimination, faithfully serve under her flag'.)

Barthes' application of a method rooted in linguistics to other systems of discourse outside language (fashion, film, food, etc.) opened up completely new possibilities for contemporary cultural studies. It was hoped that the invisible seam between language, experience and reality could be located and prised open through a semiotic analysis of this kind: that the gulf between the alienated intellectual and the 'real' world could be rendered meaningful and, miraculously, at the same time, be made to disappear. Moreover, under Barthes' direction, semiotics promised nothing less than the reconciliation of the two conflicting definitions of culture upon which Cultural Studies was so ambiguously posited—a marriage of moral conviction (in this case, Barthes' Marxist beliefs) and popular themes: the study of a society's total way of life.

This is not to say that semiotics was easily assimilable within the Cultural Studies project. Though Barthes shared the literary preoccupations of Hoggart and Williams, his work introduced a new Marxist 'problematic'[3] which was alien to the British tradition of concerned and largely untheorized 'social commentary'. As a result, the old debate seemed suddenly limited. In E. P. Thompson's words it appeared to reflect the parochial concerns of a group of 'gentlemen amateurs'. Thompson sought to replace Williams' definition of the theory of culture as 'a theory of relations between elements in a whole way of life' with his own more rigorously Marxist formulation: 'the study of relationships in a whole way of conflict'. A more analytical framework was required; a new vocabulary had to be learned. As part of this process of theorization, the word 'ideology' came to acquire a much wider range of meanings than had previously been the case. We have seen how Barthes found an 'anonymous ideology' penetrating every possible level of social life, inscribed in the most mundane of rituals, framing the most casual social encounters. But how can ideology be 'anonymous', and how can it assume such a broad significance? Before we attempt any reading of subcultural style, we must first define the term 'ideology' more precisely.

Ideology: A *lived* relation

In the *German Ideology*, Marx shows how the basis of the capitalist economic structure (surplus value, neatly defined by Godelier as 'Profit ... is unpaid work' (Godelier, 1970)) is hidden from the consciousness of the agents of production. The failure to see through appearances to the real relations which underlie them does not occur as the direct result of some kind of masking operation consciously carried out by individuals, social groups or institutions. On the contrary, ideology by definition thrives beneath consciousness. It is here, at the level of' normal common sense', that ideological frames of reference are most firmly sedimented and most effective, because it is here that their ideological nature is most effectively concealed. As Stuart Hall puts it:

> It is precisely its 'spontaneous' quality, its transparency, its 'naturalness', its refusal to be made to examine the premises on which it is founded, its resistance to change or to correction, its effect of instant recognition, and the closed circle in which it moves which makes common sense, at one and the same time, 'spontaneous', ideological and *unconscious*. You cannot learn, through common sense, *how things are*: you can only discover *where they fit* into the existing scheme of things. In this way, its very taken-forgrantedness is what establishes it as a medium in which its own premises and presuppositions are being rendered invisible by its apparent transparency. (Hall, 1977)

Since ideology saturates everyday discourse in the form of common sense, it cannot be bracketed off from everyday life as a self-contained set of 'political opinions' or 'biased views'. Neither can it be reduced to the abstract dimensions of a 'world view' or used in the crude Marxist sense to designate 'false consciousness'. Instead, as Louis Althusser has pointed out:

> ...ideology has very little to do with 'consciousness'....It is profoundly *unconscious*...Ideology is indeed a system of representation, but in the majority of cases these representations have nothing to do with 'consciousness': they are usually images and occasionally concepts, but it is above all as *structures* that they impose on the vast majority of men, not via their 'consciousness'. They are perceived-accepted-suffered cultural objects and they act functionally on men via a process that escapes them. (Althusser, 1969)

Although Althusser is here referring to structures like the family, cultural and political institutions, etc., we can illustrate the point quite simply by taking as our example a physical structure. Most modern institutes of education, despite the apparent neutrality of the materials from which they are constructed (red brick, white tile, etc.) carry within themselves implicit ideological assumptions which are literally structured into the architecture itself. The categorization of knowledge into arts and sciences is reproduced in the faculty system which houses different disciplines in different buildings, and most colleges maintain the traditional divisions by devoting a separate floor to each subject. Moreover, the hierarchical relationship between teacher and taught is inscribed in the very layout of the lecture theatre where the seating arrangements—benches rising in tiers before a raised lectern—dictate the flow of information and serve to 'naturalize' professorial authority. Thus, a whole range of decisions about what is and what is not possible within education have been made, however unconsciously, before the content of individual courses is even decided.

These decisions help to set the limits not only on what is taught but on how it is taught. Here the buildings literally *reproduce* in concrete terms prevailing (ideological) notions about what education *is* and it is through this process that the educational structure, which can, of course, be altered, is placed beyond question and appears to us as a 'given' (i.e. as immutable). In this case, the frames of our thinking have been translated into actual bricks and mortar.

Social relations and processes are then appropriated by individuals only through the forms in which they are represented to those individuals. These forms are, as we have seen, by no means transparent. They are shrouded in a 'common sense' which simultaneously validates and mystifies them. It is precisely these 'perceived-accepted-suffered cultural objects' which semiotics sets out to 'interrogate' and decipher. All aspects of culture possess a semiotic value, and the most taken-for-granted phenomena can function as signs: as elements in communication systems governed by semantic rules and codes which are not themselves directly apprehended in experience. These signs are, then, as opaque as the social relations which produce them and which they represent. In other words, there is an ideological dimension to every signification:

> A sign does not simply exist as part of reality—it reflects and refracts another reality. Therefore it may distort that reality or be true to it, or may perceive it from a special point of view, and so forth. Every sign is subject to the criteria of ideological evaluation... The domain of ideology coincides with the domain of signs. They equate with one another. Whenever a sign is present, ideology is present too. Everything ideological possesses a semiotic value. (Volosinov, 1973)

To uncover the ideological dimension of signs we must first try to disentangle the codes through which meaning is organized. 'Connotative' codes are particularly important. As Stuart Hall has argued, they ' ... cover the face of social life and render it classifiable, intelligible, meaningful' (Hall, 1977). He goes on to describe these codes as 'maps of meaning' which are of necessity the product of selection. They cut across a range of potential meanings, making certain meanings available and ruling others out of court. We tend to live inside these maps as surely as we live in the 'real' world: they 'think' us as much as we 'think' them, and this in itself is quite 'natural'. All human societies *reproduce* themselves in this way through a process of 'naturalization'. It is through this process—a kind of inevitable reflex of all social life—that *particular* sets of social relations, particular ways of organizing the world appear to us as if they were universal and timeless. This is what Althusser (1971) means when he says that 'ideology has no history' and that ideology in this general sense will always be an 'essential element of every social formation' (Althusser and Balibar, 1968).

However, in highly complex societies like ours, which function through a finely graded system of divided (i.e. specialized) labour, the crucial question has to do with which specific ideologies, representing the interests of which specific groups and classes will prevail at any given moment, in any given situation. To deal with this question, we must first consider how power is distributed in our society. That is, we must ask which groups and classes have how much say in defining, ordering and classifying out the social world. For instance, if we pause to reflect for a moment, it should be obvious that access to the means by which ideas are disseminated in our society (i.e. principally the mass media) is *not* the same for all classes. Some groups have more say, more opportunity to make the rules, to organize meaning, while others are less favourably placed, have less power to produce and impose their definitions of the world on the world.

Thus, when we come to look beneath the level of 'ideology-in-general' at the way in which specific ideologies work, how some gain dominance and others remain marginal, we can see that in advanced Western democracies the ideological field is by no means neutral. To return to the 'connotative' codes to which Stuart Hall refers we can see that these 'maps of meaning' are charged with a potentially explosive significance because they are traced and re-traced along the lines laid down by the *dominant* discourses about reality, the *dominant* ideologies. They thus tend to represent, in however obscure and contradictory a fashion, the interests of the *dominant* groups in society.

To understand this point we should refer to Marx:

> The ideas of the ruling class are in every epoch the ruling ideas, i.e. the class which is the ruling *material* force of society is at the same time its ruling *intellectual* force. The class which has the means of material production at its disposal, has control at the same time over the means of mental production, so that generally speaking, the ideas of those who lack the means of mental production are subject to it. The ruling ideas are nothing more than the ideal expression of the dominant material relationships grasped as ideas; hence of the relationships which make the one class the ruling class, therefore the ideas of its dominance. (Marx and Engels, 1970)

This is the basis of Antonio Gramsci's theory of hegemony which provides the most adequate account of how dominance is sustained in advanced capitalist societies.

Hegemony: The moving equilibrium

'Society cannot share a common communication system so long as it is split into warring classes' (Brecht, *A Short Organum for the Theatre*).

The term hegemony refers to a situation in which a provisional alliance of certain social groups can exert 'total social authority' over other subordinate groups, not simply by coercion or by the direct imposition of ruling ideas, but by 'winning and shaping consent so that the power of the dominant classes appears both legitimate and natural' (Hall, 1977). Hegemony can only be maintained so long as the dominant classes 'succeed in framing all competing definitions within their range' (Hall, 1977), so that subordinate groups are, if not controlled; then at least contained within an ideological space which does not seem at all 'ideological': which appears instead to be permanent and 'natural', to lie outside history, to be beyond particular interests (see *Social Trends*, no. 6, 1975).

This is how, according to Barthes, 'mythology' performs its vital function of naturalization and normalization and it is in his book *Mythologies* that Barthes demonstrates most forcefully the full extension of these normalized forms and meanings. However, Gramsci adds the important proviso that hegemonic power, precisely *because* it requires the consent of the dominated majority, can never be permanently exercised by the same alliance of 'class fractions'. As has been pointed out, 'Hegemony ... is not universal and "given" to the continuing rule of a particular class. It has to be won, reproduced, sustained. Hegemony is, as Gramsci said, a "moving equilibrium" containing relations of forces favourable or unfavourable to this or that tendency' (Hall et al., 1976a).

In the same way, forms cannot be permanently normalized. They can always be deconstructed, demystified, by a 'mythologist' like Barthes. Moreover commodities can be symbolically 'repossessed' in everyday life, and endowed with implicitly oppositional meanings, by the very groups who originally produced them. The symbiosis in which ideology and social order, production and reproduction, are linked is then neither fixed nor guaranteed. It can be prised open. The consensus can be fractured, challenged, overruled, and resistance to the groups in dominance cannot always be lightly dismissed or automatically incorporated. Although, as Lefebvre has written, we live in a society where ' ...objects in practice become signs and signs objects and a second nature takes the place of the first—the initial layer of perceptible reality' (Lefebvre, 1971), there are, as he goes on to affirm, always 'objections and contradictions which hinder the closing of the circuit' between sign and object, production and reproduction.

We can now return to the meaning of youth subcultures, for the emergence of such groups has signalled in a spectacular fashion the breakdown of consensus in the post-war period. In the following chapters we shall see that it is precisely objections and contradictions of the kind which Lefebvre has described that find expression in subculture. However, the challenge to hegemony which subcultures represent is not issued directly by them. Rather it is expressed obliquely, in style. The objections are lodged, the contradictions displayed (and, as we shall see, 'magically resolved') at the profoundly superficial level of appearances: that is, at the level of signs. For the sign-community, the community of myth-consumers, is not a uniform body. As Volosinov has written, it is cut through by class:

> Class does not coincide with the sign community, i.e. with the totality of users of the same set of signs of ideological communication. Thus various different classes will use one and the same language. As a result, differently oriented accents intersect in every ideological sign. Sign becomes the arena of the class struggle. (Volosinov, 1973)

The struggle between different discourses, different definitions and meanings within ideology is therefore always, at the same time, a struggle within signification: a struggle for possession of the sign which extends to even the most mundane areas of everyday life. To turn once more to the examples used in the Introduction, to the safety pins and tubes of vaseline, we can see that such commodities are indeed open to a double inflection: to 'illegitimate' as well as 'legitimate' uses. These 'humble objects' can be magically appropriated; 'stolen' by subordinate groups and made to carry 'secret' meanings: meanings which express, in code, a form of resistance to the order which guarantees their continued subordination.

Style in subculture is, then, pregnant with significance. Its transformations go 'against nature', interrupting the process of 'normalization'. As such, they are gestures, movements towards a speech which offends the 'silent majority', which challenges the principle of unity and cohesion, which contradicts the myth of consensus. Our task becomes, like Barthes', to discern the hidden messages inscribed in code on the glossy surfaces of style, to trace them out as 'maps of meaning' which obscurely represent the very contradictions they are designed to resolve or conceal.

Academics who adopt a semiotic approach are not alone in reading significance into the loaded surfaces of life. The existence of spectacular subcultures continually opens up those surfaces to other potentially subversive readings. Jean Genet, the archetype of the 'unnatural' deviant, again exemplifies the practice of resistance through style. He is as convinced in his own way as is Roland Barthes of the ideological character of cultural signs. He is equally oppressed by the seamless web of forms and meanings which encloses and yet excludes him. His reading is equally partial. He makes his own list and draws his own conclusions:

> I was astounded by so rigorous an edifice whose details were united against me. Nothing in the world is irrelevant: the stars on a general's sleeve, the stock-market quotations, the olive harvest, the style of the judiciary, the wheat exchange, the flower-beds, ...Nothing. This order ... had a meaning—my exile. (Genet, I 967)

It is this alienation from the deceptive 'innocence' of appearances which gives the teds, the mods, the punks and no doubt future groups of as yet unimaginable 'deviants' the impetus to move from man's second 'false nature' (Barthes, I 972) to a genuinely expressive artifice; a truly subterranean style. As a symbolic violation of the social order, such a movement attracts and will continue to attract attention, to provoke censure and to act, as we shall see, as the fundamental bearer of significance in subculture.

No subculture has sought with more grim determination than the punks to detach itself from the taken-for-granted landscape of normalized forms, nor to bring down upon itself such vehement disapproval. We shall begin therefore with the moment of punk and we shall return to that moment throughout the course of this book. It is perhaps appropriate that the punks, who have made such large claims for illiteracy, who have pushed profanity to such startling extremes, should be used to test some of the methods for 'reading' signs evolved in the centuries-old debate on the sanctity of culture.

Notes

1. Although Williams had posited a new, broader definition of culture, he intended this to complement rather than contradict earlier formulations:

> It seems to me that there is value in each of these kinds of definition.... the degree to which we depend, in our knowledge of many past societies and past stages of our own, on the body ofintellectual and imaginative work which has retained its major communicative power, makes the description of culture in these terms if not complete, then at least reasonable ... there are elements in the 'ideal' definition which ... seem to me valuable. (Williams, I 965)

2. In his *Course in General Linguistics*, Saussure stressed the arbitrary nature of the linguistic sign. For Saussure, language is a system of mutually related values, in which arbitrary 'signifiers' (e.g. words) are linked to equally arbitrary 'signifieds' ('concepts ... negatively defined by their relations with other terms in the system') to form signs. These signs together constitute a system. Each element is defined through its position within the rele vant system—its relation to other elements—through the dialectics of identity and difference. Saussure postulated that other systems of significance (e.g. fashion, cookery) might be studied in a similar way, and that eventually linguistics would form part of a more general science of signs —a semiology.
3. The fashionable status of this word has in recent years contributed to its indiscriminate use. I intend here the very precise meaning established by Louis Althusser: 'the *problematic* of a word or concept consists of the theoretical or ideological framework within which that word or concept can be used to establish, determine and discuss a particular range of issues and a particular kind of problem' (Althusser and Balibar, 1968; see also Bennett, 1979).

SUBCULTURES, CULTURES, AND CLASS

BY JOHN CLARKE, STUART HALL, TONY JEFFERSON, AND BRIAN ROBERTS

Parent Culture and Subculture

In modern societies, the most fundamental groups are the social classes, and the major cultural configurations will be, in a fundamental though often mediated way, "class cultures." Relative to these cultural-class configurations, *sub*-cultures are sub-sets—smaller, more localized and differentiated structures, within one or other of the larger cultural networks. We must, first, see subcultures in terms of their relation to the wider class-cultural networks of which they form a distinctive part. When we examine this relationship between a subculture and the "culture" of which it is a part, we call the latter the "parent" culture. This must not be confused with the particular relationship between "youth" and their "parents," of which much will be said below. What we mean is that a subculture, though differing in important ways—in its "focal concerns," its peculiar shapes and activities—from the culture from which it derives, will also share some things in common with that "parent" culture. The bohemian subculture of the *avant-garde* which has arisen from time to time in the modern city, is both distinct from its "parent" culture (the urban culture of the middle class intelligentsia) and yet also a part of it (sharing with it a modernizing outlook, standards of education, a privileged position vis-a-vis productive labor, and so on). In the same way, the "search for pleasure and excitement" which some analysts have noted as a marked feature of the "delinquent subculture of the gang" in the working class, also shares something basic and fundamental with it. Subcultures, then, must first be related to the "parent cultures" of which they are a sub-set. But, subcultures must *also* be analyzed in terms of their relation to the dominant culture—the overall disposition of cultural power in the society as a whole. Thus, we may distinguish respectable, "rough," delinquent and the criminal subcultures *within* working class culture: but we may also say that, though they differ amongst themselves, they *all* derive in the first instance from a "working class parent culture": hence, they are all subordinate subcultures, in relation to the dominant middle-class or bourgeois culture.

Sub-cultures must exhibit a distinctive enough shape and structure to make them identifiably different from their "parent" culture. They must be focused around certain activities, values, certain uses of material artifacts, territorial spaces etc. which significantly differentiate them from the wider culture. But, since they are sub-sets, there must also be significant things which bind and articulate them with the "parent" culture.

Sub-cultures, therefore, take shape around the distinctive activities and "focal concerns" of groups. They can be loosely or tightly bounded. Some subcultures are merely loosely-defined strands or "milieux" within the parent culture: they possess no distinctive "world" of their own. Others develop a clear, coherent identity and structure. When these tightly-defined groups are also distinguished by age and generation, we call them "youth subcultures."

John Clarke, Stuart Hall, Tony Jefferson, and Brian Roberts, "Subcultures, Cultures, and Class," *Resistance Through Rituals.* Copyright © 2006 by Taylor & Francis Group LLC. Reprinted with permission.

"Youth subcultures" form up on the terrain of social and cultural life. Some youth subcultures are regular and persistent features of the "parent" class-culture: the ill-famed "culture of delinquency" of the working-class adolescent male, for example. But some subcultures appear only at particular historical moments: they become visible, are identified and labeled (either by themselves or by others): they command the stage of public attention for a time: then they fade, disappear or are so widely diffused that they lose their distinctiveness. It is the *latter* kind of subcultural formation which primarily concerns us here. The peculiar dress, style, focal concerns, milieux, etc. of the Teddy Boy, the Mod, the Rocker or the Skin-head set them off, as distinctive groupings, both from the broad patterns of working-class culture as a whole, and also from the more diffused patterns exhibited by "ordinary" working class boys (and, to a more limited extent, girls). Yet, despite these differences, it is important to stress that, as subcultures, they continue to exist within, and coexist with, the more inclusive culture of the class from which they spring. Members of a subculture may walk, talk, act, look "different" from their parents and from some of their peers: but they belong to the same families, go to the same schools, work at much the same jobs, live down the same "mean streets" as their peers and parents. In certain crucial respects, they share the same position (vis-a-vis the dominant culture), the same fundamental and determining life-experiences, as the "parent" culture from which they derive. Through dress, activities, leisure pursuits and life-style, they may project a different cultural response or "solution" to the problems posed for them by their material and social class position and experience. But the membership of a subculture cannot protect them from the determining matrix of experiences and conditions which shape the life of their class as a whole. They experience and respond to *the same basic problematic* as other members of their class who are not so differentiated and distinctive in a "subcultural" sense. Especially in relation to the *dominant* culture, their subculture remains like other elements in their class culture—subordinate and subordinated.

In what follows, we shall try to show why this *double articulation* of youth subcultures—first, to their "parent" culture (e.g. working class culture), second, to the dominant culture—is a necessary way of staging the analysis. For our purposes, subcultures represent a necessary, "relatively autonomous," but *intermediary* level of analysis. Any attempt to relate subcultures to the "socio-cultural formation as a whole" must grasp its complex unity by way of these necessary differentiations.

"Youth Culture"

"Youth Culture," in the singular and with capital letters, is a term we borrow from and refer to in our analysis, but which we cannot and do not *use* in any but a descriptive sense. It is, of course, precisely the term most common in popular and journalistic usage. It is how the "phenomenon of Youth" in the post-war period has been most commonsensically appropriated. It appears to be a simple and common starting point, a simple concept. Actually, it presupposes already extremely complex relations. Indeed, what it disguises and represses—differences between different strata of youth, the class-basis of youth cultures, the relation of "Youth Culture" to the parent culture and the dominant culture, etc.—is more significant than what it reveals. The term is premised on the view that what happened to "youth" in this period is radically and qualitatively different from anything that had happened before. It suggests that all the things which youth got into in this period were more significant than the different kinds of youth groups, or the differences in their social class composition. It sustains certain ideological interpretations—e.g. that age and generation mattered most, or that Youth Culture was "incipiently classless"—even, that "youth" had itself become a class. Thus it identified "Youth Culture" exclusively with its most phenomenal aspect—its music, styles, leisure consumption. Of course, post-war youth did engage in distinctive cultural pursuits, and this was closely linked with the expansion of the leisure and fashion industries, directed at the "teenage market." But the term "Youth Culture" confuses and identifies the two aspects, whereas what is needed is a detailed picture of how youth groups fed off and appropriated things provided by the market, and, in turn, how the market tried to expropriate and incorporate things produced by the subcultures: in other words, the dialectic between youth and the youth market industry. The term "Youth Culture" appropriates the situation of the young almost exclusively in terms of the commercial and publicity manipulation and exploitation *of* the young. As a concept, it has little or no explanatory power. We must try to get behind this market phenomenon, to its deeper social, economic and cultural roots. In short, our aim is to de-throne or *de-construct* the term, "Youth Culture," in favor of a more complex set of categories.

We shall try, first, to replace the concept of "Youth Culture" with the more structural concept of "subculture." We then want to *reconstruct* "subcultures" in terms of their relation, first, to "parent" cultures, and, through that, to the dominant culture, or better, to the struggle between dominant and subordinate cultures. By trying to set up these intermediary levels in place of the immediate catch-all idea of "Youth Culture," we try to show how youth subcultures are related to class relations, to the division of labor and to the productive relations of the society, without destroying what is specific to their content and position.

It is essential to bear in mind that the topic treated here relates *only* to those sections of working-class or middle-class youth where a response to their situation took a distinctive subcultural form. This must in no way be confused with an attempt to delineate the social and historical position of working-class youth as a whole in the period. The great majority of working-class youth never enters a tight or coherent subculture at all. Individuals may, in their personal life-careers, move into and out of one, or indeed several, such subcultures. Their relation to the existing subcultures may be fleeting or permanent, marginal or central. The subcultures are important because there the response of youth takes a peculiarly tangible form. But, in the post-war history of the class, these may be less significant than what most young people do most of the time. The relation between the "everyday life" and the "subcultural life" of different sections of youth is an important question in its own right, and must *not* be subsumed under the more limited topic which we address here. As Howard Parker reminds us, even the "persistent offenders" of the delinquent subcultures are only occasionally preoccupied with illegal or delinquent behavior (Parker, 1974). For the majority, school and work are more structurally significant—even at the level of consciousness—than style and music.

Youth: Metaphor for Social Change

We propose to move from the most phenomenal aspects of youth subcultures to the deeper meanings. We deal, first, with the most immediate aspect—the qualitative *novelty* of Youth Culture. Then, with the most *visible* aspects of social change which were variously held to be responsible for its emergence. Finally, we look at the *wider debate*, to which the debate about Youth Culture was an important, though subsidiary appendage.

New Phenomenon?

We have said that an important element of the concept, "Youth Culture," was its post-war novelty. The following quotation from Roberts reminds us to be cautious on this account; it could almost be read as referring to any of the distinctive postwar youth culture formations, though what it describes is in fact an Edwardian youth in "the classic slum":

> The groups of young men and youths who gathered at the end of most slum streets on fine evenings earned the condemnation of all respectable citizens. They were damned every summer by city magistrates and increasingly harried by the police. In the late nineteenth century the Northern Scuttler and his "moll" had achieved a notoriety as widespread as that of any gang in modern times. He had his own style of dress—the union shirt, bell-bottomed trousers, the heavy leather belt, pricked out in fancy designs with the large steel buckle and the thick, ironshod clogs. His girl-friend commonly wore clogs and shawl and a skirt with vertical stripes. (Roberts, 1971: 123)

It is vital, in any analysis of contemporary phenomena, to think historically; the Roberts quotation clearly points to this thread of historical continuity which we cannot afford to overlook.

On the other hand, there is, also, much evidence to suggest that there were distinctively new historical features in the 1950's which should make us wary of the opposite fault: the tendency to adopt a static or circular view of history and so rob the post-war period of its historical specificity. The significance of the many visible structural and cultural changes of the post-war period were weighted differently by commentators and analysts at the time: but, in most calculations, the emergent "Youth Culture" figured prominently. It was, according to emphasis, one *product* of these changes, their *epitome*, or, most sinisterly, a *portent* of future changes. But, whatever the emphasis, Youth Culture, or aspects of it, was centrally linked to how these changes were interpreted.

One important set of inter-related changes hinged around "affluence," the increased importance of the market and consumption, and the growth of the "Youth-oriented" leisure industries. The most distinctive product of these changes was the arrival of Mark Abrams' "teenage consumer"; relatively speaking, Abrams saw "teenagers" as the prime beneficiaries of the new affluence:

> as compared with 1938, their *real* earnings (i.e. after allowing for the fall in value of money) have increased by 50% (which is double the rate of expansion for adults), and their real "discretionary" spending has probably risen by 100%. (Abrams, 1959: 9)

It was but a short step from here to the view that teenagers' collective habits of consumption constituted "distinctive teenage spending for distinctive teenage ends in a distinctive teenage world" (Abrams, 1959: 10); in other words, the economic basis for a unique, self-contained, self-generating Youth Culture.

The second nexus of changes with which Youth Culture came readily to be identified, as one unfortunate by-product, were those surrounding the arrival of *mass* communications, *mass* entertainment, *mass* art and *mass culture.*

Central to this notion was the idea that more and more people were being submitted (and the passivity implied was not accidental) to ever-more uniform cultural processes. This was the result of the spread in mass consumption, plus the "political enfranchisement" of the masses, and (above all) the growth in mass communications. The spread of mass communications was identified with the growth of the press, radio, television, mass publishing (and not with computers, internal TV and video-systems, data banks, information storage and retrieval, etc.—the commercial and managerial "uses" which provided the real infrastructure of the "communications revolution"). For those interpreting social change within the framework of what came to be called the "mass society thesis," the birth of commercial television in Britain in the mid 1950's was a watershed event.

Youth Culture was connected with this set of changes in several ways. Firstly, and most simply, the creation of a truly mass culture meant the arrival of the means of "imitation" and "manipulation" on a national scale. The notion that Youth Culture was a result of such "mindless" imitation by teenagers, fostered by shrewd and "manipulating" commercial interests, is captured indelibly by the following quotation from Paul Johnson, probably the least perceptive commentator on Youth, in a field distinctive for its bottomless mediocrity:

> Both T.V. channels now run weekly programmes in which popular records are played to teenagers and judged. While the music is performed, the cameras linger savagely over the faces of the audience. What a bottomless chasm of vacuity they reveal. Huge faces, bloated with cheap confectionery and smeared with chain-store make-up, the open, sagging mouths and glazed eyes, the hands mindlessly drumming in time to the music, the broken stiletto heels, the shoddy, stereotyped, "with-it" clothes: here, apparently, is a collective portrait of a generation enslaved by a commercial machine (Johnson, 1964).

Secondly, and more sophisticatedly, some aspects of the new Youth Culture were seen, portentously, as representing the worst effects of the new "mass culture"—its tendency to "unbend the springs" of working class action and resistance. Hoggart, in so many respects our most sensitive recorder of the experimental nuances of working-class culture, has to be counted among the offenders here; for his portrait of the "juke-box boys ... who spend their evenings listening in harshly lighted milk-bars to the nickelodeons" (Hoggart, 1958: 247) could almost—in its lack of concreteness and "felt" qualities—have been written by one of the new "hack" writers he so perceptively analyses:

> The hedonistic but passive barbarian who rides in a fifty-horse-power bus for threepence, to see a five-million-dollar film for one-and-eight-pence, is not simply a social oddity; he is a portent (Hoggart, 1958: 250).

The third set of changes which were said to have "produced" a qualitatively-distinct Youth Culture turned around a hiatus in social experience precipitated by the war. Generally, the argument maintained that the disruptive effects of the war on children born during that period—absent fathers, evacuation and other breaks in normal family life, as well as the constant violence—was responsible for the "new" juvenile delinquency of the mid 50's, typified by the Teds, which was itself seen as a precursor of a more general tendency towards violence in Youth Culture. Fyvel, for example, whilst not restricting himself to this "war" explanation, nevertheless does see the Teddy Boys as "Children of an age of violence, born during a world war ..." (Fyvel: 1963, Preface); whilst Nuttall, more simply, identifies the single fact of the dropping of the first atomic bomb as responsible for the qualitative difference between the pre- and post-war generations:

> right ... at the point of dropping bombs on Hiroshima and Nagasaki the generations became divided in a very crucial way. ... The people who had not yet reached puberty ... were incapable of conceiving of life with a future ... the so-called "generation gap" started then and has been increasing ever since (Nuttall, 1970: 20).

The fourth set of changes which provided an important context for the "emergence" of Youth Culture related to the sphere of education. This interpretation pin-pointed *two* developments above all—"secondary education for all" in age-specific schools, and the massive extension of higher education. Many things were cited as providing the impetus here: the 1944 Education Act itself, which instituted the primary/secondary division for all; the expanded "pool of talent" consequent upon both this reorganization and the post-war "bulge"; the meritocratic ideology of social mobility primarily through the education system; the attempts to make a positive correlation between the country's economic growth-rate and its number of highly-trained personnel; the increased demand in the economy for technicians and technologists. But, for our purposes, the effect was singular. Quite simply, the increasing number of young people spending an increasing proportion of their youth in age-specific educational institutions from the age of eleven onwards—a quite different situation from the pre-war period when almost half the post-eleven year olds were still receiving "secondary" education in all-age elementary schools—was seen, by some commentators, to be creating the pre-conditions for the emergence of a specifically "adolescent society." Coleman made the point most explicitly with his argument that an American high school pupil:

> is "cut off" from the rest of society, forced inwards towards his own age group. With his fellows, he comes to constitute a small society, one that has its most important interactions *within* itself, and maintains only a few threads of connections with the outside adult society (Coleman, 1961: 3).

Last, but by no means least, the arrival of the whole range of distinctive styles in dress and rock-music cemented any doubts anyone may have had about a "unique" younger generation. Here, as elsewhere, the specifics of the styles and music, in terms of who was wearing or listening to what, and why, were crucially overlooked in face of the new stylistic invasion—the image, depicted weekly in the new "teenage" television shows as a "whole scene going." Depending on how you viewed this pop-cultural explosion, either the barbarians were at the gates, or the turn of the rebel hipster had come at last. Again, Jeff Nuttall provides us with the most extravagant and indulgent example:

> The teddy boys were waiting for Elvis Presley. Everybody under twenty all over the world was waiting. He was the super salesman of mass distribution-hip ... he was a public butch god with the insolence of a Genet murderer. ... Most of all he was unvarnished sex taken and set way out in the open. ... The Presley riots were the first spontaneous gatherings of the community of the new sensibilities ... (Nuttall, 1970: 29–30).

Affluence, Consensus, and Embourgeoisment

These explanations for the appearance of a distinct Youth Culture emerged out of a much wider debate about the whole nature of post-war social change. The key terms in this debate were, of course, "affluence," "consensus" and "embourgeoisement." Affluence referred, essentially, to the boom in working class consumer spending (though it entailed the further, less tenable, proposition that the working classes not only had more to spend, but were *relatively* better off). "Consensus" meant the acceptance by both political parties, and the majority of the electorate, of all the measures—mixed economy, increased incomes, welfare-state "safety net"—taken after 1945 to draw people of all classes together, on the basis of a common stake in the system. It also entailed the proposition that a broad consensus of views on all the major issues had developed, including all classes; and hence the end of major political and social conflicts, especially those which exhibited a clear class pattern. "Embourgeoisement" gathered all these, and other social trends (in education, housing, redevelopment, the move to new towns and estates, etc.), together with the thesis that working-class life and culture was ceasing to be a distinct formation in the society, and everyone was assimilating rapidly towards middle class patterns, aspirations and values. These terms came to be woven together into an all-embracing social myth or "explanation" of post-war social change. Stated simply, the conventional wisdom was that "affluence" and "consensus" together were promoting the rapid "bourgeoisification" of the working classes. This was producing new social types, new social arrangements and values. One such type was the "affluent worker"—the "new type of bourgeois worker," family minded, home-centered, security-conscious, instrumentally-oriented, geographically mobile and acquisitive—celebrated in, for example, Zweig's work (Zweig, 1961). Another was the new "teenager" with his commitment to style, music, leisure and consumption: to a "classless youth culture."

Thus, for both parents and their children, *class* was seen, if at all, as being gradually, but inexorably, eroded as society's major structuring and dynamic factor. Other elements were seen to be replacing it as the basis of social stratification: status, a multiply-differentiated "pecking order" based on a complex of educational, employment and consumption-achievements; education, the new universally available and meritocratic route by which status, through job success, could be achieved; consumption, the new "affluence" route through which status, on the "never-never," could be bought by those failing the meritocratic educational hurdle; and age, above all age. Everything that was said and thought about working-class adults was raised to a new level with respect to the working-class young. Born during the war, they were seen as having least experience of and commitment to pre-war social patterns. Because of their age, they were direct beneficiaries of the welfare state and new educational opportunities; least constrained by older patterns of, or attitudes to, spending and consumption; most involved in a guilt-free commitment to pleasure and immediate satisfactions. Older people were, as it were, half-way between the old and the new world. But "youth" was wholly and exclusively in and of the new post-war world. And what, principally, made the difference was, precisely, their *age*. Generation defined them as the group most in the forefront of every aspect of social change in the post-war period. Youth was "the vanguard" of social change. Thus, the simple fact of when you were born displaced the more traditional category of class as a more potent index of social position; and the pre-war chasm between the classes was translated into a mere "gap" between the generations. Some commentators further compounded this myth by reconstituting class on the basis of the new gap: youth *was* a "new class" (see, for example: Musgrove, 1968; Rowntree and Rowntree, 1968; Neville, 1971).

Yet the whole debate depended crucially on the validity of the three central concepts we started out with—affluence, consensus and embourgeoisement; and here we must begin the task of disentangling the real from the constructed or ideological elements contained in these terms.

In general terms, the reality of post-war improvements in living standards—the real element in "affluence"—cannot be questioned. The years 1951–64 undoubtedly saw what Pinto-Duschinsky calls, "a steadier and much faster increase [in the average standard of living] than at any other time in this century"; using "any major indicator of performance, the 1950s and the early 1960s were a great improvement on the years between the wars and on the showing of the Edwardian period" (Pinto-Duschinsky, 1970; 56–57). However, this general rise in living standards critically *obscured* the fact that the *relative* positions of the classes had remained virtually unchanged. It was this mythical aspect of affluence, concealed under the persistent and insistent "never had it so good" ideology, which gradually emerged when poverty—and not just pockets of it—was rediscovered, from the early 1960's onwards.

The massive spending on consumer durables obscured the fact "that Britain lagged behind almost all her main industrial competitors and that she failed to solve the problem of sterling" (Pinto-Duschinsky, 1970: 58). In fact, Britain's affluent "miracle" was *constructed* on very shaky economic foundations, "upon temporary and fortuitous circumstances" (Bogdanor and Skidelsky, eds., 1970: 8), on a "miraculous" historical conjuncture. The Tory policy of "Bread and Circuses"—i.e. "the sacrifice of policies desirable for the long term well-being of a country in favor of over-lenient measures and temporary palliatives bringing in immediate political return" (Pinto-Duschinsky, 1970: 59) or, more succinctly, the promotion of private consumption at the expense of the public sector—was only *one possible response* to this situation, not an *inevitable* outcome.

Consensus, too, in general terms, had a real basis. The war period with its cross-class mobilizations, economic planning, political coalitions and enforced egalitarianism provided a base on which the social reforms of the post-war Labour government could be mounted; and both the war and the post-war reforms provided something of a platform for consensus. Official party politics were dominated in the 1950s by "the politics of the centre," whilst "the most vigorous political debates of the 1950s and 1960s were conducted independently of the party battle" (Pinto Duschinsky, 1970: 73, 74).

However, whilst political consensus (or stalemate) was the overriding feature of the 1950s and early 1960s, the fragility of this consensus was revealed "in the nature of the party struggle" during these years. Despite "the ultimate success of the Tories in retaining office for thirteen years, the political battle was desperately close throughout the whole period" (ibid: 69). In other words, the notion of a political consensus obscures the fact that the Conservative survival was predicated constantly on the most short-term expediency imaginable. For the whole thirteen years of Tory rule, despite this vote-catching "politics of bribery," practically half the electorate voted *against* the Tories of each election. Taken together with the finding by Goldthorpe and his colleagues that "the large majority [of the affluent workers in their study] were, and generally had been Labour supporters" (1969:172), echoing other sociological enquiries—it is quite possible to read "consensus" in a different way: as betokening a waiting attitude by the British working class (often mistaken at the time for "apathy") which an effective lead to the left by Labor at any point in the period might effectively have crystallized in a different direction (Goldthorpe et al. themselves make this argument: see, 1969: 190–5).

"Embourgeoisement," the third and final term in our sociological trinity, was the product of the other two. As such, it was the most constructed term of the three, since the frailties of the other two terms were compounded in it. Even so, the "embourgeoisement" notion, too, had some real basis, as even its critics insisted:

> Our own research indicates clearly enough how increasing affluence and its correlates can have many far-reaching consequences—both in undermining the viability or desirability of established

> life-styles and in encouraging or requiring the development of new patterns of attitudes, behavior and relationships. (Goldthorpe et al., 1969: 163)

Yet the overriding conclusion of the Cambridge team's research only confirmed what their earlier paper had suggested (Goldthorpe and Lockwood, 1963):

> what the changes in question predominantly entailed was not the ultimate *assimilation* of manual workers and their families into the social-world of the middle class, but rather a much less dramatic process of convergence, in certain particular respects, in the normative orientations of some sections of the working class and of some white-collar groups. (Goldthorpe et al., 1969: 26)

In other words, "embourgeoisement," if it meant anything at all, referred to something very different, and far more limited in scope, than anything which its more vigorous proponents envisaged. Even at the time, some of the political extrapolations made on the basis of the thesis seemed far-fetched, ideological rather than empirical in character (e.g. Abrams, 1969).

In sum, despite some significant real shifts in attitudes and living patterns, considerably overlaid by the sustained ideological onslaught of "affluence," what comes through most strongly is the stubborn *refusal of class*—that tired, "worn-out" category to disappear as a major dimension and dynamic of the social structure.

Scapegoated Youth

The dominant society did not calmly sit on the sidelines throughout the period and watch the subcultures at play. What began as a response of confused perplexity—caught in the pat phrase, "the generation gap"—became, over the years, an intense, and intensified struggle. In the 1950s, "youth" came to symbolize the most advanced point of social change: youth was employed as a metaphor for social change. The most extreme trends in a changing society were identified by the society's taking its bearings from what youth was "up to": youth was the vanguard party—of the classless, post-protestant, consumer society to come. This displacement of the tensions provoked by social change on to "youth" was an ambiguous maneuver. Social change was seen as generally beneficial ("you've never had it so good"); but also as eroding the traditional landmarks and undermining the sacred order and institutions of traditional society. It was therefore, from the first, accompanied by feelings of diffused and dispersed social anxiety.

The boundaries of society were being redefined, its moral contours redrawn, its fundamental relations (above all, those class relations which for so long gave a hierarchical stability to English life) transformed. As has been often remarked, movements which disturb a society's normative contours mark the inception of troubling times—especially for those sections of the population who have made an overwhelming commitment to the continuation of the status quo. "Troubling times," when social anxiety is widespread but fails to find an organized public or political expression, give rise to the displacement of social anxiety on to convenient scapegoat groups. This is the origin of the "moral panic"—a spiral in which the social groups who perceive their world and position as threatened, identify a "responsible enemy," and emerge as the vociferous guardians of traditional values: moral entrepreneurs. It is not surprising, then, that youth became the focus of this social anxiety—its displaced object. In the 1950s, and again in the early 1960s, the most visible and identifiable youth groups were involved in dramatic events which triggered off "moral panics," focusing, in displaced form, society's "quarrel with itself." Events connected with the rise of the Teds, and later, the motor-bike boys and the Mods, precipitated classic moral panics. Each event was seen as signifying, in microcosm, a wider or deeper social problem—the problem of youth as a whole. In this crisis of authority, youth now played the role of symptom and scapegoat.

Discussion Questions

1. What do the authors find problematic about the term "Youth Culture"?
2. How do "affluence, consensus, and embourgeoisment" relate to youth subculture?
3. Do you think that "youth subculture" is a useful concept for thinking about culture today? Or have social conditions changed too significantly since the 1950s and 1960s?

References

Abrams, M. 1959. *The Teenage Consumer*. London Press Exchange Ltd.

Abrams, M. 1969. *Must Labour Lose?* Penguin Special.

Bogdanor, V. and Skidelsky, R. (eds.) 1970. *The Age of Affluence*. Macmillan Papermac.

Coleman, A. 1961. *The Adolescent Society*. Free Press.

Fyvel, T.R. 1963. *The Insecure Offenders*. Chatto and Windus.

Goldthorpe, J.H., Lockwood, D., Bechhofer, F. and Platt, J. 1968. *The Affluent Worker: Industrial Attitudes and Behaviour*. Cambridge University Press.

Goldthorpe, J.H., Lockwood, D., Bechhofer, F. and Platt, J. 1969. *The Affluent Worker in the Class Structure*. Cambridge University Press.

Hoggart, R. 1958. *The Uses of Literacy*. Pelican.

Johnson, P. 1964. "The Menace of Beatlism." *New Statesman* (28th February).

Musgrove, F. 1968. *Youth and the Social Order*. Routledge and Kegan Paul.

Neville, R. 1971. *Play Power*. Paladin.

Nuttall, J. 1970. *Bomb Culture*. Paladin.

Parker, H.J. 1974. *View from the Boys*. David and Charles.

Pinto-Duschinsky, M. 1970. "Bread and Circuses: the Conservatives in Office, 1951–64." In V. Bogdanor and R. Skidelsky, eds. (1970).

Roberts, R. 1971. *The Classic Slum*. Manchester University Press.

Rowntree, J. and Rowntree, M. 1968. "Youth as Class: the Political Economy of Youth." *Our Generation*, Vol. 6, Nos. 1–2 (May/July).

Zweig, F. 1961. *The Worker in An Affluent Society*. Heinemann.

THE KNOWING CONSUMER

BY MARK PATTERSON

Sucker:
(a): a person easily cheated or deceived; **(b)**: a person irresistibly attracted by something specified <e.g. a sucker for ghost stories>

Savvy:
alteration of *sabi* know (in English-based creoles and pidgins), from Portuguese *sabe* he knows, from *saber* to know, from Latin *sapere* to be wise

We can outline two competing views of the consumer. Firstly, the consumer as rational agent who crafts their sense of personal identity, positioning themselves within a social group through the use, abuse and display of certain commodities. In other words, 'savvy'. The second view is the relatively mindless consumer, unwittingly compelled by the mass media to buy goods incessantly. A 'sucker'. This tension, between our assumed freedom of expression and the manipulation and control of the so-called mass culture industry, is something of a 'consumer paradox' (Miles, 1999). So the question to answer here is: are we *savvy*, knowing consumers, or *suckers* to the marketing and advertising industries? If the economy relies to such a large extent on consumers buying things they don't actually need, are we being manipulated for the larger purpose of the economy and existing power structures, or does the importance of individual choice and identity render the situation otherwise? The debate between rational agent (savvy) and consumer pawn (sucker) reaches back into the historical context of the Frankfurt School, and then to theorists of the creativity and power of everyday life such as Henri Lefebvre and Michel de Certeau.

Perhaps we find a path in-between, that is, *we make do*. Improvising, appropriating, making up and making do, are all everyday ways that we negotiate multiple sets of rules and systems, structures and spaces. The use, purchase, display of objects, commodities, things is an inextricable part of this process. The structure of this section is essentially threefold:

Suckers

Firstly, the notion of the consumer as 'sucker', as mindlessly manipulated by larger forces, is reviewed. Its familiarity stems from Marxist and neo-Marxist conceptions of the consumer, and connects with the Frankfurt School's deeply critical evaluation of consumption as the perpetuation of "false needs" (especially Adorno, Horkheimer, and Marcuse). Subsequently we find allies for this critical approach in more recent ideas about consumption, such as the beginnings of consumer psychology, as detailed by Bowlby, and retail psychology, the diverse ways that retail spaces are organised to make us consume more. Famously this includes the use of artificial scents such as bread smells in supermarkets, and aerosol sprays of 'new car smell'. Such smells and other subliminal

Mark Paterson, "The Knowing Consumer? Retail Psychology, Subcultures, and Identity," *Consumption and Everyday Life*. Copyright © 2005 by Taylor & Francis Group. Reprinted with permission.

cues imply the manipulation of the consumer's unconscious motivations, in shopping malls and showrooms. This will allow some interesting stories to be told, furthering the view of the control and programmability of consumers in retail spaces.

Savvy

Secondly, considering the 'savvy' or 'knowing' consumer, aware they are manipulated to a certain extent by large corporations and the mass media, but able to reclaim their own sense of identity in some way. The use of mass-produced objects in ways unintended by the manufacturer reveals a sense of irony and creative use ('appropriation') by the consumer, being a tacit acknowledgement of mass media manipulation, but simultaneously an unwillingness to blindly comply. In this section, a brief introduction to Michel de Certeau's *The Practice of Everyday Life (*1984), explores such individual 'tactics' within a larger corporate 'strategy'. Lefebvre's 'appropriation' of space by gatherings of people makes a former capitalist-consumer space (a market) into a social space, which follows from this.

'The Art of Being in Between': Consuming Youth

In order to track some of these ideas through more specific case studies we can look at the beginnings of youth cultures after World War Two to the present day. It illustrates the origins of a unique market directed specifically at young consumers, how it was targeted in terms of marketing and advertising, and how 'taste' and 'authenticity' has been negotiated and performed through consumption practices. Importantly, post-war youth cultures coincide with developments of in the history of manufacturing and mass consumption, and are at the forefront of disputes and issues of subcultures, that is, smaller social groups based on affinities and interests as opposed to more traditional structures such as school, workplace or family. Of course, consumption is central to these subcultures, as it is through the unique style and aesthetics of black clothes and purple lipstick that we 'become' Goths, or by purchasing and displaying knee-length trousers and hooded tops that we 'become' skaters. Thus, whichever subculture we identify within industrial or post-industrial societies, it will inevitably involve a negotiation between mass-produced goods and a creative 'appropriation' or misuse of them in order to reclaim a sense of authenticity and identity.

After introducing these themes we then ask: are we 'suckers' for taking part in an obvious form of conspicuous consumption, or 'savvy' in wanting to reclaim something and use it for our own ends? These complex negotiations occur within everyday activities and spaces of consumption. Whether it is purchasing jeans in order to rip them later, or buying pre-ripped jeans, our performances of self- and social identity occur as a complex set of negotiations within the everyday. Forging and maintaining our shifting and multiple identities between spaces of discipline—of home, work, or school—and spaces of leisure and consumption—such as pubs, clubs or malls—requires sophisticated understandings of the presentation of self in everyday life, and nuanced understandings of the shifting relations between self, space and consumption.

Suckers

Arguing that there is an unwanted imposition of culture and commodities into public life as a result of capitalism, Theodore Adorno and Max Horkheimer called this the "mass culture industry" in 1947. They observed the negative influence that popular culture was having on American society, especially popular music and Disney. The imposition of homogeneity and predictability, they argued, led to a depoliticised social conformity. The argument is powerful because it limits political and social transformation or alternatives only to those realisable within the framework of capitalism, which is by definition exploitative. Similarly, Herbert Marcuse had pronounced that, through the culture industry and the newly emerging mass consumer society, capitalism promotes an "ideology of control" that limits the powers of the individual. The monolithic control and exploitation of populations by the mass culture industry—the State, advertising and the mass media—all united in generating "false needs" he thought (1968:26-7), needs which were themselves forms of social control. By buying into false needs, so the story goes, we become passive consumers, manipulated by larger forces beyond our control. In other words, we become "mindless dupes" (Mackay 1997:3),

"pitiable dupes" (Bowlby 2000:132). We are taken in. Suckers. This construction of the consumer, the engineering of tastes, desires and (false) needs, is what Storey (1999:19ff) terms the model of "consumption as manipulation".

Most contemporary theorists of consumption no longer take this view, attributing to consumers a more active, creative role. But it is worth engaging in more recent developments that continue in this vein. For the same dialectic between individuality and conformity, between freedom and determinism, between resistance and domination, persists through more modern retail methods. The construction of the consumer continues with retail psychology, with psychoanalysis, and with the engineering of consumer desire and instinct continually orchestrated through advertising and marketing. Part of this history could be told through Freud's nephew, Edward Bernays, who contributed considerably to the rise of public relations and marketing in the USA after the second world war. "If we understand the mechanism and motives of the group mind, it is now possible to control and regiment the masses according to our will without their knowing it," he argued in 1928. This scientific technique of moulding public opinion, used for public relations and marketing in its early days, he called the "engineering of consent". Similarly, new techniques of marketing and the rise of retail psychology continues this theme of the engineering of consumer behaviour, and are briefly surveyed below.

Retail Psychology—Manipulating the Consumer

Retail psychology, a burgeoning branch of psychology, researches the various conditions under which consumers are more likely to purchase. Attempts at influencing the decisions of buyers started in the 1930s, when the self-service supermarket was becoming a retail phenomenon very separate from the local 'store'. For the first time, the scientific organisation of retail space was combined with aesthetics, the sensory appeal to the shopper. As Bowlby shows, this combination was reflected in a series of influential books by Carl Dipman for example, who envisioned a new epoch of modern, progressive retailing:

> The old-fashioned store was to a large extent a storeroom. The dealer was a storekeeper. But the modern grocery store must be a scientific salesroom. The grocer must be a modern sales engineer. (1931, in Bowlby 2000:143)

Unlike the general store, where visits only replenished items that were regularly required, the ethos of the modern grocery store was to actively promote new things, to try them out, treating the customer not as a known entity with predictable needs but, as Dipman wrote in 1935, as "a bundle of sales possibilities" (in Bowlby 2000:144). This could only occur through a "modern sales engineer", employing elementary retail psychology to disrupt previous patterns of consumption and to pick up and try out new items. To encourage this, thought Dipman, aesthetics must come to the forefront. Beauty, sensory appeal, these were the factors that mattered to mostly female customers:

> The grocery store today must be both pleasing to the customer—a thing of beauty—yet so constructed that work and labor are reduced to a minimum. ... The application of sight and touch, coupled with efficiency of operation, are the most important factors in the new retail salesmanship. (1931, in Bowlby 2000:144)

The American housewife was therefore partly constructed in the imagination of modern sales engineers like Dipman as discriminating, yet open to new possibilities and aware of the aesthetics and sensory appeal of objects and packages. The American housewife was therefore educated in aesthetics, and their position as consumers was to change—"They were not seen as blameworthy, but as the pitiable dupes of a malevolent environment called 'consumer society'" (2000:132). Continually looking for value in order to fulfil the role of dutiful household shopper, they were also a bundle of sales possibilities. After World War Two, the abundance of items on American supermarket shelves was arranged in vast, sometimes overwhelming displays. The pressure to buy partly arose from the sheer impressiveness of display, but also by appeal to the customer's "whims and fancies", which emanated from the customers themselves (Bowlby 2000:144). The older grocery stores merely replaced what was consumed in the everyday household's usual stock of items. The modern store, by combining aesthetics and organisation, and now with the abundance of items available after the war, was to pander to the whims and fancies of the customer, steadily encouraging impulse purchases.

In modern retail environments, more sophisticated appeals to the senses are made, such as ambient lighting, the subtle use of smell, music of the right tempo, and the visual appeal of window displays. The particularly fascinating innovations however are at the preconscious or subliminal level. It has long been known that certain smells for example trigger moods or feelings. As Marcel Proust famously realised in *Remembrance of Things Past*, smells can trigger emotions and memories, and the limbic system is the part of the brain responsible for these. But it was the British supermarket Tesco that pioneered an artificial smell of freshly baked bread that it pumped throughout its stores. Underhill, in his popular book on retailing *Why We Buy*, describes this as the "olfactory trail" from aisle to bakery, the piped smell of bread being "warm, homey scents" (2003:164). The warm, welcoming feelings evoked by the smell, especially by the entrance, either enticed customers inside or made customers feel more positively disposed towards the store. This new trend in retailing, 'atmospherics', attends to aspects of the atmosphere like this (music, smell or appearance) in order to influence consumer behaviour.

Similarly, the so-called 'new car smell' is held to be one of the most popular smells, despite being a possibly carcinogenic cocktail of chemical treatments to upholstery and materials. Nevertheless, it is desirable and powerfully evocative, and may enhance the purchasing decision. For example, a used-car showroom employed Oxford's The Aroma Company to produce an aerosol spray of the smell, and applied it to used cars in a trial:

> In the short space of time in which a person decides whether they like the car the smell plays a big part in whether they bond with the vehicle and can be a small but important factor when it comes to buying. (*Daily Post*, August 27, 2004)

Of course, smell is a particularly powerful way of guiding or influencing the consumer, its effectiveness lying in the association between scents and memories of warmth and homeliness, in the case of bread, or the brash, crisp, modern smell of the new car. In retail psychology, whether it is cunning or conning the consumer, there are various sensory cues and associative mechanisms and practical ways that customers can be channelled through space, past the special offers aisles and into luxury items in a distant corner of the store. The spatial arrangement of early supermarkets was similar to conventional stores. The introduction of turnstiles and the separation of entry and exit was initially a method of lowering lost sales through pilfering, as Bowlby (2000:141) shows. Subsequently the space within most supermarkets became similarly demarcated, where the inner aisles of the store were self-service, a free space to pick up and examine anything you like, and the exit as a 'control' point, where everyone must pay to leave.

Yet it is one thing to describe the mechanisms employed in influencing customers to pick up, touch and try a particular product, and another to actually compel the customer towards the purchase. The process leading up to the moment of decision can be influenced, but the actual decision belongs to the customer. Underhill writes about the experience of clothing store The Gap where, rather than clothes being on hangars, they are folded and arranged on tables within a large, open salesfloor. In traditional retail lore this means less stock being available within a given retail space. But the picking up of clothes, the unfolding and refolding, increases tactile contact with the commodity, and encourages staff to approach and offer human contact. "We buy things today more than ever based on trial and touch" (2003:162), he argues:

> It's the sensory aspect of the decision-making process that's most intriguing because how else do we experience anything? But it's especially crucial in this context because virtually all unplanned purchases—and many planned ones, too—come as a result of the shopper seeing, touching, smelling or tasting something that promises pleasure, if not total fulfilment. (2003:162)

To see all this as an "iron cage" of consumption, where consumers are locked into patterns of behaviour not of their own choosing, where their decisions are not their own, would be the logical development of the creation of, and compulsion towards, "false needs" that the Frankfurt School decried. Yet one of the criticisms of the Frankfurt School and critics of popular culture and mass consumption is that it grossly oversimplifies the workings of the mass culture industry. As Storey (1999:32) argues, there is not always the total and successful manipulation of passive subjects. Consumption always occurs in cultural contexts. The sciences of retail psychology with its sensory appeals and spatial arrangements may encourage us to touch and to try, but not—as yet—forcing us to buy. And, even when bought, items can be used in unforeseen and imaginative ways.

Savvy

Without denigrating the practices of 'just looking', the browsing, trying on and non-purchasing of products for recreational purposes, purchased commodities not only help to articulate our sense of identity, but can also be used in ways unintended or unforeseen by the manufacturers. Being a 'savvy' consumer is not about continually finding the best bargains, although that is a useful skill. Being a savvy consumer is to be aware of the contradictions between the marketing and advertising imposed on us, but still consuming items in intended and unintended ways in order to articulate something else—a sense of self-identity, of difference, or to express a social identity, that sense of belonging to a group based on shared tastes and values. Often the sense of belonging to a group is defined in terms of resistance, as Stuart Hall argues, this being a pervasive or even seductive attitude. Using a notion from Antonio Gramsci concerning the contested "terrain of culture", wherein ideological struggles take place, Hall continues:

> The people versus the power-bloc: this, rather than 'class-against-class', is the central line of contradiction around which the terrain of culture is polarized. Popular culture, especially, is organized around the contradiction: the popular forces versus the power bloc. (1981:238)

Popular culture, especially music, often encourages this collective sense of resistance against an ill-defined yet omnipotent force such as 'The Man', 'big business', 'capitalism', or the forces of commercialism. And it is only in resistance that identities and subcultures can form, despite the fact that these identities also involve consumption, that music and clothes are still bought. Nevertheless, in looking at youth subcultures and the way they are often organised around patterns of consumption entails a recognition that consumers are "active" and even creative, rather than the "passive 'dupes'" (Storey 1999:54) of much social theory.

Michel de Certeau

Whether we sympathise with the Frankfurt School's harsh critique of the mass culture industry, or even aspire to the celebrations of aspiration and material success that was *Dynasty* in the 1980s or *Sex and the City* in the late 1990s, we can acknowledge the viewpoint that our consumer choices are engineered by a culture industry that enforces homogenisation, conformity, a single model for us all to aspire to. Again, consumers become 'dupes' or 'suckers' by falling for this. But theorists such as Michel de Certeau (1925–1986) have suggested the opposite. In *The Practice of Everyday Life* (1984), de Certeau forthrightly argues instead that consumption practices can be reclaimed. Consumption can be creative; consumption is a way of asserting freedom or challenging the systems of power; and consumption can be a way of fighting back at capitalism itself. In other words, instead of simply being duped we can exercise our creativity, not merely straightforwardly using the products imposed on us, but misusing or altering them for our own purposes. There is a creativity in consumption that de Certeau wishes to reclaim, and this forms something of the fabric of our everyday micropolitics.

Rather than attempting to write and represent the totality of social relations in a grand theoretical mode, as does Lefebvre and others in their Marxist-influenced revolutionary backgrounds, Michel de Certeau is content to celebrate the more mundane moments of creativity and festivity within everyday life, including consumption. There is a different orientation to his more revolutionary brethren, the acknowledgement that consumer capitalism simply cannot contain the spontaneity and energies of the people, and that mass culture never contains the activities of the consumer, nor the *use* they make of commodities:

> The consumer cannot be identified or qualified by the newspapers or commercial products he assimilates: between the person (who uses them) and these products (indexes of the 'order' which is imposed on him), there is a gap of varying proportions opened by the uses he makes of them. (1984:32)

There is a perpetual "anonymous creativity" that persists, indicative of more pluralistic, spontaneous and unsystematic forms of culture that continually arise. The creativity involved in consumption in everyday life implies that there is a *production* in the acts and processes of consumption. "Consumers 'produce' through the adoption of errant or non-formalised practices, which obey internal logics that are often unintelligible to the outsider", summarises Gardiner (2000:170). In fact, consumption is the locus of production for the majority of the population, especially in late capitalism. Rather than being passive, victim-like suckers, consumer-producers exercise cunning, trickery, are truly savvy in their creative appropriation of mass-produced commodities. Economists, advertising executives, marketing people will translate the singular act of purchasing as signifi cant, and this can be captured by statistical study, tracing only the "material used by consumer practices—a material which is obviously that imposed on everyone by production". What cannot be captured is the *ways* of using those products, "the very activity of 'making do'" (1984:34).

In a way, de Certeau echoes Stuart Hall's observation, above, that popular culture often defines itself in opposition to the power bloc. For there to be any resistance to the dominant forces of our culture, thinks de Certeau, we must be like guerrillas. As such, consumption is likened to a tactical raid upon the system, the dominant forces:

> In reality, a rationalized, expansionist, centralized, spectacular and clamorous production is confronted by an entirely different kind of production, called 'consumption' and characterized by its ruses, its fragmentation (the results of the circumstances), its poaching, its clandestine nature, its tireless but quiet activity, in short by its quasi-invisibility, since it shows itself not in its own products (where would it place them?) but in an art of using those imposed on it. (1984:31)

In acknowledging that we no longer make our own products so easily, and therefore we must rely on products "imposed" upon us, a fundamental aspect of the culture of everyday life is therefore to be found in "adaptation", in "*ways of using* imposed systems"; and this he likens to "trickery—(ruse, deception, in the way one uses or cheats with the terms of social contracts" (1984:18).

The Art of Appropriation

In terms of ways of adapting the goods imposed on us through consumer capitalism, or "*ways of using* imposed systems" (1984:18), de Certeau introduces the term 'appropriation'. We appropriate mass-produced consumer goods or alter their meaning through use; we do different things with them, make them mean different things. In this way we negotiate our cultural identity and our politics through this use (or misuse) of standardised, mass-produced products, as Lunt and Livingstone explain:

> The process of negotiation is one in which the consumer transforms or appropriates the mass-produced object. They do not necessarily take on the meanings which are publicly associated with the object but work symbolically on the object's meaning, bringing objects into the home and under control, giving them local meanings, translating the object from an alienable to an inalienable condition. (1992:84)

Unlike the Frankfurt School, the acknowledgement that commodities and the products of the culture industries are woven into the fabric of everyday life is central to de Certeau. Sometimes the use of these mass-produced standardised products is artful, cunning, unusual, and transforms their meaning. In describing the art of appropriation, we can look at examples that show consumption is part of a dialogic process as opposed to the simple act of purchasing and display. This dialogue continues between consumers and producers, but also between consumers and other consumers. In terms of subcultures, one stylistic innovation does not exist in isolation. Imitation, mimicry, mutability and eventual transformation characterise this ongoing dialogue within, and between, subcultures. An example of this is described in the 'Subcultures' section below, which details the transformation of the scooter from democratic, unisex transport device to male Mod style icon.

Any analysis of consumption within subcultures is to a certain extent one of homology, that is, the recognition of patterns of similarity. Storey (1999) in looking at cultural consumption realises this similarity within a group and between groups. The way that subcultures or groups dress similarly and share core values clearly identifies them, whether they be Mods, Goths, punks, skaters or whatever. Yet while recognising the internal coherence of youth subcultures, we can also acknowledge a heterology, the patterns of difference and the accommodation of otherness. This heterology is clear when we notice that no one member of a group is exactly alike, and that there are stylistic traits or the innovative use of objects or decorations that mark out a member as different from another. The production of difference, the stylistic innovation, de Certeau thinks of as a process of *bricolage*. Bricolage is to acknowledge the plurality of meanings of commodities, even if mass-produced, through their use, misuse and appropriation by a subculture or group. In a sense, as Lury (1996:197) remarks, this is a double movement, the homology of sub-cultures yet the heterology of the different uses of products to mark out the differential practices of the subculture. The heterology, the marking out of difference between groups, is consequently pursued primarily through consumption, then. Following de Certeau a number of researchers have found that young consumers are active, creative and critical in their use and appropriation of commodities. "In a process of *bricolage*, they appropriated, re-accented, rearticulated or trans-coded the material of mass culture to their own ends, through a range of everyday creative and symbolic practices", summarises Mackay (1997:6). Appropriation, this artful, creative process of transforming commodities from their intended use into a sign-system of a subculture's own making, is examined in terms of ripping jeans by Fiske (1989), and of the use of motor scooters by Hebdige (1988; 2000). Thus paradigmatic examples of artful appropriation occur within youth culture.

'The Art of Being in Between': Consuming Youth

This section will take the debate concerning consumers as 'suckers' or 'savvy' into more complex territory, using the historical creation of youth cultures and their often ambiguous but necessary reliance on consumption to articulate these cultures as a continuous negotiation between positions. Steven Miles calls this 'the consuming paradox':

> The fact that in terms of our individual experience consumerism appears to have a fascinating, arguably fulfilling, personal appeal and yet simultaneously plays some form of an ideological role in actually controlling the character of everyday life. (1998:5)

In other words, this is to ask whether we are being creative and expressing ourselves and our identities through consumption, or whether we are being manipulated and controlled by a mass culture industry. It is to ask whether we are seducers or the seduced, or as we have portrayed it so far, whether 'suckers' or 'savvy'. Being a savvy consumer is therefore to be aware of Miles' "consuming paradox", the knowledge that our tastes and desires are manipulated by the mass media, yet simultaneously the belief that we still fi nd satisfaction and articulate our identities through consumption. Contrary to the Frankfurt School and its explicit notion that we become assimilated into what the mass culture industry dictates, we can 'poach' or 'appropriate' things for our own ends, ensuring that commodities can be assimilated into what we are, rather than the other way around.

Should we be wary of de Certeau's romanticised view of guerrilla consumption, the translation or appropriation of objects? Celebrating the everyday creativities that help fabricate culture is fine, but possibly leads to naïve and unrealistic claims concerning the importance of these acts. De Certeau is culpable of this in certain passages:

> Dwelling, moving about, speaking, reading, shopping and cooking are activities that seem to correspond to the characteristics of tactical ruses and surprises: clever tricks of the 'weak' within the order established by the 'strong,' an art of putting one over on the adversary on his own turf, hunters' tricks, maneuverable, polymorphic mobilities, jubilant, poetic and warlike discoveries. (1984:38)

In addition, the dramatic language of 'poaching', ruse, trickery is oppositional, still adhering to what Hall (1981) had declared, that popular culture is always defined against the power-bloc. In other words, minor victories against a larger foe may have the dramatic appeal of a war movie, but may just be the insignificant and sneaky victories of teenagers getting one over on the teacher. One problem is that there is an unsophisticated understanding of the economic and ideological model as monolithic or singular. This criticism is familiar from the Frankfurt School. But even for De Certeau, commodities are first imposed on us, and only then can we transform them. Yet the economic impetus behind the culture of consumption, Clarke argues, has always involved the use of alternative or oppositional creative practices; in short, it is simplistic to argue that cultural uniformity or homogenisation results, since the economic drive is towards increasing diversity in terms of objects and services for consumption (2000:288).

Youth culture means dwelling at the edges of such competing tendencies. In the case of consumption, this may be consumption with a 'knowing' or ironic edge. The competing or even contradictory tendencies between work and leisure, between the hard-working ethos of production and the hedonistic or pleasure-seeking ethos of consumption is particularly prominent in youth culture.

Subcultures and the Aestheticisation of Everyday Life

What is a subculture? A social group that uses the "detritus of a dominant culture to affirm a counterculture" say Clarke et al. (2000:136). The usual history of post-war consumption emphasises the emergence of youth cultures based on consumption. Subcultures were an attempt after world war two to hold on to the traditional working class community of the 'parent' culture, while using the opportunities afforded by the so-called 'affluent society' of post-war Britain and America that J.K. Galbraith had famously identified. As such, they started as working class phenomena, positioned between old values and new affluence. Subcultures in Dick Hebdige's formulation are "concerned first and foremost with consumption" (1979:94–5). The purchase of certain commodities such as records and clothes, aimed at emerging youth markets, entailed an increasing identification of the consumer with a chosen lifestyle pattern. This occurs in something like a 'bricolage' process, where commodities from the various culture industries are appropriated for their own purposes or meanings. A simple commodity can be transformed by an act of cultural resistance, such as the ripping of jeans as Fiske (1989) shows. But this act of resistance often leads to 'incorporation'—that is, the manufacturers will then sell the transformed commodity as a commodity, such as pre-ripped jeans. The analysis of the subcultural patterns of consumption in this way reveals the active nature of consumption, almost as part of a dialogic process, as opposed to the passive form of consumption that the Frankfurt School and other cultural critics assume. Consumers are not "passive dupes", as Storey (1999:54) remarks. An example of this is the scooter.

We usually think of the 'Mods' and the 'Rockers' as quintessential post-war youth subcultures, and indeed they neatly show the divide in terms of consumption. While the Rockers were more traditionally rebellious, basing their consumption on Americanised motorbike culture and rock music, the Mods were more attuned to the increasing aestheticisation of everyday life of continental Europe, receptive to modernist (hence 'mod') design influences, especially from Italy. As Hebdige explains, "Mod was predominantly working-class, male-dominated and centred on an obsessive clothes-consciousness", and therefore, according to sociological and marketing literature, "was largely a matter of commodity selection" (2000:154). This is reflected in their consumption of soul and rhythm and blues music, their prominent ownership of mopeds such as Vespa and Lambretta, their wearing of suits, often Italian in origin, displaying their taste and setting them in opposition to the Rockers, with their motorbikes, rock music, leather jackets and denims. If the motorcycle was resolutely masculine, the scooter was gendered as female. It was an aestheticised object, initially marketed to teenagers and women, as Hebdige (2000:131–2) shows. As their design progressed, the engine became increasingly hidden behind panelling, the design and streamlining coming to the fore. Hence, its use by young, working class, predominantly male Mods showed their preference for aesthetics rather than functionality, and placed progressive style and design as a badge of belonging to that particular subculture:

> As an everyday artefact invested with some standards of style and utility but which still managed to satisfy all the key criteria—elegance, serviceability, popularity and visual discretion—the scooter fulfilled all the modern ideals. (Hebdige 2000:150)

The appropriation of such an object, the unique use of a commodity outside its intended target market, assimilates a seemingly arbitrary object into a sign-system of the subculture's own making, and constitutes the object as emblematic, a badge signifying identity and belonging to a particular cultural group. "Value was conferred upon the scooter by the simple act of selection" is how Hebdige (2000:155) describes it, and the process of transformation of the scooter from a democratic mode of transport to a Mod style statement entailed its appropriation and subsequent modification. In a process of bricolage or hybridisation, out of the styles, images and material culture available to a subculture like the Mods, autonomy and uniqueness was pursued. Pennants, whip aerials, mirrors, horns were added to the original design, separating the object from its original target market, and just like Bourdieu's notion of distinction, using the object as a signal or marker to others with similar tastes. To differentiate both object and owner from the mainstream, through the purchase and transformation of the scooter, is simultaneously to bind consumer and commodity into a singular articulation of taste, style and identity.

The competition between such groups was not limited to transport or the boutique, of course, as newspapers often sensationally portrayed their violent confrontations en masse in seaside towns, as both Hebdige (1987; 2000) and Shields (1991) describe. This excessive energy was partly fuelled by the media. Cohen famously characterises the clashes at beach resorts like Clacton as a "moral panic" and shows how "folk devils" or deviants from the norm are portrayed in exaggerated form in the media, as a threat to institutions and normality, and must be neutralised (1972:40ff). And partly this excessive energy was accommodated by cycles of consumption, and has since spread to teenage consumption where the buying of commodities and the formations of identity within subcultural groups (Mods, Rockers, Punks,

Goths, Skaters and so on) is an index for the sheer, unbridled hedonistic pleasure in consumption that youth could enjoy after the stringent restrictions and rationing of wartime. The Mods are an exemplary hybrid, a subculture whose more European, upwardly-mobile and aesthetically aware sensibility was still rooted in British working-class life in urban housing estates, while their music taste included the black American urban soul of the Stax and Motown labels, and also the music of recent Afro-Caribbean immigrants, such as ska. Colin McInnes' 1959 novel *Absolute Beginners*, filmed by Julien Temple in 1986, shows the aestheticisation of Mod culture, the centrality of music to the formation of the social identity, the iconicity of the Vespa scooter, and the beginnings of the 'teenager' as a cultural entity and, later, as marketing category. The novelty of youth culture as a distinct category, represented by shiny espresso machines and coffee bars, away from the prosaic adult world of squalid pubs, is shown in this passage:

> Everyone had loot to spend, everyone a bath with verbena salts behind them, and nobody had broken hearts, because they all were all ripe for the easy summer evening. The rubber-plants in the espressos had been dusted, and the smooth white lights of the new-style Chinese restaurants—not the old Mah Jongg categories, but the latest thing with broad glass fronts, and dacron curtainings, and a beige carpet over the interiors—were shining a dazzle, like some monster telly screens. Even those horrible old anglo-saxon public-houses—all potato crisps and flat, stale ale, and puddles on the counter bar, and spittle—looked quite alluring, provided you didn't push those two-ton doors that pinch your arse, and wander in. In fact, the capital was a night-horse dream. (1961:87)

The emblematic scooter takes its part in a more generalised context of affluence, progressive design, the cultivation of style and distinction, separating this from the tawdry, the banal, the unimaginative. Hebdige calls this the 'aestheticisation' of everyday life: "The perfection of surfaces within Mod was part of the 'aestheticisation' of everyday life achieved through the intervention of the Image, through conflation of the 'public' and the 'personal', consumption and display" (2000:156).

While this section has concentrated on a particular historical era in order to exemplify the aestheticisation of everyday life, the appropriation and transformation of scooters within Mod culture, we can easily transpose this to a more recent subculture and set of objects. Unsurprisingly, in some respects little has changed. The fixation with Italian culture still persists in some echelons of the new 'Casuals' subculture, British working-class male groups organised around fashion, fighting and football, as described by Thornton. Reminiscent of Mod's fixation with style, a Portsmouth fan describes the uniform of his peers: "The knitwear was Italian; Armani and Valentino were the main labels" (in Thornton 2003:125). Of course, the range of commodities has diversified greatly, and footwear has featured prominently as an articulation of subcultural style and identity, as well as ethnicity.

From 'Generation X' to 'Generation Text'

'Generation X' was the title of a nationwide study of youth attitudes and opinions that Charles Hamblett and Jane Deverson conducted between 1963–1964. Originally commissioned for a British women's magazine, asking the nation's youth their opinions and printing chunks of the transcripts meant that their frank findings did not sit well with the magazine's editor, so was published in book form. In a variety of typefaces presumably indicating the variety of views, the cover has young people "talking about Education, Marriage, Money, Pops, Politics, Parents, Drugs, Drink, God, Sex, Class, Colour, Kinks and Living for Kicks" (1964). The timing was apposite. British youth was just emerging into the world's spotlight, with The Beatles as the epitome of cool. Mods were fighting against rockers, sexual liberation was in the air, and as we have seen, black music was fused with white lower-middle-class art school style. There was a sense of optimism in popular culture, and a plural but clearly identifiable voice of British youth.

The term 'Generation X' was therefore coined before Punk and before Douglas Coupland's eponymous novel of 1991. Yet so much has changed since either were written that current youth no longer have the naïve nihilism of 1960s teenagers, nor the fashionable *weltschmerz* of Coupland's 1990s. Arguably, contemporary youth has blended teens, tweens, twenty- and thirty-somethings into a single blob of consumer credit and status anxiety, and these 'kidults' or 'adultescents' are complicit with creative and innovative forms of the mass culture industry as never before. One example of this is in the use of mobile telephones, their appropriation and involvement in symbolic innovation. Hence we can call them 'Generation Text', as Hammersley (2005) does, rather than 'Generation X'. Mobile phone use does lead to symbolic and linguistic innovation, such as the commonly understood 'txt messg' forms of abbreviation, which has certainly eclipsed email in terms of spontaneity and instantaneity of communication. Frank Furedi (2003) off ers other examples of a creeping infantilisation of consumption, such as twentysomethings watching *Teletubbies*, the popularity of Sony PlayStations amongst twenty- and thirty-something professionals. Childish joys that are derived from childish toys represent a form of nostalgia that is experienced at an earlier life stage than before, and this nostalgia can easily be commodified. Some advertisers in the US have coined another term, 'Peterpandemonium', and explain: "People in their twenties and thirties are clamouring for comfort in purchases and products, and sensory experiences that remind them of a happier, more innocent time—childhood" (in Furedi 2003). One historical continuity between 'generation X' and the kidults of 'generation text' is that the celebration of youth involves consumption of key products that serve as markers of mutual belonging to a youthful, vibrant and energetic culture. Kidults however comprise a large market that involves age compression—everyone from five to forty-five can enjoy *Teletubbies*, *Bagpuss*, PlayStation games or Hello Kitty, but for different reasons.

Discussion Questions

1. If you agree that there are subconscious cues such as smells or sounds that make us more likely to buy things, are we 'suckers'? How can we be 'savvy'?
2. Have you ever appropriated something, bought a mainstream product and used it for alternative purposes? What was your reasoning?
3. If so much youth culture is influencing consumption, are we all infantilized as a result?
4. Can there be a subculture that isn't constituted through consumption practices?

REFERENCES

Bowlby, S. (2000) *Carried Away: The Invention of Modern Shopping.* London: Faber & Faber

Clarke, John (2000) 'Dupes and Guerrillas: The Dialectics of Cultural Consumption' in M. J. Lee (Ed.), *The Consumer Society Reader.* Oxford: Blackwell, pp. 288–293

Cohen, Stanley (1972) *Folk Devils and Moral Panics.* London: MacGibbon & Kee

De Certeau, Michel (1984) *The Practice of Everyday Life.* Trans. S. Rendall. Berkeley: University of California Press.

Fiske, John (1989) *Understanding Popular Culture.* London: Routledge

Furedi, Frank (2003) 'The children who won't grow up', Spiked at http://www.spiked-online.com/Articles/00000006DE8D.htm Posted 29 July, 2003. [Last accessed: 01/07/08]

Gardiner, Michael E. (2000) *Critiques of Everyday Life.* London: Routledge

Hall, Stuart (1981) 'Notes on Deconstructing "The Popular"', in R. Samuel (Ed.) *People's History and Socialist Theory.* London: Routledge, pp. 227–240

Hamblett, Charles & Deverson, Jane (1964) *Generation X.* London: Tandem

Hammersley, Ben (2005) 'Generation Text', *Guardian*, G2 Online section. January 13, 2005, pp. 23–24

Hebdige, Dick (1988) *Hiding in the Light: On Images and Things.* London: Routledge

Hebdige, Dick (2000) 'The Object as Image: The Italian scooter cycle' in Martyn J. Lee (Ed.), *The Consumer Society Reader.* Oxford: Blackwell, pp. 125–161

Lunt, Peter K. & Livingstone, Sonia M. (1992) *Mass Consumption and Personal Identity:*

Everyday economic experience. London: Open University Press

Lury, Celia (1996) *Consumer Culture*. Cambridge: Polity Press

MacInnes, Colin (1961) *Absolute Beginners*. 2nd Edition. Harmondsworth: Penguin

Mackay, Hugh (1997) 'Introduction' in H. Mackay (Ed.), *Consumption and Everyday Life*.London: Sage, pp. 1–14

Marcuse, Herbert (1968) *One Dimensional Man*. London: Sphere

Miles, Steven (1998) *Consumerism—As a Way of Life*. London: Sage

Shields, Rob (1991) *Places on the Margin: Alternative Geographies of Modernity*. London: Routledge

Storey, John (1999) *Cultural Consumption and Everyday Life*. London: Hodder Arnold

Thornton, Phillip (2003) *Casuals*. Lytham: Milo Books

Underhill, Paco (2003) *Why We Buy: The Science of Shopping*. New York: Texere

Class

Race

Gender

Intersections of Class, Race and Gender

PERSISTENT SOCIAL INEQUALITIES

CLASS

Class, Status, Party

Stupidity "Deconstructed"

CLASS, STATUS, PARTY

BY MAX WEBER

1: Economically Determined Power and the Social Order

Law exists when there is a probability that an order will be upheld by a specific staff of men who will use physical or psychical compulsion with the intention of obtaining conformity with the order, or of inflicting sanctions for infringement of it.* The structure of every legal order directly influences the distribution of power, economic or otherwise, within its respective community. This is true of all legal orders and not only that of the state. In general, we understand by "power" the chance of a man or of a number of men to realize their own will in a communal action even against the resistance of others who are participating in the action.

"Economically conditioned" power is not, of course, identical with "power" as such. On the contrary, the emergence of economic power may be the consequence of power existing on other grounds. Man does not strive for power only in order to enrich himself economically. Power, including economic power, may be valued "for its own sake." Very frequently the striving for power is also conditioned by the social "honor" it entails. Not all power, however, entails social honor: The typical American Boss, as well as the typical big speculator, deliberately relinquishes social honor. Quite generally, "mere economic" power, and especially "naked" money power, is by no means a recognized basis of social honor. Nor is power the only basis of social honor. Indeed, social honor, or prestige, may even be the basis of political or economic power, and very frequently has been. Power, as well as honor, may be guaranteed by the legal order, but, at least normally, it is not their primary source. The legal order is rather an additional factor that enhances the chance to hold power or honor; but it cannot always secure them.

The way in which social honor is distributed in a community between typical groups participating in this distribution we may call the "social order." The social order and the economic order are, of course, similarly related to the "legal order." However, the social and the economic order are not identical. The economic order is for us merely the way in which economic goods and services are distributed and used. The social order is of course conditioned by the economic order to a high degree, and in its turn reacts upon it.

Now: "classes," "status groups," and "parties" are phenomena of the distribution of power within a community.

2: Determination of Class-Situation by Market-Situation

In our terminology, "classes" are not communities; they merely represent possible, and frequent, bases for communal action. We may speak of a "class" when (1) a number of people have in common a specific causal

Max Weber, "Class, Status, Party," *Max Weber: Essays in Sociology*. Copyright © 2007 by Taylor & Francis Group LLC. Reprinted with permission.

component of their life chances, in so far as (2) this component is represented exclusively by economic interests in the possession of goods and opportunities for income, and (3) is represented under the conditions of the commodity or labor markets. [These points refer to "class situation," which we may express more briefly as the typical chance for a supply of goods, external living conditions, and personal life experiences, in so far as this chance is determined by the amount and kind of power, or lack of such, to dispose of goods or skills for the sake of income in a given economic order. The term "class" refers to any group of people that is found in the same class situation.]

It is the most elemental economic fact that the way in which the disposition over material property is distributed among a plurality of people, meeting competitively in the market for the purpose of exchange, in itself creates specific life chances. According to the law of marginal utility this mode of distribution excludes the non-owners from competing for highly valued goods; it favors the owners and, in fact, gives to them a monopoly to acquire such goods. Other things being equal, this mode of distribution monopolizes the opportunities for profitable deals for all those who, provided with goods, do not necessarily have to exchange them. It increases, at least generally, their power in price wars with those who, being propertyless, have nothing to offer but their services in native form or goods in a form constituted through their own labor, and who above all arc compelled to get rid of these products in order barely to subsist. This mode of distribution gives to the propertied a monopoly on the possibility of transferring property from the sphere of use as a "fortune," to the sphere of "capital goods"; that is, it gives them the entrepreneurial function and all chances to share directly or indirectly in returns on capital. All this holds true within the area in which pure market conditions prevail. "Property" and "lack of property" are, therefore, the basic categories of all class situations. It does not matter whether these two categories become effective in price wars or in competitive struggles.

Within these categories, however, class situations are further differentiated: on the one hand, according to the kind of property that is usable for returns; and, on the other hand, according to the kind of services that can be offered in the market. Ownership of domestic buildings; productive establishments; warehouses; stores; agriculturally usable land, large and small holdings—quantitative differences with possibly qualitative consequences—; ownership of mines; cattle; men (slaves); disposition over mobile instruments of production, or capital goods of all sorts, especially money or objects that can be exchanged for money easily and at any time; disposition over products of one's own labor or of others' labor differing according to their various distances from consumability; disposition over transferable monopolies of any kind—all these distinctions differentiate the class situations of the propertied just as does the "meaning" which they can and do give to the utilization of property, especially to property which has money equivalence. Accordingly, the propertied, for instance, may belong to the class of rentiers or to the class of entrepreneurs.

Those who have no property but who offer services are differentiated just as much according to their kinds of services as according to the way in which they make use of these services, in a continuous or discontinuous relation to a recipient. But always this is the generic connotation of the concept of class: that the kind of chance in the *market* is the decisive moment which presents a common condition for the individual's fate. "Class situation" is, in this sense, ultimately "market situation." The effect of naked possession *per se,* which among cattle breeders gives the non-owning slave or serf into the power of the cattle owner, is only a forerunner of real "class" formation. However, in the cattle loan and in the naked severity of the law of debts in such communities, for the first time mere "possession" as such emerges as decisive for the fate of the individual. This is very much in contrast to the agricultural communities based on labor. The creditor-debtor relation becomes the basis of "class situations" only in those cities where a "credit market," however primitive, with rates of interest increasing according to the extent of dearth and a factual monopolization of credits, is developed by a plutocracy. Therewith "class struggles" begin.

Those men whose fate is not determined by the chance of using goods or services for themselves on the market, e.g. slaves, are not, however, a "class" in the technical sense of the term. They are, rather, a "status group."

3: Communal Action Flowing from Class Interest

According to our terminology, the factor that creates "class" is unambiguously economic interest, and indeed, only those interests involved in the existence of the "market." Nevertheless, the concept of "class-interest" is an ambiguous one: even as an empirical concept it is ambiguous as soon as one understands by it something other than the factual direction of interests following with a certain probability from the class situation for a certain "average" of those people subjected to the class situation. The class situation and other circumstances remaining the same, the direction in which the individual worker, for instance, is likely to pursue his interests may vary widely, according to whether he is constitutionally qualified for the task at hand to a high, to an average, or to a low degree. In the same way, the direction of interests may vary according to whether or not a *communal* action of a larger or smaller portion of those commonly affected by the "class situation," or even an association among them, e.g. a "trade union," has grown out of the class situation from which the individual may or may not expect promising results. [Communal action refers to that action which is oriented to the feeling of the actors that they belong together. Societal action, on the other hand, is oriented to a rationally motivated adjustment of interests.] The rise of societal or even of communal action from a common class situation is by no means a universal phenomenon.

The class situation may be restricted in its effects to the generation of essentially *similar* reactions, that is to say, within our terminology, of "mass actions." However, it may not have even this result. Furthermore, often merely an amorphous communal action emerges. For example, the "murmuring" of the workers known in ancient oriental ethics: the moral disapproval of the work-master's conduct, which in its practical significance was probably equivalent to an increasingly typical phenomenon of precisely the latest industrial development, namely, the "slow down" (the deliberate limiting of work effort) of laborers by virtue of tacit agreement. The degree in which "communal action" and possibly "societal action," emerges from the "mass actions" of the members of a class is linked to general cultural conditions, especially to those of an intellectual sort. It is also linked to the extent of the contrasts that have already evolved, and is especially linked to the *transparency* of the connections between the causes and the consequences of the "class situation." For however different life chances may be, this fact in itself, according to all experience, by no means gives birth to "class action" (communal action by the members of a class). The fact of being conditioned and the results of the class situation must be distinctly recognizable. For only then the contrast of life chances can be felt not as an absolutely given fact to be accepted, but as a resultant from either (1) the given distribution of property, or (2) the structure of the concrete economic order. It is only then that people may react against the class structure not only through acts of an intermittent and irrational protest, but in the form of rational association. There have been "class situations" of the first category (1), of a specifically naked and transparent sort, in the urban centers of Antiquity and during the Middle Ages; especially then, when great fortunes were accumulated by factually monopolized trading in industrial products of these localities or in foodstuffs. Furthermore, under certain circumstances, in the rural economy of the most diverse periods, when agriculture was increasingly exploited in a profit-making manner. The most important historical example of the second category (2) is the class situation of the modern "proletariat."

4: Types of "Class Struggle"

Thus every class may be the carrier of any one of the possibly innumerable forms of "class action," but this is not necessarily so. In any case, a class does not in itself constitute a community. To treat "class" conceptually as having the same value as "community" leads to distortion. That men in the same class situation regularly react in mass actions to such tangible situations as economic ones in the direction of those interests that are most adequate to their average number is an important and after all simple fact for the understanding of historical events. Above all, this fact must not lead to that kind of pseudo-scientific operation with the concepts of "class" and "class interests" so frequently found these days, and which has found its most classic expression in the statement of a talented author, that the individual may be in error concerning his interests but that the "class" is "infallible" about its interests. Yet, if classes as such are not communities, nevertheless class situations emerge only on the basis of communalization. The communal action that brings forth class situations, however, is not basically action between members of the identical class; it is an action between members of different classes. Communal actions that directly determine the class situation of the worker and the entrepreneur are: the labor market, the commodities market, and the capitalistic enterprise. But, in its turn, the existence of a capitalistic enterprise presupposes that a very specific communal action exists and that it is specifically structured to protect the possession of goods *per se,* and especially the power of individuals to dispose, in principle freely, over the means of production. The existence of a capitalistic enterprise is preconditioned by a specific kind of "legal order." Each kind of class situation, and above all when it rests upon the power of property *per se,* will become most clearly efficacious when all other determinants of reciprocal relations are, as far as possible, eliminated in their significance. It is in this way that the utilization of the power of property in the market obtains its most sovereign importance.

Now "status groups" hinder the strict carrying through of the sheer market principle. In the present context they are of interest to us only from this one point of view. Before we briefly consider them, note that not much of a general nature can be said about the more specific kinds of antagonism between "classes" (in our meaning of the term). The great shift, which has been going on continuously in the past, and up to our times, may be summarized although at the cost of some precision: the struggle in which class situations are effective has progressively shifted from consumption credit toward, first, competitive struggles in the commodity market and, then, toward price wars on the labor market. The "class struggles" of antiquity—to the extent that they were genuine class struggles and not struggles between status groups—were initially carried on by indebted peasants, and perhaps also by artisans threatened by debt bondage and struggling against urban creditors. For debt bondage is the normal result of the differentiation of wealth in commercial cities, especially in seaport cities. A similar situation has existed among cattle breeders. Debt relationships as such produced class action up to the time of Cataline. Along with this, and with an increase in provision of grain for the city by transporting it from the outside, the struggle over the means of sustenance emerged. It centered in the first place around the provision of bread and the determination of the price of bread. It lasted throughout antiquity and the entire Middle Ages. The propertyless as such flocked together against those who actually and supposedly were interested in the dearth of bread. This fight spread until it involved all those commodities essential to the way of life and to handicraft production. There were only incipient discussions of wage disputes in antiquity and in the Middle Ages. But they have been slowly increasing up into modern times. In the earlier periods they were completely secondary to slave rebellions as well as to fights in the commodity market.

The propertyless of antiquity and of the Middle Ages protested against monopolies, preemption, forestalling, and the withholding of goods from the market in order to raise prices. Today the central issue is the determination of the price of labor.

This transition is represented by the fight for access to the market and for the determination of the price of products. Such fights went on between merchants and workers in the putting-out system of domestic handicraft during the transition to modern times. Since it is quite a general phenomenon we must mention here that the class antagonisms that are conditioned through the market situation are usually most bitter between those who actually and directly participate as opponents in price wars. It is not the rentier, the share-holder, and the banker who suffer the ill will of the worker, but almost exclusively the manufacturer and the business executives who are the direct opponents of workers in price wars. This is so in spite of the fact that it is precisely the cash boxes of the rentier, the share-holder, and the banker into which the more or less "unearned" gains flow, rather than into the pockets of the manufacturers or of the business executives. This simple state of affairs has very frequently been decisive for the role the class situation has played in the formation of political parties. For example, it has made possible the varieties of patriarchal socialism and the frequent attempts—formerly, at least—of threatened status groups to form alliances with the proletariat against the "bourgeoisie."

5: Status Honor

In contrast to classes, *status groups* are normally communities. They are, however, often of an amorphous kind. In contrast to the purely economically determined "class situation" we wish to designate as "status situation" every typical component of the life fate of men that is determined by a specific, positive or negative, social estimation of *honor.* This honor may be connected with any quality shared by a plurality, and, of course, it can be knit to class situations: class distinctions are linked in the most varied ways with status distinctions. Property as such is not always recognized as a status qualification, but in the long run it is, and with extraordinary regularity. In the subsistence economy of the organized neighborhood, very often the richest man is simply the chieftain. However, this often means only an honorific preference. For example, in the so-called pure modern "democracy," that is, one devoid of any expressly ordered status privileges for individuals, it may be that only the families coming under approximately the same tax class dance with one another. This example is reported of certain smaller Swiss cities. But status honor need not necessarily be linked with a "class situation." On the contrary, it normally stands in sharp opposition to the pretensions of sheer property.

Both propertied and propertyless people can belong to the same status group, and frequently they do with very tangible consequences. This "equality" of social esteem may, however, in the long run become quite precarious. The "equality" of status among the American "gentle-men," for instance, is expressed by the fact that outside the subordination determined by the different functions of "business," it would be considered strictly repugnant—wherever the old tradition still prevails—if even the richest "chief," while playing billiards or cards in his club in the evening, would not treat his "clerk" as in every sense fully his equal in birthright. It would be repugnant if the American "chief" would bestow upon his "clerk" the condescending "benevolence" marking a distinction of "position," which the German chief can never dissever from his attitude. This is one of the most important reasons why in America the German "clubby-ness" has never been able to attain the attraction that the American clubs have.

6: Guarantees of Status Stratification

In content, status honor is normally expressed by the fact that above all else a specific *style of life* can be expected from all those who wish to belong to the circle. Linked with this expectation are restrictions on "social" intercourse (that is, intercourse which is not subservient to economic or any other of business' "functional" purposes). These restrictions may confine normal marriages to within the status circle and may lead to complete endogamous closure. As soon as there is not a mere individual and socially irrelevant imitation of another style of life, but an agreed-upon communal action of this closing character, the "status" development is under way.

In its characteristic form, stratification by "status groups" on the basis of conventional styles of life evolves at the present time in the United States out of the traditional democracy. For example, only the resident of a certain street ("the street") is considered as belonging to "society," is qualified for social intercourse, and is visited and invited. Above all, this differentiation evolves in such a way as to make for strict submission to the fashion that is dominant at a given time in society. This submission to fashion also exists among men in America to a degree unknown in Germany. Such submission is considered to be an indication of the fact that a given man *pretends* to qualify as a gentleman. This submission decides, at least *prima facie,* that he will be treated as such. And this recognition becomes just as important for his employment chances in "swank" establishments, and above all, for social intercourse and marriage with "esteemed" families, as the qualification for dueling among Germans in the Kaiser's day. As for the rest: certain families resident for a long time, and, of course, correspondingly wealthy, e.g. "F. F. V., i.e. First Families of Virginia," or the actual or alleged descendants of the "Indian Princess" Pocahontas, of the Pilgrim fathers, or of the Knickerbockers, the members of almost inaccessible sects and all sorts of circles setting themselves apart by means of any other characteristics and badges … all these elements usurp "status" honor. The development of status is essentially a question of stratification resting upon usurpation. Such usurpation is the normal origin of almost all status honor. But the road from this purely conventional situation to legal privilege, positive or negative, is easily traveled as soon as a certain stratification of the social order has in fact been "lived in" and has achieved stability by virtue of a stable distribution of economic power.

7: "Ethnic" Segregation and "Caste"

Where the consequences have been realized to their full extent, the status group evolves into a closed "caste." Status distinctions are then guaranteed not merely by conventions and laws, but also by *rituals*. This occurs in such a way that every physical contact with a member of any caste that is considered to be "lower" by the members of a "higher" caste is considered as making for a ritualistic impurity and to be a stigma which must be expiated by a religious act. Individual castes develop quite distinct cults and gods.

In general, however, the status structure reaches such extreme consequences only where there are underlying differences which are held to be "ethnic." The "caste" is, indeed, the normal form in which ethnic communities usually live side by side in a "societalized" manner. These ethnic communities believe in blood relationship and exclude exogamous marriage and social intercourse. Such a caste situation is part of the phenomenon of "pariah" peoples and is found all over the world. These people form communities, acquire specific occupational traditions of handicrafts or of other arts, and cultivate a belief in their ethnic community. They live in a "diaspora" strictly segregated from all personal intercourse, except that of an unavoidable sort, and their situation is legally precarious. Yet, by virtue of their economic indispensability, they are tolerated, indeed, frequently privileged, and they live in interspersed political communities. The Jews are the most impressive historical example.

A "status" segregation grown into a "caste" differs in its structure from a mere "ethnic" segregation: the caste structure transforms the horizontal and unconnected coexistences of ethnically segregated groups into a vertical social system of super and subordination. Correctly formulated: a comprehensive societalization integrates the ethnically divided communities into specific political and communal action. In their consequences they differ precisely in this way: ethnic coexistences condition a mutual repulsion and disdain but allow each ethnic community to consider its own honor as the highest one; the caste structure brings about a social subordination and an acknowledgment of "more honor" in favor of the privileged caste and status groups. This is due to the fact that in the caste structure ethnic distinctions as such have become "functional" distinctions within the political societalization (warriors, priests, artisans that are politically important for war and for building, and so on). But even pariah people who are most despised are usually apt to continue cultivating in some manner that which is equally peculiar to ethnic and to status communities: the belief in their own specific "honor." This is the case with the Jews.

Only with the negatively privileged status groups does the "sense of dignity" take a specific deviation. A sense of dignity is the precipitation in individuals of social honor and of conventional demands which a positively privileged status group raises for the deportment of its members. The sense of dignity that characterizes positively privileged status groups is naturally related to their "being" which does not transcend itself, that is, it is to their "beauty and excellence" (καλο-κἀγαθια). Their kingdom is "of this world." They live for the present and by exploiting their great past. The sense of dignity of the negatively privileged strata naturally refers to a future lying beyond the present, whether it is of this life or of another. In other words, it must be nurtured by the belief in a providential "mission" and by a belief in a specific honor before God. The "chosen people's" dignity is nurtured by a belief either that in the beyond "the last will be the first," or that in this life a Messiah will appear to bring forth into the light of the world which has cast them out the hidden honor of the pariah people. This simple state of affairs, and not the "resentment" which is so strongly emphasized in Nietzsche's much admired construction in the Genealogy of Morals, is the source of the religiosity cultivated by pariah status groups. In passing, we may note that resentment may be accurately applied only to a limited extent; for one of Nietzsche's main examples, Buddhism, it is not at all applicable.

Incidentally, the development of status groups from ethnic segregations is by no means the normal phenomenon. On the contrary, since objective "racial differences" are by no means basic to every subjective sentiment of an ethnic community, the ultimately racial foundation of status structure is rightly and absolutely a question of the concrete individual case. Very frequently a status group is instrumental in the production of a thoroughbred anthropological type. Certainly a status group is to a high degree effective in producing extreme types, for they select personally qualified individuals (e.g. the Knighthood selects those who are fit for warfare, physically and psychically). But selection is far from being the only, or the predominant, way in which status groups are formed: Political membership or class situation has at all times been at least as frequently decisive. And today the class situation is by far the predominant factor, for of course the possibility of a style of life expected for members of a status group is usually conditioned economically.

8: Status Privileges

For all practical purposes, stratification by status goes hand in hand with a monopolization of ideal and material goods or opportunities, in a manner we have come to know as typical. Besides the specific status honor, which always rests upon distance and exclusiveness, we find all sorts of material monopolies. Such honorific preferences may consist of the privilege of wearing special costumes, of eating special dishes taboo to others, of carrying arms—which is most obvious in its consequences—the right to pursue certain non-professional dilettante artistic practices, e.g. to play certain musical instruments. Of course, material monopolies provide the most effective motives for the exclusiveness of a status group; although, in themselves, they are rarely sufficient, almost always they come into play to some extent. Within a status circle there is the question of intermarriage: the interest of the families in the monopolization of potential bridegrooms is at least of equal importance and is parallel to the interest in the monopolization of daughters. The daughters of the circle must be provided for. With an increased inclosure of the status group, the conventional preferential opportunities for special employment grow into a legal monopoly of special offices for the members. Certain goods become objects for monopolization by status groups. In the typical fashion these include "entailed estates" and frequently also the possessions of serfs or bondsmen and, finally, special trades. This monopolization occurs positively when the status group is exclusively entitled to own and to manage them; and negatively when, in order to maintain its specific way of life, the status group must *not* own and manage them.

The decisive role of a "style of life" in status "honor" means that status groups are the specific bearers of all "conventions." In whatever way it may be manifests all "stylization" of life either originates in status groups or is at least conserved by them. Even if the principles of status conventions differ greatly, they reveal certain typical traits, especially among those strata which are most privileged. Quite generally, among privileged status groups there is a status disqualification that operates against the performance of common physical labor. This disqualification is now "setting in" in America against the old tradition of esteem for labor. Very frequently every rational economic pursuit, and especially "entrepreneurial activity," is looked upon as a disqualification of status. Artistic and literary activity is also considered as degrading work as soon as it is exploited for income, or at least when it is connected with hard physical exertion. An example is the sculptor working like a mason in his dusty smock as over against the painter in his salon-like "studio" and those forms of musical practice that are acceptable to the status group.

9: Economic Conditions and Effects of Status Stratification

The frequent disqualification of the gainfully employed as such is a direct result of the principle of status stratification peculiar to the social order, and of course, of this principle's opposition to a distribution of power which is regulated exclusively through the market. These two factors operate along with various individual ones, which will be touched upon below.

We have seen above that the market and its processes "knows no personal distinctions": "functional" interests dominate it. It knows nothing of "honor." The status order means precisely the reverse, viz.: stratification in terms of "honor" and of styles of life peculiar to status groups as such. If mere economic acquisition and naked economic power still bearing the stigma of its extra-status origin could bestow upon anyone who has won it the same honor as those who are interested in status by virtue of style of life claim for themselves, the status order would be threatened at its very root. This is the more so as, given equality of status honor, property *per se* represents an addition even if it is not overtly acknowledged to be such. Yet if such economic acquisition and power gave the agent any honor at all, his wealth would result in his attaining more honor than those who successfully claim honor by virtue of style of life. Therefore all groups having interests in the status order react with special sharpness precisely against the pretensions of purely economic acquisition. In most cases they react the more vigorously the more they feel themselves threatened. Calderon's respectful treatment of the peasant, for instance, as opposed to Shakespeare's simultaneous and ostensible disdain of the *canaille* illustrates the different way in which a firmly structured status order reacts as compared with a status order that has become economically precarious. This is an example of a state of affairs that recurs everywhere. Precisely because of the rigorous reactions against the claims of property *per se,* the "parvenu" is never accepted, personally and without reservation, by the privileged status groups, no matter how completely his style of life has been adjusted to theirs. They will only accept his descendants who have been educated in the conventions of their status group and who have never besmirched its honor by their own economic labor.

As to the general *effect* of the status order, only one consequence can be stated, but it is a very important one: the hindrance of the free development of the market occurs first for those goods which status groups directly withheld from free exchange by monopolization. This monopolization may be effected either legally or conventionally. For example, in many Hellenic cities during the epoch of status groups, and also originally in Rome, the inherited estate (as is shown by the old formula for indiction against spendthrifts) was monopolized just as were the estates of knights, peasants, priests, and especially the clientele of the craft and merchant guilds. The market is restricted, and the power of naked property *per se,* which gives its stamp to "class formation," is pushed into the background. The results of this process can be most varied. Of course, they do not necessarily weaken the contrasts in the economic situation. Frequently they strengthen these contrasts, and in any case, where stratification by status permeates a community as strongly as was the case in all political communities of antiquity and of the Middle Ages, one can never speak of a genuinely free market competition as we understand it today. There are wider effects than this direct exclusion of special goods from the market. From the contrariety between the status order and the purely economic order mentioned above, it follows that in most instances the notion of honor peculiar to status absolutely abhors that which is essential to the market: higgling. Honor abhors higgling among peers and occasionally it taboos higgling for the members of a status group in general. Therefore, everywhere some status groups, and usually the most influential, consider almost any kind of overt participation in economic acquisition as absolutely stigmatizing.

With some over-simplification, one might thus say that "classes" are stratified according to their relations to the production and acquisition of goods; whereas "status groups" are stratified according to the principles of their *consumption* of goods as represented by special "styles of life."

An "occupational group" is also a status group. For normally, it successfully claims social honor only by virtue of the special style of life which may be determined by it. The differences between classes and status groups frequently overlap. It is precisely those status communities most strictly segregated in terms of honor (viz. the Indian castes) who today show, although within very rigid limits, a relatively high degree of indifference to pecuniary income. However, the Brahmins seek such income in many different ways.

As to the general economic conditions making for the predominance of stratification by "status," only very little can be said. When the bases of the acquisition and distribution of goods are relatively stable, stratification by status is favored. Every technological repercussion and economic transformation threatens stratification by status and pushes the class situation into the foreground. Epochs and countries in which the naked class situation is of predominant significance are regularly the periods of technical and economic transformations. And every slowing down of the shifting of economic stratifications leads, in due course, to the growth of status structures and makes for a resuscitation of the important role of social honor.

10: Parties

Whereas the genuine place of "classes" is within the economic order, the place of "status groups" is within the social order, that is, within the sphere of the distribution of "honor." From within these spheres, classes and status groups influence one another and they influence the legal order and are in turn influenced by it. But "parties" live in a house of "power."

Their action is oriented toward the acquisition of social "power," that is to say, toward influencing a communal action no matter what its content may be. In principle, parties may exist in a social "club" as well as in a "state." As over against the actions of classes and status groups, for which this is not necessarily the case, the communal actions of "parties" always mean a societalization. For party actions are always directed toward a goal which is striven for in planned manner. This goal may be a "cause" (the party may aim at realizing a program for ideal or material purposes), or the goal may be "personal" (sinecures, power, and from these, honor for the leader and the followers of the party). Usually the party action aims at all these simultaneously. Parties are, therefore, only possible within communities that are societalized, that is, which have some rational order and a staff of persons available who are ready to enforce it. For parties aim precisely at influencing this staff, and if possible, to recruit it from party followers.

In any individual case, parties may represent interests determined through "class situation" or "status situation," and they may recruit their following respectively from one or the other. But they need be neither purely "class" nor purely "status" parties. In most cases they are partly class parties and partly status parties, but sometimes they are neither. They may represent ephemeral or enduring structures. Their means of attaining power may be quite varied, ranging from naked violence of any sort to canvassing for votes with coarse or subtle means: money, social influence, the force of speech, suggestion, clumsy hoax, and so on to the rougher or more artful tactics of obstruction in parliamentary bodies.

The sociological structure of parties differs in a basic way according to the kind of communal action which they struggle to influence. Parties also differ according to whether or not the community is stratified by status or by classes. Above all else, they vary according to the structure of domination within the community. For their leaders normally deal with the conquest of a community. They are, in the general concept which is maintained here, not only products of specially modern forms of domination. We shall also designate as parties the ancient and medieval "parties," despite the fact that their structure differs basically from the structure of modern parties. By virtue of these structural differences of domination it is impossible to say anything about the structure of parties without discussing the structural forms of social domination *per se*. Parties, which are always structures struggling for domination, are very frequently organized in a very strict "authoritarian" fashion. …

Concerning "classes," "status groups," and "parties," it must be said in general that they necessarily presuppose a comprehensive societalization, and especially a political framework of communal action, within which they operate. This does not mean that parties would be confined by the frontiers of any individual political community. On the contrary, at all times it has been the order of the day that the societalization (even when it aims at the use of military force in common) reaches beyond the frontiers of politics. This has been the case in the solidarity of interests among the Oligarchs and among the democrats in Hellas, among the Guelfs and among Ghibellines in the Middle Ages, and within the Calvinist party during the period of religions struggles. It has been the case up to the solidarity of the landlords (international congress of agrarian landlords), and has continued among princes (holy alliance, Karlsbad decrees), socialist workers, conservatives (the longing of Prussian conservatives for Russian intervention in 1850). But their aim is not necessarily the establishment of new international political, i.e. *territorial*, dominion. In the main they aim to influence the existing dominion.[1]

Discussion Questions

1. What does Weber mean by the term "social honor"? In your opinion, is this concept more, or less, relevant in contemporary society, compared to Weber's day?

2. How does Weber define the concept of "class"? How does this differ from "community," and why is this distinction important?
3. How do the "status order" and the "economic order" differ? Give examples of ways in which they influence each other.

Notes

**Wirtschaft und Gesellschaft,* part III, chap. 4, pp. 631–40. The first sentence in paragraph one and the several definitions in this chapter which are in brackets do not appear in the original text. They have been taken from other contexts of *Wirtschaft und Gesellschaft.*

One cross-reference footnote to a passage in *Wirtschaft und Gesellschaft,* p. 277, has been omitted, and one footnote has been placed in the text. A brief unfinished draft of a classification of status groups is appended to the German text; it has been omitted here.

1. The posthumously published text breaks off here. We omit an incomplete sketch of types of "warrior estates."

STUPIDITY "DECONSTRUCTED"

BY JOANNA KADI[1]

Dozens of workers move deliberately around the building site at the University of Minnesota, driving huge machines, handling dangerous equipment, carrying heavy loads. They can barely talk over the noise, but they are communicating and working together well. A wrongly-interpreted nod, a misunderstood word, a petty quarrel could mean the loss of a hand or a life. Although that's not the only reason for cooperative efforts; they're a common working-class practice.

I connect with these workers. I've lived with people like them, worked with people like them—I'm one of them. The worst jobs I've had were made bearable thanks to our jokes, camaraderie, easy flow of conversation. The familiar sweat, dirty hands, missing teeth, and lined faces reassure me. Workers.

Workers at the university. We've built every university that has ever existed, yet we're shunned and despised within academia's hallowed halls. Explicitly and implicitly, we've been taught our place—and it's not in a student's desk or the professors' lounge. We're needed to construct the university, maintain, clean, and repair it.

Oh, we're welcome here, as long as we stay where we're supposed to. We know the monster that presents itself if we dare step out of place. *Stupid. We are too stupid to study, learn, think, analyze, critique. Because working-class people are stupid.* So much energy goes into the social lie that poor people are stupid; capitalism needs a basic rationalization to explain why things happen the way they do. So we hear, over and over, that our lousy jobs and living situations result from our lack of smarts. I internalized this lie. Rationally, I knew money and brains didn't go hand in hand. But on deep unconscious levels, I believed in my own stupidity and in the stupidity of working-class people.

I want to examine these dynamics in this essay which I titled "Stupidity 'Deconstructed'" in order to connect with construction workers and to express my irritation toward postmodernists who consistently use the term. This piece goes hand in hand with the writing of working-class people committed to theorizing about our experiences in universities and factories. It's past time for such a movement; *we* must create theory about our lives. No one else. If middle- and upper-middle-class people want to write about indoctrination into class privilege and unlearning it, great. But leave the rest to us.

A sordid history lurks here. Middle- and upper-middle class academics have traditionally sought out the experiences and stories of working-class/working-poor people for use in shaping theory. That is, we provide the raw material of bare facts and touching stories; they transform these rough elements into theory. Sound familiar? Gosh, it sounds like an exact replication of factory activity. Academics have approached me after I've given presentations on class, and said, "The stories about your family are so interesting." (*Oh, thank you so much.*) "Don't you think they'd be stronger if you let them stand on their own?" Unedited translation: give me your stories, I'll write the theory. Leave it to the experts. *It's time to forget that shit.*

Joanna Kadi, "Stupidity Deconstructed," *Thinking Class: Sketches from a Cultural Worker,* pp. 39-57. Copyright © 1996 by Joanna Kadi. Reprinted with permission by South End Press.

Yes, I'm a Worthy Person, I Have Two University Degrees.

I understand the workings of universities. I paid attention when I studied at the University of Toronto and the Episcopal Divinity School in Massachusetts. I've hung out on other campuses, and heard more than enough university stories. Levels of elitism and arrogance vary with regional difference, size, prestige, and how many misfits end up on the campus, but the core system remains: privileged people belong here.

If only I'd known this years ago! Then anger, instead of feeling crazy, alienated, and stupid, would have been uppermost. *Don't get me started. Even hearing that word makes my blood boil Even hearing the word "smart" makes my blood boil. I want to wring your neck.*

From a young age, I loved to read and write and learn. But my future in that general motors city had been mapped out, and books didn't appear anywhere. I didn't like the map; nor did I like being surrounded by people who treated me like a handy repository for muddy boots and unmitigated rage. University offered a good solution (or so I thought). I started working paid jobs at age ten and saved every penny for the endeavor.

In Mr. Smythe's math class, the third floor of that ancient high school, sun streams through windows onto old wooden desks. Test results are read out loud—no surprises. Top marks for me, the Johnson twins, Brian Kingsley, Jonathon Woodley, Amanda Britian. Their label: brain. Mine: jock and party-er. Their parents: doctor, lawyer, psychiatrist, executive. Mine: line worker. Mr. Smythe advised the Johnson twins to apply to Waterloo or Toronto but not McMaster, and the intricacies of differences between these universities went way over my head; our guidance counselor poured over pamphlets and reference books with Brian once a week; Mr. and Mrs. Woodley and Jonathon drove to a different campus each weekend. I got wrecked every Friday and Saturday night and cruised around in cars driven by boys as stoned and drunk as me.

Despite my party-er status, despite the lack of help in selecting the "right" school, despite my total cluelessness, I applied to three universities. Only my grades appeared on transcripts; no entries for parents' work history or weekend activities. Fresh out of high school, naive but steadfast, I carried my cheap vinyl suitcase up those marble steps of Queen's University. Four months. I had cash for two years, but not enough class privilege. My throat locked, my tongue twisted, I sat in back rows with arms wrapped around chest and stomach. To say I felt like a fish out of water hardly describes my overwhelming feelings of confusion, depression, inadequacy, and shame. People actually asked me the year my grandparents graduated! Not just my parents, my *grandparents*. I thought everyone's grandparents were poor. I knew everyone's parents weren't poor, but I assumed everyone in the previous generation experienced poverty. Now rich white girls with straight teeth asked, "When did your grandparents graduate?" Four months. I'm surprised I lasted that long.

Years later I returned to those hallowed halls. Not through any formal, reasonable plan—more because I was pissed off. Today the whole thing strikes me as a big joke. During a bitter separation, a lawyer told me I could get more money from my ex-husband if I enrolled in university. During our marriage, I worked and supported him while he earned a degree, and I deserved an equivalent education. "Sounds good," I told her. We got the money and I went back to school.

Women's studies, University of Toronto. Middle-class and upper-middle-class women. *I'm so stupid.* I sat surrounded by women years younger than me, women exuding poise and confidence as they discussed graduate school options and Karl Marx. (Marx. Oh, yeah, that guy those other rich[2] people I worked with at CBC Radio used to spout off about.) *What am I doing here?* I talked to janitors and I talked to Kim, the last holdout for cigarettes in the whole department. We scrunched in corners of the smoking lounge so she could indulge and the smoke gave me a headache, but I didn't care. Better a headache than crazy. Kim anchored me. A white girl, working-class, smart as a whip, skinny and tough. We sat close together in back rows and whispered comments to each other because we couldn't say them out loud. I couldn't have made it without her.

Another bizarre turn of events dropped me in graduate school. A professor at U of T actually took an interest in me. My brain flip-flopped. "You should go on to graduate school," she told me earnestly. "You're very smart. And you have such good study habits. You would do so well." Smart? No, stupid. Graduate school? No, janitor. What is graduate school? What happens there? What's an M.A.? A Ph.D.? They must be the same things with different names. I said nothing out loud; that would reveal my stupidity. A friend told me about a university with a master's program in feminist ethics. I didn't know any other graduate programs. I didn't know how to find them. *I can't believe I'm writing this down. Now people will know just how stupid I really am.* I didn't know jackshit.

I applied for the feminist ethics program and laid out stringent conditions to make it as unlikely as possible I would ever get there. If the school offered me acceptance, a scholarship covering tuition, a job on campus, housing for my lover and me. Then, and only then, would I take the leap. My divorce money had dried up, and I would never, never in a million years, take out a loan. I knew all about loans and debts. Every working-class person I grew up with laid down the law: never take out a loan for anything except a mortgage on a house. Loans are bad. Debts are bad. You'll never get rid of these horrible burdens. I'd fly to the moon before borrowing money for graduate school. *Graduate school. What is it?*

The school met my stringent conditions. Uh-oh. But once there, I found Joann and Sheri and Meck, and we laughed until we cried and cried until we laughed about academia and how stupid we felt. We didn't have Aristotle and Socrates as reference points, couldn't even spell the names. We didn't know how to use the library system. We hadn't grown up with parents and family friends waxing nostalgic about university days and cutesy pranks, thus easing our entry into this strange world.

Then, something truly amazing. A working-class professor. I studied with one of the most brilliant minds in this country, Dr. Katie Geneva Cannon, a working-class, African-American woman from the South, who pushed me and pushed me and pushed me to think critically about class. Take it apart, figure it out, analyze it, *it's just like my brother used to do when he started building stereo equipment at age ten,* pull and pull and pull, you are smart, she said, you need to write. I sat in class, sweating, tongue-tied, scared shitless, and looked at her, teaching, questioning, inspiring, her brilliance shining like a star. *She was destined to cook and clean for white people, that is, if she didn't get something worse—if she can do it, maybe I can too.*

Buildings cut from fine stone and beautiful wood. My hands ache with the remembering. The maintenance men I worked with: Tony, shy and sweet with a faint Portuguese accent; Al, tough hide covering a heart like worn flannel; Eddy, drifting from job to job, booze on his breath, twisted grin, broken front tooth. I worked with them through the summer and felt so comfortable in our little lounge, drinking coffee and smoking, smoking, always smoking—rich people have given it up but we're still puffing away.

I spent hours wrestling with voices in my head telling me "You're stupid," and listening to trusted friends telling me "You're not stupid. This system makes you feel stupid." We figured out our own analysis: the university system is intricately linked with the capitalist system. People with power at the university will do their part to reinforce and promote the capitalist explanation for class difference—smart rich people, stupid poor people—in return for continued benefits and privileges from the current structure. They don't want a motley bunch of upstart working-class urchins figuring any of this out and refusing to sit in quiet shame.

They don't want graduates of their system to end up like me: class identity and loyalties stronger than ever, angry about the others who never had a chance, who still believe they're stupid, who always will, some already in their graves. Yes, I'm angry.

Constructing/Deconstructing: Building/Hiring

For the capitalist system to continue ruthlessly grinding on (or for the capitalist system to "succeed," as you would say) those of us bred for stupid and/or dangerous work must believe we're not as smart as the people who boss us around. It's critical. Capitalism needs simple explanations about why poor people with lousy jobs take orders from men in suits. Lack of brains fits the bill. (So does the lie that rich people work harder. I'll tackle that in another essay.) Any noticeable class divisions stem from difference in intellectual capacity. Connected to this is the touting of "American ingenuity" as the doorway to upward mobility. It's as untrue as the existence of a whole class of stupid people, but if enough people believe it—even partially believe it—this idea will reinforce and strengthen capitalism. After all, if we believe brains lead to success, we'll blame ourselves for not getting ahead. Personal failure, not systemic oppression, explains why we're going nowhere so very fast.

I grew up learning the bulk of the population in our small general motors city—that is, workers—was stupid. Dumb, brutish, boring, close to animals. Did I believe it? In some ways, I knew people in my family had brains and the bosses didn't. My extended family joked about it frequently. But just as frequently, they indicated they believed it. And at deep levels, I internalized the lie and lived with it for years. It impacted my thoughts, decisions, and actions, and surfaced resoundingly when I entered university. The smugness and certainty with which upper-middle-class people paraded their brain cells jarred me; for a time I was taken in by this, and it contrasted so sharply with my inability to speak, let alone parade, that I felt I really must be stupid. Thankfully, that didn't last long. *Who knows what will happen if we realize that we're not so stupid and you're not so smart? Maybe you'll lose privileges and status. Maybe you'll have to clean up your own messes. Maybe we'll find fulfilling work and the drudge work will be shared equally. Maybe we'll remove your feet from our necks.*

Of course, I didn't feel stupid at university only because of constructions concerning stupid workers. That coupled with an unfamiliar upper-middle-class world made me feel stupid. I didn't know any of the middle-class/upper-middle-class reference points and contexts, ranging from GRE's and LSAT's to Ph.D.'s and post-doc fellowships. I couldn't swish around with the entitlement of privileged students; I crept. I liked janitors more than professors; more to the point, I identified with janitors, not professors.

Language proved crucially important in opening a door into clarity, awareness, and class pride. It happened this way: I grew up around people who built things—houses, additions on houses, large buildings. They talked about it by saying, "I built that." This meant they planned and designed something, then picked up a hammer, nails, and saw, and began constructing.

University professors used this same phrase, often when discussing summer homes. They said authoritatively, "I built that." I knew what it meant to build something and I thought they meant they must have built their summer home. But they didn't look like they knew anything about construction work. I felt confused. I was astounded when I stumbled across the translation. "I built this" really meant "I hired some of you to build this for me."

So. Privileged people misuse language in ways that distort meanings of commonplace, easy-to-understand words like "build." This told me something. Then I read articles focusing on class, usually written by university professors. I looked forward to these, because I needed to develop my class analysis and thought these articles would help. But again disappointment and shame resulted. I didn't understand most of what I read. Abstract and impersonal, these essays stood three times removed from concrete reality of working-class life.

After confusion and shame, another door opened. If they misused a simple word like build, how could I trust them? If their articles used weird words like "proletariat" and showed they didn't know the first thing about us, maybe they weren't quite so smart. *Maybe we weren't quite so stupid.*

My hunch solidified after examining academic attraction to and use of postmodern theory and language. This horrible mix of distorted language and casual appropriation of our ideas allowed me once and for all to dismiss the ideology about stupid workers. As far as I can tell, postmodern theoreticians say nothing new, but their inaccessible language makes it appear as though they do. For example, they're fascinated with the notion that multiple realities exist in society, and they've written and theorized extensively about this.

Puh-lease. Everybody in my neighborhood, including the mechanics who had to sniff carbon monoxide in tiny, enclosed garages all day long, grasped that idea with no problem. We lived it. We had our reality, the bosses had theirs, and we understood them both. Theorists like W. E. B. Du Bois wrote about double consciousness—whereby African Americans understand their reality and white people's—at the turn of this century. But I've never seen postmodernists attribute these ideas to the people of color and/or working-class people who've lived and understood them for centuries. Instead, postmodernists steal these ideas and dress them up in language so inaccessible only a tiny, elite group can discuss them.

We need to ask, and begin answering, hard, practical questions. Who defines smart and stupid, and why? Who misuses language, and for whose benefit? Who writes theory, and why? Who goes to university, and why? Who does the academy serve? Can universities be transformed into places where everyone is welcomed and respected?

In this country, the first institutions of higher learning were trade or agricultural schools and theological centers, with liberal arts colleges and medical schools following. Around the turn of this century, with the establishment of standardization and class-biased guidelines, universities took on the task of serving middle- and upper-class white men. That group enjoyed peace and quiet for several decades, until the rest of us began banging on the door. Grudgingly, after years and years of hard work, little chinks appeared in those thick, stone doors. *The doors we built, with our hands. The doors we couldn't walk through.* The misfits demanded entrance: Africans, Asians, Natives, Arabs, Latinos, women, queers, even welfare mothers. Even the sons and daughters of factory workers and miners and janitors. What's a rich white man to do? The stress must be unbelievable. Poor guys.

Capitalism exists as a human construct, not a natural or innate system. We've been steeped in lies about its inevitability, and it seems to take on its own life as its institutions reinforce each other and the system. But it *is* a human construct, carefully set up to keep a small number of people stretched out comfortably along the backs of the rest of us. Remember: human constructs can be destroyed.

Rich Equals Smart, Poor Equals Stupid

I think of the university and a swift hot anger rushes from the pit of my stomach, sweeps through my throat, bursts out of my mouth. Stone buildings beautifully carved, wooden rooms beautifully balanced. Underpaid exploited workers. Our hands next to the hands of a professor "deconstructing" ideas with strings of six-syllable words. *Stupid.* Underpaid exploited workers keeping these buildings clean. *Stupid.* I think of myself and working-class friends sitting in back rows, saying nothing, sweating, fearful that one word from these stubborn, hurt mouths will betray us, will expose ourselves/our class.

Many mechanisms have been created in this rigidly defined, class-structured society to keep poor people in our place. Our place. We crouch over and the rest of you keep your feet on our necks. You sit complacently, feet resting comfortably—"Could you move just a little bit to the left?"—crossing ankles, smiling in our direction—"Very nice." One such mechanism is the constant, cross-racial image of the worker as stupid. Growing up, I attached "stupid" to workers and "smart" to executives. This didn't happen because of a weird personal quirk. It resulted from force-fed images and words of TV shows, newspapers, magazines, and movies. Any TV show with working-class characters, first "The Honeymooners" and "I Love Lucy," then "All In the Family," covertly and overtly highlighted the stupidity of bus drivers, factory workers, and plumbers. Movies, books, and comics followed suit. At school, middle-class kids called us stupid; we hurled back "stuck up," but never "stupid." Working-class/working-poor kids failed and dropped out, but not middle-class kids. Our town newspaper consistently portrayed general motors executives as calm, rational types, while union members appeared unthinking, wild, and chaotic.

Oh, you're exaggerating. You've gone too far. Stupid merely refers to someone not terribly intelligent. You've attached all these cultural, class-based meanings. You're way out on a limb. Chill out. People are gonna think you're nuts.

I look up "stupid" in the dictionary and find: 1. slow of mind, obtuse, brutish; 2. dulled in feeling or sensation, torpid; 3. marked by or resulting from dullness, senseless; 4. lacking interest or point, vexatious, exasperating.[3] I look up stupid in the dictionary and feel: 1. recognition; 2. affirmation of what I have felt my whole life and what I am saying in this essay; 3. fury; 4. disgust.

This dictionary definition fits precisely with what I learned in my bones before I could talk. A very particular set of cultural baggage goes along with stupid. Not a mere description of how well someone thinks, stupid has become a cultural concept with a particular code and set of signifiers that describe working-class people as the middle and upper classes perceive and construct us. It doesn't truthfully describe working-class people; rather, it speaks clearly to the particular understanding rich people created and maintain with a vengeance.

Brutish, dull, senseless. *I grew up believing we're thick-skinned, slow-witted, impervious to pain, boring.* The dominant culture drove this point home relentlessly. Someone called me sensitive and I couldn't grasp her meaning. *Working-class people can't be sensitive.* Rich people construct us as stupid and brainwash us Day One to make us believe it. We read their newspapers, watch their TV shows, take in their movies, and work jobs that reinforce what we see and hear. A vicious cycle.

What's the reality? I do know working-class people who fit the stereotype. Of course, their brains have been fried from decades of drudge work. Like Howie, my partner on the assembly line. Slow, barely able to get a complete sentence out of his mouth, unable to believe I learned his job in two hours. Vacant look, hollow eyes. Couldn't read. *You try working on an assembly line, at the same station, for thirty-eight years. How interesting will you be? How much will you know about world affairs? How creative will you feel?*

It's painful to acknowledge the fact that some of our brains have been fried. Not stupid from birth, as rich people insist, but fried from decades of the most boring, idiotic, repetitive work imaginable. I've done it. I fought every minute to keep my mind away from the hovering void. The boredom, lethargy, apathy, and meaninglessness surrounding that factory, surrounding every factory, constitutes a horrible and violating reality of daily life.

Stupid. They marked my family as stupid, and this confused me. I didn't think we were, but had no tools for arguing against such an intense social construct. I grew more confused and internalized the belief in my own stupidity, as all around me, my family proceeded with their lives and used their brains. My aunt went from grade school education to neighborhood CPA; she knew all the deductions, could add numbers ridiculously quickly, and did everyone's taxes for free. My grandfather, literate in three languages, poor, steered new Lebanese immigrants through the morass of landlords, bosses, lawyers. My father and uncles, with their tenth-grade educations, filled out daily crossword puzzles with pens and painstakingly planned, calculated, measured, added rooms on small houses, with wiring, plumbing, support beams, ceilings, floor tiles, never a sixteenth of an inch out. I once helped a friend build a porch, holding boards in place as she hammered, blinking in disbelief because half-inch gaps appeared. My mother and aunts balanced budgets, paying bills with nonexistent funds, borrowing some from here, begging some from there, adding and subtracting large numbers in their heads.

Class socialization begins early. Material possessions, home environment, and neighborhood provide information about our present situation and our future. Family members' sense of/lack of entitlement and expectation provides more. Social constructions of class, put out by institutions such as media and school, are a third factor. Whether family members resist or unquestioningly take in these social constructions impacts class socialization.

For a continuous supply of expendable workers, capitalism must offer ideas and experiences that reinforce each other. If people who look, act, talk, and live like you are constantly portrayed as working particular jobs because they're too stupid to get anything better, chances are you'll believe the lie when you end up in the same factory.

Ideas help reinforce and explain different class locations. Capitalism relies on various institutions, such as the university, to pass on relevant knowledge about the system. Universities need to replicate and reinforce central ideologies. Such as poor people stupid, rich people smart—a perfect example of the kind of polarized thinking that has hindered and weakened Western thought for centuries. These categorizations feed into an either/or mentality and ignore complications and complexities. They also shore up oppressive systems of racism, sexism, and classism because of the positive meaning attached to one half of the equation and the negative meaning attached to the other—male/female, white/black, heterosexual/homosexual, virgin/whore, thinking/feeling. I always include rich/poor and smart/stupid in this list of important categories; lately I've begun to perceive the ways they map on to each other to become richsmart/poorstupid.

In the years I spent in Women's Studies, we spent hours and hours analyzing the superficial nature of dualistic thinking around men/women, white/black, and thinking/feeling, and reflected on more complicated and realistic understandings. But we never touched on the smart/stupid, rich/poor breakdown. (Of course, we were in a university classroom.) This particular ideological split goes a long way to support the dangerous, classist myth I've discussed in this essay. It's time to pay attention.

In thinking about rich smart/poor stupid, we need to analyze stupidity and intelligence. Writing this essay might play into the belief that only one kind of intelligence exists, the kind defined and revered by the ruling class in conjunction with academics, because I focus on the university, the stupid/smart dichotomy, and class oppression. That's not my intention. In the same ways I understand the category of "race" as a myth while acknowledging the reality of racism and different physical/cultural traits, I want to put "intelligence" as defined in a limited and narrow way by the ruling class into the myth category, while acknowledging a variety of mental capacities and different types of intelligence.[4]

Many different kinds of intelligence exist, and these cross class lines. Universities revere the type of intelligence that can synthesize information rapidly and understand abstract concepts. Equally valid types of intelligence enable a child to design and build a bird house, a mother to balance a budget with no money, an "uneducated" man to enthrall listeners with stories, a young woman who hasn't had music lessons to compose a piano tune, a girl to write a poem, a homeless person to comprehend the poem, a neighborhood to devise a plan to stop a company from dumping toxic waste, three young women to invent scathing responses to catcalls and whistles. These types of intelligence require creativity, humor, ability to ask questions, care, a good memory, compassion, belief in solidarity, ability to project an image of something that doesn't physically exist.

Some manual-labor jobs require intelligent, creative thinking, such as carpentry, video technology, and grounds keeping/designing. Most manual-labor jobs require little thinking of any sort, and are marked by monotony and danger. Some executive jobs require intelligence and creative thinking, and most don't. (None, however, are likely to be dangerous.) On the whole, capitalism has offered little in the way of stimulating, educational, growth-enhancing work experiences.

Can I Really Be Working-Class and Smart?

The sarcasm in this heading is an attempt to get at underlying and often unconscious beliefs about stupidity which popped up constantly after I got my master's degree. People freaked out. Working-class people with university degrees freak out ourselves and our middle-class "brothers and sisters" (more sarcasm). We ask: "Am I still working-class?" Middle-class people inform us, delicately and sensitively: "You're not working-class anymore."

Where do these reactions come from? Let me first examine what working-class people mean when we say: *am I working-class now?* I have a university degree. A secret subtext, a critical message lurks here.

One day I figured out my translation. When I asked: "Am I working-class now that I have a university degree," I meant: "Am I working-class now that I'm smart?" Back to my theory about dualistic thinking. If the stupid/smart dichotomy is a cornerstone of the academy, and if this division rests clearly along class lines (rich people smart/poor people stupid) then conferring university degrees onto middle- and upper-class people isn't only about knowledge, courses passed, GPAs, degrees, and job security. University degrees constitute a symbol, a marker, so the world understands the bearer comes from the middle/upper-class. Degrees separate this group from lowly, unprivileged, stupid workers.

Then working-class people traverse the minefield of academia and end up with initials after our names. We get confused. Very confused, because those initials symbolize the separation between rich and poor. Rich people need these degrees to feel smart, to remind themselves they are not a lowly janitor sweeping halls, a lowly cook slopping out lousy cafeteria food. They need them, but somehow we end up with them. We get confused. Are we announcing we're smart? But working-class people can't be smart. *If we are working-class, we can't be smart. Therefore, since we've earned a university degree, we are no longer working-class.*

Now, that's not true, for at least three reasons. First, whatever is going on subconsciously, consciously I know rich people aren't necessarily smart. Having cleaned their houses, read their garbled manuscripts, and "typed" (code word for "re-wrote") their incoherent essays, I'm well aware of this.

Second, whatever silly initials my friends and I carry after our names, we're still working-class.[5] We still talk the same and feel the same and work shit jobs. We don't float around thinking we're entitled to everything; we don't grab whatever we want. We don't acquire privilege, entitlement, and arrogance after slogging it out in the academy.

Third, all of this begs the question: does class location change if one factor governing class location alters? Some people say yes. For them, once working-class people make a good salary they cease being working-class. By the same standard, if working-class people earn university degrees, they leave their class of origin.

I disagree with this, since I believe class identity comes from many places: education, values, culture, income, dwelling, lifestyle, manners, friends, ancestry, language, expectations, desires, sense of entitlement, religion, neighborhood, amount of privacy.[6] If one of these, such as education, shifts dramatically, class identity doesn't change.

Let me return to the statement of "fact" made by middle-class people: "You can't be working class. You have a university degree." I want to address this because I've heard it frequently, usually after I've asserted my working-class identity.

The remark contains arrogance that goes unnoticed by the speaker *(surprise, surprise)* but not by me *(surprise, surprise)*. When a person with class privilege takes on the task of defining and articulating class location of someone from a lower class, it's arrogant and offensive.

Does this happen because working-class people claiming our identity threaten class-privileged people? In the United States, class is a taboo subject for everyone, let alone some upstart housecleaner or garbage man. Rich people need an automatic response, and seem to prefer a verbal attack that immediately silences the speaker. Discounting someone's identity usually does the trick.

This action is similar to the way white people try to shut me up when I critique racism: they question my identity as a person of color because of my light skin. Middle-class people attempt to shut me up by discrediting me, calling my identity into question, anything to stop me from claiming a working-class identity from which I might offer some criticism of their class privilege.

Implicit in middle-class people's assertion that I have indeed "moved up" is the ever popular belief that upward mobility is easily achieved and highly desirous. Neither of these is true, as far as I can tell. Some small percentage of working-class families have moved into the middle class in one or two generations, but they are the exception rather than the rule. As for upward mobility being highly desirable? Not for me. The values, ethics, simple lifestyles, and cultures of working-class people from any racial/ethnic group appeal to me more than the constrained emotional life, isolation, and gross materialism of rich people. The only aspect of class privilege I find desirable is rich people's innate belief/knowledge that options about life—from job choice to education to creative activities—really do exist. Not to mention the freedom from despair over whether the rent will be paid or whether food will appear on the table.

How Do You Spell "Class"?

Universities have changed in the last twenty years. Critiques of the system, hard questions, cross-disciplinary dialogues, new programs and departments springing up—Women's Studies, Ethnic Studies, Queer Studies. This is great, but what about class? I know the kind of rampant sexism, racism, and heterosexism progressive professors and administrators deal with as they struggle to change curricula, but it's hard to deal with the classism of this crowd because I expect more. I'm dismayed to read the advanced theories these people offer when discussing race, gender, or sexuality, and contrast that to blank looks about the c-l-a-s-s word.[7]

I've heard progressive professors present information about social change movements, and been excited to study common people's history and struggles. But I'm angry when pertinent information about participants' class location doesn't enter the discussion. In a lecture about the 1960s' Black civil rights movement, a professor carefully delineated racial issues but somehow forgot to mention that most people putting their asses on the line were poor. Another professor discussed "gay men" and "lesbians" fighting back at the Stonewall riots. I didn't learn until later that Black and Puerto Rican drag queens and white butches and femmes really carried off the honors; none of them held executive day jobs.[8] I want to call progressive professors on their failure to integrate class into the curriculum, on their failure to notice they are as out-to-lunch about class as the straight white men they criticize.

Hand in hand with changes to existing institutions, I propose the establishment of new institutions. I want Working Class Studies set up. I want working-class and working-poor histories, cultures, ideologies, theories, languages studied. I want the many worthy individuals who spent their lives working for social justice studied and examined. I want us teaching each other, want the labor halls and community centers filled with janitors, secretaries, housecleaners, garbage men, lineworkers, want us in charge of curriculum and reading lists and teaching. I envision us at the center; I don't want "experts" explaining our lives to us, standing behind a lectern and pontificating for two hours on proletarians.

Maybe I'm paranoid, but I anticipate this reaction to my idea: *You've got to be kidding.* Eyes focused on the front of the room, looking anywhere else but toward me, silence, shifting bodies, unease, a bright smile from the professor: "Thank you for that interesting suggestion. Shall we move on?" *It's happened to we before. Once I actually told a group of rich, white students I thought we should have Class Speak-Outs where only poor people could speak. No one looked at me. My words rolled into a hole in the middle of the floor and disappeared from the face of the earth.* I know what the reaction to this will be: what on earth are you suggesting? *Study a bunch of stupid rednecks?*[9] Chuckle, chuckle.

Conclusion

At 3:00 p.m., construction workers on the University of Minnesota campus finish up. Privileged university students grumble about what an easy job these guys have and how early they're leaving. They have no idea these workers arrived at 6:00 or 7:00 in the morning. They don't know how a body feels after eight hours of physical labor. They don't care.

As for me, I just watch the workers go by and feel many things. I feel at home, because these men look so familiar, from their flannel shirts, jeans, and workboots down to lunch pails and thermoses, cigarettes, and hard hats. I feel comfortable, because I like being around them. *These are my people. And we're not stupid.* I feel angry, because I know how students and professors perceive these workers. Because I know some of these workers believe the lies about who's stupid and who's smart, who has the right to think and study here and who has the right to build and clean here.

But I am clear. *I'm working-class. I'm smart. Just like the people I grew up with.* We know how to screw the system, we know how to take care of ourselves and survive when the odds are against us. We cook tasty meals with one onion, build our own stereo speakers, cut precisely-fitting pieces of wood for porches, know how to wire our houses and sew clothes, we like to read and think and talk to each other. We make music and art and tell stories. We know how to work cooperatively and we know how to give, generously, both hands open.

I've figured out I belong in the university. Not just when they need a janitor, or a cook, or a construction worker. But when I want to go. If I choose to study there, I won't let anyone make me feel stupid; I'll remember why it's so important they try. I won't let them turn me into an assimilationist, a fraud, a middle-class-identified polite girl who's grateful for all the help these nice rich people offer. I'll stay true to my roots. I'll use my brains, and my hands, to take this system apart. I'll use my brains, and my hands, to get your feet off my neck.

Notes

1. Thanks to Jan Binder, Elizabeth Clare, Cynthia Lane, Jeff Nygaard, and Susan Raffo for their help with this piece.
2. In this essay, when I use the word "rich," I mean anyone middle-class and up. Poor means anyone working-class and down. That is the way the working-class and working-poor people I grew up with use the terms. I find these categories problematic on one hand because they miss a lot of the subtleties of class. For example, they ignore my privilege of being working-class instead of working-poor. On the other hand, I still find them powerful and appropriate categories. Middle-class people, who could choose to realize they are also being duped by rich people and decide they would be better off aligning themselves with working-class and working-poor people, continually align themselves with the rich. This is another reason to include middle-class people in the "rich" group.
3. From *Webster's New Collegiate Dictionary,* 1979.
4. Thanks to Jeff Nygaard for helping me articulate this point.
5. I also know other working-class people who have earned a university degree and are no longer working-class identified. These people are intent on passing and assimilating. I'm not

sure if they are really middle-class, but they are certainly middle-class identified.

6. Thanks to Dr. Katie Cannon, for articulating all of this so clearly.
7. A notable exception to the lack of discussion/curriculum around this issue are the courses I took from Dr. Katie Cannon, which consistently dealt with critical questions relating to race, class, sex, ability, and sexuality. Dr. Cannon is continuing this groundbreaking work at Temple University in Philadelphia.
8. I want to mention here the regular inclusion, in Women's Studies, of the women's campaign to get the vote. I believe it is an important struggle to study, but I've also come to believe that part of its popularity in women's studies is that the social location of those activists reflects the social location of the women teaching in those programs in a way that other struggles usually do not.
9. For the best discussion I have ever read on the offensiveness of rich people using the term "redneck," read Elliott, "Whenever I Tell You the Language We Use is a Class Issue, You Nod Your Head in Agreement—and Then You Open Your Mouth," *Out of the Class Closet: Lesbians Speak*, Julia Penelope, editor (Freedom, CA: The Crossing Press, 1994). Elliott's article first appeared in *Lesbian Ethics*, vol. 4, no. 2 (Spring 1991).

RACE

Racial Formation

Inequality Hidden in Plain View

Whiteness as Contingent Hierarchies

RACIAL FORMATION

Understanding Race and Racism in the Post-Civil Rights Era

BY MICHAEL OMI AND HOWARD WINANT

In 1982–83, Susie Guillory Phipps unsuccessfully sued the Louisiana Bureau of Vital Records to change her racial classification from black to white. The descendent of an 18th century white planter and a black slave, Phipps was designated "black" in her birth certificate in accordance with a 1970 state law which declared anyone with at least 1/32nd "Negro blood" to be black.

The Phipps case raised intriguing questions about the concept of race, its meaning in contemporary society, and its use (and abuse) in public policy. Assistant Attorney General Ron Davis defended the law by pointing out that some type of racial classification was necessary to comply with federal record-keeping requirements and to facilitate programs for the prevention of genetic diseases. Phipps's attorney, Brian Begue, argued that the assignment of racial categories on birth certificates was unconstitutional and that the 1/32nd designation was inaccurate. He called on a retired Tulane University professor who cited research indicating that most Louisiana whites have at least 1/20th "Negro" ancestry.

In the end, Phipps lost. The court upheld the state's right to classify and quantify racial identity.[1]

Phipps's problematic racial identity, and her effort to resolve it through state action, is in many ways a parable of America's unsolved racial dilemma. It illustrates the difficulties of defining race and assigning individuals or groups to racial categories. It shows how the racial legacies of the past—slavery and bigotry—continue to shape the present. It reveals both the deep involvement of the state in the organization and interpretation of race, and the inadequacy of state institutions to carry out these functions. It demonstrates how deeply Americans both as individuals and as a civilization are shaped, and indeed haunted, by race.

Having lived her whole life thinking that she was white, Phipps suddenly discovers that by legal definition she is not. In U.S. society, such an event is indeed catastrophic.[2] But if she is not white, of what race is she? The state claims that she is black, based on its rules of classification,[3] and another state agency, the court, upholds this judgment. Despite the classificatory standards that have imposed an either-or logic on racial identity, Phipps will not in fact "change color." Unlike what would have happened during slavery times if one's claim to whiteness was successfully challenged, we can assume that despite the outcome of her legal challenge, Phipps will remain in most of the social relationships she had occupied before the trial. Her socialization, her familial and friendship networks, her cultural orientation, will not change. She will simply have to wrestle with her newly acquired "hybridized" condition. She will have to confront the "other" within.

The designation of racial categories and the assignment of race is no simple task. For centuries, this question has precipitated intense debates and conflicts, particularly in the U.S.—disputes over natural and legal rights, over the distribution of resources, and indeed, over who shall live and who shall die.

Michael Omi and Howard Winant, "Racial Formation: Understanding Race and Racism In the Post-Civil Rights Era," *Race, Class, and Gender in the United States*, ed. Paula S. Rothenberg, pp. 53-76. Copyright © 1994 by Taylor & Francis Group LLC. Reprinted with permission.

A crucial dimension of the Phipps case is that it illustrates the inadequacy of claims that race is a mere matter of variations in human physiognomy, that it is simply a matter of skin "color." But if race cannot be understood in this manner, how can it be understood? We cannot fully hope to address this topic—no less than the meaning of race, its role in society, and the forces that shape it—in one chapter, nor indeed in one book. Our goal, however, is far from modest: we wish to offer at least the outlines of a theory of race and racism.

What Is Race?

There is a continuous temptation to think of race as an essence, as something fixed, concrete and objective. And there is also an opposite temptation: to imagine race as a mere illusion, a purely ideological construct that some ideal non-racist social order would eliminate. It is necessary to challenge both these positions, to disrupt and reframe the rigid and bipolar manner in which they are posed and debated, and to transcend the presumably irreconcilable relationship between them.

The effort must be made to understand race as an unstable and "decentered" complex of social meanings constantly being transformed by political struggle. With this in mind, let us propose a definition: *race is a concept that signifies and symbolizes social conflicts and interests by referring to different types of human bodies.* Although the concept of race invokes biologically-based human characteristics (so-called "phenotypes"), selection of these particular human features for purposes of racial signification is always and necessarily a social and historical process. In contrast to the other major distinction of this type, that of gender, there is no biological basis for distinguishing among human groups along the lines of race.[4] Indeed, the categories employed to differentiate among human groups along racial lines reveal themselves, upon serious examination, to be at best imprecise, and at worst completely arbitrary.

If the concept of race is so nebulous, can we not dispense with it? Can we not "do without" race, at least in the "enlightened" present? This question has been posed often, and with greater frequency in recent years.[5] An affirmative answer would of course present obvious practical difficulties: it is rather difficult to jettison widely held beliefs, beliefs which moreover are central to everyone's identity and understanding of the social world. So the attempt to banish the concept as an archaism is at best counterintuitive. But a deeper difficulty, we believe, is inherent in the very formulation of this schema, in its way of posing race as a problem, a misconception left over from the past, and suitable now only for the dustbin of history.

A more effective starting point is the recognition that despite its uncertainties and contradictions, the concept of race continues to play a fundamental role in structuring and representing the social world. The task for theory is to explain this situation. It is to avoid both the utopian framework that sees race as an illusion we can somehow "get beyond," and also the essentialist formulation that sees race as something objective and fixed, a biological datum.[6] Thus we should think of race as an element of social structure rather than as an irregularity within it; we should see race as a dimension of human representation rather than an illusion. These perspectives inform the theoretical approach we call racial formation.

Racial Formation

We define racial formation as *the sociohistorical process by which racial categories are created, lived out, transformed, and destroyed.* Our attempt to elaborate a theory of racial formation will proceed in two steps. First, we argue that racial formation is a process of historically situated projects in which human bodies and social structures are represented and organized. Next we link racial formation to the evolution of hegemony, the way in which society is organized and ruled. Such an approach, we believe, can facilitate understanding of a whole range of contemporary controversies and dilemmas involving race, including the nature of racism, the relationship of race to other forms of differences, inequalities, and oppression such as sexism and nationalism, and the dilemmas of racial identity today.

From a racial formation perspective, race is a matter of both social structure and cultural representation. Too often, the attempt is made to understand race simply or primarily in terms of only one of these two analytical dimensions.[7] For example, efforts to explain racial inequality as a purely social structural phenomenon are unable to account for the origins, patterning, and transformation of racial difference. Conversely, many examinations of racial difference—understood as a matter of cultural attributes a la ethnicity theory, or as a society-wide signification system, a la some poststructuralist accounts—cannot comprehend such structural phenomena as racial stratification in the labor market or patterns of residential segregation.

An alternative approach is to think of racial formation processes as occurring through a linkage between structure and representation. Racial projects do the ideological "work" of making these links. A racial project is simultaneously an interpretation, representation, or explanation of racial dynamics, and an effort to reorganize and redistribute resources along particular racial lines. Racial projects connect what race means in a particular discursive practice and the ways in which both social structures and everyday experiences are racially organized, based upon that meaning. Let us consider this proposition, first in terms of large-scale or macro-level social processes, and then in terms of other dimensions of the racial formation process.

Racial Formation as a Macro-Level Social Process

To interpret the meaning of race is to frame it social structurally. Consider for example, this statement by Charles Murray on welfare reform:

> My proposal for dealing with the racial issue in social welfare is to repeal every bit of legislation and reverse every court decision that in any way requires, recommends, or awards differential treatment according to race, and thereby put us back onto the track that we left in 1965. We may argue about the appropriate limits of government intervention in trying to enforce the ideal, but at least it should be possible to identify the ideal: Race is not a morally admissible reason for treating one person differently from another. Period.[8]

Here there is a partial but significant analysis of the meaning of race: it is not a morally valid basis upon which to treat people "differently from one another." We may notice someone's race, but we cannot act upon that awareness. We must act in a "color-blind" fashion. This analysis of the meaning of race is immediately linked to a specific conception of the role of race in the social structure: it can play no part in government action, save in "the enforcement of the ideal." No state policy can legitimately require, recommend, or award different status according to race. This example can be classified as a particular type of racial project in the present-day U.S.—a "neoconservative" one.

Conversely, to recognize the racial dimension in social structure is to interpret the meaning of race. Consider the following statement by the late Supreme Court Justice Thurgood Marshall on minority "set-aside" programs:

> A profound difference separates governmental actions that themselves are racist, and governmental actions that seek to remedy the effects of prior racism or to prevent neutral government activity from perpetuating the effects of such racism.[9]

Here the focus is on the racial dimensions of social structure—in this case of state activity and policy. The argument is that state actions in the past and present have treated people in very different ways according to their race, and thus the government cannot retreat from its policy responsibilities in this area. It cannot suddenly declare itself "color-blind" without in fact perpetuating the same type of differential, racist treatment.[10] Thus, race continues to signify difference and structure inequality. Here, racialized social structure is immediately linked to an interpretation of the meaning of race. This example too can be classified as a particular type of racial project in the present-day U.S.—a "liberal" one.

These two examples of contemporary racial projects are drawn from mainstream political debate; they may be characterized as center-right and center-left expressions of contemporary racial politics.[11] We can, however, expand the discussion of racial formation processes far beyond these familiar examples. In fact, we can identify racial projects in at least three other analytical dimensions: first, the political spectrum can be broadened to include radical projects, on both the left and right, as well as along other political axes. Second, analysis of racial projects can take place not only at the macro-level of racial policy-making, state activity, and collective action, but also at the level of everyday experience. Third, the concept of racial projects can be applied across historical time, to identify racial formation dynamics in the past. We shall now offer examples of each of these types of racial projects.

The Political Spectrum of Racial Formation

We have encountered examples of a neoconservative racial project, in which the significance of race is denied, leading to a "color-blind" racial politics and "hands off" policy orientation; and of a "liberal" racial project, in which the significance of race is affirmed, leading to an egalitarian and "activist" state policy. But these by no means exhaust the political possibilities. Other racial projects can be readily identified on the contemporary U.S. scene. For example, "far right" projects, which uphold biologistic and racist views of difference, explicitly argue for white supremacist policies. "New right" projects overtly claim to hold "color-blind" views, but covertly manipulate racial fears in order to achieve political gains.[12] On the left, "radical democratic" projects invoke notions of racial "difference" in combination with egalitarian politics and policy.

Further variations can also be noted. For example, "nationalist" projects, both conservative and radical, stress the incompatibility of racially-defined group identity with the legacy of white supremacy, and therefore advocate a social structural solution of separation, either complete or partial.[13] As we saw in Chapter 3, nationalist currents represent a profound legacy of the centuries of racial absolutism that initially defined the meaning of race in the U.S. Nationalist concerns continue to influence racial debate in the form of Afrocentrism and other expressions of identity politics.

Taking the range of politically organized racial projects as a whole, we can "map" the current pattern of racial formation at the level of the public sphere, the "macro-level" in which public debate and mobilization takes place.[14] But important as this is, the terrain on which racial formation occurs is broader yet.

Racial Formation as Everyday Experience

Here too racial projects link signification and structure, not so much as efforts to shape policy or define large-scale meaning, but as the applications of "common sense." To see racial projects operating at the level of everyday life, we have only to examine the many ways in which, often unconsciously, we "notice" race.

One of the first things we notice about people when we meet them (along with their sex) is their race. We utilize race to provide clues about who a person is. This fact is made painfully obvious when we encounter someone whom we cannot conveniently racially categorize—someone who is, for example, racially "mixed" or of an ethnic/racial group we are not familiar with. Such an encounter becomes a source of discomfort and momentarily a crisis of racial meaning.

Our ability to interpret racial meanings depends on preconceived notions of a racialized social structure. Comments such as, "Funny, you don't look black," betray an underlying image of what black should be. We expect people to act out their apparent racial identities; indeed we become disoriented when they do not. The black banker harassed by police while walking in casual clothes through his own well-off neighborhood, the Latino or white kid rapping in perfect Afro patois, the unending faux pas committed by whites who assume that the nonwhites they encounter are servants or tradespeople, the belief that nonwhite colleagues are less qualified persons hired to fulfill affirmative action guidelines, indeed the whole gamut of racial stereotypes—that "white men can't jump," that Asians can't dance, etc. etc.—all testify to the way a racialized social structure shapes racial experience and conditions meaning. Analysis of such stereotypes reveals the always present, already active link between our view of the social structure—its demography, its laws, its customs, its threats—and our conception of what race means.

Conversely, our ongoing interpretation of our experience in racial terms shapes our relations to the institutions and organizations through which we are imbedded in social structure. Thus we expect differences in skin color, or other racially coded characteristics, to explain social differences. Temperament, sexuality, intelligence, athletic ability, aesthetic preferences, and so on are presumed to be fixed and discernible from the palpable mark of race. Such diverse questions as our confidence and trust in others (for example, clerks or salespeople, media figures, neighbors), our sexual preferences and romantic images, our tastes in music, films, dance, or sports, and our very ways of talking, walking, eating, and dreaming become racially coded simply because we live in a society where racial awareness is so pervasive. Thus in ways too comprehensive even to monitor consciously, and despite periodic calls—neoconservative and otherwise—for us to ignore race and adopt "color-blind" racial attitudes, skin color "differences" continue to rationalize distinct treatment of racially-identified individuals and groups.

To summarize the argument so far: the theory of racial formation suggests that society is suffused with racial projects, large and small, to which all are subjected. This racial "subjection" is quintessentially ideological. Everybody learns some combination, some version, of the rules of racial classification, and of her own racial identity, often without obvious teaching or conscious inculcation. Thus are we inserted in a comprehensively racialized social structure. Race becomes "common sense"—a way of comprehending, explaining, and acting in the world. A vast web of racial projects mediates between the discursive or representational means in which race is identified and signified on the one hand, and the institutional and organizational forms in which it is routinized and standardized on the other. These projects are the heart of the racial formation process.

Under such circumstances, it is not possible to represent race discursively without simultaneously locating it, explicitly or implicitly, in a social structural (and historical) context. Nor is it possible to organize, maintain, or transform social structures without simultaneously engaging, once more either explicitly or implicitly, in racial signification. Racial formation, therefore, is a kind of synthesis, an outcome, of the interaction of racial projects on a society-wide level. These projects are, of course, vastly different in scope and effect. They include large-scale public action, state activities, and interpretations of racial conditions in artistic, journalistic, or academic fora,[15] as well as the seemingly infinite number of racial judgments and practices we carry out at the level of individual experience.

Since racial formation is always historically situated, our understanding of the significance of race, and of the way race structures society, has changed enormously over time. The processes of racial formation we encounter today, the racial projects large and small which structure U.S. society in so many ways, are merely the present-day outcomes of a complex historical evolution. The contemporary racial order remains transient. By knowing something of how it evolved, we can perhaps better discern where it is heading. We therefore turn next to a historical survey of the racial formation process, and the conflicts and debates it has engendered.

The Evolution of Modern Racial Awareness

The identification of distinctive human groups, and their association with differences in physical appearance, goes back to prehistory, and can be found in the earliest documents—in the Bible, for example, or in Herodotus. But the emergence of a modern conception of race does not occur until the rise of Europe and the arrival of Europeans in the Americas. Even the hostility and suspicion with which Christian Europe viewed its two significant non-Christian "others"—the Muslims and the Jews—cannot be viewed as more than a rehearsal for racial formation, since these antagonisms, for all their bloodletting and chauvinism, were always and everywhere religiously interpreted.[16]

It was only when European explorers reached the Western Hemisphere, when the oceanic seal separating the "old" and the "new" worlds was breached, that the distinctions and categorizations fundamental to a racialized social structure, and to a discourse of race, began to appear. The European explorers were the advance guard of merchant capitalism, which sought new openings for trade. What they found exceeded their wildest dreams, for never before and never again in human history has an opportunity for the appropriation of wealth remotely approached that presented by the "discovery."[17]

But the Europeans also "discovered" people, people who looked and acted differently. These "natives" challenged their "discoverers'" preexisting conceptions of the origins and possibilities of the human species.[18] The representation and interpretation of the meaning of the indigenous peoples' existence became a crucial matter, one which would affect the outcome of the enterprise of conquest. For the "discovery" raised disturbing questions as to whether all could be considered part of the same "family of man," and more practically, the extent to which native peoples could be exploited and enslaved. Thus religious debates flared over the attempt to reconcile the various Christian metaphysics with the existence of peoples who were more "different" than any whom Europe had previously known.[19]

In practice, of course, the seizure of territories and goods, the introduction of slavery through the encomienda and other forms of coerced native labor, and then through the organization of the African slave trade—not to mention the practice of outright extermination—all presupposed a worldview which distinguished Europeans, as children of God, full-fledged human beings, etc., from "others." Given the dimensions and the ineluctability of the European onslaught, given the conquerors' determination to appropriate both labor and goods, and given the presence of an axiomatic and unquestioned Christianity among them, the ferocious division of society into Europeans and "others" soon coalesced. This was true despite the famous 16th-century theological and philosophical debates about the identity of indigenous peoples.[20]

Indeed debates about the nature of the "others" reached their practical limits with a certain dispatch. Plainly they would never touch the essential: nothing, after all, would induce the Europeans to pack up and go home. We cannot examine here the early controversies over the status of American souls. We simply wish to emphasize that the "discovery" signaled a break from the previous proto-racial awareness by which Europe contemplated its "others" in a relatively disorganized fashion. In other words, we argue that the "conquest of America" was not simply an epochal historical event—however unparalleled in its importance. It was also the advent of a consolidated social structure of exploitation, appropriation, domination. Its representation, first in religious terms, but soon enough in scientific and political ones, initiated modern racial awareness.

The conquest, therefore, was the first—and given the dramatic nature of the case, perhaps the greatest—racial formation project. Its significance was by no means limited to the Western Hemisphere, for it began the work of constituting Europe as the metropole, the center, of a series of empires which could take, as Marx would later write, "the globe for a theater."[21] It represented this new imperial structure as a struggle between civilization and barbarism, and implicated in this representation all the great European philosophies, literary traditions, and social theories of the modern age.[22] In short, just as the noise of the "big bang" still resonates through the universe, so the overdetermined construction of world "civilization" as a product of the rise of Europe and the subjugation of the rest of us, still defines the race concept.

From Religion to Science

After the initial depredations of conquest, religious justifications for racial difference gradually gave way to scientific ones. By the time of the Enlightenment, a general awareness of race was pervasive, and most of the great philosophers of Europe, such as Hegel, Kant, Hume, and Locke, had issued virulently racist opinions.

The problem posed by race during the late 18th century was markedly different than it had been in the age of conquest, expropriation, and slaughter. The social structures in which race operated were no longer primarily those of military conquest and plunder, nor of the establishment of thin beachheads of colonization on the edge of what had once seemed a limitless wilderness. Now the issues were much more complicated: nation-building, establishment of national economies in the world trading system, resistance to the arbitrary authority of monarchs, and the assertion of the "natural rights" of "man," including the right of revolution.[23] In such a situation, racially organized exploitation, in the form of slavery, the expansion of colonies, and the continuing expulsion of native peoples, was both necessary and newly difficult to justify.

The invocation of scientific criteria to demonstrate the "natural" basis of racial hierarchy was both a logical consequence of the rise of this form of knowledge, and an attempt to provide a more subtle and nuanced account of human complexity in the new, "enlightened" age. Spurred on by the classificatory scheme of living organisms devised by Linnaeus in *Systema Naturae* (1735), many scholars in the eighteenth and nineteenth centuries dedicated themselves to the identification and ranking of variations in humankind. Race was conceived as a biological concept, a matter of species. Voltaire wrote that "The negro race is a species of men (sic) as different from ours … as the breed of spaniels is from that of greyhounds," and in a formulation echoing down from his century to our own, declared that "If their understanding is not of a different nature from ours … it is at least greatly inferior. They are not capable of any great application or association of ideas, and seem formed neither for the advantages nor the abuses of philosophy."[24]

Jefferson, the preeminent exponent of the Enlightenment doctrine of "the rights of man" on North American shores, echoed these sentiments:

> In general their existence appears to participate more of sensation than reflection. … [I]n memory they are equal to whites, in reason much inferior … [and] in imagination they are dull, tasteless, and anomalous. … I advance it therefore … that the blacks, whether originally a different race, or made distinct by time and circumstances, are inferior to the whites. … Will not a lover of natural history, then, one who views the gradations in all the animals with the eye of philosophy, excuse an effort to keep those in the department of Man (sic) as distinct as nature has formed them?[25]

Such claims of species distinctiveness among humans justified the inequitable allocation of political and social rights, while still upholding the doctrine of "the rights of man." The quest to obtain a precise scientific definition of race sustained debates that continue to rage today. Yet despite efforts ranging from Dr. Samuel Morton's studies of cranial capacity[26] to contemporary attempts to base racial classification on shared gene pools,[27] the concept of race has defied biological definition.

In the 19th century, Count Joseph Arthur de Gobineau drew upon the most respected scientific studies of his day to compose his four-volume *Essay on the Inequality of Races* (1853–1855).[28] He not only greatly influenced the racial thinking of the period, but his themes would be echoed in the racist ideologies of the next one hundred years: beliefs that superior races produced superior cultures and that racial intermixtures resulted in the degradation of the superior racial stock. These ideas found expression, for instance, in the eugenics movement launched by Darwin's cousin, Francis Galton, which had an immense impact on scientific and sociopolitical thought in Europe and the United States.[29] In the wake of civil war and emancipation, and with immigration from southern and Eastern Europe as well as East Asia running high, the U.S. was particularly fertile ground for notions such as social darwinism and eugenics.

Attempts to discern the scientific meaning of race continue to the present day. For instance, an essay by Arthur Jensen that argued that hereditary factors shape intelligence not only revived the "nature or nurture" controversy, but also raised highly volatile questions about racial equality itself.[30] All such attempts seek to remove the concept of race from the historical context in which it arose and developed. They employ an essentialist approach that suggests instead that the truth of race is a matter of innate characteristics, of which skin color and other physical attributes provide only the most obvious, and in some respects most superficial, indicators.

From Science to Politics

It has taken scholars more than a century to reject biologistic notions of race in favor of an approach that regards race as a social concept. This trend has been slow and uneven, and even today remains somewhat embattled, but its overall direction seems clear. At the turn of the century Max Weber discounted biological explanations for racial conflict and instead highlighted the social and political factors that engendered such conflict.[31]

W. E. B. DuBois argued for a sociopolitical definition of race by identifying "the color line" as "the problem of the 20th century."[32] Pioneering cultural anthropologist Franz Boas rejected attempts to link racial identifications and cultural traits, labeling as pseudoscientific any assumption of a continuum of "higher" and "lower" cultural groups.[33] Other early exponents of social, as opposed to biological, views of race included Robert E. Park, founder of the "Chicago school" of sociology, and Alain Leroy Locke, philosopher and theorist of the Harlem renaissance.[34]

Perhaps more important than these and subsequent intellectual efforts, however, were the political struggles of racially defined groups themselves. Waged all around the globe under a variety of banners such as anti-colonialism and civil rights, these battles to challenge various structural and cultural racisms have been a major feature of 20th century politics. The racial horrors of the 20th century—colonial slaughter and apartheid, the genocide of the holocaust, and the massive bloodlettings required to end these evils—have also indelibly marked the theme of race as a political issue par excellence.

As a result of prior efforts and struggles, we have now reached the point of fairly general agreement that race is not a biologically given but rather a socially constructed way of differentiating human beings. While a tremendous achievement, the transcendence of biologistic conceptions of race does not provide any reprieve from the dilemmas of racial injustice and conflict, nor from controversies over the significance of race in the present. Views of race as socially constructed simply recognize the fact that these conflicts and controversies are now more properly framed on the terrain of politics. By privileging politics in the analysis that follows we do not mean to suggest that race has been displaced as a concern of scientific inquiry, or that struggles over cultural representation are no longer important. We do argue, however, that race is now a preeminently political phenomenon. Such an assertion invites examination of the evolving role of racial politics in the U.S. This is the subject to which we now turn.

Dictatorship, Democracy, Hegemony

For most of its existence both as a European colony and as an independent nation, the U.S. was a racial dictatorship. From 1607 to 1865—258 years—most nonwhites were firmly eliminated from the sphere of politics.[35] After the civil war there was the brief egalitarian experiment of Reconstruction which terminated ignominiously in 1877. In its wake followed almost a century of legally sanctioned segregation and denial of the vote, nearly absolute in the South and much of the Southwest, less effective in the North and far West, but formidable in any case.[36] These barriers fell only in the mid-1960s, a mere quarter-century ago. Nor did the successes of the black movement and its allies mean that all obstacles to their political participation had now been abolished. Patterns of racial inequality have proven, unfortunately, to be quite stubborn and persistent.

It is important, therefore, to recognize that in many respects, racial dictatorship is the norm against which all U.S. politics must be measured. The centuries of racial dictatorship have had three very large consequences: first, they defined "American" identity as white, as the negation of racialized "otherness"—at first largely African and indigenous, later Latin American and Asian as well.[37] This negation took shape in both law and custom, in public institutions and in forms of cultural representation. It became the archetype of hegemonic rule in the U.S. It was the successor to the conquest as the "master" racial project.

Second, racial dictatorship organized (albeit sometimes in an incoherent and contradictory fashion) the "color line," rendering it the fundamental division in U.S. society. The dictatorship elaborated, articulated, and drove racial divisions not only through institutions, but also through psyches, extending up to our own time the racial obsessions of the conquest and slavery periods.

Third, racial dictatorship consolidated the oppositional racial consciousness and organization originally framed by marronage[38] and slave revolts, by indigenous resistance, and by nationalisms of various sorts. Just as the conquest created the "native" where once there had been Pequot, Iroquois, or Tutelo, so too it created the "black" where once there had been Asante or Ovimbundu, Yoruba or Bakongo.

The transition from a racial dictatorship to a racial democracy has been a slow, painful, and contentious one; it remains far from complete. A recognition of the abiding presence of racial dictatorship, we contend, is crucial for the development of a theory of racial formation in the U.S. It is also crucial to the task of relating racial formation to the broader context of political practice, organization, and change.

In this context, a key question arises: In what way is racial formation related to politics as a whole? How, for example, does race articulate with other axes of oppression and difference—most importantly class and gender—along which politics is organized today?

The answer, we believe, lies in the concept of *hegemony*. Antonio Gramsci—the Italian communist who placed this concept at the center of his life's work—understood it as the conditions necessary, in a given society, for the achievement and consolidation of rule. He argued that hegemony was always constituted by a combination of coercion and consent. Although rule can be obtained by force, it cannot be secured and maintained, especially in modern society, without the element of consent. Gramsci conceived of consent as far more than merely the legitimation of authority. In his view, consent extended to the incorporation by the ruling group of many of the key interests of subordinated groups, often to the explicit disadvantage of the rulers themselves.[39] Gramsci's treatment of hegemony went even farther: he argued that in order to consolidate their hegemony, ruling groups must elaborate and maintain a popular system of ideas and practices—through education, the media, religion, folk wisdom, etc.—which he called "common sense." It is through its production and its adherence to this "common sense," this ideology (in the broadest sense of the term), that a society gives its consent to the way in which it is ruled.[40]

These provocative concepts can be extended and applied to an understanding of racial rule. In the Americas, the conquest represented the violent introduction of a new form of rule whose relationship with those it subjugated was almost entirely coercive. In the U.S., the origins of racial division, and of racial signification and identity formation, lie in a system of rule that was extremely dictatorial. The mass murders and expulsions of indigenous people, and the enslavement of Africans, surely evoked and inspired little consent in their founding moments.

Over time, however, the balance of coercion and consent began to change. It is possible to locate the origins of hegemony right within the heart of racial dictatorship, for the effort to possess the oppressor's tools—religion and philosophy in this case—was crucial to emancipation (the effort to possess oneself). As Ralph Ellison reminds us, "The slaves often took the essence of the aristocratic ideal (as they took Christianity) with far more seriousness than their masters."[41] In their language, in their religion with its focus on the Exodus theme and on Jesus's tribulations, in their music with its figuring of suffering, resistance, perseverance, and transcendence, in their interrogation of a political philosophy that sought perpetually to rationalize their bondage in a supposedly "free" society, the slaves incorporated elements of racial rule into their thought and practice, turning them against their original bearers.

Racial rule can be understood as a slow and uneven historical process that has moved from dictatorship to democracy, from domination to hegemony. In this transition, hegemonic forms of racial rule—those based on consent—eventually came to supplant those based on coercion. Of course, before this assertion can be accepted, it must be qualified in important ways. By no means has the U.S. established racial democracy at the end of the century, and by no means is coercion a thing of the past. But the sheer complexity of the racial questions U.S. society confronts today, the welter of competing racial projects and contradictory racial experiences that Americans undergo, suggests that hegemony is a useful and appropriate term with which to characterize contemporary racial rule.

Race, Racism, and Hegemony

Parallel to the debates on the concept of race, recent academic and political controversies about the nature of racism have centered on whether it is primarily an ideological or structural phenomenon. Proponents of the former position argue that racism is first and foremost a matter of beliefs and attitudes, doctrines and discourse, which only then give rise to unequal and unjust practices and structures.[42] Advocates of the latter view see racism as primarily a matter of economic stratification, residential segregation, and other institutionalized forms of inequality that then give rise to ideologies of privilege.[43]

From the standpoint of racial formation, these debates are fundamentally misguided. They discuss the problem of racism in a rigid "either-or" manner. We believe it is crucial to disrupt the fixity of these positions by simultaneously arguing that ideological beliefs have structural consequences, and that social structures give rise to beliefs. Racial ideology and social structure, therefore, mutually shape the nature of racism in a complex, dialectical, and overdetermined manner.

Even those racist projects that at first glance appear chiefly ideological turn out upon closer examination to have significant institutional and social structural dimensions. For example, what we have called "far right" projects appear at first glance to be centrally ideological. They are rooted in biologistic doctrine, after all. The same seems to hold for certain conservative black nationalist projects that have deep commitments to biologism.[44] But the unending stream of racist assaults initiated by the far right, the apparently increasing presence of skinheads in high schools, the proliferation of neo-Nazi websites on the Internet, and the appearance of racist talk shows on cable access channels, all suggest that the organizational manifestations of the far right racial projects exist and will endure.[45]

By contrast, even those racisms that at first glance appear to be chiefly structural upon closer examination reveal a deeply ideological component. For example, since the racial right abandoned its explicit advocacy of segregation, it has not seemed to uphold—in the main—an ideologically racist project, but more primarily a structurally racist one. Yet this very transformation required tremendous efforts of ideological production. It demanded the rearticulation of civil rights doctrines of equality in suitably conservative form, and indeed the defense of continuing large-scale racial inequality as an outcome preferable to (what its advocates have seen as) the threat to democracy that affirmative action, busing, and large-scale "race-specific" social spending would entail.[46] Even more tellingly, this project took shape through a deeply manipulative coding of subtextual appeals to white racism, notably in a series of political campaigns for high office that have occurred over recent decades. The retreat of social policy from any practical commitment to racial justice, and the relentless reproduction and divulgation of this theme at the level of everyday life—where whites are now "fed up" with all the "special treatment" received by nonwhites, etc.—constitutes the hegemonic racial project at this time. It therefore exhibits an unabashed structural racism all the more brazen because on the ideological or signification level it adheres to a principle to "treat everyone alike."

In summary, the racism of today is no longer a virtual monolith, as was the racism of yore. Today, racial hegemony is "messy." The complexity of the present situation is the product of a vast historical legacy of structural inequality and invidious racial representation, which has been confronted during the post-World War II period with an opposition more serious and effective than any it had faced before. The result is a deeply ambiguous and contradictory spectrum of racial projects, unremittingly conflictual racial politics, and confused and ambivalent racial identities of all sorts.

Discussion Questions

1. In recent years civil rights advocates have brought suit against companies like CSX railroad and Fleet Bank on the grounds that they profited from African slavery in their early years. For example, the lawsuits alleged that corporate ancestors of CSX used slave labor to lay railroad track and to build railroad facilities; they charged that corporate ancestors of Fleet Bank (which merged with Bank of America in 2004) insured plantation owners' "property" (the slaves themselves) in the antebellum South against the risk of slaves running away.

   In your view what merit do these lawsuits have? Should contemporary corporations be liable for their predecessors' collaboration with slavery? Are the descendents of slaves entitled to compensation because their ancestors' labor was (allegedly) coerced by CSX's antecedents or because their ancestors' bodies were (allegedly) insured by Fleet's corporate founders against loss to their slavemasters?

Is the black community as a whole entitled to such compensation?

2. The United States is becoming a lot less white. Projecting current population (and immigration) trends forward to the year 2050, the U.S. Census Bureau predicts that in 2050, the population will be about 25% Latino/Hispanic, 17% black, and 9% Asian American. In many of the largest cities in the U.S., whites are already a minority. The state of California, which was about 75% white in 1975, was only about 42% white in 2007.

   What are the implications of these population trends for racial formation in the United States? How in your view will the country adapt to these patterns? For example, do you foresee a greater acceptance among whites of their minority status? Or do you think there will be greater hostility to members of "other" groups? What racial projects do you expect whites to be carrying out as a result of their declining proportion of the U.S. population?

3. In 2005 white families' average net worth (the monetary value of investments, savings, and property belong to these families) was approximately 11X the average net worth of black families. This inequality in wealth distribution had grown significantly over the four decades since the passage of civil rights legislation in the 1960s.

   In your view what accounts for the continuing (and in some ways increasing) gap between blacks and whites in the present, supposedly "color-blind" era?

4. In 1997 golf star Tiger Woods referred to himself as "Cablinasian" on the Oprah Winfrey TV program. He said that it bothered him when people referred to him as black, since he is one-fourth black, one-fourth Thai, one-fourth Chinese, one-eighth white and one-eighth American Indian.

   Discuss Woods's self-identification as a racial project. In what ways is he situating himself in the U.S. racial mosaic? What are the implications for him (and for other Americans) of his invention of a "Cablinasian" identity?

5. Starting in the 1970s, and more intensively since then, many politicians, academics, and public figures have argued that the United States is becoming a "color-blind" society. (The term actually goes back to Justice Harlan's dissent in the landmark *Plessy v. Ferguson* decision of 1896.) Yet survey results continue to show persistent beliefs in black inferiority, laziness, and criminality.

   Is there a discrepancy here, or can these two trends be reconciled? Discuss these views on race as conflicting or overlapping racial projects.

Notes

1. *San Francisco Chronicle*, September 14, 1982, May 19, 1983. Ironically, the 1970 Louisiana law was enacted to supersede an old Jim Crow statute which relied on the idea of "common report" in determining an infant's race. Following Phipps' unsuccessful attempt to change her classification and have the law declared unconstitutional, a legislative effort arose which culminated in the repeal of the law. See *San Francisco Chronicle*, June 23, 1983.
2. Compare the Phipps case to Andrew Hacker's well-known "parable" in which a white person is informed by a mysterious official that "the organization he represents has made a mistake" and that "... [a]ccording to their records ... , you were to have been born black: to another set of parents, far from where you were raised." How much compensation, Hacker's official asks, would "you" require to undo the damage of this unfortunate error? See Hacker, *Two Nations: Black and White, Separate, Hostile, Unequal* (New York: Charles Scribner's Sons, 1992), pp. 31–32.
3. On the evolution of Louisiana's racial classification system, see Virginia Dominguez, *White By Definition: Social Classification in Creole Louisiana* (New Brunswick: Rutgers University Press, 1986).
4. This is not to suggest that gender is a biological category while race is not. Gender, like race, is a social construct. However, the biological division of humans into sexes—two at least, and possibly intermediate ones as well—is not in dispute. This provides a basis for argument over gender divisions—"how natural?" etc.—which does not exist with regard to race. To ground an

argument for the "natural" existence of race, one must resort to philosophical anthropology.

5. "The truth is that there are no races; there is nothing in the world that can do all we ask race to do for us. ... The evil that is done is done by the concept, and by easy—yet impossible—assumptions as to its application." (Kwame Anthony Appiah, *In My Father's House: Africa in the Philosophy of Culture* [New York: Oxford University Press, 1992.]) Appiah's eloquent and learned book fails, in our view, to dispense with the race concept, despite its anguished attempt to do so; this indeed is the source of its author's anguish. We agree with him as to the non-objective character of race, but fail to see how this recognition justifies its abandonment. This argument is developed below.
6. We understand essentialism as *belief in real, true human essences, existing outside or impervious to social and historical context.* We draw this definition, with some small modifications, from Diana Fuss, *Essentially Speaking: Feminism, Nature, & Difference* (New York: Routledge, 1989), p. xi.
7. Michael Omi and Howard Winant, "On the Theoretical Status of the Concept of Race," in Warren Crichlow and Cameron McCarthy, eds., *Race, Identity, and Representation in Education* (New York: Routledge, 1993).
8. Charles Murray, *Losing Ground: American Social Policy, 1950–1980* (New York: Basic Books, 1984), p. 223.
9. Justice Thurgood Marshall, dissenting in *City of Richmond v. J.A. Croson Co.*, 488 U.S. 469 (1989).
10. See, for example, Derrick Bell, "Remembrances of Racism Past: Getting Past the Civil Rights Decline," in Herbert Hill and James E. Jones, Jr., eds., *Race in America: The Struggle for Equality* (Madison: The University of Wisconsin Press, 1993), pp. 75–76; Gertrude Ezorsky, *Racism and Justice: The Case for Affirmative Action* (Ithaca: Cornell University Press, 1991), pp. 109–111; David Kairys, *With Liberty and Justice for Some: A Critique of the Conservative Supreme Court* (New York: The New Press, 1993), pp. 138–41.
11. Howard Winant has developed a tentative "map" of the system of racial hegemony in the U.S. circa 1990, which focuses on the spectrum of racial projects running from the political right to the political left. See Winant, "Where Culture Meets Structure: Race in the 1990s," in idem, *Racial Conditions: Theories, Politics, Comparisons* (Minneapolis: University of Minnesota Press, 1994).
12. A familiar example is use of racial "code words." Recall George Bush's manipulations of racial fear in the 1988 "Willie Horton" ads, or Jesse Helms's use of the coded term "quota" in his 1990 campaign against Harvey Gantt.
13. From this perspective, far right racial projects can also be interpreted as "nationalist." See Ronald Walters, "White Racial Nationalism in the United States," *Without Prejudice* I, 1 (Fall, 1987).
14. Howard Winant has offered such a "map" in "Race: Theory, Culture, and Politics in the United States Today," in Marcy Darnovsky et al., eds., *Contemporary Social Movements and Cultural Politics* (Philadelphia: Temple University Press, 1994).
15. We are not unaware, for example, that publishing this work is in itself a racial project.
16. Although the Inquisition pioneered racial anti-semitism with its doctrine of "limpieza de sangre" (the claim that Jews could not be accepted as converts because their blood was "unclean"), anti-semitism only began to be seriously racialized in the 18th century, as George L. Mosse shows in *Toward the Final Solution: A History of European Racism* (New York: Howard Fertig, 1978).
17. As Marx put it:

    > The discovery of gold and silver in America, the extirpation, enslavement, and entombment in mines of the aboriginal population, the beginning of the conquest and looting of the East Indies, the turning of Africa into a warren for the commercial hunting of blackskins, signalized the rosy dawn of the era of capitalist production. These idyllic proceedings are the chief momenta of primitive accumulation. (Karl Marx, *Capital*, Vol. I (New York: International Publishers, 1967), p. 751.)

    David E. Stannard argues that the wholesale slaughter perpetrated upon the native peoples of the Western hemisphere is unequalled in history, even in our own bloody century. See his *American Holocaust: Columbus and the Conquest of the New World* (New York: Oxford University Press, 1992).

18. Winthrop Jordan provides a detailed account of the sources of European attitudes about color and race in *White Over Black: American Attitudes Toward the Negro, 1550-1812* (New York: Norton, 1977 [1968]), pp. 3–43.
19. In a famous instance, a 1550 debate in Valladolid pitted the philosopher and translator of Aristotle, Gines de Sepulveda, against the Dominican Bishop of the Mexican state of Chiapas, Bartolome de Las Casas. Discussing the native peoples, Sepulveda argued that

    > In wisdom, skill, virtue and humanity, these people are as inferior to the Spaniards as children are to adults and women to men; there is as great a difference between them as there is between savagery and forbearance, between violence and moderation, almost—I am inclined to say, as between monkeys and men (Sepulveda, "Democrates Alter," quoted in Tsvetan Todorov, *The Conquest of America: The Question of the Other* (New York: Harper and Row, 1984), p. 153).

    In contrast, Las Casas defended the humanity and equality of the native peoples, both in terms of their way of life—which he idealized as one of innocence, gentleness, and generosity—and in terms of their readiness for conversion to Catholicism, which for him as for Sepulveda was the true and universal religion (Las Casas, "Letter to the Council of the Indies," quoted ibid, p. 163). William E. Connolly interrogates the linkages proposed by Todorov between early Spanish colonialism and contemporary conceptions of identity and difference in *Identity/Difference: Democratic Negotiations of Political Paradox* (Ithaca: Cornell University Press, 1991), pp. 40–48).
20. In Virginia, for example, it took about two decades after the establishment of European colonies to extirpate the indigenous people of the greater vicinity; 50 years after the establishment of the first colonies, the elaboration of slave codes establishing race as prima facie evidence for enslaved status was well under way. See Jordan, *White Over Black*.
21. *Capital*, p. 751.
22. Edward W. Said, *Culture and Imperialism* (New York: Alfred A. Knopf, 1993).
23. David Brion Davis, *The Problem of Slavery in The Age of Revolution* (Ithaca: Cornell University Press, 1975).
24. Quoted in Thomas F. Gossett, *Race: The History of an Idea in America* (New York: Schocken Books, 1965), p. 45.
25. Thomas Jefferson, "Notes on Virginia" [1787], in Merrill D. Peterson, *Writings of Thomas Jefferson* (New York: The Library of America, 1984), pp. 264–66, 270. Thanks to Prof. Kimberly Benston for drawing our attention to this passage.
26. Proslavery physician Samuel George Morton (1799–1851) compiled a collection of 800 crania from all parts of the world which formed the sample for his studies of race. Assuming that the larger the size of the cranium translated into greater intelligence, Morton established a relationship between race and skull capacity. Gossett reports that "In 1849, one of his studies included the following results: the English skulls in his collection proved to be the largest, with an average cranial capacity of 96 cubic inches. The Americans and Germans were rather poor seconds, both with cranial capacities of 90 cubic inches. At the bottom of the list were the Negroes with 83 cubic inches, the Chinese with 82, and the Indians with 79." Gossett, *Race: The History of an Idea in America*, p. 74. More recently, Steven Jay Gould has reexamined Morton's data, and shown that his research data were deeply, though unconsciously, manipulated to agree with his "a priori conviction about racial ranking." Gould, *The Mismeasure of Man* (New York: W. W. Norton, 1981), pp. 50–69.
27. Definitions of race founded upon a common pool of genes have not held up when confronted by scientific research which suggests that the differences *within* a given human population are every bit as great as those *between* populations. See L. L. Cavalli-Sforza, "The Genetics of Human Populations," *Scientific American*, (September 1974), pp. 81–89.
28. A fascinating summary critique of Gobineau is provided in Tsvetan Todorov, *On Human Diversity: Nationalism, Racism, and Exoticism in French Thought*, trans. Catherine Porter (Cambridge, MA: Harvard University Press, 1993), esp. pp. 129–40.

29. Two good histories of eugenics are Allen Chase, *The Legacy of Malthus* (New York: Knopf, 1977); Daniel J. Kelves, *In the Name of Eugenics: Genetics and the Uses of Human Heredity* (New York: Knopf, 1985).
30. Arthur Jensen, "How Much Can We Boost IQ and Scholastic Achievement?" *Harvard Educational Review*, 39 (1969), pp. 1–123.
31. See Weber, *Economy and Society*, Vol. I (Berkeley: University of California Press, 1978), pp. 385–87; Ernst Moritz Manasse, "Max Weber on Race," *Social Research*, Vol. 14 (1947), pp. 191–221.
32. Du Bois, *The Souls of Black Folk* (New York: Penguin, 1989 [1903]), p. 13. Du Bois himself wrestled heavily with the conflict between a fully sociohistorical conception of race, and the more essentialized and deterministic vision he encountered as a student in Berlin. In "The Conservation of Races" (1897) we can see his first mature effort to resolve this conflict in a vision which combined racial solidarity and a commitment to social equality. See Du Bois, "The Conservation of Races," in Dan S. Green and Edwin D. Driver, eds., *W. E. B. Du Bois On Sociology and the Black Community* (Chicago: University of Chicago Press, 1978), pp. 238–49; Manning Marable, *W. E. B. Du Bois: Black Radical Democrat* (Boston: Twayne, 1986), pp. 35–38. For a contrary, and we believe incorrect reading, see Appiah, *In My Father's House*, pp. 28–46.
33. A good collection of Boas's work is George W. Stocking, ed., *The Shaping of American Anthropology, 1883–1911: A Franz Boas Reader* (Chicago: University of Chicago Press, 1974).
34. Robert E. Park's *Race and Culture* (Glencoe, IL: Free Press, 1950) can still provide insight; see also Stanford H. Lyman, *Militarism, Imperialism, and Racial Accommodation: An Analysis and Interpretation of the Early Writings of Robert E. Park* (Fayetteville: University of Arkansas Press, 1992); Locke's views are concisely expressed in Alain Leroy Locke, *Race Contacts and Interracial Relations*, ed. Jeffrey C. Stewart (Washington, DC: Howard University Press, 1992), originally a series of lectures given at Howard University.
35. Japanese, for example, could not become naturalized citizens until passage of the 1952 McCarran-Walter Act. It took over 160 years, since the passage of the Naturalization Law of 1790, to allow all "races" to be eligible for naturalization.
36. Especially when we recall that until around 1960, the majority of blacks, the largest racially-defined minority group, lived in the South.
37. The construction of whiteness and its tropes of identity is explored in numerous studies, far too many to cite here. Some outstanding examples are Toni Morrison, *Playing In The Dark: Whiteness and the Literary Imagination* (Cambridge, MA: Harvard University Press, 1992); Michael Paul Rogin, *Fathers and Children: Andrew Jackson and the Subjugation of the American Indian* (New York: Knopf, 1975); Richard Drinnon, *Facing West: The Metaphysics of Indian-hating and Empire-building* (Minneapolis: University of Minnesota Press, 1980).
38. This term refers to the practice, widespread throughout the Americas, whereby runaway slaves formed communities in remote areas, such as swamps, mountains, or forests, often in alliance with dispossessed indigenous peoples.
39. Antonio Gramsci, *Selections from the Prison Notebooks*, edited and translated by Quintin Hoare and Geoffrey Nowell Smith (New York: International Publishers, 1971), p. 182.
40. Anne Showstack Sassoon, *Gramsci's Politics*, 2nd. ed. (London: Hutchinson, 1987); Sue Golding, *Gramsci's Democratic Theory: Contributions to Post-Liberal Democracy* (Toronto: University of Toronto Press, 1992).
41. Ralph Ellison, *Shadow and Act* (New York: New American Library, 1966), p. xiv.
42. See Miles, *Racism*, p. 77. Much of the current debate over the advisability and legality of banning racist hate speech seems to us to adopt the dubious position that racism is primarily an ideological phenomenon. See Mari J. Matsuda et al, *Words That Wound: Critical Race Theory, Assaultive Speech, and the First Amendment* (Boulder, CO: Westview Press, 1993).

43. Or ideologies which mask privilege by falsely claiming that inequality and injustice have been eliminated. See Wellman, *Portraits of White Racism*.
44. Racial teachings of the Nation of Islam, for example, maintain that whites are the product of a failed experiment by a mad scientist.
45. Elinor Langer, "The American Neo-Nazi Movement Today," *The Nation*, July 16/23, 1990.
46. Such arguments can be found in Nathan Glazer, *Affirmative Discrimination*, Charles Murray, *Losing Ground*, and Arthur M. Schlesinger, Jr., *The Disuniting of America*, among others.

INEQUALITY HIDDEN IN PLAIN VIEW:

Implications for how State Lotteries Redistribute Tax Liability along Racial Lines

BY KASEY HENRICKS

Many Chicagoans are getting shortchanged, particularly when it comes to money exchange between the Illinois Lottery (IL) and Illinois State Board of Education (ISBE). A significant portion of lottery sales are earmarked for education in Illinois. Because these revenues are not generated equally, however, some contribute more to education than others. When money is distributed in a way that transfers it from one community to another, one community's fiscal gain comes at another's expense. So the question stands: Who plays, and who pays?

To answer this question, I use the metro area of Chicago as a case study to measure the racial incidence of the IL and ISBE. In other words, I simultaneously compare the generation and appropriation of lottery revenues with respect to a community's racial profile. My wager is that this money exchange transfers resources from marginalized to mainstream communities and that this process is inherently organized along lines of race. In other words, I estimate that lottery revenues disproportionately come from communities composed predominantly of people of color and then are redistributed across other communities throughout the state.

At face value, money exchange between the IL and ISBE may seem race neutral. No one is required to play the lottery after all, and provisions governing the IL and ISBE are not racially explicit. This, however, does not negate how consequences of this exchange can be deeply raced, particularly when money is taken from communities of color and allotted to other communities. If my wager is correct, then Illinois' process for funding public education represents policy that produces race inequalities.

LOTTERY PROLIFERATION IN THE MODERN AMERICAN CONTEXT

Today lotteries are everywhere. Their emergence, however, is a recent historical development. If we time-travelled to a year as recent as 1963, the pervasively familiar imagery of lotteries would be nonexistent. This is because for over 70 years, they were outlawed in the United States (Clotfelter & Cook, 1989). That is, until New Hampshire broke the streak. Confronted with one of the country's least-funded public education systems (largely as a result of no state income or sales tax in addition to resistance to property tax hikes), its state legislators had few options other than to establish a lottery for much-needed funds (Nibert, 2000). On March 13, 1964, Governor John W. King became the first player of the modern state lottery. Soon after that, New York adopted its own lottery in 1967. Then, during the 1970s and 1980s, state lotteries spread like wildfire across the nation. In just these two decades, the number of state lotteries, including the District of Columbia, increased thirteenfold—from two to 26. As I write these words, all but six states operate their own lotteries. Though much ink has been spilled on how this trend came to be, few lotto scholars connect it to broader trends in government finance. More specifically, what remains less understood is the obscure role lotteries play in the changing composition of American taxation. Even less is known about the role of race in this great transformation.

The proliferation of state lotteries is a part of a broader trend in America's rearranging tax composition (see also Henricks & Embrick, 2017). In part, the change in how the government goes about paying for itself was initiated by White homeowners who resisted desegregation efforts (e.g., busing) and revolted against their property tax dollars being funneled toward public education for children of color (Bonastia, 2012; Hohle, 2015; Seamster & Henricks, 2015). Once these rebellions culminated in numerous legislative reforms, including property tax relief and reductions in state spending, local finance was forever changed. The traditional tax base of government had been eroded, and policymakers no longer could depend upon once reliable forms of revenue like property taxes. Confronted with massive budgetary shortfalls, governments have been compelled to entertain new ways to replace the missing revenue. Lotteries represent one viable alternative that helps make up the difference (Clotfelter & Cook, 1989; Nibert, 2000; Peppard, 1987).

The Scope of Lotteries and Their Implicit Form of Taxation

Modern state lotteries lie at a strange crossroads of government operations. On the one hand, they seem like another regulatory agency, but on the other hand, they act more like private industry. Bureaucratically speaking,"[lotteries] are held out to be just another square on the organizational charts of government, and allegedly are designed to be vaguely 'regulatory' in nature" (Karcher, 1989, p. 47). As David Nibert (2000) argues, they live up to this description in some ways by establishing guidelines to preserve the integrity and accountability of their daily operations and, perhaps most importantly, to prevent corruption. The regulatory nature of lotteries helps preserve their own legitimacy in the public's eye, but at the end of the day, these institutions exist to maximize tax revenues and increase the bottom line.

The lottery is an anomalous form of taxation. Because of its unimposing nature and reliance on voluntary participation, some lottery scholars like Charles Clotfelter and Philip Cook (1989) have labeled it a "painless tax" (p. 215). Contrary to conventional definitions offered by the new fiscal sociologists who conceptualize a tax as an "obligation to contribute money or goods to the state" (Martin et al., 2009, p. 3), people purchase lottery tickets as consumer products out of their own volition. The state then implicitly retains a fraction of the proceeds while simultaneously avoiding political backlash often associated by sheer mention of the "t-word." In fact, this lottery tax is so implicit that those who purchase lottery tickets are not referred to as taxpayers. They go by another name. As former New Jersey State Senator Alan J. Karcher (1989) argues: "Lottery advocates have devised other euphemisms to shield the playing public from realizing they are being taxed. Ticket buyers are always referred to as 'players,' never as taxpayers" (p. 38). Regardless of how these lottery revenues are collected, though, they carry the same value as do any other taxes. For these reasons, among others, the lottery can be defined as a form of taxation (Beckert& Lutter, 2009; Clotfelter & Cook 1989; Nibert, 2000).

The amount of money generated from lottery sales is consequential. Clotfelter and Cook (1989) have shown, for instance, that lotteries generate more money than all other forms of gambling combined, are more profitable than any other public enterprise operated by state governments, and trump most excise taxes in their ability to generate state income. In 2011 alone, lottery proceeds generated more than $18 billion for state governments, which then spent this money to finance nearly every public service imaginable (U.S. Census Bureau, 2011). According to census data, about half the gross sales of lottery tickets are returned to players through prize winnings, slightly more than 10% cover operating costs, and proceeds directed to states' public services represent about one-third of all lottery sales in any given year. Today, state governments find themselves in positions of dependency. They are confronted with budgetary shortfalls, the contemporary economic outlook is uncertain, and no alternatives for generating large sums of money are readily available. States become "instant winners" when they can avoid tax increases and tap lotteries for money.

TABLE 5.4.1. ILLINOIS PUBLIC EDUCATION EXPENDITURES AND ENROLLMENTS, 1975—1984

	Rates of Decline in Percentages	
	Real Net Education Expenditures	Total Public Education Enrollments
1976	-3.1	-1.2
1977	-4.8	-1.5
1978	-1.7	-2.6
1979	-5.2	-3.4
1980	-4.5	-3.4
1981	-16.2	-3.0
1982	-13.6	-3.1
1983	-5.3	-2.3
1984	-2.8	-1.5

Sources: The Illinois real net education expenditures were drawn from Borg and Mason (1990), and the Illinois total public education enrollments were drawn from ISBE (2004).

Without these funds, public services like education would likely suffer. For reasons like these, lotteries show no sign of being abandoned any time soon.

THE ILLINOIS LOTTERY: AN EXAMPLE OTHERS HAVE FOLLOWED

In many ways, Illinois is a model lottery state. It was among the first states to adopt a lottery (in 1973), and through trials and tribulations, its history offers a cautionary tale for other states that have adopted their own. The Illinois Lottery was passed on the promise of money for K–12 public education. A few years after its adoption, however, it became clear to policymakers and the public alike that the state's lottery did not deliver what had been promised. This is especially true as it relates to the kids of Illinois and additional funds for their schooling. Economists Mary Borg and Paul Mason (1990) have shown that real net expenditures on public education declined for a 10-year period after the Illinois Lottery's initiation. Whereas the annual education budget totaled about $3.2 billion in 1975, it had declined to less than $1.8 billion by 1984. Some of the downward trend can be attributed to other factors like lower student enrollments, but lower student enrollments only offer so much explanation for declining education budgets. For most years between 1975 and 1984, dwindling expenditures on public education outpaced declining enrollments by rates that were frequently double, triple, or even more. The greatest disparities occurred in the early 1980s (see Table 5.4.1), an era marked by great divestment from public services throughout most of America (Piven & Cloward, 1982).

Perhaps it was figures like these that prompted legal reform so that the original promise of the Illinois Lottery (i.e., additional funds for education) could be met. Part of the problem with the existing Illinois Lottery Law (in 1973) was that it directed net lottery proceeds to the general revenue fund rather than the common school fund. This meant that no mechanism was in place to ensure lottery money would go to education, and instead legislatures could effectively exercise much discretion in spending lottery money however they saw fit. The Illinois Lottery Law was amended in 1985 to prevent this from happening, as it explicitly required net lottery proceeds to be "earmarked" for the state's common school fund. Even with this addition, the Illinois Lottery has not added funding but merely displaced alternative sources of revenue that once financed public education (Borg & Mason, 1988; 1990). The lottery tax represents a regressive turn of education finance, whereby lottery revenues have essentially replaced progressive forms of taxation like corporate, property, and income taxes. Illinois is no anomaly, however. On the contrary, it is a symbolic example of the situation confronting many states across America (Borg & Mason, 1990).

The ways in which lotteries are framed as a boon to education finance can cause unforeseen adverse consequences. Because lotteries were initiated to

FIGURE 5.4.1. WHERE DOES ILLINOIS LOTTERY MONEY GO? A BREAKDOWN FOR FISCAL YEAR 2011

Prize Winnings: $1,368 Million

60.3 %

Retailer and Vender
Commissions/Bonuses: $161 Million

7.1 %

Other Operating Expenses
(e.g., Salaries, Advertisements): $72 Million

3.2 %

Proceeds Allocated to the
Common School Fund and
Other Select State Funds: $668 Million

29.4 %

Source: Henricks and Embrick, 2017.

supplement school funds, many people may be led to believe that schools are now swimming in more lottery money than they know what to do with. Though this is hardly the truth, sometimes facts do not matter as much as perception. James Smith, a former Belleville, Illinois school superintendent, knows this lesson all too well. In an interview for *Time* magazine, he complained that he could not "get a bond issue authorized because local officials think that schools are rolling in the lottery money" (Donoghue, 1989, p. 19). Of course, this is hardly true. The Illinois Lottery's real financial benefit to schools has been, at best, negligible from a budgetary standpoint. Nonetheless, when distorted information is acted upon as though it were accurate and truthful, then this false information becomes real in its consequences (see Thomas & Thomas, 1928). In the case of Illinois, it is ultimately the institution of education, and all those people embedded within it, that are most detrimentally affected. Many of these schools are in extreme need of resources and bare necessities, yet lotteries have ways of painting pictures that suggest just the opposite.

HOW MUCH ILLINOIS LOTTERY MONEY ARE WE TALKING ABOUT?

Year after year in the 2000s, the Illinois Lottery boasted record-breaking sales (Illinois Lottery, 2010), so much so that later years of the 2000s amounted to sales surpassing the $2 billion mark. In any given year, about a third, or $600 million, was allocated to the Illinois Common School Fund—the primary source of funding for the state's public primary and secondary schools (Illinois Lottery, 2005; 2009). In 2011, the Illinois Lottery's contribution to education approximated $668 million and represented nearly 10% of the state's education budget (State of Illinois, 2011). The remaining money was designated to cover prize winnings, operating costs, and other expenses. Over $1.3 billion (60.3%) was reserved for prize winnings. About $161 million (7.1%) went to retailers or vendors. And approximately $72 million (3.2%) was spent on other expenses like advertising. (See Figure 5.4.1 for a breakdown of how each lottery dollar was spent in 2011.)

While lottery proceeds are spread across Illinois, most of this money was generated from one area of the state: the Chicago metro area. To illustrate this further, I turn to data from the 2010 Census and integrate it with 2011 records obtained from the Illinois Department of Revenue. This information was collected by performing an audit that followed guidelines of the state's Freedom of Information Act (FOIA), or §5-140 of the Illinois Compiled Statutes. Most states have adopted freedom of information laws like these, which are commonly referred to as "sunshine" laws among journalists and legal scholars, so that members of the public can access a broad range of government documents and records. These include the various budgetary items that drive this study. According to records collected from the Illinois Department of Revenue, nearly 70% of the over $2.1 billion in lottery sales for fiscal year 2011 came from tickets sold within the Chicago Metropolitan Statistical Area. This means that a vast majority of the lottery tickets sold in Illinois came from eight of the state's 102 counties.

When taking a closer look at the zip codes that comprise the counties within the Chicago Metropolitan Statistical Area, it is apparent that much of this lottery money comes from certain pockets of Cook County (see Figure 5.4.2). These pockets represent communities within the densely populated city limits of Chicago, especially those in the South and West Sides. In 2011, for example, it was not uncommon for many of these communities to generate over $10 million in lottery sales. Meanwhile, the further one gets from the city's central business district, the less lottery sales that were generated. Sales for communities at the outer edges of McHenry, Kane, and Will Counties, for example, struggled to surpass $2 million in annual lottery sales.

The Illinois Lottery Tax: Generated From Whom?

The Illinois Lottery is like a reverse Robin Hood tax with racial implications. It swindles money from marginal groups and then redistributes it by financing public services to which most all people are entitled. Using the Chicago Metropolitan Statistical Area as a case study, I measure the extent to which lottery revenues disproportionately come from communities composed of non-White residents. Because Chicago remains among the most segregated cities in the nation, space represents a de facto proxy measure for race (see Henricks et al., 2017). This type of measurement is problematic in terms of precision, given the fact that no Chicago community is composed of only one group. I am willing to live with this limitation, however, on at least two counts. One, data alternatives are unavailable. And two, the metro area's level of hypersegregation means that many of Chicago's communities are composed mainly of only one group—especially when it comes to its Black residents.

The unit of analysis for comparing lottery sales between communities is a zip code tabulation area. This is a census unit generalized from areal representations of the United States Postal

FIGURE 5.4.2. A SPATIAL OVERVIEW OF ILLINOIS LOTTERY REVENUES BY ZIP CODE, 2011 FISCAL YEAR. SELECT COUNTIES OF THE CHICAGO METRAPOLOTIN AREA

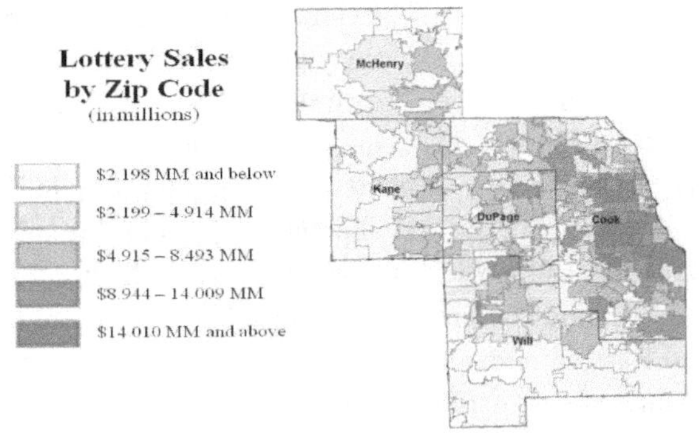

Source: Henricks and Embrick, 2017.
**Note: The map illustrates data derived from the 2010 Census and the illinois Department of Revenue*

TABLE 5.4.2. A SOCIODEMOGRAPHIC PROFILE OF THE CHICAGO METRO AREA BY ZIP CODE, 2010-2011

	Mean	Min..	Max.	Std.
Deviation				
Lottery Revenues				
Sales for Fiscal Year	5,233,105	35,192	26,805,228	4,758,807
Racial Composition				
Percent of White Residents	61.7	0.3	96.8	27.9
General Demographics				
Total Population	27,454	493	113,916	20,712
Median Years of Age	37.4	23.8	57.0	5.0
Percent Over 17 Years Old	75.6	63.1	97.4	5.9
Mean HH Size	2.7	1.5	4.1	0.4
Housing Characteristics				
Percent of Vacant Units	7.8	1.3	75.0	5.9
Percent of Renter-Occupied	29.2	4.4	75.6	18.0
N (ZCs)				285

Source: Henricks and Embrick, 2017
****Note: The data presented here derives from the 2010 Census and the Illinois Department of Revenue***

Service zip code service areas. In total, the Chicago Metropolitan Statistical Area is composed of about 300 zip codes. Most of these are neighborhoods that people call home, but a slim minority consist of airports, business districts, or other restricted areas where next to no one lives. Once these sparsely populated areas are omitted for statistical reasons, we are left with 285 zip codes for our final analysis. (See Table 5.4.2 for a descriptive summary of the sociodemographic characteristics regarding these zip codes.) Total lottery revenues generated by these zip codes in 2011 ranged from a low of $35,000 to a high of nearly $27 million. The average zip code, however, amassed about $5.2 million in lottery sales. When lottery revenues are further examined by a community's racial composition, considerable variation becomes obvious.

Predominantly non-White communities, by and large, generate millions of dollars more than do communities composed predominantly of White people. Compare the five highest- and lowest-grossing communities in 2011, for example (see Figure 5.4.3). At least $19 million in lottery sales separate these communities. The five communities that sold the least amount of lottery tickets were majority White spaces. Aside from the top-grossing community, which was composed of 61.2 White residents and had sales of over $35,000, the remaining four lowest-selling zip codes consisted of populations that were 90% or more White. At the other end of the spectrum, the highest-grossing communities were those where mostly people of color lived. Two of the highest-grossing zip codes, which respectively sold about $27 billion and $21 billion worth of lottery tickets, had Black populations of 96.8 and 94.2%. The third-highest-grossing zip code had a Black population of 62.2% and a Latinx population of 33.9%, while the fourth-highest-grossing zip code was predominantly Latinx (75.9%).

Though comparing the five highest- and lowest-grossing zip codes along with their racial compositions offers a quite suggestive interpretation regarding from whom lottery money comes, it remains limited as a form of analysis. Namely, it only accounts for two variables at once, but other factors might explain the trends I observe. It is entirely possible, for instance, that the communities with the highest-grossing sales are also those with the largest population size. If this is the case, then these communities would likely have a larger base of potential ticket buyers, and it would make good sense that sales are higher. To account for potential criticisms like these and to better show the direct impact a community's racial composition has on lottery sales, I perform a linear regression (i.e., ordinary least squares) analysis. Like our logistic regression analysis in the previous chapter, this permits us to gain a more nuanced understanding of how multiple variables simultaneously and

FIGURE 5.4.3. HOW DO LOTTERY REVENUES RANGE BY ZIP CODE AND RACIAL COMPOSITION?*

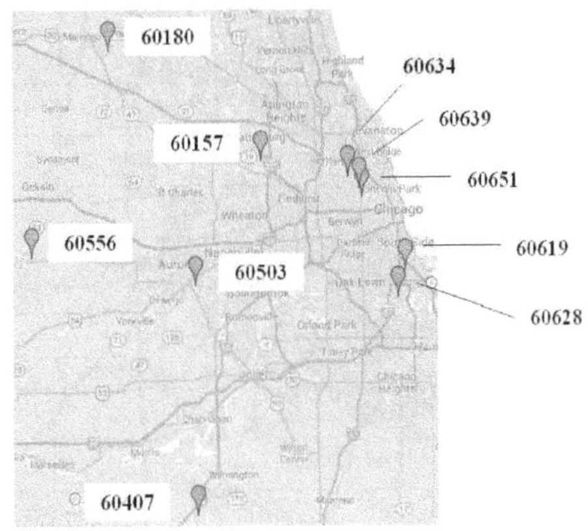

Five Zip Codes With the Lowest Sales	Total Sales	Percent White	Percent Black	Percent Latinx
1. 60503	35,192	61.2	8.8	12.4
2. 60157	39,106	90.6	0.1	5.3
3. 60180	104,899	93.4	0.3	4.1
4. 60407	113,454	93.6	0.5	3.1
5. 60556	123, 394	90.2	1.1	5.7

Five Zip Codes With the Lowest Sales	Total Sales	Percent White	Percent Black	Percent Latinx
1. 60619	26,805,228	0.5	96.8	1.1
2. 60628	20,964,146	1.2	94.2	3.3
3. 60651	20,036,300	2.8	62.2	33.9
4. 60639	19,844,372	7.1	15.2	75.9
5. 60634	19,333,370	60.1	1.0	33.5

Source: Henricks and Embrick, 2017
**Note: The data presented h in the above map and crosstabulation derive from the 2010 Census an the Illinois Department of Revenue*

independently affect lottery sales. A linear regression analysis yields several results that are of interest to us. Most importantly, it permits me to measure the effects of independent variables, disassociated from other independent variables, on the dependent variable of lottery sales. It also allows researchers to assess how race operates alongside other variables, since social factors do not exist in an isolated vacuum.

I begin with a race-only model, given that the analysis is race centered, and from there, I supplement this model with two others that progressively subtract other variables that might explain away any observed racial differences. In this analysis, however, race is measured differently, since my unit of analysis is a spatial, not an individual, unit. It is measured by the percentage of White residents within a zip code, which permits me to estimate how much lottery sales increase for each percent increase in White residents. The characteristics I consider include most of those available in the 2010 Census, which include measures of racial composition, population size, age, household size, and various housing attributes.

The main entries listed in Table 5.4.3 include unstandardized regression coefficients. These represent the predicted change in the dependent variable associated with a one-unit change in a particular independent variable, when all other independent variables are held constant (Lewis-Beck, 1980). According to my final model (Model 3), each one percent increase in a community's White residents decreases sales by $44,746. This is the effect race has on a zip code's

TABLE 5.4.3. WHAT DETERMINES LOTTERY SALES PER ZIP CODE WITHIN THE CHICAGO METRO AREA?*

	Model 1	Model 2	Model 3
Racial Composition			
Percent of White Residents	-92,799	-56,477	-44,746
General Demographics			
Total Population		156	157
Median Years of Age		74,122	131,819
Percent Over 17 Years Old		433,489	964,748
Mean HH Size*	2.7	1.5	4.1
Housing Characteristics			
Percent of Vacant Units			94,748
Percent of Renter-Occupied			15,143
Constant	10,962,162	-15,219,203	-17,705,592
Model Summary			
R^2	.30	.71	.72
N (ZCs)			285

Source: Henricks and Embrick, 2017
**Note: The main entries listed are unstandarized regerssion coefficients (β).*

lottery sales, when holding constant all other factors. These factors include the total population size, median years of age, percentage of residents over 17 years of age, mean household size, the percentage of vacant units, and the number of renter-occupied units in a community. Below the main entries are various other statistics that summarize the model. Namely, this includes the coefficient of determination (R^2) statistic, which refers to amount of variance the model explains. Essentially, this statistic is a comparison of the actual observations versus predicted observations. It "tells you what proportion of the variability of the dependent variable is 'explained' by the regression model" (Norušis 2008, p. 43). For the final model, this statistic is .72. This means that Model 3 explains 72% of the variability for annual lottery revenues.

Substantively, what do the models illustrate? They paint a consistent picture of how race independently and simultaneously "colors" annual lottery revenues. Annual lottery revenues per zip code decrease accordingly: by White racial composition, annual lottery sales decrease by

- $894,920 when a community consists of 20% White residents,
- $1,789,840 when a community consists of 40% White residents,
- $2,684,760 when a community consists of 60% White residents,
- $3,579,680 when a community consists of 80% White residents, and
- $4,474,600 when a community consists of 100% White residents.

What the evidence from the regression analysis confirms is that my original observation remains true. Most lottery revenues are not generated by predominately White communities. Rather, they tend to come from predominately Black and Latinx communities. Given this fact, the Illinois Lottery can also be understood as a racially regressive source of revenue for the state's primary and secondary education system.

The Lottery Tax: Expended on Whom?

Following Illinois Public Act 90–548, proceeds from the Illinois Lottery are directed to the common school fund. Once there, the Illinois Department of Revenue draws upon this revenue to finance the Illinois State Board of Education, which then determines funding levels for school districts across the state (Illinois State Board of Education, 2011; State of Illinois, 2009). Alongside the lottery money in this pool are sums of cash generated from other sources, which can broadly range from private-sector money to money from the state and federal governments (Johnson, 1999; State of Illinois, 2009). Placement of money in this common fund makes it difficult, if not impossible, for analysts to "follow the money" and trace how lottery dollars are spent. Similar to how money-laundering schemes work, the way Illinois government finances education obscures the origin of how expenditures for this public service originate. This lack of transparency could be demystified, however, if the state created a ledger to show where lottery money is spent with respect to where it originated. As it is, no such document exists. I wish I could say this is uncommon.

It is not. The state of Illinois is similar to the rest of the country in how it pays for education. Drawing money from a common fund, the amount of money a school district receives is largely dependent on three criteria: district property taxes, student enrollment, and average daily attendance (McKoy & Vincent, 2006). These criteria are outlined in the general state aid (GSA) formula, which is provided in Figure 5.4.4. The first criterion requires funding to be based upon measures of local wealth. This primarily consists of money from property taxes, which is also known as equalized assessed value (EAV). Depending upon levels of wealth, each district is allotted a foundational level of funds. Impoverished districts are allocated more money than the wealthiest districts, which receive a flat rate. The second criterion accounts for average daily attendance (ADA). Districts with high attendance rates receive more money, while those with lower rates receive less money. The wealthiest school districts, however, are capped by this criterion and receive a flat rate for high attendance. The third criterion considers an additional provision for poverty-stricken districts. Districts with high poverty counts can receive additional state funding, which is determined by the number of low-income residents and the average daily attendance of the district's pupils.

At face value, it seems as though the GSA formula embodies an education finance policy that is both race neutral and economically progressive. Each district's financial ability, without regard to race, is considered before state aid is appropriated. The three criteria outlined above show the state's attempt to ensure that districts that lack resources, as determined by the property tax base, have a basic level of funding, while more affluent areas are obligated to fund their own districts' education. For those that do not have ample resources, the state intervenes to make up the difference and guarantee a minimum level of funding. As stated on the Illinois State Comptroller's (n.d.) website: "The formula is designed to distribute more aid to poorer districts

FIGURE 5.4.4. GENERAL STATE AID FORMULA: HOW THE ILLINOIS STATE BOARD OF EDUCATION FINANCES PRIMARY AND SECONDARY SCHOOLS

GENERAL STATE AID FORMULA = EAV + ADA + HIGH POVERTY

EAV stands for Equalized Assessed Value, which refers to local wealth. This is measured by local property taxes. The wealthiest districts receive a flat rate, while impoverished districts are appropriated more money.

ADA stands for Average Daily Attendance, which is defined by the prior year's best attendance rate during any 3-month span. Higher ADA rates translate into higher state appropriations. The wealthiest districts, however, receive a flat rate.

The high-poverty criterion refers to an additional provision that provides supplemental funding for districts confronted with significant levels of poverty. This is measured by two factors: 1) the number of low-income residents per district and 2) the ADA of a district's pupils.

Source: ISBE, 2011

and a minimum amount to wealthier districts" (para. 1). Progressive intentions, however, do not translate into progressive outcomes.

Because the GSA formula guarantees only a basic level of funding, inequities remain due to compounding factors of segregation and disparate wealth gaps across districts. Critics like Gary Orfield and Chungmei Lee (2005) as well as Pamela Walters (2001) argue that such a formula relies too much on local property taxes, and this perpetuates de facto disparities between communities and what they can contribute to education. Residential segregation by race (and class) inevitably leads to "inequalities in tax revenues among school districts [that] produce inequalities in educational resources, facilities, programs, and opportunities" (Walters, 2001, p. 44). Wealthier districts, which are disproportionately White, can often pour more money into education than poorer districts, even when they receive substantially less state aid.

Progressive intentions are further displaced when lottery revenues are redistributed without considering from whom they originated. Roughly 70% of all lottery money comes from the Chicagoland area, which means that lottery players in this area contributed over $438 million of the total $668 million allocated to the state's common fund for education. That said, our regression analysis shows that this money is not generated equally across communities. In the Chicagoland area, non-White communities contribute considerably more money to education via the lottery than do White communities. Such unequal contributions offset a finance scheme intended to be race neutral and economically progressive. Because marginalized communities are the primary source for lottery revenues, the formula ends up circulating this money out of these communities and spreads it across all communities.

It is the Illinois State Board of Education's omission of any lottery criterion—like from where and whom this money comes—for determining state aid for education that mobilizes minority money out of minority communities. In a worst-case scenario, racially marginalized communities end up subsidizing public education, a service to which all state residents are entitled. The formula permits such an outcome to occur when it does not consider lottery revenues (and from where they come) as a criterion for funding each district. Non-White communities could collectively contribute more capital to education through the lottery (in addition to other sources of earmarked revenues for education) than predominantly White communities. When this occurs, financing public education becomes more of a racially inequitable obligation—regardless of progressive intent.

THE ILLINOIS LOTTERY:

STATE-SPONSORED (RE)PRODUCTION OF RACIAL INEQUALITY

During the Reconstruction era that followed the Civil War, students of color began enrolling in public schools in unprecedented numbers, but they faced much resistance from Whites who refused to fund education for laboring classes, let alone racial minorities (Anderson, 1988). White elites responded by restructuring education financeand shifting the burden to people of color. In their view, as W.E.B. Du Bois (1935/1992) noted, it was "an unjustifiable waste of private property for public disaster" (p. 641). Not only were Blacks levied taxes that paid for general public education, but their schools were also self-supported without tax contributions from the White population (Anderson, 1988; Du Bois, 1935/1992). Such practices were standard throughout the South but also spanned much of the nation.

What type of education did their money buy? It bought an education that was subpar and grossly inferior (Anderson, 1988). Black students and other students of color attended schools that were segregated and underfunded. Such schools were often overcrowded, lacked qualified instructors, and provided inadequate learning materials. Much of the curriculum came to emphasize a vocational focus that presupposed that Blacks occupied a position of political and economic subordination (Anderson, 1988; Du Bois, 1935/1992). In the words of Du Bois (1935/1992): "Every cent spent on [these schools] was taken from Negro rents and wages, and came back to property holders tenfold in increased opportunities for exploitation" (p. 665).

What has changed in education since Du Bois' days is that racial inequalities persist in pervasively insidious ways that are institutional, covert, and seemingly nonracial but no less effective (Bonilla-Silva, 2001). The institution of education remains not a democratizing institution but one that sustains social control and constrains opportunity for mobility (Lewis, 2003). Contemporary problems of segregation, tracking, and high-stakes standardized testing culminate in outcomes of disparity (Orfield & Lee, 2005). How schools are financed is another contributing factor, but most scholars have yet to study how the lottery supplements these other discriminatory mechanisms to maintain racial inequality. When it comes to financing public education, lotteries exemplify old perfume in a new bottle.

In the case of Illinois, the lottery did not provide additional funding to education as promised but displaced other progressive sources of tax revenue (Borg & Mason, 1988; 1990). Such infrastructural redesign quintessentially frees elite interests of their fiscal responsibility to public finance, all the while displacing the tax burden of public education—a service that helps make capital accumulation possible—onto those who play the lottery most: people of color. It is crucial to understand who this money comes from to understand how fiscal responsibility has been shifted from some groups to others. The evidence we offer shows that reliance on the lottery for education finance discretely shifts the tax burden onto groups marginalized by their racial status. Public education is increasingly supported by regressive taxation of the lottery, which exacerbates racial inequality when it transfers resources from marginalized to mainstream communities. Under the worst circumstances, such communities are burdened with subsidizing public education. This is especially true when lottery tax contributions eclipse other sources of money used to finance public education. When lottery-generated revenues are distributed in such a way, inequitable distributions of economic capital by race are preserved. One community's enrichment comes at the expense of another's impoverishment. It represents a state-sponsored money exchange that captures one mechanism for the reproduction of racial inequality.

REFERENCES

Anderson, J. D. (1988). *The education of blacks in the South, 1860–1935.* Chapel Hill, NC: University of North Carolina Press.

Beckert, J., & Lutter, M. (2013). Why the poor play the lottery: Sociological approaches to explaining class-based lottery play." *Sociology, 47*(6), 1152–1170.

Bonastia, C. (2012). *Southern stalemate: Five years without public education in Prince Edward County, Virginia.* Chicago, IL: University of Chicago Press.

Bonilla-Silva, E. (2001). *White supremacy and racism in the post-civil rights era.* Boulder, CO: Lynne Rienner.

Borg, M. O., & Mason, P. M. (1988). The budgetary incidence of a lottery to support education. *The National Tax Journal, 41*(1), 75–86.

Borg, M. O., & Mason, P. M. (1990). Earmarked lottery revenues: Positive windfalls or concealed redistribution mechanisms. *Journal of Education Finance, 15*(3), 289–301.

Clotfelter, C. T., & Cook, P. J. (1989). *Selling hope: State lotteries in America.* Cambridge, MA: Harvard University Press.

Du Bois, W.E.B. (1992). *Black reconstruction in America.* New York, NY: Atheneum. (Original work published in 1935.)

Henricks, K., & Embrick, D. G. (2017). *State lotteries: Historical continuity, rearticulations of racism, and American taxation.* New York, NY: Routledge.

Henricks, K., Lewis, A. E., Arenas, I., & Lewis, D. G. (2017). *A tale of three cities: The state of racial justice in Chicago.* Chicago, IL: University of Illinois at Chicago, Institute for Research on Race and Public Policy.

Hohle, R. (2015). *Race and the origins of neoliberalism.* New York, NY: Routledge.

Illinois Department of Revenue. (2011). *Sales report SLS989-01, IDOR FY2011 lottery sales by zip code.* Springfield, IL: Illinois Department of Revenue.

Illinois Lottery. (2005). *Winning big: Illinois lottery annual report 2005.* Retrieved from http://www.illinoislottery.com/subsections/PR/FY05AnRpt.pdf

Illinois Lottery. (2009). *Dream by numbers: Illinois lottery annual report 2008.* Retrieved from http://www.illinoislottery.com/subsections/PR/ FY08AnRpt.pdf

Illinois Lottery. (2010). *A charmed life. Illinois lottery annual report 2009.* Retrieved from http://www.illinoislottery.com/subsections/PR/FY09AnRpt.pdf

Illinois State Board of Education. (2004). *Illinois public school enrollment projections: 2004–05–2012–13.* Springfield, IL: Illinois State Board of Education.

Illinois State Board of Education. (2011). *General state aid—FY 2011 overview.* Retrieved from http://www.isbe.state.il.us/funding/pdf/gsa_overview.pdf

Johnson, D. R. (1999). Public school finance programs of the United States and Canada 1998–1999. *U.S. Department of Education: National Center for Education Statistics.* Retrieved from http://nces.ed.gov/edfin/ pdf/StFinance/Illinois.pdf

Karcher, A. J. (1989). *Lotteries.* New Brunswick, NJ: Transaction Publishers.

Lewis, A. E. (2003). *Race in the schoolyard: Negotiating the color line in classrooms and communities.* New Brunswick, NJ: Rutgers University Press.

Lewis-Beck, M. S. (1980). *Applied regression: An Introduction.* Beverly Hills, CA: Sage.

Martin, I. W., Mehrotra, A. K., & Prasad, M. (Eds.). (2009). *The new fiscal sociology: Taxation in comparative and historical perspective.* Cambridge, UK: Cambridge University Press.

McKoy, D. L., & Vincent, J. M. (2006). Housing and education: The inextricable link. In James H. Carr and Nandinee K. Kutty (Eds.), *Segregation: The rising costs for America* (pp. 125–150). New York, NY: Routledge.

Nibert, D. (2000). *Hitting the lottery jackpot: Government and the taxing of dreams.* New York, NY: Monthly Review Press.

Norušis, M. J. (2008). *SPSS statistics 17.0 guide to data analysis.* Upper Saddle River, NJ: Prentice Hall.

Orfield, G., & Lee, C. (2005). *Why education matters: Poverty and educational inequality.* Cambridge, MA: The Civil Rights Project, Harvard University.

Peppard, D. M., Jr. (1987). Government as bookie: Explaining the rise of lotteries for revenue." *Review of Radical Political Economics, 19*(3), 56–68.

Piven, F. F., & Cloward, R. A. (1982). *The new class war.* New York, NY: Pantheon Books.

Seamster, L., & Henricks, K. (2016). The second redemption: Backlash politics and public education." *Humanity & Society, 39*(4), 363–375.

State of Illinois. (2009). *Illinois state budget: Fiscal year 2010.* Retrieved from http://www.state.il.us/budget/FY2010/FY2010_Operating_Budget.pdf

Thomas, W.I., & Thomas, D. S. (1928). *The child in America: Behavior problems and programs.* New York, NY: Knopf.

U.S. Census Bureau. (2011). *Income and apportionment of state-administered lottery funds: 2011.* Washington, D.C.: U.S. Census Bureau.

Walters, P. B. (2001). Education access and the state: Historical continuities and discontinuities in racial inequality in American education." *Sociology of Education, 74*(1), 35–49.

WHITENESS AS CONTINGENT HIERARCHIES

Who Counts as White and Why

BY STEVE GARNER

What is the Point of Using "Whiteness" as an Analytical Tool?

So far we have observed that whiteness has been conceptualized in a number of complementary ways. In this chapter I will focus on the idea that in addition to a set of borders between people categorized as "white" and "non white," there is another set of internal borders produced by racialization. In other words, there are socially observable degrees of whiteness between the groups that seem to be unproblematically white. Examples here include Southern, Central and Eastern European immigrant groups, Jews, Gypsy-Travellers/Roma, as well as the numerous and important divisions based on class, gender, sexuality, region, etc., identified in the literature on both America and Britain (Hartigan 2005, Nayak 2003, Daniels 1997). The reader may well be experiencing trepidation about the extent to which we are encroaching onto other areas of work. We already have concepts like "anti-semitism," "sexism" and "homophobia." Class divisions are already covered in other literatures. Considering that European migrants are white anyway, how is this to do with "race"? Isn't it ethnicity, another area abundantly, if not excessively, analyzed already? I do not want to be proscriptive. There are plenty of perspectives that can bring fruitful analyses to bear on these identities and social hierarchies, and using the whiteness problematic is one of them. However, I hope to convince you of its utility through the use of three of the broad areas of study dealt with in the literature: immigration into America in the nineteenth and early twentieth century (the "in-between peoples" thesis); the "White Australia" policy (1901–1972); and the related ideas of "white trash" in America, and the working class in the U.K.

Before we look at those case studies, I want to provide a brief outline of the history of "white" as a racial identity, in order to put them into perspective. We have to keep in mind that we are dealing with social interpretations of physical and cultural phenomena, and these interpretations can change over time and place, reflecting the political, economic and cultural distinctiveness of the context.

Where Did Whiteness Come From?

Primarily we have looked so far at the intersection of whiteness and its Others, those racialized identities created by white world's military, commercial and ideological domination of the globe since the sixteenth century. That is the story of how Europeans simultaneously created whiteness and otherness as collective identities. Although from the vantage point of the twenty-first century, the terms "white" and "black" seem to go without saying, these words have not always been used to identify human beings. Indeed use of the term "white" to describe people dates back only to the sixteenth century. At that time however it was one of

Steve Garner, "Whiteness as Contingent Hierarchies: Who Counts as White and Why," *Whiteness: An Introduction*, pp. 63-79. Copyright © 2007 by Taylor & Francis Group LLC. Reprinted with permission.

a range of labels, and not the one most frequently used. Religion, nation, and social class were all deployed more than color. The literature on the period from 1500 to the end of the seventeenth century arrives at a rough consensus: the co-existence of religious labels of identity; "Christian" and "heathen" in the American colonies (Jordan 1968, Frederickson 1988) rendered color distinctions redundant until slaves began to convert to Christianity. Elsewhere in the New World, V.S. Naipaul (1969) notes that after the slave revolt in Berbice (then in Dutch Guiana, South America) in 1764, the dead were divided up in official reports neither as "black" and "white," nor even as "slave" and "free," but as "Christians" and "heathens."

Slavery is now irrevocably linked in popular understandings of history to the transatlantic slave trade and its institutions in the Americas, with Africans as its principal population. However, vital to the development of whiteness is the acknowledgement that in the Anglophone colonies, it was the end of the seventeenth century before the status of "free" and "unfree" labor corresponded perfectly to European and African workers respectively. This is because in the earlier days of colonization, white indentured laborers[1] were employed before, and then alongside Africans. When these indentured laborers became numerically inferior due to their access to landownership after indentureship, then the numbers of enslaved Africans started to rapidly over take them. So it was around the last decade of the seventeenth century that the only unfree laborers were Africans. There were free Blacks as well as free white laborers, and it is at this point that we see the emergence of colony-level legislation against voting rights for Blacks; "race" mixing; and the introduction of restrictions on property ownership for Black people. We can thus start the clock of "whiteness" as an explicit legitimized collective identity in North America and the Anglophone Caribbean from around that point. This was clearly not a historical coincidence. The sixteenth and seventeenth centuries was the period when Europeans were beginning to encounter people from Africa, the Americas and Asia on an ongoing basis, and notice the obvious if cosmetic physical differences between groups alongside the cultural ones.

In the period between then and the mid nineteenth century, the idea that some people's identities were "white" came to be attached to the new ways of understanding mankind that developed out of the Enlightenment (Eze 1997). These understandings were enshrined in elite scientific discourse as empirically provable racial differences explaining cultural, political and technological inequalities. While earlier eras had noted that physical appearance, climate and culture differed from place to place, there was no sustained intellectual effort to link these in a coherent philosophy of difference. This changed during the Enlightenment. Climate, it was argued, determined physical appearance, and in turn these determined the capacity of different people to evolve, that is, toward the goal of European norms. However, the mainstream discourse fixed the relationship of climate to civilizational capacity: only those living in temperate climates, that is, white Europeans, could properly attain the heights of civilization, and the others trailed behind. Versions of this logic appeared throughout the eighteenth and early nineteenth centuries. By the mid nineteenth century, this was no longer up for discussion, but was itself the basis for further discussion.

Indeed, as racial science and philosophy garnered credence, increasingly complex schemas were produced, in which there were subdivisions of whiteness. Notions of Anglo-Saxon supremacy (within the multi-layered "white race") began to gain intellectual support, bolstered by an amalgam of the press, a network of scientists engaged in somatic measurements (Horsman 1981) and internationally read work. Robert Knox and Joseph Arthur Comte de Gobineau developed the notion that within the white "race," Anglo-Saxons were particularly capable of civilization in comparison to Celts, Slavs and Latins[2]. This hierarchy within a hierarchy is the basis of the thesis developed by U.S. labor historians David Roediger and James Barrett, whose work we shall look at next.

Case Study 1: "Inbetween people"?

In a set of influential publications (Roediger 1991, Barrett and Roediger 1997, 2004, 2005), Roediger and Barrett argue that in the period from the 1850s to the 1910s, incoming migrant Europeans were exposed to a situation where the American mainstream racialized values exerted forces that pushed Europeans to claim whiteness for themselves, in order to gain privileged access to resources, and psychological and social capital (Du Bois's "wages of whiteness")[3]. Barrett and Roediger (1997, 2004) maintain two principal and connected points. Firstly, "Whiteness" is to do with cultural and political power and, secondly, not all those who appear phenotypically white are incorporated equally into the dominant group.

Catholic and Jewish migrants from the various Southern, Eastern and Central European countries, they argue, were not immediately accepted socially and culturally as white. Differential access to this resource was sought by successive waves of migrants learning the rules of the game, or "this racial thing," as one of Barrett and Roediger's respondents puts it (1997: 6). They label these groups of less dominant Europeans, who were temporarily disadvantaged in the U.S. context by class and culture, "inbetween people": not white, but not black either.

Scholarship in dialogue with the writers above has debated the extent to which various ethnic groups such as Jewish- (Brodkin 1994, 1998) and Italian-Americans (Guglielmo and Salerno 2003) can be considered "white." These arguments posit some parallels between the Irish and the Italians in America, suggesting that over time they "became" white. However, there is a counter-argument developed by some historians such as Eric Arnesen (2001) and Tom Guglielmo (2003) that European immigrants did not actually have to "become" white, relative to Blacks and Mexicans, for example, and that the "inbetween people" theory does not withstand scrutiny. I think the keys to unravelling this knot are reasonably straightforward. They are to do with understanding the priorities and assumptions of the protagonists. The first thing to realize is that the "inbetween people" thesis does not claim that Irish, Italian and other European immigrants were really "black," but that they were literally "denigrated," that is, likened to black Americans (in terms of civilization and social status), and they temporarily occupied the lowest positions on the economic and social ladder of free labor. This social, occupational and often geographical proximity to Free Blacks gave rise to the imperative for these migrant groups to distance themselves from them. The further they moved from blackness, the closer they got to whiteness. This strategy was executed in some cases through the urban equivalent of ethnic cleansing (Bernstein, 1990; Ignatiev, 1996).

So the point is not to suggest that certain groups of immigrants were not phenotypically white, which is why Tom Guglielmo (2003) correctly identifies "race" and color as often separate but overlapping criteria in late nineteenth- and early twentieth-century American institutional definitions, but that ideologically and culturally they were indeed considered different and lesser "white races." The corollaries of this categorization were not a set of life chances equivalent to those of Blacks, Native Americans or Hispanics, rather the obligation to define themselves as "white" in a society where that mattered a great deal, whereas in their countries of origin, it had mattered scarcely at all. European immigrants thus "became" white on arrival in the New World, runs the argument, because they disembarked into a new set of social identities that articulated with those they had brought with them, and one overarching identity was whiteness.

I think this conclusion needs qualification. Not being white, and being black, are two very different things: the Catholic Irish were always salvageable for whiteness in a way that African, Mexican, Asian and Native Americans were not (Garner 2003). This is because legally they were definitely white, in as far as they could become naturalized citizens, and were not treated as imports (Haney-López 1996, Jacobson 1998). The second problem is an interesting one that illustrates a divergence of interpretations of identical material. The protagonists in this debate prioritize different arenas as the source of their claims. On one side, Barrett and Roediger see the cultural domain as the one in which perceptions of "inbetweenness" are made explicit, while Arnesen and Guglielmo pragmatically see the legal domain as predominant. Whatever people said or did, argue the latter, in law all white people were white. However, this reasoning is open to the criticism that in sociological terms, the law can just as easily be deconstructed as can popular culture: it is not a superior level of discourse. The legal domain, argues Cheryl Harris (1993), was utilized from the nineteenth century to inject scientific rationality into decisions about who belonged to which race: and these decisions had material impacts. Yet the basis of the law was spurious, reliant as it was on unfeasibly accurate records about people's ancestry, and understandings of definitions of "race" that were not empirically provable. The result of this was that the legal concept of "blood" was no more objective than that which the law dismissed as subjective and unreliable (Harris 1993: 1740). Guglielmo (2003), for example, refers to material suggesting that Italians (especially from the South) were subject to the same kind of racializing discourses, placing them at a lower level of civilization vis-à-vis Anglo-Saxons, as were the Irish. Yet it is worth reiterating that "not white" does not mean "black." Even if it did, how can we explain the court ruling referred to by Jacobson (1998: 4) in which an Alabama court found that the State had not proved beyond doubt that a Sicilian woman was white?

Used sociologically, the term "white" can be interpreted as encompassing non-material and fluid dominant norms and boundaries. Within the white racialized hierarchy were, as Guglielmo rightly points out, a number of "races." Indeed, using the distinction between "white" and "non white" as a starting point is a legitimate historical argument. In the USA, white migrants were people with rights, while Blacks were property without rights, for example. Yet this approach regards the terms "white" and "black" themselves as natural entities or givens, whose existence is then transposed into law. A sociologist however, ought to view these terms and the social relations they cover as part of the puzzle itself, that is, as products of the processes of racialization.

What emerges from this is that there are various contexts: economic, social, legal, cultural, for example, in which meaning is attributed to types of difference. In practice, it is impossible to completely separate these dimensions, but it is useful to start from this basis as a way of thinking through these issues. Moreover, the period covered, around 70 years from the mid nineteenth century to the First World War, enables us to see that understandings of who fits where in the social hierarchies can change. Why this happens when it happens can only be answered by reference to the historical record. We might put forward a few important structural items here, such as the Irish Famine, which altered the complexion of Irish migration to America; the Civil War, Reconstruction and after, which provided the framework both for black/white relations and for the formation of a "white vote" in American politics; the development of the U.S. economy to a stage which required so many manual workers that the labor supply was exhausted within the country and meant that there was plentiful work available for migrants; the consequent slump at the end of the nineteenth century experienced by Western Europe, which meant that the availability of employment that had absorbed some of the workers from Southern and Eastern Europe was diminished. Place all these together with the framework for understanding difference established by racial science in the nineteenth century, and outlines of the problem we have seen conceptualized, using the shorthand "inbetween peoples," or the process of "becoming white," emerge more clearly. Bear in mind that being white was not just about a certain range of phenotypes, but also about claims on culture and values.

Case Study 2: "White Australia"

The Australian colonies were founded, much like the American colonies, as separate entities. Their foundation at the end of the eighteenth century, under the British Crown, proceeded on the legal principle that Australia was empty, uninhabited and unsettled land (*terra nullius*). Thus the white European settlers founded the colonies on the contradictory basis that the Aboriginal populations (now referred to as "First Australians") did not exist, yet their collective relations with them were, as for the European settlers in North America, frequent and necessary. By the mid nineteenth century, the Australian colonies were absorbing migrant labor from the Pacific Islands, China and India. Between 1901 (when the Commonwealth of Australia became a dominion, with its own federal government) until 1972, Australia's immigration policy was based on the objectives of:

1. Protecting indigenous (i.e. white) labor from competition with Asian and Pacific Island labor, and
2. Preserving an Anglo-Celtic majority in the country.

The term "White Australia" was coined in 1906, as an assertion of these twin objectives. The point of looking at this policy and the problems it ran into later in the twentieth century is firstly, to highlight both the haziness around who is considered white at a given moment and why; and secondly, to give an idea of some of the contextual, structural considerations that frame such changes within a hierarchy.

"White Australia" then was not a single piece of legislation, but a doctrine underlying an accumulation of laws and practices that restricted immigration from outside the country (except Europe) and excluded foreign nationals within Australia from various benefits and elements of citizenship. The 1901 Commonwealth Immigration Restriction Act (IRA) was the first piece of legislation passed by the new Federal Government. Its most well-known features were its provision for a written test in any European language, at the discretion of an immigration officer, to determine a prospective immigrant's fitness for approval; and the categories of person whose entry was prohibited. These were: the physically or mentally ill, categories of criminal other than political prisoner, prostitutes, those living on prostitutes' earnings, and those likely to be a charge on the communal purse (Tavan 2005: 7–8). In addition, various other laws provided for the repatriation of foreigners (Pacific Island Labourers Act 1901), excluded foreigners from voting (Commonwealth Franchise Act 1902; Naturalization Act 1903) and from benefits like pensions (Old-Age and Invalid Pensions Act 1908) and the Commonwealth maternity bonus (1912).

However, to properly understand the compound anxieties about being usurped by foreign labor and facing "racial contamination," as Labor Party leader John Christian Watson put it during parliamentary debate in 1901, it should be noted that blueprints of White Australia were already embodied in the legislation of the various Australian colonies before they combined to form the Commonwealth of Australia in 1900. Asian and Pacific Islanders had been working in Australia since the first half of the nineteenth century, primarily in the mining and sugar industries respectively. Hostile political agitation as a response to the migration of Indian, Chinese and Pacific Islanders into various parts of the country had led to state governments passing restrictions in a number of waves during the second half of the century. This became particularly intense in the late 1880s. By the end of the century, a model of indirectly discriminatory policies had been introduced. The 1901 IRA was therefore the endorsement, on a national level, of a set of practices ongoing across Australia. What was at stake was a conception of Australia as a unique civilization of Europeans encountering and overcoming a natural environment that other Europeans did not have to tame. The combination of whiteness, Britishness and embryonic Australianness that this embodied was most clearly defined in its dealings with First Australians and with the Chinese, not only through the physical differences shorthanded as racial, but the underlying values that Australians saw themselves as having and the other groups as lacking: vitality, industriousness, purity, cleanliness. The idea of geographical vulnerability added urgency to turn-of-the-century Australians' view of themselves as the pioneers of civilization surrounded by potential adversaries. In the prevailing social Darwinist ideological context, they were the spearhead of the white race forced into proximity with lesser races. In the ensuing struggle, they would prevail as the stronger, fitter race[4]. This is why although non-Europeans had their uses, mixing with them and allowing them citizenship was seen as counter-productive. Governments did not attempt the mass deportations provided for in the IRA, and particular industries such as pearl diving enjoyed, de facto, special dispensation to employ Pacific Islanders and Chinese, who were seen as "naturally" more suited to this work. Gwenda Tavan (2005: 15) interprets White Australia as a populist and popular device for generating nationalism in a fledgling society. It garnered support from all interest groups despite tensions of gender, class and religion. She goes on to contextualize it as central to the specific form of social liberalism that was the national ideology of the emergent State. This required state intervention to mitigate the excesses of the market, ensure fairer distribution of wealth, and provide minimum living conditions. The cultural homogeneity putatively anchoring this set of values was seen as essential to successfully building a civilization geographically remote from the epicenter of world civilization (Europe). Within this, the labor movement's opposition to the conditions of Kanaka (Pacific Island) workers in the sugar industry, on the grounds of their virtual slavery, was not viewed as contradictory to its support for repatriation of the foreign element of the workforce.

Indeed, it was the tropical part of Australia, the Northern Territories, that most exercised elite Australians' minds in the first half of the twentieth century. While the baseline for Australian immigration was to build on British and, to a lesser extent, Irish stock, the idea of "race" and its relationship to climate and space proved problematic. Simply put, the association of different "races" with particular types of climate, and with innate characteristics militated against Northern Europeans flourishing in this tropical environment (Anderson 2006). Yet with the departure of the Pacific Islanders in the first decades of the twentieth century, the North required a substitute labor force. The settlement of the North needed not just white supervisors, as had been the case in other tropical areas of colonial expansion, but a tropical white male laboring workforce. Was this a contradiction in terms? Alison Bashford (2000: 255) argues that tropical medicine debated the question, "Is White Australia possible?" between 1900 and the 1930s. The problem revolved not around white men colonizing other people in the tropics, but "as colonizers of a difficult and resilient space" (2000: 258). In this debate, First Australians had again been made invisible. The focus was on how whiteness could be adapted to overcome the tropical environment. Indeed, suggestions of how to accomplish this contributed, maintains Bashford, to producing "an idea that whiteness was not only a characteristic of skin and color, but was also about how one lived, how one arranged one's moment by moment existence in space and time [...] the capacity to live in the tropics had to be learnt in minute, detailed and constant ways" (2000: 266).

At least for those engaged in the public health discourse, the solution was to apply science and rationality to impose order on the environment (Anderson 2006). A more pressing problem for employers in the Queensland and Northern Territories sugar plantations was to remain economically viable. Here, the niceties of the public health debate were ignored by workers intent on retaining a standard of living promised by the dismissal of competition in the form of Pacific Island labor. Yet in the mid 1920s, migrants from Italy began arriving in their thousands to work on the estates. This triggered a hostile campaign led by the Brisbane-based *Worker* newspaper against Italian immigration (Sheills 2006). The Italians occupied a position straddling the lines of whiteness. Officially categorized as "white aliens," they became the object of a discourse aimed at presenting them as a threat not just to jobs, but to living standards (being willing to work for lower wages) and the cultural future of Australia (due to their clannishness, corruption, backward civilization and unfitness for vigorous pioneer activity required to settle and develop empty land). By 1925, the Queensland government had set up a Royal Commission to investigate the impact of the increased number of aliens in North Queensland. The Commissioner charged with producing a report made a sharp distinction between Northern and Southern Italians, castigating the latter vis-à-vis their Northern counterparts, for their clannishness, resistance to assimilation and propensity towards crime and violence. He was not alone in thinking this, either in Australia or elsewhere. Italians themselves debated the North–South divide in terms of culture and civilization (Verdicchio 1997), and the characterization of the Sicilians as "inferior types" represented a boundary line between white and less white aliens.

Indeed, while the 1901 Immigration Act had been primarily aimed at keeping out the Chinese, the second- and third-largest groups of "prohibited" immigrants (i.e. those refused the right to land in Australia) were Southern Europeans: Maltese and Italians. Distinctions within the "white race" meant that Latins were lower down the racial pecking order than Anglo-Saxons, Alpines and Nordic peoples. Added to this complication was the reclassification of Axis member nationals (from Bulgaria, the Austro-Hungarian Empire, Germany and Turkey) during World War I as hostile aliens. There was even a temporary internment camp in New South Wales, and bans continued until at least 1923. Between 1912 and 1946 (the period when separate figures on the Maltese were kept), the prevailing practice of immigration officers was to question the right of Southern Europeans to land, even if, as in the case of the Maltese, they had British passports. Perceived racial difference here overrode nationality. In the most well-known case, 208 Maltese were kept out of Australia in 1916 (York 1990) by Melbourne immigration officials who gave them the dictation test in Dutch: all failed.

What this reveals about the workings of whiteness is its lack of solidity and stability. Even the taken-for-granted visible signs can be misleading, or be irrelevant to those wielding power in precise situations. Cultural and political factors can override the phenotypical ones. Moreover, the capacity to centre problems around whiteness per se can make other people invisible. Despite First Australians living in Northern Territories and Northern Queensland for millennia, public discourse obliterated them from the picture. The land was read through white eyes as "empty" because it was neither owned according to private land-ownership laws, nor cultivated in ways that made sense in agrarian norms (planting, cultivation and harvest).

The basis for anxiety about shades of whiteness is expressed again through competition, or at least perceived competition, for work and conditions within international labor markets. It is not feasible to extricate the material from the cultural aspects of whiteness if we seek to understand it in its lived context.

Case Study 3: The Racialization of Working-Class Cultures

"Abject Whites" in the U.K.

Ethnographic writing on white racialized identities in the U.K. has focused disproportionately, as has much of the academic work on class, on working-class men. This can be seen as a reflection of the academy's middle-class composition and of ethnography's colonial heritage. Since Victorian times, middle-class academics and philanthropists have conducted surveys of the poor, the work of Friedrich Engels (1969[1844]), Henry Mayhew (1967[1861]) and Charles Booth (1902) being the best-known examples. The objective of such projects may have been to reform, politicize or evangelize the working classes, but the common strands were the revelation of their failings, and the creation of an inventory of what they did not have. In describing them, researchers drew parallels between them and colonized peoples. Anthony Wohl, on the web resource "Victorian Web"[5] notes that a number of characteristics were applied by British commentators to the nineteenth-century working classes, Irish immigrants and colonial subjects. They were: unreasonable, irrational, and easily excited, childlike, superstitious (not religious), criminal (with neither respect for private property, nor notions of property), excessively sexual, filthy, inhabited unknown dark lands or territories and shared physical qualities. Wohl has clearly identified an overlap between the language of "race" and that of class, locating both as being fixed on the body and culture.

The key point to grasp in the discourse on whiteness is that behavior, appearance and culture are linked. There has to be an explanation for why some of the "race" placed at the top of the hierarchy clearly do not match the criteria established for superiority: bad genes and dysfunctional culture. From this viewpoint, the language and frames used in order to discursively distinguish (or make) classes, class fractions and "races," are very similar.

This process of negatively evaluating working-class habitus and behavior has become so dominant a discourse that in the post-industrial era of structural un- and underemployment, studies demonstrate that such values have to some extent become internalized. Bev Skeggs (1997) observes that the working-class women she interviews themselves often dis-identify from the working class. They define "working class" by reference to values they personally do not or no longer have, or to economic predicaments they do not face. Indeed, the age of readily-sanctioned reference to a working-class "us" appears, outside particular work milieux, to have disappeared from their social world. The anxiety around owning white working-class subject positions can be read as a reflection of white middle- and ruling-class attempts to pathologize and racialize them as an "underclass." Although the "underclass" is rarely used as a sociological term in twenty-first century British scholarship (after intensive use in the late 80s and 90s), parts of the underclass debate map onto groups within the working class who are perceived as lacking in respectability: in the contemporary period these are "Chavs" (Haywood and Yar, 2005; Nayak, 2003), or more abstractly, in Chris Haylett's (2001) argument, "abject whites."

She contends that sections of a white "underclass" are constructed in turn-of-the-century Britain as "people who are outside/beyond/beneath the nation" (2001: 358). This process involves devaluing social actions carried out by them. The protagonists in the Autumn 1993 "white" riots (in Oxford, Cardiff and Newcastle) "were not hailed as class revolutionaries or even righteously angered disenfranchised minorities, rather they were an embarrassing sign of what the white working-class poor had become—a disorganized, racist and sexist detritus" (ibid.: 358). Indeed, in the de-unionized post-Fordist landscape, blame for this "decline" in the working class is placed on the working class themselves, or at least the poorest sections of it.

Over time, argues Haylett, explanations of decline have become increasingly less structural, and more individual, and fixed around pathological working-class masculinities and backwardness. In short the poor emerge as the exact opposite of the expanding multicultural, cosmopolitan middle classes. Indeed, Haylett stresses that the identity work accomplished in this discourse is relational, that is the multicultural modern group (the British middle classes) depend on the "abject unmodern" white working class (ibid.: 365) for their own identity.

This "power-evasive discourse" (Frankenberg, 1994) is picked up in specific relation to "race," in for example the work on "color-blind racism" (Bonilla-Silva, 2002) in the USA. Like minorities, with whom they are often compared, working-class Whites in these narratives are culturally disposed to degeneracy, crime, over-fecundity, fecklessness, etc.

"White Trash" in the USA

Similar themes resonate throughout the new studies and problematization of "white trash" in the USA (Wray and Newitz 1997, Hartigan 2005, 1999, 1997a, b, Wray 2006). In these accounts, whiteness is significantly mediated by class (Bettie 2000, Gibbons 2004, Morris 2005). The polarized pairing of productiveness–unproductiveness is also central. Hartigan's tracing of the development of the phenomenon of "white trash" in the USA (2005) demonstrates some interesting points of comparison between "race" and class on one hand, and the U.K. and the USA on the other. Using the conclusion of nineteenth-century travel writer James Gilmore[6] he distinguishes between elements of the working class: "The *poor* white man labors, the *mean* white man does not labor: and labor makes the distinction between them."

Again, echoes of the underclass debate resonate loudly, with a moral categorization of the working class into productive and unproductive groups: the deserving and undeserving poor. Writing from the 1860s, says Hartigan, evidenced the struggle between those for whom such "meanness" was in the blood and those who recognized a degree of environmental input. These competing logics developed into the twentieth century. Racial theorist Madison Grant, for example, understood "white trash" as a combination of natural habitat and bloodlines: to do with sexuality, urbanization and crime, rather than just immigration (Grant 1916). Eugenics discourse stressed the perils of mixing good with bad genes, and responsibility for policing the genetic border. It argued that a host of antisocial and expensive behavior derived from poor family etiquette and practices. The result of this discourse in popular outlets, contends Hartigan, was heightened middle-class awareness of their racial selves, and of threat from below. In the scenarios popularized in the press, the idea of "racial poisons" dominated discourse, with the weaker blood multiplying faster than the stronger. Gertrude Davenport (the wife of leading eugenicist Charles Davenport) wrote in a popular magazine in April 1914 that "the greatest menace of imbecility is not that the imbecile may break into our house and steal our silver, or that he might set fire to our barn, but that he may be born of our flesh" (Hartigan 2005: 95).

Similarly, in Winthrop Stoddard's (1922) Freudian fight for civilization taking place within the Self, class status coincides with racial value:

> Let us understand once and for all [he warns] that we have among us a rebel army—the vast host of the inadaptable, the incapable, the envious, the discontented, filled with instinctive hatred of civilization and progress, and ready on the instant to rise in revolt. Here are foes that need watching. Let us watch them (1922: 87).

The overlap with contemporaneous American eugenics discourse on immigrants from Southern and Eastern Europe is very similar to Stoddard's comments here, and underscores the idea that "race" and class are intimately connected in discourse of hierarchization. People's culture and behavior is in the blood, these theories argue, and within the dominant "race" there are those whose culture and behavior is more like those of subordinate races than those of the dominant. The struggle is for the dominant to remain pure and unpolluted, a theme pivotal to discourse on "race." The white trash figure then is marked as an excessive body that pollutes others. It displays the innate behavior that both confirms the depths to which the working class has collapsed (so far from work, so far from respectability), and at the same time emphasizes the industriousness and respectability of the middle-class subjects that fill the signifier "white trash" with meaning.

Plural Trajectories of Whiteness

I began this chapter by floating the idea that there are a set of internal borders within the ostensibly homogenous "white" group, and that these borders are contingent on political, economic and social factors that make them more or less relevant. In this final section, I want to draw out some of the complexity involved in the social relations that white working-class people maintain with minorities in Britain, as illustrated through empirical fieldwork.

Ethnographic fieldwork has illuminated what we could call the "plural trajectories" of whiteness. In other words, how white people in broadly similar class positions make sense of the social material used to understand "race" in differing ways. We are going to look briefly at two pieces of British ethnographic fieldwork to demonstrate some aspects of these "plural trajectories": Katherine Tyler's discussions with residents of a former mining town in the English Midlands (2004), and Les Back's study of young people on the "Riverview" estate in South London (1996).

Tyler's (2004) inter-generational dialogue among small-town Leicestershire inhabitants shows how personal biographies profoundly shape the ways in which people perceive "Others." Among the interviewees, no homogenous representative voice is expressed: white superiority is contested by some, just as it is accepted unthinkingly by more. Identification can take the form of empathy. "Sarah's" experience of growing up working in her Czech immigrant father's shop gives her empathy with the people working in family-run Asian businesses when she hears criticisms of Asian corner shops, for example (Tyler 2004: 304). Moreover, a person may develop a critical angle through mobility and return. Another of Tyler's respondents, "Jim," returns to the town after three years at university in a small, more multicultural city. He reports that his recognition and awareness of racism increased dramatically after he was reabsorbed into family circles and heard the types of discourse that he previously listened to uncritically. He can now reflect on the older generation's assumptions and dissect them. When his grandmother died, the house she had lived in was bought by an Asian family, something that his uncles were unhappy about. "The presence of Asians in the home where they were brought up," paraphrases Tyler (2004: 299), "signifies an intolerable and unacceptable transformation." Here we see a crucial element of the mechanism of enacting whiteness. A perceived negative change (in this case the retrospective tainting of the family) is attached to an effect (the Asian buyer) rather than a cause (the grandmother's death, the psychological toll of memories of childhood in that home, the broader global changes that brought the family in question from Asia to Britain).

Inter-generational and gendered differences are also revealed by this study. The older people are generally less reflexive about whiteness and quicker to deploy racialized discourse, as are men as compared to women, many of whom see more positives where the men see only negatives.

There are clearly a number of places to be located ideologically in the racialization process, which becomes even more evident in the London housing estates where Les Back worked in the early 1990s. Back's (1996) ethnography of youth culture on South London estates suggests that values determine the salient borders of identity, and that culture becomes the "modality" (following Stuart Hall) through which they are racialized. Black and white youths there put aside sporadic but real differences in order to ally against Vietnamese and Bangladeshi newcomers (1996: 240–241) in what Back terms "neighborhood nationalism." This alliance assumes the form of verbal and occasionally physical attacks. While the black youths are well aware that in other circumstances they could, and indeed have been, the victims of such aggression from their white counterparts, in the context of defining membership of the estate, their secular, linguistic and music-based coalition with white youth in "Riverview" estate appears to predominate. They thus become what Back terms "contingent insiders" (1996: 240), while their counterparts in "Southgate" estate seemed to enjoy a qualitatively different relationship with their white peers, who had "vacated concepts of whiteness and Englishness … in favor of a mixed ethnicity that was shared" (ibid.: 241). So while there is frequently tension, there is also often alliance, through personal relationships drawing on shared knowledge and experiences.

Indeed, a recurrent topic in British ethnographic studies is the heterogeneity and elasticity of the category "white" in its members' affiliations with black and Asian cultures, to the point where, in some specific contexts, terms such as "black" or "white" culture become almost ideal-types.[7]

These groups of young people illustrate a paradox that resurfaces elsewhere in British fieldwork. In their survey of shopkeepers in a London borough, Wells and Watson (2005) find that not all those championing "white values" are white, while some champions of white rights include their black neighbors in their embattled and beleaguered "we." In these cases the "Other" is usually Muslim. Clearly, the power relationships at a personal and local level allow for whiteness to be expanded to incorporate those not phenotypically white beneath its cultural canopy for the enactment of both rhetorical and physical violence. People who are not white can be absorbed into honorary whiteness in particular circumstances, yet this invariably involves othering different groups. In fact this othering appears constitutive of the process of redrawing the boundary of whiteness in terms of values, so that it embraces British black or Asian people, depending on the context. In confirming shared values, the groups that share and do not share them are defined.

Conclusions: Overlapping Hierarchies of Class and Whiteness

In previous chapters, I focused on the borders between white and non-white. Here, the concentration has been on the other end of whiteness, between the constituent groups of the white whole. I want to emphasize that these latter borders are contingent, that is, open to political and social change. A group might be considered unproblematically white at one stage in one place, but not in another place at another time. Or, this might change for a specific group in the same place over different periods. Changing economic and social conditions led to different appraisals of who was allowed into Australia and why: what were the criteria? The design and application of the White Australia strategy, as well as the example of the "inbetween peoples" thesis, are clearly about the parallel boundaries of whiteness; the one separating white from its non-white Other, and those separating the really white from the less so.

While groups such as Jews, Gypsies and immigrants frequently find themselves marginalized within the social relations of "race," I want to encourage you to think of how the process works in relation to class. We have already noted that for a long time, the way in which membership of classes and "races" was conceptualized was very similar. One function of the internal borders of whiteness is to isolate a group of Whites as being the sole agents of negative and un-modern behaviors and attitudes, thus removing responsibility for discrimination from the others. As Hartigan concludes:

> "Part of what the epithet white trash expresses is the general view held by whites that there are only a few extreme, dangerous whites who are really racist or violently misguided, as opposed to recognizing that racism is an institutional problem pervading the nation and implicating all whites in its operation" (Hartigan 2005: 118–119).

I am tempted here to paraphrase Orwell, and suggest that in the process of racialization, all Whites are nominally equal, but some are more equal than others. This is true not only of how people express racism, but in the representations of how racism is expressed. The idea of portraying, or representing some groups as not-quite-white is part of the same power imbalance as the one that enables racism to function at a collective level. The discourse of "race" and class are intimately connected.

Indeed, while racist ideas do abound in the working-class communities studied—although this label is contested in Chicago's Midtown (Kefalas 2003), and Detroit's Corktown and Warrendale (Hartigan 1999)—academics and media professionals play a significant role in creating a selective picture in which only the working class express such ideas and live in segregated neighborhoods. This is not borne out, even by the often questionable opinion poll results. Studies of whiteness in middle-class circles, residential areas or workplaces, or at all, are unfortunately few and far between[8]. Whiteness is neither just for the wealthy, nor just the poor. Yet the people who have engaged in defining the desirability of including particular segments of their compatriots in the civilized, right-thinking mainstream have been middle- and upper-class British and Americans.

Moreover, under certain conditions, whiteness (as a dominant set of values and assumptions that make various groups problematic) is not even always only for white people. It is clear from survey research that minorities generally have more sympathy for immigrants and asylum seekers, and more of them tend to understand racism as structural rather than individually generated (Lamont 2000, Weis and Fine 1996), yet from the examples of Back (1996), Wells and Watson (2005) and Hoggett *et al.* (1992, 1996) there is enough to suggest that there might occasionally be a strategic overlap of values between white and black people that coalesce around defending neighborhoods, and possibly jobs. Moreover, minorities do engage to a degree with power-evasive discourse such as color-blind racism (Bonilla-Silva, 2002), just as many of Skeggs' respondents defined "working class" as not them, but somebody else. There is a great deal of complexity on view in the fieldwork done on white working-class communities, and a number of individual biographical pathways that lead people also to be anti-racist. If this work teaches us anything, it is that attitudes cannot be read off simplistically from class positions.

We should recognize throughout that hierarchies are always in the process of construction, deconstruction and reconstruction: nothing is fixed, not even racialized boundaries. The hierarchies I refer to are expressed in terms of patterns of power relations; that is, the power to name, the power to control and distribute resources. While the group defined as "white" has historically monopolized this sort of power, who counts as "white" at a given moment and at a given time is far less certain. This requires us to understand political, social, cultural and economic factors as a messy whole, rather than as easily distinguishable and analyzable components: a challenge, but a worthwhile one.

Discussion Questions

1. What do class and racial identities have in common and what distinguishes them?
2. What role to specific national contexts play in the way class and race get linked and unlinked?
3. When we define our own group, we define another implicitly. What evidence of this emerges from the discussion of class and "race" here?
4. What does the author mean by "… in the process of racialization, all Whites are nominally equal, but some are more equal than others" in this context?

Notes

1. Indenture was a form of labor whereby the worker generally signed up to work for a specified period without pay on the basis that s(he) would receive a lump sum or a parcel of land at the expiry of the contract. However, political and other types of prisoners were also made into indentured laborers in the British Empire, particularly in the seventeenth century.
2. Scottish surgeon Robert Knox's *The Races of Men* (1850), and French aristocrat de Gobineau's *Essai sur l'inégalité des races humaines* (1853–55) are key works in this regard.
3. W.E.B. Du Bois' much referred to passage in *Black Reconstruction (1998: 700),* his history of class and race relations in post-bellum America, attempts to find a reason why otherwise poor and oppressed white Southerners sided with the landed elite against the freed slave population in the 1870s. His answer is that it was not merely a question of economics, but of psychology. The status effect of feeling racially superior was equivalent to a "public and psychological wage" (of whiteness) that they were paid in excess of their meager financial rewards. Barrett and Roediger are not alone in positing whiteness as an overarching mainstream value of Americanness; Horsman (1981), Saxton (1990), Bernstein (1990), Almaguer (1994), Allen (1994), Ignatiev (1996) and Jacobson (1998) all suggest this.
4. "Social Darwinism" was a framework for understanding the social world, developed from Darwin's research into plants and animals and

particularly popular during the last quarter of the nineteenth century. Evolution is cast in social Darwinism as an ongoing struggle for survival with the best-adapted and powerful species surviving at the cost of the weaker ones. It was used to justify imperialism, the class order of society and gender inequalities among other things.

5. "Victorian Web" is accessible at: <http://www.victorianweb.org/history/race/rcov.html>. On the overlap of "race" and class, see also Lorimer (1978).
6. Gilmore, J. *Down in Tennessee*, 1864: 188–89.
7. In their study of the East End of London, Paul Hoggett *et al.* (1996: 113) remark on a similar set of provisional allegiances, noting the large Afro-Caribbean presence in a demonstration following the fatal stabbing of a white schoolboy by a Bangladeshi boy:

   "The paradox is that whilst Afro-Caribbean soccer players can still be the object of crude racial abuse at nearby Millwall Football Club, Afro-Caribbeans can nevertheless also be included in an imaginary community of English-speaking Christian Eastenders which stands opposed to the alien Muslim threat."
8. Hall 1992; Ware 1992; Pierce 2003; Johnson and Shapiro 2003; Hartigan (1999); Forman and Lewis, 2006; Reay *et al.*, 2007; Clarke and Garner (forthcoming).

References

Allen, T. (1994) *The Invention of the White Race (Vol. 2)* New York: Verso.

Almaguer, T. (1994) *Racial Fault Lines: The origins of white supremacy in California* Berkeley: University of California Press.

Anderson, W. (2006) *Cultivating Whiteness: Science, Health and Racial Destiny in Australia* Cambridge: Cambridge University Press.

Arnesen, E. (2001) "Whiteness and the Historians' Imagination" *International Labor and Working Class History* 60:3–32.

Back, L. (1996) *New Ethnicities and Urban Culture: Social Identity and Racism in the Lives of Young People* London: UCL Press.

Barrett, J. and Roediger, D. (2005) "The Irish and the 'Americanization' of the 'New Immigrants' in the Streets and in the Churches of the Urban United States, 1900–1930" *Journal of American Ethnic History* 24(4): 4–33.

——— (2004) "Making new immigrants inbetween: Irish hosts and white pan-ethnicity, 1890–1930" in Foner, N. and Frederickson, G. (eds) *Not Just Black and White: Immigration and Race, Then and Now* New York: Russell Sage Foundation Press, pp. 167–196.

——— (1997) "Inbetween Peoples: Race, Nationality and the 'New Immigrant' Working Class" *Journal of American Ethnic History* Spring, 1997:3–44.

Bashford, A. (2000) ""Is White Australia possible"? Race, colonialism and tropical medicine *Ethnic and Racial Studies* 23(2): 248–71.

Bernstein, I. (1990) *The New York Draft Riots of 1863: their Significance for American Society in the Civil War Period* New York: Oxford University Press.

Bettie, J. (2000) "Women without Class: Chicas, Cholas, Trash, and the Presence/Absence of Class Identity" *Signs* 26(1): 1–35.

Bonilla-Silva, (2002).

Booth, C. (1902) *Labour and life of the people of London* London: MacMillan.

Brodkin, K. (1994) "How Did Jews Become White Folks?" in Gregory, S. and Sanjck, R. (eds) *Race* New Brunswick, NJ: Rutgers University Press.

——— (1998) *How Jews became White Folks: And What That Says About Race in America* New Brunswick, NJ: Rutgers University Press.

Clarke, S. and Garner, S. (forthcoming) *White Identities* London: Pluto.

Daniels, J. (1997) *White Lies: Race, class, gender, and sexuality in white supremacist discourse* New York: Routledge.

Du Bois, W.E.B. (1998 [1935]) *Black Reconstruction in the United States, 1860–1880* New York: Free Press.

Engels, F. (1969 [1844]) *The Condition of the Working Class in England: From Personal Observation and Authentic Sources* St.Albans: Panther.

Eze, E. (1997) *Race and the Enlightenment: A Reader* Boston: Blackwell.

Forman, T. and Lewis, A. (2006) "Racial Apathy and Hurricane Katrina: The Social Anatomy of Prejudice in the Post-Civil Rights Era," *Du Bois Review: Social Science Research on Race,* 3: 175–202.

Frankenberg, R. (1994) *White Women, Race Matters* Madison: University of Wisconsin Press.

Frederickson, G. (1988) *The Arrogance of Race: Historical perspectives on slavery, racism and social inequality* Hanover NH: Wesleyan University Press.

Garner, S. (2003) *Racism in the Irish Experience* London: Pluto.

Gibbons, M. (2004) "White Trash: A Class Relevant Scapegoat for the Cultural Elite" *Journal of Mundane Behaviour* 5(1). Online <http://www.mundanebehavior.org/issues/v5n1/gibbons.htm> Accessed on 25 June 2008.

Grant, M. (1916) *The Passing of The Great Race; or, The racial basis of European history* New York: Charles Scribner and Sons.

Guglielmo, T. (2003) "Rethinking Whiteness Historiography: the Case of Italians in Chicago, 1890–1945" in Doane and Bonilla-Silva (eds), pp. 49–61.

Guglielmo, J. and Salerno, S. (2003) *Are Italians white? How race is made in America* New York: Routledge.

Hall, C. (1992) *White, Male and Middle Class: explorations in feminism and history* Cambridge: Cambridge University Press.

Haney-López, I. (1996) *White by Law: The Legal Construction of Race* New York: New York University Press.

Harris, C. (1993) "Whiteness as Property" *Harvard Law Review* 106(8): 1707–93.

Hartigan, J. (2005) *Odd Tribes: toward a cultural analysis of white people* Durham, NC: Duke University Press.

——— (1999) *Racial Situations: class predicaments of whiteness in Detroit* Princeton NJ: Princeton University Press.

——— (1997a) "Locating White Detroit" in Frankenberg (ed) pp.180–213.

——— (1997b) "Name Calling: Objectifying 'Poor Whites' and 'White Trash' in Detroit" in Wray and Newitz (eds), pp.41–56.

Haylett C. (2001) "Illegitimate Subjects?: Abject Whites, Neo-Liberal Modernization and Middle Class Multiculturalism" *Environment and Planning D: Society and Space* 19(3): 351–70.

Hayward, K. and Yar, M. (2005) "The "chav" phenomenon: consumption, media and the construction of a new underclass," *Crime, Media and Society* 2(1): 9–28.

Hoggett, P. (1992) "A place for experience: a psychoanalytic perspective on boundary, identity and culture" *Environment and Planning D: Society and Space* 10:345–356.

Hoggett, P., Jeffers, S., and Harrison, L. (1996) "Race, ethnicity and community in three localities," *New Community* 22(10):111–125.

Horsman, R. (1981) *Race and Manifest Destiny: the Origins of American Anglo-Saxonism* Cambridge: CUP.

Ignatiev, N. (1996) *How the Irish Became White* New York: Routledge.

Jacobson, M. (1998) *Whiteness of a Different Colour: European Immigrants and the Alchemy of Race* Cambridge, MA: Harvard University Press.

Johnson, H., and Shapiro, T. (2003) "Good Neighborhoods, Good Schools: Race and the 'Good Choices' of White Families in Doane and Bonilla-Silva (eds), *White Out: the continuing significance of racism* New York: Routledge, pp. 173–88.

Jordan, W. (1968) *White over Black: American Attitudes Toward the Negro, 1550–1812* Chapel Hill: University of North Carolina Press.

Kefalas, M. (2003) *Working-class Heroes: Protecting Home, Community and Nation in a Chicago Neighborhood* Berkeley: UCLA Press.

Lamont, M. (2000) *The Dignity of Working Men* Cambridge, MA: Harvard University Press.

Lorimer, D. (1978) *Color, Class, and the Victorians: English Attitudes to the Negro in the Mid-Nineteenth Century.* Leicester: Leicester University Press.

Mayhew, H. (1967 [1861]) *London Labour and the London Poor: A Cyclopaedia of the Condition and Earnings of Those That Will Work, Those That Cannot Work, and Those That Will Not Work* New York: A.M. Kelley.

Morris, E. (2005) "From 'Middle Class' to 'Trailer Trash': Teachers' Perceptions of White Students in a Predominantly Minority School" *Sociology of Education* 78: 99–121.

Naipaul, V.S. (1969) *The Middle Passage* London: Penguin.

Nayak, A. (2003) "Ivory Lives: Economic Restructuring and the Making of Whiteness in a Post-industrial Youth Community" *European Journal of Cultural Studies* 6(3): 305–25.

Pierce, J. (2003) "Racing for Innocence": Whiteness, Corporate Culture and the Backlash against Affirmative Action" in Doane and Bonilla-Silva (eds), pp. 199–214.

Reay, D., Hollingworth, S., Williams, K., Crozier, G., Jamieson, F., James, D., and Beedell, P. (2007). "A Darker Shade of Pale?" Whiteness, the Middle Classes and Multi-Ethnic Inner City Schooling," *Sociology*, 41(6): 1041–1060.

Roediger, D. (1991) *The Wages of Whiteness: race and the making of the American working class* London: Verso.

Saxton, A. (1990) *The Rise and Fall of the White Republic: Class Politics and Mass Culture in Nineteenth Century America* New York: Verso.

Shiells, G. (2006) "A Different Shade of White" *National Library of Australia News*, August. Online: <http://www.nla.gov.au/pub/nlanews/2006/aug06/article4.html> (Accessed on 25 June 2008).

Skeggs, B. (1997) *Formations of Class and Gender: Becoming Respectable* London: Routledge.

Stoddard, W. (1922) *Revolt Against Civilization* New York: Scribner.

Tavan, G. (2005) *The Long Slow Death of White Australia* Carlton, VA: Scribe.

Tyler, K. (2004) "Reflexivity, tradition and racism in a former mining town" *Ethnic and Racial Studies* 27(2): 290–302.

Verdicchio, P. (1997) *Bound by Distance: Rethinking Nationalism Through the Italian Diaspora* Madison, NJ: Fairleigh Dickinson University Press.

Ware, V. (1992) *Beyond the Pale: White Women, Racism and History* Verso: London.

Weis, L. and Fine, M. (1996) "Narrating the 1980s and 1990s: Voices of Poor and Working-Class White and African-American Men" *Anthropology and Education Quarterly* 27(4): 493–516.

Wells, K. and Watson, S. (2005) "A Politics of Resentment: Shopkeepers in a London Neighbourhood" *Ethnic and Racial Studies* 28(2): 261–77.

Wohl, A. (187) "Race and Class Overview: Parallels in Racism and Class Prejudice," <http://www.victorianweb.org/history/race/rcov.html>.

Wray, M. (2006) *Not Quite White: White Trash and the Boundaries of Whiteness* Durham, NC: Duke University Press.

Wray, M. and Newitz, A. (1997) (eds) *White Trash: Race, and class in America* New York: Routledge.

York, B (1990) *Empire and Race: The Maltese in Australia, 1881–1949* Kensington, NSW: University of New South Wales Press.

GENDER

Women's Perspective as a Radical Critique of Sociology

Black Sexual Thought

LGBT Identity and Activism

WOMEN'S PERSPECTIVE AS A RADICAL CRITIQUE OF SOCIOLOGY

BY DOROTHY E. SMITH

1. The women's movement has given us a sense of our right to have women's interests represented in sociology, rather than just receiving as authoritative the interests traditionally represented in a sociology put together by men. What can we make of this access to a social reality that was previously unavailable, was indeed repressed? What happens as we begin to relate to it in the terms of our discipline? We can of course think, as many do, merely of the addition of courses to the existing repertoire—courses on sex roles, on the women's movement, on women at work, on the social psychology of women and perhaps somewhat different versions of the sociology of the family. But thinking more boldly or perhaps just thinking the whole thing through a little further might bring us to ask first how a sociology might look if it began from the point of view of women's traditional place in it and what happens to a sociology which attempts to deal seriously with that. Following this line of thought, I have found, has consequences larger than they seem at first.

From the point of view of "women's place" the values assigned to different aspects of the world are changed. Some come into prominence while other standard sociological enterprises diminish. We might take as a model the world as it appears from the point of view of the afternoon soap opera. This is defined by (though not restricted to) domestic events, interests, and activities. Men appear in this world as necessary and vital presences. It is not a women's world in the sense of excluding men. But it is a women's world in the sense that it is the relevances of the women's place that govern. Men appear only in their domestic or private aspects or at points of intersection between public and private as doctors in hospitals, lawyers in their offices discussing wills and divorces. Their occupational and political world is barely present. They are posited here as complete persons, and they are but partial—as women appear in sociology predicated on the universe occupied by men.

But it is not enough to supplement an established sociology by addressing ourselves to what has been left out, overlooked, or by making sociological issues of the relevances of the world of women. That merely extends the authority of the existing sociological procedures and makes of a women's sociology an addendum. We cannot rest at that because it does not account for the separation between the two worlds and it does not account for or analyze for us the relation between them. (Attempts to work on that in terms of biology operate within the existing structure as a fundamental assumption and are therefore straightforwardly ideological in character.)

The first difficulty is that how sociology is thought—its methods, conceptual schemes, and theories—has been based on and built up within the male social universe (even when women have participated in its doing). It has taken for granted not just that scheme of relevances as an itemized inventory of issues or subject matters (industrial sociology, political sociology, social stratification, etc.) but the fundamental social and political structures under which these become relevant

Dorothy E. Smith, "Women's Perspective as a Radical Critique of Sociology," *The Feminist Standpoint Theory Reader: Intellectual and Political Controversies*. Copyright © 2003 by Taylor & Francis Group. Reprinted with permission.

and are ordered. There is a difficulty first then of a disjunction between how women find and experience the world beginning (though not necessarily ending up) from their place and the concepts and theoretical schemes available to think about it in. Thus in a graduate seminar last year, we discussed on one occasion the possibility of a women's sociology and two graduate students told us that in their view and their experience of functioning in experimental group situations, theories of the emergence of leadership in small groups, etc., just did not apply to what was happening as they experienced it. They could not find the correlates of the theory in their experiences.

A second difficulty is that the two worlds and the two bases of knowledge and experience don't stand in an equal relation. The world as it is constituted by men stands in authority over that of women. It is that part of the world from which our land of society is governed and from which what happens to us begins. The domestic world stands in a dependent relation to that other and its whole character is subordinate to it.

The two difficulties are related to one another in a special way. The effect of the second interacting with the first is to impose the concepts and terms in which the world of men is thought as the concepts and terms in which women must think their world. Hence in these terms women are alienated from their experience.

The profession of sociology is predicated on a universe which is occupied by men and is itself still largely appropriated by men as their "territory." Sociology is part of the practice by which we are all governed and that practice establishes its relevances. T us the institutions which lock sociology into the structures occupied by men are the same institutions which lock women into the situations in which they fi nd themselves oppressed. To unlock the latter leads logically to an unlocking of the former. What follows then, or rather what then becomes possible—for it is of course by no means inevitable—is less a shift in the subject matter than a different conception of how it is or might become relevant as a means to understand our experience and the conditions of our experience (both women's and men's) in corporate capitalist society.

2. When I speak here of governing or ruling I mean something more general than the notion of government as political organization. I refer rather to that total complex of activities differentiated into many spheres, by which our kind of society is ruled, managed, administered. It includes that whole section which in the business world is called "management." It includes the professions. It includes of course government more conventionally defined and also the activities of those who are selecting, training, and indoctrinating those who will be its governors. The last includes those who provide and elaborate the procedures in which it is governed and develop methods for accounting for how it is done and predicting and analyzing its characteristic consequences and sequences of events, namely the business schools, the sociologists, the economists, etc. These are the institutions through which we are ruled and through which we, and I emphasize this we, participate in ruling.

Sociology then I conceive as much more than ideology, much more than a gloss on the enterprise which justifies and rationalizes it, and, at the same time as much less than "science." The governing of our kind of society is done in concepts and symbols. The contribution of sociology to this is that of working up the conceptual procedures, models, and methods by which the immediate and concrete features of experience can be read into the conceptual mode in which the governing is done. What is actually observed or what is systematically recovered by the sociologist from the actualities of what people say and do, must be transposed into the abstract mode. Sociology thus participates in and contributes to the formation and facilitation of this mode of action and plays a distinctive part in the work of transposing the actualities of people's lives and experiences into the conceptual currency in which it is and can be governed.

Thus the relevances of sociology are organized in terms of a perspective on the world which is a view from the top and which takes for granted the pragmatic procedures of governing as those which frame and identify its subject matter. Issues are formulated as issues which have become administratively relevant not as they are significant first in the experience of those who live them. The kinds of facts and events which are facts for us have already been shaped up and given their character and substance as facts, as relations, etc., by the methods and practice of governing. Mental illness, crimes, riots, violence, work satisfaction, neighbors and neighborhoods, motivation, etc., these are the constructs of the practice of government. In many instances, such as mental illness, crimes, neighborhoods, etc., they are constituted as discrete phenomena primarily by administrative procedures and others arise as problems in relation to the actual practice of government, as for example concepts of motivation, work satisfaction, etc.

The governing processes of our society are organized as social entities constituted externally to those persons who participate in and perform them. The managers, the bureaucrats, the administrators, are employees, are people who are used. They do not own the enterprises or otherwise appropriate them. Sociologists study these entities under the heading of formal organization. They are put together as objective structures with goals, activities, obligations, etc., other than those which its employees can have as individuals. The academic professions are also set up in a mode which externalizes them as entities vis-à-vis their practitioners. The body of knowledge which its members accumulate is appropriated by the discipline as its body. The work of members aims at contributing to that body of knowledge.

As graduate students learning to become sociologists, we learn to think sociology as it is thought and to practice it as it is practiced. We learn that some topics are relevant and some are not. We learn to discard our experienced world as a source of reliable information or suggestions about the character of the world; to confine and focus our insights within the conceptual frameworks and relevances which are given in the discipline. Should we think other kinds of thoughts or experience the world in a different way or with edges and horizons that pass beyond the conceptual, we must practice a discipline which discards them or find some procedure which makes it possible to sneak them in. We learn a way of thinking about the world which is recognizable to its practitioners as the sociological way of thinking.

We learn to practice the sociological sumption of the actualities of ourselves and of other people. We find out how to treat the world as instances of a sociological body of knowledge. The procedure operates as a sort of conceptual imperialism. When we write a thesis or a paper, we learn that the first thing to do is to latch it on to the discipline at some point. This may be by showing how it is a problem within an existing theoretical and conceptual framework. The boundaries of inquiry are thus set within the framework of what is already established. Even when this becomes, as it happily often does, a ceremonial authorization of a project which has little to do with the theory used to authorize it, we still work within the vocabularies and within the conceptual boundaries of what we have come to know as "the sociological perspective."

An important set of procedures which serve to constitute the body of knowledge of the discipline as something which is separated from its practitioners are those known as "objectivity." The ethic of objectivity and the methods used in its practice are concerned primarily with the separation of the knower from what he knows and in particular with the separation of what is known from any interests, "biases," etc., which he may have which are not the interests and concerns authorized by the discipline. I must emphasize that being interested in knowing something doesn't invalidate what is known. In the social sciences the pursuit of objectivity makes it possible for people to be paid to pursue a knowledge to which they are otherwise indifferent. What they feel and think about society can be taken apart from and kept out of what they are professionally or academically interested in.

3. The sociologist enters the conceptually ordered society when he goes to work. He enters it as a member and he enters it also as the mode in which he investigates it. He observes, analyzes, explains, and examines as if there were no problem in how that world becomes observable to him. He moves among the doings of organizations, governmental processes, bureaucracies, etc., as a person who is at home in that medium. The nature of that world itself, how it is known to him and the conditions of its existence or his relation to it are not called into question. His methods of observation and inquiry extend into it as procedures which are essentially of the same order as those which bring about the phenomena with which he is concerned, or which he is concerned to bring under the jurisdiction of that order. His perspectives and interests may differ, but the substance is the same. He works with facts and information which have been worked up from actualities and appear in the form of documents which are themselves the product of organizational processes, whether his own or administered by him, or of some other agency.

He fits that information back into a framework of entities and organizational processes which he takes for granted as known, without asking how it is that he knows them or what are the social processes by which the phenomena which correspond to or provide the empirical events, acts, decisions, etc., of that world, may be recognized. He passes beyond the particular and immediate setting in which he is always located in the body (the office he writes in, the libraries he consults, the streets he travels, the home he returns to) without any sense of having made a transition. He works in the same medium as he studies.

But like everyone else he also exists in the body in the place in which it is. This is also then the place of his sensory organization of immediate experience, the place where his coordinates of here and now before and after are organized around himself as center; the place where he confronts people face to face in the physical mode in which he expresses himself to them and they to him as more and other than either can speak. It is in this place that things smell. The irrelevant birds fly away in front of the window. Here he has indigestion. It is a place he dies in. Into this space must come as actual material events, whether as the sounds of speech, the scratchings on the surface of paper which he constitutes as document, or directly, anything he knows of the world. It has to happen here somehow if he is to experience it at all.

Entering the governing mode of our kind of society lifts the actor out of the immediate local and particular place in which he is in the body. He uses what becomes present to him in this place as a means to pass beyond it to the conceptual order. This mode of action creates then a bifurcation of consciousness, a bifurcation of course which is there for all those who participate in this mode of action. It establishes two modes of knowing and experiencing and doing, one located in the body and in the space which it occupies and moves into, the other which passes beyond it. Sociology is written in and aims at this second mode. Vide Bierstedt:

> Sociology can liberate the mind from time and space themselves and remove it to a new and transcendental realm where it no longer depends upon these Aristotelian categories. (1966)

Even observational work aims at its description in the categories and hence conceptual forms of the "transcendental realm."

4. Women are outside and subservient to this structure. They have a very specific relation to it which anchors them into the local and particular phase of the bifurcated world. For both traditionally and as a matter of occupational practices in our society, the governing conceptual mode is appropriated by men and the world organized in the natural attitude, the home, is appropriated by (or assigned to) women (Smith, 1973).

It is a condition of a man's being able to enter and become absorbed in the conceptual mode that he does not have to focus his activities and interests upon his bodily existence. If he is to participate fully in the abstract mode of action, then he must be liberated also from having to attend to his needs, etc., in the concrete and particular. The organization of work and expectations in managerial and professional circles both constitutes and depends upon the alienation of man from his bodily and local existence. The structure of work and the structure of career take for granted that these matters are provided for in such a way that they will not interfere with his action and participation in that world. Providing for the liberation from the Aristotelian categories of which Bierstedt speaks, is a woman who keeps house for him, bears and cares for his children, washes his clothes, looks after him when he is sick, and generally provides for the logistics of his bodily existence.

The place of women then in relation to this mode of action is that where the work is done to create conditions which facilitate his occupation of the conceptual mode of consciousness. The meeting of a man's physical needs, the organization of his daily life, even the consistency of expressive background, are made maximally congruent with his commitment. A similar relation exists for women who work in and around the professional and managerial scene. They do those things which give concrete form to the conceptual activities. They do the clerical work, the computer programming, the interviewing for the survey, the nursing, the secretarial work. At almost every point women mediate for men the relation between the conceptual mode of action and the actual concrete forms in which it is and must be realized, and the actual material conditions upon which it depends.

Marx's concept of alienation is applicable here in a modified form. The simplest formulation of alienation posits a relation between the work an individual does and an external order which oppresses her, such that the harder she works the more she strengthens the order which oppresses her. This is the situation of women in this relation. The more successful women are in mediating the world of concrete particulars so that men do not have to become engaged with (and therefore conscious of) that world as a condition to their abstract activities, the more complete man's absorption in it, the more effective the authority of that world and the more total women's subservience to it. And also the more complete the dichotomy between the two worlds, and the estrangement between them.

5. Women sociologists stand at the center of a contradiction in the relation of our discipline to our experience of the world. Transcending that contradiction means setting up a different land of relation than that which we discover in the routine practice of our worlds.

The theories, concepts, and methods of our discipline claim to account for, or to be capable of accounting for and analyzing the same world as that which we experience directly. But these theories, concepts, and methods have been organized around and built up out of a way of knowing the world which takes for granted the boundaries of an experience in the same medium in which it is constituted. It therefore takes for granted and subsumes without examining the conditions of its existence. It is not capable of analyzing its own relation to its conditions because the sociologist as an actual person in an actual concrete setting has been cancelled in the procedures which objectify and separate him from his knowledge. Thus the linkage which points back to its conditions is lacking.

For women those conditions are central as a direct practical matter, to be somehow solved in the decision to take up a sociological career. The relation between ourselves as practicing sociologists and ourselves as working women is continually visible to us, a central feature of experience of the world, so that the bifurcation of consciousness becomes for us a daily chasm which is to be crossed, on the one side of which is this special conceptual activity of thought, research, teaching, administration, and on the other the world of concrete practical activities in keeping things clean, managing somehow the house and household and the children, a world in which the particularities of persons in their full organic immediacy (cleaning up the vomit, changing the diapers, as well as feeding) are inescapable. Even if we don't have that as a direct contingency in our lives, we are aware of that as something that our becoming may be inserted into as a possible predicate.

It is also present for us to discover that the discipline is not one which we enter and occupy on the same terms as men enter and occupy it. We do not fully appropriate its authority, i.e., the right to author and authorize the acts and knowing and thinking which are the acts and knowing and thinking of the discipline as it is thought. We cannot therefore command the inner principles of our action. That remains lodged outside us. The frames of reference which order the terms upon which inquiry and discussion are conducted originate with men. The subjects of sociological sentences(if they have a subject) are male. The sociologist is "he." And even before we become conscious of our sex as the basis of an exclusion (they are not talking about us), we nonetheless do not fully enter ourselves as the subjects of its statements, since we must suspend our sex, and suspend our knowledge of who we are as well as who it is that in fact is speaking and of whom. Therefore we do not fully participate in the declarations and formulations of its mode of consciousness. The externalization of sociology as a profession which I have described above becomes for women a double estrangement.

There is then for women a basic organization of their experience which displays for them the structure of the bifurcated consciousness. At the same time it attenuates their commitment to a sociology which aims at an externalized body of knowledge based on an organization of experience which excludes theirs and excludes them except in a subordinate relation.

6. An alternative approach must somehow transcend this contradiction without reentering Bierstedt's "transcendental realm" (1966). Women's perspective, as I have analyzed it here, discredits sociology's claim to constitute an objective knowledge independent of the sociologist's situation. Its conceptual procedures, methods, and

relevances are seen to organize its subject matter from a determinate position in society. This critical disclosure becomes, then, the basis for an alternative way of thinking sociology. If sociology cannot avoid being situated, then sociology should take that as its beginning and build it into its methodological and theoretical strategies. As it is now, these separate a sociologically constructed world from that which is known in direct experience and it is precisely that separation which must be undone.

I am not proposing an immediate and radical transformation of the subject matter and methods of the discipline nor the junking of everything that has gone before. What I am suggesting is more in the nature of a reorganization which changes the relation of the sociologist to the object of her knowledge and changes also her problematic. This reorganization involves first placing the sociologist where she is actually situated, namely at the beginning of those acts by which she knows or will come to know; and second, making her direct experience of the everyday world the primary ground of her knowledge.

We would reject, it seems to me, a sociology aimed primarily at itself. We would not be interested in contributing to a body of knowledge the uses of which are not ours and the knowers of whom are who knows whom, but generally male—particularly when it is not at all clear what it is that is constituted as knowledge in that relation. The professional sociologist's practice of thinking it as it is thought would have to be discarded. She would be constrained by the actualities of how it happens in her direct experience. Sociology would aim at offering to anyone a knowledge of the social organization and determinations of the properties and events of their directly experienced world. Its analyses would become part of our ordinary interpretations of the experienced world, just as our experience of the sun's sinking below the horizon is transformed by our knowledge that the world turns. (Yet from where we are it seems to sink and that must be accounted for.)

The only way of knowing a socially constructed world is knowing it from within. We can never stand outside it. A relation in which sociological phenomena are objectified and presented as external to and independent of the observer is itself a special social practice also known from within. The relation of observer and object of observation, of sociologist to "subject" is a specialized social relationship. Even to be a stranger is to enter a world constituted from within as strange. The strangeness itself is the mode in which it is experienced.

When Jean Briggs (1970) made her ethnographic study of the ways in which an Eskimo people structure and express emotion, what she learned and observed emerged for her in the context of the actual developing relations between her and the family with whom she lived and other members of the group. Her account situates her knowledge in the context of those relationships. Affections, tensions, and quarrels were the living texture in which she learnt what she describes. She makes it clear how this context structured her learning and how what she learnt and can speak of became observable to her. Briggs tells us what is normally discarded in the anthropological or sociological telling. Although sociological inquiry is necessarily a social relation, we have learned to disattend our own part in it. We recover only the object of its knowledge as if that stood all by itself and of itself. Sociology does not provide for seeing that there are always two terms to this relation. An alternative sociology must be reflexive (Gouldner, 1971), i.e., one that preserves in it the presence, concerns, and experience of the sociologist as knower and discover.

To begin from direct experience and to return to it as a constraint or "test" of the adequacy of a systematic knowledge is to begin from where we are located bodily. The actualities of our everyday world are already socially organized. Settings, equipment, "environment," schedules, occasions, etc., as well as the enterprises and routines of actors are socially produced and concretely and symbolically organized prior to our practice. By beginning from her original and immediate knowledge of her world, sociology offers a way of making its socially organized properties first observable and then problematic.

Let me make it clear that when I speak of "experience" I do not use the term as a synonym for "perspective." Nor in proposing a sociology grounded in the sociologist's actual experience, am I recommending the self-indulgence of inner exploration or any other enterprise with self as sole focus and object. Such subjectivist interpretations of "experience" are themselves an aspect of that organization of consciousness which bifurcates it and transports us into mind country while stashing away the concrete conditions and practices upon which it depends. We can never escape the circles of our own heads if we accept that as our territory. Rather the sociologist's investigation of our directly experienced world as a problem is a mode of discovering or rediscovering the society from within. She begins from her own original but tacit knowledge and from within the acts by which she brings it into her grasp in making it observable and in understanding how it works. She aims not at a reiteration of what she already (tacitly) knows, but at an exploration through that of what passes beyond it and is deeply implicated in how it is.

7. Our knowledge of the world is given to us in the modes in which we enter into relations with the object of knowledge. But in this case the object of our knowledge is or originates in a "subject." The constitution of an objective sociology as an authoritative version of how things are is done from a position and as part of the practices of ruling in our kind of society. It has depended upon class and sex bases which make it possible for sociology to evade the problem that our kind of society is known and experienced rather differently from different positions within it. Our training teaches us to ignore the uneasiness at the junctures where transitional work is done—for example, the ordinary problems respondents have of fitting their experience of the world to the questions in the interview schedule. It is this exclusion which the sociologist who is a woman cannot so easily preserve, for she discovers, if she will, precisely that uneasiness in her relation to her discipline as a whole. The persistence of the privileged sociological version (or versions) relies upon a substructure which has already discredited and deprived of authority to speak, the voices of those who know the society differently. The objectivity of a sociological version depends upon a special relation with others which makes it easy for the sociologist to remain outside the other's experience and does not require her to recognize that experience as a valid contention.

Riding a train not long ago in Ontario I saw a family of Indians, woman, man, and three children standing together on a spur above a river watching the train go by. There was (for me) that moment—the train, those five people seen on the other side of the glass. I saw first that I could tell this incident as it was, but that telling as a description built in my position and my interpretations. I have called them a family; I have said they were watching the train. My understanding has already subsumed theirs. Everything may have been quite other for them. My description is privileged to stand as what actually happened, because theirs is not heard in the contexts in which I may speak. If we begin from the world as we actually experience it, it is at least possible to see that we are located and that what we know of the other is conditional upon that location as part of a relation comprehending the other's location also. There are and must be different experiences of the world and different bases of experience. We must not do away with them by taking advantage of our privileged speaking to construct a sociological version which we then impose upon them as their reality. We may not rewrite the other's world or impose upon it a conceptual framework which extracts from it what fits with ours. Our conceptual procedures should be capable of explicating and analyzing the properties of their experienced world rather than administering it. Their reality, their varieties of experience must be an unconditional datum.

8. My experience on the train epitomizes a sociological relation. The observer is already separated from the world as it is experienced by those she observes. That separation is fundamental to the character of that experience. Once she becomes aware of how her world is put together as a practical everyday matter and of how her relations are shaped by its concrete conditions (even in so simple a matter as that she is sitting in the train and it travels, but those people standing on the spur do not) the sociologist is led into the discovery that she cannot understand the nature of her experienced world by staying within its ordinary boundaries of assumption and knowledge. To account for that moment on the train and for the relation between the two experiences (or more) and the two positions from which those experiences begin involves positing a total socioeconomic order "in back" of that moment. The coming together which makes the observation possible as well as how we were separated and drawn apart as well as how I now make use of that here—these properties are determined elsewhere than in that relation itself.

Further, how our knowledge of the world is mediated to us becomes a problem. It is a problem in knowing how that world is organized for us prior to our participation as knowers in that process. As intellectuals we ordinarily receive it as a media world, of documents, images, journals, books, talk, as well as in other symbolic modes. We discard as an essential focus of our practice other ways of knowing. Accounting for that mode of knowing and the social organization which sets it up for us again leads us back into an analysis of the total socioeconomic order of which it is part. It is not possible to account for one's directly experienced world or how it is related to the worlds which others directly experience who are differently placed by remaining within the boundaries of the former.

If we address the problem of the conditions as well as the perceived forms and organization of immediate experience, we should include in it the events as they actually happen or the ordinary material world which we encounter as a matter of fact—the urban renewal project which uproots 400 families; how it is to live on welfare as an ordinary daily practice; cities as the actual physical structures in which we move; the organization of academic occasions such as that in which this paper originated. When we examine them, we find that there are many aspects of how these things come about of which we have little as sociologists to say. We have a sense that the events which enter our experience originate somewhere in a human intention, but we are unable to track back to find it and to find out how it got from there to here. Or take this room in which I work or that room in which you are reading and treat that as a problem. If we think about the conditions of our activity here, we could track back to how it is that there are chairs, table, walls, our clothing, our presence; how these places (yours and mine) are cleaned and maintained, etc. There are human activities, intentions, and relations which are not apparent as such in the actual material conditions of our work. The social organization of the setting is not wholly available to us in its appearance. We bypass in the immediacy of the specific practical activity, a complex division of labor which is an essential precondition to it. Such preconditions are fundamentally mysterious to us and present us with problems in grasping social relations in our land of society with which sociology is ill equipped to deal. Our experience of the world is of one which is largely incomprehensible beyond the limits of what is known in a common sense. No amount of observation of face-to-face relations, no amounts of analysis of commonsense knowledge of everyday life, will take us beyond our essential ignorance of how it is put together. Our direct experience of it constitutes it (if we will) as a problem, but it does not offer any answers. The matrix of direct experience as that from which sociology might begin discloses that beginning as an "appearance" the determinations of which lie beyond it.

We might think of the "appearances" of our direct experience as a multiplicity of surfaces, the properties and relations among which are generated by a social organization which is not observable in its effects. The structures which underlie and generate the characteristics of our own directly experienced world are social structures and bring us into unseen relations with others. Their experience is necessarily different from ours. Beginning from our experienced world and attempting to analyze and account for how it is, necessitates positing others whose experience is different.

Women's situation in sociology discloses to her a typical bifurcate structure with the abstracted conceptual practices on the one hand and the concrete realizations, the maintenance routines, etc., on the other. Taking each for granted depends upon being fully situated in one or the other so that the other does not appear in contradiction to it. Women's direct experience places her a step back where we can recognize the uneasiness that comes in sociology from its claim to be about the world we live in and its failure to account for or even describe its actual features as we fi nd them in living them. The aim of an alternative sociology would be to develop precisely that capacity from that beginning so that it might be a means to anyone of understanding how the world comes about for her and how it is organized so that it happens to her as it does in her experience.

9. Though such a sociology would not be exclusively for or done by women it does begin from the analysis and critique originating in their situation. Its elaboration therefore depends upon a grasp of that which is prior to and fuller than its formulation. It is a little like the problem of making a formal description of the grammar of a language. The linguist depends and always refers back to the competent speakers' sense, etc. In her own language she depends to a large extent upon her own competence. Women are native speakers

of this situation and in explicating it or its implications and realizing them conceptually, they have that relation to it of knowing it before it has been said.

The incomprehensibility of the determinations of our immediate local world is for women a particularly striking metaphor. It recovers an inner organization in common with their typical relation to the world. For women's activities and existence are deter-mined outside them and beyond the world which is their "place." They are oriented by their training and by the daily practices which confirm it, toward the demands and initiations and authority of others. But more than that, the very organization of the world which has been assigned to them as the primary locus of their being is determined by and subordinate to the corporate organization of society (Smith, 1973). Thus, as I have expressed her relation to sociology, its logic lies elsewhere. She lacks the inner principle of her own activity. She does not grasp how it is put together because it is determined elsewhere than where she is. As a sociologist then the grasp and explora-tion of her own experience as a method of discovering society restores to her a center which in this enterprise at least is wholly hers.

Discussion Questions

1. What difficulties in seeing women's interest represented in sociology does Smith discuss?
2. Smith speaks of the bifurcation of consciousness, and argues that sociology aims to reach a "transcendental realm." How does this aspiration benefit male sociologists over female sociologists?
3. What alternative does the author offer in order to address women sociologists' "double estrangement?"
4. For Smith, why is our necessarily mediated knowledge of the world a problem? What are the consequences?

Note

This paper was originally prepared for the meetings of the American Academy for the Advancement of Science (Pacific Division) Eugene, Oregon, June, 1972. The original draft of this paper was typed by Jane Lemke and the final version by Mildred Brown. I am indebted to both of them.

REFERENCES

Bierstedt, Robert. 1966. "Sociology and general education." In Charles H. Page (ed.), *Sociology and Contemporary Education*. New York: Random House.

Briggs, Jean L. 1970. *Never in Anger*. Cambridge, Mass.: Harvard University Press.

Gouldner, Alvin. 1971. *The Coming Crisis in Western Sociology*. London: Heinemann Educational Books.

Smith, Dorothy E. 1973. "Women, the family and corporate capitalism." In M. L. Stephenson (ed.), *Women in Canada*. Toronto: Newpress.

BLACK SEXUAL THOUGHT

The New Racism

BY PATRICIA HILL COLLINS

Over one hundred years ago, African American intellectual William E.B. DuBois predicted that the problem of the twentieth century would be the presence of the color line. By that, DuBois meant that the policies of colonialism and racial segregation were designed to create, separate, and rank the various "races" of man. Until legally outlawed in the 1950s and 1960s, the color line policies of Jim Crow racial segregation kept the vast majority of African Americans from quality educations, good jobs, adequate health care, and the best neighborhoods. In contrast, the problem of the twenty-first century seems to be the seeming absence of a color line. Formal legal discrimination has been outlawed, yet contemporary social practices produce virtually identical racial hierarchies as those observed by DuBois. By whatever measures used in the United States or on a global scale, people of African descent remain disproportionately clustered at the bottom of the social hierarchy. The effects of these historical exclusions persist today under a new racism.[1]

It is important to note that the new racism of the early twentieth century has not replaced prior forms of racial rule, but instead incorporates elements of past racial formations. As a result, ideas about race, gender, sexuality and Black people as well as the social practices that these ideas shape and reflect remain intricately part of the new racism, but in changed ways. The new racism thus reflects a situation of permanence and change. Just as people of African descent were disadvantaged within prior forms of economic organization, a similar outcome exists today. On a global scale, wealth and poverty continue to be racialized. This is permanence. At the same time, racial hierarchy is produced in a context of massive economic, political, and social change that organizes racial hierarchy differently. The processes used to maintain the same outcome are also different. In a similar fashion, ideas about sexuality and gender that were very much a part of prior forms of racial rule remain as important today. They too are differently organized to produce remarkably similar results.

First, new forms of global capitalism frame the new racism. Globalization itself is certainly not new—it was a core characteristic of former patterns of racism. The African Slave Trade had a global reach and its legacy created the contemporary African Diaspora. The colonial wealth of Europe was based on a global system of racial subordination of people of color. Yet the increasing concentration of capital in the hands of fewer and fewer corporations distinguishes the contemporary global capitalism from its nineteenth century counterpart. Today, relatively few transnational corporations are driving the world economy and their decisions affect the global distribution of wealth and poverty. These new forms of global organization have polarized world populations. On one end are elites who are wealthy beyond the imagination, and who have the freedom to come and go as they please, wherever and whenever they want. The locals, the people who are stuck in one place, without jobs, and for whom time seems to creep by, populate the other end.[2]

Patricia Hill Collins, "Black Sexual Thought," Black Sexual Politics: African Americans, Gender, and the New Racism. Copyright © 2005 by Taylor & Francis Group. Reprinted with permission.

People of African descent are routinely disadvantaged in this global economy where corporations make the decisions, and where "the company is free to move; but the consequences of the move are bound to stay."[3] Within a global context, Black people and other people of color are those more likely to lose jobs in local labor markets. They are the ones who lack control over oil, mineral wealth, or other natural resources on their land; who lose their land to global agribusiness; and who are denied basic services of electricity and clean water, let alone the luxury goods of the new information age. The benefits of telecommunications and other new technologies have had a far greater impact on Whites than on people of African descent and other people of color. For example, though Europe and North America constitute twenty percent of the world's population, two-thirds of all televisions and radios are owned and controlled in these two regions.[4]

The new racism is also characterized by a changing political structure that disenfranchises people, even if they appear to be included. In the United States, for example, people may vote, but corporations and other propertied entities wield tremendous influence in deciding the outcome of elections because they fund campaigns. All levels of government have been affected by a growing concentration of economic power that has fostered corporate influence over public policy. This same process operates in a transnational context. Global corporations increasingly dominate national, regional and local governance. This concentrated economic power erodes the authority of national governments and has created unprecedented migrations of people and jobs both within and between nation-states. The ineffectiveness of transnational governance and domestic policies of racial desegregation in reducing Black poverty suggests an important link joining the experiences of people of African descent with post-colonial governance and the experiences of African Americans in the United States with racial desegregation. The outcome is reconfigured social hierarchies of race, class, gender and sexuality, with people of African descent clumped at the bottom. Patterns of desegregation and subsequent resegregation of African Americans in the United States resemble the decolonization and recolonization that characterizes the global context.[5]

The new racism also relies more heavily on mass media to reproduce and disseminate the ideologies needed to justify racism. There are two themes here—the substance of racial ideologies under the new racism, and the forms in which ideologies are created, circulated and resisted. Ideas about Black sexuality certainly appear in contemporary racial ideologies. But the growing significance of Black popular culture and mass media as sites for creating and resisting racial ideologies is also striking. The films, music, magazines, music videos and television shows of global entertainment, advertising and news industries that produce superstars like Jennifer Lopez help manufacture the consent that makes the new racism appear to be natural, normal and inevitable.[6]

The challenges of the new racism have been especially pronounced for African American women and men, the subjects of this text. The issues associated with the politics of the new racism and with the manipulation of ideologies within them, in the case of African Americans, the discourse on Black sexuality, affect everyone. But the specific form that race, sexuality, and politics take for African Americans can serve as an important site for examining these larger issues. Moreover, the African American community contains a crucial subpopulation in these debates. A generation of young African American men and women who were born after the struggles for civil rights, Black power, and African nation-state independence has come of age under this new racism. Referred to as the hip-hop generation, this group has encountered, reproduced and resisted new forms of racism that continue to rely on ideas about Black sexuality. Expecting a democratic, fair society with equal economic opportunities, instead, this group faced disappearing jobs, crumbling schools, drugs, crime and the weakening of African American community institutions. The contradictions of the post-civil rights era affect all African Americans, yet have been especially pronounced for Black youth.[7]

America—A Sexually Repressive Society?

Sexualized Black bodies seem to be everywhere in contemporary mass media, yet within African American communities, understanding sexual politics remains elusive. In a social context that routinely depicts men and women of African descent as the embodiment of deviant sexuality, African American politics has remained curiously silent on issues of gender and sexuality. As a result, African Americans lack a vibrant, public discussion of the complex issues that the prevailing discourse on Black sexuality has raised for African American men and women. In more candid moments, however, some African American thinkers stress how damaging the absence of a self-defined

Black sexual politics can be. As African American cultural critic Cheryl Clarke pointed out over twenty years ago:

> Like all Americans, black Americans live in a sexually repressive culture. And we have made all manner of compromise regarding our sexuality in order to live here. We have expended much energy trying to debunk the racist mythology which says our sexuality is depraved. Unfortunately, many of us have overcompensated and assimilated the Puritan value that sex is for procreation, occurs only between men and women, and is only valid within the confines of heterosexual marriage. ... Like everyone else in America who is ambivalent in these respects, black folk have to live with the contradictions of this limited sexual system by repressing or closeting any other sexual/erotic urges, feelings, or desires.[8]

Given the saturation of American mass media with sexual themes, and the visibility of sexualized spectacles that include men and women of African descent within movies, music videos, and popular music in particular, Clarke's comments may seem to be odd. How can American culture be "sexually repressive" when sexuality seems to be everywhere? White actresses routinely play roles that include graphic sex scenes. Moreover, Black women are not downtrodden rape victims, but instead, also seem to be in control of their own sexuality. Director Spike Lee's African American leading lady Nola Darling seemed to be calling the shots in *She's Gotta Have It*, Lee's groundbreaking film about Black female sexuality. Destiny's Child and Jennifer Lopez certainly do not seem "repressed." How can African Americans be sexually "closeted" when Black sexuality itself serves as an icon for sexual freedom?

For African Americans, these questions are crucial, especially in the context of the post-civil rights era where Black popular culture and mass media are increasingly important for racial rule. Sexual regulation occurs through repression, both by eliminating sexual alternatives and by shaping the public debates that do exist. In order to prosper, systems of oppression must regulate sexuality, and often do so by manufacturing ideologies that render some ideas commonsensical while obscuring others. The expanding scope of mass media makes this process more visible and more importantly, in the United States, does seem to have produced a "sexually repressive culture."

The treatment of human sexuality in American society reflects a curious combination of censorship and excessive visibility (e.g., hypervisibility), of embarrassed silences and talk-show babble. On the one hand, since colonial times, selected groups within U.S. society have striven to suppress a wide range of sexual ideas and practices.[9] American colonists paid close attention to the sexual behavior of individuals, not to eliminate sexual expression, but to channel it into what they thought was its proper setting and purpose: as a "duty and a joy within marriage, and for purposes of procreation."[10] More recently, the election of conservative Republican Ronald Reagan in 1980 emboldened the Christian Right to advance a fundamentalist family values discourse. Resembling the colonial discourse from the 1600s, the contemporary family values position argues 1) all sexual practices should occur only within the confines of heterosexual marriage; 2) the fundamental purpose of sexuality is procreation; and 3) children should be protected from all sexual information with the exception of abstinence as the preferred form of birth control before marriage.

This historical and contemporary agenda that has suppressed and often censored a range of ideas concerning human sexuality has made it difficult to have open, candid and fact-based public debates. This censorship not only affects public dialogues, it influences research on human sexuality.[11] Heterosexism, with its ideas about what constitutes normal and deviant sexuality holds sway to the point where significant gaps exist in the social science literature on human sexuality. Despite the conservative thrust since 1980, the suppression of a range of ideas about human sexuality is not new. Research done in the 1950s by Alfred Kinsey and his colleagues at Indiana University provides a textbook case of sexual censorship. Kinsey's work treated all sexual practices, including homosexuality and bisexuality, as inherently "normal" and defined the array of sexual practices reported by study participants as benign indicators of human difference. But Kinsey's work virtually ground to a halt when funding for this line of scientific research dried up.

It has taken the field some time to recover from this censorship. In essence, heterosexism and its accompanying assumptions of heterosexuality operate as a hegemonic or taken-for-granted ideology that is willingly chosen or imposed upon research on human sexuality. Societal norms that install heterosexuality as the only way to be normal still hold sway.[12] For example, the term *sexuality* itself is used so synonymously with heterosexuality that schools, churches, and other social institutions treat heterosexuality as natural, normal and inevitable. Studying sexual practices that stray too far from prevailing norms, for example, sex outside of marriage, adolescent sexuality, homosexuality, and formerly taboo sexual practices such as anal and oral sex, become situated within a social problems framework. This approach not only stigmatizes individuals and groups who engage in alternative sexual practices, it also reinforces views of human sexuality itself as being a problem that should not be discussed in public. Alternately, research on human sexuality is often annexed to bona fide social problems, for example, adolescent pregnancy and the people living with HIV/AIDS. Sexuality seems to be everywhere, but research that investigates variations in human sexuality outside of a social problems framework has only recently come to the forefront.

The treatment of sex education in American public schools illustrates how a sexually repressive culture strives to render human sexuality invisible. Sex education remains a hot topic, with students receiving spotty information at best. Topics that are important to adolescents have been difficult to include within sex education programs. Despite high student interest and a growing recognition that comprehensive sex education might save lives, programs tend to shy away from discussing sexuality before marriage, the use of contraception, homosexuality, and other controversial topics. Ironically, the checkered pattern of research on human sexuality offers a good case for how heterosexism operates as a system of power that negatively affects straight and lesbian, gay, bisexual and transgendered (LGBT) students alike. Because adolescents of all sexual orientations are in the process of forming sexual identities, they are especially affected by heterosexism. For example, despite a high adolescent pregnancy rate, worrisome increases in the rate of HIV infection among American adolescents, and emerging research demonstrating that high school students grappling with LGBT identities are more prone to depression and suicide, the reluctance to talk openly about human sexuality within U.S. schools places students at risk. Similarly, a special report on adolescent sexuality points to the difficulties of collecting data on adolescent conceptions of abstinence.[13] Anecdotal reports suggest that many adolescents who engage in oral sex think that they are practicing abstinence because they are refraining from genital sexual intercourse. These practices may protect them from pregnancy, but they also expose adolescents to risks of sexually transmitted diseases, including HIV.[14]

Despite these repressive practices, on the other hand, sexual ideas and images within contemporary U.S. society enjoy a visibility that would have been unheard of in Kinsey's 1950s America. Recognizing that sex sells, corporations increasingly use it to sell cars, toothpaste, beer and other consumer goods. This media saturation has made sexual spectacles highly visible within American popular culture. Soap operas, prime time television, billboards, music videos, movies, and the Internet all contain explicit sexual material. Making sex highly visible in marketplace commodity relations becomes important to maintaining profitability within the U.S. capitalist political economy. The goal is neither to stimulate debate nor to educate, but to sell products.

In the absence of other forums, talk shows on network television provide one important public medium for gaining sexual information. Unfortunately, such shows foster the commodification of sexuality. Stressing sexually explicit conversations that titillate rather than instruct, talk shows illustrate how marketplace relations profit from sexual spectacles. By the early 2000s, this market had segmented into a variety of shows, each carving out its specific identity, often based on distinctive norms regarding race, class, gender and sexuality[15]. For example, the Montel Williams Show routinely trumpets the benefits of the heterosexual family, primarily by extolling the role of fathers in their children's lives. By itself, this message is fairly innocuous. However, the show's format creates sexual spectacles that function as modern day morality plays about race, gender and sexuality. Mr. Williams, an African American, routinely conducts paternity tests for women who are not "sure" who fathered their babies. The potential fathers are invited to hear the results of the paternity test on the air, with a stern talk by Mr. Williams concerning their "responsibility" to those branded as fathers by DNA evidence. This family drama is played out repeatedly, with Mr. Williams readying himself to deliver the message to wayward young men—if you take it out of your pants, you need to take care of your babies. Moreover, as an African American man married to a White woman, Mr. Williams's shows repeatedly bring on working-class, interracial couples where young White mothers try to get their sexually irresponsible Black boyfriends to claim paternity. If this weren't enough, Mr. Williams also devotes shows to the pain experienced by biracial children in search of their wayward parents.

The Maury Povich Show also trades in this racial family drama, but with more emphasis on race and sexuality. Not only does Mr. Povich, a White American, do shows where White women seek paternity tests for their Black male partners, Mr. Povich presents Black women and Black men in an especially stark light. One show, for example, featured a Black woman who brought on nine Black men as candidates for her six-month-old daughter's "baby daddy."[16] All nine failed the paternity test. After the revelation, with cameras rolling in search of the all-important "money shot,"[17] Mr. Povich followed the distraught young mother backstage, and volunteered to keep working with her until she had tracked down the Black deadbeat dad. Like Mr. Williams, Mr. Povich delivers a message about responsibility to the DNA-branded fathers. Via the choice of topic, and showing the African American woman whose sexuality was so out of control that she had no idea who had fathered her child, Mr. Povich panders to longstanding societal beliefs about Black sexuality.

The crying and raw emotion solicited on Mr. Williams's and Mr. Povich's shows pales in comparison to the staged sexual spectacles of the Jerry Springer Show. Mr. Springer's shows routinely combine sexuality and violence, two sure-fire audience builders. Here participants are invited to come on the air and reveal "secrets" to seemingly unsuspecting spouses, lovers and friends. The "secrets" routinely involve cheating, lying and false paternity. By his choice of guests, Mr. Springer's show also takes sexual spectacles to an entirely new level. Morbidly obese women parade across the stage in bikinis, verbally taunting the audience to comment on their appearance. In a context where women's bodies are routinely sexualized, displaying seemingly hideous female bodies is designed to shock and solicit ridicule. These confessional talk shows also routinely conduct paternity tests, show pictures of babies who lack legal fathers, discuss sexual infidelity, and display audience members in sexually explicit clothing (or lack thereof). For many Americans, these shows substitute for public discussions of sexuality because few other outlets are available.

African Americans are well represented in the public spectacles provided by Mr. Williams's, Mr. Povich's and Mr. Springer's talk shows. Guests on all three programs are clearly working-class, with many of them Black and Latino. These shows are not just about sexuality, they also signal clear messages about race and class. They depict the challenges of explaining a new, interracial class structure that can no longer rely on biological notions of race to differentiate poor people (assumed to be Black) from middle-class people (assumed to be White). In the new multicultural America, Blacks can be middle-class (the hugely popular *Cosby Show* broke that barrier in the 1980s) and, in fact, a certain degree of Black middle-class visibility is needed to buttress arguments of equal opportunity (Oprah Winfrey and Montel Williams both exemplify this need for visible, accomplished Blacks). But how does one explain the persistence of poverty among *White* Americans if poverty has long been attributed to Black biological inferiority? They are not biologically Black, but their poverty and downward mobility can be explained if they are seen as being culturally or socially Black. Whites who embrace Black culture become positioned closer to Blacks and become stigmatized. In the context of the new racism, cultural explanations for economic success and poverty substitute for biological arguments concerning intelligence or genetic dispositions for immorality or violence.

Viewing stories about historically taboo interracial sexuality between White women and Black men becomes the new sexual spectacle, where working class White women become "darkened" by their sexual relationships with irresponsible working-class Black men.[18] When accused of paternity by these "trashy" White women, Black men are depicted as proud of their irresponsible sexual behavior. Certainly White men are given paternity tests on these shows, but typically these are working-class or poor White men who are hauled in by working-class White mothers of their alleged children. In contrast to the White women who point the finger of paternity at both Black and White men, Black women rarely identify White men as the potential fathers of their babies. Given the history of interracial, institutionalized rape of Black women by White men, White fathers of Black children would hardly be newsworthy. Instead, Black women are presented as being so reckless that they do not know who fathered their children or, sharing a common fate with their White sisters, they point the finger at irresponsible Black men. Despite similarities that link all three shows, they do offer different scripts for solving the problems of these sexual spectacles. Part of the appeal of the Montel Williams Show lies in his role in this family drama—Williams plays the part of the caring yet stern Black patriarch who provides the fatherly discipline that so many of his guests seemingly lack. In contrast, Mr. Povich presents himself as a kindly White father, showing concern for his emotional albeit abnormal guests. Mr. Springer is merely a ringmaster—he doesn't get near his guests, preferring instead to watch the cursing and chair throwing from a safe distance. Discipline them, listen to them, or dismiss them—all three solutions apply to working-class and poor guests. Apparently middle-class Americans (even Black ones) have little difficulty identifying which sexual partner conceived their children. Affluent, thirty-something White women awaiting the results of paternity tests for their biracial babies just do not appear on any of these shows.

Much more is at stake here than the accuracy of the depictions of African American women and men within talk shows and other forms of mass media. African Americans and Black culture are highly visible within the American movies, music, sports, dance, and fashion that help shape contemporary ideologies of race, gender, sexuality and class in a global context. Sexual spectacles travel, and they matter. Historical context disappears, leaving seemingly free-floating images in its wake that become the new vocabulary that joins quite disparate entities. Terms such as "primitive," "backward," "jungle," "wild," and "freak" uncritically cycle through contemporary global culture, leaving undisturbed the pejorative historical meanings associated with this vocabulary. But history hides in the shadows of these terms, because these concepts are incomprehensible without a social context to give them meaning. For example, the pervasive use of animal imagery persists within some expressions of contemporary Black popular culture, as suggested by the decision to clothe Destiny's Child in animal skin bikinis on their 2000 *Survivor* album cover. These depictions eerily resemble past practices of associating Africans with animals, particularly apes, monkeys and chimpanzees. The choice of animal may change—no longer apes, Black men have taken on new identities as "dogs" energetically engaged in chasing the (kitty) "cat"—but associating Black men and women with lusty, animal sexual practices apparently has not. Although different meanings may be associated with animal imagery, Snoop Doggy Dog, Bow Wow, and the classic phrase "you my main dog" all invoke this same universe of animal imagery. Moreover, representations of Black men as "dogs" who have replaced the cool "cats" of prior eras of African American jazzmen, as well as the video "hos" who populate rap music videos suggest the emergence of an increasingly sophisticated gender-specific expression of ideas about Blackness sold in the global marketplace. Josephine Baker's 1925 topless banana skirt dance and Destiny's Child's "bootylicious" would be meaningless without this history, even if those enjoying the images do not consciously see the connections.

African American theorist Cornel West identifies the paradox of a sexually repressive culture that on the one hand, seems saturated with sexuality, but that on the other hand, suppresses education and open dialogue concerning human sexuality. To West, race matters: "the paradox of the sexual politics of race in America is that, behind closed doors, the dirty, disgusting, and funky sex associated with Black people is often perceived to be more intriguing and interesting, while in public spaces talk about Black sexuality is virtually taboo."[19] Black sexuality is routinely invoked within American society, namely, the alleged sexual prowess of the Black men accused of fathering babies with White women, but analyzing it is discouraged. The result is a society fraught with contradictions. For example, well-off White teenagers can drive expensive cars to racially segregated high schools and college campuses that admit only a few handpicked African Americans, all the while booming the latest sexually explicit lyrics of their favorite Black hip-hop artist. American viewers can sit in their living rooms viewing talk shows that censure the African American man accused of fathering three out-of-wedlock children with two different White women, yet still be intrigued by his sexual prowess. Legions of young American men can wonder what it would be like to get Beyoncé from Destiny's Child or Jennifer Lopez in bed.

Like other Americans, African Americans must make sense of this curious sexual climate that accompanies the new racism. This task is made even more difficult by that fact that African Americans are included in these debates, often serving as examples of what *not* to be or, alternately, as icons of sexual freedom served up as the antidote to American sexual repression. As part of the colorblind racism that has accompanied the erasure of the color line, the ubiquitous *inclusion* of images of Black sexuality that permeate contemporary movies, television shows, and music videos can replicate the power relations of racism today just as effectively as the *exclusion* of Black images in these same media did prior to the 1960s. Thus, Cheryl Clarke's observation that African Americans live in a sexually repressive culture speaks less to the prominence of representations of Black sexuality within an increasingly powerful mass media than to the *function* of these images in helping to construct a "limited sexual system."

Gender, Sexuality, and African American Politics

African Americans typically think that gender relations are a private concern, mainly reflecting the love relationships between heterosexual men and women. Those who see the harmful effects of gender oppression on African Americans still wish to define issues of gender and sexuality solely within the context of Black community politics, a domestic issue among Black people. Place the "public" issue of race first, they counsel, and leave the more "private" issues of gender and sexuality for us to work out among ourselves. Relying on ideas about family to construct ideas about race, this approach sees African Americans as participating in a large, imagined racial family. In service to the race, each individual African American should put on a good face for the critical White public that sits in judgment outside African American communities. The adage "don't air dirty laundry in public" speaks to this African American community norm of keeping these and other family problems hidden. [20]

What these approaches fail to grasp is that common-sense notions about differences of gender and sexuality that allegedly distinguish Whites (carriers of "normal" gender ideology and sexual practices) from Blacks (carriers of "deviant" gender ideology and sexual practices) have long served as the fulcrum for constructing racial difference. Within white/black binary thinking, ideas about racial normality and deviancy draw heavily upon ideas about gender and sexuality for meaning. Moreover, because racial normality has been defined in gender-specific terms, African American progress or lack thereof in achieving the gender norms attributed to Whites has long been used as a marker of racial progress. Stated differently, African Americans have been evaluated within a context of a sex role theory that by its very nature disadvantages Black people.[21] Within a Western sex role ideology premised on ideas of strong men and weak women, on active, virile masculinity and passive, dependent femininity, the seeming role reversal among African Americans has been used to stigmatize Black people.[22] This ideology not only identifies a reversed, damaged gender ideology as a sign of racial difference, it further claims that flawed ideas concerning Black masculinity and Black femininity reflect equally problematic conceptions of sexuality.

The new racism does present some formidable puzzles for African American politics. In prior periods where biological theories were used to justify racist practices, racism and anti-racism had a seemingly organic and oppositional relationship. One could either be *for* racism by believing that Blacks were biologically inferior and deserved the treatment that they received. Or one could be *against* it by rejecting these beliefs and pointing to racial prejudice and institutional discrimination as more important in explaining Black disadvantage. These distinctions no longer hold for many White and Black Americans. Under the new color-blind racism that erases the color line, racism itself seems to have disappeared. As French sociologist Michel Wieviorka points out, "this clear-cut polarity between racists and anti-racists no longer exists."[23] With the exception of largely discredited right-wing groups, few American organizations openly advocate theories of Black inferiority based on outdated racial biology. As a result, groups holding vastly different perspectives on what constitutes antiracist political activism can claim that they are the true antiracists.

African American politics is buffeted by the same trends that afflict antiracist practices overall. In the context of new U.S. racial formations and of conflicting approaches to Black empowerment and social justice, African American antiracist politics seems stuck between two ineffective ideological options. On one side stands a threadbare civil rights agenda that continues to preach racial integration to an African American population so incarcerated in extensive inner city ghettos that few Whites are left to integrate schools, neighborhoods, and public facilities.[24] Whites have voted with their feet and their pocketbooks, and few attend the annual Martin Luther King Day rally any more. On the other side stands a largely symbolic Black Nationalist agenda that shapes the gender politics of controversial organizations such as the Nation of Islam. Black Nationalist ideology also appears as a faux radical politics in some hip-hop culture, for example, in the work of Public Enemy or Ice T, primarily because African American youth quite rightly perceive few other options. Neither choice has been especially effective in addressing the social problems of the inner cities or in fostering a broader social justice agenda within the United States.

Black Americans must figure out how to deal with the contours of the new racism and must do so with an increased sensitivity to issues of gender and sexuality. Political theorist Cathy J. Cohen's schema of consensus and crosscutting political issues provides a useful model for understanding current African American antiracist politics. Consensus issues affect all identifiable group members, in this case, all who claim or are assigned a Black identity. Consensus issues may affect all group members, but they may not take the same form for all group members. In contrast, crosscutting issues disproportionately and directly affect only certain segments of a group. Cohen suggests that current African American politics treat race as a consensus issue while relegating gender and sexuality the secondary status as crosscutting issues. Within this thinking, Black women are affected by gender and Black men are not, and lesbian, gay, bisexual and transgendered Black people are affected by sexuality and heterosexual Blacks are not.

Gender and sexuality have historically both been crosscutting issues within the frame-work of an overarching antiracist political project. This has been a problem because, within Black political arenas, crosscutting issues are often deemed to be secondary to the greater good of the group.[25] In a context where gender has been associated with Black women and where sexuality has been the province of Black (LGBT) people, these groups have often been encouraged to take a back seat for the greater good of racial solidarity. Many have not gone willingly. The explosion of Black feminism since the 1970s was spurred on, in large part, by the refusal of Black women activists to take a back seat to men within both the civil rights and Black Nationalist political movements. Similar catalysts stimulated the increasing visibility of Black lesbians and gays. These groups point out that, without serious attention to contemporary Black sexual politics, African Americans may uncritically circulate ideas about race, class, gender and sexuality that bear striking resemblance to those long advanced by White elites.

An antiracist politics that does not reframe the consensus issue of race in terms of class, gender, sexuality, and age will remain incapable of responding to the complexities of the new racism. Take, for example, the pressing issue of violence that confronts people of African descent. African Americans are all affected by violence, but by different manifestations. Regardless of social class, Black men are more likely to encounter state-sanctioned violence at the hands of police whereas Black women are more likely to experience intimate violence of battering and rape at the hands of fathers, brothers, spouses, boyfriends, and men in their neighborhoods. Black youth and children witness this violence and are profoundly affected by it. Black LGBT people encounter hate crimes of verbal and physical harassment that stem from homophobia. Young Black men often kill one another, a form of internecine violence that reflects the significance of age. Poor and working class Black people are more vulnerable to certain types of violence than their more affluent counterparts. Violence represents a potentially divisive issue if one form of violence is deemed to be more important than others because the segment of Black people who experience it are deemed more worthy of attention and help. Rather than viewing violence as a crosscutting issue, each group member would recognize the importance of all forms of anti-violence political action, even if particular forms of violence, for example, police harassment, or wife battering, or rape, did not directly affect him or her.

Given these challenges, it is vital that the notion of antiracist politics be expanded beyond more traditional notions of political parties, social movements, and grass-roots political organizations. Political anthropologist James C. Scott uses the term "infrapolitics" to describe the hidden behaviors of everyday resistance. Despite appearances of consent, people challenge inequalities of race, class, gender and sexuality through conversations, jokes, songs, folklore, theft, foot-dragging and a multitude of everyday behaviors.[26] As African American historian Robin D.G. Kelley points out, "the political history of oppressed people cannot be understood without reference to infrapolitics, for these daily acts have a cumulative effect on power relations."[27] Everyday life contains many opportunities for resistance, if individual thoughts and actions can be conceptualized in this fashion. Infrapolitics provide important insights concerning the political possibilities for oppressed groups that seemingly lack political options. For example, within African American communities, men and women have different degrees of access to formal power. Men are more likely to engage in traditional politics of office-holding whereas women have been more involved in the day to day infrapolitics of bringing about change. Moreover, because infrapolitics and traditional politics are interdependent, neither is sufficient as the sole form of political resistance.

Contemporary forms of oppression do not routinely force people to submit. Instead, they manufacture consent for domination so that we lose our ability to question and thus collude in our own subordination. Images of Jennifer Lopez, Destiny's Child, and Montel Williams, are all part of this process of reproduction and contestation. In this context of oppressions occurring through the normal structures of society, within contemporary nation-states such as the United States, oppression becomes expressed as a routinized violence or normalized war within one society. Within the United States, oppression now takes a new form, one where society itself is saturated with the relations of warfare against selected members of society itself. Routinized violence can break through into open conflict (1992 Los Angeles and 2001 in Cincinnati), but more often, this normalized war also operates through the infrapolitics of everyday life, through a series of mini-assaults that convince each one of us to stay in our place.[28] Black people are under assault, and the racial and gender meanings assigned to Black bodies as well as the social meanings of Black sexuality in American society overall constitute sites of contestation in an uncivil civil war against Black people.

Developing a Progressive Black Sexual Politics

African Americans express quite diverse and often contradictory responses to the challenges raised by prevailing Black sexual politics. How can Jennifer Lopez and Destiny's Child be independent women and bootylicious at the same time? If African American women can be convinced to perceive themselves solely in terms of the value of their bootys in marketplace relations, then oppression may be complete. If African American men accept the images of themselves as sexually irresponsible boys as depicted on the Montel Williams, Maury

Povich, and Jerry Springer Shows, then they too participate in structuring their own oppression. But is anyone ever without agency to this degree?

The antidote to a gender-specific racial oppression that advances controlling images of deviant Black sexuality does not lie in embracing a conservative politics of respectability that mimics the beliefs of those responsible for the sexually repressive culture in the first place. Rather, in the context of a new racism, men and women who rescue and redefine sexuality as a source of power rooted in spirituality, expressiveness, and love can craft new understandings of Black masculinity and Black femininity needed for a progressive Black sexual politics. When reclaimed by individuals and groups, redefined ideas about sexuality and sexual practices can operate as sources of joy, pleasure and empowerment that simultaneously affirm and transcend individual sexual pleasure for social good.

Black feminist poet Audre Lorde certainly knew this when, almost thirty years ago, she identified the power of the erotic as an important source of energy for resisting gender oppression.[29] Lorde redefined the erotic as the deep feelings within each of us in search of love, affirmation, recognition and a spiritual and/or physical connection to one another. Lorde argued that impoverished notions of love of self and others lie at the heart of oppression. Reclaiming the erotic as a domain of exploration, pleasure, and human agency is thus vital to individual empowerment. Lorde associated erotic power with women and with female sexuality. But the power of the erotic need not be reserved for women, nor is it synonymous with physical sexual expression. Such power is available to all human beings, including men.

For women and men alike, and for *individuals* from diverse race, ethnic, sexual, age and national backgrounds, claiming such power remains easier said than done. Expressing individual agency and challenging the Black sexual politics that shape everyday life is complicated; linking the individual agency expressed in these social locations to a *collective* group politics may seem unattainable. The dialectical relationship between oppression and activism makes all politics difficult, including this one. A fundamental contradiction lies at the juncture where intersecting oppressions grounded in dominance confront a resistance nourished by expansive notions of care, eroticism, spirituality and politicized love. On the one hand, perverting the power of the erotic by manipulating ideas about sexuality has been and continues to be an important dimension of oppressions of race, gender, class and sexuality. For African Americans, these manipulations take myriad forms and continue to affect contemporary Black sexual politics. On the other hand, because deeply held feelings, especially those that have bodily expression, constitute one of the most important sources of energy available to human beings, people who are able to reclaim the power of the erotic gain a crucial weapon in resisting these intersecting oppressions. Despite these challenges, for African Americans, the struggle is essential.

Discussion Questions

1. What are the three characteristics of the new racism?
2. What are the implications of a sexually repressive society for Black sexuality?
3. What are consensus and crosscutting political issues? How do these issues apply to Black sexual politics?
4. What does Collins suggest is needed for a progressive Black sexual politics?

Notes

1. The changes generated by postcoloniality, global capitalism, and new technologies have sparked a lively debate about the contours and meaning of the new racism in the United States. Some scrutinize the transformation of contemporary US society as a racialized social system composed of structural and ideological dimensions (Bonilla-Silva 1996). When it comes to African Americans, structurally, American society has not made the gains in desegregating its housing, schools, and employment promised by the civil rights movement (Massey and Denton 1993). One study of Atlanta, GA revealed that neighborhood-level racial resegregation is emerging as a new spatial pattern within major American cities, even those with a politically enfranchised

and highly visible Black middle class (Orfield and Ashkinaze 1991). Other research points to the growth of a prison-industrial complex as an important new site for institutionalized racism confronting working-class and poor African Americans and Latinos (Miller 1996). Ideologically, a belief in upholding "colorblindness" masks the continued inequalities of contemporary racism. By proclaiming that equal treatment of *individuals* under the law is sufficient for addressing racism, this ideology redefines group-based, anti-racist remedies such as affirmative action as being "racist" (Crenshaw 1997). For a critique of colorblindness and an analysis of how this racial ideology merits rethinking in the United States, see (Guinier and Torres 2002).

2. For a thorough analysis of how globalization shapes contemporary racial formations, see Winant's analysis of the United States, South Africa, Brazil and Europe in the post-World War II era (Winant 2001). Feminist analysis has also produced a broad literature on globalization and women's economic status, some of it focused on how racism, sexism and issues of globalization. For representative theoretical work in this tradition, see (Alexander 1997; Mohanty 1997). African American scholars have also focused more attention on the global political economy. For representative works in this tradition, see (Wilson 1996) (Brewer 1994) (Squires 1994).
3. Bauman 1998, 9.
4. Lusane 1997, 114.
5. M. Jacqui Alexander's discussion of the tourist industry in the Bahamas provides an especially insightful analysis of the effects of globalization on nation-state autonomy and on social problems within the Bahamas (Alexander 1997).
6. Cultural studies and studies of mass media underwent massive growth after 1980. For general work on the media, see (Gitlin 2001). For race and media, see (Entman 2000). The field of Black cultural studies has generated a range of literature. For representative works, consult (Bobo 1995; Kelley 1994; Kelley 1997; Rose 1994; Wallace 1990; Gilroy 2000; Ransby and Matthews 1993; Gates 1992; Neal 2002; Watkins 1998; Cashmore 1997; Caponi 1999; Dent 1992b; Hall 1992; Dyson 1996).
7. Kitwana 2002.
8. Clarke 1983, 199.
9. D'Emilio and Freedman suggest that the suppression of a range of sexual practices was part of colonization. Comparing the sexual practices of Native Americans, which varied widely, with European colonialist perceptions of such practices, in every region where Europeans and indigenous peoples came into contact, Europeans judged the sexual life of natives as "savage" and their own practices as "civilized. For example, most indigenous peoples did not associate either nudity or sexuality with sin. They accepted premarital intercourse, polygamy, or institutionalized homosexuality, all practices that were condemned by European church and state (D'Emilio and Freedman 1997, 6–7). They point out, "perhaps the most striking contrast between English and Indian sexual systems was the relative absence of sexual conflict among native Americans, due in part to their different cultural attitudes toward both property and sexuality ... In cultures in which one could not 'own' another person's sexuality, prostitution—the sale of sex—did not exist prior to the arrival to European settlers. Rape—the theft of sex—only rarely occurred, and it was one of the few sexual acts forbidden by Indian cultures" (D'Emilio and Freedman 1997, 8).
10. D'Emilio and Freedman 1997, 16.
11. A 1995 report published by the Social Science Research Council charts the political difficulties that have plagued scientific studies of sexuality within American social science (di Mauro 1995).
12. Hegemony is also a mode of social organization wherein the dissent of oppressed groups is absorbed and thereby rendered politically useless. Moreover, in hegemonic situations, power is diffused throughout a social system such that multiple groups police one another and suppress each other's dissent. For example, if African Americans come to believe the dominant ideology and accept ideas about Black masculinities and Black femininities constructed within the dominant framework, then Black political dissent about gender and about all things tied to gender become weakened. Because they are used to justify existing social hierarchies, hegemonic ideologies may

seem invincible. But ideologies of all sorts are never static. Instead, they are always internally inconsistent and are always subject to contestation (Magubane 2001).

13. Remez 2000.
14. Of suppression of sex education and the limits on discussions that do exist have an especially negative impact on African American adolescents. HIV/AIDS has had a significant impact on African American youth. For statistics, see http://www.cdc.gov/hiv/pubs/Facts/afam.pdf.
15. For an analysis of talk shows, especially the production of "trashy" talk shows, see (Grindstaff 2002). Grindstaff does not emphasize race, but her study of how talk shows replicate and reproduce ideas about social class and gender provides insight into the general process of ideology construction and contestation. She notes that talk shows are typically geared to women, feature working-class guests, and aim to display ordinary people engaged in extraordinary behavior.
16. Mark Anthony Neal and Hortense Spillers offer two different interpretations of the emergence of the term "baby daddy" to describe unmarried fatherhood among African American men. Neal's chapter "Baby Mama (Drama) and Baby Daddy (Trauma): Post-Soul Gender Politics uses Black popular culture (Neal 2002, 57-97). In contrast, Spillers' essay "Mama's Baby, Papa's Maybe: An American Grammar Book," also examines unmarried fatherhood in the context of American race relations and the exploitation of Black bodies under slavery (Spillers 2000).
17. Grindstaff borrows the phrase the "money shot" from pornography to describe the efforts of producers to get ordinary people to deliver strong emotions such as joy, sorrow, rage, or remorse that can be seen in visible, bodily terms. Crying, shaking, running, and other evidence of emotion besides just talk are solicited. As Grindstaff points out, "Like pornography, daytime talk is a narrative of explicit revelation in which people 'get down and dirty' and 'bare it all' for the pleasure, fascination, or repulsion of viewers. Like the orgasmic cum shot of pornographic films, the money shot of talk shows makes visible the precise moment of letting go, of losing control, of surrendering to the body and its 'animal' emotions" (Grindstaff 2002, 19). This is why Mr. Povich followed the woman backstage—he was in search of an authentic money shot.
18. Sociologist Abby Ferber describes how White supremacist literature remains obsessed with this theme of interracial sexuality generally and of protecting the body of the White woman (and thus the White race) from Black penetration. White women who willingly partner with Black men become redefined as "darkened," trashy women (Ferber 1998a).
19. West 1993, 83.
20. The works of Black women writers repeatedly identify how they are encouraged to keep silent about gender problems within African American communities. For example, African American scholars Johnnetta Cole and Beverly Guy-Sheftall recount how their volume on the struggle for women's equality within African American communities goes against racial discourse that counsels Black women not to "air dirty laundry" about gender and sexuality (Cole and Guy-Sheftall 2003, xxiii–xxxviii). They name their book *Gender Talk* in an effort to reverse these silences.
21. Sex role theory has generated considerable critique. Michael Messner summarizes five common problems with sex role theory: 1) it focuses on individualistic, voluntary levels of analysis that minimize institutional power relations; 2) it implies a false symmetry between men and women that masks gender oppression; 3) it uses the male sex role to create a falsely universalized (middle-class, White, heterosexual) norm and measures deviance using this standard; 4) it relies on binary ideas about gender that reify biological notions of male and female sex categories; and 5) it is inadequate for examining changes in gender ideology, especially resistance (Messner 1998, 258). Messner points out that sociologists do not use the terms "race roles" or "class roles" when describing other social inequalities: "we may speak of race or class *identities*, but we do so within the context of an understanding of the historical dynamics of race and class *relations*" (Messner 1998, 258). R.W. Connell offers a comparable critique: "the conceptualization of gender through role theory ... reifies expectations and self-descriptions, exaggerates consensus, marginalized questions of power,

and cannot analyze historical change" (Connell 1992, 735). By the 1980s, a more historicized and politicized language of gender relations virtually supplanted the language of sex role theory within sociology, although not within psychology, education, social work and other disciplines.

22. In his classic work on stigma, Erving Goffman examines the strategies used by people who are stigmatized to manage a "spoiled identity" (Goffman 1963). While scholars often use Goffman's work to explore the management of stigma by individuals, here I use the concept to explore how Blacks as a group respond to the stigma of Blackness that is evidenced by a seemingly deviant Black sexuality.
23. Wieviorka 1997, 139.
24. In 1999, 55 percent of Blacks but only 22 percent of non-Hispanic Whites lived in the central cities of metropolitan areas (McKinnon and Humes 2000, 2).
25. Cohen 1999, 14–15.
26. Scott 1990.
27. Kelley 1994, 8.
28. Gilroy 2000.
29. Lorde 1984, 53–59.

REFERENCES

Alexander, M. Jacqui. 1997. "Erotic Autonomy as a Politics of Decolonization: An Anatomy of Feminist and State Practice in the Bahamas Tourist Industry." *Feminist Genealogies, Colonial Legacies, Democratic Futures*. Ed. M. Jacqui Alexander and Chandra Talpade Mohanty, 63–100. New York: Routledge.

Bauman, Zygmunt. 1998. *Globalization: The Human Consequences*. New York: Columbia University Press.

Bobo, Jacqueline. 1995. *Black Women as Cultural Readers*. New York: Columbia University Press.

Bonilla-Silva, Eduardo. 1996. "Rethinking Racism: Toward a Structural Interpretation." American Sociological Review 62 (June): 465–480.

Brewer, Rose. 1994. "Race, Class, Gender and U.S. State Welfare Policy: The Nexus of Inequality for African American Families." *Color, Class and Country: Experiences of Gender*. Ed. Gay Young and Bette J. Dickerson, 115–127. London: Zed.

Caponi, Gena Dagel, ed. 1999. *Signifyin(g), Sanctifyin', & Slam Dunking; A Reader in African American Expressive Culture*. Amherst: University of Massachusetts Press.

Cashmore, Ellis. 1997. *The Black Culture Industry*. New York: Routledge.

Clarke, Cheryl. 1983. "The Failure to Transform: Homophobia in the Black Community." *Home Girls: A Black Feminist Anthology*. Ed. Barbara Smith, 197–208. New York: Kitchen Table Press

Cohen, Cathy J. 1999. *The Boundaries of Blackness: AIDS and the Breakdown of Black Politics*. Chicago: University of Chicago Press.

Cole, Johnetta Betsch, and Beverly Guy-Sheftall. 2003. *Gender Talk: The Struggle for Women's Equality in African American Communities*. New York: Ballantine.

Connell, R. W. 1992. "A Very Straight Gay: Masculinity, Homosexual Experience, and the Dynamics of Gender." *American Sociological Review* 57 (December): 735–751.

Crenshaw, Kimberlé Williams. 1997. "Color Blindness, History, and the Law." *The House That Race Built*. Ed. Wahneema Lubiano, 280–288. New York: Pantheon.

D'Emilio, John, and Estelle B. Freedman. 1997. *Intimate Matters: A History of Sexuality in America*. Chicago: University of Chicago Press.

Dent, Gina. ed. 1992. *Black Popular Culture*. Seattle: Bay Press.

di Mauro, Diane. 1995. *Sexuality Research in the United States: An Assessment of the Social and Behavioral Sciences*. New York: Social Science Research Council, Sexuality Research Assessment Project.

Dyson, Michael Eric. 1996. *Between God and Gangsta Rap: Bearing Witness to Black Culture*. New York: Oxford University Press.

Entman, Robert M., and Rojecki Andrew. 2000. *The Black Image in the White Mind: Media and Race in America*. Chicago: University of Chicago Press

Ferber, Abby L. 1998. *White Man Falling: Race, Gender, and White Supremacy*. Lanham, Md.: Rowman & Littlefield.

Gates, Henry Louis. 1992. *Loose Canons: Notes on the Culture Wars*. New York: Oxford University Press.

Gilroy, Paul. 2000. *Against Race: Imagining Political Culture Beyond the Color Line*. Cambridge, Mass: Belknap Press of Harvard University Press.

Gitlin, Todd. 2001. *Media Unlimited: How the Torrent of Images and Sounds Overwhelms Our Lives*. New York, Henry Holt.

Goffman, Erving. 1963. Stigma: *Notes on the Management of Spoiled Identity*. Englewood Cliffs, N.J.: Prentice Hall.

Grindstaff, Laura. 2002. T*he Money Shot: Trash, Class, and the Making of TV Talk Shows*. Chicago: University of Chicago Press.

Guinier, Lani, and Gerald Torres. 2002. *The Miner's Canary: Enlisting Race, Resisting Power, Transforming Democracy*. Cambridge, Mass.: Harvard University Press.

Hall, Stuart. 1992. "What Is This 'Black' in Black Popular Culture?" *Black Popular Culture*. Ed. Gina Dent, 21–33. Seattle: Bay Press.

Kelley, Robin D. G. 1994. *Race Rebels: Culture, Politics, and the Black Working Class*. New York: Free Press.———. 1997. *Yo' Mama's DisFUNKtional!: Fighting the Culture Wars in Urban America*. Boston: Beacon Press.

Kitwana, Bakari. 2002. *The Hip Hop Generation: Young Blacks and the Crisis in Africa-American Culture*. New York: Basic Books.

Lorde, Audre. 1984. *Sister Outsider: Essays and Speeches*. Freedom, Calif.: Crossing Press.

Lusane, Clarence. 1997. *Race in the Global Era: African Americans at the Millennium*. Boston: South End Press.

Magubane, Zine. 2001. "Which Bodies Matter? Feminism, Poststructuralism, Race, and the Curious Theoretical Odyssey of the 'Hottentot Venus.'" *Gender and Society* 15, no. 6: 816–834.

Massey, Douglas S., and Nancy Denton. 1993. *American Apartheid: Segregation and the Making of the Underclass*. Cambridge, Mass.: Harvard University Press.

McKinnon, Jesse, and Karen Humes. 2000. *The Black Population in the United States:* March 1999. Current Population Reports, Series P20-530. U.S. Census Bureau. Washington, D.C.: U.S. Government Printing Office.

Messner, Michael A. 1990. "When Bodies Are Weapons: Masculinity and Violence in Sport." *International Review of the Sociology of Sport* 25: 203–217.

Miller, Jerome G. 1996. *Search and Destroy: African-American Males in the Criminal Justice System*. New York: Cambridge University Press.

Mohanty, Chandra Talpade. 1997. "Women Workers and Capitalist Scripts: Ideologies of Domination, Common Interests, and the Politics of Solidarity." *Feminist Genealogies, Colonial Legacies, Democratic Futures*. Ed. M. Jacqui Mohanty Chandra and Talpade Alexander, 3–29. New York: Routledge.

Neal, Mark Anthony. 2002. *Soul Babies: Black Popular Culture and the Post-Soul Aesthetic*. New York: Routledge.

Orfield, Gary, and Carole Ashkinaze. 1991. *The Closing Door: Conservative Policy and Black Opportunity*. Chicago: University of Chicago Press.

Ransby, Barbara, and Tracye Matthews. 1993. "Black Popular Culture and the Transcendence of Patriarchal Illusions." Race and Class 35, no. 1: 57–68.

Remez, Lisa. 2000. "Oral Sex among Adolescents: Is It Sex or Abstinence?" *Family Planning Perspectives* 32, no. 6: 298–304.

Rose, Tricia. 1994. *Black Noise: Rap Music and Black Culture in Contemporary America*. Hanover, N.H.:

Scott, James C. 1990. *Domination and the Arts of Resistance: The Hidden Transcripts*. New Haven, Conn.: Yale University Press.

Spillers, Hortense J. 2000. "Mama's Baby, Papa's Maybe: An American Grammar Book." *The Black Feminist Reader*. Ed. Joy James and T. Denean Sharpley-Whiting, 57–87. Malden, Mass.: Blackwell.

Squires, Gregory D. 1994. *Capital and Communities in Black and White: The Intersections of Race, Class, and Uneven Development*. Albany: State University of New York Press.

Wallace, Michele. 1990. I*nvisibility Blues: From Pop to Theory*. New York: Verso.

Watkins, S. Craig. 1998. *Representing: Hip Hop Culture and the Production of Black Cinema*. Chicago: University of Chicago Press.

West, Cornel. 1993. *Race Matters*. Boston: Beacon Press.

Wieviorka, Michel. 1997. "Is It So Difficult to Be an Anti-Racist?" *Debating Cultural Hybridity: Multi-cultural Identities and the Politics of Anti-racism*. Ed. Pnina Werbner and Tariq Modood, 139–53. London: Zed.

Winant, Howard. 2001. *The World Is a Ghetto: Race and Democracy since World War II*. New York: Basic Books.

THE FACEBOOK REVOLUTION

LGBT Identity and Activism

BY MARGARET COOPER AND KRISTINA DZARA

Using Facebook (2009), a popular worldwide social networking site with millions of members, is just one way that people stay in touch with old friends and meet new ones. Although Facebook was originally created as a site for college students, it has since expanded so that anyone with a valid email address can join. There is one key difference between Facebook and other online social networks. Facebook is one of the few social network sites where those who are friends online are also friends or at least acquaintances in real life (Ellison et al. 2007; Ross et al. 2009). Thus, Facebook serves as an additional way that a user can interact with friends and loved ones.

In this article, we dissect Facebook as a tool that LGBT users employ to construct, maintain, and sometimes hide their identities. We do this because Facebook is an innovative social tool that enables users to attempt to reflect to their friends who they believe themselves to be. Although this sense of and management of identity begins with the individual, it may be encouraged or discouraged by other Facebook users, potentially creating conflict. Below, we draw on broad-ranging social psychological principles to explore, analyze, and explain the use of Facebook by those under the LGBT umbrella.

Methods and Analysis

In her work with rural lesbians, Cooper (1990, 2007, and forthcoming) recently discovered a change in the way these women could acquire information. Where formerly isolated by geography, rural lesbians were able now to go online and seek out communities where they could gain information and support from others in similar situations. Cooper then became interested in the internet, and was led to the topic of Facebook by her LGBT college students. She then joined Facebook herself and became a member of many LGBT groups. Her co-author had been a member of Facebook since 2006 and has joined a number of political and social Facebook groups. Together Cooper and Dzara explored the site as participant observers, analyzing profiles available to all users for constructions of identity and obtaining anecdotal information from users. In addition, we conducted an academic search of journal articles and books related to Facebook as well as a Lexis Nexis search on Facebook articles in the popular press.We also reviewed academic research conducted on the topics of Facebook, internet activism and issues of personality and identity (Ellison et al. 2007; Pempek et al. 2009; Raacke and Bonds-Raacke 2008; Ross et al. 2009; Seder and Oishi 2009; Valkenburg et al. 2006; Zhao et al. 2008).

Our observations led us to three areas of constructionist analysis. These are: 1) identity construction, 2) identity management and negotiation, and 3) collective

Margaret Cooper and Kristina Dzara, "The Facebook Revolution: LGBT Identity and Activism," *LGBT Identity and Online New Media*. Copyright © 2010 by Taylor & Francis Group. Reprinted with permission.

identity, activism, and the construction of issues as social problems.

Identity Construction

> They (Facebook) allow people to display themselves not just as self-made individual persons, but as individuals. In one way, they give everyone the chance to be individuals in the sense of being unique, because any person can be shown as being in the centre of a social universe—their own. No matter who you are, your Facebook website has you as the one in focus. (Dalsgaard 2008, p. 9)

Buhrmester and Prager (1995) developed a "model of self-disclosure" in which adolescents can achieve "identity development"and "intimacy development"both through the process of revealing their thoughts and feelings to their peers. Today's generation of youth possesses a new and different tool for self-revelation through Facebook. In fact, according to Pempek et al. (2009, p. 228), "such contacts (on Facebook) may foster the development of identity and intimate relationships, including friendships as well as romantic relationships." The internet, overall, has changed communication for most (Raacke and Bonds-Raacke 2008).

For the Facebook user, self-revelation is not merely an act of sharing personal details, but is also an active construction of one's perception of who one is. Through Facebook, the user creates a social artifact expressing one's self. This involves developing a profile which states basic information about the individual (however much he or she desires to reveal), possibly posting pictures, reporting a current "status" based upon what the user is doing at any selected time and posting music or news events on their "walls." In addition, users post messages on the walls of other members.

Users have the ability to limit views of their profiles to just "friends" or to anyone in all of their "networks." Networks represent typically a geographical region or a college or university to which the individual chooses. According to a study by Pempek et al. (2009, p. 233),"61.96% of respondents allowed their profile page to be seen by all of their networks and all of their 'friends ...' Put simply, most students provide open access to personal information."

In Pempek et al.'s 2009 study, respondents were asked about the development of their profiles and the reasons for including information in various categories. "Interestingly," Pempek et al. (2009, p. 233) wrote,"students often posted media preferences—favorite books, music and movies—as a way to express identity." Often these selections were viewed as symbolic representations of how they wish others to perceive them. Pempek et al. (2009, p. 233) wrote that the "About Me" section "was also commonly chosen as an expression of their identity. In this section, college students sometimes write funny facts, clever statements, or provide links to pictures and websites that they like." Each of these entries by students can act as deliberate markers by which they present themselves (Goffman 1959).

Users also may provide information about their religious and political views (Dalsgaard 2009). According to Pempek et al. (2009), however, students more often presented their media favorites instead of these religious and political preferences. Some users, however, use their profiles to link to others with similar political views. LGBT users often join groups within the gay and lesbian virtual community which then become a part of the user's profile. In addition, LGBT users may actively seek to construct an "out" identity by presenting news on gay and lesbian events, information about social or political activities, or news stories relating to some topic of interest to the LGBT audience.

Facebook allows the opportunity for the user to choose his or her relationship status and to list the name of the individual whom he or she is seeing.An email is then sent to that individual to confirm the relationship and upon confirmation, the status of the relationship and the partner's name are posted on the user's Facebook website. Some users of the site have recently started a group to complain that Facebook does not allow "civil union" as a relationship status. This limits the LGBT individual in a civil union to choose "married to"or "in a relationship with," or simply,"it's complicated."

There have also been complaints by the transgendered and their allies that Facebook forces a choice between only "male" and "female" for one's sex. While Facebook now allows the option of not showing one's sex in the profile, a transgendered option is not available. In contrast to MySpace, another popular social networking site, Facebook does not ask nor present the user's sexual orientation but allows it to be ignored,implied,or directly presented by the user. While Facebook can be seen as multiplying options for networking among LGBT individuals, in other ways it may be seen as perpetuating the hegemonic discourse by its creation of a structure that does not permit total flexibility in self-identification.

Facebook allows users to invite "friends" to their page. Once someone is invited, they must confirm that they are indeed friends with the person who sent the invitation. When this is done, they appear on the user's page under the "friends" section and are allowed to post messages on their "wall." Ellison et al.(2007) and Steinfield et al. (2008) have studied the number of friends and how this often acts as an indicator of social capital or popularity. Not only does the friend list contribute to identity presentation of the user in this way, the individuals the one selects as friends often contribute to the identity construction. If a person is known to be gay and out,"friending" this individual also makes a statement to the others on the friend list. Thus some who are gay and out may discover a hesitance of others to "friend" them on Facebook, even when these individuals may interact in "real-life." Not only does your friend list contribute to your identity construction, but your presence on another's list contributes to the messages he or she wishes to present, or not present, based upon his or her own identity. As Goffman (1963) indicated, one may become stigmatized simply by association with one who bears a discredited identity.

Users may post photos of themselves as identity markers. In these photos, some may choose to display themselves with romantic partners, or in other situations. For example, one young man changed his profile picture to show himself participating at a recent drag event. Photos also allow for the presentation of gender identity. Users may also "tag," or identify other Facebook users, in his or her pictures as well. If one's picture is "tagged" by another user, a notice is posted that this individual is in the picture.A user has the option of "untagging"his or her own picture. However, this does not remove the picture from the other's website. According to Pempek et al., (2009, p. 233), "the most common reason for females to untag a photo was displeasure with their appearance in the photo (88.88% of females who untagged photos), indicating how they looked was an important part of their self-presentation to others." Males, according to Pempek et al. (2009), were likely to "untag" photos for this reason, but also "because the photos depicted them engaging in an act that they did not wish for others to see, such as underage drinking." For the LGBT community, there has been no specific research about how the "tagging" of pictures by others may influence the LGBT individual's identity construction, although it most certainly has the potential to influence the perception of one's identity by others. This issue could directly be linked to concern about disclosure of one's orientation and the difficulty of managing and negotiating stigmatized identity (Goffman 1963) in a virtual setting.

Identity Management and Negotiation

> To display or not to display; to tell or not to tell; to let on or not to let on; to lie or not to lie; and in each case, to whom, how, when and where. (Goffman 1963)

Erving Goffman wrote about the decision-making strategies which occur in daily interactions for those who possess potentially discrediting identities. In face-to-face interactions, an individual has the ability and power to discern the possible acceptance level of the other and choose what (and how much) information to reveal at any one time.This can be particularly crucial for those who reside in rural, conservative areas with a possibility of resultant discrimination and violence.

In contrast to the one-to-one interactions, Facebook represents a "one-to-many style of communication" (Pempek et al. 2009, p. 227). Facebook presents new opportunities for LGBT individuals in the possibility of finding networks, social support and information. It, however, also presents new challenges as well. For a gay individual, how much information does she or he present to others? How much of this is directly given and how much is implicit? What strategies does one develop to manage the data about oneself?

Many are often mistaken in the assumption that "coming out" is a simple event, completed totally and irrevocably. Instead, "coming out" is rather a process, and one by which a gay individual may choose to reveal bits of his or her identity and to manage the flow of this information. Goffman (1963) called this "information control." In this case, a gay person may choose how much information to give to any selected individual at one time, interpret the reaction of the individual, and then decide, based upon the other's response, whether to contribute more information about one's identity. In addition, a person may choose to give some information to one individual, much more to another, and still little or no information to someone else. In day-to-day interactions, this constitutes an active negotiation of identity (Goffman 1963) based upon management and control of information given. When someone chooses to post information about one's self on Facebook, a special challenge is presented. How much information does one present about one's sexual identity? And in what matter does one do so, knowing that this will be seen by a multitude of "friends," likely with varying degrees of comfort with the user's sexuality.

Each of us represents a multiplicity of identities, from those of a sibling, son or daughter, classmate, or employee, among others. Facebook can create a conflict about how to present oneself in a way that is not detrimental to oneself in any of these categories. Popular news stories have told of those who lost their jobs, were denied promotions, or were not hired due to their Facebook profiles. In addition, gay individuals may experience family members wanting them to "friend" them. Each of life's roles may be seen as having scripts, along with acceptable norms and guidelines. What is acceptable for one role is potentially not for another. These challenges are present for everyone. For an LGBT individual, the negotiation of these may be even more crucial, and even potentially hazardous.

The following scenarios are based upon anecdotal information given by LGBT Facebook users:

- Rob is "out" to friends in real-life. He is not out on Facebook, however, since not all of his family members know. He plans a secret trip with his new boyfriend, who posts how he can't wait for their romantic European vacation.
- Sarah is also "out" in everyday life but has not posted this, or any indicator of this, on Facebook, due to the fact that she may face discrimination at work. Several coworkers have added her to their friends list. She states in a status update that she can't wait to go to a movie on Saturday night. One real-life friend posts, "Can't wait to meet your new lover!" Another friend posts,"You guys will like her! She's really nice!"
- Cary is out to friends and family. Yet some of his family members are conservative and uncomfortable with public displays of affection between Cary and a partner. A friend of Cary's posts pics of him and his boyfriend in an embrace at a party. Another pic posted shows Cary's boyfriend in drag at a fundraiser.

In scenario one, Rob may be able to delete the message from his new boyfriend so that it does not appear on his wall. However there is no guarantee that others have not seen it before Rob has. If this is the case, the information has already been revealed. If Rob does choose to delete it, he then must explain to his new boyfriend why he did so. While these are discussions that often enter into gay relationships, about who will know about the relationship, etc., in the case of the internet these conversations often arise before the individual is ready to have them. Simply because of the nature of "one-to-many" communication, everyone will know what you know, sometimes before you do.

In the second scenario, Sarah is out to her friends but not to her coworkers. This is not an unusual situation when someone fears discrimination at work. In these cases, an individual typically is able to decide in which coworker to confide, if any, and on what basis. Yet with the Facebook scenario, she has been outed to coworkers and has lost control over the information regarding her identity.

In our third case, Cary has been out to his family and friends. Yet his relationships with some had functioned best when little personal information was given regarding the romantic nature of his partnership. Some considered it a "don't ask, don't tell" situation. Cary was comfortable with this setup because it allowed him to share his basic identity with others important to them, yet did not risk losing them due to their personal unease with the issue of homosexuality. Now Cary is seen in a different light due to the romantic embrace with his partner and the picture of his partner in drag. While sexual identity may have been revealed to others, the individual may have had control over what kind of information was conveyed and in what manner the recipient could hear and accept. Now he must renegotiate identity with those concerned, not only about being gay, but what it means to be gay, how he lives his life, and the role gender identity plays with regard to his partner. Even if Cary "untags" these pictures from his profile, the photos will still be available on his friend's website, to which family and friends may have access. Another possible threat resulting from these postings would be the reaction of an employer who may be uncomfortable with such a presentation online.

In another case, Randy, who is married and not out to his wife, joined a gay sexual identity group on Facebook. A note appeared on his friends' pages, including his wife's, that he had joined this group. If he then chose to leave the group hoping to cover his tracks, a note would be sent that he had just left a gay group (Facebook no longer typically sends these messages). The name of the group also appears on one's page.

The internet presents quite a unique opportunity for those who desire to "come out online." Facebook allows for the individual to post their revelation for all to see, and some young people may choose this option for "coming out."

Yet others may be out in their everyday lives and out on Facebook, and then face the decision of confirming friends who did not know of their orientation, perhaps an old friend from high school or a former teacher or pastor. If they don't confirm the friend based upon this, there will likely be hard feelings. If they do, the new information will be now thrown into the mix of their relationship, sometimes changing its nature.

Facebook users may choose to allow anyone in their "network" to view their pages, or to only allow friends to do so. Still most people have a diverse group of friends entailing many aspects and realms of their lives. Recalling the quote from Goffman (1963) at the beginning of this section, Facebook presents new and different challenges, some possibly even more complicated than those before.

Collective Identity, Activism, and the Construction of Social Problems

> The Internet has done more than simply change the distribution of information and reduce the cost of movement activity and development. Perhaps the most significant contribution the Internet offers social movements is the expansion of where activism happens. The Internet has developed into more than a tactic or tool social movements employ: it has become a space—albeit a virtual one—within which organizing and activism can happen. (Shapiro 2004, p. 172)

The ability to join LGBT groups on Facebook creates access to information and resources. For many, especially those in isolated, rural areas, these groups may be the individual's first contact with others who share similar identities. Many groups post pertinent information related to LGBT political issues and community social events. In addition, members may access message boards whereby they are able to read posts by others, ask questions, and gather information. Through online communities,not only may a personal identity be tested and accepted, but the connection between the individual identity and the collective identity develops (Hunt and Benford 2004; Melucci 1995; Taylor and Whittier 1992; Valocchi 2001). The young gay person can gain a sense of not being alone and of belonging to a community larger than oneself. Through online communities and through the social and political events and activities they promote, cultural markers of community can be learned by the individual. These may include the knowledge of the rainbow flag, the pink triangle, and other symbols and customs of a community.

In addition to advertising social events in the LGBT community, these online groups also serve as valuable transmitters for issues of concern within the community itself. Many Facebook groups have developed in tribute to those who have been victims of hate crimes or abuse due to their orientations. News regarding cases such as these is often posted and sent to group members. Messages also are sent directly, in many cases, to the member's Facebook message inbox, with an email to the person alerting him or her to the presence of this message. This system has been used effectively by those who seek to mobilize regarding a social issue.

Social constructionists' views of social problems (Benford and Hunt 2003; Davis 2005; Loseke 2007; Spector and Kitsuse 1987) focus on the process by which an issue becomes considered an actual problem. According to Loseke (2007, p. 20), "social problems work is the human activity needed to construct social problems and to do something about social problems." This is because "people create meaning because meaning is not inherent in objects" (Loseke 2007, p. 25). Just as identity is negotiated, so is the process of social problems identification. Consider that issues such as child abuse, domestic violence (Loseke 2007) and hate crimes (Jenness and Broad 1997) have always existed,but only lately have they been considered a recognizable kind of social problem. For this to have occurred, claims-makers (Loseke 2007; Spector and Kitsuse 1987) have developed the concepts which portray these issues as problems, engage in framing of information and messages (Snow and Benford 1988), and attempt to attach meaning to various events and ideas in a which will be culturally specific (Loseke 2007) and resonant (Snow and Benford 1988).

Through "causes," on Facebook, anyone may create a "cause" which is of concern. They engage in framing the message of this cause, promote it to potential sympathizers, and gather supporters or "members." These practices assist in legitimating an issue as a social problem to the Facebook membership. As users join the cause, the potential for change becomes even greater. In this way, Facebook "cause" creators and their adherents work to validate issues as social problems and often offer corrective measures (e.g. petitions, rallies, boycotts, etc.). Holstein and Miller (2003, p. 78) note that "social problems work is interactive as well as rhetorical." According to Loseke (2007, p. 20) "the goal of the social problems game is to persuade people to worry about a condition and to do something to resolve it."

Joel Best (1990) once wrote that for social claims to be taken seriously, there is a competition among those claims-makers to make their issues heard. Benford and Hunt (2003) also discussed how these issues become part of the "public problems marketplace,"where "the point of most of this work is to use public arenas to persuade particular audiences to accept specific definitions of imputed problem conditions."(2003,p.155) To Best, however,"there is nothing even-handed about this competition …

> In general, the advantage belongs to the insiders, the owners of well-established social problems, with ready access to the policymakers and the media. Outsiders are at a disadvantage. Their chances are particularly remote in some arenas; legislatures are far more likely to respond to the concerns of lobbyists and other insiders than to claims from outsiders. In comparison, the media, with their constant need for fresh material ("news"), are more receptive to outsiders' claims.But because the media offer the best hope for many outsider claims-makers, the competition for media attention can be fierce. (1990, p. 16)

Facebook goes a long way toward leveling these playing fields. With Facebook, the user does not have to have access to traditional means of communication or media, he or she can develop a cause for concern, market it to its potential audience, and direct interventions from behind his or her own computer. Users have established groups to support hate crime legislation, have organized protests to California's Proposition 8 and have supported rallies for gay marriage rights. In these ways, Facebook users have subverted the traditional structures which act as gatekeepers of dissent.

Yet while Facebook has greatly increased the ability of LGBT connections and the possibilities for collective identity, social problem construction,and activism, Michael Shernoff (2006, p. 21) worries the internet is:

> ... lulling us into a false sense of security. Because if we're sitting at home, we can't be out in the street carrying signs or running the risk of getting gay-bashed outside a bar, or hearing someone yell "Faggot!" when we walk home with a lover. Are we forgetting about the realities of homophobia while we sit at home forwarding petitions or talking dirty with strangers? ... At what point do we trade our slippers in for walking shoes and go back out into the physical gay world, which has been shrinking in recent years? (Shernoff 2006, p. 21)

Sally Kohn, a community organizer, concurs. In a June 8, 2008 article for the *Christian Science Monitor,* she wrote,"Internet activism is individualistic. It's great for a sense of interconnectedness, but the Internet does not bind individuals in shared struggle the same as the face-to-face activism of the 1960s and '70s did. It allows us to channel our individual power for good, but it stops there." Kohn added that the "real challenges in our society ...won't politely go away with a few clicks of the mouse."

Are these writers identifying unique challenges presented by internet activism or are they simply nostalgic for a bygone era and underestimating the subversive impact of a new medium? Does Facebook create an entirely new way of being, complete with new norms for belonging and innovative tactics for activism?

While the arena of internet activism is certainly new and, to some degree, relatively untested, we can not deny its potential force and impact. Through its ability to connect those from geographically disparate or isolated areas, assist with the construction of a personal identity and an awareness of collective identity, its power can not be dismissed. Internet activism goes straight to the source: the potential audience. It does not have to court traditional sources of access for media-play or attention and basically subverts the hegemonic system of competition written of by Joel Best (1990).

As with anything new, there will be unforeseen challenges. The points raised by Shernoff and Kohn are valid ones. True success, while initiated in virtual space, will be measured by change in the world around us. Facebook, however, has created a place for activism to occur and has empowered those who seek to create a cause to do so, to promote it, educate about it, and enlist members. Eve Shapiro, writing of transgender activism on the internet, states that:

> There are two central ways in which the Internet has transformed transgender organizing. First, the Internet has become a tool for activists and organizations to use to reduce organizations' upstart and maintenance costs and to provide quick and efficient information distribution. Second, the Internet has become a *space* within which to facilitate networking and collective identity development and employ new tactics, leading to the further development, growth and success of the transgender movement. (Shapiro 2004, p. 171)

Conclusion

> ... with social networking sites, users are now the creators of content, and they view one another's profiles and information rather than viewing mass-produced content made by large corporations. They also became the stars of their own productions. (Pempek et al. 2009)

Facebook has created a new realm of interaction in our society. While research on internet social networking sites is still new, we can, without a doubt, assert that it has revolutionized our means of communication and our possibilities for connecting with others. Since it is such a new cultural fixture, those of us who are Facebook users create, learn, and modify norms of its use.We learn new forms of etiquette and find new ways to stay in touch with those who matter to us.

As we create our identities online, constructing ourselves as we wish others to perceive us, we clarify to ourselves who we are and what matters most to us. We ask ourselves the questions: Who do I want to be? How do I want others to see me? We create and transmit these images to others, as we interact with those which they have designed as well. Through Facebook, youth face an opportunity to construct themselves in a way unknown to prior generations of young.

For the gay individual, we see not only the opportunities for self-presentation and social networking. We also see the challenges of identity negotiation and information control. While gays and lesbians have faced these dilemmas for generations, Facebook presents an entirely new arena with no known or verifiable strategies for management. Each individual must test the waters for him- or her-self. A fertile ground for future research will be on the topic of just how LGBT individuals negotiate and manage information in these new virtual settings.

As we've seen,the internet can present a huge potential for activism. Facebook offers exciting and unique ways in which to make social change. As we have seen in this chapter, Facebook members take part in "social problems work," creating and legitimating causes in our "public problems marketplace." In these ways, Facebook offers an unprecedented opportunity for networking and activism. Anyone can create a cause, market it, and educate others. By taking the issues directly to the audiences,Facebook subverts traditional paths to social change and eliminates the hegemonic gatekeepers.

While our chapter on Facebook is not meant to be exhaustive and comprehensive, we feel that we have raised some important topics for further discussion. We hope that others will continue to research Facebook to discover how LGBT groups grow and develop, how collective identities are acquired and how Facebook has changed the nature of social activism.

As Facebook grows and matures, we will undoubtedly continue to be fascinated by its opportunities and challenges. We have entered into a reflexive relationship whereby we will be influenced while we are indeed influencing others. The LGBT community will still negotiate identities, both personally and collectively. Facebook will offer new and exciting ways to learn about ourselves, others, and the issues which most affect those under the LGBT umbrella. Our world has been changed by Facebook. No doubt it will continue to be so.

References

Benford, R. D. and Hunt, S. A. 2003. Interactional dynamics in public problems marketplaces: Movements and the counterframing and reframing of public problems. *In Challenges and choices: Constructionist perspectives on social problems,* edited by J. A. Holstein and G. Miller. Hawthorne, NY: Aldine de Gruyter: 153–186.

Best, J. 1990. *Threatened children: Rhetoric and concern about child-victims.* Chicago: University of Chicago Press.

Buhrmester, D. and Prager, K. 1995. Patterns and functions of self-disclosure during childhood and adolescence. *In Disclosure processes in children and adolescents,* edited by K. J. Rotenberg. Cambridge: Cambridge University Press, 10–56.

Cooper, M. 1990. R*ejecting femininity: Research notes on gender identity in lesbians.* Deviant Behavior 11: 371–380.

Cooper, M. 2007. What is it like to be a rural lesbian? I*n Readings in deviant behavior,* edited by A. Thio, T. Calhoun, and A. Conyers. Needham Heights, MA: Allyn and Bacon, 171–175.

Cooper, M. forthcoming. *Rural popular culture and its impact on lesbian identity.* In Queer identities/political realities, edited by K. German and B. Drushel. Oxford: Oxford Scholars Press.

Dalsgaard, S. 2008. Facework on Facebook: The presentation of self in virtual life and its role in the U.S. elections. *Anthropology Today* 24(6): 8–12.

Davis, J. E. 2005. *Accounts of innocence: Sexual abuse, trauma and the self.* Chicago: University of Chicago Press.

Ellison, N. B., Steinfield, C., and Lampe, C. 2007. The benefits of Facebook "friends": Social capital and college students' use of online social network sites. *Journal of Computer-Mediated Communication* 12(4): 1143–1168.

Facebook. 2009. http://www.facebook.com/ [Accessed August 24, 2009]

Goffman, E. 1959. *Presentation of self in everyday life.* Garden City, NY: Doubleday.

Goffman, E. 1963. *Stigma: Notes on the management of a spoiled identity.* London: Pelican Books.

Holstein, J. A. and Miller, G. 2003. Social constructionism and social problems work. In

Challenges and choices: Constructionist perspectives on social problems, edited by J. A. Holstein and G. Miller. Hawthorne, NY: Aldine de Gruyter, 70–91.

Hunt, S. A. and Benford, R. D. 2004. Collective identity, solidarity, and commitment. *In The Blackwell companion to social movements,* edited by D. A. Snow, S. A. Soule, and H. Kriesi. Malden, MA: Blackwell, 433–457.

Jenness, V. and Broad, K. 1997. *Hate crimes: New social movements and the politics of violence.* Hawthorne, NY: Aldine de Gruyter.

Kohn, S. 2008. Real change happens off-line. *Christian Science Monitor,* June 30.

Loseke, D. R. 2007 *Thinking about social problems: An introduction to constructionist perspectives.* New Brunswick, NJ and London: Aldine Transaction.

Melucci, A. 1995. The process of collective identity. *In Social movements and culture,* edited by H. Johnston and B. Klandermans. Minneapolis: University of Minnesota Press, 41–63.

Pempek, T. A., Yermolayeva, Y. A., and Calvert, S. L. 2009. College students' social networking experiences on Facebook. *Journal of Applied Developmental Psychology* 30: 227–238

Raacke, J. and Bonds-Raacke, J. 2008. MySpace and Facebook: Applying the uses and gratifications theory to exploring friend-networking sites. *Cyberpsychology and Behavior* 11(2): 169–174.

Ross, C., Orr, E. S., Arseneault, J. M., Simmering, M. G. and Orr, R. R. 2009. Personality and motivations associated with Facebook use. *Computers in Human Behavior* 25: 578–586.

Seder, J. P. and Oishi, S. 2009. Ethnic/racial homogeneity in college students' Facebook friendship networks and subjective well-being. *Journal of Research in Personality* 43: 438–443.

Shapiro, E. 2004. Transcending barriers: Transgender organizing on the internet. Journal of Gay and Lesbian Social Services 16(3/4): 165–179.

Shernoff, M. 2006. The heart of a virtual hunter. *Gay and Lesbian Review.* (January–February): 20–22.

Snow, D. A. and Benford, R. D. 1988. Ideology, frame resonance, and participant mobilization. *International Social Movement Research* 1: 197–217.

Spector, M. and Kitsuse, J. I. 1987. *Constructing social problems.* Hawthorne, NY: Aldine de Gruyter.

Steinfield, C., Ellison, N. B., and Lampe, C. 2008. Social capital, self-esteem, and use of online social network sites: A longitudinal analysis. *Journal of Applied Developmental Psychology* 29: 434–445.

Taylor, V. and Whittier, N. E. 1992. Collective identity in social movement communities: Lesbian feminist mobilization. *In Social movements: Perspectives and issues,* edited by S. M. Buechler and F. K. Cylke. Mountain View, CA: Mayfield Publishing, 505–519.

Valkenburg, P. M., Peter, J., and Schouten, A. P. 2006. Friend networking sites and their relationship to adolescents' well being and social self-esteem. *CyberPsychology* 9: 584–590.

Valocchi, S. 2001. Individual identities, collective identities, and organizational structure: The relationship of the political left and gay liberation in the United States. *Sociological Perspectives* 44(4): 445–467.

Zhao, S., Grasmuck, S., and Martin, J. 2008. Identity construction on Facebook: Digital empowerment in anchored relationships. *Computers in Human Behavior* 24: 1816–1836.

INTERSECTIONS OF CLASS, RACE, AND GENDER

When You Get Laid Off, It's Like You Lose a Part of Yourself

Making Sense of Race, Class, and Gender

Moving Past Race and Gender

WHEN YOU GET LAID OFF, IT'S LIKE YOU LOSE A PART OF YOURSELF

BY LILLIAN RUBIN

For Larry Meecham, "downsizing" is more than a trendy word on the pages of the *Wall Street Journal* or the business section of the *New York Times*. "I was with the same company for over twelve years; I had good seniority. Then all of a sudden they laid off almost half the people who worked there, closed down whole departments, including mine," he says, his troubled brown eyes fixed on some distant point as he speaks. "One day you got a job; the next day you're out of work, just like that," he concludes, shaking his head as if he still can't believe it.

Nearly 15 percent of the men in the families I interviewed were jobless when I met them. Another 20 percent had suffered episodic bouts of unemployment—sometimes related to the recession of the early 1990s, sometimes simply because job security is fragile in the blue-collar world, especially among the younger, less experienced workers. With the latest recession, however, age and experience don't count for much; every man feels at risk.

Tenuous as the situation is for white men, it's worse for men of color, especially African-Americans. The last hired, they're likely to be the first fired. And when the axe falls, they have even fewer resources than whites to help them through the tough times. "After kicking around doing shit work for a long time, I finally got a job that paid decent," explains twenty-nine-year-old George Faucett, a black father of two who lost his factory job when the company was restructured—another word that came into vogue during the economic upheaval of the 1990s. "I worked there for two years, but I didn't have seniority, so when they started to lay guys off, I was it. We never really had a chance to catch up on all the bills before it was all over," he concludes dispiritedly.

I speak of men here partly because they're usually the biggest wage earners in intact families. Therefore, when father loses his job, it's likely to be a crushing blow to the family economy. And partly, also, it's because the issues unemployment raises are different for men and for women. For most women, identity is multi-faceted, which means that the loss of a job isn't equivalent to the loss of self. No matter how invested a woman may be in her work, no matter how much her sense of self and competence are connected to it, work remains only one part of identity—a central part perhaps, especially for a professional woman, but still only a part. She's mother, wife, friend, daughter, sister—all valued facets of the self, none wholly obscuring the others. For the working-class women in this study, therefore, even those who were divorced or single mothers responsible for the support of young children, the loss of a job may have been met with pain, fear, and anxiety, but it didn't call their identity into question.

For a man, however, work is likely to be connected to the core of self. Going to work isn't just what he does, it's deeply linked to who he is. Obviously, a man is also father, husband, friend, son, brother. But these are likely to be roles he assumes, not without depth and meaning, to be sure, but not self-defining in the same way as he experiences work. Ask a man for a statement of his identity, and he'll almost always respond

Lillian Rubin, "When You Get Laid Off, It's Like You Lose a Part of Yourself," *Families on the Fault Line: America's Working Class Speaks About the Family, the Economy, Race, and Ethnicity*, pp. 103-125. Copyright © 1994 by Lillian B. Rubin. Reprinted with permission by HarperCollins Publishers.

by telling you first what he does for a living. The same question asked of a woman brings forth a less predictable, more varied response, one that's embedded in the web of relationships that are central to her life.

Some researchers studying the impact of male unemployment have observed a sequenced series of psychological responses. The first, they say, is shock, followed by denial and a sense of optimism, a belief that this is temporary, a holiday, like a hiatus between jobs rather than joblessness. This period is marked by heightened activity at home, a burst of do-it-yourself projects that had been long neglected for lack of time. But soon the novelty is gone and the projects wear thin, ushering in the second phase, a time of increasing distress, when inertia trades places with activity and anxiety succeeds denial. Now a jobless man awakens every day to the reality of unemployment. And, lest he forget, the weekly trip to the unemployment office is an unpleasant reminder. In the third phase, inertia deepens into depression, fed by feelings of identity loss, inadequacy, hopelessness, a lack of self-confidence, and a general failure of self-esteem. He's tense, irritable, and feels increasingly alienated and isolated from both social and personal relationships.

This may be an apt description of what happens in normal times. But in periods of economic crisis, when losing a job isn't a singular and essentially lonely event, the predictable pattern breaks down. During the years I was interviewing families for this book, millions of jobs disappeared almost overnight. Nearly everyone I met, therefore, knew someone—a family member, a neighbor, a friend—who was out of work. "My brother's been out of a job for a long time; now my brother-in-law just got laid off. It seems like every time I turn around, somebody's losing his job. I've been lucky so far, but it makes you wonder how long it'll last."

At such times, nothing cushions the reality of losing a job. When the unbelievable becomes commonplace and the unexpected is part of the mosaic of the times, denial is difficult and optimism impossible. Instead, any layoff, even if it's defined as temporary, is experienced immediately and viscerally as a potentially devastating, cataclysmic event.

It's always a shock when a person loses a job, of course. But disbelief? Denial? Not for those who have been living under a cloud of anxiety—those who leave work each night grateful for another day of safety, who wonder as they set off the next morning whether this is the day the axe will fall on them. "I tell my wife not to worry because she gets panicked about the bills. But the truth is, I stew about it plenty. The economy's gone to hell; guys are out of work all around me. I'd be nuts if I wasn't worried."

It's true that when a working-class man finds himself without a job he'll try to keep busy with projects around the house. But these aren't undertaken in the kind of holiday spirit earlier researchers describe. Rather, building a fence, cleaning the garage, painting the family room, or the dozens of other tasks that might occupy him are a way of coping with his anxiety, of distracting himself from the fears that threaten to overwhelm him, of warding off the depression that lurks just below the surface of his activity. Each thrust of the saw, each blow of the hammer helps to keep the demons at bay. "Since he lost his job, he's been out there hammering away at one thing or another like a maniac," says Janet Kovacs, a white thirty-four-year-old waitress. "First it was the fence; he built the whole thing in a few days. Then it was fixing the siding on the garage. Now he's up on the roof. He didn't even stop to watch the football game last Sunday."

Her husband, Mike, a cement finisher, explains it this way: "If I don't keep busy, I feel like I'll go nuts. It's funny," he says with a caustic, ironic laugh, "before I got laid off my wife was always complaining about me watching the ball games; now she keeps nagging me to watch. What do you make of that, huh? I guess she's trying to make me feel better."

"Why didn't you watch the game last Sunday?" I ask.

"I don't know, maybe I'm kind of scared if I sit down there in front of that TV, I won't want to get up again," he replies, his shoulders hunched, his fingers raking his hair. "Besides, when I was working, I figured I had a right."

His words startled me, and I kept turning them over in my mind long after he spoke them: "When I was working, I figured I had a right." It's a sentence any of the unemployed men I met might have uttered. For it's in getting up and going to work every day that they feel they've earned the right to their manhood, to their place in the world, to the respect of their family, even the right to relax with a sporting event on TV.

It isn't that there are no gratifying moments, that getting laid off has no positive side at all. When unemployment first hits, family members usually gather around to offer support, to buoy a man's spirits and their own. Even in families where conflict is high, people tend to come together, at least at the beginning. "Considering that we weren't getting along so well before, my wife was really good about it when I got laid off," says Joe Phillips, an unemployed black truck driver. "She gave me a lot of support at first, and I appreciate it."

"You said 'at first.' Has that changed?" I ask.

"Hell, yes. It didn't last long. But maybe I can't blame it all on her. I've been no picnic to live with since I got canned."

In families with young children, there may be a period of relief—for the parents, the relief of not having to send small children off to child care every day, of knowing that one of them is there to welcome the children when they come home from school; for the children, the exhilarating novelty of having a parent, especially daddy, at home all day. "The one good thing about him not working is that there's someone home with the kids now," says twenty-five-year-old Gloria Lewis, a black hairdresser whose husband has been unemployed for just a few weeks. "That part's been a godsend. But I don't know what we'll do if he doesn't find work soon. We can't make it this way."

Teenagers, too, sometimes speak about the excitement of having father around at first. "It was great having my dad home when he first got laid off," says Kevin Sollars, a white fourteen-year-old. "We got to do things together after school sometimes. He likes to build ship models—old sailing ships. I don't know why, but he never wanted to teach me how to do it. He didn't even like it when I just wanted to watch; he'd say, 'Haven't you got something else to do?' But when he first got laid off, it was different. When I'd come home from school and he was working on a ship, he'd let me help him."

But the good times usually don't last long. "After a little while, he got really grumpy and mean, jumped on everybody over nothing," Kevin continues. "My mom used to say we had to be patient because he was so worried about money and all that. Boy, was I glad when he went back to work."

Fathers may also tell of the pleasure in getting to spend time with their children, in being a part of their daily life in ways unknown before. "There's a silver lining in every cloud, I guess. I got to know my kids like I never did before," says Kevin's father, who felt the sting of unemployment for seven months before he finally found another job. "It's just that being out of work gets old pretty fast. I ran out of stuff to do around the house; we were running out of money; and there I was sitting on my keister and stewing all day long while my wife was out working. I couldn't even enjoy building my little ships."

Once in a while, especially for a younger man, getting laid off or fired actually opens up the possibility of a new beginning. "I figured, what the hell, if I'm here, I might as well learn how to cook," says twenty-eight-year-old Darnell Jones, a black father of two who, until he was laid off, had worked steadily but always at relatively menial, low-paying jobs in which he had little interest or satisfaction. "Turned out I liked to cook, got to be real good at it, too, better than my wife," he grins proudly. "So then we talked about it and decided there was no sense in sitting around waiting for something to happen when there were no good jobs out there, especially for a black man, and we figured I should go to cooking school and learn how to do it professionally. Now I've got this job as a cook; it's only part-time, right now, but the pay's pretty good, and I think maybe I'll go full-time soon. If I could get regular work, maybe we could even save some money and I could open my own restaurant someday. That's what I really want to do."

But this outcome is rare, made possible by the fact that Darnell's wife has a middle-management position in a large corporation that pays her $38,000 a year. His willingness to try something new was a factor, of course. But that, too, was grounded in what was possible. In most young working-class families of any color or ethnic group, debts are high, savings are nonexistent, and women don't earn nearly enough to bail the family out while the men go into a training program to learn new skills. A situation that doesn't offer much encouragement for a man to dream, let alone to believe his dream could be realized.

As I have already indicated, the struggles around the division of labor shift somewhat when father loses his job. The man who's home all day while his wife goes off to work can't easily justify maintaining the traditional household gender roles. Therefore, many of the unemployed men pick up tasks that were formerly left to their wives alone. "I figure if she's working and I'm not, I ought to take up some of the slack around here. So I keep the place up, run the kids around if they need it, things like that," says twenty-nine-year-old Jim Andersen, a white unemployed electrician.

As wives feel their household burdens eased, the strains that are almost always a part of life in a two-job family are somewhat relieved. "Maybe it sounds crazy to you, but my life's so much easier since he's out of work, I wish it could stay this way," says Jim's wife, Loreen, a twenty-nine-year-old accounting clerk. "If only I could make enough money, I'd be happy for him to stay home and play Mr. Mom."

But it's only a fantasy—first because she can't make enough money; second, and equally important, because while she likes the relief from household responsibilities, she's also uneasy about such a dramatic shift in family roles. So in the next breath, Loreen says, "I worry about him, though. He doesn't feel so good about himself being unemployed and playing house."

"Is it only him you worry about? Or is there something that's hard for you, too?" I ask.

She's quiet for a moment, then acknowledges that her feelings are complicated: "I'm not sure what I think anymore. I mean, I don't think it's fair that men always have to be the support for the family; it's too hard for them sometimes. And I don't mind working; I really don't. In fact, I like it a lot better than being home with the house and the kids all the time. But I guess deep down I still have that old-fashioned idea that it's a man's job to support his family. So, yeah, then I begin to feel—I don't know how to say it—uncomfortable, right here inside me," she says, pointing to her midsection, "like maybe I won't respect him so much if he can't do that. I mean, it's okay for now," she hastens to reassure me, perhaps herself as well. "But if it goes on for a real long time like with some men, then I think I'll feel different."

Men know their wives feel this way, even when the words are never spoken, which only heightens their own anxieties about being unemployed. "Don't get me wrong; I'm glad she has her job. I don't know what we'd do if she wasn't working," says Jim. "It's just that ... ," he hesitates, trying to frame his thoughts clearly. "I know this is going to sound pretty male, but it's my job to take care of this family. I mean, it's great that she can help out, but the responsibility is mine, not hers. She won't say so, but I know she feels the same way, and I don't blame her."

It seems, then, that no matter what the family's initial response is, whatever the good moments may be, the economic and psychological strains that attend unemployment soon overwhelm the good intentions on all sides. "It's not just the income; you lose a lot more than that," says Marvin Reed, a forty-year-old white machinist, out of work for nearly eight months. He pauses, reflects on his words, then continues. "When you get laid off, it's like you lose a part of yourself. It's terrible; something goes out of you. Then, on top of that, by staying home and not going to work and associating with people of your own level, you begin to lose the sharpness you developed at work. Everything gets slower; you move slower; your mind works slower.

"It's a real shocker to realize that about yourself, to feel like you're all slowed down and ... ," he hesitates again, this time to find the words. "I don't know how to explain it exactly, maybe like your mind's pushing a load of mud around all the time," he concludes, his graying head bowed so as not to meet my eyes.

"Everything gets slower"—a sign of the depression that's so often the unwelcome companion of unemployment. As days turn into weeks and weeks into months, it gets harder and harder to believe in a future. "I've been working since I was fourteen," says Marvin, "and I was never out of work for more than a week or two before. Now I don't know; I don't know when I'll get work again. The jobs are gone. How do you find a job when there's none out there anymore?"

The men I talked with try to remind themselves that it's not their fault, that the layoffs at the plant have nothing to do with them or their competence, that it's all part of the economic problems of the nation. But it's hard not to doubt themselves, not to wonder whether there's something else they could have done, something they might have foreseen and planned for. "I don't know; I keep thinking I could have done something different," says Lou Coltrane, a black twenty-eight-year-old auto worker, as he looks away to hide his pain. "I know it's crazy; they closed most of the plant. But, you know, you can't help thinking, maybe this, maybe that. It keeps going round and round in my head:

Maybe I should have done this; maybe I should have done that. Know what I mean?"

But even when they can accept the reality that they had no control over the situation, there's little surcease in the understanding. Instead, such thoughts increase their feelings of vulnerability and helplessness—feelings no one accepts easily. "I worked nineteen years for this damned company and how do they pay me back?" asks Eric Hueng, a forty-four-year-old unemployed Asian factory worker, as he leaves his chair and paces the room in a vain attempt to escape his torment. "They move the plant down to some godforsaken place in South America where people work for peanuts and you got no choice but to sit there and watch it happen. Even the government doesn't do a damn thing about it. They just sit back and let it happen, so how could I do anything?" he concludes, his words etched in bitterness.

For American men—men who have been nurtured and nourished in the belief that they're masters of their fate—it's almost impossible to bear such feelings of helplessness. So they find themselves in a cruel double bind. If they convince themselves that their situation is beyond their control, there's nothing left but resignation and despair. To fight their way but of the hopelessness that follows, they begin to blame themselves. But this only leaves them, as one man said, "kicking myself around the block"—kicks that, paradoxically, allow them to feel less helpless and out of control, while they also send them deeper into depression, since now it's no one's fault but their own.

"I can't believe what a fool I was," says Paul Santos, a forty-six-year-old Latino tool and die maker, his fingers drumming the table nervously as he speaks. "I was with this one company for over fifteen years, then this other job came along a couple of years ago. It seemed like a good outfit, solid, and it was a better job, more money and all. I don't know what happened; I guess they got overextended. All I know is they laid off 30 percent of the company without a day's notice. Now I feel stupid; if I had stayed where I was, I'd still be working."

Shame, too, makes an appearance, adding to the self-blame, to Paul's feeling that he did something wrong, something stupid—that if he'd somehow been better, smarter, more prescient, the outcome would be different. And the depression deepens. "I've been working all my life. Now it's like I've got nothing left," Paul explains, his eyes downcast, his voice choked with emotion. "When you work, you associate with a group of people you respect. Now you're not part of the group anymore; you don't belong anywhere. Except," he adds with disgust, "on the unemployment line."

"Now that's a sad sight, all these guys shuffling around, nobody looking at anybody else. Every time I go there, I think, *Hey, what the hell am I doing here? I don't belong here, not with these people. They're deadbeats.* Then I think, *Yeah, well you're here, so it looks like you're no better than them, doesn't it?*"

Like so many other men, Paul hasn't just lost a job; he's lost a life. For his job meant more than a living wage. It meant knowing he had an identity and a place in the world—a place where his competence was affirmed, where he had friends who respected and admired him, men with whom he could share both the frustrations and satisfactions of life on the job.

It's not just for men that the job site is a mirror in which they see themselves reflected, a mirror that reflects back an image that reassures them that they're valued contributors to the social world in which they live. It functions this way for all of us. But it's particularly important for men because when the job disappears, all this goes too, including the friendships that were so important in the validation of the self.

In my earlier research on friendship, the men I interviewed spoke repeatedly about how, once they left the job, they lost contact with the friends they had made at work. Sometimes these men acknowledged that it was "out of sight, out of mind." But others insisted that, even though they might never see each other again, these friendships represented lasting bonds. "Maybe they don't continue to see each other once the activity [or job] doesn't keep them together," said one man I interviewed then, "but that doesn't mean they don't share very deep and lasting bonds, does it?"[10] Perhaps. But the bonds, if they exist, can't replace the face-to-face interactions that are so important to the maintenance of the self.

"I don't see anybody anymore," mourns Bill Costas, a thirty-four-year-old unemployed white meat packer who had worked in the same plant for nine years. "The guys I worked with were my buddies; after all those years of working together, they were my friends. We'd go out after work and have a beer and shoot the bull. Now I don't even know what they're doing anymore."

For wives and children, it's both disturbing and frightening to watch husband and father sink ever deeper into despair. "Being out of work is real hard on him; it's hard to see him like this, so sad and jumpy all the time," laments Bill's wife, Eunice, a part-time bank teller who's anxiously looking for full-time work. "He's always been a good provider, never out of work hardly a day since we got married. Then all of a sudden this happens. It's like he lost his self-respect when he lost that job."

His self-respect and also the family's medical benefits, since Eunice doesn't qualify for benefits in her part-time job. "The scariest part about Bill being out of a job is we don't have any medical insurance anymore. My daughter got pneumonia real bad last winter and I had to borrow money from my sister for the doctor bill and her medicine. Just the medicine was almost $100. The doctor wanted to put her in the hospital, but we couldn't because we don't have any health insurance."

Her husband recalls his daughter's illness, in a voice clogged with rage and grief. "Do you know what it's like listening to your kid when she can't breathe and you can't send her to the hospital because you lost your benefits when you got laid off?"

In such circumstances, some men just sit, silent, turned inward, enveloped in the gray fog of depression from which they can't rouse themselves. "I leave to go to work in the morning and he's sitting there doing nothing, and when I come home at night, it's the same thing. It's like he didn't move the whole day," worries thirty-four-year-old Deidre Limage, the wife of a black factory worker who has been jobless for over a year.

Other men defend against feeling the pain, fear, and sadness, covering them over with a flurry of activity, with angry, defensive, often irrational outbursts at wife and children—or with some combination of the two. As the financial strain of unemployment becomes crushing, everyone's fears escalate. Wives, unable to keep silent, give voice to their concerns. Their husbands, unable to tolerate what they hear as criticism and blame—spoken or not—lash out. "It seems like the more you try to pull yourself up, the more you get pushed back down," sighs Beverly Coleride, a white twenty-five-year-old cashier with two children, whose husband has worked at a variety of odd jobs in their seven-year marriage. "No matter how hard we try, we can't seem to set everything right. I don't know what we're going to do now; we don't have next month's rent. If Kenny doesn't get something steady real quick, we could be on the street."

"We could be on the street"—a fear that clutches at the hearts and gnaws at the souls of the families in this study, not only those who are unemployed. Nothing exemplifies the change in the twenty years since I last studied working class families than the fear of being "on the street". Then, homelessness was something that happened somewhere else, in India or some other far-off and alien land. Then, we wept when we read about the poor people who lived on the streets in those other places. *What kind of society doesn't provide this most basic of life's needs?* we asked ourselves. Now, the steadily increasing numbers of homeless in our own land have become an ever-present and frightening reminder of just how precarious life in this society can be. Now, they're in our face, on our streets, an accepted category of American social life—"the homeless."

Just how readily accepted they are was brought home to me recently when my husband, who volunteers some time in the San Francisco schools, reported his experience with a sixth-grade class there. He had been invited to talk to the children about career opportunities and, in doing so, talked about his own past as a restaurateur. The students listened, engrossed. But instead of the questions he had expected when he finished, they were preoccupied with how he managed the problem of the homeless. Did he feed homeless people when they asked for food, they wanted to know. He explained that at the time he had restaurants in the Bay Area, there were no homeless on the streets. Undaunted, they wanted to know what he did when he found a homeless person sleeping in the doorway of the restaurant. He reminded them that he had just told them that homelessness wasn't an issue when he was in business. They listened, he said, but they couldn't really grasp the idea of a world without the homeless. How could it be otherwise? At their age, homelessness is so much a part of their daily world that they take it for granted, a phenomenon not of their time but of all times.

As homelessness has increased, even those of us who remember when it was unthinkable have become inured to the sight of the men and women who make their home on the streets. Inured, and also anxious. We recoil as we walk by, trying not to see, unable to meet their eyes, ashamed of our own good fortune, anger and sympathy tugging us in opposite directions. Neither feels good. The anger is a challenge to our belief that we're kind, humane, caring. But the sympathy is even more threatening. To allow ourselves to feel compassion is to open the floodgates of our own vulnerability, of our denied understanding of how delicately our lives and fortunes are balanced.

For Beverly Coleride, as for the other women and men I met, sustaining the denial has become increasingly difficult. No matter how much they want to obliterate the images of the homeless from consciousness, the specter haunts them, a frightening reminder of what's possible if they trip and fall. Perhaps it's because there's so much at stake now, because the unthinkable has become a reality, that anxieties escalate so quickly. So as Beverly contemplates the terror of being "on the street," she begins to blame her husband. "I keep telling myself it's not his fault, but it's real hard not to let it get you down. So then I think, well, maybe he's not trying hard enough, and I get on his case, and he gets mad, and, well, I guess you know the rest," she concludes with a harsh laugh that sounds more like a cry of pain.

She doesn't *want* to hurt her husband, but she can't tolerate feeling so helpless and out of control. If it's his fault rather than the workings of some impersonal force, then he can do something about it. For her husband, it's an impossible bind. "I keep trying, looking for something, but there's nothing out there, leastwise not for me. I don't know what to do anymore; I've tried everything, every place I know," he says disconsolately.

But he, too, can't live easily with such feelings of helplessness. His sense of his manhood, already under threat because he can't support his family, is eroded further by his wife's complaints. So he turns on her in anger: "It's hard enough being out of work, but then my wife gets on my case, yakking all the time about how we're going to be on the street if I don't get off my butt, like it's my fault or something that there's no work out there. When she starts up like that, I swear I want to hit her, anything just to shut her mouth," he says, his shoulders tensed, his fists clenched in an unconscious expression of his rage.

"And do you?" I ask.

The tension breaks; he laughs. "No, not yet. I don't know; I don't want to," he says, his hand brushing across his face. "But I get mad enough so I could. Jesus, doesn't she know I feel bad enough? Does she have to make it worse by getting on me like that? Maybe you could clue her, would you?"

"Maybe you could clue her"—a desperate plea for someone to intervene, to save him from his own rageful impulses. For Kenny Coleride isn't a violent man. But the stress and conflict in families where father loses his job can give rise to the kind of interaction described here, a dynamic that all too frequently ends in physical assaults against women and children.

Some kind of violence—sometimes against children only, more often against both women and children—is the admitted reality of life in about 14 percent of the families in this study. I say "admitted reality" because this remains one of the most closely guarded secrets in family life. So it's reasonable to assume that the proportion of families victimized by violence could be substantially higher.

Sometimes my questions about domestic violence were met with evasion: "I don't really know anything about that."

Sometimes there was outright denial, even when I could see the evidence with my own eyes: "I was visiting my sister the other day, and I tripped and fell down the steps in front of her house."

And sometimes teenage children, anguished about what they see around them, refused to participate in the cover-up. "I bet they didn't tell you that he beats my mother up, did they? Nobody's allowed to talk about it; we're supposed to pretend like it doesn't happen. I hate him; I could kill him when he does that to her. My mom, she says he can't help it; it's because he's so upset since he got fired. But that's just her excuse now. I mean, yeah, maybe it's worse than it was before, but he did it before, too. I don't understand. Why does she let him do it to her?"

"Why does she let him do it to her?" A question the children in these families are not alone in asking, one to which there are few satisfactory answers. But one thing is clear: The depression men suffer and their struggle against it significantly increase the probability of alcohol abuse, which in turn makes these kinds of eruptions more likely to occur.

"My father's really changed since he got laid off," complains Buddy Truelman, the fifteen-year-old son of an unemployed white steel worker. "It's like he's always mad about something, you know, ready to bite your head off over nothing. I mean, he's never been an at-ease guy, but now nothing you do is okay with him; he's always got something to say, like he butts in where it's none of his business, and if you don't jump to, he gets mad as hell, carries on like a crazy man." He pauses, shifts nervously in his chair, then continues angrily, "He and my mom are always fighting, too. It's a real pain. I don't hang around here any more than I have to."

Buddy's mother, Sheila, a thirty-four-year-old telephone operator, echoes her son. "He's so touchy; you can't say anything without him getting mad. I don't mind so much if he takes it out on me, but he's terrible to the kids, especially to my son. That's when I get mad," she explains, passing a hand over her worried brow. "He's got no right to beat up on that kid the way he does."

"Do you mean he actually hits him?" I ask.

She hesitates and looks away, the torment of memory etched on her face. Finally, brushing away the tears that momentarily cloud her vision, she replies, "Yeah, he has. The last time he did it, he really hurt him—twisted his arm so bad it nearly broke—and I told him I'd leave if he ever hit Buddy again. So it's been okay for a while. But who knows? He has a few beers and it's like he goes crazy, like he can't control himself or something."

Many of the unemployed men admit turning to alcohol to relieve the anxiety, loneliness, and fear they experience as they wait day after day, week after week for, as one man put it, "something to happen." "You begin to feel as if you're going nuts, so you drink a few beers to take the edge off," explains thirty-seven-year-old Bill Anstett, a white unemployed construction worker.

It seems so easy. A few beers and he gets a respite from his unwanted feelings—fleeting, perhaps, but effective in affording some relief from the suffering they inflict. But a few beers often turn out to be enough to allow him to throw normal constraints to the wind. For getting drunk can be a way of absenting the conscious self so that it can't be held responsible for actions undertaken. Indeed, this may be as much his unconscious purpose as the need to rid himself of his discomfort. "I admit it, sometimes it's more than a few and I fall over the edge," Bill grants. "My wife, she tells me it's like I turn into somebody else, but I don't know about that because I never remember."

With enough alcohol, inhibitions can be put on hold; conscience can go underground. "It's the liquor talking," we say when we want to exempt someone from responsibility for word or deed. The responsibility for untoward behavior falls to the effects of the alcohol. The self is in the clear, absolved of any wrongdoing. So it is with domestic violence and alcohol. When a man gets drunk, the inner voice that speaks his failure and shame is momentarily stilled. Most men just relax gratefully into the relief of the internal quiet. But the man who becomes violent needs someone to blame, someone onto whom he can project the feelings that cause him such misery. Alcohol helps. It gives him license to find a target. With enough of it, the doubts and recriminations that plague him are no longer his but theirs—his wife's, his children's; "them" out there, whoever they may be. With enough of it, there's nothing to stay his hand when his helpless rage boils over. "I don't know what happens. It's like something I can't control comes over me. Then afterward I feel terrible," Peter DiAngelo, an unemployed thirty-two-year-old truck driver, says remorsefully.

One-fifth of the men in this study have a problem with alcohol, not all of them unemployed. Nor is domestic violence perfectly correlated with either alcohol abuse or unemployment. But the combination is a potentially deadly one that exponentially increases the likelihood that a man will act out his anger on the bodies of his wife and children. "My husband drinks a lot more now; I mean, he always drank some, but not like now," says Inez Reynoso, a twenty-eight-year-old Latina nurse's aide and mother of three children who is disturbed about her husband's mistreatment of their youngest, child, a three-year-old boy. "I guess he tries to drink away his troubles, but it only makes more trouble. I tell him, but he doesn't listen. He has a fiery temper, always has. But since he lost his job, it's real bad, and his drinking doesn't help it none.

"I worry about it; he treats my little boy so terrible. He's always had a little trouble with the boy because he's not one of those big, strong kids. He's not like my older kids; he's a timid one, still wakes up scared and crying a lot in the night. Before he got fired, my husband just didn't pay him much attention. But now he's always picking on him; it's like he can't stand having him around. So he makes fun of him something terrible, or he punches him around."

The mother in me recoils at Inez's story. But the psychotherapist understands at least something of what motivates Ramon Reynoso's assault on his young son. For this father, this man who's supposed to be the pillar on which the family rests, who defines himself as a man by his ability to support his family, the sight of this weak and puny little boy is like holding up a mirror to his now powerless self. Unable to tolerate the feelings of self-hatred the image engenders, he projects them outward, onto the child, and rains blows down on him in an effort to distance himself from his own sense of loss and diminishment.

"Does he hit you, too?" I ask Inez.

She squirms in her chair; her fingers pick agitatedly at her jeans. I wait quietly, watching as she shakes her head no. But when she speaks, the words say something else. "He did a couple of times lately, but only when he had too many beers. He didn't mean it. It's just that he's so upset about being out of work, so then when he thinks I protect the boy too much he gets real mad."

When unemployment strikes, sex also becomes an increasingly difficult issue between wives and husbands. A recent study in Great Britain found that the number of couples seeking counseling for sexual problems increased in direct proportion to the rise in the unemployment rate. Anxiety, fear, anger, depression—all emotions that commonly accompany unemployment—are not generators of sexual desire. Sometimes it's the woman whose ardor cools because she's frightened about the future: "I'm so scared all the time, I can't think about sex." Or because she's angry with her husband: "He's supposed to be supporting us and look where we are." More often it's the men who lose their libido along with their jobs—a double whammy for them since male identity rests so heavily in their sexual competence as well as in their work.

This was the one thing the men in this study couldn't talk about. I say "couldn't" because it seemed so clearly more than just "wouldn't." Psychologically, it was nearly impossible for them to formulate the words and say them aloud. They had no trouble complaining about their wives' lack of sexual appetite. But when it was they who lost interest or who become impotent, it was another matter. Then, their tongues were stilled by overwhelming feelings of shame, by the terrible threat their impotence posed to the very foundation of their masculinity.

Their wives, knowing this, are alarmed about their flagging sex lives, trying to understand what happened, wondering what they can do to be helpful. "Sex used to be a big thing for him, but since he's been out of work, he's hardly interested anymore," Dale Meecham, a white thirty-five-year-old waitress says, her anxiety palpable in the room. "Sometimes when we try to do it, he can't, and then he acts like it's the end of the world—depressed and moody, and I can't get near him. It's scary. He won't talk about it, but I can see it's eating at him. So I worry a lot about it. But I don't know what to do, because if I try to, you know, seduce him and it doesn't work, then it only makes things worse."

The financial and emotional turmoil that engulfs families when a man loses his job all too frequently pushes marriages that were already fragile over the brink. Among the families in this study, 10 percent attributed their ruptured marriages directly to the strains that accompanied unemployment. "I don't know, maybe we could have made it if he hadn't lost his job," Maryanne Wallace, a twenty-eight-year-old white welfare mother, says sadly. "I mean, we had problems before, but we were managing. Then he got laid off, and he couldn't find another job, and, I don't know, it was like he went crazy. He was drinking; he hit me; he was mean to the kids. There was no talking to him, so I left, took the kids and went home to my mom's. I thought maybe I'd just give him a scare, you know, be gone for a few days. But when I came back, he was gone, just gone. Nobody's seen him for nearly a year," she says, her voice limping to a halt as if she still can't believe her own story.

Economic issues alone aren't responsible for divorce, of course, as is evident when we look at the 1930s. Then, despite the economic devastation wrought by the Great Depression, the divorce rate didn't rise. Indeed, it was probably the economic privations of that period that helped to keep marriages intact. Since it was so difficult to maintain one household, few people could consider the possibility of having to support two.

But these economic considerations exist today as well, yet recent research shows that when family income drops 25 percent, divorce rises by more than 10 percent. Culture and the institutions of our times make a difference. Then, divorce was a stigma. Now, it's part of the sociology and psychology of the age, an acceptable remedy for the disappointment of our dreams.

Then, too, one-fourth of the work force was unemployed—an economic disaster that engulfed the whole nation. In such cataclysmic moments, the events outside the family tend to overtake and supersede the discontents inside. Now, unemployment is spottier, located largely in the working class, and people feel less like they're in the middle of a social catastrophe than a personal one. Under such circumstances, it's easier to act out their anger against each other.

And finally, the social safety net that came into being after the Great Depression—social security, unemployment benefits, public aid programs targeted specifically to single-parent families—combined with the increasing numbers of women in the work force to make divorce more feasible economically.

Are there no families, then, that stick together and get through the crisis of unemployment without all this trauma? The answer? Of course there are. But they're rare. And they manage it relatively well only if the layoff is short and their resources are long.

Almost always, these are older families where the men have a long and stable work history and where there are fewer debts, some savings, perhaps a home they can refinance. But even among these relatively privileged ones, the pressures soon begin to take their toll. "We did okay for a while, but the longer it lasts, the harder it gets," says forty-six-year-old Karen Brownstone, a white hotel desk clerk whose husband, Dan, lost his welding job nearly six months ago. "After the kids were grown, we finally managed to put some money by. Dan even did some investments, and we made some money. But we're using it up very fast, and I get real scared. What are we going to do when his unemployment runs out?

"I tell him maybe he has to get in a different line of work because maybe they don't need so many welders anymore. But he just gets mad and tells me I don't know what I'm talking about. Then there's no point talking to him at all; he just stamps around and hollers. Or else he leaves, gets in the car and goes screeching away. But I *do* know what I'm talking about. I read in the paper about how these companies are cutting back, and they're not going to need so many workers anymore. He knows it, too; he reads the paper all the time. He just won't try something else; it's like he's too proud or something."

When I talk with Karen's husband, Dan, he leans forward in his chair and says angrily, "I can't go out and get one of those damn flunky jobs like my wife wants me to. I've been working all my life, making a decent living, too, and I got pride in what I do. I try to tell her, but she won't listen." He stops, sighs, puts his head in his hands and speaks more softly: "I'm the only one in my whole family who was doing all right; I even helped my son go to college. I was proud of that; we all were. Now what do I do? It's like I have to go back to where I started. How can you do that at my age?"

He pauses again, looks around the room with an appraising eye, and asks: "What's going to happen to us? I know my wife's scared; that's why she's on my case so much. I worry, too, but what can I do if there's no work? Even she doesn't think I should go sling hamburgers at McDonald's for some goddamn minimum wage."

"There's something between minimum wage jobs and the kind you had before you were laid off, isn't there?" I remark.

"Yeah, I know; you sound like her now," he says, his features softening into a small smile. "But I can't, not yet. I feel like I've got to be ready in case something comes up. Meanwhile, it's not like I'm just sitting around doing nothing. I've hustled up some odd jobs, building things for people, so I pick up a little extra change on the side every now and then. It's not a big deal, but it helps, especially since it doesn't get reported. I don't know, I suppose if things get bad enough, I'll have to do something else. But," he adds, his anger rising again, "dammit, why should I? The kind of jobs you're talking about pay half what I was making. How are we supposed to live on that, tell me that, will you?"

Eventually, men like Dan Brownstone who once held high-paying skilled jobs have no choice but to pocket their pride and take a step down to another kind of work, to one of the service jobs that usually pay a fraction of their former earnings—that is, if they're lucky enough to find one. It's never easy in our youth-oriented society for a man past forty to move to another job or another line of work. But it becomes doubly difficult in times of economic distress when the pool of younger workers is so large and so eager. "Either you're overqualified or you're over the hill," Ed Kruetsman, a forty-nine-year-old unemployed white factory worker, observes in a tired voice.

But young or old, when a man is forced into lower-paying, less skilled work, the move comes with heavy costs—both economic and psychological. Economically, it means a drastic reduction in the family's way of life. "Things were going great. We worked hard, but we finally got enough together so we could buy a house that had enough room for all of us," says thirty-six-year-old Nadine Materie, a white data processor in a bank clearing center. "Tina, my oldest girl, even had her own room; she was so happy about it. Then my husband lost his job, and the only thing he could find was one that pays a lot less, *a lot less*. On his salary now we just couldn't make the payments. We had no choice; we had to sell out and move. Now look at this place!" she commands, with a dismissive sweep of her hand. Then, as we survey the dark, cramped quarters into which this family of five is now jammed, she concludes tearfully, "I hate it, every damn inch of it; I hate it."

For Tina Materie, Nadine's fifteen-year-old daughter, her father's lost job has meant more than the loss of her room. The comforts and luxuries of the past are gone, and the way of fife she once took for granted seems like a dream. For a teenager whose sense of self and place in the world is so heavily linked to peer group acceptance and to, in Tina's own words, "being like the other kids," the loss is staggering. "We can't afford anything anymore; and I mean *anything*," she announces dramatically. "I don't even go to the mall with the other kids because they've got money to buy things and I don't. I haven't bought a new record since we moved here. Now my mom says I can't get new school clothes this year; I have to wear my cousin's hand-me-downs. How am I going to go to school in those ugly things? It's bad enough being in this new school, but now … ," she stops, unable to find the words to express her misery.

Worst of all for the children in the Materie family, the move from house to apartment took them to a new school in a distant neighborhood, far from the friends who had been at the center of their lives. "My brother and me, we hate living here," Tina says, her eyes misting over as she speaks. "Both of us hate the kids who live around here. They're different, not as nice as the kids where we used to live. They're tough, and I'm not used to it. Sometimes I think I'll quit school and get a job and go live where I want," she concludes gloomily.

Psychologically, the loss of status can be almost as difficult to bear as the financial strain. "I used to drive a long-distance rig, but the company I worked for went broke," explains Greg Northsen, a thirty-four-year-old white man whose wife is an office worker. "I was out of work for eleven and a half months. Want to know how many days that is? Maybe, how many hours? I counted every damn one," he quips acidly.

"After all that time, I was ready to take whatever I could get. So now I work as an orderly in a nursing home. Instead of cargo, I'm hauling old people around. The pay's shit and it's damn dirty work. They don't treat those old people good. Everybody's always impatient with them, ordering them around, screaming at them, talking to them like they're dumb kids or something. But with three kids to feed, I've got no choice."

He stops talking, stares wordlessly at some spot on the opposite wall for a few moments, then, his eyes clouded with unshed tears, he rakes his fingers through his hair and says hoarsely, "It's goddamn hard. This is no kind of a job for a guy like me. It's not just the money; it's …" He hesitates, searching for the words, then, "It's like I got chopped off at the knees, like … aw, hell, I don't know how to say it." Finally, with a hopeless shrug, he concludes, "What's the use? It's no use talking about it. It makes no damn difference; nothing's going to make a difference. I don't understand it. What the hell's happening to this country when there's no decent jobs for men who want to work?"

Companies go bankrupt; they merge; they downsize; they restructure; they move—all reported as part of the economic indicators, the cold statistics that tell us how the economy is doing. But each such move means more loss, more suffering, more families falling victim to the despair that comes when father loses his job, more people shouting in rage and torment: "What the hell's happening to this country?"

MAKING SENSE OF RACE, CLASS, AND GENDER

The Discursive Construction of Class

BY CELINE-MARIE PASCALE

The gap between rich and poor in the United States has arguably exceeded the capacity to sustain meaningful democracy. Congressional Budget Office data show that, after adjusting for inflation, the average after-tax income of the top one percent of the population rose by $576,000—or 201 percent—between 1979 and 2000; the average income of the middle fifth of households rose $5,500, or 15 percent; and the average income of the bottom fifth rose $1,100, or 9 percent (Center on Budget and Policy Priorities 2003).[1] In daily, life this disparity is embodied in the struggles of African American, Native American, Native Alaskan, and Hispanic families that, according to the U.S. Census, have *median* household incomes $10–20,000 below government-based calculations for self-sufficiency. The disparity also is embodied in the struggles faced by 40 percent of poor single-parent working mothers who paid at least half of their income for child care in 2001(Center on Budget and Policy Priorities 2003); in the struggles of 4.9 million families who paid half of their income in rent in 2002 (National Alliance to End Homelessness 2002); and, in the struggles of more than 3.7 million adults with disabilities living on federal Supplemental Security Income (SSI), which now provides less than one-third the income needed for a one-bedroom apartment (O'Hara and Cooper 2003:11). Minimum-wage workers, in 2002, were unable to afford a one-bedroom apartment in any city in the nation. If the increase in poverty is apparent, the tremendous increase in wealth accruing to the top 1% of the population is more extremely hard to track. While conditions of poverty may make the evening news, thorough reports on conditions of affluence are more unusual. The affluence and poverty that variously shape life in the United States are not part of a sustained or routine public conversation. In the United States, economic inequality—arguably one of the most *material* sites of "difference"—is often one of the least visible.

If commonsense leads people to believe that we can recognize race and gender on sight, even if we might sometimes find ourselves confused or mistaken, commonsense about class operates quite differently. While people living in the extreme poverty of homeless make class visually recognizable, generally class is not apparent "just by looking" at a person, or in passing encounters. The presence of people who are homeless is arguably the most consistently clear display of class in daily life. If the observable presence of race and gender means that each can be made relevant at potentially any moment, the relative invisibility of class renders it far less likely to be made relevant.

I do not mean to suggest that wealth and poverty are simply a matter of language and representation but rather, I argue that because material conditions and discursive practices are not distinct, understandings of class need to be rooted to language, as well as economics. All objects and events are made meaningful through language. An earthquake may be understood as a geological phenomenon or an act of god; a stone may be a marker, a sculpture, or geological evidence, depending on the meaning we give to it (Hall 1997).

Celine-Marie Pascale, "Making Sense of Race, Class, and Gender: The Discursive Construction of Class," *Making Sense of Race, Class, and Gender: Commonsense, Power, and Privilege in the U.S.*, pp. 79-108. Copyright © 2007 by Taylor & Francis Group LLC. Reprinted with permission.

We must interpret experience in order for it to become meaningful. The cultural discourses that enable people in the U.S. to make sense of wealth and poverty cannot be separated from the material conditions of that production. While the word "discourse" often is used as a synonym for "talk," here it has a more specialized meaning. Discourses are cultural frameworks for understanding what knowledge is useful, relevant or true in a specific context. For example, a scientific discourse enables scientists to "recognize" a stone as a kind of geological evidence.

In my initial analysis of interviews, talk about class appeared to be so completely dislocated from economics as to lack *any* concrete mooring. Indeed, everyday assumptions about class appeared to be idiosyncratic. Scholars have often raised the specter of "false consciousness" to describe a lack of class-consciousness. Yet it is important to recall there was a time in U.S. history when cogent class analyses shaped public discourse. The disappearance of public discourse cannot be separated from a class history shaped by the U.S. government's consistent willingness to use deadly violence against workers and unions through deployment of the National Guard and federal troops between 1870 and 1930. Although we "forget" it, we begin talking about wealth and poverty within a pre-existing discourse shaped by class struggle.

We live in a country that appears to be devoted to the ideal of democratic equality, yet is divided by disparities that are produced through a commitment to competitive prosperity. I begin by focusing my analysis on the simple questions: In what ways, and on what terms, does commonsense knowledge make class positions (our own and others) recognizable? In order for class differences to be generally invisible, there must be a systematic detachment between the social displays and economic productions of class. How is that people recognize, or fail to recognize, themselves and others as members of socio-economic classes? I examine how commonsense knowledge about class in the United States leads people to engage in practices that systematically disorganize the presence of social and economic capital. By analyzing commonsense understandings of class, I unsettle economic determinism and move toward more complex, fluid conceptualizations that incorporate discursive aspects of class.

Belonging to the Middle Class

Most people I interviewed characterized themselves as middle-class—regardless of whether they were multimillionaires or blue-collar workers. While this might strike readers as itself a matter of commonsense, rather than as a point of analytic interest, it is possible to understand this information as something more than a cliché. Toward that end, let me begin by saying that four of the five multimillionaires I interviewed characterized themselves as middle class and asserted that perceptions of them as wealthy were mistaken. (I will come back to this exception a bit later.) For example, Brady, a white attorney specializing in estate planning explained: "I guess we define class by wealth since we don't have nobility here. So … I guess I'm in the middle, based our tests, our society, probably middle class."[2] I found it difficult to think of Brady, with assets of nearly $5 million dollars, as "in the middle" of the economic spectrum. As Brady continued, he described upper-class people as "pretentious" and added: "I don't feel class is that important and I don't care for folks who think it is." Brady's dismissal of class is not so much a denial of his wealth but a dismissal of the "folks" who make wealth the measure of a person. Similarly, Polard, a white commercial real estate developer, distinguished his wealth from his personality. He talked about himself as "middle class" and called himself "an average kinda joe" who "eats hamburgers at McDonalds." Polard did not just call himself "average" but invoked a discourse that links him to a certain kind of masculinity. Polard elaborated: "I don't feel a connection to I guess what one would consider upper class. I don't feel connected to that. You know, my friends—my relationships—and that, are middle America." Throughout the interview Polard reinforced a distinction between the kind of person he is and the wealth that he has. For instance, Polard said:

> When uh you live in this house … the average person driving down the street will view the big house with all the land sitting on an expensive street, [and think] he must be very rich. But I mean that's not me, it isn't my personality. … I'm just an ordinary kinda guy.

Polard is not denying his wealth; on the exit interview form, he valued his assets at over $100 million. Yet Polard displaces economic considerations of class by centering personal values. From eating at McDonald's to his personal relationships, Polard lays claim to a *class* identity that stands apart, or is made to stand apart, from his wealth.

Polard and Brady talk about "being middle-class" as being *a particular kind of person*—rather than as being a particular level of income or assets. Certainly, the routine nature of daily life leads most people to think of themselves as average (Sacks 1992). While it would be quite easy to press the claim that Polard is deluding himself (or me) by characterizing himself as "middle class," such a claim would foreclose important questions. In particular, on what terms, or in what contexts, do people characterize themselves by a *class* category that is independent of their economic resources? How might such misrecognition of class (willful or not) create a cultural quarantine that prevents critical questions, and opposing interpretations, from arising, or being seriously engaged?

While the rhetoric people invoke when talking about class may be race and/or gender specific (eg., "an average joe"), I sought and examined patterns of commonsense about class that transcended boundaries of race and gender. So, it is important to note that white men were not the only multi-millionaires to characterize themselves as middle class. Two women, one Latina and one American Indian, who were self-made multimillionaires expressed similar sentiments. Marisol Alegria owned two burger franchises at the time of our interview. Marisol explained:

> In the community here, um, I find that there's a lotta respect for that [owning and operating fast food franchises]. Sometimes it's a misconceived respect, I think, an' especially in my case, because the perception is, "Oh my gosh, there's a lady that must be a multimillionaire." Or, you know, "That lady's just making beaucoup bucks," you know, and—and that kind of a thing. But it really, um—and there ARE some out there. I mean, because most of my counterparts throughout, are REALLY in the big buck category.

Marisol talks about herself as the object of "misconceived respect" based on a false perception. Yet, she is a self-made multimillionaire with assets just under $10 million. It seems possible that Marisol can argue that perceptions of her as wealthy are "misconceived" by comparing herself to even wealthier peers. Certainly, "beaucoup bucks" and "big bucks" are relative terms that avoid any fixed notion of wealth. However, Marisol also resists being perceived by others as a multimillionaire—a very specific category and one that is consistent with her own characterization of her assets. It seems unlikely then that Marisol is invoking a purely relative notion of wealth, or that she is trying to conceal her wealth in the interview. Since Marisol objects to the *perception* of her as a multimillionaire, it seems possible that she does not believe that she is *recognizable* as a multimillionaire—that in social environments she does not stand out as different. It is not just that class, seen from within, can be imagined to be invisible but that *markers of class can be disorganized in such a way as to make class unintelligible.* Indeed, Marisol later talked about the care that she takes with her appearance so that she does not stand out.

> *Marisol:* I have a wonderful, and I really feel very good about this, I have a wonderful experience at mixing very well. I could be with the richest of the rich and not drop the beat, not feel intimidated, or uncomfortable.
> *Celine-Marie:* Mmhmm.
> *Marisol:* You know, I know that I have an outfit or two that would wear just as well. And if were going to ... uh, one of my employee's baptismals, out in Las Viejas I know that I could wear, you know, something there to not intimidate or feel ... you know, as though I'm out of ... out of class there.
> *Celine-Marie:* Mmhmm.
> *Marisol*: or would intimidate the guests or anything else.
> *Celine-Marie:* Mmhmm.
> *Marisol:* I think I can do that very well. So ... for that reason, I think I ... I just kinda ... mesh very well.

Here one can better see why Marisol might object to the *perception* that she is a multimillionaire. Marisol talks about herself as someone in the middle. She can socialize with the "richest of the rich" and not "feel intimidated" and can attend a social gathering hosted by one of her fast food employees without intimidating the other guests. Marisol talks about class as a social category based on interaction; to intimidate or be intimidated is "to be out of class."

Lorraine Doe, an American Indian who worked as a tribal administrator, also talked about herself as being middle class based on being an "average" person. At the time of our interview, she held assets of over $500 million dollars. It is not just that Marisol, Lorraine, Polard, and Brady think of class in purely personal terms but that in order to maintain their "ordinariness," they *must* think of class in this way. And in this sense their personal identity as ordinary people is in conflict with a class location based on extraordinary wealth.

In order to produce and maintain the appearance of a class identity, people must understand and manipulate complex meanings attached to work, wealth, consumer goods and other commodified cultural forms. Recall, for instance, that Polard described himself as "an average joe who eats hamburgers at McDonalds" and Brady referred to "folks" rather than to "people."

Outside of the Middle Class

Among the five multimillionaires I interviewed, Charlie Chin, a land and business developer, stood as the exception. Charlie identified himself as a first-generation Chinese-American and talked about himself as anything BUT ordinary. Charlie, with assets over $10 million, was the only multimillionaire to categorize himself as "around the top" in terms of class. He described himself as a person who enjoys socializing among university presidents, hospital administrators, and government officials. Whereas other multimillionaires articulated a gap between the way others might perceive them based on wealth, and the kind of person they really are, Charlie made no such distinction. Charlie was also the only multimillionaire to talk about wealth as a means to overcome the vulnerabilities of racism, immigration, and poverty. For instance, Charlie explained:

> I think that if you were a Mexican or Chinese immigrant and you don't have a great command of the language or let's say you have a command of the language but you slip up a little bit with your words or your tenses, things like that and you go to a hospital … you're treated differently than if I go in there.…
>
> So I'll go into the hospital and I'll KNOW the doctor. Ok? Or, I'll know the other doctors there. I'll know the HEAD of the HOSPITAL. Ok? … Whereas if you go in and you look like you don't belong or you can't pay your bill or um or you're not going to cause them a problem if they leave an instrument in your stomach or something like that … it's just, it's just COMPLETELY different. … I think you will live longer. … I think you will be cheated less, you will be treated with more respect, you will get faster service and they will make sure that YOU don't die. … That's why I work hard so I can take care of myself and my family and my extended family [big inhale] in that, in that manner. Also I KNOW that that's rotten and so I like to do things so that everybody gets a certain type of respect and care and consideration, too. Because what kind of society do you live in if it's too, too far that way?

Charlie Chin's strong identification with the experiences of immigrants, racism and poverty produces *disidentification* with dominant class discourse, even as he celebrates the benefits of wealth. Disidentification is more than a lack of identification; it is a process of challenging a dominant (i.e., hegemonic) discourse in ways that expose what the hegemonic discourse conceals. Indeed it is the work of disidentification that makes Charlie Chin's class privilege visible. His celebratory success emerges from a history of legal exclusions in the U.S. that once prevented his parents, aunts, and uncles from the rights of citizenship, property ownership, and fair employment. In addition, Charlie's family was consistently vulnerable to the physical, emotional, and economic violence of racists. While one might say Charlie Chin is a poster child for the American Dream, in his talk about class, he does not identify with the notions of equality and fairness that permeate the mythology of the American Dream. Nor does he identify with the mythic middle class. Rather, Charlie effectively resists hegemonic class discourses and resituates the competitive prosperity of the American Dream within historical processes of racism and economic oppression. This particular practice of disidentification is possible because class identification is constituted within various, often competing, systems of representation that carry forward different parts of histories.

Excepting Charlie Chin, people who did not identify themselves as middle-class resisted characterizing themselves by class at all—regardless of whether they eventually categorized themselves as above or below "middle class." For example, Lana Jacobs, a highly successful artist who held assets of nearly a million dollars at the time of our interview, illustrates this point. Lana continued to make her home and studio in the working-class community of color, where she had lived before her success as an artist. While she freely characterized herself as an artist, as black, and as a woman, Lana refused to characterize herself by class. Lana explained:

> I guess I am a universal person. I don't see myself fitting into a group. I am not a group-minded kind of person. ... I feel stifled by groups because I have my own ... my own attitude about uh what I feel what I know I lived. ... I try not to judge. I work on my judgments about people.

Lana talked about class as a voluntary social category—something she could refuse to join. If Lana experiences being a woman, an artist, or black, as a social *fact,* she talks about class as a social *judgment*. However, the unwillingness of the people I interviewed to characterize themselves as wealthy or poor should not be confused with their willingness to characterize others as such. Lana had no difficulty characterizing her grandparents as "a little below middle class." Yet being *a little* above or below the middle is an assessment comparatively free of judgment since to be "in the middle" is to be like most other people. By contrast, if Lana were to characterize herself by assets and wealth, she would be far more than "a little above" her family and community. By resisting class categorization, Lana implicitly asserts her long-standing connections to family, neighbors, and friends.

Similarly, when I asked Cuauhtemoc, a part-time stock clerk, if he had a class identity, he explained:

> I consider myself a full-blooded Mexican but as far as a class ... money's not a big thing to me, yeah we need it and everything but you know if it wasn't around or whatever, things would be a lot better. You know uhm ... I think, I don't really consider myself a class, I think I'm more, I think I'm really ... how would you say it, privilege who I am and what I have you know, because no, I don't have a lot of money but I have what I need.

Cuauhtemoc advances his identity as "full-blooded Mexican" yet, like Lana, dismisses the importance of class identification. Interestingly he explains that he "privileges" who he is and what he has *because* he doesn't have a lot of money. If "not having a lot of money" conjures images of need or poverty, Cuauhtemoc also quickly dispels those images by saying "I have what I need." The class identifications most readily available to him through U.S. hegemonic discourse would be poor or lower class—identifications more likely to diminish, than enhance, a sense of self.

All of the people I interviewed who experienced daily economic hardship resisted hegemonic class categories, sometimes by inventing new categories. Emerson Piscopo was unemployed at the time of our interview. He offered a surprising response to my question about class.

> *Celine-Marie:* Uh-huh. Do you have a class identity?
> *Emerson*: Uh, meaning where, where I fit in to society?
> *Celine-Marie:* Mhmm.

> *Emerson*: Um, I guess fore … forefront, I'm a transsexual,
> *Celine-Marie:* Mhmm.
> *Emerson:* transgender, transgender um, I'm since I'm still, I'm it just using hormones right now, and I have had surgery though, a hysterectomy, I guess I'm PART of the way there.

Initially, I was flummoxed by his answer. Had he misunderstood the question? Was he subverting a question he didn't want to answer? Was he refocusing the conversation to a topic more important to him? I came back to the issue later in the interview and reintroduced a question about his class identity. Emerson explained his family's economic circumstances this way:

> I'm starting out, I just, I had that major surgery so I'm not backed by a year's worth of work and it affected us [short pause] financially greatly, and we are both trying to catch up. We're, we're doin' it, but we're struggling, basically. We're in the struggling class. Not, not POOR but somewhere in between poor and okay.

Emerson introduces his family's economic difficulties through news of his surgery and his loss of work; he offers an *explanation* even before mentioning the economic hardship. Emerson talks about "trying to catch up"—indicating that ordinarily, his family had more resources and then frames their efforts to "catch up" as successful, if incomplete. In this way, Emerson is able to describe economic hardship while resisting identification with poverty. He underscores this resistance by saying "Not POOR but somewhere in between poor and okay." Thus Emerson not only defines the conceptual space between being poor and okay as one of personal struggle, he constitutes the meaning of his experience in a broader economic and social context.

If Emerson's response appears to be an anomaly, or a strategy that might be adopted only by people in economic transition, consider this exchange with Captain Ahab, a senior partner in a successful law firm:

> *Celine-Marie:* Uh-huh. Where would you place yourself in terms of class?
> *Captain Ahab:* I am first of all an immigrant. I moved to the United States at age six from Canada but um moved from Canada to Florida so it was a fairly long move. And so I arrived in Florida, again you know as an immigrant, and with an accent and so went through that type of displacement. Was exposed to discrimination issues at that age. I can remember very clearly driving through the southern United States and having my parents explain to me uh about the situation involving segregation in the South. This would have been in 1952. …
> *Celine-Marie:* That's interesting. Where do you put yourself today in terms of class?
> *Ahab:* Uh … upper-middle class.

Captain Ahab, like Emerson, responded to my question in a way that deferred or deflected a discussion of class. Both men also displaced my question about class identity by responding with features of their identity that each felt to be more central than class: Captain Ahab as an immigrant and Emerson as a transsexual. If class is important to either man, they seem anxious to privilege a representation of self that is not class-based.

When I pursued the conversation about class, Captain Ahab described his class identity this way:

> My wife is superintendent and principal of a school district, a one-school school district. She has a master's degree. I have a BA, an MA and a JD. And probably we're more upper-middle class by education, than by finances. Uh but uh still I think in the overall scale, we'd probably be considered upper-middle class.

Ahab underscores education as the determining factor in his assessment of class and then seems to capitulate to an unwanted characterization as upper-middle class. While one might argue that hegemonic notions of class can be produced through education, in Captain Ahab's talk about class, educational attainments are made to eclipse economic ones.

Overall, the people I interviewed understood class as a social judgment, not just an evaluation of someone's economic resources, but of their "self." When talking about their own *class* identities, everyone (except Charlie Chin) used discursive practices invoking social criteria that masked, distorted, or rendered invisible, their economic circumstances—even though they each volunteered their income and assets on the interview form. Class—construed in very personal terms, as something social—depends upon corresponding discourses of free will, personal values, and individual choices. In asserting the *primary importance* of a "me" that stands apart from one's economic conditions, talk about class systematically hid from view the cultural, social, and economic conditions that structure access to jobs, income, and wealth.

Concluding Remarks

At stake in class identities is the capacity for self-recognition (the source of agency) and the capacity of *others* to recognize us—the capacity for collective identities. So it is especially important to note that the very discourses through which people articulated class identities disorganized the presence and meaning of social and economic capital. To the extent that people can and do talk about class *as if* it is unrelated to power and wealth, they shrouded the political dimensions of daily life with commonsense knowledge. The discursive production of class obscured the networks of power that emerge through wealth. These networks of power extend beyond resources that are owned to the *potential* to control resources and people. And, in this sense the everyday "doing of class" (West and Fenstermaker 1995), and the discursive formations upon which such doing relies, occluded not only visible displays of wealth and poverty but also the history and politics of class and class struggle.

The discursive practices regarding class constituted that which they purported to describe: the relative irrelevance of class. Hegemonic discourse effectively subverts the capacity for collective identity based on class interests because class subjects are produced through discourses that conceal class positions, interests, and relationships. Class functions as it does in the United States, not because people are engaged in fictional performances of passing or because they are beset by false consciousness. Rather, class must be understood as performative precisely because discourse—as a kind of societal speech—is a practical part of what people think and feel—how we see the world.

The language of class is performative (i.e., constitutive) in that discursive practices produce the appearance of "classlessness" that they purport to describe. The relationship between material economic circumstances and the social meanings of those circumstances are not completely distinct. While capitalism has always relied on global and local relations of production, it also has produced—and required—particular forms of consciousness. Because relations of exploitation are never lived in economic terms alone, understandings of language in general—and discursive practices in particular—are critical to understanding class struggle. As mentioned at the start, we *begin* talking about class within a pre-existing discourse shaped by class struggle. Like all hegemonic discursive practices, the discursive production of class secures institutionalized relations of power. One of the most important goals of power is to prevail in determining the agenda of the struggle, to determine which questions can be raised and on what terms. Class conflict is pre-empted by the hegemonic discursive practices through which class is constituted.

Hegemonic discourse—not material circumstances—shaped class categorizations and subverted the capacity for collective identity/agency based on economic interests. While theories of class offer insight into important aspects of capitalism, within sociology much of this theory is used to reify categories of class and center debates on the adequacy and limitations of various categorization efforts. However, even if one thinks of class in purely economic terms, it exceeds existing frameworks for understanding class. Is it reasonable to think of someone with $450,000 in assets as wealthy? What if those assets are equity accrued through 40 years of real estate inflation on a small house owned by someone who works in a small factory making jewelry? How is one to understand the class position of a person who earns $70,000 a year as an independent contractor in the technology industry and who is unable to afford to buy a home because of inflated housing prices? If working-class jobs once provided workers and others with the ability to buy not only homes and cars but also boats and vacation property, this is no longer the case. Today, even people with upper-income professional careers do not necessarily experience the benefits of what was once considered wealth; rather, many now refer to themselves as "house poor" because all of their income is tied up in homeownership. This is not to equate those who are "house poor" with those who are living on minimum wage in a rented apartment, but to argue that historical categories of class are inadequate for understanding the contemporary distribution of wealth, the kinds of work and remuneration available, and the potential for social justice organizing. We are in need of new ways of conceptualizing class.

Understanding how identity and subjectivity are constituted within language provides an opportunity to re-theorize economic inequalities and the possibilities for social change. The imagined communities of class are not distinguished by truth or falsity but by the styles in which they are imagined which allow us to recognize different parts of our histories, and to construct points of identification.

The work of disidentification requires resituating the politics that personalize poverty and wealth into the historical conditions that make each possible and apparently natural. This would require the re-membering of self and others by calling into question the identities we have come to inhabit as members of a "classless" nation. As scholars, one means through which we can advance an agenda of social justice is by working at the constitutive frontiers of language to imagine new socialities, new subjectivities. In the beginning of the 21st century, resistance to hegemonic economic forces in the United States requires an understanding of the performativity of language in relation to material conditions lived experience.

Discussion Questions

1. Pascale argues that material conditions and discursive practices are not distinct. What does this mean?
2. Why does Pascale place the word 'recognize' in single quotes when she writes "... a scientific discourse enables scientists to 'recognize' a stone as a kind of geological evidence"?
3. What discourse(s) do you use to describe your own (or your parents') class location? Does this reading challenge any assumptions that you have held?
4. Have you ever experienced class location used as a social judgment against yourself or others? Have you ever used it as a social judgment?

Notes

1. The Census Bureau does not publish data on the incomes of the top one percent; the Congressional Budget Office supplements Census data with IRS data to capture gains and losses among the top one percent of the population.
2. My racial characterization of interviewees comes from self-identifications on the interview exit form. All names are pseudonyms chosen by the interviewees.

References

Hall, Stuart. 1997. "The Work of Representation." Pp. 1–74 in *Representation: Cultural representations and signifying practices*, edited by S. Hall. Thousand Oaks: Sage Publications, Inc.

Homelessness, National Alliance to End. 2002, Retrieved 2005 http://www.endhomelessness.org/).

O'Hara, Ann and Emily Cooper. 2003, "Priced Out," May. Retrieved July 7, 2005 (http://www.tacinc.org/).

Priorities, Center on Budget and Policy. 2003, "Poverty Increases and Median Income Declines for Second Consecutive Year," Retrieved Fall 2005, 2006 (http://www.cbpp.org/9-26-03pov.htm).

Sacks, Harvey. 1992. "On Doing "Being Ordinary."" Pp. 413–440 in *Structures of Social Action: Studies in conversation analysis*, edited by J. M. Atkinson and J. Heritage. Cambridge: Cambridge University Press.

West, Candace and Sarah Fenstermaker. 1995. "Doing Difference." *Gender and Society* 9: 8–37.

MOVING PAST RACE AND GENDER

BY BELL HOOKS

In these times of extreme anti-feminist backlash, of mounting fascism, and its concomitant support of war and all things that are like war, it is vital that we celebrate the strength of sustained feminist movement, of Women's Studies. Its very existence, its survival, its continued growth and development is a testament to the power of solidarity between progressive women and men, especially the solidarity of individual visionary black women who have had to work against the conservative history rooted in sexist biases that once were the absolute foundation of feminist education.

In the introduction to her book *We Are the Ones We Have Been Waiting For*, Alice Walker shares this insight:

> It is the worst of times because it feels as though the very earth is being stolen from us...: the land and air poisoned, the water polluted, the animals disappeared, humans degraded and misguided. War is everywhere. It is the best of times because we have entered a period...of great clarity as to cause and effect. A blessing when we consider how much suffering human beings have endured, in previous millennia, without a clue to its cause.... Because we can now see into every crevice of the globe and because we are free to explore previously unexplored crevices in our own hearts and minds, it is inevitable that everything we have needed to comprehend in order to survive, everything we have needed to understand in the most basic of ways will be illuminated now.... We live in a time of global enlightenment. This alone should make us shout for joy.

As feminist educators we can shout for joy. And yet we must also arouse our collective will to continue freedom's struggle, to continue to use our intellect and our imaginations to forge new and liberatory ways of knowing, thinking, and being, to work for change. We must revitalize our critical consciousness, to rekindle the seeds of militant radicalism that are the roots of every Women's Studies and Feminist Studies program and Women's Research Center in our nation. To do that, we must dare to make feminist meetings both times to celebrate and times to expand our consciousness. Let us honor the insight of Audre Lorde who once asked all of us, in all our diversity and differences of race, class, nationality, religion, sexual practice, to "remember what is dark and ancient and divine within ourselves that it may aid our speaking, our dreaming, our way of life."

When we speak of the ancient dark divine the intent is not to re-inscribe some folksy image of the all-knowing strong black female. Our intent is not re-mammification or the evocation of any racialized sexist thinking that would render exotic the bodies and beings of black women by suggesting that we are

bell hooks, "Moving Past Race and Gender," *Teaching Critical Thinking: Practical Wisdom*. Copyright © 2009 by Taylor & Francis Group. Reprinted with permission.

innately more in tune with the earth, more soulful, more nurturing, more caring, more ethical than other groups of women or that we represent a feminine alternative to patriarchy. Patriarchy has no gender.

When we speak radically of the dark divine, the invitation is for each and every one of us to transcend race and gender, to move beyond categories, and into the interior spaces of our psyches to encounter there the ground of our being, the place of mystery, creativity, and possibility. For it is there that we can construct the mind that can resist, that can revision, that can create the maps that when followed will liberate us. To embrace the ancient dark divine is to engage the political and the spiritual; engaging the dark divine, we are all called to empathic identification with black females globally. We are called to see clearly that the fate of black females in the world is the mirror into which everyone can look and see all our destinies unfolding.

During the early stages of contemporary feminist movement it was common to talk about black women as experiencing double jeopardy because we were likely to be victimized by both sexism and racism. Then, as the movement progressed, class was added to this equation and a discussion of triple jeopardy ensued. In actuality, black females are assailed on all sides, on so many fronts that words like "double" or "triple jeopardy" are simply inadequate descriptions. We face exploitation and/or oppression. We face dehumanization from so many locations that the feminist strategies for our continued survival envisioned so far are nowhere near as complex and as clearly defined as they must be if we are to thrive.

For black females globally and here in our nation, these are dangerous times. To create lives of optimal well-being and, most fundamentally, just to survive, we require a feminist theory and practice that not only raises consciousness but offers new and different ways to think and be, activist strategies that can only be radical and/or revolutionary because there is no place in the existing structure of imperialist white-supremacist capitalist patriarchy where we are truly safe, individually or collectively. When we come together to celebrate, for some of us, those of us who were engaged with Women's Centers from the inception find that our shouts of joy also must make way for moments of mourning, of ritual remembrance.

For in this unsafe world, we have witnessed untimely loss, the deaths of so many powerful black female voices, writers, thinkers, activists, artists, and visionary feminists. And for some of us, colleges and universities were the place where we first gathered, met one another face to face, and made our voices heard, experienced our first taste of a solidarity so sweet, so soul-nurturing that we were, indeed, literally carried away, ecstatically transported by the power of silences broken, by the sound of our decolonized speech. This is what Audre Lorde describes in conversation with Adrienne Rich when she declares: "What understanding begins to do is to make knowledge available for use, and that's the urgency, that's the push, that's the drive." In those heady days we were learning how to do just that. We needed the Women's Center and Women's Studies then, and we need them now. Much vital feminist theory/black feminist theory emerged in conversations and debates in these locations.

In the early days of the feminist movement, Toni Cade Bambara was with us, a leftist, social commentator, writer, leader of a black feminist vanguard, and lover of blackness. It was her voice that told us in the anthology *The Black Woman* that we needed to:

> set up a comparative study of the woman's role...in all the third world nations; to examine the public school and blueprint some viable alternatives; to explore ourselves and set the record straight on the matriarch and the Evil Black Bitch; to delve into history and pay tribute to all [black female] warriors...; to outline work that has been done and remains to be done in the area of consumer education and cooperative economics;[and] that we needed to get into the whole area of sensuality and sex.

These are just some of the insights we must remember and use.

Wisely, Bambara was telling us that we would need to move beyond simplistic categories like masculine and feminine because, as she explains,

> I have always found the either/or implicit in those definitions antithetical to what...revolution for self is all about—the whole person... that the usual notions of sexual differentiation in roles is an obstacle to political consciousness...that a revolutionary must be capable, of above all, total self-autonomy.

Bambara writes these words in 1970 and yet audiences and other black women engaged in feminist theory and practice still ask me, "Are you black first or a woman?" We know that when we ask them what feminist thinkers do you read and study, the answer is almost always "none." This is why archives are important and why the continual study of our work is crucial. This is why it is important that work by visionary black thinkers be collected in archives, ones that are, first and foremost, accessible to those who are engaged in the process of decolonization.

We know how easily and how quickly our words are forgotten, our histories buried. We all know that students, even our Women's Studies students, often show no hint of recognition when we talk about the works of Pat Parker, Lorraine Hansberry, Barbara Christian, Endesha Mae Holland, June Jordan, Octavia Butler, and even Audre Lorde. We know that feminist thinker Michelle Wallace has theorized the nature and substance of our continued invisibility because she has lived with the fear of erasure. In *Invisibility Blues* she reminds us:

> I have come to see the difficulties black women writers encounter as structural and systemic.... Because black women are perceived as marginal to the production of knowledge, their judgment cannot be trusted.... As a consequence black women are not allowed (by themselves as well as by others) to make definitive statements about the character of power, agency, and resistance within and beyond the black community. If and when they persist in doing so, the discouragement is great.

Wallace's insight is yet another reminder of why it is important that our papers be gathered, respected, used. As we all know, there are a small number of individual black women writers who have managed to engage in the insurrection of subjugated knowledge in such a way that our work is read more broadly, studied in classrooms, and quoted in a variety of texts (I place my writing among this work). Yet this inclusion does not ensure lasting presence, continued visibility, or sustained recognition.

On one hand, it is awesome that the critique of race and racism by women of color, many of us black women, brought to feminist movement fundamentally altered the nature of feminist theory. Yet we can still read celebrated theory by white women that builds on this work without any mention of the individual black women thinkers who laid the foundation. To resist this erasure, we must do all we can to document, to highlight, to study, to celebrate, and most importantly to create work that is cutting-edge, that breaks through silences and the different walls that have been erected to block our vision, of ourselves and of our futures.

Ironically, as more work by black women has received attention, much of that work has become more conservative, reformist, and not radical. We get gender without feminism. We are offered womanism as though it is the antidote to a powerful poison, that dangerous substance being feminism. When we connect Wallace's writing on invisibility with the constant demand Lorde makes in her work that silences be broken, then we claim our power to make ourselves visible because we have both a theory that enables us to understand what hems us in and a theory that conceptualizes our power to set ourselves and our words free. Lorde challenges us to not be trapped by fear. In The Transformation of Silence she declares:

> We can learn to work and speak when we are afraid in the same way we have learned to work and speak when we are tired. For we have been socialized to respect fear more than our own needs for language and definition, and while we wait in silence for that finial luxury of fearlessness, the weight of that silence will choke us...there are many silences to be broken.

At times we want to be silent about how grave our circumstances are. We do not want to speak about how difficult it has become for black females of all classes to garner support in all areas of our lives. We want to be silent about how hard it is to raise consciousness, to critique, challenge, and change sexism, within and beyond black communities (particularly when the forms of black community that once placed us in meaningful solidarity with progressive black men are eroding daily). All black females, irrespective of class positionality, know how difficult it is to constructively change our lives so that we can have the necessary health and well-being to fuel revolutionary visions of social change.

Significantly, Toni Bambara, Audre Lorde, and June Jordan were all critical thinkers who dared to be militant, to speak when silence would have afforded them greater comfort. They all wrote about the need for black females to claim the space of becoming whole. Speaking openly of her commitment to feminist movement in the essay "Where Is the Love," Jordan testifies:

> I am a feminist, and what that means to me is much the same as the meaning of the fact that I am Black: it means that I must undertake to love myself and to respect myself as though my very life depends upon self-love and self-respect. It means that I must everlastingly seek to cleanse myself of the hatred and contempt that surrounds and permeates my identity.... It means that the achievement of self-love and self-respect will require inordinate, hourly vigilance, and that I am entering my soul into a struggle that will most certainly transform the experience of all the peoples of the earth, as no other movement can, in fact hope to claim: because the movement into self-love, self-respect, and self-determination is the movement now galvanizing the true, the unarguable majority of human beings everywhere.

It is essential to our struggle for self-determination that we speak of love, as love is the necessary foundation enabling us to survive the wars, the hardships, and the sickness and the dying with our spirits intact. It is love that allows us to survive whole.

When I began to write books on love for a more popular audience, I would often hear from readers that I was no longer as radical, as militant as I appeared to them to have been. To those who would limit and define black female intellect, imprison us in academies where our teaching cannot reach the masses of people who are seeking life-changing theory and practice, love has no meaning. Hence they will not understand that it is the most militant, most radical intervention anyone can make to not only speak of love, but to engage the practice of love. For love as the foundation of all social movements for self-determination is the only way we create a world that domination and dominator thinking cannot destroy. Anytime we do the work of love we are doing the work of ending domination.

We, black females globally, have a long history of struggling through brokenness, of enduring great pain, and yet holding on. This is still the history of victimhood. The history that visionary radical black women are making in our lives and in our work, here today, is not a history that begins with brokenness. It is a history that begins with the recognition that the work of love is our revolutionary starting point, that to love ourselves no matter our circumstance is already to stand in the place of victory.

Power and Politics

Media

Education

Prison Industrial Complex

SOCIAL INEQUALITIES WITHIN INSTITUTIONS

POWER AND POLITICS

The Power Elite

Political Power and Power Over the Media

THE POWER ELITE

BY C. WRIGHT MILLS

The powers of ordinary men are circumscribed by the everyday worlds in which they live, yet even in these rounds of job, family, and neighborhood they often seem driven by forces they can neither understand nor govern. 'Great changes' are beyond their control, but affect their conduct and outlook none the less. The very framework of modern society confines them to projects not their own, but from every side, such changes now press upon the men and women of the mass society, who accordingly feel that they are without purpose in an epoch in which they are without power.

But not all men are in this sense ordinary. As the means of information and of power are centralized, some men come to occupy positions in American society from which they can look down upon, so to speak, and by their decisions mightily affect, the everyday worlds of ordinary men and women. They are not made by their jobs; they set up and break down jobs for thousands of others; they are not confined by simple family responsibilities; they can escape. They may live in many hotels and houses, but they are bound by no one community. They need not merely 'meet the demands of the day and hour'; in some part, they create these demands, and cause others to meet them. Whether or not they profess their power, their technical and political experience of it far transcends that of the underlying population. What Jacob Burckhardt said of 'great men,' most Americans might well say of their elite: 'They are all that we are not.'

The power elite is composed of men whose positions enable them to transcend the ordinary environments of ordinary men and women; they are in positions to make decisions having major consequences. Whether they do or do not make such decisions is less important than the fact that they do occupy such pivotal positions: their failure to act, their failure to make decisions, is itself an act that is often of greater consequence than the decisions they do make. For they are in command of the major hierarchies and organizations of modern society. They rule the big corporations. They run the machinery of the state and claim its prerogatives. They direct the military establishment. They occupy the strategic command posts of the social structure, in which are now centered the effective means of the power and the wealth and the celebrity which they enjoy.

The power elite are not solitary rulers. Advisers and consultants, spokesmen and opinion-makers are often the captains of their higher thought and decision. Immediately below the elite are the professional politicians of the middle levels of power, in the Congress and in the pressure groups, as well as among the new and old upper classes of town and city and region. Mingling with them in curious ways are those professional celebrities who live by being continually displayed but are never, so long as they remain celebrities, displayed enough. If such celebrities are not at the head of any dominating hierarchy, they do often have the power to distract the attention of the public or afford sensations to the masses, or, more directly, to gain the ear of those who do occupy positions of direct

C. Wright Mills, from *The Power Elite,* pp. 3-18, 20-23, 365-367. Copyright © 1956, 2000 by Oxford University Press. Reprinted with permission.

power. More or less unattached, as critics of morality and technicians of power, as spokesmen of God and creators of mass sensibility, such celebrities and consultants are part of the immediate scene in which the drama of the elite is enacted. But that drama itself is centered in the command posts of the major institutional hierarchies.

1

The truth about the nature and the power of the elite is not some secret which men of affairs know but will not tell. Such men hold quite various theories about their own roles in the sequence of event and decision. Often they are uncertain about their roles, and even more often they allow their fears and their hopes to affect their assessment of their own power. No matter how great their actual power, they tend to be less acutely aware of it than of the resistances of others to its use. Moreover, most American men of affairs have learned well the rhetoric of public relations, in some cases even to the point of using it when they are alone, and thus coming to believe it. The personal awareness of the actors is only one of the several sources one must examine in order to understand the higher circles. Yet many who believe that there is no elite, or at any rate none of any consequence, rest their argument upon what men of affairs believe about themselves, or at least assert in public.

There is, however, another view: those who feel, even if vaguely, that a compact and powerful elite of great importance does now prevail in America often base that feeling upon the historical trend of our time. They have felt, for example, the domination of the military event, and from this they infer that generals and admirals, as well as other men of decision influenced by them, must be enormously powerful. They hear that the Congress has again abdicated to a handful of men decisions clearly related to the issue of war or peace. They know that the bomb was dropped over Japan in the name of the United States of America, although they were at no time consulted about the matter. They feel that they live in a time of big decisions; they know that they are not making any. Accordingly, as they consider the present as history, they infer that at its center, making decisions or failing to make them, there must be an elite of power.

On the one hand, those who share this feeling about big historical events assume that there is an elite and that its power is great. On the other hand, those who listen carefully to the reports of men apparently involved in the great decisions often do not believe that there is an elite whose powers are of decisive consequence.

Both views must be taken into account, but neither is adequate. The way to understand the power of the American elite lies neither solely in recognizing the historic scale of events nor in accepting the personal awareness reported by men of apparent decision. Behind such men and behind the events of history, linking the two, are the major institutions of modern society. These hierarchies of state and corporation and army constitute the means of power; as such they are now of a consequence not before equaled in human history—and at their summits, there are now those command posts of modern society which offer us the sociological key to an understanding of the role of the higher circles in America.

Within American society, major national power now resides in the economic, the political, and the military domains. Other institutions seem off to the side of modern history, and, on occasion, duly subordinated to these. No family is as directly powerful in national affairs as any major corporation; no church is as directly powerful in the external biographies of young men in America today as the military establishment; no college is as powerful in the shaping of momentous events as the National Security Council. Religious, educational, and family institutions are not autonomous centers of national power; on the contrary, these decentralized areas are increasingly shaped by the big three, in which developments of decisive and immediate consequence now occur. …

Within each of the big three, the typical institutional unit has become enlarged, has become administrative, and, in the power of its decisions, has become centralized. Behind these developments there is a fabulous technology, for as institutions, they have incorporated this technology and guide it, even as it shapes and paces their developments.

The economy—once a great scatter of small productive units in autonomous balance—has become dominated by two or three hundred giant corporations, administratively and politically interrelated, which together hold the keys to economic decisions.

The political order, once a decentralized set of several dozen states with a weak spinal cord, has become a centralized, executive establishment which has taken up into itself many powers previously scattered, and now enters into each and every cranny of the social structure.

The military order, once a slim establishment in a context of distrust fed by state militia, has become the largest and most expensive feature of government, and, although well versed in smiling public relations, now has all the grim and clumsy efficiency of a sprawling bureaucratic domain.

In each of these institutional areas, the means of power at the disposal of decision-makers have increased enormously; their central executive powers have been enhanced; within each of them modern administrative routines have been elaborated and tightened up.

As each of these domains becomes enlarged and centralized, the consequences of its activities become greater, and its traffic with the others increases. The decisions of a handful of corporations bear upon military and political as well as upon economic developments around the world. The decisions of the military establishment rest upon and grievously affect political life as well as the very level of economic activity. The decisions made within the political domain determine economic activities and military programs. There is no longer, on the one hand, an economy, and, on the other hand, a political order containing a military establishment unimportant to politics and to money-making. There is a political economy linked, in a thousand ways, with military institutions and decisions. On each side of the world-split running through central Europe and around the Asiatic rim-lands, there is an ever-increasing interlocking of economic, military, and political structures. If there is government intervention in the corporate economy, so is there corporate intervention in the governmental process. In the structural sense, this triangle of power is the source of the interlocking directorate that is most important for the historical structure of the present.

The fact of the interlocking is clearly revealed at each of the points of crisis of modern capitalist society—slump, war, and boom. In each, men of decision are led to an awareness of the interdependence of the major institutional orders. In the nineteenth century, when the scale of all institutions was smaller, their liberal integration was achieved in the automatic economy, by an autonomous play of market forces, and in the automatic political domain, by the bargain and the vote. It was then assumed that out of the imbalance and friction that followed the limited decisions then possible a new equilibrium would in due course emerge. That can no longer be assumed, and it is not assumed by the men at the top of each of the three dominant hierarchies.

For given the scope of their consequences, decisions—and indecisions—in any one of these ramify into the others, and hence top decisions tend either to become coordinated or to lead to a commanding indecision. It has not always been like this. When numerous small entrepreneurs made up the economy, for example, many of them could fail and the consequences still remain local; political and military authorities did not intervene. But now, given political expectations and military commitments, can they afford to allow key units of the private corporate economy to break down in slump? Increasingly, they do intervene in economic affairs, and as they do so, the controlling decisions in each order are inspected by agents of the other two, and economic, military, and political structures are interlocked.

At the pinnacle of each of the three enlarged and centralized domains, there have arisen those higher circles which make up the economic, the political, and the military elites. At the top of the economy, among the corporate rich, there are the chief executives; at the top of the political order, the members of the political directorate; at the top of the military establishment, the elite of soldier-statesmen clustered in and around the Joint Chiefs of Staff and the upper echelon. As each of these domains has coincided with the others, as decisions tend to become total in their consequence, the leading men in each of the three domains of power—the warlords, the corporation chieftains, the political directorate—tend to come together, to form the power elite of America.

2

The higher circles in and around these command posts are often thought of in terms of what their members possess: they have a greater share than other people of the things and experiences that are most highly valued. From this point of view, the elite are simply those who have the most of what there is to have, which is generally held to include money, power, and prestige—as well as all the ways of life to which these lead. But the elite are not simply those who have the most, for they could not 'have the most' were it not for their positions in the great institutions. For such institutions are the necessary bases of power, of wealth, and of prestige, and at the same time, the chief means of exercising power, of acquiring and retaining wealth, and of cashing in the higher claims for prestige.

By the powerful we mean, of course, those who are able to realize their will, even if others resist it. No one, accordingly, can be truly powerful unless he has access to the command of major institutions, for it is over these institutional means of power that the truly powerful are, in the first instance, powerful. Higher politicians and key officials of government command such institutional power; so do admirals and generals, and so do the major owners and executives of the larger corporations. Not all power, it is true, is anchored in and exercised by means of such institutions, but only within and through them can power be more or less continuous and important. ...

If we took the one hundred most powerful men in America, the one hundred wealthiest, and the one hundred most celebrated away from the institutional positions they now occupy, away from their resources of men and women and money, away from the media of mass communication that are now focused upon them—then they would be powerless and poor and uncelebrated. For power is not of a man. Wealth does not center in the person of the wealthy. Celebrity is not inherent in any personality. To be celebrated, to be wealthy, to have power requires access to major institutions, for the institutional positions men occupy determine in large part their chances to have and to hold these valued experiences.

3

The people of the higher circles may also be conceived as members of a top social stratum, as a set of groups whose members know one another, see one another socially and at business, and so, in making decisions, take one another into account. The elite, according to this conception, feel themselves to be, and are felt by others to be, the inner circle of 'the upper social classes.' They form a more or less compact social and psychological entity; they have become self-conscious members of a social class. People are either accepted into this class or they are not, and there is a qualitative split, rather than merely a numerical scale, separating them from those who are not elite. They are more or less aware of themselves as a social class and they behave toward one another differently from the way they do toward members of other classes. They accept one another, understand one another, marry one another, tend to work and to think if not together at least alike.

Now, we do not want by our definition to prejudge whether the elite of the command posts are conscious members of such a socially recognized class, or whether considerable proportions of the elite derive from such a clear and distinct class. These are matters to be investigated. Yet in order to be able to recognize what we intend to investigate, we must note something that all biographies and memoirs of the wealthy and the powerful and the eminent make clear: no matter what else they may be, the people of these higher circles are involved in a set of overlapping 'crowds' and intricately connected 'cliques.' There is a kind of mutual attraction among those who 'sit on the same terrace'—although this often becomes clear to them, as well as to others, only at the point at which they feel the need to draw the line; only when, in their common defense, they come to understand what they have in common, and so close their ranks against outsiders.

The idea of such ruling stratum implies that most of its members have similar social origins, that throughout their lives they maintain a network of informal connections, and that to some degree there is an interchangeability of position between the various hierarchies of money and power and celebrity. We must, of course, note at once that if such an elite stratum does exist, its social visibility and its form, for very solid historical reasons, are quite different from those of the noble cousinhoods that once ruled various European nations.

That American society has never passed through a feudal epoch is of decisive importance to the nature of the American elite, as well as to

American society as a historic whole. For it means that no nobility or aristocracy, established before the capitalist era, has stood in tense opposition to the higher bourgeoisie. It means that this bourgeoisie has monopolized not only wealth but prestige and power as well. It means that no set of noble families has commanded the top positions and monopolized the values that are generally held in high esteem; and certainly that no set has done so explicitly by inherited right. It means that no high church dignitaries or court nobilities, no entrenched landlords with honorific accouterments, no monopolists of high army posts have opposed the enriched bourgeoisie and in the name of birth and prerogative successfully resisted its self-making.

But this does *not* mean that there are no upper strata in the United States. That they emerged from a 'middle class' that had no recognized aristocratic superiors does not mean they remained middle class when enormous increases in wealth made their own superiority possible. Their origins and their newness may have made the upper strata less visible in America than elsewhere. But in America today there are in fact tiers and ranges of wealth and power of which people in the middle and lower ranks know very little and may not even dream. There are families who, in their well-being, are quite insulated from the economic jolts and lurches felt by the merely prosperous and those farther down the scale. There are also men of power who in quite small groups make decisions of enormous consequence for the underlying population.

The American elite entered modern history as a virtually unopposed bourgeoisie. No national bourgeoisie, before or since, has had such opportunities and advantages. Having no military neighbors, they easily occupied an isolated continent stocked with natural resources and immensely inviting to a willing labor force. A framework of power and an ideology for its justification were already at hand. Against mercantilist restriction, they inherited the principle of *laissez-faire*; against Southern planters, they imposed the principle of industrialism. The Revolutionary War put an end to colonial pretensions to nobility, as loyalists fled the country and many estates were broken up. The Jacksonian upheaval with its status revolution put an end to pretensions to monopoly of descent by the old New England families. The Civil War broke the power, and so in due course the prestige, of the antebellum South's claimants for the higher esteem. The tempo of the whole capitalist development made it impossible for an inherited nobility to develop and endure in America.

No fixed ruling class, anchored in agrarian life and coming to flower in military glory, could contain in America the historic thrust of commerce and industry, or subordinate to itself the capitalist elite—as capitalists were subordinated, for example, in Germany and Japan. Nor could such a ruling class anywhere in the world contain that of the United States when industrialized violence came to decide history. Witness the fate of Germany and japan in the two world wars of the twentieth century; and indeed the fate of Britain herself and her model ruling class, as New York became the inevitable economic, and Washington the inevitable political capital of the western capitalist world.

4

The elite who occupy the command posts may be seen as the possessors of power and wealth and celebrity; they may be seen as members of the upper stratum of a capitalistic society. They may also be defined in terms of psychological and moral criteria, as certain kinds of selected individuals. So defined, the elite, quite simply, are people of superior character and energy.

The humanist, for example, may conceive of the 'elite' not as a social level or category, but as a scatter of those individuals who attempt to transcend themselves, and accordingly, are more noble, more efficient, made out of better stuff. It does not matter whether they are poor or rich, whether they hold high position or low, whether they are acclaimed or despised; they are elite because of the kind of individuals they are. The rest of the population is mass, which, according to this conception, sluggishly relaxes into uncomfortable mediocrity.

This is the sort of socially unlocated conception which some American writers with conservative yearnings have recently sought to develop. But most moral and psychological conceptions of the elite are much less sophisticated, concerning themselves not with individuals but with the stratum as a whole. Such ideas, in fact, always arise in a society in which some people possess more than do others of what there is to possess. People with advantages are loath to believe that they just happen to be people with advantages.

They come readily to define themselves as inherently worthy of what they possess; they come to believe themselves 'naturally' elite; and, in fact, to imagine their possessions and their privileges as natural extensions of their own elite selves. In this sense, the idea of the elite as composed of men and women having a finer moral character is an ideology of the elite as a privileged ruling stratum, and this is true whether the ideology is elite-made or made up for it by others.

In eras of equalitarian rhetoric, the more intelligent or the more articulate among the lower and middle classes, as well as guilty members of the upper, may come to entertain ideas of a counter-elite. In western society, as a matter of fact, there is a long tradition and varied images of the poor, the exploited, and the oppressed as the truly virtuous, the wise, and the blessed. Stemming from Christian tradition, this moral idea of a counter-elite composed of essentially higher types condemned to a lowly station, may be and has been used by the underlying population to justify harsh criticism of ruling elites and to celebrate utopian images of a new elite to come.

The moral conception of the elite, however, is not always merely an ideology of the overprivileged or a counter-ideology of the underprivileged. It is often a fact: having controlled experiences and select privileges, many individuals of the upper stratum do come in due course to approximate the types of character they claim to embody. Even when we give up—as we must—the idea that the elite man or woman is born with an elite character, we need not dismiss the idea that their experiences and trainings develop in them characters of a specific type. …

5

These several notions of the elite, when appropriately understood, are intricately bound up with one another, and we shall use them all in this examination of American success. We shall study each of several higher circles as offering candidates for the elite, and we shall do so in terms of the major institutions making up the total society of America; within and between each of these institutions, we shall trace the interrelations of wealth and power and prestige. But our main concern is with the power of those who now occupy the command posts, and with the role which they are enacting in the history of our epoch.

Such an elite may be conceived as omnipotent, and its powers thought of as a great hidden design. Thus, in vulgar Marxism, events and trends are explained by reference to 'the will of the bourgeoisie'; in Nazism, by reference to 'the conspiracy of the Jews'; by the petty right in America today, by reference to 'the hidden force' of Communist spies. According to such notions of the omnipotent elite as historical cause, the elite is never an entirely visible agency. It is, in fact, a secular substitute for the will of God, being realized in a sort of providential design, except that usually non-elite men are thought capable of opposing it and eventually overcoming it.

The opposite view—of the elite as impotent—is now quite popular among liberal-minded observers. Far from being omnipotent, the elites are thought to be so scattered as to lack any coherence as a historical force. Their invisibility is not the invisibility of secrecy but the invisibility of the multitude. Those who occupy the formal places of authority are so check-mated—by other elites exerting pressure, or by the public as an electorate, or by constitutional codes—that, although there may be upper classes, there is no ruling class; although there may be men of power, there is no power elite; although there may be a system of stratification, it has no effective top. In the extreme, this view of the elite, as weakened by compromise and disunited to the point of nullity, is a substitute for impersonal collective fate; for, in this view, the decisions of the visible men of the higher circles do not count in history.

Internationally, the image of the omnipotent elite tends to prevail. All good events and pleasing happenings are quickly imputed by the opinion-makers to the leaders of their own nation; all bad events and unpleasant experiences are imputed to the enemy abroad. In both cases, the omnipotence of evil rulers or of virtuous leaders is assumed. Within the nation, the use of such rhetoric is rather more complicated: when men speak of the power of their own party or circle, they and their leaders are, of course, impotent; only 'the people' are omnipotent. But, when they speak of the power of their opponent's party or circle, they impute to them omnipotence; 'the people' are now powerlessly taken in.

More generally, American men of power tend, by convention, to deny that they are powerful. No American runs for office in order to rule or even govern, but only to serve; he does not become a bureaucrat or even an official, but a public servant. And nowadays, as I have already pointed out, such postures have become standard features of the public-relations programs of all men of power. So firm a part of the style of power-wielding have they become that conservative writers readily misinterpret them as indicating a trend toward an 'amorphous power situation.'

But the 'power situation' of America today is less amorphous than is the perspective of those who see it as a romantic confusion. It is less a flat, momentary 'situation' than a graded, durable structure. And if those who occupy its top grades are not omnipotent, neither are they impotent. It is the form and the height of the gradation of power that we must examine if we would understand the degree of power held and exercised by the elite.

If the power to decide such national issues as are decided were shared in an absolutely equal way, there would be no power elite; in fact, there would be no *gradation* of power, but only a radical homogeneity. At the opposite extreme as well, if the power to decide issues were absolutely monopolized by one small group, there would be no gradation of power; there would simply be this small group in command, and below it, the undifferentiated, dominated masses. American society today represents neither the one nor the other of these extremes, but a conception of them is none the less useful: it makes us realize more clearly the question of the structure of power in the United States and the position of the power elite within it.

Within each of the most powerful institutional orders of modern society there is a gradation of power. The owner of a roadside fruit stand does not have as much power in any area of social or economic or political decision as the head of a multi-million-dollar fruit corporation; no lieutenant on the line is as powerful as the Chief of Staff in the Pentagon; no deputy sheriff carries as much authority as the President of the United States. Accordingly, the problem of defining the power elite concerns the level at which we wish to draw the line. By lowering the line, we could define the elite out of existence; by raising it, we could make the elite a very small circle indeed. In a preliminary and minimum way, we draw the line crudely, in charcoal as it were: By the power elite, we refer to those political, economic, and military circles which as an intricate set of overlapping cliques share decisions having at least national consequences. In so far as national events are decided, the power elite are those who decide them. ...

6

It is not my thesis that for all epochs of human history and in all nations, a creative minority, a ruling class, an omnipotent elite, shape all historical events. Such statements, upon careful examination, usually turn out to be mere tautologies, and even when they are not, they are so entirely general as to be useless in the attempt to understand the history of the present. The minimum definition of the power elite as those who decide whatever is decided of major consequence, does not imply that the members of this elite are always and necessarily the history-makers; neither does it imply that they never are. We must not confuse the conception of the elite, which we wish to define, with one theory about their role: that they are the history-makers of our time. To define the elite, for example, as 'those who rule America' is less to define a conception than to state one hypothesis about the role and power of that elite. No matter how we might define the elite, the extent of its members' power is subject to historical variation. If, in a dogmatic way, we try to include that variation in our generic definition, we foolishly limit the use of a needed conception. If we insist that the elite be defined as a strictly coordinated class that continually and absolutely rules, we are closing off from our view much to which the term more modestly defined might open to our observation. In short, our definition of the power elite cannot properly contain dogma concerning the degree and kind of power that ruling groups everywhere have. Much less should it permit us to smuggle into our discussion a theory of history.

During most of human history, historical change has not been visible to the people who were involved in it, or even to those enacting it. Ancient Egypt and Mesopotamia, for example, endured for some four hundred generations with but slight changes in their basic structure. That is six and a half times as long as the entire Christian era, which has only prevailed some sixty generations; it is about eighty times as long as the five generations of the United States' existence. But now the tempo of change is so rapid, and the means of observation so accessible, that the interplay of event and decision seems often to be quite historically visible, if we will only look carefully and from an adequate vantage point.

When knowledgeable journalists tell us that 'events, not men, shape the big decisions,' they are echoing the theory of history as Fortune, Chance, Fate, or the work of The Unseen Hand. For 'events' is merely a modern word for these older ideas, all of which separate men from history-making, because all of them lead us to believe that history goes on behind men's backs. History is drift with no mastery; within it there is action but no deed; history is mere happening and the event intended by no one.

The course of events in out time depends more on a series of human decisions than on any inevitable fate. The sociological meaning of 'fate' is simply this: that, when the decisions are innumerable and each one is of small consequence, all of them add up in a way no man intended—to history as fate.

But not all epochs ate equally fateful. As the circle of those who decide is narrowed, as the means of decision are centralized and the consequences of decisions become enormous, then the course of great events often rests upon the decisions of determinable circles. This does not necessarily mean that the same circle of men follow through from one event to another in such a way that all of history is merely their plot. The power of the elite does not necessarily mean that history is not also shaped by a series of small decisions, none of which are thought out. It does not mean that a hundred small arrangements and compromises and adaptations may not be built into the going policy and the living event. The idea of the power elite implies nothing about the process of decision-making as such: it is an attempt to delimit the social areas within which that process, whatever its character, goes on. It is a conception of who is involved in the process.

The degree of foresight and control of those who are involved in decisions that count may also vary. The idea of the power elite does not mean that the estimations and calculated risks upon which decisions are made are not often wrong and that the consequences are sometimes, indeed often, not those intended. Often those who make decisions are trapped by their own inadequacies and blinded by their own errors.

Yet in our time the pivotal moment does arise, and at that moment, small circles do decide or fail to decide. In either case, they are an elite of power. The dropping of the A-bombs over Japan was such a moment; the decision on Korea was such a moment; the confusion about Quemoy and Matsu, as well as before Dienbienphu were such moments; the sequence of maneuvers which involved the United States in World War II was such a 'moment.' Is it not true that much of the history of our times is composed of such moments? And is not that what is meant when it is said that we live in a time of big decisions, of decisively centralized power?

Most of us do not try to make sense of our age by believing in a Greek-like, eternal recurrence, nor by a Christian belief in a salvation to come, nor by any steady march of human progress. Even though we do not reflect upon such matters, the chances are we believe with Burckhardt that we live in a mere succession of events; that sheer continuity is the only principle of history. History is merely one thing after another; history is meaningless in that it is not the realization of any determinate plot. It is true, of course, that our sense of continuity, our feeling for the history of our time, is affected by crisis. But we seldom look beyond the immediate crisis or the crisis felt to be just ahead. We believe neither in fate nor providence; and we assume, without talking about it, that 'we'—as a nation—can decisively shape the future but that we as individuals somehow cannot do so.

Any meaning history has, 'we' shall have to give to it by our actions. Yet the fact is that although we are all of us within history we do not all possess equal powers to make history. To pretend that we do is sociological nonsense and political irresponsibility. It is nonsense because any group or any individual is limited, first of all, by the technical and institutional means of power at its command; we do not all have equal access to the means of power that now exist, nor equal influence over their use. To pretend that 'we' are all history-makers is politically irresponsible because it obfuscates any attempt to locate responsibility for the consequential decisions of men who do have access to the means of power.

From even the most superficial examination of the history of the western society we learn that the power of decision-makers is first of all limited by the level of technique, by the *means* of power and violence and organization that prevail in a given society. In this connection we also learn that there is a fairly straight line running upward through the history of the West; that the means of oppression and exploitation, of violence and destruction, as well as the means of production and reconstruction, have been progressively enlarged and increasingly centralized.

As the institutional means of power and the means of communications that tie them together have become steadily more efficient, those now in command of them have come into command of instruments of rule quite unsurpassed in the history of mankind. And we are not yet at the climax of their development. We can no longer lean upon or take soft comfort from the historical ups and downs of ruling groups of previous epochs. In that sense, Hegel is correct: we learn from history that we cannot learn from it.

POLITICAL POWER AND POWER OVER THE MEDIA

BY GADI WOLFSFELD

Power has made Reality its Bitch
—Mark Danner

Think about two political actors, each trying to get into the news. For now let's talk only about the traditional news media (the new media will come into play a bit later). Assume, for the sake of argument that both are from the same political party, both have similar political views, and both look equally good in front of the camera. But there's one small difference between them: one is the president of the United States and the other is a new congressman from North Dakota. Presidents have a huge number of journalists assigned to them and can appear in the news any time they want. The congressman, on the other hand, has to compete with a horde of other politicians and convince reporters that he has something newsworthy to say. The president never has any problem getting into the national news, while the new congressman will be lucky if he gets covered in the local news.

Other powerful people in the government, whether it be the U.S. secretary of state, the secretary of defense, or the Speaker of the House also have little trouble getting into the news. If we were to build a ladder of influence from the most powerful people in Washington to the least important, we would have a pretty accurate measure of their chance of getting into the national news. Here's a good illustration of how political power leads to power over the media. Anybody who is reading this book probably knows the name of the secretary of state. Now try to name the secretary of Veterans Affairs. Unless you have some reason to be concerned with veteran issues, chances are you have no idea.

The reason, of course, is that the secretary of Veterans Affairs is simply not considered newsworthy, unless (s)he gets in trouble. A good rule of thumb is that journalists run after the politically powerful and politically weak run after journalists. This brings us to the first of the five principles. *Political power can usually be translated into power over the news media.*

One reason journalists consider the powerful more newsworthy is that these are the people who are most likely to have an impact on the country and the world. The president, after all, can go to war. The chance that an individual member of Congress can have a major impact on the political process is slim unless they are the deciding vote in an important piece of legislation. Even then, their fame is likely to be brief and they will quickly return to obscurity.

Here's another way to think of this idea. The relationship between journalists and political leaders can be considered a *competitive symbiosis*. It is a symbiotic relationship because each depends on the other in order to achieve their goals. Leaders want publicity and the journalists want interesting information they can turn into news. The reason the relationship is also competitive is that each wants to get the most from the other while "paying" as little as possible. Leaders want to get lots of publicity without having to reveal too much and reporters want to get the juiciest information without having to give a free ride to the politician. The more

Gadi Wolfsfeld, "Political Power and the Power Over the Media," *Making Sense of Media & Politics*, pp. 9-22. Copyright © 2011 by Taylor & Francis Group LLC. Reprinted with permission.

powerful leaders have the best information to "sell" and that's why journalists compete for the privilege of getting it, especially if they can get first crack at the story.

The fact that political power can be translated into power over the news media does not mean that the weaker political actors never get into the news. The news media have a preference for conflicts that is just as important as their preference for power. There is also an expectation that journalists will attempt to maintain a certain balance in news coverage. This means that even if they give a great deal of coverage to a presidential speech they will then allow the opposition to respond. Many talk shows also encourage a lively debate because that always makes the show more appealing.

Nevertheless, there is still something inherently elitist about these debates. Political movements and groups outside of the Washington Beltway are rarely invited to participate. So the journalists' notion of balance really means finding a balance between Republican and Democratic leaders. Political scientist Lance Bennett has done extremely important work on this issue and he argues that the best way to understand this is to think of this process as a form of "indexing." The news media mostly focus on what these elites are saying and doing and they record it. If neither the government nor the opposition is talking about an issue, even an important issue, the news media will likewise, simply ignore it. Equally important, claims Bennett, this obsession with elites also severely limits the *range* of opinions that are talked about in the news media. Researcher Jonanthan Mermin makes a similar point suggesting that the news media often seem to serve as "transcribers of official utterances."

This reluctance of the press to express any independent opinion about issues can have serious consequences for public debates about issues. A useful example has to do with the public debate over the Iraq War. The major argument for going to war was the firm belief in Washington that Saddam Hussein had developed Weapons of Mass Destruction (WMD). Within a relatively short amount of time, it became clear that this was not the case, yet public support for the war remained surprisingly high.

Research on this topic suggests one of the reasons was the lack of much critical coverage in the press. In a book entitled *Why the Press Failed* Lance Bennett, Regina Lawrence, and Steven Livingston attempted to explain this anomaly. One of the more important explanations was that the Democratic leadership in Congress and the Senate was extremely uncomfortable criticizing the president about the war until much later in the conflict. There were plenty of critics outside of Washington, but the media's overdependence on elite opinion apparently prevented them from providing the American public with an alternative perspective.

Mermin has a wonderful quote by TV journalist Jim Lehrer that provides a telling demonstration of this point with regard to the war in Iraq:

> The word occupation ... was never mentioned in the run-up to the war. It was liberation. This was [talked about in Washington as] a war of liberation, not a war of occupation. So as a consequence, those of us in journalism never even looked at the issue of occupation.

In other words, unless the political leadership is debating an issue, journalists are rarely able to bring other perspectives to the table. Some might argue that this is how representative democracy should work. These are after all the people who were elected to lead. True democracies however must have a genuinely independent press who present a wide range of viewpoints for us to consider.

Power Comes in Many Forms

The idea that power leads to media access is not limited to politicians. There are also individuals, organizations, and companies that are inherently newsworthy because, among other reasons, they have vast resources that also allow them to have a major impact on society. When Microsoft or Google speak about political issues that affect their industry, the news media listen. The same is true about political organizations and even protest movements. An organization the size of Greenpeace—which has offices in over forty countries—may not have the type of access afforded a major U.S. cabinet member, but they are much more likely to get reporters to their events than a small local group of environmentalists protesting against a factory accused of polluting their water.

The fact that power translates into access to the news media can also be applied to cities, states, and even countries. One is much more likely to hear news that comes from the richest and more populated states (e.g., New York, California) than from the poorer states (e.g., Arkansas). And people living in Europe are more likely to hear what is happening in the United States than anything happening in Africa. It is sad but true that Europeans are more likely to know what is happening with Paris Hilton, Britney Spears, and the late Michael Jackson than about political leaders in Nigeria. One of the most important rules of international news is that there is always a flood of information that flows from the haves to the have-nots and a mere trickle that runs in the opposite direction.

Not Just More Coverage But Usually More Positive

Does the fact that powerful elites get covered *more* mean that they get covered more positively? The answer, for the most part, is yes. There are basically two doors for getting into the news. The front door is reserved for VIPs: the people with political power. When these people enter, they are usually treated with respect. They are covered because of who they are as much as for what they are doing or saying. Here is a typical front door story from the *New York Times* that appeared in September 2009.

> **White House Scraps Bush's Approach to Missile Shield**
>
> WASHINGTON—President Obama scrapped his predecessor's proposed antiballistic missile shield in Eastern Europe on Thursday and ordered instead the development of a reconfigured system designed to shoot down short- and medium-range Iranian missiles. In one of the biggest national security reversals of his young presidency, Mr. Obama canceled former President George W. Bush's plan to station a radar facility in the Czech Republic and 10 ground-based interceptors in Poland. Instead, he plans to deploy smaller SM-3 interceptors by 2011, first aboard ships and later in Europe, possibly even in Poland or the Czech Republic. Mr. Obama said that the new system "will provide stronger, smarter and swifter defenses of American forces and America's allies" to meet a changing threat from Iran.

In these types of stories political leaders are basically using the press as an electronic bulletin board. They announce what they are going to do and provide carefully prepared explanations about why they are doing it. Now this doesn't mean that every new organ will be equally accommodating. Thus the Fox News story for the same day covered the announcement much more negatively. Generally, however, unless there is major controversy about what is being said, heads of state are given much more latitude to pass their messages to the public. As noted, the opposition is usually given a chance to respond but being able to respond to an event is very different than being able to initiate it. One has to add to all this the ability to produce endless amounts of soft stories such as the media frenzy that accompanied the debate about which dog would be lucky enough to be adopted by the Obamas. Dominating the headlines is one of the important advantages that come with political power.

Those with power and resources have the added advantages of being able to hire "spin doctors" who are experts at promoting stories to the news media. While many pundits often exaggerate the influence of these advisors, the ability to place potential news stories in an attractive package does make a difference. Advisors are also experts at preparing stories in ways that make it easier to turn them into news stories. Reporters are always pressed for time. Public relations people make journalists' lives much easier because they provide easy access to information and events, deal with technical details such as lighting and camera angles, and even prepare news releases that need little editing before being turned into news. Having a large staff and a bit of money also allows powerful political actors to hire a talented web team who are responsible for keeping journalists (and supporters) in the loop and preparing interesting videos for general distribution. This means that political power can also be translated into power over the new Internet-based media.

This doesn't mean that every journalist and news medium will provide positive coverage of such announcements. There are certain newspapers, television stations, and especially blogs that are either generally opposed to the president or certain policies. In addition, journalists often frame stories about the powerful with a certain degree of cynicism and reporters are also always on the lookout for scandals. Powerful leaders also fail, and the media are more than happy to talk about these shortcomings in great detail. Even with regard to negative stories, political power can be critical when it comes to damage control. Reporters who come down too hard on powerful leaders may find themselves at the back of the line for getting information. So journalists have no choice but to think very carefully before they go to war against their most important sources. A White House reporter that reveals a presidential scandal is like a magician who burns himself alive on stage. It's a wonderful trick, but you can only do it once.

The other way to get into the news is through the back door. This door is reserved for weaker political actors who only become newsworthy if they do something especially weird or deviant. The powerful can be pretty boring and still get into the news. But if you are not important you better be interesting.

One way weaker groups become interesting enough to get into the news is to take their clothes off. Naked protests have been carried out by groups ranging from People for the Ethical Treatment of Animals ("I'd rather go naked than wear fur") to firefighters demanding higher wages. Naked protesters are not only deviant enough to be considered news, they also provide great visuals. But like all groups that use exceptional actions to attract media attention, those who undress pay a heavy price in terms of legitimacy. Take, for example, the following two news stories about naked bicyclists. The first took place in Seattle in June 2004 and the second in Denver in June 2009 (it was probably not a total coincidence that both took place in June rather than February).

Naked Bicyclists Ride in Protest Over Environmental Abuse

A group of between 50 and 60 naked bicyclists took to the streets of Seattle on Saturday, and a few were seen in Olympia, police said. The event was a protest but it was not immediately clear whether it was linked to a radical environmentalist group known as the Earth Liberation Front. Protesters in Seattle said that they were protesting the use of cars, which increases pollution ... The FBI on Friday warned law enforcement agencies across the country that radical environmentalists might be staging protests this weekend to show their support for a jailed arsonist. The FBI bulletin said the Earth Liberation Front reportedly was planning a "day of action and solidarity" that could include acts of eco-terrorism, according to Tor Bjornstad, a police commander in Olympia, one of the cities mentioned as a likely target.

Boulder Police will be Scrutinizing Naked Bicyclists in Saturday Protest

The Boulder Police Department has a reminder for riders planning to participate Saturday in the World Naked Bike Ride: Indecent-exposure laws will be enforced. Participants not covering their genitals are subject to arrest and, if convicted under this statute, may be required to register as sexual offenders, the department said in a release Wednesday. The department said it also has reached out to organizers of the event to advise them about ways participants may avoid arrest. These include wearing undergarments that cover genitalia or otherwise obscuring those body parts from public view. Participants are strongly urged to be mindful of the requirements of the law.

Both news stories put a special emphasis on what can be called the "Law and Order" frame. In the Seattle story the bicyclists were probably protesting against car pollution and were somehow turned into terrorists (which makes the story far more interesting). The Denver story—which was written before the protest—was initiated by the police and warned protesters that they might be registered as sex offenders. These two stories exemplify two major modes for covering these types of protests: they are covered as either weird, dangerous, or both.

The fact that journalists often focus on the issue of law and order provides important advantages to the authorities because this often fits the message they are promoting. In many conflicts the weaker side (let's call them the challenger) is attempting to talk about some type of injustice while the more powerful side wants to stress the need for law and order. This is true about workers' strikes, protests about issues such as discrimination and human rights, and even when a weaker country (say Iran) challenges a more powerful country (the U.S.). The challenger wants to talk about their demands while the news media are interested in the action. When workers shut down an airline, the major part of the story has to do with the masses of people stranded at airports; the workers' demands for more money are neither interesting nor photogenic. The same is true when protesters use some form of disorder to attract media attention. Any damage they cause is far more newsworthy than the stories they tell about the dangers of (say) global warming. Whatever the personal sympathies of the reporters the old adage remains true: "if it bleeds it leads."

Now to be fair, not every protest gets negative coverage. If, for example, a group can mobilize a very large demonstration for what is generally seen as a legitimate cause, journalists are much more likely to provide sympathetic coverage. In these cases it is the size of the protest that provides the necessary drama. But here, too, only the more powerful political movements can pull of an event of that magnitude and even they can't do it too often. Any publicity they achieve is likely to be fleeting.

Another problem of getting in the news through the back door is that even if you've only put on a weird costume to get in, you're not allowed to change clothes once you get inside. So there you are being filmed in a Polar Bear costume to protest global warming. You want to talk about the environment and the reporters keep asking you about the costume ("How hot is it in there"?). If you decide you've had enough and step outside to change into a jacket and tie, you won't be allowed back in the news room. Peering through the small, dirty window above the locked door in the back you find you've been replaced by naked jugglers protesting prayer in schools.

Is There a Side Door?

There is one strategy that weaker groups can sometimes use to provide news people with drama without completely sacrificing legitimacy: *civil disobedience*. Take, for example, a sit-in that blocks an entrance to a factory accused of polluting the water in a particular city. This too is an act of disorder but being dragged of or beaten by police can turn the protesters into victims rather than aggressors. This tactic provides drama with a minimal amount of downside. The relative success of such tactics depends on three factors: the level of violence that the authorities use against the group, the extent to which people can identify with your cause, and the level of violence you use. If you decide to block a road in order to get a raise in salary, for example, you'll probably be covered as a bunch of trouble makers. This is a reminder of how political context and breadth of support can make a major difference in news coverage.

One of the most successful examples of the civil disobedience strategy was used in the civil rights struggle in the 1960s. Martin Luther King had stressed to his followers and the public that the struggle for racial equality would be nonviolent. Even when the protesters were beaten with clubs they refused to respond in kind. An historic protest took place in Birmingham, Alabama, on May 4, 1963. The Police Commissioner Eugene "Bull" Conner decided to set attack dogs on the protesters leading to some terrible pictures of police brutality. One of the most famous pictures was published on the front page of the *New York Times* and showed a fifteen-year old boy being viciously attacked by German Shepherds.

In an important book on the role of the press in the civil rights struggle, Gene Roberts and Hank Klibanoff described the impact the photos had on the political environment surrounding the struggle.

> The police response and the images it produced had an instant impact in two places where it mattered most, Birmingham and Washington. In Birmingham Negro leaders who had been negotiating quietly with moderate whites and who had been reluctant to support [Martin Luther] King quickly fell in line behind him ... The images had a far more important impact in Washington ... That afternoon, [President John] Kennedy sent Burke Marshall of the Justice Department's civil rights division to Birmingham.

The fact that the civil rights movement received so much sympathetic coverage was much more than a question of mere strategy. It was also a reflection of the fact that American public opinion about race issues was beginning to change. This was a case where journalists—at least in the North—were making editorial *choices* to cover the story as a clear case of injustice. It tells us that, despite the close association between power and media access, there are cases in which the news media play a more independent role in political conflicts. We also learn that shocking visual images can have an important effect on the political process and that this was true even before the creation of the Internet and YouTube.

Cumulative Inequality

Another ramification of our first principle is the idea of *cumulative inequality*. Not only does political power translate to power over the media, but the political actors who most need access to the news are the ones that find it the most difficult to obtain. As in many areas of life, when it comes to exposure in the news media, the rich generally get richer and the poor remain poor. Those with real political power certainly enjoy getting good publicity (who doesn't?) and it also helps them achieve their political goals. But because they *have* power, they are less *dependent* on the news media than others; they can get things done directly (say by passing a law or sending troops somewhere).

The powerless, on the other hand, have little chance of achieving anything without some public attention. It doesn't matter if it is a protest group trying to recruit members, a member of the political opposition who is trying to speak out against the government, a third party presidential candidate trying to get on the ballot, or a developing country launching a campaign to attract tourism. In each of these cases getting into the news is essential to their cause. But these are the actors who are the least likely to be invited to attend the party; the only way they can get in is if they hide inside the cake and jump out when least expected.

To illustrate this point let's think about two organizations who are pressuring the government concerning different pieces of legislation. One is Microsoft who is concerned about a new law that will limit its ability to include its software as part of every computer that is sold. The other is the Ostrich Liberation League (OLL) who is attempting to get a law passed that makes it illegal to sell ostrich meat, to ride ostriches, or to produce ostrich saddles or hats.

Microsoft has enormous resources that can allow it to work almost entirely behind the scenes using an army of lawyers, lobbyists, and maybe even a few politicians who have received campaign support. From Microsoft's perspective, the less the press writes about the issue the better. The OLL, on the other hand, has no chance at all of getting anywhere unless they attract media attention. But let's face it, Ostriches will never be considered big news. The only way the OLL will get into the news is by doing something outrageous knowing full well that they will be covered as a bunch of wacky eccentrics, to put it mildly.

It is important to emphasize that the level of power should be seen as a continuum rather than a dichotomy. While this discussion has referred to the powerful and the powerless, the truth is that there are political organizations, interest groups, and think tanks that fall somewhere in between these two extremes. The ability of these various actors to promote themselves to the media without resorting to extreme tactics is directly related to their place on the power continuum.

In general however, the news media are major agents for maintaining and even intensifying the power gaps in society. The rules of access insure that the powerful are constantly seen as more important and in many cases more respectable than the weak. This in turn makes it easier for them to maintain or change their preferred policies. As discussed, these rules are not set in stone. There are times when the news media serve as advocates of the weak.

What About the New Media?

Some readers probably think that everything said to this point is simply out of date. They would argue that in the age of cell phones with cameras, YouTube, and the Blogosphere political power becomes less important. Today, even the weakest groups can get their message out to everyone through the Internet and social networking platforms. All it takes is for one good political story to go viral and everyone—including the mainstream media—is paying attention.

The new technology does make a difference, sometimes even a huge difference. But in addition to the new opportunities that have become available because of the new media, there are also some important limitations. The new advantages and the limitations of this new technology can be understood by looking at the type of challenger that could most benefit from these changes: political movements.

Political Movements and the New Media

Most political movements are the classic "back door" challengers. Even the largest movements are usually not considered inherently newsworthy. They still must do something dramatic if they hope to get covered by the traditional media and, as said, this more often than not translates into negative coverage. The question that needs to be asked is how much the new communication technology changes the ability of these movements to become more powerful, to get their message out to supporters and the general public, and to bring about political change.

There are four major goals political movements attempt to achieve where the new Internet media could be useful. The first, and most obvious, is that it should help movements in their efforts to mobilize supporters to their cause. The second goal is to have their messages and news stories appear in the traditional media which will allow them to reach a much wider audience. Related to that amplification effect, the third goal is to have an influence on public opinion so the wider audience becomes more sympathetic with the movement. And ultimately, the fourth is to have an impact on politics. These four goals can be seen as four stations that movements have to pass in their attempts to climb an extremely steep mountain whose peak is called political success. It turns out that not only does it become increasingly difficult to pass each station, but one finds that the new technology becomes less and less helpful as one gets closer to the top.

The first station movements need to pass has to do with their ability to mobilize supporters and other resources in order to become more powerful. Here is where political movements receive their greatest boost from the new media technology. Here, the changes that have taken place with the advent of the new media are nothing short of revolutionary. The Internet and SMS technology provides movements with the potential to communicate instantly with millions of people around the world. Compare the cost and effectiveness of mailing leaflets to supporters as opposed to sending out emails that include both a video presentation and the opportunity to respond to what they've received. Think about the ability to remind people continually of a protest taking place, of being able to ask people to electronically sign a petition and pass it on to their friends, of allowing people to make a donation using a credit card while sitting in their pajamas in front of the computer, or of sending an inspiring speech by your leader to people living in thirty different countries. Now let's supercharge all of this by allowing every movement to put links on its web site that allows it to communicate and build coalitions with other similar movements around the country and the world. When you put all of these assets together you begin to understand the potential the new media represent for mobilizing people and groups for the cause.

The major thing to remember is that all of this revolutionary technology provides movements with the *potential* to exponentially increase their membership and resources. Whether it actually does depends, among many other things, on how much the movement's messages and leaders resonate with a large segment of the public. Here too it's a question of political context. There are tens of thousands of movements demanding our attention. The amount of time and attention any of us can or will devote to any one movement is still extremely limited. Thus, even if a movement has the best technology available it will remain small and obscure unless it appeals to a relatively large number of people who are willing to devote time and money to the cause. Even in the digital age, it is hard to get Americans excited about the preservation of historical sites in Albania.

Movement leaders also find that the fact that people are willing to sign an electronic petition about something does not mean they will either give money or come to a demonstration. In fact, because electronic participation is so easy it may give some people a sense that "they've done their part" and thus even lower the number of people who are willing to get out of their pajamas and do something active for the movement. Perhaps it is no coincidence that in May 2009 one of the oldest American social activists, Ralph Nader, made an extremely aggressive attack on Internet activism. He called the Internet "a huge waste of trivial time." He asked his audience of college students to consider what they were going to tell their grandchildren:

> You know. The world is melting down. They're nine years old. They're sitting on your lap. They've just become aware of things that are wrong in the world: starvation, poverty, whatever. And they ask you, what were you doing when all this was happening: Grandma? Grandpa? That you were too busy updating your profile on Facebook ?

A similar point was made by Evgeny Morozov who coined an extremely useful term for this: *slacktivism*. Slacktivism is a combination of the words slacker and activism. The idea is that there are quite a number of digital activities people can carry out that make them feel good about themselves but have absolutely no impact on either society or politics. One of the examples he gives is a Facebook group called "Saving the Children of Africa." Morozov points out that at first glance the organization looks very impressive because it has over 1.2 million members. At the time he wrote however, the organization had raised a paltry $6,000 (about a half a penny a person). As he puts it: "The problem, however, is that the granularity of contemporary digital activism provides too many easy way-outs: too many people decide to donate a penny where they may otherwise want to donate a dollar."

As we move up the mountain of political success, the air gets increasingly thin and the new technology becomes much less helpful. The reason can be summed up in one word: *competition*. Consider attempting to just get past the second station of trying to get favorable coverage of your group in the traditional media. Generating buzz on the Internet about your cause can certainly make a difference, but it is no substitute for generating an investigative report on *CBS Evening News* or *Sixty Minutes*. There are tens of thousands of politicians, organizations, movements, companies, and (let us not forget) celebrities all competing to make it into these news and current events programs. All of these competitors use Twitter and many of them can use the new technology to produce newsworthy events. But the traditional media still have only so much space and time to allocate, even if their web sites provide more space than in the past. Younger journalists probably spend more time actively searching political blogs and Internet sites but they too only have so much time and energy to look. And guess what? They will be especially interested in spending time trying to find stories about the politically powerful.

It also turns out that only a small fraction of major news stories come from the blogosphere. Researchers Jure Leskovec, Lars Backstrom, and Jon Kleinberg employed a powerful computer program to search the web over a fairly large period of time to study the rise and fall of the biggest news stories. They tracked an amazingly large 1.6 million mainstream media sites and blogs. The finding that is most relevant to this discussion was that a mere 3.5 percent of all major news cycles were initiated in the blogosphere and then moved to the other media. The vast majority of news stories ran in the opposite direction: the blogs and alternative news sites were following stories that first appeared in the traditional news media. This should tell you something important about how difficult it is for all political actors to use the new media as a means of breaking into the mainstream media. It should also tell you that traditional media remains the best tool for generating political waves about an issue.

The competition becomes even fiercer when an organization attempts to move beyond gaining news coverage and attempts to interest the broad public or to get policy makers to actually make changes. Starting with having an impact on public opinion, it is almost impossible for a small group to be heard above the crowd. There are, of course, people—you know who you are—who spend hours every day reading political blogs. But even they have no choice but to confine themselves to those issues that interest them. In that case, we are moving from the age of broadcasting to what many have called *narrowcasting*.

Getting the attention of political leaders and policy makers is even harder and needless to say they have their own agendas to promote. Here's a good example that comes from Amnesty International working in Britain. I interviewed one of the people involved in media relations, and he was talking about both the great advantages provided by the web and some limitations. As an example of some of the problems he faced, he talked about an electronic petition they had organized against an anti-terrorism law that allowed the police to lock up terrorist suspects for six weeks before they have to charge them with any offense. They organized a fairly successful campaign to get people to sign a petition on the Prime Minister's web site. The Amnesty spokesperson talked about his frustration.

> We got a reasonable number of people to sign up. The failure was that there were so many populist issues that are being petitioned and we were maybe the 15th most popular. Some of the things that were more popular than us were ridiculous. One of them was whether to allow the Red Arrows [a display troop of the Royal Aircraft] to fly over London to mark the Olympics. The other had to do with demanding that a right-wing television presenter who had a show about cars became Home Secretary [one of the Ministers]. It was a joke and it received I think 5 times as many signatures as we did.

Perhaps a metaphor would be helpful. Your organization has just purchased a megaphone so your leaders will be especially loud. The problem is that every group has a megaphone. To make things worse, those with political power not only have more megaphones, they also have sophisticated sound systems so their speeches are heard all over the country.

Despite all these limitations, there are two very different types of movements who seem to have benefited the most from the emergence of the Internet. The first are what are known as Transnational Advocacy Networks (TANs). Groups dealing with climate change, the dangers of globalization, nuclear proliferation, cruelty to animals, and human rights are all examples of movements who have far more power and influence now than in the past because of their ability to mobilize supporters and resources from around the world. Researchers, governments, and international companies have all begun to think about how these groups' increasing power is having an impact on the world. In fact researchers Sean Aday and Steve Livingston even go so far as to claim that in some cases the impact of these movements can be compared to that of countries.

The second type of group that has seen a major change in their fortunes due to the Internet is terrorist organizations. The Internet provides these groups with a number of important advantages. Terrorist organizations can instantly exchange information—including technical information about weapons—from and to any place on the planet. They can also distribute inspirational material and videos to supporters and potential supporters. The videos can include inspiring speeches from their leaders, threats to carry out terrorist attacks, and actual footage from the attacks they have carried out. Because such videos are considered newsworthy many Western journalists end up showing them to the broader public and in doing so unintentionally help the terrorists spread fear.

The Internet can also be used by terrorists to coordinate tactics and strategy. One of the most important traits of the Internet is that individuals around the world can create *communities* that give them a sense of belonging. While this can, in most cases, be seen as a positive development there are some communities the world could live without. The reason why terrorist groups are especially likely to be empowered by the new media is because mobilization—especially international mobilization—is such a central element in their overall strategy. Unlike more conventional movements, they are not usually attempting to convince the broad public or Western leaders about the legitimacy of their cause. Their goals are to intimidate their opponents. Terrorist groups don't enter the news media through the back door, they simply blow it open.

The Internet also provides terrorists with an extremely effective and anonymous method for doing strategic research before an attack. A good example of this new found power can be seen in the report about the planning of the 9/11 attack that was published by the National Commission on Terrorist Attacks Upon the United States. The leaders of Al-Qaeda were able to use the Internet to find flight schools that might accept them and to find routes and flight paths of various airlines and of course to communicate with each other. In fact, learning how to use the Internet was an important part of their terrorist training.

So in some ways the new media have radically changed the relationship between political and media power. But due to the rules of political competition, these cases remain the exception rather than the rule. When it comes to the ability of movements and other challengers to organize and mobilize it is certainly a new age. On the other hand, the new technologies appear to be less revolutionary when it comes to getting a message to the broad public or bringing about real change. Equally important, the ability of political actors to successfully exploit the new media depends first and foremost on who they represent, their goals, and the political environment in which they are operating. The powerful, it turns out, still have the upper hand.

So if things are so great for the political powerful, why are they constantly whining about news coverage? It turns out that despite their many advantages even the most powerful lose control over news stories. This brings us to the next part of our story.

Questions for Thought and Discussion

1. Bearing in mind what was said about political power over the news media, record and watch the national or local news on television. How many stories involve powerful people or groups and how many items include weaker actors? What are the differences between the kinds of news stories that are constructed about powerful and less powerful political actors?
2. Think of a political group with which you identify. Based on what you learned in this chapter, think about the following questions: What are some of the activities the group could carry out in order to generate some positive publicity? What are the characteristics of the group that either increase or decrease its chances of getting this type of publicity? Is there anything the group has done that you consider a mistake because of the bad publicity it produced?

MEDIA

The Media and Class Warfare

South Asians in U.S. Television and Film

THE MEDIA AND CLASS WARFARE

BY NORMAN SOLOMON

A few decades ago, upwards of one-third of the American workforce was unionized. Now the figure is down around 10 percent. And news media are central to the downward spiral.

As unions wither, the journalistic establishment has a rationale for giving them less ink and air time. As the media coverage diminishes, fewer Americans find much reason to believe that unions are relevant to their working lives.

But the media problem for labor goes far beyond the fading of unions from newsprint, television and radio. Media outlets aren't just giving short shrift to organized labor. The avoidance extends to unorganized labor, too.

So often, when issues of workplaces and livelihoods appear in the news, they're framed in terms of employer plights. The frequent emphasis is on the prospects and perils of companies that must compete.

Well, sure, firms need to compete. And working people need to feed and clothe and house themselves and their families. And workers hope to receive adequate medical care.

The issue of health insurance is a political talking point for many candidates these days. But meanwhile, unionized workers are finding themselves in a weakened position when they try to retain whatever medical coverage they may have. And non-unionized workers often have little or none.

With all the media discussion of corporate bottom-line difficulties, the human element routinely gets lost in the shuffle. In day-to-day business news and in general reporting, the lives of people on the line are apt to be rendered as abstractions. Or they simply go unmentioned.

The topic of war in Iraq is huge in the media. I can't say much for the quality of that coverage, but at least it keeps reporting that a military war is happening overseas. But what about the economic war that's happening at home?

Phrases like "class war" have been discredited in American news media—tarred as too blunt, too combative, too rhetorical. But, call it what you will, the clash of economic interests is with us always.

Waged from the top down, class war is a triumphant activity—and part of the success involves the framing and avoidance of certain unpleasant realities via corporate-owned media outlets. You don't need to be a rocket scientist or a social scientist to grasp that multibillion-dollar companies are not going to own, or advertise with, media firms that challenge the power of multibillion-dollar companies.

One of the dominant yet little-remarked-upon shifts in the media landscape over the past couple of decades has been the enormous upsurge in business news as general news. A result is that tens of millions of low-income people are seeing constant news stories about challenges and opportunities for well-to-do investors.

The reverse, of course, is not the case. The very affluent of our society don't often pick up a newspaper or tune in the evening news and encounter waves of stories and commentaries about the dire straits of America's poor people and what it's like to be one of them. And it's even more rare to see coverage of ways that a few people grow obscenely wealthy as a direct result of the further impoverishment of the many.

"Class war"? The nation's most powerful editors cringe at the phrase. But every day, millions of Americans are painfully aware that—by any other name—class warfare is going on, and they're losing.

Norman Solomon, "The Media and Class Warfare," *The Humanist*, vol. 68, no. 1, pp. 42. Copyright © 2008 by American Humanist Association. Reprinted with permission. Provided by ProQuest LLC. All rights reserved.

SOUTH ASIANS IN U.S. TELEVISION AND FILM

Trends in Ethnic Media Representations

BY BHOOMI K. THAKORE

This chapter covers the importance of understanding diversity in media representation, specifically in terms of the images we see in our popular media. As an agent of socialization, the media has a profound impact on how we understand our society and the people who live in it. Diverse representations that accurately reflect our social world help us with these understandings in order to improve our social interactions and promote differences in experiences and identities.

The South Asian[1] population in the United States largely reflects migration patterns that allowed for the entrance of two different groups. The first group, composed of highly skilled technical migrants, arrived under permissions granted with the passing of the 1965 Immigration and Nationality Act (Takaki, 1989; Prashad, 2000; Wu, 2002). These Asian immigrants are often perceived in U.S. society as the stereotypical "model minority" for their high education levels and occupational statuses. However, as with any stereotype, this one is equally problematic for its limiting assumptions about the professional pursuits of Asian Americans (McGee, Thakore, & LaBlance, 2016; Takaki, 1989; Tuan, 1999). The second group, which arrived under family reunification policies as relatives of those naturalized citizens from the first group, is much more diverse in their educational and occupational backgrounds. In the 21st century, most South Asians in the United States are either the 1.5- or second-generation children of immigrants or newly immigrated family members of naturalized citizens (Maira, 2002; Prashad, 2000; Purkayastha, 2005; Shankar, 2008).[2]

Throughout the 20th century, representations of South Asians in U.S. film and television were limited to exotic foreigners or nameless taxi drivers and background convenience store owners. In many ways, these representations relied heavily on their characterization of South Asians as foreign and ethnic minorities who are unable to assimilate into mainstream U.S. society. In the 21st century, media representations of South Asians are now reflecting the changing demographics of this population. Indeed, this has some historical precedent. For example, beginning in the 1970s, there were increasing examples of Black and Latinx characters in U.S. film and television. As scholars have suggested, the increase in these diverse representations was due in large part to advertising and the perceived purchasing power of these groups (Coltrane &

---

1 I define "South Asian" as those whose ethnic origins are from such countries as India, Pakistan, Bangladesh, Sri Lanka, Nepal, and Bhutan.

2 As discussed by Rumbaut and Portes (2001) and others, the second generation is those children who are born in the United States to first-generation parents who themselves immigrated. The 1.5 generation is those who immigrate to the United States as young children.

Messineo, 2000; Cortese, 2008). However, as with most representations of people of color, these early examples tended to rely heavily on stereotypical representations and beauty ideals that perpetuated the racial social order (Beltran & Fojas, 2008; Hall, 1997; Thakore, 2016; Vera & Gordon, 2003). In the 21st century, the popularity of Bollywood films (films produced in India) and the U.K.-produced film *Slumdog Millionaire* among U.S. audiences helped propel South Asians to becoming the next big ethnicity in popular media. Additionally, most South Asians are used as the "honorary White" (Bonilla-Silva, 2004) minority to round out color-blind social circles in popular films and television shows (Rastogi, 2010). South Asians are also a good stand-in for Arabs and Muslims in this post-9/11 reality of fear (Alsultany, 2012; Nacos & Torres-Reyna, 2007). The only major requirements are that they be experienced and, of course, good-looking.

In this chapter, I identify the most common types of South Asian characters in U.S. film and television. My research utilizes two rounds of data. First, I distributed an online survey in the fall of 2010 to students at and affiliated with a private university in Chicago. Respondents answered a variety of questions about their basic demographics, media-consumption habits, and perceptions of South Asian characters (both historically and contemporarily) as positive, negative, or both. Next, I conducted 50 interviews between May 2011 and January 2012. Interview respondents answered questions about their background, their social networks, their media consumption, their perceptions of South Asians in the media and in society, and their perceptions on the future of media representations. Here, I present the most frequently reported representations to understand the types of South Asian characters prevalent on the U.S. screen (Thakore, 2016), the kinds of South Asian representations that resonate with this sample of media consumers, and suggestions about what these representations mean for the perception of South Asians in the 21st century.

Relevant Literature

The Racial Formation of South Asians

As Omi and Winant (2014) argued, racial *formations* are the result of social, political, and economic forces that have determined the status and perceptions of people of color. These statuses have formed over time depending on social and historical circumstances. Black–White relations have been strained for centuries, due in large part to allegiances to Social Darwinism. For other groups, including Asian Americans, the dynamics have been similar. Indeed, Asian Americans of all origins have struggled for decades in mainstream U.S. society to define and defend their racial, ethnic, and national origins. The most important struggle took place in the U.S. Census, in which Asian Americans were unable to identify as one of nine Asian/Pacific Islander groups until 1990 (Omi, 1999; Zhou & Lee, 2003).

In the early 20th century, South Asians were considered a part of the Aryan category in the United States during the migration of Punjabi Indians to the West Coast. However, contentious legal fights for citizenship by individuals like Bhagat Singh Thind in California changed this categorization quickly. In 1923, the U.S. Supreme Court ruled that Thind, a World War I veteran, was categorically Aryan but understood (by them) to be Indian and thus could not apply for citizenship. Soon after, the United States began strong limitations on Indian immigration to the West and the legal rights of those Indians already settled. It was not until 1946 that these early Indian immigrants were able to become citizens (Leonard, 1997; Prashad, 2000; Takaki, 1985). In 1965, President Johnson signed the Immigration and Nationality Act, allowing highly educated migrants from Asia to immigrate to the United States. From 1966 to 1977, 83% of immigrants from India were professional and technical workers, including approximately 20,000 science PhDs, 40,000 engineers, and 25,000 doctors (Prashad, 2000, p. 75).

The racial formation of South Asians has also been influenced in part by media representations, which in turn have been influenced by South Asian immigration in the 1960s and 1970s that brought these highly educated and professional migrants (Prashad, 2000; Takaki, 1985; Wu, 2002). The rhetoric of Asians as "model minorities" in the United States has been popular since the mid-1980s, with news stories following President Reagan's remarks in 1984 about the high educational achievements of Asian Americans. Within a few years, there were stories about Asians as the model minority on *60 Minutes* and in the publications *U.S. News and World Report*, *Fortune*, *The New Republic*, and *Newsweek* (Takaki, 1989, p. 474). To some extent, this rhetoric was true for the time. In 1980, 36% of foreign-born Asians had college degrees, compared to 11% of Whites. In 1990, this increased to 42% of Asians, compared to 25% of Whites (Wu, 2002, pp. 50–51).

However, even for being model minorities, Asians have still been unable to achieve the same economic and professional standing as Whites. When factoring in education, gender, ethnicity, and working hours, the average personal income of Asian Americans still tends to be less than Whites (Takaki, 1989, p. 475). Additionally, race relations in the United States continue to be segmented for immigrants due to their cultural differences. The extent to which new groups can assimilate into society will be determined by the extent to which they let go of their ethnic culture to assimilate into mainstream society (Alba & Nee, 2003; Gordon, 1964; Park, 1950; Steinberg, 1979).

South Asian Americans are also subjected to the same practices of institutional and interactional racism as other groups of color. As many race scholars have noted, race relations in the United States have shifted from overt practices of separation and inequality to more covert actions and attitudes that promote inclusivity on the surface but maintain a racial hierarchy (Bonilla-Silva, 2014; Doane & Bonilla-Silva, 2003; Feagin, 2000; Pager & Shepard, 2008). Kim (1999) argued that Asian Americans are "triangled" between Whites and Blacks, in terms of their social status and perceived assimilation into society. Bonilla-Silva (2004) argued that the U.S. racial hierarchy is developing into the kind of triracial system that is present in many Latin American countries in which color and socioeconomic status determine one's social position. In the United States, this is composed of the White group, which includes European Whites, assimilated Latinos, and light-skinned multiracials; the honorary White group, which includes light-skinned Latinos and East and South Asians; and the collective Black group, which includes Southeast Asians and dark-skinned people of color. For Bonilla-Silva, skin tone and money will largely inform an individual's ability to move up this racial ladder. These dynamics will have larger impacts on how South Asians are perceived and represented.

A Brief History of South Asian Media Representations

Stuart Hall (1997, 2003) argued that representations of racial and ethnic minorities tend to be either overtly or covertly racist. Historically, overt representations use negative characterizations to convey the "inferiority" of people of color. As many scholars have argued, overtly racist representations have been phased out for everything from consumer protests to perceptions of political correctness (Beltran & Fojas, 2008; Chito Childs, 2009; Cortese, 2008; Davé, 2013; Entman & Rojecki, 2000; Gray, 2004; Jhally & Lewis, 1992; Larson, 2006; Vera & Gordon, 2003; Wilson et al., 2003). Today, covert representations are not as obvious but still tend to do this in more subtle ways. In the media, non-White characters are integrated into storylines alongside White actors and characters but remain secondary characters who have at least some stereotypical characteristics.

During the early days of film, representations of Indians were limited to those in India. In her analysis of representations of India in feature films from the early 20th century, Dorothy Jones (1955) found that most Indian representations were some variation of primitive tribesman, cultured native, or stalwart soldier. Overall, these portrayals perpetuated the same Orientalist understanding of the East as a mystical and mysterious land (Jones, 1955; Said, 1979). This continued within other examples from the early 20th century, including those in the film *Gunga Din* (1939) and minor characters like Punjab from *Annie* (1982).

In 1952, the Indian film *Mother India* received an Academy Award nomination for Best Foreign Film. The film symbolized the struggle of India as a country after the British granted independence in 1947, represented as a woman named Radha (played by Nargis) who struggled as a widow with three children. One of these children was played by actor Sajid Khan[3], who appeared at age 15 on U.S. television on the NBC show Maya (1967). The show revolved around a 15-year-old English boy looking for his father with a local Indian boy, Raji, and his elephant, Maya (Brooks & Marsh, 2007). The show only lasted until February of the 1967–1968 season. The stark differences between the two are emphasized in ways that reinforce the White Savior role (Hughey, 2014; Vera & Gordon, 2003) and in portraying India as an Orientalized Other. The representations of India as a foreign and exotic land where everyone has an elephant are simply reinforcing stereotypes about people who are Indian and what life is like in India. They are essentialized for audience entertainment and interest. There were similarly Orientalized representations in the 1984 film *Indiana Jones and the Temple of Doom,* directed by Steven Spielberg. Set in 1935 India, the film chronicled the adventures of the epitomized White Savior, Indiana Jones (Harrison Ford), who is tasked with saving a sacred Sankara stone from members of the Thuggee cult. The South Asian actors in this film included Om Puri and Roshan Seth, who are established actors in Indian and British cinema but were typecast for these particular roles as savage Indians who eat monkey brains.

Beginning in the 1980s, Indians/South Asians (men) were portrayed as background characters in films and televisions shows (with mostly White casts) set in New York City or similar urban areas. These "actors" were most likely the actual drivers of taxicabs or employees/owners of the convenience stores the stories were set in and who may have received a little bit of cash for the filming rights. Again, South Asian women were virtually absent in these films and programs. Actual South Asian actors did not begin to pop up in popular television until the 1980s and 1990s, with actors such as Jori Colemant (*Head of the Class*), Brian George (*Seinfeld*), and Iqbal Theba (*Married With Children*, and others). These were among those popular shows in which there were other recurring non-White characters, like *Married with Children* (1987–1997) and *Roseanne* (1988–1997), but these characters had limited storylines and screen time.

Indian director Mira Nair, who began her career with documentaries about India, such as the international-award-winning *Salaam Bombay*! (1988), released her first feature film in 1991, *Mississippi Masala.* The film is about the developing relationship between a twice-migrant Indian Ugandan woman, Meena (played by Sarita Choudhury) and a local African American man, Demetrius (played by Denzel Washington). Not only did the film portray the frustrations of parents and families on both sides, but it was also set within the racialized space of Mississippi. This film was revolutionary as the first to represent this kind of interracial relationship in the United States.

South Asian-inspired cinema was also more available in the United States and Canada, mostly within art house theaters. In the 1990s, Indian Canadian director Deepa Mehta produced her Elements Trilogy, which included *Fire* (1996), *Earth* (1998), and *Water* (2005), the latter of which was nominated for the Academy Award for Best Foreign Language Film. In 2002, U.K. director Gurinder Chadra produced the film *Bend it Like Beckham,* which followed the struggles of Jess (played by Parminder Nagra), a Punjabi British teenager playing with a football team against the wishes of her parents.[4] Bollywood-produced films were increasingly available in select theaters for nonresident Indians and later became more widely available on video/DVD. These images appealed not only to the South Asian immigrant experience but also to the up-and-coming generation of young South Asians who were consuming these images and struggling to blend into their host societies (Desai, 2004; Sharma, 2010.

A film that arguably changed the landscape of South Asian media representations in the 21st century was the 2008 film *Slumdog Millionaire.* The film portrayed the life of Jamal Malik (played by Dev Patel), who is a finalist on the Indian version of the show *Who Wants to Be a Millionaire?* The film juxtaposes Jamal's life as a young boy in the slums with his brother Salim and his childhood love Latika (played by Freida Pinto). The audience

3 Sajid Khan also released a music album in the late 1960s with a few singles that almost made the Billboard Top 100. He was quite the heartthrob among girls around this time and appeared in teen magazines of the day.

4 It is noteworthy that in 2003, the year after *Bend It Like Beckham* was released, actress Parminder Nagra was cast in her recurring role in the NBC show ER (1994–2009).

is exposed to the experiences in Jamal's life that allowed him to correctly answer questions that even the most educated person would get wrong. Overall, the characters in *Slumdog Millionaire* are perceived as "third world" others who have significantly different experiences than Westerners. As a result, the actual life circumstances of Indians in India who face extreme poverty, child exploitation, and abuse against women is sugar-coated and ignored. The assumption that this story is not only believable but also normal and common suggests that there is a disconnect between the perceptions of this film by mainstream Western audiences and the realities of the story being told about India, a story that displays the realities of the slums but uses fantasy to soften the blow in many ways (Thakore, 2012).

On television, the next 21st-century example was by way of the NBC show *Outsourced* (2010–2011), a sitcom about a White call center manager whose job and department are outsourced to India. One of the most noteworthy aspects of this show was the fact that the cast was majority non-White. Five of the main characters on the show were of Indian/South Asian descent. These characters, and the other South Asian characters in the background of the show, were played by trained and well-established South Asian actors from the United States, Canada, and India. Additionally, one-third of the writing team was Indian American (*The Times of India*, 2011). For these reasons in particular, *Outsourced* was revolutionary in U.S. prime time television. At first, the show received positive reviews for its "diversity" and was signed for a second season soon after the premiere of the first episode. However, by the end of the first season, *Outsourced* was cancelled (*The Times of India*, 2011). As I discussed elsewhere (Thakore, 2016), a show like this did not have the (mainstream) viewership necessary to make it profitable for the producers and financiers, due in large part to its dependence on overt stereotypes of foreignness.

While there have been many empirical studies examining the experiences of South Asians in the United States (Maira, 2002; Purkayastha, 2005; Shankar, 2008), there have been fewer that examine the ways in which South Asians are being represented in popular media and the ways in which these representations are being perceived. This is particularly relevant today as these representations are increasing. In the next section, I discuss some of the findings from my research on the most frequently reported South Asian media characters of the 21st century.

Findings

Forever Foreigner: Apu

One of the most popular characters identified by my respondents was Apu Nahasapeemapetilon from the FOX sitcom *The Simpsons*. This long-running show revolves around the working-class Simpson family and the cast of characters that make up their town of Springfield, USA. Apu is the longtime owner and manager of the local Kwik-E-Mart. Respondents in the study overwhelmingly describe Apu's character as a negative representation. For example, respondents used words and phrases such as *stereotypical, convenience store clerk, business owner, cheap, foreign, heavily accented, having lots of children, ignorant, stupid, dumb, and the butt of jokes.* None of the respondents in the study described Apu as a solely positive character, but those who described him as both positive and negative pointed to his PhD in Engineering, his representation as a family man, and his sympathetic portrayal.

When respondents talked about Apu, they did so in very overtly ethnic ways, with references to his practice of Hinduism, his wedding ceremony, his vegetarianism, and his statue of Ganesh in his store. These representations of well-understood aspects of Indian culture are practically required when portraying a person of Indian descent on U.S. television. The character also represents a traditional immigrant, with heavily accented or limited English, having an occupation that is associated with a segment of South Asians in the United States. As one respondent said, "Not his personality but what he does for a living, that's something that I definitely see in the neighborhood. So I get it. I'm sure there are people who live in certain neighborhoods who don't get outside the neighborhood who think that's an accurate portrayal just cos [sic] they don't know." (Interview Respondent Ayo, female, 29, Black). These negative perceptions of Apu as an immigrant and a small business owner suggest that perceptions of South Asians in these professions are generally negative. This corresponds to the kinds of attitudes that many Americans have toward new immigrants, particularly those who they perceive as foreign, ethnic, and most importantly, not assimilated.

Respondents perceived Apu negatively because of his stereotypical characteristics—specifically, as a convenience store owner and accented foreigner. When referencing these stereotypes, respondents also characterized him as dumb, ignorant, and an easy target for ridicule. One described Apu as "Thickly accented, bumbling, owner of a dilapidated, marginal convenience store, clearly different in culture, appearance, and language from everyone else, at one point had something like eight kids all at once" (Survey Respondent #57, male, 25, White/ Latino). In particular, the (negative) perception of Apu as a convenience store clerk and business owner suggests that media representation of those South Asians who reflect the demographic shift in the 1980s and 1990s of less educated South Asians immigrating to America (Prashad, 2000). Thus, those immigrants who are more likely to work in such positions are considered negative representations, with negative stereotypes. These negative perceptions of Apu as an immigrant and a small business owner suggest that perceptions of South Asians in these professions are generally negative. This corresponds to the kinds of attitudes that many Americans have toward new immigrants, particularly those who they perceive as foreign, ethnic, and most importantly, not assimilated (Rumbaut & Portes, 2001; Alba & Nee, 2003; Waters & Jimenez, 2005).

The Model Minority: Kumar

One character who was portrayed as both professional and tied to cultural traditions was Kumar Patel from the *Harold and Kumar* film series. The 2004 film *Harold and Kumar Go to White Castle* follows the comedic exploits of Kumar, an Indian American prospective medical student, and Harold, a Korean American finance officer, smoking marijuana and looking for a White Castle. Overt representations of ethnicity and stereotypes were present through the representation of Kumar as a prospective doctor. Professionally, Kumar "played into many different stereotypes of South Asians. He played a 'silly Asian' character who was going to be a doctor" (Survey Respondent #136, 22, female, White). The representation of Kumar as a medical student reflects the well-established stereotype of South Asians as high-achieving, model minorities (McGee et al., 2016; Takaki, 1985; Wu, 2000).

One element of Kumar's character development was the culture clash he experienced with his family over attending medical school and becoming a doctor. As one respondent said, "I would say definitely in *Harold and Kumar,* Kumar's dad pushing him to be a doctor would definitely kind of fall into what I had talked about, everybody's parents pushing them to be working in the professional doctor, lawyer kind of jobs" (Interview Respondent Lauren, female, 34, White/Latina). The representation of Kumar's struggles with his family over pursuing a career as a doctor speaks to how the model minority stereotype influences identity formation for the younger second-generation children of South Asian immigrants (Purkayastha, 2005; Shankar, 2008). Not only do parents and families encourage success; the external pressure of what it means to be "Asian" or "Indian" is also reflected off of them. For Lauren, Kumar's characterization reflected her perceptions of the pressure college-aged South Asians feel from their parents to pursue advanced degrees. These reflect the real-life challenges for Asian Americans navigating two cultural worlds. As a result, education and profession become a part of South Asian identity.

Asian Americans (mostly East Asian and South Asian) have long been stereotyped as the model minority, and it is assumed that all members of this racial/ethnic group are highly intelligent and successful (Takaki, 1985; Wu, 2000). However, as scholars have established, this stereotype not only falsely presupposes a racial hierarchy that is genetic (McGee et al., 2016) but also fails to acknowledge contemporary educational and legal policies that once allowed only a cross-section of educated Asians to immigrate to the United States (Prashad, 2000; Purkayastha, 2005). Further, this stereotype has played an important role in the placement of Asians and South Asians into the "honorary White" category, which positions them as more acceptable than collective Blacks but still not good enough as Whites (Bonilla-Silva, 2004; Feagin, 2001; Kim, 1999).

Just Like Everyone Else: Kelly and Tom

The most popular character reported by respondents in this study was one that did not have any kind of overt ethnic characteristics: Kelly Kapoor (played by Mindy Kaling) from the NBC show *The Office*. In the show, Kelly worked as a customer service employee in a small paper company in Scranton, PA. Originally, Mindy Kaling started as a writer and director for the show. She literally wrote the character for herself in the episode called "Diversity Day" (1.02) and became a member of the cast after that. Kaling had continued her roles as writer, executive producer, and occasional director until 2012, when she left *The Office* for her own show, *The Mindy Project*. Respondents similarly characterized the character of Tom Haverford (played by Aziz Ansari), from Parks and Recreation. In the show, Tom played an assistant in the Pawnee (Indiana) Parks Department. At the time of casting, Ansari was best known as a comedian who had appeared as secondary characters in a variety of films and television shows.

Both Kelly Kapoor and Tom Haverford were portrayed as characters that were not stereotypical. As one respondent said, "Aziz Ansari in all of his [roles] has never played any kind of stereotypical or negative character" (Survey Respondent #98, 18, male, White). In *The Office*, Kelly came off as celebrity obsessed and boy crazy. As one respondent said, "Instead of pigeon-holing [sic] her into a token racial-minority [*sic*] her character is more identifiable as a Nuevo valley girl or kinda ditzy everyday 20-something. She is funny and employed" (Survey Respondent #179, 31, female, White). What is most noteworthy is that respondents perceived both of these characters as positive for breaking some of the preexisting stereotypes of South Asians as either accented foreigners or highly educated medical professionals.

Over the years, South Asian representations have moved away from the traditional and stereotypical examples of Apu to ones that are well-rounded and, most significantly, are *not* identifiable by ethnicity. These contemporary South Asian representations fit into Herman Gray's (2005) category of assimilationist representations, in which non-White characters are portrayed similarly to White characters in the lack of any overt references to the character's ethnic culture. As one respondent said, "[Tom] is sort of similar to *The Office* with Kelly's character, just kind of breaking stereotypes, from ... representations of what I've seen as South Asian, as mostly serious professionals in the medical field, or like physics or doctors, things like that. So I guess positive in that way" (Interview Respondent Ethan, male, 31, White). For Ethan, Tom is portrayed similar to Kelly as outside of well-established stereotypes of the model minority. Interestingly, both of these characters were on shows that were back-to-back on NBC's Thursday-night lineup during the early 2010s. Anyone who watched that block of television during that time period was exposed to two very similar South Asian representations, both of which exist in stark contrast to the previously mentioned representations.

Many of the South Asian respondents in this study also discussed how the characters' *lack* of ethnic characteristics resonated with them on a personal level. While discussing Kelly from *The Office*, one respondent said, "I never really thought of her as being Indian, I just thought her character was fine, she was just stupid and annoying sometimes. And that's how she was being represented because it's not like she has an accent or anything. And to me it's just like someone who grew up here and looks like that. So I don't know if other people got that from that" (Interview Respondent Priya, female, 24, second-generation South Asian American). As Priya said, Kelly's lack of accent was the most salient characteristic that identified Kelly as not Indian, which refers back to the significance of the accented "brown voice," which Shilpa Davé (2013) identified as the overt ethnic accent used to otherize South Asians on-screen. Thus, it can be inferred that positive South Asian representations are those who have assimilated and do not present overtly ethnic characteristics. As Rumbaut and Portes (2001) suggested, the extent to which an immigrant can assimilate is based on their family's human capital, acculturation into language and everyday cultural practices, and economic stability through resources. With regard to generations of South Asians, these factors are particularly important for the ways that others perceive them through media and in society.

Conclusion

In this chapter, I examined audience perceptions of the most popular South Asian characters discussed among media consumers. From this analysis, I developed a historical trajectory of South Asian characters that have existed in U.S. media: the forever foreigner, the model minority, and the average American. The average American archetype is most prevalent in popular TV and film today and appears to be well integrated into the social circles of the fellow characters. This historical trajectory of South Asians on the screen is important for a few key reasons. Representations of South Asians have undergone a racial formation in both their characterization on the screen and their perception by audiences. This trajectory also speaks to the changing nature of stereotypes associated with South Asians in the United States. While traditional representations relied on characterizations as the foreigner or the model minority, contemporary examples rely less on these overt ethnic characteristics. In fact, these Americanized representations tend to play up the fact that these characters know little about their ethnic culture and are thus assimilated and acceptable.

Mainstream film and television audiences are aware of the effect attempted by portraying a character with a heavy accent. For example, a character like Apu, with a thick Indian accent and a stereotypically Indian profession, is more likely to be perceived negatively, compared to a character like Kumar, a second-generation Indian American medical student. Additionally, a character like Kumar, who is less "Indian" but still portrays the stereotype of the Indian doctor, is seen as more stereotypical than characters like Kelly and Tom, who break the molds. Americanized South Asian characters are portrayed in ways that emphasize assimilated identity through interracial relationships, diverse social networks, and even Western names and reinforce the whitewashed characteristics of other non-White characters we have seen in popular television and film.

Today, non-White characters are integrated into mainstream popular media alongside White actors and characters but remain essentialized and in secondary storylines (Beltran & Fojas, 2008; Chito Childs, 2009; Gray, 2004; Jhally & Lewis, 1992; Nacos & Torres-Reyna, 2007; Vera & Gordon, 2003). In the 21st century, South Asian media representations are just one part of the larger browning of Main Street, USA represented in television and film. In real life, South Asians tend to live in urban areas and are thus absent from most rural communities. The only South Asians these people know are the ones on television. Even the most popular actors and characters in 2017, including Priyanka Chopra in *Quantico* (2015–present), Aziz Ansari in *Master of None* (2015–present), and Kunal Nayyar in *The Big Bang Theory* (2007–present), continue to be surrounded by nearly all White actors. This reproduces a dynamic where South Asians are a sufficient stand-in for representations of "diversity."

Many of the contemporary media representations of South Asians have been portrayed in ways that are seemingly devoid of any ethnic or gendered stereotypical characteristics. Accent tends to be at the essence of how these South Asian actors are written (Davé, 2012). These whitewashed, assimilationist representations reflect a color-blind ideology in which it is assumed that minorities are equal to Whites on the surface but does not acknowledge the inherent inequality underneath. Additionally, the degree to which these limited opportunities are the only ones available to South Asian actors have larger implications for the livelihood of South Asians in Hollywood.

South Asian media representations are not created in a vacuum but are part of deliberate decisions made by media producers and executives to maintain noncritical characterizations of South Asians on-screen. Only through cable and streaming entertainment do we get nonnormative representations, but these only remain popular among niche audiences. Additionally, while South Asian media characters today have significantly improved from the overt caricatures of the past, these characterizations subtly maintain idealized (White) characteristics. The actors in these roles exist at one extreme of the *foreigner* or *whitewashed* spectrum.

References

Alba, R., & Nee, V. (2003). *Remaking the American mainstream.* Cambridge, MA: Harvard University Press.

Alsultany, E. (2012). *Arabs and Muslims in the media: Race and representation after 9/11.* New York, NY: New York University Press.

Beltran, M., & Fojas, C. (Eds.) (2008). *Mixed race Hollywood.* New York, NY: New York University Press.

Bonilla-Silva, E. (2004). From bi-racial to tri-racial: Towards a new system of racial stratification in the USA. *Ethnic and Racial Studies,* 27(6), 931–50.

Bonilla-Silva, E. (2013). *Racism without racists: Color-blind racism and the persistence of racial inequality in the United States* (4th ed.). Lanham, MD: Rowman and Littlefield.

Brooks, T., & Marsh, E. (2007). *The complete directory to prime time network TV shows, 1946–present* (9th ed.). New York, NY: Ballantine Books.

Chito Childs, E. (2009). *Fade to Black and White: Interracial images in popular culture.* Lanham, MD: Rowman and Littlefield.

Coltrane, S., & Messineo, M. (2000). The perpetuation of subtle prejudice: Race and gender imagery in 1990s television advertising. *Sex Roles,* 42(5/6), 363–389.

Cortese, A. (2008). *Provocateur: Images of women and minorities in advertising.* Lanham, MD: Rowman and Littlefield.

Davé, S. (2013). *Indian accents: Brown voice and racial performance in American television and film.* Champaign, IL: University of Illinois Press.

Doane, A. W., & Bonilla-Silva, E. (Eds.). (2003). *White out: The continuing significance of racism.* New York, NY: Routledge.

Entman, R., & Rojecki, A. (2000). *The Black image in the White mind.* Chicago, IL: University of Chicago Press.

Feagin, J. (2000). *Racist America: Roots, current realities, and future reparation.* New York, NY: Routledge.

Gordon, M. (1964). *Assimilation in American life: The role of race, religion and national origin.* New York, NY: Oxford University Press.

Gray, H. (2004). *Watching race: Television and the struggle for Blackness.* Minneapolis, MN: University of Minnesota Press.

Hall, S. (1997). *Representation: Cultural representations and signifying practices.* Thousand Oaks, CA: Sage.

Hall, S. (2003). The whites of their eyes: Racist ideologies and the media. In G. Dines and J. Humez (Eds.), *Gender, race and class in media: A text-reader* (pp. 89–93). Thousand Oaks: Sage.

Hughey, M. W. (2014). *The White savior film: Content, critics, and consumption.* Philadelphia, PA: Temple University Press.

Jones, D. (1955). *The portrayal of China and India on the American screen, 1896–1955: The evolution of Chinese and Indian themes, locales, and characters as portrayed on the American screen.* Cambridge, MA: MIT Center for International Studies.

Jhally, S., & Lewis, J. (1992). *Enlightened racism: The Cosby Show, audiences and the myth of the American dream.* Oxford, U.K.: Westview Press.

Kim, C. J. (1999). The racial triangulation of Asian Americans. *Politics and Society, 27*(1), 105–138.

Larson, S. G. (2006). *Media and minorities: The politics of race in news and entertainment.* Lanham, MD: Rowman and Littlefield.

Leonard, K. I. (1997). *The South Asian Americans.* Westport, CT: Greenwood Press.

Maira, S. (2002). *Desis in the house: Indian American youth culture in New York City.* Philadelphia, PA: Temple University Press.

McGee, E. O., Thakore, B. K., & LaBlance, S. S. (2016). The burden of being model: Racialized experiences of Asian STEM college students. *Journal of Diversity in Higher Education.* Online First, doi: 10.1037/DHE0000022.

Nacos, B. L., & Torres-Reyna, O. (2007). *Fueling our fears: Stereotyping, media coverage and public opinion of Muslim Americans.* Lanham, MD: Rowman and Littlefield.

Omi, M. (1999). Racial identity and the state: Contesting the federal standards for classification. In P. Wong (Ed.), *Race, ethnicity and nationality in the United States* (pp. 25–33). New York, NY: Westview Press.

Omi, M., & Winant, H. (2014). *Racial formation in the United States: From the 1960s to the 1990s* (3rd ed.). New York, NY: Routledge.

Park, R. E. (1950). Race and culture. Glencoe, IL: The Free Press.

Pager, D., & Shepard, H. (2008). The sociology of discrimination: Racial discrimination in employment, housing, credit, and consumer markets." *Annual Review of Sociology*, 34(1), 181–209.

Prashad, V. (2000). The karma of brown folk. Minneapolis, MN: University of Minnesota Press.

Purkayastha, B. (2005). *Negotiating ethnicity: Second-Generation South Asian Americans traverse a transnational world.* New Brunswick, NJ: Rutgers University Press.

Rastogi, N. S. (2010). Beyond Apu: Why are there suddenly so many Indians on television? *Salon.* Retrieved from http://www.slate.com/id/2255937/

Rumbaut, R., & Portes, A. (2001). *Ethnicities: Children of immigrants in America.* Berkeley, CA: University of California Press.

Said, E. (1979). *Orientalism.* New York, NY: Vintage.

Shankar, S. (2008). *Desi land: Teen culture, class and success in Silicon Valley.* Durham, NC: Duke University Press.

Sharma, N.T. (2010). *Hip hop Desis: South Asian Americans, blackness, and a global race consciousness.* Durham, NC: Duke University Press.

Steinberg, S. (1979). *The ethnic myth: Race, ethnicity and class in America.* Boston, MA: Beacon Press.

Takaki, R. (1989). *Strangers from a different shore: A history of Asian Americans.* Boston, MA: Little, Brown and Company.

Thakore, B. K. (2012). Rags-to-riches in the 21st century: The reality behind representations in *Slumdog Millionaire. Humanity and Society, 36*(1), 93–95.

Thakore, B. K. (2016). *South Asians on the U.S. screen: Just like everyone else?* Lanham, MD: Lexington Books.

The Times of India. (2011, May 21). NBC cancels 'Outsourced': First TV show set in India. Retrieved from http://articles.timesofindia.indiatimes.com/2011-05-21/us-canada-news/29568095_1_outsourced-show-ben-rappaport

Tuan, M. (1999). *Forever foreigners or honorary Whites? The Asian ethnic experience today.* New Brunswick, NJ: Rutgers University Press.

Vera, H., & Gordon, A. (2003). *Screen saviors: Hollywood fictions of Whiteness.* Lanham, MD: Rowman and Littlefield.

Waters, M., & Jimenez, T. (2005). Assessing immigrant assimilation: New empirical and theoretical challenges. *Annual Review of Sociology, 31*, 105–25.

Wilson, C. C., Guiterrez, F., & Lena Chou. (2003). *Racism, sexism and the media: The rise of class communication in multicultural America.* Thousand Oaks, CA: Sage.

Wu, F. (2002). *Yellow: Race in America beyond Black and White.* New York, NY: Basic Books.

Zhou, M., & Lee, J. (2004). Introduction: The making of culture, identity and ethnicity among Asian American youth. In Jennifer Lee and Min Zhou (Eds.), *Asian-American youth: Culture, identity and ethnicity* (pp. 1–32). New York, NY: Routledge.

EDUCATION

Education and Social Inequality
Schooling in Capitalist America

SCHOOLING IN CAPITALIST AMERICA

Educational Reform and the Contradictions of Economic Life

BY SAMUEL BOWLES AND HERBERT GINTIS

Education and Inequality

> Universal education is the power, which is destined to overthrow every species of hierarchy. It is destined to remove all artificial inequality and leave the natural inequalities to find their true level. With the artificial inequalities of caste, rank, title, blood, birth, race, color, sex, etc., will fall nearly all the oppression, abuse, prejudice, enmity, and injustice, that humanity is now subject to.
>
> Lester Frank Ward, *Education* c. 1872

A review of educational history hardly supports the optimistic pronouncements of liberal educational theory. The politics of education are better understood in terms of the need for social control in an unequal and rapidly changing economic order. The founders of the modern U.S. school system understood that the capitalist economy produces great extremes of wealth and poverty, of social elevation and degradation. Horace Mann and other school reformers of the antebellum period knew well the seamy side of the burgeoning industrial and urban centers. "Here," wrote Henry Barnard, the first state superintendent of education in both Connecticut and Rhode Island, and later to become the first U.S. Commissioner of Education, "the wealth, enterprise and professional talent of the state are concentrated … but here also are poverty, ignorance, profligacy and irreligion, and a classification of society as broad and deep as ever divided the plebeian and patrician of ancient Rome."[1] They lived in a world in which, to use de Tocqueville's words, "… small aristocratic societies … are formed by some manufacturers in the midst of the immense democracy of our age [in which] … some men are opulent and a multitude … are wretchedly poor."[2] The rapid rise of the factory system, particularly in New England, was celebrated by the early school reformers; yet, the alarming transition from a relatively simple rural society to a highly stratified industrial economy could not be ignored. They shared the fears that de Tocqueville had expressed following his visit to the United States in 1831:

> When a work man is unceasingly and exclusively engaged in the fabrication of one thing, he ultimately does his work with singular dexterity; but at the same time he loses the general faculty of applying his mind to the direction of the work. … [While] the science of manufacture lowers the class of workmen, it raises the class of masters. … [If] ever a permanent inequality of conditions … again penetrates into the world, it may be predicted that this is the gate by which they will enter.[3]

Samuel Bowles and Herbert Gintis, "Schooling in Capitalist America," *Schooling in Capitalist America: Educational Reform and the Contradictions of Economic Life*, pp. 26-37, 124-131. Copyright © 1976 by Samuel Bowles and Herbert Gintis. Reprinted with permission by Basic Books, a Member of Perseus Books Group.

While deeply committed to the emerging industrial order, the far-sighted school reformers of the mid-nineteenth century understood the explosive potential of the glaring inequalities of factory life. Deploring the widening of social divisions and fearing increasing unrest, Mann, Barnard, and others proposed educational expansion and reform. In his Fifth Report as Secretary of the Massachusetts Board of Education, Horace Mann wrote:

> Education, then beyond all other devices of human origin, is the great equalizer of the conditions of men—the balance wheel of the social machinery. … It does better than to disarm the poor of their hostility toward the rich; it prevents being poor.[4]

Mann and his followers appeared to be at least as interested in disarming the poor as in preventing poverty. They saw in the spread of universal and free education a means of alleviating social distress without redistributing wealth and power or altering the broad outlines of the economic system. Education, it seems, had almost magical powers.

> The main idea set forth in the creeds of some political reformers, or revolutionizers, is, that some people are poor because others are rich. This idea supposed a fixed amount of property in the community … and the problem presented for solution is, how to transfer a portion of this property from those who are supposed to have too much to those who feel and know that they have too little. At this point, both their theory and their expectation of reform stop. But the beneficient power of education would not be exhausted, even though it should peaceably abolish all the miseries that spring from the coexistence, side by side of enormous wealth, and squalid want. It has a higher function. Beyond the power of diffusing old wealth, it has the prerogative of creating new.[5]

The early educators viewed the poor as the foreign element that they were. Mill hands were recruited throughout New England, often disrupting the small towns in which textile and other rapidly growing industries had located. Following the Irish potato famine of the 1840s, thousands of Irish workers settled in the cities and towns of the northeastern United States. Schooling was seen as a means of integrating this "uncouth and dangerous" element into the social fabric of American life. The inferiority of the foreigner was taken for granted. The editors of the influential *Massachusetts Teacher*, a leader in the educational reform movement, writing in 1851, saw "… the increasing influx of foreigners …" as a moral and social problem:

> Will it, like the muddy Missouri, as it pours its waters into the clear Mississippi and contaminates the whole united mass, spread ignorance and vice, crime and disease, through our native population?
>
> If … we can by any means purify this foreign people, enlighten their ignorance and bring them up to our level, we shall perform a work of true and perfect charity, blessing the giver and receiver in equal measure. …
>
> With the old not much can be done; but with their children, the great remedy is *education*. The rising generation must be taught as our own children are taught. We say *must be* because in many cases this can only be accomplished by coercion.[6]

Since the mid-nineteenth century the dual objectives of educational reformers—equality of opportunity and social control—have been intermingled, the merger of these two threads sometimes so nearly complete that it becomes impossible to distinguish between the two. Schooling has been at once something done for the poor and to the poor.

The basic assumptions which underlay this co-mingling helps explain the educational reform movement's social legacy. First, educational reformers did not question the fundamental economic institutions of capitalism: Capitalist ownership and control of the means of production and dependent wage labor were taken for granted. In fact, education was to help preserve and extend the capitalist order. The function of the school system was to accommodate workers to its most rapid possible development. Second, it was assumed that people (often classes of people or "races") are differentially equipped by nature or social origins to occupy the varied economic and social levels in the class structure. By providing equal opportunity, the school system was to elevate the masses, guiding them sensibly and fairly to the manifold political, social, and economic roles of adult life.

Jefferson's educational thought strikingly illustrates this perspective. In 1779, he proposed a two-track educational system which would prepare individuals for adulthood in one of the two classes of society: the "laboring and the learned."[7] Even children of the laboring class would qualify for leadership. Scholarships would allow "… those persons whom nature hath endowed with genius and virtue …" to "… be rendered by liberal education worthy to receive and able to guard the sacred deposit of the rights and liberties of their fellow citizens."[8] Such a system, Jefferson asserted, would succeed in "… raking a few geniuses from the rubbish."[9] Jefferson's two-tiered educational plan presents in stark relief the outlines and motivation for the stratified structure of U.S. education which has endured up to the present. At the top, there is the highly selective aristocratic tradition, the elite university training future leaders. At the base is mass education for all, dedicated to uplift and control. The two traditions have always coexisted although their meeting point has drifted upward over the years, as mass education has spread upward from elementary school through high school, and now up to the post-high-school level.

Though schooling was consciously molded to reflect the class structure, education was seen as a means of enhancing wealth and morality which would work to the advantage of all. Horace Mann, in his 1842 report to the State Board of Education, reproduced this comment by a Massachusetts industrialist:

> The great majority always have been and probably always will be comparatively poor, while a few will possess the greatest share of this world's goods. And it is a wise provision of Providence which connects so intimately, and as I think so indissolubly, the greatest good of the many with the highest interests in the few.[10]

Much of the content of education over the past century and a half can only be construed as an unvarnished attempt to persuade the "many" to make the best of the inevitable.

The unequal contest between social control and social justice is evident in the total functioning of U.S. education. The system as it stands today provides eloquent testimony to the ability of the well-to-do to perpetuate in the name of equality of opportunity an arrangement which consistently yields to themselves disproportional advantages, while thwarting the aspirations and needs of the working people of the United States. However grating this judgment may sound to the ears of the undaunted optimist, it is by no means excessive in light of the massive statistical data on inequality in the United States. Let us look at the contemporary evidence.

We may begin with the basic issue of inequalities in years of schooling. As can be seen in figure 2–1 [removed from this anthology], the number of years of schooling attained by an individual is strongly associated with parental socioeconomic status. This figure [removed from this anthology] presents the estimated distribution of years of schooling attained by individuals of varying socioeconomic backgrounds. If we define socioeconomic background by a weighted sum of income, occupation, and educational level of the parents, a child from the ninetieth percentile may expect, on the average, five more years of schooling than a child in the tenth percentile.[11]

A word about our use of statistics is in order. Most of the statistical calculations which we will present have been published with full documentation in academic journals. We provide some of the relevant technical information in our footnotes and appendix. However, those interested in gaining a more detailed understanding of our data and methods are urged to consult our more technical articles.

The data, most of which was collected by the U.S. Census Current Population Survey in 1962, refers to "non-Negro" males, aged 25–64 years, from "non-farm" background in the experienced labor force.[12] We have chosen a sample of white males because the most complete statistics are available for this group. Moreover, if inequality for white males can be documented, the proposition is merely strengthened when sexual and racial differences are taken into account.

Additional census data dramatize one aspect of educational inequalities: the relationship between family income and college attendance. Even among those who had graduated from high school in the early 1960s, children of families earning less than $3,000 per year were over six times as likely *not* to attend college as were the children of families earning over $15,000.[13] Moreover, children from less well-off families are *both* less likely to have graduated from high school and more likely to attend inexpensive, two-year community colleges rather than a four-year B.A. program if they do make it to college.[14]

Not surprisingly, the results of schooling differ greatly for children of different social backgrounds. Most easily measured, but of limited importance, are differences in scholastic achievement. If we measure the output of schooling by scores on nationally standardized achievement tests, children whose parents were themselves highly educated outperform the children of parents with less education by a wide margin. Data collected for the U.S. Office of Education Survey of Educational Opportunity reveal, for example, that among white high school seniors, those whose parents were in the top education decile were, on the average, well over three grade levels in measured scholastic achievement ahead of those whose parents were in the bottom decile.[15]

Given these differences in scholastic achievement, inequalities in years of schooling among individuals of different social backgrounds are to be expected. Thus one might be tempted to argue that the close dependence of years of schooling attained on background displayed in the left-hand bars of Figure 2–1 [removed from this anthology] is simply a reflection of unequal intellectual abilities, or that inequalities in college attendance are the consequences of differing levels of scholastic achievement in high school and do not reflect any additional social class inequalities peculiar to the process of college admission.

This view, so comforting to the admissions personnel in our elite universities, is unsupported by the data, some of which is presented in Figure 2–1 [removed from this anthology]. The right-hand bars of Figure 2–1 [removed from this anthology] indicate that even among children with identical IQ test scores at ages six and eight, those with rich, well-educated, high-status parents could expect a much higher level of schooling than those with less-favored origins. Indeed, the closeness of the left-hand and right-hand bars in Figure 2–1 [removed from this anthology] shows that only a small portion of the observed social class differences in educational attainment is related to IQ differences across social classes.[16] The dependence of education attained on background is almost as strong for individuals with the same IQ as for all individuals. Thus, while Figure 2–1 [removed from this anthology] indicates that an individual in the ninetieth percentile in social class background is likely to receive five more years of education than an individual in the tenth percentile; it also indicated that he is likely to receive 4.25 more years schooling than an individual from the tenth percentile with the same IQ. Similar results are obtained when we look specifically at access to college education for students with the same measured IQ. Project Talent data indicates that for "high ability" students (top 25 percent as measured by a composite of tests of "general aptitude"), those of high socioeconomic background (top 25 percent as measured by a composite of family income, parents' education, and occupation) are nearly twice as likely to attend college than students of low socioeconomic background (bottom 25 percent). For "low ability" students (bottom 25 percent), those of high social background are more than four times as likely to attend college as are their low social background counterparts.[18]

Inequality in years of schooling is, of course, only symptomatic of broader inequalities in the educational system. Not only do less well-off children go to school for fewer years, they are treated with less attention (or more precisely, less benevolent attention) when they are there. These broader inequalities are not easily measured. Some show up in statistics on the different levels of expenditure for the education of children of different socioeconomic backgrounds. Taking account of the inequality in financial resources for each year in school and the inequality in years of schooling obtained, Jencks estimated that a child whose parents were in the top fifth of the income distribution receives roughly twice the educational resources in dollar terms as does a child whose parents are in the bottom fifth.[19]

The social class inequalities in our school system, then, are too evident to be denied. Defenders of the educational system are forced back on the assertion that things are getting better; the inequalities of the past were far worse. And, indeed, there can be no doubt that some of the inequalities of the past have been mitigated. Yet new inequalities have apparently developed to take their place, for the available historical evidence lends little support to the idea that our schools are on the road to equality of educational opportunity. For example, data from a recent U.S. Census survey reported in Spady indicate that graduation from college has become no less dependent on one's social background. This is true despite the fact that high-school graduation is becoming increasingly equal across social classes.[20] Additional data confirm this impression. The statistical association (coefficient of correlation) between parents' social status and years of education attained by individuals who completed their schooling three or four decades ago is virtually identical to the same correlation for individuals who terminated their schooling in recent years.[21] On balance, the available data suggest that the number of years of school attained by a child depends upon family background as much in the recent period as it did fifty years ago.

Thus, we have empirical reasons for doubting the egalitarian impact of schooling. But what of those cases when education has been equalized? What has been the effect? We will investigate three cases: the historical decline in the inequality among individuals in years of school attained, the explicitly compensatory educational programs of the War on Poverty, and the narrowing of the black/white gap in average years of schooling attained.

Although family background has lost none of its influence on how far one gets up the educational ladder, the historical rise in the minimum legal school-leaving age has narrowed the distance between the top and bottom rungs. Inequality of educational attainments has fallen steadily and substantially over the past three decades.[22] And has this led to a parallel equalization of the distribution of income? Look at Figure 6.6.1. The reduction in the inequality of years of schooling has not been matched by an equalization of the U.S. income distribution.[23] In fact, a recent U.S. Labor Department study indicates that as far as labor earnings (wages and salaries) are concerned, the trend since World War II has been unmistakenly away from equality. And it is precisely inequality in labor earnings which is the target of the proponents of egalitarian school reforms.[24] But does the absence of an overall trend toward income equality mask an equalizing thrust of schooling that was offset by other disequalizing tendencies? Perhaps, but Jacob Mincer and Barry Chiswick of the National Bureau of Economic Research, in a study of the determinants of inequality in the United States, concluded that the significant reduction in schooling differences among white male adults would have had the effect—even if operating in isolation—of reducing income inequality by a negligible amount.[25]

Next, consider that group of explicitly egalitarian educational programs brought together in the War on Poverty. In a systematic economic survey of these programs, Thomas Ribich concludes that with very few exceptions, the economic payoff to compensatory education is low.[26] So low, in fact, that in a majority of cases studied, direct transfers of income to the poor would have accomplished considerably more equalization than the educational programs in question. The major RAND Corporation study by Averch came to the same conclusion.

Lastly, consider racial inequalities. In 1940, most black male workers (but a minority of whites) earned their livelihoods in the South, by far the poorest region; the education gap between nonwhites and whites was 3.3 years (38 percent of median white education).[27] By 1972, blacks had moved to more affluent parts of the country, and the education gap was reduced to 18 percent (4 percent for young men aged 25–34 years).[28] Richard Freeman has shown that this narrowing of the education gap would have virtually achieved black/white income equality had blacks received the same benefits from education as whites.[29] Yet the income gap has not closed substantially: The income gap for young men is 30 percent, despite an education gap of only 4 percent.[30] Clearly as blacks have moved toward educational (and regional) parity with whites, other mechanisms—such as entrapment in center-city ghettos, the suburbanization of jobs, and perhaps increasing segmentation of labor markets—have intensified to maintain a more-or-less constant degree of racial income inequality. Blacks certainly

FIGURE 6.6.1. EQUALIZATION OF EDUCATION HAS NOT BEEN ASSOCIATED WITH EQUALIZATION OF INCOME

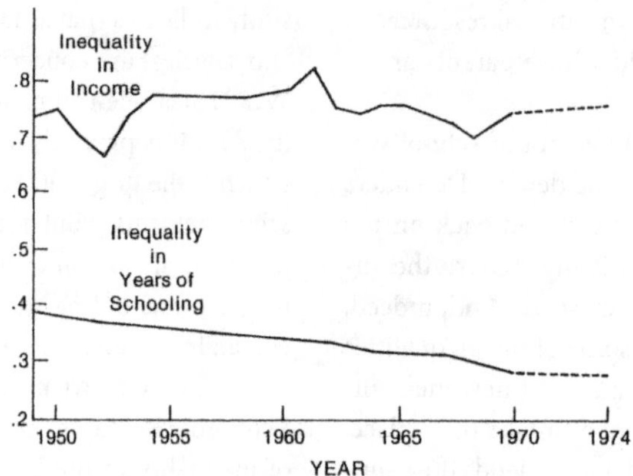

Notes: The upper line shows the trend over time in the degree of inequality of income, as measured by the standard deviation of the natural logarithm of annual income of males aged twenty-five or older. The lower line shows the trend over time in the degree of inequality of years of schooling, as measured by the coefficient of variation (the standard deviation divided by the mean) of the years of schooling attained by males aged twenty-five and older. Data for 1970 to 1974 are estimates based on U.S. Census data.

Source: Barry Chiswick and Jacob Mincer, "Time Series Changes in Personal Income Inequality in the U.S.," *Journal of Political Economy*, Vol. 80, No. 3, Part II (May–June 1972).

suffer from educational inequality, but the root of their exploitation lies outside of education, in a system of economic power and privilege in which racial distinctions play an important role.

The same must be concluded of inequality of economic opportunity between men and women. Sexual inequality persists despite the fact that women achieve a level of schooling (measured in years) equivalent to men.

We conclude that U.S. education is highly unequal, the chances of attaining much or little schooling being substantially dependent on one's race and parents' economic level. Moreover, where there is a discernible trend toward a more equal educational system—as in the narrowing of the black education deficit, for example—the impact on the structure of economic opportunity is minimal at best. As we shall presently see, the record of the U.S. school system as a promoter of full human development is no more encouraging.

Education and Personal Development: The Long Shadow of Work

> Every child born into the world should be looked upon by society as so much raw material to be manufactured. Its quality is to be tested. It is the business of society, as an intelligent economist, to make the best of it.
>
> Lester Frank Ward, *Education, c.* 1872

It is not obvious why the U.S. educational system should be the way it is. Since the interpersonal relationships it fosters are so antithetical to the norms of freedom and equality prevalent in American society, the school system can hardly be viewed as a logical extension of our cultural heritage. If neither technological necessity nor the bungling mindlessness of educators explain the quality of the educational encounter, what does?

Reference to the educational system's legitimation function does not take us far toward enlightenment. For the formal, objective, and cognitively oriented aspects of schooling capture only a fragment of the day-to-day social relationships of the educational encounter. To approach an answer, we must consider schools in the light of the social relationships of economic life. In this chapter, we suggest that major aspects of educational organization replicate the relationships of dominance and subordinancy in the economic sphere. The correspondence between the social relation of schooling and work accounts for the ability of the educational system to produce an amenable and fragmented labor force. The experience of schooling, and not merely the content of formal learning, is central to this process.

In our view, it is pointless to ask if the net effect of U.S. education is to promote equality or inequality, repression or liberation. These issues pale into insignificance before the major fact: The educational system is an integral element in the reproduction of the prevailing class structure of society. The educational system certainly has a life of its own, but the experience of work and the nature of the class structure are the bases upon which educational values are formed, social justice assessed, the realm of the possible delineated in people's consciousness, and the social relations of the educational encounter historically transformed.

In short, and to return to a persistent theme of this book, the educational system's task of integrating young people into adult work roles constrains the types of personal development which it can foster in ways that are antithetical to the fulfillment of its personal developmental function.

Reproducing Consciousness

> ... children guessed (but only a few
> and down they forgot as up they grew
> autumn winter spring summer). ...
>
> e e cummings, 1940

Economic life exhibits a complex and relatively stable pattern of power and property relationships. The perpetuation of these social relationships, even over relatively short periods, is by no means automatic. As with a living organism, stability in the economic sphere is the result of explicit mechanisms constituted to maintain and extend the dominant patterns of power and privilege. We call the sum total of these mechanisms and their actions the reproduction process.

Amidst the sundry social relations experienced in daily life, a few stand out as central to our analysis of education. These are precisely the social relationships which are necessary to the security of capitalist profits and the stability of the capitalist division of labor. They include the patterns of dominance and subordinacy in the production process, the distribution of ownership of productive resources, and the degrees of social distance and solidarity among various fragments of the working population—men and women, blacks and whites, and white- and blue-collar workers, to mention some of the most salient.

What are the mechanisms of reproduction of these aspects of the social relations of production in the United States? To an extent, stability is embodied in law and backed by the coercive power of the state. Our jails are filled with individuals who have operated outside the framework of the private-ownership market system. The modern urban police force as well as the National Guard originated, in large part, in response to the fear of social upheaval evoked by militant labor action. Legal sanction, within the framework of the laws of private property, also channels the actions of groups (e.g., unions) into conformity with dominant power relationships. Similarly, force is used to stabilize the division of labor and its rewards within an enterprise: Dissenting workers are subject to dismissal and directors failing to conform to "capitalist rationality" will be replaced.

But to attribute reproduction to force alone borders on the absurd. Under normal conditions, the effectiveness of coercion depends at the very least on the inability or unwillingness of those subjected to it to join together in opposing it. Laws generally considered illegitimate tend to lose their coercive power, and undisguised force too frequently applied tends to be self-defeating. The consolidation and extension of capitalism has engendered struggles of furious intensity. Yet instances of force deployed against a united and active opposition are sporadic and have usually given way to détente in one form or another through a combination of compromise, structural change, and ideological accommodation. Thus it is clear that the consciousness of workers—beliefs, values, self-concepts, types of solidarity and fragmentation, as well as modes of personal behavior and development—are integral to the perpetuation, validation, and smooth operation of economic institutions. The reproduction of the social relations of production depends on the reproduction of consciousness.

Under what conditions will individuals accept the pattern of social relationships that frame their lives? Believing that the long-term development of the existing system holds the prospect of fulfilling their needs, individuals and groups might actively embrace these social relationships. Failing this, and lacking a vision of an alternative that might significantly improve their situation, they might fatalistically accept their condition. Even with such a vision they might passively submit to the framework of economic life and seek individual solutions to social problems if they believe that the possibilities for realizing change are remote. The issue of the reproduction of consciousness enters each of these assessments.

The economic system will be embraced when, first, the perceived needs of individuals are congruent with the types of satisfaction the economic system can objectively provide. While perceived needs may be, in part, biologically determined, for the most part needs arise through the aggregate experiences of individuals in the society. Thus the social relations of production are reproduced in part through a harmony between the needs which the social system generates and the means at its disposal for satisfying these needs.

Second, the view that fundamental social change is not feasible, unoperational, and utopian is normally supported by a complex web of ideological perspectives deeply embedded in the cultural and scientific life of the community and reflected in the consciousness of its members. But fostering the "consciousness of inevitability" is not the office of the cultural system alone. There must also exist mechanisms that systematically thwart the spontaneous development of social experiences that would contradict these beliefs.

Belief in the futility of organizing for fundamental social change is further facilitated by social distinctions which fragment the conditions of life for subordinate classes. The strategy of "divide and conquer" has enabled dominant classes to maintain their power since the dawn of civilization. Once again, the splintered consciousness of a subordinate class is not the product of cultural phenomena alone, but must be reproduced through the experiences of daily life.

Consciousness develops through the individual's direct perception of and participation in social life.[31] Indeed, everyday experience itself often acts as an inertial stabilizing force. For instance, when the working population is effectively stratified, individual needs and self-concepts develop in a correspondingly fragmented manner. Youth of different racial, sexual, ethnic, or economic characteristics directly perceive the economic positions and prerogatives of "their kind of people." By adjusting their aspiration accordingly, they not only reproduce stratification on the level of personal consciousness, but bring their needs into (at least partial) harmony with the fragmented conditions of economic life. Similarly, individuals tend to channel the development of their personal powers—cognitive, emotional, physical, aesthetic, and spiritual—in directions where they will have an opportunity to exercise them. Thus the alienated character of work, for example, leads people to guide their creative potentials to areas outside of economic activity: consumption, travel, sexuality, and family life. So needs and need-satisfaction again tend to fall into congruence and alienated labor is reproduced on the level of personal consciousness.[32]

But this congruence is continually disrupted. For the satisfaction of needs gives rise to new needs. These new needs derive from the logic of personal development as well as from the evolving structure of material life, and in turn undercut the reproduction of consciousness. For this reason the reproduction of consciousness cannot be the simple unintended by-product of social experience. Rather, social relationships must be consciously organized to facilitate the reproduction of consciousness.

Take, for instance, the organization of the capitalist enterprise. Power relations and hiring criteria within the enterprise are organized so as to reproduce the workers' self-concepts, the legitimacy of their assignments within the hierarchy, a sense of the technological inevitability of the hierarchical division of labor itself, and the social distance among groups of workers in the organization. Indeed, while token gestures towards workers' self-management may be a successful motivational gimmick, any delegation of real power to workers becomes a threat to profits because it tends to undermine patterns of consciousness compatible with capitalist control. By generating new needs and possibilities, by demonstrating the feasibility of a more thoroughgoing economic democracy, by increasing worker solidarity, an integrated and politically conscious program of worker involvement in decision-making may undermine the power structure of the enterprise. Management will accede to such changes only under extreme duress of worker rebellion and rapidly disintegrating morale, if at all.

But the reproduction of consciousness cannot be insured by these direct mechanisms alone. The initiation of youth into the economic system is further facilitated by a series of institutions, including the family and the educational system, that are more immediately related to the formation of personality and consciousness. Education works primarily through the institutional relations to which students are subjected. Thus schooling fosters and rewards the development of certain capacities and the expression of certain needs, while thwarting and penalizing others. Through these institutional relationships, the educational system tailors the self-concepts, aspirations, and social class identifications of individuals to the requirements of the social division of labor.

The extent to which the educational system actually accomplishes these objectives varies considerably from one period to the next. Recurrently through U.S. history these reproduction mechanisms have failed, sometimes quite spectacularly. In most periods—and the present is certainly no exception—efforts to use the schools to reproduce and extend capitalist production relations have been countered both by the internal dynamic of the educational system and by popular opposition.

We have identified the two main objectives of dominant classes in educational policy: the production of labor power and the reproduction of those institutions and social relationships which facilitate the translation of labor power into profits. We may now be considerably more concrete about the way that educational institutions are structured to meet these objectives. First, schooling produces many of the technical and cognitive skills required for adequate job performance. Second, the educational system helps legitimate economic inequality. The objective and meritocratic orientation of U.S. education, reduces discontent over both the hierarchical division of labor and the process through which individuals attain position in it. Third, the school produces, rewards, and labels personal characteristics relevant to the staffing of positions in the hierarchy. Fourth, the educational system, through the pattern of status distinctions it fosters, reinforces the stratified consciousness on which the fragmentation of subordinate economic classes is based.

What aspects of the educational system allow it to serve these various functions? We shall suggest in the next section that the educational system's ability to reproduce the consciousness of workers lies in a straight-forward correspondence principle: For the past century at least, schooling has contributed to the reproduction of the social relations of production largely through the correspondence between school and class structure.

Upon the slightest reflection, this assertion is hardly surprising. All major institutions in a "stable" social system will direct personal development in a direction compatible with its reproduction. Of course, this is not, in itself, a critique of capitalism or of U.S. education. In any conceivable society, individuals are forced to develop their capacities in one direction or another. The idea of a social system which merely allows people to develop freely according to their "inner natures" is quite unthinkable, since human nature only acquires a concrete form through the interaction of the physical world and preestablished social relationships.

Our critique of education and other aspects of human development in the United States fully recognizes the necessity of some form of socialization. The critical question is: What for? In the United States the human development experience is dominated by an undemocratic, irrational, and exploitative economic structure. Young people have no recourse from the requirements of the system but a life of poverty, dependence, and economic insecurity. Our critique, not surprisingly, centers on the structure of jobs. In the U.S. economy work has become a fact of life to which individuals must by and large submit and over which they have no control. Like the weather, work "happens" to people. A liberated, participatory, democratic, and creative alternative can hardly be imagined, much less experienced. Work under capitalism is an alienated activity.

To reproduce the social relations of production, the educational system must try to teach people to be properly subordinate and render them sufficiently fragmented in consciousness to preclude their getting together to shape their own material existence. The forms of consciousness and behavior fostered by the educational system must themselves be alienated, in the sense that they conform neither to the dictates of technology in the struggle with nature, nor to the inherent developmental capacities of individuals, but rather to the needs of the capitalist class. It is the prerogatives of capital and the imperatives of profit, not human capacities and technical realities, which render U.S. schooling what it is. This is our charge.

Discussion Questions

1. How has Jefferson's proposed "two-track" system endured in modern education?
2. Do you think mandatory college attendance, hypothetically, would narrow the income gap between rich and poor citizens? Why or why not?

Notes

1. Henry Barnard, *Papers for the Teacher: 2nd Series* (New York: F. C. Brownell, 1866), pp. 293–310.
2. Alexis de Tocqueville, as quoted in Jeremy Brecher, *Strike!* (San Francisco: Straight Arrow Books, 1972), pp. xi, xii.
3. *Ibid.*, p. 172.
4. Horace Mann as quoted in Michael Katz, ed., *School Reform Past and Present* (Boston: Little, Brown and Company, 1971), p. 141.
5. *Ibid.*, p. 145.
6. *The Massachusetts Teacher* (October 1851), quoted in Katz (1971), *loc. cit.*, pp. 169–170.
7. David Tyack, *Turning Points in American Educational History* (Waltham, Mass.: Blaisdell, 1967), p. 89.
8. *Ibid.*, p. 109.
9. *Ibid.*, p. 89.
10. Mann, quoted in Katz (1971), *loc. cit.*, p. 147.
11. This calculation is based on data reported in full in Samuel Bowles and Valerie Nelson, "The 'Inheritance of IQ' and the Intergenerational Transmission of Economic Inequality," *The Review of Economics and Statistics*, Vol. LVI, No. 1, February 1974. It refers to non-Negro males from non-farm backgrounds, aged 35–44 years. The zero-order correlation coefficient between socioeconomic background and years of schooling was estimated at 0.646. The estimated standard deviation of years of schooling was 3.02. The results for other age groups are similar.
12. See Appendix A, footnote 14, in Chapter 4 and the following sources: Bowles and Nelson (1974), *op. cit.;* Peter Blau and Otis D. Duncan, *The American Occupational Structure* (New York: John Wiley, 1967); Otis D. Duncan, D. C. Featherman, and Beverly Duncan, *Socioeconomic Background and Occupational Achievement, Final Report,* Project No. S-0074 (EO-191) (Washington, D.C.: Department of Health, Education and Welfare, Office of Education, 1968); Samuel Bowles, "Schooling and Inequality from Generation to Generation," *The Journal of Political Economy,* Vol. 80, No. 3, Part II, May–June 1972.
13. These figures refer to individuals who were high-school seniors in October, 1965, and who subsequently graduated from high school. College attendance refers to both two- and four-year institutions. Family income is for the twelve months preceding October 1965. Data is drawn from U.S. Bureau of the Census, *Current Population Reports,* Series P-60, No. 183, May 1969.
14. For further evidence, see U.S. Bureau of the Census (1969), *op. cit.*; and Jerome Karabel, "Community Colleges and Social Stratification," *Harvard Educational Review,* Vol. 424, No. 42, November 1972.
15. Calculation based on data in James S. Coleman *et al., Equality of Educational Opportunity* (Washington, D.C.: U.S. Government Printing Office, 1966), and Bowles and Gintis (1972), *loc. cit.*
16. The data relating to IQ are from a 1966 survey of veterans by the National Opinion Research Center; and from N. Bayley and E. S. Schaefer, "Correlations of Maternal and Child Behaviors with the Development of Mental Ability: Data from the Berkeley Growth Study," *Monographs of Social Research in Child Development,* 29, 6 (1964).
17. This figure [removed from this anthology] is based on data reported in full in our Appendix

A and in Bowles and Nelson (1974), *op. cit.* The left-hand bars of each pair were calculated using the estimated correlation coefficient between socioeconomic background and education of 0.65. The results for other age groups were similar: 0.64 for ages 25–34 and 44–54, and 0.60 for ages 55–64 years. The right-hand bars were calculated from the normalized regression coefficient on socioeconomic background from an equation using background and early childhood IQ to predict years of schooling, which was estimated at 0.54. The results for other age groups were similar: 0.54 for ages 25–34 and 45–54, and 0.48 for ages 55–64.

18. Socioeconomic background is defined as normalized sum of father's education, father's occupational status, and parents' income. The mean and standard deviation of years of schooling were estimated at 11.95 and 3.02, respectively.
19. Based on a large sample of U.S. high-school students as reported in: John C. Flannagan and William W. Cooley, *Project Talent, One Year Follow-up Study,* Cooperative Research Project, No. 2333, University of Pittsburgh: School of Education, 1966.
20. Christopher Jencks *et al., Inequality: A Reassessment of the Effects of Family and Schooling in America* (New York: Basic Books, 1972), p. 48.
21. William L. Spady, "Educational Mobility and Access: Growth and Paradoxes," in *American Journal of Sociology,* Vol. 73, No. 3, November 1967; and Blau and Duncan, *op. cit.* (1967). More recent data support the evidence of no trend toward equality. See U.S. Bureau of Census (1969), *op. cit.*
22. Blau and Duncan (1967), *op. cit.* See the reported correlations in Appendix A.
23. We estimate the coefficient of variation of years of schooling at about 4.3 in 1940 (relying on Barry Chiswick and Jacob Mincer, "Time Series Changes in Personal Income Inequality in the U.S.," *Journal of Political Economy,* Vol. 80, No. 3, Part II [May–June 1972], Table 4 for the standard deviation of schooling and the Decennial Census for the mean), and at 2.95 in 1969 (relying on Chiswick and Mincer [1972], Table B10).
24. Calculated from Table B1 and Table B10 in Chiswick and Mincer (1972), *op. cit.*
25. Peter Henle, "Exploring the Distribution of Earned Income," *Monthly Labor Review,* Vol. 95, No. 12, December 1972. Inequalities in income (profit, rent interest, and transfer payments plus labor earnings) may also have increased if the unmeasured income from capital gains and other tax shelters for the rich are taken into account. See Jerry Cromwell, "Income Inequalities, Discrimination and Uneven Development," unpublished Ph.D. dissertation, Harvard University, May 1974.
26. Chiswick and Mincer (1972), *loc. cit.*
27. Thomas I. Ribich, *Education and Poverty* (Washington, D.C.: Brookings Institution, 1968).
28. United States Bureau of the Census, *Current Population Reports,* Series P-60, October 1970, Table 75, p. 368.
29. *Ibid.* (November 1972), Table 1, p. 14.
30. Michael Reich, *Racial Discrimination and the Distribution of Income,* Ph.D. dissertation, Harvard University, May 1973.
31. Herbert Gintis, "Welfare Criteria with Endogenous Preferences: The Economics of Education," *International Economic Review,* June 1974; Alfred Schutz and Thomas Luckmann, *The Structure of the Life-World* (Evanston, Illinois: Northwestern University Press, 1973); and Peter L. Berger and Thomas Luckmann, *The Social Construction of Reality: A Treatise in the Sociology of Knowledge* (Garden City, L.I., N.Y.: Doubleday and Co., 1966).
32. For an extended treatment of these issues, see Herbert Gintis, "Alienation and Power," in *The Review of Radical Political Economics,* Vol. 4, No. 5, Fall 1972.

EDUCATION AND SOCIAL INEQUALITY

What Schools are Supposed to Do, and What Schools Really Do

BY JUDSON G. EVERITT

Introduction: Expectations and Realities in Education

In the United States and abroad alike, education has been the aspect of society with the highest expectations. Education has been considered the remedy to almost any social problem one can imagine, such as preparing people for employment, creating good national citizens, eliminating racial discrimination, alleviating poverty, instilling good moral character, preventing the spread of disease, strengthening local communities, minimizing teenage pregnancy, integrating diverse cultures, adapting to technological change, developing nation-states—and the list could go on and on. Simultaneously, education has been the aspect of society that has drawn an enormous amount of criticism, such as: teachers are underqualified, standardized testing is horribly biased, schools fail to teach strong moral values, students are apathetic and often dangerous, Black/White achievement gaps persist, schools fail to promote cultural diversity, illiterate students are simply promoted through the grades, getting bachelor's and graduate degrees does not guarantee jobs, grade inflation is rampant—this list could also go on and on. Given that so much is at stake in education and that there are so many apparent failures in education, we must ask ourselves: Why do we entrust so much to a social institution that we do not believe delivers on its promises?

The answers are many and complex. In fact, there are far too many to explain adequately in one introductory chapter. Yet sociologists who look at systems of education from a critical theoretical perspective offer us insights into how and why our schools often fail to live up to our expectations. The short answer is that our expectations for public education rest on false assumptions. Many of us believe that schools are capable of transforming our society into a better one. Yet, to understand how and why public schools do not solve all of the social problems we believe they are capable of solving, we must turn our attention to the ways that public schools are themselves influenced and constrained by structured systems of social inequality in society. A critical theoretical perspective in sociology helps us do that.

Viewing Education Through a Critical Lens

Who does well in school, and who does not, is most strongly influenced by the socioeconomic background of students as well as their race and gender. Over sixty years of research has documented in various ways the importance of class and race in determining inequalities in education and the related inequalities in occupational and social-class status into adulthood (Blau & Duncan, 1967; Featherman & Hauser, 1978; Entwisle, Alexander, & Olson, 1997; Roscigno, 1995). In addition, more recent research has consistently

Judson Everitt, "Education and Social Inequality: What Schools are Supposed to Do, and What Schools Really Do." Copyright © 2012 by Judson Everitt. Reprinted with permission.

found that girls are now outperforming boys at all levels of schooling (Entwisle et al., 2007). Just to give an example, take the issue of students' social-class background. According to the United States Department of Education (1995), at the point of entering kindergarten, 95% of kids whose parents are college graduates could identify the colors red, blue, yellow, and green, compared to only 51% of kids whose parents dropped out of high school. Moreover, at the point of entering kindergarten, 42% of kids whose parents are college graduates knew all the letters of the alphabet, compared to only 9% of kids whose parents dropped out of high school. These inequalities persist into later grades and affect college attendance as well. Of the high school graduates who enroll in college, 88% of the students who have parents who graduated from college go on to college themselves, and only 27% of the students who have parents who dropped out of high school make it to college.

Notice that schools themselves do not determine any of these factors. Teachers and principals have no control over the socioeconomic background or the racial and gender statuses of the students they receive. But schools are supposed to be places where anyone can succeed, right? Education is supposed to be the avenue available to all people, regardless of their background, that prepares and propels them to a quality standard of living into adulthood. Why does it appear to be working this way for some students but not for others? Moreover, why has there been very little change for so long in this state of affairs?

There are many competing answers out there to these questions, but this chapter focuses on those offered to us by a critical theoretical perspective in sociology. Namely, if we view public education from a critical perspective, we see it as part of a larger social system that structures inequality into our society. This perspective on education was most notably argued by Bowles and Gintis in their classic book Schooling in *Capitalist America* (1976), and Bourdieu and Passeron offered a similar perspective in their book Reproduction in *Education, Society, and Culture* (1977). Bowles and Gintis (1976) discuss the relationship between education and our capitalist economy. They theorize that there is a widely accepted idea that competition in capitalist economies is fair for all members of society and that those who are successful earned it, while those who are not somehow failed in the competition. The critical perspective challenges this widely held assumption, and Bowles and Gintis argue that competition is not always fair. Some people have advantages that others do not in the competition for everything from good grades to college admission to employment, and these advantages and disadvantages fall along lines of social class, race, and gender. They argue that schools are a part of this wider social system of inequality that privileges some more than others. Because people often assume that success in school is based solely on individual intelligence, hard work, and initiative—in other words, that some people earn it and other people do not—Bowles and Gintis argue that schools do more to legitimize and reproduce existing inequality rather than reduce it. How do schools do this, and how are they constrained by inequalities that already exist in society? In the next section, I discuss some key elements of public education where we see some answers to these questions.

Schooling Practices That Reproduce Inequality

Sociologists who have studied education over the years have identified a great many ways in which the relationship between schools and the wider society serves to aggravate social inequality rather than to reduce social inequality. For the purposes of this chapter, I am going to introduce just a few of the key things that schools commonly do that contribute to persistent inequality in who does well in school. The first involves rules for how schools are funded; the second involves rules for how schools educate kids with different skill levels; and the third involves common expectations that teachers have about students that influence the ways they teach children of different backgrounds.

Money Matters: School-Finance Law in the United States

Think for a moment about what a good school looks like. Most readers of this book are students, likely within your first 2 years of college. So you know a lot about schools: by now, you have spent at least 12 years of your life going to school on a daily basis for roughly 180 days out of each year. You know what is supposed to happen in schools and what kinds of supplies and resources schools should have. Given your knowledge and experience in schools, make a list of all the things that a good school should have in order to effectively educate students. What would that list include, and how long would it be? The school would need a building, for starters, one that is safe, clean, and has electricity and plumbing. A teaching staff would be good too, preferably effectively trained teachers. It would need a curriculum, textbooks, desks, and lockers. It would need classrooms with blackboards (or dry-erase boards), labs with computers, and a library with books, maps, and other resources. It would need offices for the administration, an auditorium, a gymnasium, a cafeteria, athletic facilities, an art room, and a teachers' lounge. It would need school buses to transport students and the drivers and gasoline to keep them running. And it would need an endless list of supplies: classroom supplies, office supplies, food supplies, maintenance supplies, athletic supplies, art supplies, science-lab supplies, and computing supplies, just to name a few. Clearly, schools need a lot of resources to accomplish their key tasks, and this raises at least one very practical question: Who pays for all of this stuff?

In short, you and your families pay for it. If it is a private school, then you pay for it with tuition dollars. If it is a public school, you pay for it with tax dollars. The system through which public schools are funded in this country is based largely on property taxes. Since the origin of public education in the United States, it has been locally controlled. In other words, public education is controlled mostly by state governments and local districts. This includes how education is funded. On the one hand, the specific details of how schools are funded vary from state to state (i.e., funding laws in Illinois differ slightly from those in Indiana, Ohio, and Texas, etc.). On the other hand, there is enough similarity between state funding laws that we can identify an overall system of how schools receive funding in this country. Generally, this system is known as "the Foundation Program" (Kozol, 1991).

The way this system works is really quite simple. There are three main components: 1) The property in local school districts is taxed at a certain rate, and a large slice of the property tax revenue in the district is spent on the public schools in that district. 2) The amount of property tax revenue that is generated in the district depends on the value of the property in the district. For example, if the average home in one school district is worth $1 million and it is taxed at a rate of 5%, that generates $50,000 of property tax revenue for the local school per home. If, however, the average home in a poorer district is worth $100,000 and it is taxed at the same rate, this generates only $5,000 of property tax revenue for the local school per home. For districts where the overall property value is relatively high, this system usually generates plenty of money to fund the needs of the local school. For those districts where the overall property value is low, however, the property tax revenue will likely not provide sufficient funds for local schools. 3) For poorer districts, the state government will supplement their district with additional funds up to a state-determined minimum level of funding for all school districts. In other words, the state government makes sure that all school districts in the state are operating with a minimum level of funding to support their schools.

Notice, however, that "minimum" does not mean "equal." Wealthier districts often fund their schools very well with the property tax revenue they can generate in their districts. Some public high schools have immaculate facilities that rival those of many college campuses, including the most up-to-date technology in almost all aspects of their schooling. The poorest districts in our country, however, have schools that are lucky to have running water and sanitary cafeterias. Class sizes range up to 35–40 students per teacher, many of those teachers are full-time substitutes who can be paid as little as $15,000 per year, and large closets double as classrooms. Admittedly, the majority of public schools lie somewhere between the two examples I have just described, but such examples exist throughout the country, and they are, in part, a product of these funding laws (Kozol, 1991).

Such inequality in funding is a problem, but it is aggravated by another law in the system: compulsory-attendance laws. No matter where you live in this country, if you are 16 years old or younger, you are required by law to attend school. This law exists for good reason: ideally, we want all of our children to learn the skills and knowledge necessary to be good citizens and productive workers. However, if you factor in the Foundation Program for school finance, compulsory-attendance law then serves to force—by law—our children into unequal schools, given the way that our public schools are funded. Such inequality may or may not be the explicit intent of these laws, but the effect is unequal access to schooling resources for children, depending upon where they live. Given the high degree of residential segregation in our country by social class as well as race (Massey & Denton, 1994), the structured system through which we provide public education itself creates drastic differences in the educational resources that kids from different backgrounds can access. As such, kids from poor family backgrounds are far less likely to have adequate schools, reducing their chances for the educational success necessary for them to be upwardly mobile.

Tracking: Different Knowledge, Different Behaviors, Different Outcomes

Resources and funding, however, are just one piece of the inequality puzzle. In fact, there remains debate as to how much money really matters in determining educational success. Some studies have found that funding matters very little in determining whether or not students will do well in school (Jencks et al., 1972). More recent studies have shown that funding is quite important to student performance, but its effectiveness depends upon how schools spend their finances (Fitzpatrick & Yoels, 1992) and how different families access these resources (Klugman, 2008). Indeed, how schools themselves manage both their resources and their students is of central concern when assessing how effectively, and how equitably, they are educating students. When it comes to how schools actually deliver instruction to students, there is a very common practice called "tracking" that many scholars argue is another key way in which existing inequality gets reproduced in education.

The practice of tracking (also known as ability grouping), on the surface, seems to make good sense. Essentially, it is the process by which teachers and schools group students of similar ability and skill level. Depending on grade level and subject matter, this practice can happen among students in the same classroom (remember those reading groups in elementary school?) or it can entail grouping students into different classrooms (like regular versus advanced placement classes in high school). The intent of such grouping practices is to make instruction more efficient, both for teachers and students. Imagine for a moment that you are a high school language arts teacher. Your curriculum requires that you teach the classic American novel, *The Grapes of Wrath* by John Steinbeck, to a class of 30 10th graders. Ten of your 30 students are outstanding students with college-level literacy skills. Ten more are average students who are reading at grade level. The remaining 10 students, however, are behind, and most of them are barely reading at a 6th-grade level. How do you teach this novel to all of these students simultaneously? If you teach at a level sufficient to challenge your best students, most of the others will be completely lost. Conversely, if you teach at a level that offers the much-needed skill remediation to your lower-performing students that is necessary for them to understand the complex themes and imagery of the novel, then many of your remaining students will be bored to tears. Teaching to the middle group might alleviate these two problems a bit, but then both remain problems to a degree. Tracking is the common practice intended to address this type of instructional dilemma. By grouping students based on ability, many educators argue, everyone is on the same page, and teachers can more efficiently address the specific needs of different groups of students. Not surprisingly, teachers prefer this practice to the all-inclusive alternative (Hallinan, 1994), and studies find that teachers strongly prefer to teach the high-track classes (Finley, 1984).

But does tracking actually provide more efficient instruction to all students? Most of the available research shows us that it does not. While it often works well for high-performing students, it does little for midrange students. More importantly, it does not help low-performing students "catch up" to their peers. On the contrary, most studies find that tracking actually inhibits low-performing students' performance, and this problem persists throughout their educational careers. For example, studies of ability grouping in first-grade reading instruction find that low-performing students are put in low-track groups, due as much to their behavior as to their actual literacy skill (Eder, 1981). As such, the kids themselves are more disruptive during their reading instruction, and the teacher's efforts to manage their behavior also disrupt instructional time. Placing these students together, then, itself renders the instruction that these students receive highly inefficient, and many of them do not develop their literacy skills at a pace that would bring them up to the same level as their higher-performing peers. Additional research shows that kids who fall behind early in their schooling remain behind throughout their schooling, and ability grouping is one key way in which this problem persists (Entwisle, Alexander, & Olson, 2005).

Kids who start behind stay behind in later grades, and the problems of tracking do not go away. In addition, there is clear consensus among scholars that poor and minority children are overrepresented in low-track classes at all levels of schooling, so they are more likely to be disadvantaged by tracking than their wealthier, and Whiter, peers (Hallinan, 1994; Lucas, 1999; Oakes, 1985). In later grades, into middle and high school, the differences in what students learn in high-track versus low-track classes become even more severe. As you might imagine, students in high-track classes are receiving knowledge and skills at a level that prepares them for college. They are learning subject matter like literature, math, science, and foreign language, but they are also learning advanced writing, interpretation, and critical-thinking skills as well. They are encouraged by their teachers to think independently and creatively about how to solve problems, and they are taught how to express themselves effectively (Oakes, 1985). Students in low-track classes, on the other hand, often learn very different skills and values. Obviously, the content of their classes is not as advanced as that of high-track classes, and many of them take courses that teach a variety of vocational skills. Moreover, the types of behaviors they are encouraged to engage in are quite different as well. Rather than learning to think critically and independently, they are more likely to be encouraged to respect authority and follow directions (Oakes, 1985). In other words, students in high-track classes learn the knowledge and skills that put them on track for college and the types of occupations one can expect with undergraduate and graduate degrees, and low-track students learn the knowledge and skills that put them on track to enter the labor market in jobs that are lower in pay, prestige, authority, and stability.

Scholars disagree on what should be done about the problems with tracking. Some argue that tracking is inherently unequal, disadvantages poor and minority students, and is therefore discriminatory (Oakes, 1985). Others feel that we should not throw the baby out with the bathwater, so to speak. They point to evidence that many students go through their schooling taking high-track classes in some subject matters and regular or low-track classes in other subject matters, so it is not the case that students are only either in low- or high-track classes (Hallinan, 1994). Regardless, the practice of tracking continues to have discriminatory effects, with poor and minority students more likely to be placed into lower tracks that funnel them into working- and lower-class positions into adulthood (Entwisle, Alexander, & Olson, 2006). As such, tracking, in its current practice, is a key mechanism through which we see evidence of what Bowles and Gintis (1976) warned us about: that public education does more to reproduce inequalities that already exist rather than overcome them. From their point of view, it is not just that public education is attempting to overcome wider forms of social inequality in society and is failing to do so. Rather, the ways that schools operate actively contribute to the persistence of social inequality over time.

Seeing What You Expect to See: The Role of Teachers

Whenever discussing how schools function, it is necessary to discuss the people who work inside them and who are responsible for carrying out the daily tasks of instruction. Teachers have very difficult jobs to do, and this chapter is not intended to be an indictment of teachers in the United States. Yet teachers are human beings like the rest of us and, like the rest of us, have their own backgrounds, experiences, perspectives, and, inevitably, their own biases that shape the ways they view the world. They, like their students, bring with them into school buildings perspectives, skills, and experiences that are shaped by the wider society in which they live. Teachers, like all of us, are shaped by their gender, their race, and their social-class status. When looking at these characteristics across the occupation of teaching, we see that the overwhelming majority of teachers are very similar:

by and large, they are middle-class White women. Overall, more than 75% of all public school teachers in the Unites States are women, more than 83% of all teachers are White, and in most all cases, being a teacher places one within middle-class status (National Center for Education Statistics, 2004; U.S. Department of Education, 2015).

We must take these demographic characteristics of teachers into account when making sense of much of the research on what teachers expect from their students and how those expectations affect student outcomes. For many years, research has shown that teachers have different expectations for student behavior, and this affects their assessments of student academic performance. Indeed, it has been shown that as much as 50% of the variance in the way teachers grade students is explained by students' classroom behavior (Farkas, Grobe, Sheehan, & Yuan, 1990). In other words, teachers grade more negatively the kids who disrupt class than they do students who do not disrupt class or who do it less often. Such links between behavior and academic evaluation are particularly hard on poor minority boys, with whom teachers—on average—are more likely to have more negative interactions and grade negatively as well (Entwisle, Alexander, & Olson, 2007). This impacts which students are more likely to be retained for 1 year or more in their academic careers, and low-income students are at greater risk of retention, with low-income boys at the greatest risk. Given that additional research shows that those students who are retained are more likely to drop out of school (Alexander et al., 2003), we see another means by which the everyday decisions made in schools about who does well, and who does not, impact the life chances of students from different backgrounds.

Conversely, the interactions that teachers have with middle-class students and their parents can often lead to these students gaining educational advantages. Middle-class parents largely share the perspective that they are peers, or equals, of their children's teachers. They share this perspective, given that those among the middle class are going to have at least the same, or higher, educational attainment and occupational prestige. As such, they feel it is perfectly appropriate for them to talk with their kids' teachers and ask for special accommodations for their kids and their schooling (such as extra time to complete assignments or opportunities to retake tests to improve their scores). When they do, teachers and other school figures usually accommodate them. Working- and lower-class parents do not view their kids' teachers as equals. Rather, they largely view teachers as experts in education, due in large part to the fact that teachers have completed more schooling and have higher occupational status than most working- and lower-class parents. They do not feel it is appropriate to intervene in their child's schooling because they feel that teachers are more qualified to address their children's educational needs than they are. As a result, working-class and lower-class children do not benefit from the same individual accommodations that middle-class students often receive and therefore do not have access to the same benefits to their schooling (Lareau, 2011). Moreover, teachers, among others, often mistakenly interpret the behavior of working- and lower-class parents as evidence that they do not care about their children's education. Annette Lareau (2011) shows us that this is not the case. She finds in her research that these parents do care very much about their kids' education and, instead, the differences in parenting strategies are a product of what she and Bourdieu call "cultural capital" differences that influence their perspectives on the appropriate relationship between schools and families. These differences among parents of different social-class background, and the ways that teachers and school authorities interact with them in ways that reward middle-class students, serve as another contributing factor in why family socioeconomic background is the largest determinant of educational performance.

Education Policy: Missing the Target

What has been done in an effort to remedy the persistent inequalities in education? Given that such inequalities are largely reflections of wider social inequalities in society, it would stand to reason that alleviating them would require addressing these larger inequalities in social class, race, and gender. Indeed, such an approach is the one proposed by Bowles and Gintis (1976). As we have seen in this chapter, resources for different schools reflect inequalities in property values in different communities; tracking is an instructional response to differences in prior skills that kids bring with them to schools; and social-class background, race, and gender shape the interactions that teachers have with students and their parents. As such, many scholars argue that change in education must happen in conjunction with, not prior to, comprehensive change in socially structured inequalities. At the very least, policies intended to improve overall schooling outcomes for all students must address the social sources of the problem.

We have had some education policies that have attempted to alleviate the inequalities that students bring with them from outside schools. The Elementary and Secondary Education Act (ESEA), passed originally in 1965, had as one of its key components what is referred to as Title I funding for schools. This is additional federal funding for districts and schools with relatively high proportions of low-income students. Such funding does not eliminate the differences in school funding discussed earlier, but it does help poorer schools to a degree, and this program continues to exist. We also have a National Free and Reduced Lunch Program that provides funding to offset the cost of buying lunch for low-income students. This program has also become the way in which we commonly measure the proportion of students in a school who are from a lower socioeconomic background. Such programs help, but as we have discussed throughout this chapter, they do not overcome persistent inequalities.

We have also had a variety of desegregation policies in public schools throughout the country since the '60s and '70s. Such policies were intended to alleviate the problems created by residential segregation by race and social class, and the most common method of desegregation was to bus students of different backgrounds (usually poor and minority students) to schools outside their immediate neighborhoods so as to increase the racial diversity of schools in the overall community and to increase access to better-funded schools for many poor and minority students. These programs varied widely from state to state and district to district, but nearly all generated a great deal of controversy. White families tended to leave districts that imposed such policies, opting to live in more segregated suburban areas (a trend commonly referred to as "White flight"). Also, over the years, desegregation policies were challenged in court on the basis that they were unconstitutional by virtue of the fact that students were being placed in schools based on racial status, which meant in some cases students were denied access to a certain school on the basis of race. There were many such cases over the last two decades, and by and large, the courts have agreed that they have been unconstitutional. With the most recent of these cases, in 2004, the Supreme Court made such a ruling on the desegregation policies in Louisville, KY, and Seattle, WA, and since then, desegregation policies in public education have largely become a thing of the past.

Education in an Era of Accountability

Recent education policy has attempted to address persistent inequalities in education and improve public schooling overall by holding teachers and schools more accountable for performance. The No Child Left Behind Act (NCLB), passed in 2002, was the first law to establish accountability mandates at the federal level in the United States. Under the law, schools are required to make sure that their students reach the "proficient" level, usually as measured by standardized testing, over a certain period of time (all students by 2014, for all schools). Moreover, under NCLB, schools are measured each year to make sure they are making "adequate yearly progress" (AYP) toward the goal of getting all students proficient in their required subject matters. If schools fail to meet their AYP goals for 3 years in a row, they can be sanctioned by the state in a number of ways: students have the option to transfer to a different school; funding can be taken away from the schools; and in the most extreme case, the administration of the school can be taken over in attempt to "turn around" the school. In more recent years, schools and districts have developed ways of trying to measure individual teacher performance and base teaching effectiveness by the degree to which teachers improve their students' academic performance.

Accountability policies have changed in recent years. First through its "Race to the Top" initiative and later through waivers that allowed states to avoid sanctions under NCLB, the United States Department of Education began offering states incentives to more closely tie teacher evaluation to student academic performance. As such, accountability shifted from holding schools accountable to holding individual teachers accountable. This policy shift contributed to an increase in the use of "value-added" models as a component of teacher evaluation in states and districts across the country. Value-added models attempt to measure the impact of individual teachers on student performance over time, controlling for, among other factors, students' prior skill levels (Harris, 2011). While using these and other ways of measuring teacher influence on student performance has become widespread (Porter, 2015; U.S. Dept. of Education, 2014), it has been a controversial policy practice, especially when value-added measures have been used as the basis to reward or sanction individual teachers. Among the more problematic issues in using value-added measures for evaluating teachers, such models are unable to account for student motivation, which decidedly influences their performance, varies a great deal among students, and is largely beyond the control of individual teachers (Kelly, 2012).

Accountability underwent another change with the passage of the Every Student Succeeds Act in late 2015, which was a reauthorization of NCLB that turned over a significant amount of control to individual states to determine exactly how they do accountability. Nonetheless, accountability is here to stay in many ways. More importantly, accountability policies rely upon the assumption that the source of the problems in education lies exclusively with teachers and schools. We know that it is more complicated than that. If there is one consistent finding in many decades of sociological theory and research on education, it is that public schools are socially situated within wider systems of inequality, and differential outcomes for kids are a reflection of this condition of schools. Current accountability policies largely fail to take this into account. Certainly, we can and should improve schools and the teachers who work within them, but simply punishing them when their students do not perform as highly as we would like is unlikely to get at the root of the problem.

Despite the passage of accountability mandates, schools remain funded through the Foundation Program; tracking remains a very common instructional practice; and relationships between teachers, students, and parents remain differentiated by race, class, and gender. Until we begin directly addressing the types of social conditions of schooling discussed in this chapter, the common expectation that our public schools will begin to reduce persistent inequalities in society is unlikely to become a widespread reality.

References:

Blau, P., & Duncan, O. D. (1967). The American occupational structure. New York, NY: John Wiley & Sons.

Bourdieu, P., & Passeron, C. (1977). *Reproduction in education, society, and culture*. London: Sage.

Bowles, S., & Gintis, H. (1976). *Schooling in capitalist America: Educational reform and the contradictions of economic life*. New York, NY: Basic Books.

Eder, D. (1981). Ability grouping as a self-fulfilling prophecy: A micro-analysis of teacher–student interaction. *Sociology of Education, 54,* 151–162.

Entwisle, D. R., Alexander, K. L., & Olson, L. (1997). *Children, schools, and inequality.* New York, NY: Westview.

Entwisle, D. R., Alexander, K. L., & Olson, L. (2005). First grade and educational attainment by age 22: A new story. *American Journal of Sociology, 110,* 1458–1502.

Entwisle, D. R., Alexander, K. L., & Olson, L. (2006). Educational tracking within and between schools: From the first grade through middle school and beyond. In A. Huston and M. Ripke (Eds.), *Developmental contexts in middle childhood* (pp. 173–97). New York, NY: Cambridge University Press.

Entwisle, D. R., Alexander, K. L., & Olson, L. (2007). Early schooling: The handicap of being poor and male. *Sociology of Education, 80(2),* 114–38.

Farkas, G., Grobe, R., Sheehan, D., & Shuan, Y. (1990). Cultural resources and school success: Gender, ethnicity, and poverty groups within an urban school district. *American Sociological Review, 55,* 46–61.

Featherman, D., & Hauser, R. (1978). *Opportunity and change*. New York, NY: Academic Press.

Fitzpatrick, K., & Yoels, W. (1992). Policy, school structure, and sociodemographic effects on statewide high school dropout rates. *Sociology of Education, 65,* 76–93.

Hallinan, M. T. (1994). Tracking: From theory to practice. *Sociology of Education, 67,* 79–84.

Jencks, C., et al. (1972). *Inequality: Reassessment of the effect of family and schooling in America.* New York, NY: Harper & Row.

Kelly, S. (2012). Understanding teacher effects: Market versus process models of educational improvement. In S. Kelly (Ed.), *Assessing teacher quality: Understanding teacher effects on instruction and achievement* (pp. 7-32). New York, NY: Teacher College Press.

Kozol, J. (1991). *Savage inequalities: Children in America's schools.* New York, NY: Harper Collins.

Lareau, A. (2011). *Unequal childhoods: Class, race, and family life* (2nd ed.). Berkeley, CA: University of California Press.

Lucas, S. R. (1999). *Tracking inequality: Stratification and mobility in American high schools.* New York, NY: Teachers College Press.

National Center for Education Statistics. (2004). *Schools and staffing survey: 2003–2004.* Retrieved from https://nces.ed.gov/pubs2003/2003409.pdf

Oakes, J. (1985). *Keeping track: How schools structure inequality.* New Haven, CT: Yale University Press.

Porter, E. (2015, March 24). Grading teachers by the test. *New York Times.* Available at https://www.nytimes.com/2015/03/25/business/economy/grading-teachers-by-the-test.html

Roscigno, V. (1998). Race and reproduction of educational disadvantage. *Social Forces, 76,* 1033–1061.

United States Department of Education. (2014). *Laws & guidance.* Retrieved from http://www2.ed.gov/policy/eseaflex/secretary-letters/cssoltr8212014.html

United States Department of Education, National Center for Education Statistics. (2015). *Digest of education statistics, 2013.* Washington, DC: NCES.

PRISON INDUSTRIAL COMPLEX

Disproportionate Minority Contact

Pathways to Downward Mobility

DISPROPORTIONATE MINORITY CONTACT

How Race/Ethnicity Impacts the Juvenile Justice System

BY PAUL KETCHUM, B. MITCHELL PECK, AND PATRICK POLASEK

Introduction

The most visible role of the justice system is to dispense sanctions against those who break certain rules of society. In a truly impartial system, sanctions would be meted out based only upon the rate and severity of breaking those codified rules. This chapter will critically examine how race impacts the juvenile justice system through an examination of disproportionate minority contact (DMC), the term used to describe minority overrepresentation in the juvenile justice system.

The juvenile justice system began with the Progressive movement at the turn of the 20th century. The Progressives envisioned a country where all Americans were to enter the ranks of the middle class. Everyone was to respect private property, send their children to school, and give up whatever vices that they might have brought with them as they immigrated so that they might become hardworking and law-abiding. The juvenile courts, along with schools and other governmental agencies, were used to Americanize, assimilate, and acculturate immigrants (Feld, 1999). Giving the state the right and responsibility to substitute its own control over children for that of the natural parents when the latter appeared unable or unwilling to meet their responsibilities or when the child posed a problem for the community proved a powerful tool for imposing assimilation. In essence, the legal concept of *parens patriae* provided the formal justification for intervening in the lives of immigrants and the poor. It was a tool to control "other people's children," a theme continued by the juvenile courts today.

The United States has attempted to appear to be racially neutral on crime while Black, Hispanic, and other racial/ethnic minorities are socially, politically, and economically emasculated by the criminal and juvenile justice systems, resulting in largely disenfranchised communities. While minority youth have always been overrepresented in the juvenile and criminal justice systems, in our modern era of purported color-blindness, we have achieved a level of inequality that would make any old-fashioned overt racist proud. An overwhelming amount of research shows that minority youth are overrepresented at every stage of the juvenile justice system, from initial police contact to incarceration (Snyder & Sickmund, 2006; Feld, 1999; Kempf Leonard, Pope, & Feyerherm, 1995), and that this overrepresentation continues into the criminal court system.

Black males face roughly a 30% likelihood of incarceration in their lives (Petit & Western, 2004; Bonczar & Beck, 1997). On any given day, about one-third of Black males in their 20s are under official criminal justice supervision (Mauer, 1999). Despite consistently making up less than 15% of the overall population, Blacks have grown from 29% of the prison population in 1950 to about 50% of the prison population (Russell, 1998), ironically at a time of purported growing racial equality. By 1978, the arrest rate for Blacks had grown to almost 100 arrests for every 1,000 Blacks (Mauer, 1999). At the same time, the arrest rate for Whites was

Paul Ketchum, B. Mitchell Peck, and Patrick M. Polasek, "Disproportionate Minority Contact: The Impact of Race/Ethnicity in the Juvenile Justice System." Copyright © 2012 by Paul Ketchum, B. Mitchell Peck, and Patrick M. Polasek. Reprinted with permission.

35 arrests per 1,000 Whites, or about two-thirds less. Juvenile rates are almost as lopsided (Mauer, 1999). In 1995, Blacks composed only 15% of the overall juvenile population but 34% of all youth in the juvenile justice system, including 26% of juvenile arrests, 32% of delinquency referrals to juvenile court, 41% of the juveniles detained, 46% of the juveniles in correctional facilities, and 52% of the juveniles transferred to adult court (Mauer, 1999). During this period, Whites made up 80% of the total juvenile population but only 63% of those in the juvenile justice system (Walker, Spohn, & DeLone, 2000).

That minority youths, most notably Black youths, are overrepresented in the juvenile justice system is beyond dispute. The data overwhelmingly show Black youths in the juvenile justice system in numbers well beyond proportional representation.

According to Office of Juvenile Justice and Delinquency Preventions (OJJDP) juvenile court records, Black youth, compared to other racial groups, are

- 4–8 times more likely to be arrested for an indexed violent crime;
- 2–4 times more likely to be arrested for a property crime;
- involved in 28% of delinquency cases but result in 35% of detained cases;
- involved in 22% of drug cases but 37% of detained drug cases;
- among delinquency cases involving Black juveniles, more likely to be petitioned than were cases involving White youth or youth of other races;
- disproportionately petitioned—78% of drug cases involving Black youth were petitioned, compared to 57% for other non-Whites and 56% for Whites (including Hispanics);
- more likely than other groups to have their case waived to criminal court/certified as an adult; and
- more likely to be placed in out-of-home placement than other groups (Snyder & Sigmund, 1999).

Many theories have tried to explain this significant overrepresentation of minority youth. While all have added to the body of knowledge, the two most prominent are those explaining DMC as the result of *differential involvement* and those alternatively explaining DMC as the result of *differential treatment.*

Differential Involvement and Differential Treatment

Differential Involvement

Differential involvement contends that minority overrepresentation at any level in the justice system is due to minorities committing more crimes. Differential involvement in offending is a result of individual traits or choices either 1) independent of social problems or 2) attributable as a result of social problems. D'Sousa (1995) aligns himself with the first possibility when he states that those who are especially cautious of young Black men are simply employing rational discrimination based on prudent statistics that use racial or ethnic identity combined with gender, demeanor, and other factors to exclude interaction with young Black men when possible because it is "known" that these individuals commit more crimes, especially violent and drug-related crimes. A number of scholars have suggested that juveniles of color offend at higher rates than do other individuals, simply by choice (D'Sousa, 1995; Herrnstein & Murray, 1994; Wilbanks, 1986; Wilson & Herrnstein, 1985).

Overrepresentation in the justice system is perceived as fallacy from this view, as observed inequities in the justice system reflect the realities of which individuals actually offend rather than focusing on social problems that lead certain groups to be more or less likely to commit a crime. This concept assumes that each individual a) has the ability to choose whether or not to commit a crime and b) that social forces take a back seat to individual choice. Though this view lacks rigorous empirical support, we include it here, as it stubbornly retains public support.

There is an alternative view of differential involvement that suggests that higher levels of offending from the young living in poor minority neighborhoods are rooted in environmental factors (Huizinga, Thornberry, Knight, & Lovegrove, 2007; Martinez, 2002; Anderson, 1999). This perspective suggests that issues such as poverty, disrupted home life, relative disadvantage, limited economic and educational opportunity, disenfranchisement, and limited community policing are among those factors that influence both the prevalent types of crime as well as the crime rate. From this view, minorities' differential involvement in crime is due to environmental factors encouraging or otherwise rewarding criminal behavior. For instance, the Oklahoma Office of Juvenile Affairs (Damphousse, Davis, & Charish, 2004) found that Black and Hispanic youths committed more crime than did White youth; however, once environmental conditions were controlled for, the difference disappeared.

Differential involvement is ideologically grounded in blame assigned to the offender, either fully (individual choice) or partially (rooted in social problems), based on arrest and conviction rates. It further assumes that arrest and conviction rates of minorities as compared to Whites are reflective of actual rates of commission of delinquent and criminal acts. If minorities actually commit delinquent and criminal acts at rates well above those of Whites, the only rational policy course is to address how to limit minorities' involvement in delinquent and criminal acts.

The 2003 juvenile arrest records and 2000 juvenile court records from OJJDP clearly show significant overrepresentation of Black male youths in almost every category of juvenile court records, including arrests. However, the discrepancy in arrest and conviction rates for Blacks and Whites cannot be easily explained as different rates of offending between White and Black juveniles (Snyder & Sickmund, 1999). For example, Wordes and Bynum (1995) found in their study of the juvenile justice system in Michigan, both through official police records and interviews with officers, that race or race-related factors, such as being in the wrong neighborhood or hanging out on the street, heavily contributed to a decision by officers to initiate contact. Many of the officers interviewed also noted that boys need a father figure in their lives and that single mothers (statistically a more common living situation for Blacks) cannot adequately control delinquent behavior. Similarly, in Pennsylvania, Kempf Leonard and Sontheimer (1995) discovered that "... offense-related, system-related, and social history factors are accorded different weight depending on race" (p. 120).

Differential Treatment

Differential involvement, be it dependent on or independent of social problems, appears to play a role in DMC but doesn't fully explain the issue. Differential treatment suggests that minorities receive disproportionate punishment for offending. Potential causes of differential treatment resulting in DMC range from indirect racial effect to overt racism. Indirect racial effect could be caused by juvenile justice officials focusing on factors that are strongly correlated to race, such as socio-economic status, demeanor, family structure, and school status, resulting in racialized outcomes (Pope & Snyder, 2003; Pope & Feyerherm, 1990). Along these lines, Wordes and Bynum (1995) found that police officers sometimes formed decisions based on expectations tinged by racial/ethnic stereotypes. Bridges and Steen (1998) found the same of court officials. In fact, a number of studies have found that while the type of current offense and prior record explain much of the observed minority overrepresentation in the juvenile justice system, these do not explain all of the racial differences (Fagan et al., 1987; Krisberg et al., 1987; McCarthy & Smith, 1986). Feld (1999) argues that "A system of justice in which the most powerful explanatory legal variables—present offense and prior record—account for only about 25% of the variance in sentencing remains a highly discretionary and perhaps discriminatory one" (p. 94).

Differing rates of official placement of juvenile offenders itself creates de facto segregation, as 1) Latinos are more likely to be placed in public facilities, 2) Blacks and Latinos are more often placed in private residential care, and 3) White offenders are most likely to be placed in privately run group homes and private drug and alcohol treatment centers (Kempf Leonard & Sontheimer, 1995). Another cause of differential treatment is what Feld (1999) refers to as "justice by geography." Feld (1999) noted that "... individualized discretion is often synonymous with racial disparities in sentencing juveniles" (p. 72). Urban and, to a lesser degree, suburban courts tend to be more formalized in structure, allowing less judicial discretion. According to Feld, this is due to the larger caseloads found in urban courts, which, in turn, forces reliance upon standardized bureaucratic measures.

By any measurement, minorities are overrepresented in the juvenile justice system. This overrepresentation has remained fairly constant in the last decade, as 1993 figures from the FBI show that African Americans, though only 12% of the general population (about 15% of the juvenile population), accounted for 27% of all juvenile arrests, 49% of juvenile arrests for violent crime, and 26% of arrests for property crime (Joseph, 1995). Significantly, the further they move through the system, the greater the disproportionate representation (Kempf Leonard et al., 1995). At the juvenile court level, in 1993, about 20% of all youths referred to juvenile court were detained. Of that 20%, however, judges detained about 18% of White juveniles and 26% of Black juveniles (Feld, 1999).

Juvenile courts are not immune to racial bias. In fact, due to the amplification effect (Walker et al., 2000; Feld, 1999; Kempf Leonard et al., 1995), because minority youth are more likely to be arrested in the first place and a prior record is a major determining factor for further arrests, at each stage (initial contact, juvenile court, detention, criminal court, and incarceration), the percentage of minority youth climbs as one moves through the system (Hendricks & Byers, 2000).

The OJJDP has concluded that "… institutional bias or racism occurs from the initial contact the juvenile makes with law enforcement up through the juvenile court system itself" (Lardiero, 1997). Other evidence similarly suggests that race is frequently a factor at different points throughout the juvenile justice system. Bishop and Frazier (1996), using both analysis of case histories and interviews with officials at all levels of the juvenile justice system, conclude that race is the dominant factor at every stage of processing but most important at the initial arrest stage. Free (1996) found that African Americans were less likely than Whites to be released by the police. Both the case history analysis and the interviews support the idea that race is more of a determining factor for the police than any other part of the juvenile system, likely due to a lack of public oversight, as officers have significant latitude in deciding to commit to initial contact and then whether or not to make the contact official, such as with a citation or arrest (Kempf Leonard et al., 1995).

The practice of racial profiling also makes African American youth more susceptible to initial contact (Jackson and Pabon, 2000). The concepts of differential treatment and differential involvement collide most publicly with the issue of racial profiling. Key to the concept of mistrust of the justice system for many minorities is the concept of racial profiling, or the "out-of-place" doctrine. Kathryn Russell (1998) points out that the "out-of-place" doctrine, which a number of courts have upheld as legal, gives police a legal justification for stopping and questioning Blacks when they are in a predominantly White neighborhood. Studies indicate that Black males are stopped for questioning by the police at a rate much higher than any other racial or ethnic group. According to Russell, this creates a problem in that Black males are stopped and questioned *at a rate much higher than the level of Black involvement in crime*. Of course, racial targeting for the purpose of enhancing the efficiency of the criminal justice system (racial profiling) has effects upon the minority community well beyond the scope of the justice system. For instance, Coates (2011) explains:

> How racial non-elites respond to racial profiling may be the difference between life and death. In cities across the nation, increased levels of incarceration, fear, and even death have resulted as these non-elites have found their opportunities for freedom and security impaired … repeated episodes of racial intimidation, profiling, and discrimination may produce increased levels of stress, hypertension, and other related health conditions (256).

Racial profiling targets minorities and damages their lives, yet many Whites see it as, at worst, a necessary evil, while programs that target the enhancement of Black lives are seen negatively by Whites (Bobo & Kluegel, 1993).

There is evidence that suggests that many minority youth and their parents may not fully understand their options in juvenile court or trust those representing their interests (Joseph, 1995; Kempf Leonard et al., 1995). This may be related to research that shows that Blacks are significantly more likely to be represented by public defenders rather than private attorneys, which may, in turn, play a role in the overrepresentation of minority youth in detention facilities (Hendricks & Byers,

2000). However, a lack of private attorneys does not explain overrepresentation of minority juveniles at other stages of the juvenile justice system, such as initial police contact or arrest. Within the juvenile justice continuum, beginning with initial police contact at the least severe end of the juvenile justice system and ending with juvenile waivers (moving juvenile cases to criminal court to be tried as an adult) as the most severe end of the juvenile justice continuum, there is a constant growth in overrepresentation of Black youths, with the greatest level of disproportional representation in juvenile waivers to criminal court (Kempf Leonard et al., 1995). Interestingly, there is no rational evidence to support the disparities in sentencing or in waivers between minority and White offenders (Hendricks & Byers, 2000; Free, 1996; Joseph, 1995; Kempf Leonard et al., 1995).

Bridges, Conley, Engen, and Price-Spratlen (1995) found, during their interviews with juvenile court judges, a tendency for judges to decide that it was in the best interest of many minority youths to place them in a detention facility, as it was preferable to their home life, though they did not extend this same decision to White (non-Hispanic) youths (Kempf Leonard et al., 1995). The specter of single-parent families, or more specifically of Black women raising children alone, appears to play a significant role in the juvenile justice decision-making process. The problem with the stereotypes and assumptions, particularly those involving parental ability and involvement, is that in an overworked system, shortcuts, in the form of decisions made using stereotypes, may be used (Feld, 1999; Singer, 1996).

Few juvenile court judges believe racial disparities in confinement to be racially based (Bridges & Steen, 1998). Instead, most judges (Bridges & Steen, 1998; Secret & Johnson, 1997; Kempf Leonard et al., 1995) attributed the disparities with regard to Blacks and other minorities as "... substantial ethnic and racial differences in criminal behavior" (institutionalized discrimination) or the fact that youths from wealthier families have access to nonadjudicated facilities that the poor do not (contextual discrimination). Essentially, judges may use extralegal characteristics like race to create "a mental map of the accused person's underlying character" (Secret & Johnson, 1997) and to predict his/her future behavior. Alternatively, the harsher treatment of African American and Hispanic juveniles might reflect both class and race biases on the part of juvenile court judges (Secret & Johnson, 1997). In other words, "the individual's economic and social class and the color of his skin ... determine his relationship to the legal system" (Feld, 1999).

Bridges and Steen's (1998) study of probation officers examined 233 narrative reports written by juvenile probation officers in three different counties in the state of Washington in 1990 and 1991. Each narrative included the probation officer's description of the crime and an assessment of the factors that motivated the crime as well as an evaluation of the youth's background to assess his or her likelihood of recidivism. The probation officers "... tended to attribute crimes committed by Whites to negative environmental factors (poor school performance, delinquent peers, dysfunctional family, use of drugs or alcohol) ... [yet] ... they tended to attribute crimes committed by Black youths to negative personality traits and 'bad attitudes' (refusal to admit guilt, lack of remorse, failure to take offense seriously, lack of cooperation with court officials). They also found probation officers judged Black youth to have a significantly higher risk of reoffending than White youth" (p. 174).

In this post–civil rights era, we are used to rules and laws designed to correct racial inequities. Further, we have largely come to believe that either measures used at the institutional level can correct lingering racism or that racism is so institutionalized that it can never be overcome. Theories supporting differential involvement either 1) rest upon the absurd premise that crime and delinquency are purely a result of "free will" and that minority overrepresentation is due to the failings of minority groups, either through learned attitudes or genetic predisposition, or 2) that issues of class and only coincidentally of race are the cause of minority overrepresentation in the juvenile and criminal justice systems, essentially ruling out the influence or even existence of subtle discrimination. Current theories of differential treatment similarly fall short, as they also tend to focus on institutional factors. While the existing literature has added much to our understanding of how race and ethnicity impact the juvenile justice system, each perspective tends to assign primary responsibility for DMC to a particular group: either the offenders or those who make decisions at each contact point within the juvenile justice system. From a theoretical standpoint, this debate is of limited use, as the end result is likely more reflective of ideological perspective. From a policy perspective, the debate is equally frustrating, as those who attempt to implement policies to minimize DMC are faced with focusing policy on decision makers or offenders. As Piquero (2008) notes, understanding the degree to which differential offending or differential processing contribute to DMC doesn't matter as much as how they combine to create minority overrepresentation in the juvenile justice system.

The Larger Picture: Minority Overrepresentation and the Racialized Social System

Almost forgotten in the debate about differential treatment and differential involvement in the juvenile justice system is the larger problem illustrated by *any* statistically significant minority overrepresentation. If, as some have suggested, we live in a postracial society, then race should never be statistically relevant. In other words, if 12% of a given population is Black, then we would expect, in a postracial society, that 12% of the doctors, lawyers, prisoners, janitors, teachers, criminals, accountants, out of work, wealthy, poor, etc. would be Black. The very existence of minority overrepresentation in the juvenile justice system means that the scales and blindfold of Lady Justice don't exist, leaving only the sword to punish "others" or, in the case of juvenile court, "other peoples' children."

Researchers of racial and ethnic relations recognize how firmly race is embedded in the structural foundations of American society (Bonilla-Silva, 2001, 2003; Feagin, 2006; Omi & Winant, 1994). In the past 20 years, more race scholars have come to recognize that while overt racial prejudice continues to manifest itself in our society, contemporary forms of racial discrimination are often more subtle, covert, and nonapparent. According to these scholars, in a post–civil rights era that is governed by strict laws and regulations—specifically aimed at deterring overt racial discrimination—new forms of racism have emerged that allow actors to explain existing racial inequality as the result of nonracial dynamics. Scholars have labeled these forms of discrimination as laissez-faire racism (Bobo & Kluegal, 1993), colorblind racism (Bonilla-Silva, 2003), symbolic racism (Henry & Sears, 2002), and aversive racism (Sears & Henry, 2003). We draw here primarily on the works of Joe Feagin's systemic racism and White racial frame theories and Eduardo Bonilla-Silva's racialized social system framework.

Racialized social system explains racism as a global phenomenon that has impacted all societies that came into contact with colonizing European Whites (Bonilla-Silva, 2001). The racialization of the world system is based on social, economic, political, and psychological relations of domination and subordination between social groups defined as superior "races" and groups defined as inferior "races" (Omi & Winant, 1994; Bonilla-Silva, 2001; see also Feagin, 2006). Bonilla-Silva (2001) argues that the racialization of the world created "racialized social systems" where the dominant race has developed various practices and mechanisms to maintain its social standing and subjected racial groups have struggled to attempt to change their position in the social order. Racism has a material or structural foundation; that is, "racial" matters in societies reflect the interests of the parties in conflict. Thus, Bonilla-Silva (2001, 2006) argues that while prejudice in all its variants can be regarded as an expression of dominant-group interests, effective racial control benefits not from a plurality of highly racialized individuals in society but from the passive and tacit support of the racial order by most members of the dominant race—in the case of the United States, Whites. Because racialized social systems work to preserve White privilege, progressive attempts to create a more balanced and egalitarian society are often ideal in theory yet failures in practice. For example, although there is debate surrounding the notion that schools and educators are necessarily privileged sites or actors for progressive social change, in truth, they usually function, despite contradictions, to reproduce the racialized social system (Althusser, 1977; see also Lewis, 2003).

A particularly important concept in the racialized social system theory is Bonilla-Silva's (2006) "White habitus," which he defines as "a racialized, uninterrupted socialization process that conditions and creates Whites' racial taste, perceptions, feelings, and emotions and their views on racial matters" (p. 104). According to Bonilla-Silva, the White habitus not only promotes strong group ties (White solidarity), but it also creates, promotes, and maintains negative views about non-Whites. Although Bonilla-Silva discusses White habitus in the context of Whites' social relationship with Blacks (e.g., neighborhood interaction, interracial friendship or relationship), one could think about the exclusive space that is dominated by White males in the U.S. court system that promotes strong group ties (i.e., White male solidarity). Consequently, this White (male) habitus creates, promotes, and maintains negative views about non-Whites.

In his book *Racist America: Roots, Realities, and Future Reparations*, Feagin (2000, 2010; see also Feagin, 2005) develops a conceptual framework that explains the current conditions of Blacks in the United States—a theory he refers to as systemic racism. Systemic racism emphasizes the structural, institutional, and systemic elements present in a racialized and oppressive system. In essence, Feagin (2000) argues that the present state of Blacks and other non-Whites in the United States is a result of a system that has deep historical roots in preserving White privilege through the exploitation and discrimination of non-Whites. Systemic racism, according to Feagin (2000) includes "a diverse assortment of racist practices; the unjustly gained economic and political power of Whites; the continuing resource inequalities; and the White-racist ideologies, attitudes, and institutions created to preserve White advantages and power" (p. 16). The adverse effects of systemic racism manifest themselves not only in Blacks' everyday lives and Whites' group identity, but it is also ever changing so that the structural and institutional vestiges of racial discrimination against non-Whites continue to evolve, and therefore persist, with society. Thus, major institutions such as the criminal justice system continue to hold on to racial stereotypes and engage in racial practices that negatively impact the lives of racial minorities.

Recently, Feagin (2009, 2010) has introduced his concept of the "White racial frame" as a way to help us understand not only why but also how it is that many folks, especially White Americans, are unable to fully understand the past or present racially oppressive system in which we live. According to Feagin (2010), most White Americans have adopted a racial frame that "interprets and defends White privileges and advantaged conditions as meritorious and accents White virtues as well as the alleged inferiority and deficiencies of those people of color who are oppressed" (p. 25). Such allegiance to this racial frame creates a worldview that allows Whites, and minorities who adopt such a view, to justify Whites' positions in society as "superior" to other "inferior" groups. Minorities, therefore, are deserving of their inferior place in society. Further, Feagin notes that, once embedded in the institutions and minds of folks in society, the "White racial frame" becomes a "concrete force" in that society that works to help reinforce and maintain racial stereotypes, narratives, images, emotions, and even discrimination.

Viewed through the lens of racialized social systems theory, DMC emerges as an expected outcome for a society where prejudice is regarded as an expression of dominant-group interests, supported by most members of the dominant race. Differential treatment and differential involvement, in turn, become two sides of the same coin, maintaining the racial status quo through the marginalization of minority children. Simply put, a juvenile justice system in which Whites are significantly underrepresented serves to reinforce Whites' narratives of moral superiority and minority inferiority. Maintaining the facade of White moral superiority is achieved from tacit, subtle stacking of the deck through 1) marginalizing minorities and therefore limiting sources of traditional success and 2) hypervigilance for minority failure to "toe the line," as established by the dominant White society.

DMC in Oklahoma

The authors of this chapter conducted research for the Oklahoma Office of Juvenile Affairs (OJA), a brief overview of which will be used here to illustrate the different ways in which bias creates DMC. The OJA study measured official crime data from police and courts; self-report data from juveniles from urban, suburban and rural schools; and coded in-depth interviews with juvenile justice professionals from Oklahoma. Police data showed non-Whites (with the exception of Asians) as significantly more likely to be stopped, arrested, and prosecuted than Whites. For example, the odds of arrest versus being cited, as compared to Whites, show that Black youth are 2.06 times,

Native American youth 2.57 times, and "other/don't know" (which is mostly made up of Latinos) 1.84 times more likely than White youth to be arrested. However, self-report data showed that non-White youth and White youth commit crime at rates with no statistically significant difference, yet non-Whites were 5.33 times more likely to be "detained, questioned, handcuffed" by police and nine times as likely as Whites to be transported by police to a detention center. The self-report data also confirmed the increased likelihood of non-Whites to be arrested rather than cited by police.

In an effort to understand causes for this discrepancy, the authors conducted 176 interviews of police officers, juvenile court lawyers and judges, and juvenile probation officers. Almost of the participants subscribed to stereotypes of non-White families having significantly different value systems and involvement as parents, neither of which is supported by research. Racial isolation increased this tendency, as those who live and/or were raised in White, segregated communities, tended to be stronger in their belief in racial/ethnic family differences.

Works Cited

Althusser, L. (1977). On the Twenty-Second Congress of the French Communist Party. *New Left Review*, (104), 3.

Anderson, E. (1999). *Code of the street: Decency, violence, and the moral life of the inner city.* New York, NY: W. W. Norton.

Bishop, D. & Frazier, C. (1996). Race effects in juvenile justice decision-making: Findings of a statewide analysis. *Journal of Criminal Law and Criminology, 86,* 392–413.

Bobo, L., & Kluegel, J. (1993). Opposition to race-targeting: Self-interest, stratification ideology or racial attitudes? *American Sociological Review, 58,* 443–464.

Bonczar, T. P., & Beck, A. J. (1997). Lifetime likelihood of going to state or federal prison (Bureau of Justice Statistics Special Report, U.S. Department of Justice Publication No. NCJ 160092). Washington, DC: U.S. Department of Justice, Bureau of Justice Statistics.

Bonilla-Silva, E. (2001). *White supremacy and racism in the post-civil rights era.* Boulder, CO: Lynne Rienner.

Bonilla-Silva, E. (2003). *Racism without racists: Color-blind racism and the persistence of racial inequality in the United States.* Lanham, MD: Rowman & Littlefield.

Bonilla-Silva, E., & Embrick, D. G. (2006). Black, honorary White, White: The future of race in the United States? Pp. 33-48 in D. L. Brunsma (Ed.), *Mixed messages: Doing race in the color-blind era.* Boulder, CO: Lynne Rienner.

Bonilla-Silva, E., & Forman, T. (2000). I'm not a racist but …: Mapping White college students' racial ideology in the USA. *Discourse and Society, 11,* 50–85.

Bridges, G., Conley, D., Engen, R., & Price-Spratlen, T. (1995). Racial disparities in the confinement of juveniles: Effects of crime and community social structure on punishment. Pp. 128-152 in K. Kempf Leonard, C. Pope, and W. Feyerherm (Eds.), *Minorities in juvenile justice.* Thousand Oaks, CA: Sage.

Bridges, G., & Steen, S. (1998). Racial disparities in official assessments of juvenile offending: Attributional stereotypes as mediating mechanisms. *American Sociological Review, 65,* 554–570.

Coates, R. (2011). *Covert racism: Theories, institutions, and experiences.* Boston, MA: Brill.

Damphousse, K., Charish, C., & Davis, S. (2004). *Race/ethnicity and gender effects on juvenile system processing.* Oklahoma City, OK: Oklahoma Office of Juvenile Affairs.

D'Souza, D. (1995). *The end of racism.* New York, NY: Free Press.

Fagan, J., Piper, E., & Moore, M. (1987). Violent delinquents and urban youth. *Criminology, 24,* 439–471.

Feagin, J. (2000, 2010). *Racist America: roots, current realities, and future reparations.* New York, NY: Routledge.

Feagin, J. (2006). *Systemic racism: A theory of oppression.* New York, NY: Taylor and Francis Group.

Feagin, J., & McKinney, K. (2005). *The many costs of racism.* Lanham, MD: Rowman & Littlefield.

Feld, B. (1999). *Bad kids: Race and the transformation of the juvenile court*. New York, NY: Oxford University.

Forman, T. (2004). *Color-blind racism and racial indifference: The role of racial apathy in facilitating enduring inequalities in the changing terrain of race and ethnicity*. In Marian Krysan and Amanda Lewis (Eds.). New York, NY: Russell Sage Foundation.

Free, M. (1996). *African Americans and the criminal justice system*. New York, NY: Garland.

Hendricks, J., & Byers, B. (Eds.). (2000). *Multicultural perspectives in criminal justice and criminology* (2nd ed.). Springfield IL: Charles C. Thomas.

Henry, P., & Sears, D. O. (2002). The symbolic racism 2000 scale. *Political Psychology, 23,* 253–283.

Herrnstein, R., & Wilson, J. Q. (1985). Crime and human nature. New York: Simon and Schuster.

Huizinga, D., Thornberry, T., Knight, K., & Lovegrove, P. (2007). *Disproportionate minority contact in the juvenile justice system: A study of differential minority arrest/referral to court in three cities.* OJJDP Document No. 219743.

Jackson, R., & Pabon, E. (2000). Race and treating other people's children as adults. *Journal of Criminal Justice, 28,* 507–515.

Joseph, J. (1995). *Black youths, delinquency, and juvenile justice*. Westport, CT: Greenwood.

Kempf Leonard, K., & Sontheimer, H. (1995). Racial disparities in the confinement of juveniles: Effects of crime and community social structure on punishment. Pp. 98-127 in K. Kempf Leonard, C. Pope, and W. Feyerherm (Eds.), *Minorities in juvenile justice*. Thousand Oaks, CA: Sage.

Kempf Leonard, K., Pope, C., & Feyerherm, W. (Eds.). (1995). *Minorities in juvenile justice.* Thousand Oaks, CA: Sage.

Krisberg, B., Schwartz, I., Fishman, G., Eisikovits, Z., Guttman, E., & Joe, K. (1987). The incarceration of minority youth. *NPPA Journal, 33*(2), 173-205.

Lardiero, C. (1997). Of disproportionate minority confinement. *Corrections Today, 59,* 14–15.

Lewis, A. E. (2003). *Race in the schoolyard: Negotiating the color line in classrooms and communities*. Rutgers University Press.

Martinez, R., Jr. (2002). *Latino homicide: Immigration, violence, and community*. New York, NY: Routledge.

Mauer, M. (1999). The crisis of the young African American male and the criminal justice system. *Impacts of incarceration on the African American family, 199.*

McCarthy, B. R., & Smith, B. L. (1986, February). The conceptualization of discrimination in the juvenile justice process: The impact of administrative factors and screening decisions on juvenile court dispositions. *Criminology, 24*(1), 41–64.

Murray, C., & Herrnstein, R. (1994). The bell curve. *Intelligence and Class Structure in American Life,* New York: Free Press.

Omi, M., & Winant, H. (1994). *Racial formation in the United States: From the 1960s to the 1990s* (2nd ed.). New York, NY: Routledge.

Pettit, B. and Western, B. (2004). Mass imprisonment and the life course: Race and class inequality in U.S. incarceration. *American Sociological Review,* 69(2): 151-169.

Picca, L.H., & Feagin, J. P. (2007). *Two-faced racism: Whites in the backstage and frontstage.* New York, NY: Routledge.

Piquero, A. R. (2008). Disproportionate minority contact: The future of children. *Juvenile Justice, 18*(2), 59–79.

Pope, C., & Snyder, H. (2003). *Race as a factor in juvenile arrests* (OJJDP Juvenile Justice Bulletin). Washington DC: U.S. Department of Justice.

Pope, C., & Feyerherm, W. (1990). Minority status and juvenile justice processing: An assessment of the research literature. *Criminal Justice Abstracts, 22,* 327–335 (part 1); 527–542 (part 2).

Russell, K. (1998). *The color of crime: Racial hoaxes, White fear, Black protectionism, police harassment, and other macroaggressions.* New York, NY: University Press.

Sears, D.O., & Henry, P. J. (2003). The origins of symbolic racism: Interpersonal relations and group processes. *Journal of Personality and Social Psychology, 85*(2), 259–275.

Secret & Johnson. (1997). The effect of race on juvenile justice decision making in Nebraska: Detention, adjudication, and disposition, 1988–1993. *Justice Quarterly, 14,* 445–478.

Singer, S. I. (1996). Merging and emerging systems of juvenile and criminal justice. Law & Policy, 18(1-2), 1-15.

Snyder, H. N., & Sickmund, M. (2006). *Juvenile offenders and victims: 2006 national report.* Washington, DC: U.S. Department of Justice, Office of Justice Programs, Office of Juvenile Justice and Delinquency Prevention.

Walker, S., Spohn, C., & DeLone, M. (2000). *The color of justice* (2nd ed.). Belmont, CA: Wadsworth/Thompson Learning.

Wordes, M., & Bynum, T. S. (1995). Policing juveniles: Is there bias against youths of color? Pp. 47-65 in K. Kempf Leonard, C. Pope, and W. Feyerherm (Eds.), *Minorities in juvenile justice.* Thousand Oaks, CA: Sage.

PATHWAYS TO DOWNWARD MOBILITY

The Impact of Schools, Welfare, and Prisons on People of Color

BY ROGELIO SAENZ, KAREN M. DOUGLAS, DAVID G. EMBRICK, AND GIDEON SJOBERG

Throughout the course of American society, racial stratification has been a fact of life. Indeed, the founding of the nation occurred alongside the extermination and subjugation of indigenous people. Through the centuries other groups, most notably blacks, have been subjugated and oppressed. While race is well embedded in the foundation of American society, organizational arrangements and the occupants of positions within them have contributed to continued stratification.

W.E.B. Du Bois predicted that the major issue of the 20th century in the United States would be the color line. Little did Du Bois realize that his prediction would be realized into the 21st century (Darling-Hammond 2004). The 20th century began with the clear demarcation of the races with people of color cut off completely from societal opportunity structures. The period extending from the late 1950s to the early 1970s witnessed a ray of hope for minorities, particularly in the areas of education and civil rights. These gains, however, were short-lived as the closing decades of the 20th century and the beginning of the 21st century have involved significant retrenchment to earlier epochs.

While such trends have occurred across all societal institutions, we focus on three that have experienced especially grave changes over the last few decades—education, welfare, and prisons. These institutions are intimately linked, with education thought to be the great equalizer (or enabler), welfare the safety net, and prisons the social control. In recent times, the educational and welfare institutions have decreasingly served their designated functions while increasingly being subjected to social control.

This chapter has three objectives. First, we provide a theoretical overview, drawing on perspectives from the race/ethnic and organization literatures, to ground our analysis. Second, we provide an in-depth overview of each of the three institutions focusing on changing trends and the significance of race. Finally, we close with a discussion of the implications of our analysis.

Theoretical Framework

Scholars of racial and ethnic relations recognize how firmly race is embedded in the structural foundations of American society. We draw here primarily on the works of Joe Feagin's systemic racism and Eduardo Bonilla-Silva's racialized social systems perspectives.

Systemic Racism

In his book, *Racist America: Roots, Realities, and Future Reparations*, Feagin (2000; see also Feagin 2005) develops a conceptual framework that explains the current conditions of blacks in the United States—a theory he refers to as systemic racism. Systemic racism emphasizes the structural, institutional, and systemic elements present in a racialized and oppressive system. In essence, Feagin (2000) argues that the present state

Rogelio Saenz, Karen Douglas, David Embrick and Gideon Sjoberg, "Pathways to Downward Mobility: The Impact of Schools, Welfare, and Prisons on People of Color," *Handbook of the Sociology of Racial and Ethnic Relations*, ed. Hernán Vera and Joe R. Feagin, pp. 373-409. Copyright © 2007 by Springer Science+Business Media LLC. Reprinted with permission.

of blacks and other non-whites in the United States is a result of a system that has deep historical roots in preserving white privilege through the exploitation and discrimination of non-whites. Systemic racism, according to Feagin (2000:16), includes "a diverse assortment of racist practices; the unjustly gained economic and political power of whites; the continuing resource inequalities; and the white-racist ideologies, attitudes, and institutions created to preserve white advantages and power." The adverse effects of systemic racism do not merely manifest themselves in blacks' everyday lives and whites' group identity, but systemic racism is also ever changing so that the structural and institutional vestiges of racial discrimination against non-whites continue to evolve, and therefore persist, with society. Thus, major institutions such as education, prisons, and welfare systems in the United States continue to hold on to racial stereotypes and engage in racial practices that negatively impact the lives of racial minorities.

The Racialized Social System

The racialized social system theory, according to Bonilla-Silva (2001), explains racism as a global phenomenon that affected all societies that came into contact with European whites. The racialization of the world system was, and still is, based on social, economic, political, and psychological relations of domination and subordination between social groups defined as superior "races" and groups defined as inferior "races" (Omi and Winant 1994; Bonilla-Silva 2001). Bonilla-Silva (2001) argues that the racialization of the world created "racialized social systems" where the dominant race has developed various practices and mechanisms to maintain its social standing and subjugated racial groups have struggled to attempt to change their position in the social order. Racism has a material or structural foundation, that is, "racial" matters in societies reflect the interests of the parties in conflict. Thus, Bonilla-Silva (2001, 2006) notes that while prejudice in all its variants can be regarded as an expression of dominant group interests, effective racial control benefits not from a plurality of highly racialized individuals in society, but from the passive and tacit support of the racial order by most members of the dominant race—in the case of the United States, whites. Because racialized social systems work to preserve white privilege, progressive attempts to create a more balanced and egalitarian society are often ideals in theory, yet failures in practice. For example, although there is debate surrounding the notion that schools and educators are necessarily privileged sites or actors for progressive social change, in truth, they usually function, despite contradictions, to reproduce the racialized social system (Althusser 1977).

The Need for Organizational Understanding in Race and Ethnicity

The foundational elements of race in societal institutions are well established. However, in order to delve deep in understanding how racial inequality is sustained, we turn to insights from the organizational literature. Our conception of organizations moves beyond Weber, so as to incorporate the role of human agency as elaborated by John Dewey and George Herbert Mead (see Sjoberg et al. 2002). In brief we find that human agents within organizations shape and are shaped by the nature of organizational structures; so too human agents (e.g., clients) who interact with organizations shape and are shaped by the complex organizational arrangements in question. While attentive to the larger organizational complexes, we focus primarily on how impoverished minorities interact with the lower echelons of organizations such as education, welfare, and prisons.

Formal organizations are characterized by rules and norms (formal and informal), and typically these rules or norms are organized so that some persons have more knowledge and power than do others. Modern-day organizations are typified by, for instance, hierarchy, a complex division of labor, and standardization and routinization of many everyday activities. Assuredly the manner in which hierarchy, the division of labor, and routinization are put together can vary considerably. Still the principles remain rather intact. There is a great deal of talk nowadays about the leveling of organizational hierarchy, but that thesis does not square with the fact that managers—in large corporations and even in universities—are rewarded, socially and economically, more handsomely than ever before.

The hierarchical patterns generally mean that the leadership of organizations strives to sustain a monopoly of knowledge about how the system actually works. Concomitantly, school, prison, or welfare officials are keenly aware of their larger constituency. And persons outside organizations who interact with members of organizations vary considerably in the social and cultural capital they possess as they strive to cope with the rather technical rules to which educational, welfare, and prison personnel are expected to adhere.

One defining characteristic of educational, welfare, and prison organizations is that the rules and norms are fewer and vaguer for the managers of organizational power than for the personnel who staff lower-level positions, the latter typically being engulfed by rules or norms that are more constraining and confining. This pattern is heightened by leadership's delegation to personnel below of blameability under the guise of responsibility. A simple illustration may clarify our argument. The managers of school systems theoretically delegate responsibility to street-level workers below—to teachers in particular—who must interact with students and often family members. But if the school is criticized for its performance, it is often the teachers or other lower-level personnel, not the upper-level personnel, who bear the brunt of the attack—in part because the lower-level personnel interact directly with the clients, in part because the leadership is able to deflect attention away from its own failings.

A salient feature of organizations such as schools, prisons, and welfare agencies is that persons who are most bound by the rules are those who most frequently interact with the poor from racial and ethnic minority groups. Consequently, impoverished minorities, who are the least knowledgeable about how the system functions, are called upon to interact with persons who are the least able to bend the rules. Certainly, street-level workers are constantly called upon to interpret the rules relating to how they should cope with clients (rules do not interpret themselves), but street-level workers possess only limited freedom to reinterpret the rules so as to accommodate the special circumstances in which poor people find themselves. Yes, it is said that the cop on the beat has considerable discretion. But this is typically carefully bounded. We know that the police in Texas are prone to stop, often in an arbitrary manner, Latino drivers in Texas, and they are far less likely to arbitrarily stop privileged whites. The latter command the economic resources along with social and cultural capital to challenge the system, their views being looked upon favorably by judges and others who would resent being hassled by officers in the manner racial and ethnic minorities are hassled.

Clearly, middle-class parents typically understand that administrators are less bound by the rules, and thus their children's special needs are more likely to be addressed by upper-echelon administrators rather than by lower-level employees. In the case of public schools, middle-class parents can, come election time, contribute money to candidates for the school board (and mobilize so as to elect the candidates that support their views), and in the case of private schools, the parents pay the bill rather directly and often expect to receive privileged treatment. Put simply, according to business protocol, "the customer is always right."

What we should recognize is that persons who interact with the educational, welfare, and prison systems do so in terms of their social and cultural capital—concepts that Pierre Bourdieu (1986) introduced into the sociological lexicon. We use "social capital" to refer to the social networks that persons are able to tap for learning about how to cope with organizations, whereas "cultural capital"—as we employ the term—involves knowledge (formal and tacit) as to how organizations operate. Clearly impoverished minorities are embedded in social networks, but these, while supportive of their everyday activities, often cannot be relied upon to provide knowledge of how to understand and cope with the rules of formal organizations. Lacking such resources, economically strapped minorities find themselves vulnerable in societal institutions as they are forced to interact directly with lower-level occupants of organizations who have little power and are positioned to apply the rules in a rather narrow manner. The data strongly suggest that organizations, even those in the areas of education and welfare, which are designed to assist economically strapped minorities improve themselves, may also serve to keep them in their place. Although ideal values or beliefs call for equal treatment and equality, actual practices vary considerably from these ideals.

We shall also briefly introduce a more specialized topic relating to social organizations—namely privatization, which has received little attention by scholars who write about racial and ethnic minorities. When the general public or sociologists discuss privatization, they generally think about the private sector taking over activities traditionally defined as governmental in nature. This pattern has been widespread in the past quarter-century, as we have witnessed major efforts to privatize schools, prisons, and the welfare system. Further, it is frequently assumed that the governmental sector is bureaucratized and the private sector is not. But that thesis is unsustainable empirically. Large corporations—including those whose business is education, prisons, and welfare—are typified by hierarchy (note the power and earnings of managers), a complex division of labor, and routinization and standardization (the ideal of efficiency being widely invoked). Admittedly, private- and public-sector organizations differ considerably in their objectives, but significant organizational similarities between the private and public sectors can be delineated. In addition to moving educational, welfare, and prison activities from the public to the private sector, we can isolate another feature to privatization, overlooked by most sociologists. Although we are unable to pursue the issue in detail herein, students of race relations will need to address the matter of transferring risk from both public and private organizations onto individuals. In recent decades sociologists such as Anthony Giddens (1998) and Ulrich Beck (1992) have, in a highly innovative manner, highlighted the need to investigate the issue of risk. What they have not done (given their inattention to formal organizations) is to examine how we have witnessed a systematic effort to shift risk—regarding, for instance, health insurance and retirement benefits—from organizations onto individuals with potentially grave implications for racial and ethnic minorities. This effort was highlighted by the intense political debate in the United States in 2005 regarding the future of social security, during which time strategic elements of the U.S. public acknowledged that it is easier for organizations (in this instance the government) to bear the burden of risk for future payment of retirement benefits than it is for individuals to do so.

In sum, we envisage our discussion of formal organizations as a loose framework (having drawn on Sjoberg et al. 1966, 2002; and Tan and Sjoberg 2005) within which we analyze the research that has emerged with respect to how impoverished minorities are called upon to interact and cope with schools, welfare agencies, and prisons. After an overview of the literature and historical trends, we draw out more fully, in the concluding sector of this chapter, the implications of our analysis for the study of race and ethnic relations in the United States and elsewhere.

The Sweet Enchantment Of Color-Blind Education

Education has historically been viewed as the great equalizer or enabler—the route through which people can gain access to societal opportunity structures and through which inequality can be reduced. It is viewed as the primary vehicle through which people achieve upward mobility. Human capital theory, for example, emphasizes the importance of education in maximizing benefits from labor markets. It is commonly assumed that everyone has equal access to education. Thus, educational outcomes are seen in personal terms, with blame placed on students and their families when they fail or drop out of school.

Despite the notion that education is the great equalizer, the reality is much different, particularly in the case of minorities. At the beginning of the 20th century, the schooling of blacks occurred in apartheid conditions—separate schools for blacks and whites. Today, despite efforts to provide minority students—primarily black and Latino—with greater access to education, these students continue to be schooled in apartheid-like environments. The color line in American education is alive and well in the beginning of the 21st century.

The Reproduction of Inequality in Education

Sociologists recognize the intergenerational stratification of education (see Feagin 2005). For example, status attainment scholars have noted the importance of parental socioeconomic status (SES) on the educational, occupational, and earnings outcomes of their offspring (Blau and Duncan 1967; Sewell and Hauser 1975). Economists have also indicated that people with greater socioeconomic resources have relatively few children, but invest heavily in their education (Becker and Lewis 1973; Blake 1981). Hence, well-off parents pass on their advantages to their children.

Yet, affluent parents invest in their children in other ways, too. Bourdieu and Passeron (1990) demonstrate how these parents provide their children with social connections and cultural sophistication, which can help them navigate the educational system. Thus, well-off parents give their children access to valuable social capital (social connections) which they can tap to succeed in schools. For instance, these children live in prosperous neighborhoods and have friends who are affluent and have high academic aspirations. They also have a wide network of adult role models who can assist them in countless ways. Such students can bank on these social connections to take advantage of educational opportunities that are beyond the reach of poor and minority students.

Moreover, well-to-do parents also invest in the cultural capital (knowledge, preferences, skills, and cultural tastes) of their children. For example, such parents can enroll their children in specialized academic programs; take them on trips domestically and abroad; take them to museums; and provide them access to books, newspapers, magazines, and computers. These students also gain the cultural polish (e.g., clothing, speech, and manners) that makes them acceptable to mainstream society, including their teachers and administrators (Morris 2005). In sum, high-SES children possess cultural capital that can help them succeed in the educational system.

Furthermore, affluent parents can draw on their own social and cultural capital in managing their children's educational careers (Lareau 2000; Useem 1992). They have themselves succeeded in the educational system and know the "ropes" of the system and how the "game" is played (Ainsworth and Roscigno 2005; Laureau and Horvat 1999). Due to their high SES, these parents represent a powerful voice that educators cannot easily dismiss. Such parents can advocate for their children's place in the educational system, as they have been shown to intervene to place their children in higher academic tracks (Baker and Stevenson 1986; Laureau 2000; Lucas 1999, 2001).

While we have emphasized above the advantages that parents transmit to their children, it is apparent that such transmissions extend back numerous generations. Feagin (2005) has eloquently described how the racist foundational aspects of American society allowed whites to gain economic resources that were easily transmitted to their children and to future generations. Indeed, European immigrants in the establishment of the United States and later on gained valuable economic resources as well as land that provided advantages for themselves and for their progeny, advantages that continue to place whites in the higher spheres of the contemporary stratification system. On the other hand, Feagin (2005) points out that blacks did not have access to economic resources and land because of the institution of slavery, Jim Crow, and racism. As such, blacks did not have the valuable economic, social, and cultural capital that whites possessed that allowed them to provide their progeny with economic and social advantages. The result is that the disadvantaged position of African Americans—as well as those of Mexican Americans, Puerto Ricans, and Native Americans—today reflects the transmission of economic and social disadvantages across numerous generations extending back centuries.

We now turn to a discussion of efforts that have been made to decrease the inequities in the educational system. We will see how many whites—in conjunction with the courts—marshaled resources to reverse gains in school desegregation made following the landmark *Brown* decision.

The Politics of School Racial Desegregation

There has historically been a deep chasm between blacks and whites in the South, reflecting the deep structural elements manifested in Jim Crow policies and customs that kept the races apart (Myrdal 1944). Racially separate schools existed throughout the South for a large part of the 20th century. Although the segregation of the races occurred in a *de jure* fashion in the South, it largely took place on a *de facto* basis outside this region. Note that Mexican schools emerged in the 1910s in much of the Southwest, notably in Texas and California.

Many supporters of school segregation justified the separation of the races in public schools by arguing that schools could be separate but equal. Yet, Clotfelter (2004) shows that separate schools were unequal with respect to funding, facilities, class sizes, and course offerings. He notes that in most Deep South states, the per-pupil spending in black public schools was less than half of that in white public schools in 1940. In Mississippi, the funding of black schools was only 17 percent that of white schools. Clotfelter (2004) indicates that public school segregation was also significant in the North during the early 1950s.

This is the backdrop that existed when, on May 17, 1954, the Supreme Court announced its historic *Brown* decision, which sought to dismantle the separation of the races in public schools. Immediate resistance to the ruling arose throughout the South. Thus, southern governors tenaciously resisted desegregating public schools, with Alabama's governor, George Wallace, exemplifying this in 1963 (Clotfelter 2004:13): "I draw the line in the dust and toss the gauntlet before the feet of tyranny and I say segregation now, segregation tomorrow, segregation forever." Southern congressional members signed the Southern Manifesto, condemning the *Brown* decision (Clotfelter 2004; Feagin 2005). Further, white parents and school officials viciously opposed the implementation of the law.

Because the *Brown* decision was weak in enforcement, it allowed southern officials to stall desegregation, resulting in little progress during the 1954–1964 period in the region (Clotfelter 2004). However, increasing pressure from all three branches of government prompted significant change in the 1965–1973 period. Clotfelter (2004) highlights the 1969–1972 period as a time that saw particularly rapid change in desegregation. The percentage of blacks in the South attending schools where blacks accounted for 90 percent or more of the student body fell from 78 percent in 1968 to 25 percent in 1972 (Clotfelter 2004). The South shifted from being the most segregated region in terms of public education in 1968 to the least segregated region in 1972.

Nonetheless, dramatic changes, namely the *Milliken v. Bradley* decision in 1974, stemmed this trend not only in the South but also nationally (Clotfelter 2004). In this case involving Detroit, the Supreme Court ruled that students could not be moved across school districts to achieve school desegregation. Thus, black students could not be moved from central cities to suburbs, where whites were increasingly settling. Clotfelter (2004:31) asserts that *Milliken* "marked the beginning of a retreat from the proactive pursuit of racial balance as a judicial objective."

The early 1990s brought a series of additional Supreme Court rulings that further reversed school desegregation: *Board of Education of Oklahoma v. Dowell* (1991), *Freeman v. Pitts* (1992), and *Missouri v. Jenkins* (1995). These cases generally allowed school districts to end desegregation orders. Orfield and Eaton (1996:5) claim that:

> The significance of the *Dowell, Pitts*, and *Jenkins* decisions ... is best understood within the historical context of this long, difficult and yet unfinished post-*Brown* struggle toward desegregated schools. The quiet, gradual movement from the holdings of *Brown* to those of *Dowell, Pitts*, and *Jenkins*, expressed allegiance to *Brown* while chipping away at its spirit and its power. In many communities, *Brown* is left intact today in theory only.

Frankenberg et al. (2003:4) summarize the reversing trend in school desegregation:

> At the beginning of the twenty-first century, American public schools are now 12 years into the process of continuous resegregation. The desegregation of black students, which increased continuously from the 1950s to the late 1980s, has now receded to levels not seen in three decades. Although the South remains the nation's most integrated region for both blacks and whites, it is the region that is most rapidly going backwards as the courts terminate many major and successful desegregation orders.

Across regions, the percentage of blacks attending schools that are at least 50 percent or 90 percent nonwhite has risen. The South leads this trend, with the percentage of blacks going to schools where nonwhites compose at least 90 percent of the student body increasing from 23 percent in 1980 to 31 percent in 2000. The segregation of blacks is especially noticeable in the Northeast, where slightly more than half go to schools that are 90-100 percent nonwhite (see Kozol 2005). Also, across regions, between two thirds and four fifths of blacks attend public schools where nonwhites are the majority (data not shown here). Additionally, Latino students are now the most segregated group in public schools (Frankenberg et al. 2003).

While the courts played a major role in the reversal of the integration of public schools in the post-*Brown* period, white parents also played an active role. Clotfelter (2004) asserts that many white parents preferred not to send their children to mixed-race schools and used numerous options at their disposal—including help from state and local officials—to avoid enrolling their children in integrated schools. Clotfelter (2004) identifies strategies that averted integration including private schools, migration to suburbs, academic tracking within schools, gerrymandering of school districts, allowance of student transfers, and the siting of new schools. White parents used all of the resources at their disposal to realize their desires. Illustratively, Ladson-Billings and Tate (1995:60), drawing on Harris' (1993) concept of "whiteness as property" (the *right* that whiteness provides), argue that:

> In schooling, the absolute right to exclude was demonstrated initially by denying blacks access to schooling altogether. Later, it was demonstrated by the creation and maintenance of separate schools. More recently it has been demonstrated by white flight and the growing insistence on vouchers, public funding of private schools, and schools of choice. Within schools, absolute right to exclude is demonstrated by resegregation via tracking.

The Color Line of Public School Funding

Not only do minority students increasingly attend schools that have few white students, but their schools are also ill-financed. Kozol (1991) vividly portrays the massive inequities in the funding of public education.

As in the case of school desegregation, the courts have debated the funding issue. Kozol (2005) notes the significance of the date of March 21, 1973, when the Supreme Court overruled a Texas district court that had declared unconstitutional the funding of Texas public schools. The case involved Edgewood, a poor largely Latino district. At the time, despite having one of the highest property rates in the area, the district eked out only $37 per pupil, which rose to $231 with a grant from the state (Kozol 2005). In contrast, the richest district in the area, a predominantly white district, raised $543 per student. In the ruling, Justice Powell wrote that education "is not a fundamental interest" in that it "is not among the rights afforded explicit protection under our Federal Constitution" and continued "the argument here is not that the children in districts having relatively low assessable property values are receiving no public education; rather, it is that they are receiving a poor quality of education than that available to children in districts having more assessable wealth" (Kozol 2005:242).

Huge disparities in public-school funding persist. The Educational Trust (2005) analyzed public school funding data for 49 states to compare the funding disparities in 2003 between the top and bottom quartiles on the levels of poverty and minority enrollment. Overall, 27 of the 49 states spent less on poorer school districts than they did on richer school districts, with the average gap being $907 per pupil. The gap was greatest in New York (–$2,280) and Illinois (–$2,065). In addition, 30 of the 49 states provided less funding to school districts with the highest percentages of minority students than they did to those with the highest shares of white students, with the average gap being $614 across the states. The gap was greatest in Wyoming (–$2,416), North Dakota (–$2,046), and New York (–$1,965).

Schools with largely poor and minority student bodies suffer in other ways as well (see Bracey 2002). For example, such schools are more likely than richer schools to have inadequate facilities, curricula, educational materials, and technology. They are also more likely to have inexperienced and uncertified teachers (Hochschild 2003; Kozol 2005). Kozol (2005) provides a litany of examples showing the inferior education of minority students. Kozol (2005:163) laments that in the era of testing and accountability, there is not a "misery index for the children of apartheid education." To illustrate, Cooper (2001), in reporting on court documents on a lawsuit against the state of California, describes "young children picking up beer bottles, condoms and bullets on school grounds," "special education students assigned to no teacher and roaming the halls," "rats in cafeterias, one carrying fruit in its mouth, others scurrying around a bread rack," "chemistry labs with no chemicals at all," "literature classes without books," and "computer classes where, according to one student, 'we sit there and talk about what we would be doing if we had computers.'" Such conditions would be intolerable in schools with largely white and affluent students.

Inequality Within School Walls

Inequality is, however, embedded at varying levels of geography, what Hochschild (2003) refers to as "nested inequalities." Thus, not only does it exist across states, school districts, and schools, but it also occurs within schools. Tracking within schools is fairly widespread, as research indicates that it was used in roughly three fifths of elementary schools and in four fifths of secondary schools in the mid-1990s (Strum 1993).

While popular, tracking reproduces existing inequities (Ainsworth and Roscigno 2005; Ansalone 2001). Indeed, white and affluent students are most likely to be tracked into higher levels, with minority and poor students more likely to be placed in lower tracks (Darling-Hammond 1997; Hochschild 2003; Lucas 1999; Oakes 1995). Ansalone (2001) points out that although tracking may not be done directly on the basis of race and SES, the criteria commonly used are correlated with these attributes. For instance, children entering kindergarten are tracked based on their ability to read upon entering school, with minority and lower-SES youngsters being least likely to read at that stage. Moreover, students are tracked in other ways including cultural norms, language, and disciplinary records, all related to race and social class (Ansalone 2001).

As minority students are sorted into lower tracks, their options narrow tremendously. They do not have access to courses that can prepare them for college, but take courses that train them for low-wage jobs. They interact mostly with students who are similar to themselves. They are not likely to be identified by their teachers for awards or for academic opportunities. Research shows that academic tracking is beneficial to students in higher tracks, but harmful—or not helpful—to those in lower tracks (Ansalone 2001; Hochschild 2003; Lucas 1999). In sum, the cards are stacked against lower-track minority students (Lipman 2003). As Ansalone (2001:44) concludes, tracking "impedes the achievement and future life chances of less-advantaged students."

Accountability and High-Stakes Testing

One of the major trends affecting education concerns the increasing push for accountability and high-stakes testing. Many states have implemented such corporate-based models (Lipman 2003), which aim to hold schools accountable for the education of their students with the evaluation based solely on student performance on high-stakes tests. Despite the wide disparity in the funding and resources of public schools, all schools and students are assumed to be on an equal playing field. The models emphasize one output (students' scores) without taking into account inputs. The framework became etched nationally in 2002 when President George W. Bush's No Child Left Behind program was implemented.

While accountability programs emphasize academic excellence and the reduction of academic disparities across selected groups of students, the outcome has been far from favorable for many students, especially minorities. There are several ways in which high-stakes tests have especially hurt students of color (see McNeil 2005). First, students who fail high-stakes tests or exit exams are likely to drop out of school, while administrators have incentives to "push" low-achieving students out of school to produce high scores (Lipman 2003; McNeil 2005). Second, students who fail high-stakes exams are subject to grade retention (Lipman 2003), increasing their odds of dropping out. Third, with the emphasis on preparing students for high-stakes exams (Lipman 2003), there is a significant loss in the curriculum. As McNeil (2005:88) points out, "The work of classrooms under the accountability system has shifted from learning content, ideas, and skills to learning how to take a standardized exam." The result is that students, particularly minorities, are shortchanged academically.

In contrast, higher-SES students, primarily whites, are shielded from the drudgery of high-stakes tests, as their parents can use their social and cultural capital to intervene on their behalf. For example, Lipman (2003) notes how a predominantly white parental organization consistently pressed school administrators for the highest-quality education for their children, thus minimizing the importance of high-stakes exams on their schooling.

It is important to note that the No Child Left Behind program is based on the Texas model of accountability and high-stakes exams (Valenzuela 2005b). As Texas governor, Bush championed the model. Subsequently, in his presidential administration his two secretaries of the Department of Education were key players in the Texas model. Bush's first secretary of education, Roderick Paige, was superintendent of the Houston Independent School District (HISD) and received praise for his leadership in the district's supposed success in the state's high-stakes exams and low dropout rates. Paige's successor, Margaret Spellings, was Governor Bush's senior advisor. She was important in the development of the governor's educational policy, which is the foundation for the No Child Left Behind program. Because of its role as a model for the nation, we now examine the Texas program.

The Texas Mirage

Texas is a national leader in the accountability and high-stakes testing of public education. Indeed, the state received wide praise for the "Texas Miracle" reflecting high scores on the Texas Assessment of Academic Skills (TAAS) test alongside low dropout rates. Upon closer inspection, however, the results were far less positive than what was presented (Haney 2000; McNeil 2005). The mirage is due to various problems including the failure to take into account "missing students"—likely dropouts—and exploiting ways of classifying students to keep them from negatively affecting scores (Haney 2000).

A critical assessment of the Texas program reveals more illusion (see Valenzuela 2005a). We draw here on the analysis of McNeil (2005). The illusion stems, in part, from the use of a sole measure—performance on the TAAS—to assess academic achievement (McNeil 2005; Valenzuela 2005b). Using this indicator, scores rose steadily from 53 percent of students passing the TAAS in 1994 to 85 percent passing in 2002 (McNeil 2005), a trend that occurred across all designated categories of students.

However, McNeil (2005:57) reveals that "*On every other indicator of academic achievement,* Texas children are not only showing weak academic performance, but also growing increasingly weak over time" (italics in original). She highlights several indicators. First, Texas students have declining scores on the Texas Academic Skills Performance (TASP) exam, a less challenging test than the SAT and ACT, which most students applying to Texas public universities need to take. The percentage of test-takers passing the TASP fell from 52 percent in 1995 to 29 percent in 1999, with the percentages of beginning college students requiring remedial training increasing over the course of high-stakes testing (McNeil 2005). Second, the modest gains of Texas students on the SAT I over a 10-year period fell below national trends (Haney 2000), with Texas students ranked near the bottom nationally on SAT I scores. Third, while Texas has tried to validate its rising TAAS scores with its increasing scores on the National Assessment of Educational Progress (NAEP) (a low-stakes exam that states do not need to administer), there is need for caution (McNeil 2005). While a random sample of students is selected to take the NAEP, administrators are allowed to exclude students from taking the exam (Amrein and Berliner 2002). Haney (2000) notes that Texas has the highest percentage of students excluded from taking the NAEP and that its percentage of students excluded from taking the exam increased concomitantly with its rising NAEP scores. Finally, Texas continues to have high dropout rates. Overall, two fifths or fewer of students in the six largest school districts graduated in 1999, with Latino students in five of the districts being about half to three fourths as likely as white students to complete high school (McNeil 2005). In sum, the Texas miracle turns out to be a mirage and one that has been detrimental to the education of students, most notably minority students.

Having overviewed the structural forces operating in the educational sphere which set the parameters for the education of students, we now turn our attention to the micro world where students operate. As Reay (2004:1019) asserts, inequalities are "made and remade at the micro level, in and through innumerable everyday practices."

The Micro World of Minority Students

The schools where minority students disproportionately attend, the curricula that guide their studies, the courses that they take, and the school environments all work to marginalize them at many levels. They tend to be marginalized from the larger society, schools they attend, high-achieving peers, and teachers and administrators. Minority students tend to bear the stigma of their segregated schools and their lower academic tracks. In the era of high-stakes testing, many bear the label of "failure" either directly or through the schools that they attend. Delgado (1995) reveals the extreme forms of marginalization that some minority students experience through the notion that society sees some kids as being "beyond love." For example, Delgado (1995:49) asserts that blacks, particularly the poor:

> ... have so few chances, so little interaction with majority society, that they might as well be exiles, outcasts, permanent black sheep who will never be permitted into the fold. Majority society has, in effect, written them off.

Minority students tend to be unduly labeled as low achievers and at-risk students and to be sorted into lower academic tracks. Undoubtedly, these labels influence the opinions and expectations that teachers and administrators form of them (Ansalone 2001; Rosenbloom and Way 2004; Wheelock 1992). Because minority students tend to lack mainstream forms of social and cultural capital, they are unable to avert the low opinions and expectations that many educators have of them. In the case of students who are "written off," educators shift the focus from academics to discipline (Fernandez 2002). Accordingly, students are taught skills that will make them reliable and obedient workers who will hold low-skill, low-wage jobs when they leave school (see Kozol 2005).

Reyes (2006) examines the links between race and discipline and its consequences which question the democratic nature of education. Drawing on data from the National Center for Educational Statistics, Reyes (2006) points out that African American and Latino students are disproportionately disciplined in schools and receive harsher discipline than do white students. Indeed, Ansalone (2001) reports that teachers in lower tracks spend twice as much time disciplining students as do those in higher tracks. He notes that it is, thus, not surprising that higher-track students tend to view their teachers as "warm" and "fair," while lower track students see their teachers as "punitive" and "unenthusiastic." In addition, in the mid-1990s as part of accountability policies, the Chicago Public Schools (CPS) started the first two military high schools in the country (located in African American neighborhoods), started a military middle school, infused military programs in high schools, and initiated zero-tolerance discipline rules (Lipman 2003; see also Reyes 2006). Yet, another example of discipline imposed on minority students derives from their clothing and mannerisms. Morris (2005) observes that African American girls are constantly told to "act like young women," while Latino boys, who receive the harshest discipline, are consistently told to "tuck in that shirt!" Similarly, Ferguson (2000) shows how educators target African American males for discipline due to their clothing and behavior.

Critical race theory (CRT) and Latino critical theory (LatCrit), with their emphasis on giving "voice" to marginalized people, offer another glimpse of the world of minority students. We highlight here the counter-story of Pablo from the work of Fernández (2002). Pablo, a student at a Midwestern university, provides a personal account of his experience as a student in the Chicago public schools. He recalls that many of the mostly white teachers did not care whether students learned, did not enjoy their jobs, and exhibited racist views. Pablo also observes that the focus of schools was on vocational skills and discipline rather than on academics. He also describes how students resisted their treatment at school by skipping classes.

Yet, Pablo reports that there were some teachers who cared about students. For example, he credits a certain teacher for assisting him in getting the courses he needed to prepare for college after the teacher recognized Pablo's math skills. Moreover, he remarks that some teachers had high expectations of them and tried to focus more on academics than on discipline. This is reminiscent of the "authentic care" that Valenzuela identifies as key in teachers making true connections with their students. However, Pablo mentions that caring teachers encountered barriers related to curricular requirements and resistance from colleagues and students. This is a story that is repeated in the literature. The agency, professionalism, and integrity of teachers, overwhelmingly those in predominantly poor and minority schools, are restricted severely by school administrators who place emphasis on preparing students to do well on high-stakes exams. Indeed, policies are made by administrators who are shielded by numerous levels of subordinates in the system. In the end, it is students themselves and their teachers—those at the bottom of the hierarchy—that are held accountable for the outcome on high-stakes tests.

In sum, while the educational system has been seen as the great equalizer and the vehicle for upward mobility, the reality is quite different. Minority students have faced tremendous obstacles in attaining an equitable education. They continue to lag significantly behind and have been disproportionately tracked into low-skill, low-wage jobs that do not offer social mobility. We turn our attention now to the welfare system, which has been seen as the safety net that can cushion the fall of the poor and help them get back on their feet.

The Racial Dimensions Of The American Welfare State

The body of scholarship on the American welfare system is immense and most is beyond the scope of this chapter. Instead, we focus on illustrating the racial dimensions that are explicitly and implicitly embodied within social welfare programs and the ways that organizations reproduce and structure interactions in order to maintain the racial status quo. As we will document, race has always been a factor in social policies and programs although not one that has been readily acknowledged. Quadagno (1994:3) makes the point that "...during the 1960s social policy became linked to race in consequential ways." Indeed the social policies of the civil rights era were linked to race in consequential ways. But so were the social policies of Roosevelt's New Deal during the 1930s and 1940s as were the Civil War pensions of the 1870s before that were linked to race in consequential ways. As Katz (2000:117) explains:

> Although the history of the American welfare state is not primarily a story about race, race remains deeply imbricated in its origins and development. ... The programs and agencies of America's public and private welfare states have served African Americans both identically to and differently from whites. The original structure of some key programs guaranteed blacks different treatment while debased images of African Americans have dominated discourse around welfare reform.

Early Forms of Social Support in the United States

While many scholars date the advent of social welfare in the United States to the New Deal policies of Franklin Delano Roosevelt (FDR) during the 1930s, as the works of Katz (1986), Skocpol (1992), Gordon (1994), and Goodwin (1997) expand upon, federal social welfare programs existed in the United States well in advance of the New Deal policies during the 1930s. In fact, between 1880 and 1910 the federal government dispensed some one quarter of its annual expenditures to Civil War veterans and their widows (Skocpol 1992). Further, while the organization responsible for administering war pensions was not formally racist, racial disparities were apparent nonetheless. In actuality, in that day, as today, racism appears most fully, not in the formal legislation, but in its implementation.

In the period prior to the New Deal, the issue of gender also came to the fore in a variety of ways. Gordon documents how white, middle-class female reformers shared the conservative position with male politicians in defining two categories of women: those most deserving of aid such as widows (largely white), who, through misfortune, were left alone to care for their children in contrast to the undeserving women, divorced or deserted women (largely black), many of whom were wage-earners. Not surprisingly, social policies relating to welfare encouraged men to be wage-earners and women to be stay-at-home mothers.

It is not our intent to flesh out the details of the racial and gender disparities in the pre–New Deal welfare programs. Rather, we note only that scholars have documented in fine detail their presence in the pre–New Deal welfare programs.

Race and the New Deal Policies of FDR

In *When Affirmative Action Was White*, Katznelson (2005) explicates the ways that race shaped Franklin Delano Roosevelt's New Deal programs. He argues that assessing the impact of affirmative action by looking only at policies instituted during the 1960s' civil rights era obscures the ways the economic playing field had already been tilted in favor of whites well before this time. Katznelson provides an answer to the paradox of how during one of the most prosperous periods in U.S. history (post–WWII) the racial gap between whites and blacks grew. The answer, per Katznelson, lies in the political leverage held by racist southern Democrats during the crafting of the New Deal policies.

> The New Deal, beholden to southern votes, … could not, undercut segregation and the ancillary denial of civil and political rights. There would be no anti-lynching law on President Roosevelt's watch; nor would racial hierarchies in the armed forces or federal agencies be disturbed in any basic way. The administration was trapped … by the pervasive legacy of Jim Crow. Any crusade to break out of its power restraints would have been doomed to fail. … Such a campaign would have risked undercutting the wide array of social and economic programs the New Deal advanced. So a trade-off seemed an offer to black America: abjure too strident a claim for civil and political inclusion in exchange for assured and concrete material benefits. (p. 29)

Many programs that emerged from FDR's administration—from the highly touted GI Bill to workplace protection provisions—were deeply embedded in racist ideology. Katznelson documents that in each case, southern Democrats were able to minimize the social safety net for African Americans by either limiting the scope of the program, limiting its reach, or both. In the case of assistance for the elderly poor, for example, southern Democrats were able to get the administration of this program, including the determination of benefit levels, shifted to state and local levels. With all-white local staffs administering benefits, program acceptance rates for African Americans in the South were considerably lower than for whites despite their higher levels of need.

Southern Democrats also left their calling card on the Aid to Dependent Children's (ADC) program. ADC nationalized the state-level mothers' pension programs. ADC was structured as an entitlement program—anyone meeting the eligibility criteria was entitled to receive assistance (Mink 2003). However, because administration of the program was left to states, many states introduced restrictions on eligibility (Katznelson 2005). State officials designed qualifications around white, widowed women with children adopting "suitable" home requirements to limit black enrollment. Additional ploys used by southern politicians to exclude blacks from assistance included seasonal employment policies that cut ADC recipients off welfare rolls during cotton-picking season and "man of the house" rules that allowed social workers to make unannounced home visits and purge from welfare rolls women found living with a man (Quadagno 1994). The policies worked. In the South, black families, despite greater hardships, were underrepresented on ADC rolls (Quadagno 1994).

The 1960s' War on Poverty and Social Welfare

The enduring legacy of racial prejudice and discrimination significantly impacted the lives of African Americans—most acutely in the southern states where poverty rates were high but public assistance rates were low.

> For more than a century, the southern welfare system had reinforced the racial caste system. Fifty-five percent of Mississippi residents had incomes below the poverty level but only 14 percent received assistance; less than 10 percent of Mississippians participated in federal free lunch programs. In 1970 929,000 Alabamians lacked the income necessary for a marginal diet, yet only 277,000 benefited from the Department of Agriculture's (USDA) food-assistance programs (Quadagno 1994:128).

Southern officials used black poverty as a mechanism of social control that was neither benign nor accidental. Whites warned blacks to "surrender their uppity ideas about changing the local balance of power" (Quadagno 1994:129). Blacks would be systematically terminated from welfare rolls and other forms of assistance for registering to vote. Blacks were "relegated to decrepit housing in the worst sections of cities, forced to send their children to inferior schools, and locked out of opportunities with upward mobility ..." (Quadagno 1994:29). Instead of uplifting a poor population, southern-style welfare "reinforced social cleavages" and maintained the racial, social, and economic stratification system.

LBJ's War on Poverty offered corrective measures to the racist policies of the New Deal. At best, Quadagno argues, FDR's New Deal policies "frustrated" anti-poverty efforts. Only by removing social programs from the yoke of "old-line" agencies could the "apathy and resistance existing institutions generated be transcended" (Quadagno 1994:30).

Further, it was during the 1960s that welfare rights groups began agitating for "increased benefits, jobs, and the removal of a host of odious statutes that prevented women from receiving benefits" (Quadagno 1994:120). Consequently, Congress loosened the restrictions for assistance. However, continuing the trend begun with mothers' pensions, the notion that welfare mothers should work was solidified with an amendment to the Social Security Act in 1962 to allow states to use ADC funds to pay for child care, and the enactment of the Work Incentive Program (WIP) in 1967 served as an inducement for mothers to work.

As a result of policy liberalization, welfare rolls increased from 7.8 to 8.4 million in one year. For the first time, many of those receiving assistance were black, Latina, urban, single, and divorced mothers—all groups which had previously been limited. Johnson's programs opened doors for blacks that had previously been shut. The percentage of blacks enrolled in college and their representation in white-collar jobs increased significantly; and the wage differential between whites and blacks began to narrow (Quadagno 1994).

"We have just lost the South for a generation," folklore says LBJ muttered to an aide after signing the Civil Rights Act. Provision of basic democratic rights to a group long denied these rights sparked a backlash that welfare reform is but one manifestation.

Pre-1996 Welfare Reform Debates

The backlash against social welfare policies began before the ink had even dried. Criticisms that welfare fostered dependency, usurped fathers' responsibilities, rewarded laziness, and promoted immoral behavior emerged even before the first piece of legislation was passed. Between 1967 and 1988, federal welfare policy was modified six times—each time getting progressively moralistic and punitive for policy noncompliance—this despite already harsh penalties for noncompliance in most states. Most states already had laws enabling welfare agencies to end non-marital motherhood by sterilizing mothers. Southern states were particularly punitive. For example, in 1958 Mississippi policy denied welfare benefits to children whose parents were not married; in Louisiana and Mississippi, unmarried mothers could be subject to criminal penalties for having a child out of wedlock. By the 1960s, half of the U.S.

states could limit welfare to those deemed "morally unfit" (Mink 1998).

Beginning in 1950, federal welfare laws began requiring states to report to law enforcement officials when a child who had been abandoned by one of the parents (presumably the father) received welfare benefits. Some states categorized welfare recipients into one of two categories—employable mothers (minorities) and unemployable mothers (whites). In some instances, employable mothers were disqualified from receiving welfare, or as in the case of Arkansas, welfare grants to employable mothers were suspended during planting and harvest times (Mink 1998:37). The ensuing years saw a steady move toward requiring all welfare recipients to work, but ambivalence remained for women with small children. Per Mink (1998:38),

> From the 1960s to the present, work provisions in national welfare policy have equivocated about recipient mothers' work outside the home, mandating maternal employment in principle while exempting mothers of young children and emphasizing the wage work obligations of fathers.

The ambivalence between mothering and working continued into the 1980s. A change in welfare legislation in 1981 required certain welfare recipients to "work off their benefits" via workfare programs (work, education, or employment-related training programs). However, the Family Support Act (FSA) of 1988 exempted poor married women from work requirements and entitled welfare recipients of preschool-aged children or younger to child care if the mother could not participate in workfare programs as a result. As Mink points out, many of the FSA provisions, particularly the child care provision one, "codified the assumption that poor single mothers *should* work outside the home" (Mink 1988:41).

The long-waged war to "end welfare as we know it" ended in 1996 when President Clinton signed into law the Personal Responsibility and Work Opportunity Reconciliation Act of 1996 (PRWORA), replacing Aid to Families with Dependent Children (AFDC) with Temporary Assistance to Needy Families (TANF). We turn to this radical transformation in social welfare next.

1996 Welfare Reform

Keeping his 1992 campaign promise to "end welfare as we know it," President Clinton passed the Personal Responsibility and Work Opportunity Reconciliation Act (PRWORA) in 1996, ushering in a new era of Temporary Assistance for Needy Families (TANF). Four main purposes of TANF include: (1) to provide assistance to needy families so that children may be cared for in their own homes or in the homes of relatives; (2) to end the dependence of needy parents on government benefits by promoting job preparation, work, and marriage; (3) to prevent and reduce the incidence of out-of-wedlock pregnancies and establish annual numerical goals for preventing and reducing the incidence of these pregnancies; and (4) to encourage the formation and maintenance of two-parent families (Mink and Solinger 2003).

Welfare reform shifted funding from open-ended dollar-per-dollar matching grants in AFDC to block grants in which the federal government allocated a fixed annual dollar amount to states to administer the TANF program. In that TANF block grants are fixed with no inflation adjustments built in, so over time they lose value. Between 1997 and 2002, TANF block grants lost 12 percent of their value and are projected to be 22 percent lower in value in 2007 than in 1997 (Weaver 2002).

Most radically, PRWORA replaced federal entitlement to assistance with temporary, time-limited participation: "This part shall not be interpreted to entitle any individual or family to assistance under any State program funded under this part" (Mink and Solinger 2003:645). Administration of welfare is now largely at the discretion of each state—in essence creating 50 separate programs.

Welfare reform resolved the ambivalence between mothering and working squarely in favor of work. Indeed, the law requires a state to reduce a household's TANF grant for failure to comply with work requirements. Furthermore, federal law requires that at least half of the families receiving TANF must be engaged in some kind of work-related activity for at least 30 hours a week. Single parents with children under the age of six must engage in work-related activities for at least 20 hours per week. States not meeting these thresholds can lose 5 percent or more of their TANF grant. However, states can offset these work requirements with caseload reduction credits (Center for Budget and Policy Priorities 2002).

The act specifies the parameters for receiving TANF assistance. There is no federal assistance for more than five years; for a teenage parent who does not attend high school (or its equivalent); for a teenage parent who is not living under some type of adult supervision; for those convicted of felony drug charges; or for immigrants. Further, households may lose assistance if children fail to attend school on a regular basis; or, if they, or anyone in the household, fail to comply with their individual responsibility plan.

Welfare reform disqualified from food stamps all able-bodied adults without dependents who had received food stamps for at least three months over a preceding 36-month period but had worked less than 20 hours per week. The act also required that the states remove from food stamp rolls most permanent resident aliens also previously eligible under AFDC provisions.

States are provided financial incentives to decrease illegitimacy rates (without a concomitant rise in abortion) and reduce welfare caseloads. However, states can be penalized for failing to meet work participation rate thresholds; failing to comply with paternity establishment and child-support enforcement requirements; or, failing to limit overall cash assistance to 60 months. And in keeping with the broader trend toward the privatization of governmental services, PRWORA authorized states to contract with charitable, religious, or private organizations for the provision of TANF, food stamp, and Medicaid services.

TANF Programmatic Features and Organizational Culture

Most states strongly endorsed the principles of welfare reform—both the promotion of work and the programmatic leeway it allowed. This section highlights some of the common features of states in the development of their TANF programs. Unless noted otherwise, the Welfare Rules Database developed by the Urban Institute and the Committee on Ways and Means' *2004 Green Book* are the source of the data discussed here.

Work-First Policies. Work programs vary widely from state to state regarding who must work, how much work is required, and what activities constitute work. States may (but are not required to) exempt certain individuals or groups from participating in work-related activities. States have broad discretion in determining noncompliance with work-related requirements as well as in the type of sanction to impose for failing in this area. Work-related activities include job skills training, job readiness activities, job development and placement, and job search. Education and training are allowed in most states to satisfy work-related activities but generally for a restricted period of time.

While welfare reform mandates work as a requirement of receiving cash assistance, many states have adopted "work-first" policies that "emphasize the expedient placement of recipients in whatever jobs are available" (Hays 2003:27). Texas provides a procedural illustration of "work first." Qualitative interviews conducted with welfare caseworkers, supervisors, and administrative personnel in San Antonio reveal that "work first" equates to strong informal diversion away from cash assistance (see also Hays 2003; Hancock 2002). Before potential clients can apply for TANF, they must complete a detailed work history and availability form and are then directed to a Resource Room or Career Center where a caseworker assists them with interviewing skills, helps them with resumes, and assists in locating job vacancy information from the Internet (Bell 2001).

Sanctions. TANF law requires states to penalize families for refusing to engage in work-related activities without good cause. Additionally, federal law requires that states reduce a family's TANF benefit by at least 25 percent (or remove them altogether) for not cooperating with establishing paternity or ongoing efforts in this regard. The severity of the sanction for noncompliance with work requirements varies from written warnings to reductions in household benefits. The most severe sanction for noncompliance is permanent forfeiture of cash assistance.

The adoption of family-cap policies is another sanction on welfare recipients. In an attempt to legislate and regulate sexual norms, family caps hold constant a household's TANF benefit in the event of the birth of a child while a mother is already receiving TANF. As a further deterrent, some states reduce cash assistance amounts in the event of a new birth. Some states do not allow pregnant women without other children to be eligible for cash benefits until after the child is born; other states restrict enrollment anywhere from one to nine months into the pregnancy.

Welfare Diversion Policies. Diversion programs are designed to discourage application for cash benefits. At present, more than half of the states have created formal diversion programs. One diversion from benefits is the one-time payment program. Families can choose to receive a lump-sum cash payment in lieu of monthly TANF benefits but are then barred from TANF for a specified period of time. Requiring a job search upon application is another diversion mechanism. To encourage work, many states have instituted a job-search application provision either before a TANF application is submitted or while the application is in process.

In addition to formal diversion mechanisms, states also employ a variety of informal diversion methods. In Texas "work-first" policies translate into "redirecting" the needy from cash assistance. As incentive, the regional office that "redirected" the most potential clients away from TANF was rewarded with the Commissioner's Cup (Bell 2001).

Time-limiting welfare benefits are the penultimate deterrent to cash assistance (Fitzgerald 2004). Procedures requiring onerous time commitments or excessive documentation reduce program participation (Zedlewski et al. 2006). "Work-first" policies mandate that potential recipients enter work-related activities within a specified period of time or forsake assistance. The TANF application process is itself time-consuming with some extreme cases taking upwards of half a day spent in the welfare office (see Hays 2003; Schexnayder et al. 2002; Waterhouse1992).

Life Under Welfare Reform: Caseworkers and Clients

The welfare experience itself is best described by Sharon Hays (2003) in a chapter entitled "Fear, Hope, and Resignation in the Welfare Office," within her book *Flat Broke with Children: Women in the Age of Welfare Reform*: "The world of welfare is a world of mirrored dualisms—the Work Plan and the Family Plan, the punishments and rewards, cold bureaucracy and caring maternalism, individualism and family ties, social inclusion and exclusion" (p. 95). The fundamental shift in welfare necessitated significant changes in the administration of welfare itself. "Texas adjusting to welfare rule shift," declares a July 9, 2006, headline of the Austin American-Statesman online (MacLaggan 2006:B1) as the state attempts to adjust yet again to additional changes to the PRWORA that occurred as a result of its reauthorization in late 2005. The job titles assigned to welfare caseworkers reflect this changed environment as well. For example, welfare caseworkers are now "financial planners" in New York and "work advisors" in Texas.

Accordingly, the process for determining welfare eligibility was modified to reflect a changed welfare culture of work, family (narrowly defined by politicians as two-parent traditional families), and social control. Adding to the complexity for both caseworkers and clients alike is that historically each time the rules for welfare were reformed, very few of the rules that were in place before the reform actually changed and instead were simply built upon. The results of the 1996 reform were significantly increased rules and regulations that almost doubled the size of state procedural manuals (Hays 2003:47). Bell (2001:8) provides an illustrative example of what these new procedures translate into in Texas:

> Mandated clients first went to WOA, Workforce Orientation, a three-hour session where they heard about time limits, the hours of mandated participation (35 hours/week for two parents, 30 hours/week for single parents) and the activities in which they must participate, such as job readiness and job search. At the end of the WOA, they were then given a written appointment letter/notice for a two-hour EPS (Employment Planning Session), which included further assessment and planning for employment including the Test of Adult Basic Education (TABE) to assess their skill level in math, language, and reading. At that time each was assigned to an E & T caseworker that conducted a more thorough assessment of the client's history, goals, and abilities.

Qualitative interviews conducted in Texas confirm that the time requirement for determining welfare eligibility (and re-eligibility) is particularly problematic for clients seeking services: "... the hardest thing about it is the amount of time you have to take off [work] in order to get it. And I mean even if you have an appointment, it still takes about five hours" explains one respondent (quoted in Schexnayder et al. 2002:75). These onerous, diversionary tactics are effective. As Hays notes, many women simply leave the welfare office without making an application; only the truly needy (and hardy) actually go through the process.

In addition to the time needed to make a welfare application, the process itself is also unpleasant for many caseworkers and clients. For welfare recipients, their experiences in navigating the system differed depending upon their "education, health, employment history, childcare situation, and other circumstances" (Hays 2003:96)—in short, their social and capital skills. Clients face a barrage of discomforting and intrusive requests. For example, they are asked to produce many documents—e.g., children's social security cards, birth certificates, immunization records, and school enrollment records; rent receipts, utility receipts; bank statements; insurance statements; child care contracts; to name a few. In addition, they encounter great redundancy in requested information between the application and questions asked by the caseworker (part of the verification process that caseworkers must undertake). Moreover, they face a multitude of highly intrusive questions—e.g., do you have any cash in your purse at this time? do you receive income from farming, fishing, raking leaves, mowing lawns, any kind of odd jobs like that? does your mother receive welfare? (Hays 2003:45). Caseworkers, fairly low-level employees in the welfare administrative hierarchy, have little choice but to ask what they consider in many instances to be "completely unnecessary" questions but are bound by the rules to do so anyway (Hays 2003).

Further, the privatization of some services and particularly the lack of control over any aspect of these outsourced services were also problematic for caseworkers. As Hays documents, caseworkers knew that outsourced programs were ineffective for welfare women but had little authority to do anything about it. Bell also documents problems in Texas with privatization of some services: "... Too many middle men. Too many chiefs and not enough Indians, is what it boils down to" is how one caseworker described the results (as quoted in Bell 2001:12).

The results of this process are a fairly high turnover rate for welfare caseworkers as they realized their capacity to actually make a difference in the lives of the women they were attempting to help was limited, and that the system itself was more harsh and punitive. Per Hays (2003:101), the "caseworkers who remained tended to be those with thicker skins." Further, as the disconnect between the ideals of welfare reform (largely supported by caseworkers and clients alike) and the reality of its implementation, optimism was soon replaced with resignation that little had actually changed except their work load, which had increased and gotten more complicated by the additional layers of bureaucracy imposed by welfare's reform. Coping mechanisms involved a redefinition of their original optimism of self-sufficiency to more modest goals like finding any job or increasing levels of sanctions as a means of shock therapy for welfare mothers who seemed to be in denial about welfare's time limits (Hays 2003). Bell (2001) documents that Texas caseworkers defined welfare "successes" and "failures" largely along client motivational lines—those more motivated left welfare, leaving behind the unmotivated—all of which justified the increasingly punitive interactions that resulted from those still on the rolls.

Overall, as Hays (2003:97) describes "the story of welfare reform is ... simultaneously a tale of hassles, hardships, and the road to resignation, and a vivid cultural representation of the lengths to which people will go to discover and enact shared ideals." Despite the numerous and onerous eligibility requirements, welfare recipients remained by and large supportive of welfare reform, reaffirming what has been confirmed in numerous other studies of welfare recipients: namely, that "failure to embrace the values of the nation is clearly not the malady from which these women suffer" (Hays, 2003:53). Instead, Hays continues, "the problem for most welfare clients ... is finding a job that pays enough to bring them out of poverty, offers benefits, and is flexible enough to make room for the circumstances of single parenting" (2003:55) and in an environment which continues to discriminate on the basis of both race and gender. With the welfare population overwhelmingly female and increasingly non-white, the odds of achieving anything close to the American Dream remain as illusive post-welfare reform as prior.

Understanding Welfare Reform

"A nation's laws reflect a nation's values" intones Sharon Hays (2003:3) in *Flat Broke with Children: Women in the Age of Welfare Reform*. The signing of PRWORA signaled that what FDR had begun 60 years prior with the passage of Aid to Dependent Children was no longer—the federal government was getting out of the social welfare business and returning it to the states. The nation was being indoctrinated into the southern way of life.

Historically, expansion of the American welfare state has occurred during times of both economic recession and economic growth. It was the Depression of the 1930s with its massive levels of unemployment and human suffering that provided the backdrop for passage of the first federal social welfare programs. Such massive levels of unemployment and human suffering temporarily halted the "poverty as moral failing" arguments. Over subsequent years, federal budget surpluses provided justification for increased social welfare spending; budget deficits provided the rationale for social spending retrenchment. How then to explain a radical retrenchment in social welfare during a time of federal budget surpluses?

Katznelson shows that in the negotiations surrounding FDR's policies, southern legislators were able to safeguard the racial status quo and economic stratification system through several mechanisms including exclusion and devolution of program administration to state and local levels. He also details the complicity of others in this shaping of the political landscape. With regards to welfare reform, we see similar features.

As Alice O'Connor (2001) documents, social scientists have been muzzled in criticizing the redefinition of poverty assistance either because they agreed with cultural characterizations of poor people or because they were caught in a funding treadmill that kept them responding to a changing political climate that forsook their own independent policy agenda in exchange for continued federal support.

Support for reforming welfare cut across both political party and gender lines. Despite top officials in Clinton's Department of Health and Human Services resigning their positions in protest of welfare reform, their voices came too late to stem the groundswell of public support favoring welfare reform. Similar to the split noted first during the mothers' pension debates between women, Mink (2003) documents the ways that feminists jumped aboard the welfare reform bandwagon, noting that four of five Democratic women in the Senate voted for welfare reform, as did 26 of 31 women in the House.

It is impossible to divorce social welfare legislation from race relations. The urgency to reform welfare received its greatest momentum after welfare became an entitlement for previously excluded minorities. From that point, cash aid has been reduced; fraud deterrence efforts increased; and racial stereotyping of welfare recipients has become commonplace (Hancock 2004). As Hancock demonstrates, in the charge to reform welfare a "politics of disgust" campaign was waged that demonized welfare recipients in general and black women in particular. In fact, as Lynell Hancock (2002:6) points out, "disparagement of welfare was so accepted that members of Congress were calling recipients 'alligators' and 'wolves' on the floor of the House of Representatives." Indeed, racial stereotypes provided welfare reformers with much currency. Clinton capitalized on racial stereotypes to move his agenda of "ending welfare as we know it" forward.

One assumption motivating welfare reform was that unless forced to do so, women simply will not take "personal responsibility" and work to support their children. Numerous studies (Edin and Lein 1996; Ehrenreich 2001; Hancock 2002; Hays 2003; Seccombe 1999) reveal the falsity of these assumptions, showing instead that women cycle into and out of work (and cash assistance) as their personal conditions dictate. Because the experience at the welfare office itself is so unpleasant, it is *only* for the sake of their children that women endure the demeaning treatment to which they are routinely subjected.

Welfare reform replaced universalism with particularism and continues the trend of shifting the societal risks previously borne by the federal government to individuals. Indeed, welfare no longer offers the safety net it once did. As Katz documents, while touted as highly successful because it dramatically reduced welfare rolls, welfare reform exacerbates the problems for both the poor and working poor. According to an Urban Institute report (2005), in 2000, about half of all eligible families were receiving cash assistance compared to 85 percent in 1994. According to the Center for Public Policy (2004), between 2000 and 2003, the percentage of single mothers living in poverty increased while the percentage of employed single mothers fell. Additionally, poverty among children rose while the number of children living below half the poverty line increased by nearly one million. In response, food stamp and Medicaid rolls rose but TANF rolls continued to decline, providing assistance to 845,000 *fewer* people in 2003 than in 2000.

According to Katz (2000), "the American welfare state has sustained an attack that has not only rolled back some benefits but, even more important, redefined the principles on which it rests." Citizenship, he points out, is now determined by market participation rather than birthright. Women of color are particularly impacted. During the 1994–2001 period, the percentage of non-white TANF recipients grew from 58.7 percent in 1994 to 67.8 percent in 2001 (Committee on Way and Means 2004). And another report found that blacks are the only racial group to have experienced a growth in the number of non-welfare-receiving poor (Peterson et al. 2002). Invoking the preoccupations of W.E.B. Du Bois, Katz (2000) points out that if alive today, Du Bois would "… confront the paradox that a welfare state scarred by institutional racism remains essential to the survival of millions of African Americans with minimal comfort and dignity, and he would surely worry about the impact of its transformation" (p. 126).

In December 2005, the TANF program was reauthorized until 2010. The policies were made more restrictive. The message is clear: "shape up or ship out." But to where? As the next section illustrates, for some prison is the likely destination.

The Rise Of The Prison Business

The phenomenal rate at which the United States is imprisoning segments of its population is both unprecedented and alarming. According to the Bureau of Justice Statistics' website, as of June 20, 2005, there were almost 2.2 million prisoners in federal or state prisons or in local jails—some 488 inmates per 100,000 U.S. residents. In 2002 the rate of sentenced males in state and federal prisons was a phenomenal 906 males per 100,000 males in the population. This compares to 191 per 100,000 in 1970.

According to Marc Mauer of The Sentencing Project, indeed, the United States leads the world in overall incarceration rates, which in 2004 stood at 725 incarcerations per 100,000 residents, outpacing Russia and South Africa (400). Walmsley (2005) reaches the similar conclusion. Still, Wacquant (2002) goes somewhat further in averring that the prison population of the United States appears to be larger than for the Russian gulag and the South African apartheid regime at their height.

In fact, the incarceration rates of black men resemble apartheid-like conditions. The rate of incarceration is especially alarming for black males.

For example, in 1980, the rate of black male incarceration was already a phenomenal 1,111 men per 100,000 in the population—almost seven times higher than the rate of white male incarceration (168 per 100,000). However, by 2004, the black male incarceration rate exploded to an astounding 3,218 black males per 100,000. White male incarcerations rates have also increased substantially, from 168 per 100,000 in 1980 to 463 white males per 100,000 in 2004. Nevertheless, black males are still incarcerated at seven times the rate of whites.

The sharp rise in incarceration rates in America has had a number of major consequences. One is the massive re-entry of ex-prisoners into communities, particularly certain metropolitan centers, in the United States. Although we shall not pursue the social implications of this particular transformation herein, we should take note of several patterns. When talking about the massive rise in the prison population, we also must consider a flood of ex-prisoners returning to American communities. Only recently have scholars begun to piece together the social consequences of this return. We rely upon a recent Urban Institute report titled "Understanding the Challenges of Prisoner Reentry" (Solomon et al. 2006). The report indicates that:

> In 2003 alone, more than 656,000 state and federal prisoners returned to communities across the country, affecting public safety, public health, economic and community well-being, and family

> networks. The impact of prisoner reentry is further compounded by the returning jail population with its distinctive challenges and opportunities. (p. 2)

The report goes on to state:

> Two-thirds of released prisoners are rearrested within three years of release. One and a half million children have a parent in prison. Four million citizens have lost their right to vote. (p. 2)

That these ex-prisoners by and large encounter almost insurmountable economic and social obstacles is founded on firm sociological principles.

The Transformation of Prisons and the Role of Race

The negative consequences of imprisonment are all the more reason for attempting to understand the reasons for the transformation in the nature of punishment. There is general agreement regarding the evidence on the historic explosion in the United States of the prison population in the past quarter-century or so. Admittedly scholars disagree about certain features of the data presented above, for, as Chambliss (1999) and others have reasoned, criminal justice system data often contain built-in biases. One of the difficulties concerns the lack of any substantial data on what Dow (2004), a journalist, contends is the secret immigration prisons that have emerged in recent years. With these caveats in mind, scholars agree on the general contours of the prison population as outlined above. At the same time fundamental disagreements are rife among sociologists, criminologists, and legal scholars regarding explanations for the dramatic increase in the number of inmates in the United States. This issue leads us to consider, theoretically and empirically, the nature of punishment in advanced modernity.

Janet Lauritsen and Robert J. Sampson (1998) have provided us with an instructive overview of the empirical findings contained in the vast literature on minority experiences with the criminal justice system. One of their objectives is to:

> summarize the research on minorities in the criminal justice system, emphasizing the conditions under which differential treatment is most likely to occur and the various theoretical approaches for understanding such differences. (p. 58)

Although Lauritsen and Sampson did not zero in on the rise of the prison population per se, their analysis of the larger criminal justice system is relevant for coming to terms with the rise of prisons.

However, it is Lauritsen and Sampson's general conclusion that captures our attention.

> Our review of the literature on minorities and criminal justice suggests that racial discrimination emerges some of the time at some stages of the system in some locations, but there is little evidence that racial disparities reflect systemic, overt bias on the part of the criminal justice decision makers. Rather the most compelling evidence concerning racial discrimination in the administration of justice involves community and moral constructions of "moral panics" and political responses to those contexts. (pp. 77–78)

After advancing their thesis they appear to back off from it somewhat when they contend that "Although overt race discrimination in criminal justice processing appears to be a problem restricted to specific spatial and temporal contexts, the fact remains that racial disparities in serious crimes have reached a critical state in the United States" (Lauritsen and Sampson 1998:78).

We have dwelt on the views of Lauritsen and Sampson for several reasons. Sampson is a highly distinguished sociologist/criminologist. More to the point Lauritsen and Sampson articulate, in soft terms, a view of the criminal justice system that is rather embedded in an important sector of the scholarly and legal literature.

In part the authors articulate their perspective because they are working within the presuppositions of the narrow confines of the criminal justice system. The ideals of the criminal justice system are founded on the presupposition underlying the rule of law: in effect the legal system is fair and just. Indeed a number of members of the criminal justice system are reluctant to question its foundational premises.

Courts, in examining the criminal justice system, are often called upon to address the matter of intent, and intent (or motive) is difficult to ascertain with respect to racial matters. Moreover, Cole (1999), a legal scholar, highlights another facet of belief in a color-blind legal order, as he examines the case of *McClesky v. Kemp*. In this case the Supreme Court ruled (in the face of massive statistical evidence regarding discrimination against blacks) that Georgia could continue to enforce the death penalty. The Court (in a 5–4 decision) acknowledged that if it had accepted McClesky's claim, then this reasoning "carried to its logical conclusion, throws into question the principles that underlie the entire criminal justice system." If the Court had ruled in behalf of McClesky, it would have been called upon to address the structural (or racial) arrangements of power that inhere in the criminal justice system itself and to reshape the manner in which racism undermines the claims of fairness and equality that are the basis of its legitimacy in a democratic order. In actual practice we can expect the leadership of few formal organizations in modern society to fess up to racial discrimination.

David Garland (1990), a sociologist/legal scholar, has been in the forefront of scholarship regarding punishment, having written an outstanding book in which he examines various sociologically grounded theories of punishment. In another of his works Garland (2001) attempts to account for the increased concern with crime in the United States and Great Britain. Although he does not focus on the statistical evidence per se, his analysis bears on our understanding of the criminal justice system and the rise in the number of prison inmates. While Garland weighs the role of both cultural and structural factors, he places, by his own definition, a cultural explanation in the forefront of his analysis. His is a highly nuanced account of changes in the cultural system that have occurred over the past half-century. One of Garland's strengths is his review not only of changes in the cultural patterns but also of some of the built-in contradictions that have accompanied this transformation.

Garland speaks of the declining influence of social expertise, the increased salience of crime, and the new middle-class attitudes toward crime and control. Regarding the latter, he observes that in the postwar years "the structure of everyday life became more porous, more open-textured, more generative of opportunities for criminal victimization" (Garland 2001:155), with crime becoming a source of anxiety. He is attentive to how the increase in the crime rate (which other authors raise questions about) has been fostered by an anxiety generated by the mass media. Garland also singles out the rising concern with victims' rights and a growing definition of the perpetrator as a distant "other." Within this context he writes of the reinvented prison. More generally he perceives a decline in state control and the rise of private security arrangements, an issue to which we return below. In the main, Garland slides by racial and ethnic relations as he grapples with how to understand the growing culture of control in the United States and Great Britain.

Other sociologists have also sought to account for the massive growth of the prison population. Western et al. (2004a) draw upon Rusche and Kirchheimer (1939), early Frankfort School theorists, for inspiration in understanding the "whys" and "wherefores" of punishment. Rusche and Kirchheimer relied heavily upon class, emphasizing that the prison system had become a repository for members of society who had no means of effective employment in the community. Western et al. (2004b) conclude, with due qualifications, that social class is a major factor in understanding the burgeoning of the prison population in recent decades. What is troubling about their analysis, however, is that early in their essay they present data highlighting the fact that, based on their time-series analysis, "black men were about seven to eight times more likely to be in prison or jail than white men" (p. 774). In their reliance on class analysis as a basis for explaining the rise in the prison population, they gloss over this racial component. Such reasoning follows the logic of Rusche and Kirchhemer, who, like other members of the Frankfort School, were influenced by Marx. These scholars have been unable to square class stratification with racial stratification.

However, intensive reviews of the published literature reveal that the majority of studies published in the 1969–1989 period (Pope and Feyerherm 1990) and the 1989–2001 period (Pope et al. 2002) indicate that race has a significant effect on the treatment of juveniles in the criminal justice system. In addition, sociologists have confronted the role of race with respect to the criminal justice system and the burgeoning prison population. Chambliss (1994) has highlighted some of the observations that he and his students made of police encounters with blacks in Washington, DC. Certain groups of blacks were singled out by the police in a discriminatory fashion. In his book on the impact of power and politics on crime, Chambliss (1999:63) states:

> The poor, especially, urban poor African Americans, are disproportionately the subjects of how enforcement activities at all levels, from arrest to imprisonment. … The poor, especially urban poor African Americans, are disproportionately the subjects of law enforcement. … The urban poor minorities are stereotyped as inherently criminogenic. … [C]rime in the ghetto is a self-fulfilling prophecy.

Chambliss understands what few sociologists discuss: when the police sweep up the poor, particularly poor blacks, they do so with impunity. The poor lack the economic, social, and cultural capital by which to effectively resist the system. Serious challenges to the system would clog the courts in ways unacceptable to the management of the criminal justice system. Such challenges are costly and also contain the potential for exposing questionable police practices, something managers of the criminal justice system prefer to avoid.

On a more macro level Chambliss is sensitive to the odd coalition of southern conservatives who left the Democratic party with more traditional Republicans in the political arena, as well as the role of the mass media and the criminal justice establishment in advancing the prison agenda.

Chambliss' critical stance seems to be sidestepped by a number of mainstream scholars. For Chambliss the focus on street crime and young black men as superpredators serves to deflect attention from the crimes of enforcement officials, politicians, and corporations.

Wacquant (2002) conducts an excellent analysis of the prison system. In his reading of the data, he finds that "since 1989 and for the first time in national history, African Americans make up a majority of those entering prison each year," despite the fact that the actual crime rate of African Americans has been fairly stable over a few decades (see Tonry 1995). If we are to grapple with this phenomenon, we need to break out of the narrow "crime and punishment" framework and instead analyze the role of the penal system in managing dispossessed and disadvantaged groups within the social order. To achieve this objective, Wacquant examines how historical forces have shaped current arrangements. Nowadays, in Wacquant's view, we are witnessing the prisonization of the ghetto and the ghettoization of the prison, as the ghetto has lost its capacity to buffer its residents from the powerful external forces afoot in the nation and the global sphere. The length of sentences appears today longer than ever, and surveillance over ex-cons appears to be continually extended. The new system intensifies the centuries-old association of blackness with criminality and violence.

We note here the importance of social and cultural capital in negotiating the criminal justice system, focusing particularly on juveniles. Minority youth are disproportionately represented among youth offenders at almost every step of the process from committing a crime, to being arrested, to being processed through the criminal justice system, to being sentenced (see Pope and Feyerherm 1990; Pope et al. 2002). Certainly, white parents are using their human, social, and cultural capital to free their children from facing severe forms of punishment compared to minority parents who lack such resources. Furthermore, as in the case of education, white youth as well as adult offenders are able to tap into their social and capital arsenal to conform to the expectations of the criminal justice system. On the other hand, minority youth tend to lack such resources, which places them at greater vulnerability to reaching the sentencing stages of the system compared to their white counterparts. Indeed, racial profiling plays a significant role to begin with in placing minorities in the grasp of the criminal justice system.

Hence, impoverished minorities interact more frequently than whites with the lower levels of the criminal justice system (the police, bailiffs, jail-house lawyers, etc.), and they do so without the requisite social and cultural capital to grasp the meaning of the organizational rules. Members of their social networks possess limited technical knowledge of how the system operates. This brings us back to our theme that persons who command the least knowledge of the rules of the criminal justice system, for instance, are called upon to interact with the different layers of the criminal justice system most committed to applying the rules in a rather narrow manner.

The Rise of Corporate Prisons

What we find missing from the current analysis of the prison system is a general failure to explore the relationship between the modern economy, dominated by large corporations and the prevailing ideology of individualism and the free market—both salient features of the neo-liberal model (cf. Garland 2001:174ff). In this section we outline only the barebones features of this argument.

We begin with the matter of corporations. Joseph Hallinan (2001), a world-class journalist, has written a highly instructive work on prisons in the United States. In it he captures a crucial facet of the prison system that tends to be left out of current writings by sociologists, criminologists, and legal scholars we have read. Hallinan (2001:174), rather dramatically, paints a picture of what he observed, "The appearance of the prison millionaire marked a turning point in American penology. Never before had it been possible in this country to become rich by incarcerating other people. Now, it is commonplace." Furthermore, he continues:

> The consequence of this change has been subtle but profound. The staffs of public prisons have, in effect, become farm teams for private prisons. Public prisons are now places where the ambitious can hone their financial skills before moving on to really big money in the private sector. No longer is it solely in the interest of the state to run a profitable prison—it is in the self-interest of the warden as well. The blending of personal and public interest has changed the way the country's prisons are run. Public prisons now openly emulate private ones.

Using Hallinan's observations as a point of departure, we find that the prison industry is increasingly populated by large-scale corporations. Private prisons are owned and managed not by individual entrepreneurs but by corporate entities that are bureaucratic in nature. With respect to public prisons, the contracts for supplying the prison population with food and clothing are typically let to large corporate organizations not to lone individuals. In the latter case in particular, the taxpayers foot the bill for the costs of incarceration, not the lowly prisoners who inhabit the lower reaches in the social order. Yet, as Hallinan (2001) emphasizes, we are also witnessing the rise of private prisons as well as the rise of prison labor, as prisons become production units out to make a profit, with prisoners being extremely low wages (cf. Price 2006). Hallinan (2001:147) contends that the prison-industry program in South Carolina is self-sustaining (though we must be careful here, for the supply of prisoners seems largely the product of the state apparatus).

Nils Christie (2000), a Norwegian criminologist, has spoken of the new social arrangements as the "crime control industry." In practice this pattern is a sub-feature of a larger social process occurring internationally wherein one finds the rise of a corporate control industry whose activities range from carrying out key supportive activities in Iraq to managing law and order in a number of "failed states" (cf. Singer 2004; Koppel 2006). The above patterns reflect the privatization of social control not only in the United States but also globally.

The rapid rise of prisons has occurred at a time when individuals are expected to assume increasingly greater responsibility for their own social destiny—to bear the risks of modern industrial-urban life. The privatization movement in the neo-liberal era has been accompanied by the re-emergence of utilitarianism—particularly as expressed nowadays in neo-classical economics and rational choice theorizing. In idealized terms, individuals are called upon to assume greater risks for their own employment, their own health care, etc. Such ideals are articulated in a social order that idealizes "free market relations," including the widespread flow of free labor.

We use the concept of utilitarianism (a rather unfashionable term today) to encompass both Adam Smith's thinking (with his emphasis on the natural identity of interests) and the thinking of Jeremy Bentham (with his stress on the artificial identity of interests). A version of utilitarianism dominates neo-classical economics and has become a part of the overall ideology (or belief or value system) in the United States. It is reflected in sociology by the theorizing of James Coleman (1990). To his lasting credit, Coleman acknowledges the power of large corporate actors (be these states or corporations); nonetheless individuals (or natural actors) are the foundation stone of his theorizing.

Within this intellectual tradition, human beings are characterized by their search for pleasure and their avoidance of pain. In practice the activities of individuals derive not from their social or cultural circumstances but from their inherent biopsychological condition. Thus punishment tends to be grounded in the fact that persons act in terms of their basic biopsychological dispositions. This perspective pervades the influential work of Wilson and Herrnstein (1986). With this as a premise we should not be surprised that one version of this intellectual heritage nowadays, as it has in the past, conceives of a criminogenic personality. Once committed to a biopsychological perspective, scholars and the broader citizenry can rather readily perceive of different racial and ethnic groups as characterized by different dispositions to commit criminal acts. That rehabilitation has declined as an ideal in the criminal justice system is in keeping with this overall emphasis on the individualism associated with the market model and a biopsychological conception of human nature.

Perhaps we should elaborate somewhat more fully on these two processes: the emergence of profitable large corporations that thrive on the commitment to a market and the call for individuals to assume responsibility for their actions. Briefly, there is a general assumption afoot that privatizing formerly governmental functions (whether in the educational, prison, or welfare spheres) will generate greater efficiency. But is efficiency, as judged by corporate profits, a major consideration for evaluating effective prisons? A profitable market appears to call for more and more prisoners and punishing persons for longer and longer periods of time, rather than rehabilitating them. Indeed, from a narrow empirical perspective it seems apparent that keeping persons behind bars is safer for the community than in rehabilitating them and running the risk of possible recidivism. Rehabilitation is, after all, future-oriented and more open-ended with respect to risk than locking people up and throwing away the key. Moreover, a commitment to human nature as founded on basic biopsychological conditions serves to justify the premise that criminological types exist, and their rightful place is the prison. Contrast this with a more thoroughgoing social-cultural view of criminal activity, wherein, if we broaden the scope of the ideas in, say, Matza and Sykes (1961), we discover that criminal activity is generally only a small part of the everyday routines that persons engage in. The violent criminal who holds up a 7-11 store spends most of his (her) waking hours engaged in normal everyday activities—cooking and eating, sleeping, talking with friends and acquaintances, etc. We shall need to reject the narrow biopsychological principles so widely accepted today if we are to understand the complex social and cultural processes that shape the manner in which humans beings (including criminals) come to act as they do.

In a more general sense, the so-called laws of supply and demand, when applied to prisons and prisoners, lead corporations to develop a vested interest in expanding the prison population. Larger numbers of prisoners enhance profits (whether the taxpayers pay the bill or monies are generated via prison labor), not only for the lowly guards but particularly for the managerial sector (and of course investors). A critical analysis of the perverse application of supply and demand principles with regard to prisons is long overdue. Profit making based on prison labor, for instance, appears to undermine the traditional definition of free labor in a free market. Furthermore, corporate vested interests, we would hypothesize, are coming to play a considerable role in the formation and development of the prison system, in ways yet to be explored (Price 2006). Price (2006:127) suggests that the impact of the corporate lobby has been especially effective in the South. After all, large-scale corporate organizations are not organized according to the market model and the pleasure/pain principle; instead they are characterized by hierarchy, division of labor, and an emphasis on routinization. They are oriented toward sustaining not only economic but also political power, illustrated by the monies provided political campaigns and by lobbying (Price 2006).

If our thinking is reasonably correct, the problems faced in downsizing the current prison system have become far more formidable than three decades ago. Powerful vested economic interests have a major stake in the economic survival (even expansion) of a large prison system and its own form of racism. Any substantial reduction in the size of the prison population will involve restructuring not only the larger criminal justice system but also fundamental social arrangements within the broader social order, including the creation of alternative forms of employment and profit for a crucial sector of American society. Any effective resolution of the "ex-prisoner problem" must, it appears to us, reduce the size of the prison population in the United States.

Concluding Remarks

We have provided an overview of the literature related to three institutions—education, welfare, and prison—that have undergone significant transformations over the last few decades. The literature clearly demonstrates the strong role that race and ethnicity play in the positioning of people in these institutions. Not surprisingly, minorities (African Americans, Latinos, and Native Americans) find themselves at the bottom of the stratification structure of each of the institutions examined. This is the story that we have observed for centuries in this country, as these groups were initially incorporated into American society.

The enduring position of minorities in the United States is consistent with expectations of race/ethnicity and political economy theorists. For example, Feagin (2005) argues that the current plight of African Americans was sealed centuries ago as whites were given access to economic and land resources while blacks were enslaved and completely shut out from attaining resources. Whites were able to accumulate further riches and to pass these on to future generations, while African Americans did not have such resources. In addition, the current position of minorities in the stratification system reflects their exclusion from the economic spoils that were distributed in the New Deal era, resources that went largely to whites (Katznelson 2005; Quadagno 1994). Civil rights legislation attempted to correct the inequalities that such historical forces had produced. Yet, as our overview of the literature demonstrates, the exigencies of corrective measures gave way to forces that attempted to bring back the "tried-and-true" white-privilege model that sent minorities back to the end of the line, consistent with Bonilla-Silva's (2001, 2006) argument that the post–civil rights era shifted the American lexicon to overturn the limited gains that minorities made during the short-lived civil rights era.

We find unprecedented and consistent changes in the American educational, welfare, and prison institutions over the last several decades which have served to overturn the small gains that minorities had achieved during the 1960s and 1970s. These draconian, punitive changes have come in the guise of "accountability," "morality," and "zero tolerance"—tough talk pushed into laws by conservative forces. The result is that impoverished minorities—the most vulnerable segments of American society—have been placed on a path of downward mobility via the education, welfare, and prison systems. Because of the dramatic changes that have taken place in the educational, welfare, and prison institutions and the increasing privatization that has ensued over the last few decades, we suggest that scholars in race and ethnicity will need to incorporate insights from the organizational literature to better understand—and alleviate—how inequality is supported and furthered by occupants at different levels of organizations.

When we speak of organizations we are not only concerned with the organizational rules but how persons in the organization and outside it come to shape and are shaped by the nature of such organizations. Our concern is on how minority poor who possess the least knowledge about the nature of organizations are called upon to interact with persons who staff the lower echelons of complex organizations where the rules are the most constraining.

A review of the literature reveals that the minority group poor must interact with the organizational arrangements in the spheres of education, welfare, and prisons, and in the process confront the complex interrelationships among these spheres. We find a "circular causation" among educational, prison, and welfare complexes that have yet to be sorted out by sociologists. Unfortunately, only limited data and studies exist on how economically strapped minority group members cope with, much less understand, these organizational complexes. For example, Alice O'Connor (2001) has written a wonderful book on the knowledge social scientists have acquired about the poor, but it is flawed in a striking way. Her work *Poverty Knowledge* examines the study of poverty almost solely from the perspective of the experts. The knowledge that impoverished minorities possess about the social organizations in which they are embedded is hidden from view.

The matter of the earned income tax credit underscores the saliency of technical knowledge as poor racial and ethnic minorities strive to acquire much needed economic resources to which they have a rightful claim. Persons with limited education find the rules undergirding this notion so difficult to comprehend that they typically are obliged to seek out someone with a knowledge of accounting if they are to secure the funds that are their due, and there is a segment of the poor who do not know of the monies provided by the earned income tax credit.

More generally, if social scientists take human agency seriously, they must necessarily consider in some depth how the lack of social knowledge undermines the lives of economically disadvantaged minorities. By doing so, sociologists will come to understand how various organizational complexes can assist the poor and so often keep the poor, notably racial and ethnic minorities, in their place. As social scientists come to detail these patterns, they will find, we aver, how the formal and informal rules of organizations often are employed to sustain built-in patterns of race and ethnic discrimination.

Early on we raised the issue of privatization, which has moved forward at a rapid pace in recent decades with far-reaching consequences for impoverished minorities. There are several dimensions to this process, and these have yet to be sorted out sociologically. First, there is the matter of shifting activities from the public to private sector—this process having received the bulk of attention. Privatization is well along in the realm of welfare, prisons, and schools (with, say, its voucher system). Although most state organizations have never lived up to their ideals, the increased privatization of schools, welfare, and prisons has resulted in these organizations being less accountable to the "public interest" than ever before, with deep-seated consequences for economically strapped minorities.

The paradoxes involving privatization are brought starkly to the fore in the prison industry. At one time prisons occupied a marginal role in the social order, but nowadays prisons have become big business, with a managerial sector that thrives economically at the expense of black males and increasingly Latino males. Still this prison takeover by the private sector does not square with the law of supply and demand in any meaningful way. For instance, if one makes the case that inexpensive prison labor should be employed to create goods and services that pay (at least in part for the cost of the prisons), then one undercuts the principle of free labor. Alternatively, if prison labor is not productive, the public must pay the bill (either directly or indirectly) for the private prison industry. Either way, free-market principles appear more as a convenient justification for privatization, for the economy of the prison has little or no relation to the laws of supply and demand—except that the private sector has a considerable vested interest in sustaining a sizeable supply of prisoners.

Second, there is another dimension to privatization that has received almost no attention by sociologists (though some journalists and a few political scientists have written on the topic)—notably the shifting of future risk from the governmental sector to individuals. Unquestionably this has occurred in the area of welfare, where the government no longer is expected to assist impoverished minorities who encounter major economic crises. Instead the emphasis is placed on individual—or personal—responsibility. Admittedly a commitment to personal or individual responsibility is advantageous in the formation of a disciplined labor force and is necessary when individuals are faced with decision-making in complex social situations. However, the personal responsibility of the privileged is founded not only on economic resources but on social and cultural capital. The privileged set the standards for the nature of personal responsibility, and the codes of conduct that are associated with individual responsibility are enforced within the context of organizational complexes. While many minority poor may be deeply committed to personal responsibility, they lack the economic capital and above all the social and cultural capital (e.g., social knowledge of organizational rules) to adhere to the standards espoused by the privileged middle class. This issue is underlined in the educational system wherein sizeable sectors of drop-outs and pushed-outs are minorities.

Let us for a moment examine the issues we have raised from a different vantage point—in this instance, the interrelationship of educational, welfare, and prisons systems. Certainly the impact of the prison system on destitute minority males (especially blacks and increasingly Latinos) appears to be disastrous. The labeling of persons as "convicts" or "ex-cons" (and their resultant social and legal ostracism) places a special burden on the educational system. And we surmise that the educational system will reinforce—rather than overcome—existing racism. The isolation of indigent minorities from the mainstream social order is in the process of being accentuated rather than lessened as a result of the incarceration pattern during the last few decades. The plight of impoverished minorities becomes more severe as the government has retreated from providing financial assistance in times of crises. The patterns we have isolated lend support to Joe Feagin's (2005) conception of systemic racism.

The rise of the prison industry reflects the current harshness of American society toward economically impoverished minorities. And for anyone concerned with the furtherance of a democratic order, current imprisonment arrangements require special consideration. We believe it is difficult to justify the principle that democracy is being furthered by the fact that the United States has the largest prison population, on a per-capita basis, in the world. The current prison system poses a grave social crisis for U.S. society and calls for fundamental restructuring. To do so, however, requires that members of society think carefully about the risks that result from how crime is defined and punished. Present-day practices of incarceration—sweeping as they are in their ramifications—pose grave risks for the foundations of democracy itself.

The Modern World-System

Slamming the Door on History

THE SOCIOLOGY OF DEVELOPMENT AND GLOBALIZATION

THE MODERN WORLD-SYSTEM

Social Theory: The Multicultural and Classical Readings

BY IMMANUEL WALLERSTEIN

In order to describe the origins and initial workings of a world system, I have had to argue a certain conception of a world-system. A world-system is a social system, one that has boundaries, structures, member groups, rules of legitimation, and coherence. Its life is made up of the conflicting forces which hold it together by tension, and tear it apart as each group seeks eternally to remold it to its advantage. It has the characteristics of an organism, in that it has a life-span over which its characteristics change in some respects and remain stable in others. One can define its structures as being at different times strong or weak in terms of the internal logic of its functioning.

What characterizes a social system in my view is the fact that life within it is largely self-contained, and that the dynamics of its development are largely internal. The reader may feel that the use of the term "largely" is a case of academic weaseling. I admit I cannot quantify it. Probably no one ever will be able to do so, as the definition is based on a counterfactual hypothesis: If the system, for any reason, were to be cut off from all external forces (which virtually never happens), the definition implies that the system would continue to function substantially in the same manner. Again, of course, substantially is difficult to convert into hard operational criteria. Nonetheless the point is an important one and key to many parts of the empirical analyses of this book. Perhaps we should think of self-containment as a theoretical absolute, a sort of social vacuum, rarely visible and even more implausible to create artificially, but still and all a socially-real asymptote, the distance from which is somehow measurable.

Using such a criterion, it is contended here that most entities usually described as social systems—"tribes," communities, nation-states—are not in fact total systems. Indeed, on the contrary, we are arguing that the only real social systems are, on the one hand, those relatively small, highly autonomous subsistence economies not part of some regular tribute-demanding system and, on the other hand, world-systems. These latter are to be sure distinguished from the former because they are relatively large; that is, they are in common parlance "worlds." More precisely, however, they are defined by the fact that their self-containment as an economic-material entity is based on extensive division of labor and that they contain within them a multiplicity of cultures.

It is further argued that thus far there have only existed two varieties of such world-systems: world-empires, in which there is a single political system over most of the area, however attenuated the degree of its effective control; and those systems in which such a single political system does not exist over all, or virtually all, of the space. For convenience and for want of a better term, we are using the term "world-economy" to describe the latter.

Finally, we have argued that prior to the modern era, world-economies were highly unstable structures which tended either to be converted into empires or to disintegrate. It is the peculiarity of the modern world-system that a world-economy has survived for 500

Immanuel Wallerstein, from *The Modern World-System: Capitalist Agriculture and the Origins of the European World-Economy in the Sixteenth Century*, pp. 229-233. Copyright © 1976 by Elsevier Science and Technology. Reprinted with permission.

years and yet has not come to be transformed into a world-empire—a peculiarity that is the secret of its strength.

This peculiarity is the political side of the form of economic organization called capitalism. Capitalism has been able to flourish precisely because the world-economy has had within its bounds not one but a multiplicity of political systems.

I am not here arguing the classic case of capitalist ideology that capitalism is a system based on the noninterference of the state in economic affairs. Quite the contrary! Capitalism is based on the constant absorption of economic loss by political entities, while economic gain is distributed to "private" hands. What I am arguing rather is that capitalism as an economic mode is based on the fact that the economic factors operate within an arena larger than that which any political entity can totally control. This gives capitalists a freedom of maneuver that is structurally based. It has made possible the constant economic expansion of the world-system, albeit a very skewed distribution of its rewards. The only alternative world-system that could maintain a high level of productivity and change the system of distribution would involve the reintegration of the levels of political and economic decision-making. This would constitute a third possible form of world-system, a socialist world government. This is not a form that presently exists, and it was not even remotely conceivable in the sixteenth century.

The historical reasons why the European world-economy came into existence in the sixteenth century and resisted attempts to transform it into an empire have been expounded at length. We shall not review them here. It should however be noted that the size of a world-economy is a function of the state of technology, and in particular of the possibilities of transport and communication within its bounds. Since this is a constantly changing phenomenon, not always for the better, the boundaries of a world-economy are ever fluid.

We have defined a world-system as one in which there is extensive division of labor. This division is not merely functional—that is, occupational—but geographical. That is to say, the range of economic tasks is not evenly distributed throughout the world-system. In part this is the consequence of ecological considerations, to be sure. But for the most part, it is a function of the social organization of work, one which magnifies and legitimizes the ability of some groups within the system to exploit the labor of others, that is, to receive a larger share of the surplus.

While, in an empire, the political structure tends to link culture with occupation, in a world-economy the political structure tends to link culture with spatial location. The reason is that in a world-economy the first point of political pressure available to groups is the local (national) state structure. Cultural homogenization tends to serve the interests of key groups and the pressures build up to create cultural-national identities.

This is particularly the case in the advantaged areas of the world-economy—what we have called the core-states. In such states, the creation of a strong state machinery coupled with a national culture, a phenomenon often referred to as integration, serves both as a mechanism to protect disparities that have arisen within the world-system, and as an ideological mask and justification for the maintenance of these disparities.

World-economies then are divided into core-states and peripheral areas. I do not say peripheral *states* because one characteristic of a peripheral area is that the indigenous state is weak, ranging from its nonexistence (that is, a colonial situation) to one with a low degree of autonomy (that is, a neo-colonial situation).

There are also semiperipheral areas which are in between the core and the periphery on a series of dimensions, such as the complexity of economic activities, strength of the state machinery, cultural integrity, etc. Some of these areas had been core-areas of earlier versions of a given world-economy. Some had been peripheral areas that were later promoted, so to speak, as a result of the changing geopolitics of an expanding world-economy.

The semiperiphery, however, is not an artifice of statistical cutting points, nor is it a residual category. The semiperiphery is a necessary structural element in a world-economy. These areas play a role parallel to that played, *mutatis mutandis*, by middle trading groups in an empire. They are collection points of vital skills that are often politically unpopular. These middle areas (like middle groups in an empire) partially deflect the political pressures which groups primarily located in peripheral areas might otherwise direct against core-states and the groups which operate within and through their state machineries. On the other hand, the interests primarily located in the semiperiphery are located outside the political arena of the core-states, and find it difficult to pursue the ends in political coalitions that might be open to them were they in the same political arena.

The division of a world-economy involves a hierarchy of occupational tasks, in which tasks requiring higher levels of skill and greater capitalization are reserved for higher-ranking areas. Since a capitalist world-economy essentially rewards accumulated capital, including human capital, at a higher rate than "raw" labor power, the geographical maldistribution of these occupational skills involves a strong trend toward self-maintenance. The forces of the marketplace reinforce them rather than undermine them. And the absence of a central political mechanism for the world-economy makes it very difficult to intrude counteracting forces to the maldistribution of rewards.

Hence, the ongoing process of a world-economy tends to expand the economic and social gaps among its varying areas in the very process of its development. One factor that tends to mask this fact is that the process of development of a world-economy brings about technological advances which make it possible to expand the boundaries of a world-economy. In this case, particular regions of the world may change their structural role in the world-economy, to their advantage, even though the disparity of reward between different sectors of the world-economy as a whole may be simultaneously widening. It is in order to observe this crucial phenomenon clearly that we have insisted on the distinction between a peripheral area of a given world-economy and the external arena of the world-economy. The external arena of one century often becomes the periphery of the next—or its semiperiphery. But then too core-states can become semiperipheral and semiperipheral ones peripheral.

While the advantages of the core-states have not ceased to expand throughout the history of the modern world-system, the ability of a particular state to remain in the core sector is not beyond challenge. The hounds are ever to the hares for the position of top dog. Indeed, it may well be that in this kind of system it is not structurally possible to avoid, over a long period of historical time, a circulation of the elites in the sense that the particular country that is dominant at a given time tends to be replaced in this role sooner or later by another country.

We have insisted that the modern world-economy is, and only can be, a capitalist world-economy. It is for this reason that we have rejected the appellation of "feudalism" for the various forms of capitalist agriculture based on coerced labor which grow up in a world-economy. Furthermore, although this has not been discussed in this volume, it is for this same reason that we will, in future volumes, regard with great circumspection and prudence the claim that there exist in the twentieth century socialist national economies within the framework of the world-economy (as opposed to socialist movements controlling certain state-machineries within the world-economy).

If world-systems are the only real social systems (other than truly isolated subsistence economies), then it must follow that the emergence, consolidation, and political roles of classes and status groups must be appreciated as elements of this *world*-system. And in turn it follows that one of the key elements in analyzing a class or a status-group is not only the state of its self-consciousness but the geographical scope of its self-definition.

Classes always exist potentially (*an sich*). The issue is under what conditions they become class-conscious (*fur sich*), that is, operate as a group in the politico-economic arenas and even to some extent as a cultural entity. Such self-consciousness is a function of conflict situations. But for upper strata open conflict, and hence overt consciousness, is always *faute de mieux*. To the extent that class boundaries are not made explicit, to that extent it is more likely that privileges be maintained.

Since in conflict situations, multiple factions tend to reduce to two by virtue of the forging of alliances, it is by definition not possible to have three or more (conscious) classes. There obviously can be a multitude of occupational interest groups which may organize themselves to operate within the social structure. But such groups are really one variety of status-groups, and indeed often overlap heavily with other kinds of status-groups such as those defined by ethnic, linguistic, or religious criteria.

To say that there cannot be three or more classes is not however to say that there are always two. There may be none, though this is rare and transitional. There may be one, and this is most common. There may be two, and this is most explosive.

We say there may be only one class, although we have also said that classes only actually exist in conflict situations, and conflicts presume two sides. There is no contradiction here. For a conflict may be defined as being between one class, which conceives of itself as the universal class, and all the other strata. This has in fact been the usual situation in the modern world-system. The capitalist class (the *bourgeoisie*) has claimed to be the universal class and sought to organize political life to pursue its objectives against two opponents. On the one hand, there were those who spoke for the maintenance of traditional rank distinctions despite the fact that these ranks might have lost their original correlation with economic function. Such elements preferred to define the social structure as a non-class structure. It was to counter this ideology that the bourgeoisie came to operate as a class conscious of itself. ...

The European world-economy of the sixteenth century tended overall to be a one-class system. It was the dynamic forces profiting from economic expansion and the capitalist system, especially those in the core-areas, who tended to be class-conscious, that is to operate within the political arena as a group defined primarily by their common role in the economy. This common role was in fact defined somewhat broadly from a twentieth-century perspective. It included persons who were farmers, merchants, and industrialists. Individual entrepreneurs often moved back and forth between these activities in any case, or combined them. The crucial distinction was between these men, whatever their occupation, principally oriented to obtaining profit in the world market, and the others not so oriented.

The "others" fought back in terms of their status privileges—those of the traditional aristocracy, those which small farmers had derived from the feudal system, those resulting from guild monopolies that were outmoded. Under the cover of cultural similarities, one can often weld strange alliances. Those strange alliances can take a very activist form and force the political centers to take account of them. We pointed to such instances in our discussion of France. Or they can take a politically passive form that serves well the needs of the dominant forces in the world-system. The triumph of Polish Catholicism as a cultural force was a case in point.

The details of the canvas are filled in with the panoply of multiple forms of status-groups, their particular strengths and accents. But the grand sweep is in terms of the process of class formation. And in this regard, the sixteenth century was indecisive. The capitalist strata formed a class that survived and gained *droit de cité*, but did not yet triumph in the political arena.

The evolution of the state machineries reflected precisely this uncertainty. Strong states serve the interests of some groups and hurt those of others. From however the standpoint of the world-system as a whole, if there is to be a multitude of political entities (that is, if the system is not a world-empire), then it cannot be the case that all these entities be equally strong. For if they were, they would be in the position of blocking the effective operation of transnational economic entities whose locus were in another state. And obviously certain combinations of these groups control the state. It would then follow that the world division of labor would be impeded, the world-economy decline, and eventually the world-system fall apart.

It also cannot be that *no* state machinery is strong. For in such a case, the capitalist strata would have no mechanisms to protect their interests, guaranteeing their property rights, assuring various monopolies, spreading losses among the larger population, etc.

It follows then that the world-economy develops a pattern where state structures are relatively strong in the core areas and relatively weak in the periphery. Which areas play which roles is in many ways accidental. What is necessary is that in some areas the state machinery be far stronger than in others.

What do we mean by a strong state-machinery? We mean strength vis-à-vis other states within the world-economy including other core-states, and strong vis-à-vis local political units within the boundaries of the state. In effect, we mean a sovereignty that is *de facto* as well as *de jure*. We also mean a state that is strong vis-à-vis any particular social group within the state. Obviously, such groups vary in the amount of pressure they can bring to bear upon the state. And obviously certain combinations of these groups control the state. It is not that the state is a neutral arbiter. But the state is more than a simple vector of given forces, if only because many of these forces are situated in more than one state or are defined in terms that have little correlation with state boundaries.

A strong state then is a partially autonomous entity in the sense that it has a margin of action available to it wherein it reflects the compromises of multiple interests, even if the bounds of these margins are set by the existence of some groups of primordial strength. To be a partially autonomous entity, there must be a group of people whose direct interests are served by such an entity: state managers and a state bureaucracy.

Such groups emerge within the framework of a capitalist world-economy because a strong state is the best choice between difficult alternatives for the two groups that are strongest in political, economic, and military terms: the emergent capitalist strata, and the old aristocratic hierarchies.

For the former, the strong state in the form of the "absolute monarchies" was a prime customer, a guardian against local and international brigandage, a mode of social legitimation, a preemptive protection against the creation of strong state barriers elsewhere. For the latter, the strong state represented a brake on these same capitalist strata, an upholder of status conventions, a maintainer of order, a promoter of luxury.

No doubt both nobles and bourgeois found the state machineries to be a burdensome drain of funds, and a meddlesome unproductive bureaucracy. But what options did they have? Nonetheless they were always restive and the immediate politics of the world-system was made up of the pushes and pulls resulting from the efforts of both groups to insulate themselves from what seemed to them the negative effects of the state machinery.

A state machinery involves a tipping mechanism. There is a point where strength creates more strength. The tax revenue enables the state to have a larger and more efficient civil bureaucracy and army which in turn leads to greater tax revenue—a process that continues in spiral form. The tipping mechanism works in other direction too—weakness leading to greater weakness. In between these two tipping points lies the politics of state-creation. It is in this arena that the skills of particular managerial groups make a difference. And it is because of the two tipping mechanisms that at certain points a small gap in the world-system can very rapidly become a larger one.

In those states in which the state machinery is weak, the state managers do not play the role of coordinating a complex industrial-commercial-agricultural mechanism. Rather they simply become one set of landlords amidst others, with little claim to legitimate authority over the whole.

These tend to be called traditional rulers. The political struggle is often phrased in terms of tradition versus change. This is of course a grossly misleading and ideological terminology. It may in fact be taken as a general sociological principle that, at any given point of time, what is thought to be traditional is of more recent origin than people generally imagine it to be, and represents primarily the conservative instincts of some group threatened with declining social status. Indeed, there seems to be nothing which emerges and evolves as quickly as a "tradition" when the need presents itself.

In a one-class system, the "traditional" is that in the name of which the "others" fight the class-conscious group. If they can encrust their values by legitimating them widely, even better by enacting them into legislative barriers, they thereby change the system in a way favorable to them.

The traditionalists may win in some states, but if a world-economy is to survive, they must lose more or less in the others. Furthermore, the gain in one region is the counterpart of the loss in another.

This is not quite a zero-sum game, but it is also inconceivable that all elements in a capitalist world-economy shift their values in a given direction simultaneously. The social system is built on having a multiplicity of value systems within it, reflecting the specific functions groups and areas play in the world division of labor.

We have not exhausted here the theoretical problems relevant to the functioning of a world-economy. We have tried only to speak to those illustrated by the early period of the world-economy in creation, to wit, sixteenth-century Europe. Many other problems emerged at later stages and will be treated, both empirically and theoretically, in later volumes.

In the sixteenth century, Europe was like a bucking bronco. The attempt of some groups to establish a world-economy based on a particular division of labor, to create national states in the core areas as politico-economic guarantors of this system, and to get the workers to pay not only the profits but the costs of maintaining the system was not easy. It was to Europe's credit that it was done, since without the thrust of the sixteenth century the modern world would not have been born and, for all its cruelties, it is better that it was born than that it had not been.

It is also to Europe's credit that it was not easy, and particularly that it was not easy because the people who paid the short-run costs screamed lustily at the unfairness of it all. The peasants and workers in Poland and England and Brazil and Mexico were all rambunctious in their various ways. As R. H. Tawney says of the agrarian disturbances of sixteenth-century England: "Such movements are a proof of blood and sinew and of a high and gallant spirit. … Happy the nation whose people has not forgotten how to rebel."

The mark of the modern world is the imagination of its profiteers and the counter-assertiveness of the oppressed. Exploitation and the refusal to accept exploitation as either inevitable or just constitute the continuing antinomy of the modern era, joined together in a dialectic which was far from reached its climax in the twentieth century.

SLAMMING THE DOOR ON HISTORY

A Crisis in Poland, A Massacre in China

BY NAOMI KLEIN

> I live in a Poland that is now free, and I consider Milton Friedman to be one of the main intellectual architects of my country's liberty.
> —Leszek Balcerowicz, former finance minister of Poland, November 2006

> There's a certain chemical that gets released in your stomach when you make ten times your money. And it's addictive.
> —William Browder, a U.S. money manager, on investing in Poland in the early days of capitalism

> We certainly must not stop eating for fear of choking.
> —*People's Daily*, the official state newspaper, on the need to continue free-market reforms after the Tiananmen Square massacre

Before the Berlin Wall fell, becoming the defining symbol of the collapse of Communism, there was another image that held out the promise of Soviet barriers coming down. It was Lech Walesa, a laid-off electrician with a handlebar moustache and disheveled hair, climbing over a steel fence festooned with flowers and flags in Gdańsk, Poland. The fence protected the Lenin shipyards and the thousands of workers who had barricaded themselves inside to protest a Communist Party decision to raise the price of meat.

The workers' strike was an unprecedented show of defiance against the Moscow-controlled government, which had ruled Poland for thirty-five years. No one knew what would happen: Would Moscow send tanks? Would they fire on the strikers and force them to work? As the strike wore on, the shipyard became a pocket of popular democracy within an authoritarian country, and the workers expanded their demands. They no longer wanted their work lives controlled by party apparatchiks claiming to speak for the working class. They wanted their own independent trade union, and they wanted the right to negotiate, bargain and strike. Not waiting for permission, they voted to form that union and called it Solidarność, Solidarity. That was 1980, the year the world fell in love with Solidarity and with its leader, Lech Walesa.

Walesa, then thirty-six, was so in tune with the aspirations of Poland's workers that they seemed in spiritual communion. "We eat the same bread!" he bellowed into the microphone in the Gdańsk shipyard. It was a reference not only to Walesa's own unassailable blue-collar credentials but also to the powerful role that Catholicism played in this trail-blazing new movement. With religion frowned upon by party officials, the workers wore their faith as a badge of courage, lining up to take Communion behind the barricades. Walesa, a bracing mix of bawdy and pious, opened the Solidarity office with a wooden crucifix in one hand and a bouquet of flowers in the other. When it came

Naomi Klein, "Slamming the Door on History: A Crisis in Poland, A Massacre in China," *The Shock Doctrine: The Rise of Disaster Capitalism*, pp. 215-244. Copyright © 2007 by Naomi Klein. Reprinted with permission by Henry Holt & Company.

time to sign the first landmark labor agreement between Solidarity and the government, Walesa marked his name with "a giant souvenir pen bearing the likeness of John Paul II." The admiration was mutual; the Polish pope told Walesa that his prayers were with Solidarity.

Solidarity spread through the country's mines, shipyards and factories with ferocious speed. Within a year, it had 10 million members—almost half of Poland's working-age population. Having won the right to bargain, Solidarity started making concrete headway: a five-day work week instead of six, and more say in the running of factories. Tired of living in a country that worshipped an idealized working class but abused actual workers, Solidarity members denounced the corruption and brutality of the party functionaries who answered not to the people of Poland but to remote and isolated bureaucrats in Moscow. All the desire for democracy and self-determination suppressed by one-party rule was being poured into local Solidarity unions, sparking a mass exodus of members from the Communist Party.

Moscow recognized the movement as the most serious threat yet to its Eastern empire. Inside the Soviet Union, opposition was still coming largely from human rights activists, many of whom were on the political right. But Solidarity's members couldn't easily be dismissed as stooges of capitalism—they were workers with hammers in their hands and coal dust in their pores, the people who should, according to Marxist rhetoric, have been the party's base.[1] Even more threatening, Solidarity's vision was everything the party was not: democratic where it was authoritarian; dispersed where it was centralized; participatory where it was bureaucratic. And its 10 million members had the power to bring Poland's economy to a standstill. As Walesa taunted, they might lose their political battles, "but we will not be compelled to work. Because if people want us to build tanks, we will build streetcars. And trucks will go backward if we build them that way. We know how to beat the system. We are pupils of that system."

Solidarity's commitment to democracy inspired even party insiders to rebel. "Once I was so naive as to think that a few evil men were responsible for the errors of the party," Marian Arendt, a member of the Central Committee, told a Polish newspaper. "Now I no longer have such illusions. There is something wrong in our whole apparatus, in our entire structure."

In September 1981, Solidarity's members were ready to take their movement to the next stage. Nine hundred Polish workers gathered once again in Gdańsk for the union's first national congress. There, Solidarity turned into a revolutionary movement with aspirations to take over the state, with its own alternative economic and political program for Poland. The Solidarity plan stated, "We demand a self-governing and democratic reform at every management level and a new socioeconomic system combining the plan, self-government and the market." The centrepiece was a radical vision for the huge state-run companies, which employed millions of Solidarity members, to break away from governmental control and become democratic workers' cooperatives. "The socialized enterprise," the program stated, "should be the basic organizational unit in the economy. It should be controlled by the workers council representing the collective and should be operatively run by the director, appointed through competition and recalled by the council." Walesa opposed this demand, fearing it was such a challenge to party control that it would provoke a crackdown. Others argued that the movement needed a goal, a positive hope for the future, not just an enemy. Walesa lost the debate, and the economic program became official Solidarity policy.

Walesa's fears of a crackdown turned out to be well founded. Solidarity's mounting ambition frightened and infuriated Moscow. Under intense pressure, Poland's leader, General Wojciech Jaruzelski, declared martial law in December 1981. Tanks rolled through the snow to surround factories and mines, Solidarity's members were rounded up in the thousands, and its leaders, including Walesa, were arrested and imprisoned. As *Time* reported, "Soldiers and police used force to clear out resisting workers, leaving at least seven dead and hundreds injured when miners in Katowice fought back with axes and crowbars."

Solidarity was forced underground, but during the eight years of police-state rule, the movement's legend only grew. In 1983, Walesa was awarded the Nobel Peace Prize, although his activities were still restricted and he could

---

1 One of the popular Solidarity slogans in 1980 was "Socialism—YES, Its distortions—NO" (which no doubt works better in Polish).

not accept the prize in person. "The Peace Prize laureate's seat is empty," the representative from the Nobel Committee said at the ceremony. "Let us therefore try even harder to listen to the silent speech from his empty place."

The empty space was a fitting metaphor because, by that time, everyone seemed to see what they wanted in Solidarity: the Nobel Committee saw a man who "espoused no other weapon than the peaceful strike weapon." The left saw redemption, a version of socialism that was not tainted by the crimes of Stalin or Mao. The right saw evidence that Communist states would meet even moderate expressions of dissent with brutal force. The human rights movement saw prisoners jailed for their beliefs. The Catholic Church saw an ally against Communist atheism. And Margaret Thatcher and Ronald Reagan saw an opening, a crack in the Soviet armor, even though Solidarity was fighting for the very rights that both leaders were doing their best to stamp out at home. The longer the ban lasted, the more powerful the Solidarity mythology became.

By 1988, the terror of the initial crackdown had eased, and Polish workers were once again staging huge strikes. This time, with the economy in free fall, and the new, moderate regime of Mikhail Gorbachev in power in Moscow, the Communists gave in. They legalized Solidarity and agreed to hold snap elections. Solidarity split in two: there was now the union and a new wing, Citizens' Committee Solidarity, that would participate in the elections. The two bodies were inextricably linked; Solidarity leaders were the candidates, and because the electoral platform was vague, the only specifics of what a Solidarity future might look like were provided by the union's economic program. Walesa himself didn't run, choosing to maintain his role as head of the union wing, but he was the face of the campaign, which ran under the slogan "With us, you're safer." The results were humiliating for the Communists and glorious for Solidarity: of the 261 seats in which Solidarity ran candidates, it won 260 of them.[2] Walesa, maneuvering behind the scenes, had the post of prime minister filled by Tadeusz Mazowiecki. He had little of Walesa's charisma, but as the editor of the Solidarity weekly newspaper, he was considered one of the movement's leading intellectuals.

2 The elections, while a breakthrough, were still rigged: from the outset, the Communist Party was guaranteed 65 percent of the seats in parliament's lower house, and Solidarity was allowed to contest only the remaining ones. Nevertheless, the win was so sweeping that Solidarity gained effective control of the government.

The Shock of Power

As Latin Americans had just learned, authoritarian regimes have a habit of embracing democracy at the precise moment when their economic projects are about to implode. Poland was no exception. The Communists had been mismanaging the economy for decades, making one disastrous, expensive mistake after another, and it was at the point of collapse. "To our misfortune, we have won!" Walesa famously (and prophetically) declared. When Solidarity took office, debt was $40 billion, inflation was at 600 percent, there were severe food shortages and a thriving black market. Many factories were making products that, with no buyers in sight, were destined to rot in warehouses. For Poles, the situation made for a cruel entry into democracy. Freedom had finally come, but few had the time or the inclination to celebrate because their paychecks were worthless. They spent their days lining up for flour and butter if there happened to be any in the stores that week.

All summer following its triumph at the polls, the Solidarity government was paralyzed by indecision. The speed of the collapse of the old order and the sudden election sweep had been shocks in themselves: in a matter of months, Solidarity activists went from hiding from the secret police to being responsible for paying the salaries of those same agents. And now they had the added shock of discovering that they barely had enough money to make the payroll. Rather than building the post-Communist economy they had dreamed of, the movement had the far more pressing task of avoiding a complete meltdown and potential mass starvation.

Solidarity's leaders knew they wanted to put an end to the state's viselike grip on the economy, but they weren't at all clear about what could replace it. For the movement's militant rank and file, this was the chance to test their economic program: if the state-run factories were converted to workers' cooperatives, there was a chance they could become economically viable again—worker management could be more efficient, especially without the added expense of party bureaucrats. Others argued for the same gradual approach to transition that Gorbachev was advocating at the time in Moscow—slow expansion of the areas in which supply-and-demand monetary rules apply (more legal shops and markets), combined with a strong public sector modeled on Scandinavian social democracy.

But as had been the case in Latin America, before anything else could happen, Poland needed debt relief and some aid to get out of its immediate crisis. In theory, that's the central mandate of the IMF: providing stabilizing funds to prevent economic catastrophes. If any government deserved that kind of lifeline it was the one headed by Solidarity, which had just pulled off the Eastern Bloc's first democratic ouster of a Communist regime in four decades, Surely, after all the Cold War railing against totalitarianism behind the Iron Curtain, Poland's new rulers could have expected a little help.

No such aid was on offer. Now in the grips of Chicago School economists, the IMF and the U.S. Treasury saw Poland's problems through the prism of the shock doctrine. An economic meltdown and a heavy debt load, compounded by the disorientation of rapid regime change, meant that Poland was in the perfect weakened position to accept a radical shock therapy program. And the financial stakes were even higher than in Latin America: Eastern Europe was untouched by Western capitalism, with no consumer market to speak of. All of its most precious assets were still owned by the state—prime candidates for privatization. The potential for rapid profits for those who got in first was tremendous.

Confident in the knowledge that the worse things got, the more likely the new government would be to accept a total conversion to unfettered capitalism, the IMF let the country fall deeper and deeper into debt and inflation. The White House, under George H. W. Bush, congratulated Solidarity on its triumph against Communism but made it clear that the U.S. administration expected Solidarity to pay the debts accumulated by the regime that had banned and jailed its members—and it offered only $119 million in aid, a pittance in a country facing economic collapse and in need of fundamental restructuring.

It was in this context that Jeffrey Sachs, then thirty-four, started working as an adviser to Solidarity. Since his Bolivian exploits, the hype surrounding Sachs had reached feverish levels. Marveling at how he could serve as economic shock doctor to half a dozen countries and still hold down his teaching job, the *Los Angeles Times* pronounced Sachs—who still looked like a member of the Harvard debate team—the "Indiana Jones of Economics."

Sachs's work in Poland had begun before Solidarity's election victory, at the request of the Communist government. It started with a one-day trip, during which he met with the Communist government and with Solidarity. It was George Soros, the billionaire financier and currency trader, who had enlisted Sachs to play a more hands-on role. Soros and Sachs traveled to Warsaw together, and as Sachs recalls, "I told the Solidarity group and the Polish government that I would be willing to become more involved to help address the deepening economic crisis." Soros agreed to cover the costs for Sachs and his colleague David Lipton, a staunch free-market economist then working at the IMF, to set up an ongoing Poland mission. When Solidarity swept the elections, Sachs began working closely with the movement.

Though he was a free agent, not on the payroll of either the IMF or the U.S. government, Sachs, in the eyes of many of Solidarity's top officials, possessed almost messianic powers. With his high-level contacts in Washington and legendary reputation, he seemed to hold the key to unlocking the aid and debt relief that was the new government's only chance. Sachs said at the time that Solidarity should simply refuse to pay the inherited debts, and he expressed confidence that he could mobilize $3 billion in support—a fortune compared with what Bush had offered. He had helped Bolivia land loans with the IMF and renegotiated its debts; there seemed no reason to doubt him.

That help, however, came at a price: for Solidarity to get access to Sachs's connections and powers of persuasion, the government first needed to adopt what became known in the Polish press as "the Sachs Plan" or "shock therapy."

It was an even more radical course than the one imposed on Bolivia: in addition to eliminating price controls overnight and slashing subsidies, the Sachs Plan advocated selling off the state mines, shipyards and factories to the private sector. It was a direct clash with Solidarity's economic program of worker ownership, and though the movement's national leaders had stopped talking about the controversial ideas in that plan, they remained articles of faith for many Solidarity members. Sachs and Lipton wrote the plan for Poland's shock therapy transition in one night. It was fifteen pages long and, Sachs claimed, was "the first time, I believe, that anyone had written down a comprehensive plan for the transformation of a socialist economy to a market economy."

Sachs was convinced that Poland had to take this "leap across the institutional chasm" right away because, in addition to all its other problems, it was on the verge of entering hyperinflation. Once that happened, he said, it would be "fundamental breakdown ... just pure, unmitigated disaster."

He gave several one-on-one seminars explaining the plan to key Solidarity officials, some lasting up to four hours, and he also addressed Poland's elected officials as a group. Many of Solidarity's leaders didn't like Sachs's ideas—the movement had formed in a revolt against drastic price increases imposed by the Communists—and now Sachs was telling them to do the same on a far more sweeping scale. He argued that they could get away with it precisely because "Solidarity had a reservoir of trust of the public, which was absolutely phenomenal and critical."

Solidarity's leaders hadn't planned to expend that trust on policies that would cause extreme pain to their rank and file, but the years spent in the underground, in jail and in exile had also alienated them from their base. As the Polish editor Przemyslaw Wielgosz explains, the top tier of the movement "became effectively cut off ... their support came not from the factories and industrial plants, but the church." The leaders were also desperate for a quick fix, even if it was painful, and that was what Sachs was offering. "Will this work? That's what I want to know. Will this work?" demanded Adam Michnik, one of Solidarity's most celebrated intellectuals. Sachs did not waver: "This is good. This will work."[3]

Sachs often held up Bolivia as the model that Poland should emulate, so often that the Poles grew tired of hearing about the place. "I would love to see Bolivia," one Solidarity leader told a reporter at the time. "I'm sure it's very lovely, very exotic. I just don't want to see Bolivia *here*." Lech Walesa developed a particularly acute antipathy to Bolivia, as he admitted to Gonzalo Sánchez de Lozada (Goni) when the two men met years later at a summit, when they were both presidents. "He came up to me," Goni recalled, "and said, 'I've always wanted to meet a Bolivian, especially a Bolivian president, because they're always making us take this very bitter medicine, saying you have to do it because this is what the Bolivians did. Now I know you, you're not that bad a guy, but I sure used to hate you.'"

In Sachs's talk of Bolivia, he failed to mention that in order to push through the shock therapy program, the government had imposed a state of emergency and, on two separate occasions, kidnapped and interned the union leadership—much as the Communist Party secret police had snatched and imprisoned Solidarity's leaders under a state of emergency not so long before.

What was most persuasive, many now recall, was Sachs's promise that if they followed his harsh advice, Poland would cease being exceptional and become "normal"—as in "a normal European country." If Sachs was right, and they really could fast-forward to becoming a country like France or Germany simply by hacking off the structures of the old state, wasn't the pain worth it? Why take an incremental route to change that could well fail—or pioneer a new third way—when this insta-Europe version was right there, calling out? Sachs predicted that shock therapy would cause "momentary dislocations" as prices spiked. "But then they'll stabilize—people will know where they stand."

He formed an alliance with Poland's newly appointed finance minister, Leszek Balcerowicz, an economist at the Main School of Planning and Statistics in Warsaw. Little was known of Balcerowicz's political leanings when he was appointed (all economists were officially socialist), but it would soon become clear that he saw himself as an honorary Chicago Boy, having pored over an illegal Polish edition of Friedman's *Free to Choose*. It helped "to inspire me, and many others, to dream of a future of freedom during the darkest years of communist rule," Balcerowicz later explained.

Friedman's fundamentalist version of capitalism was a long way from what Walesa had been promising the country that summer. He was still

3 Michnik later observed bitterly that "the worst thing about Communism is what comes after."

insisting that Poland was going to find that more generous third way, which he described in an interview with Barbara Walters as "a mixture. … It won't be capitalism. It will be a system that is better than capitalism, that will reject everything that is evil in capitalism."

Many did argue that the sudden fix that Sachs and Balcerowicz were selling was a myth, that, rather than jolting Poland into health and normalcy, shock therapy would create an even bigger mess of poverty and deindustrialization than before. "This is a poor, weak country. We simply cannot take the shock," a leading doctor and health care advocate told the *New Yorker* journalist Lawrence Weschler.

For three months after their historic victory at the polls and their abrupt transition from outlaws to lawmakers, the Solidarity inner circle debated, paced, yelled and chain-smoked, unable to decide what to do. Every day, the country fell deeper into economic crisis.

A Very Hesitant Embrace

On September 12, 1989, the Polish prime minister, Tadeusz Mazowiecki, rose before the first elected parliament. The Solidarity caucus had at last decided what it was going to do about the economy, but only a handful of people knew the final decision—was it the Sachs Plan, the Gorbachev gradualist route or Solidarity's platform of workers' cooperatives?

Mazowiecki was on the verge of announcing the verdict, but in the middle of his momentous speech, before he could confront the country's most burning question, something went terribly wrong. He started to sway, clasped the lectern and, according to one witness, "grew pale, gasped for breath and was heard to mutter under his breath, 'I'm not feeling too well.'" His aides whisked him out of the chamber, leaving the 415 deputies to trade rumors. Was it a heart attack? Had he been poisoned? By the Communists? By the Americans?

One floor below, a team of doctors examined Mazowiecki and administered an electrocardiogram. It wasn't a heart attack or poison. The prime minister was simply suffering from "acute fatigue," from too little sleep and too much stress. After almost an hour of tense uncertainty, he reentered the parliamentary chamber, where he was greeted with thunderous applause. "Excuse me," said the bookish Mazowiecki. "The state of my health is the same as the state of the Polish economy."

At long last, the verdict: the Polish economy would be treated for its own acute fatigue with shock therapy, a particularly radical course of it that would include "privatization of state industry, the creation of a stock exchange and capital markets, a convertible currency, and a shift from heavy industry to consumer goods production" as well as "budget cuts"—as fast as possible and all at once.

If the dream of Solidarity began with Walesa's energetic vault over the steel fence in Gdańsk, then Mazowiecki's exhaustedly succumbing to shock therapy represented the end of that dream. Finally, the decision came down to money. Solidarity's members did not decide that their vision for a cooperatively run economy was wrongheaded, but their leaders became convinced that all that mattered was winning relief from the Communist debts and immediately stabilizing the currency. As Henryk Wujec, one of Poland's leading advocates of cooperatives, put it at the time, "If we had enough time, we might even be able to pull it off. But we don't have time." Sachs, meanwhile, could deliver the money. He helped Poland negotiate an agreement with the IMF and secured some debt relief and $1 billion to stabilize the currency—but all of it, particularly the IMF funds, was strictly conditional on Solidarity's submitting to shock therapy.

Poland became a textbook example of Friedman's crisis theory: the disorientation of rapid political change combined with the collective fear generated by an economic meltdown to make the promise of a quick and magical cure—however illusory—too seductive to turn down. Halina Bortnowska, a human rights activist, described the velocity of change in this period as "the difference between dog years and human years, the way we're living these days … you start witnessing these semi-psychotic reactions. You can no longer expect people to act in their own best interests when they're so disoriented they don't know—or no longer care—what those interests are."

Balcerowicz, the finance minister, has since admitted that capitalizing on the emergency environment was a deliberate strategy—a way, like all shock tactics, to clear away the opposition. He explained that he was able to push through policies that were antithetical to the Solidarity vision in both content and form because Poland was in what he dubbed a period of "extraordinary politics." He described that condition as a short-lived window in which the rules of "normal politics" (consultation, discussion, debate) do not apply—in other words, a democracy-free pocket within a democracy.

"Extraordinary politics," he said, "by definition is a period of very clear discontinuity in a country's history. It could be a period of very deep economic crisis, of a breakdown of the previous institutional system, or of a liberation from external domination (or end of war). In Poland, all three phenomena converged in 1989." Because of those extraordinary circumstances, he was able to shunt aside due process and force "a radical acceleration of the legislative process" to pass the shock therapy package.

In the early nineties, Balcerowicz's theory about periods of "extraordinary politics" attracted considerable interest among Washington economists. And no wonder: only two months after Poland announced that it would accept shock therapy, something happened that would change the course of history and invest Poland's experiment with global significance. In November 1989, the Berlin Wall was joyously dismantled, the city was turned into a festival of possibility and the MTV flag was planted in the rubble, as if East Berlin were the face of the moon. Suddenly it seemed that the whole world was living the same kind of fast-forward existence as the Poles: the Soviet Union was on the verge of breaking apart, apartheid in South Africa seemed on its last legs, authoritarian regimes continued to crumble in Latin America, Eastern Europe and Asia, and long wars were coming to an end from Namibia to Lebanon. Everywhere, old regimes were collapsing, and the new ones rising in their place had yet to take shape.

Within a few years it seemed as if half the world was in a period of "extraordinary politics," or "in transition," as liberated countries came to be called in the nineties—suspended in an existential in-betweenness of past and future. According to Thomas Carothers, a leader in the U.S. government's so-called democracy-promotion apparatus, "in the first half of the 1990s … the set of 'transitional countries' swelled dramatically, and nearly 100 countries (approximately 20 in Latin America, 25 in Eastern Europe and the former Soviet Union, 30 in sub-Saharan Africa, 10 in Asia, and 5 in the Middle East) were in some kind of dramatic transition from one model to another."

Many were claiming that all of this flux, and the fall of real and metaphorical walls, would lead to an end of ideological orthodoxy. Freed from the polarizing effects of dueling superpowers, countries would finally be able to choose the best of both worlds—some hybrid of political freedom and economic security. As Gorbachev put it, "Many decades of being mesmerized by dogma, by a rule-book approach, have had their effect. Today we want to introduce a genuinely creative spirit."

In Chicago School circles, such talk of mix-and-match ideologies was met with open contempt. Poland had clearly shown that this kind of chaotic transition opened up a window for decisive men, acting swiftly, to push through rapid change. Now was the moment to convert former Communist countries to pure Friedmanism, not some mongrel Keynesian compromise. The trick, as Friedman had said, was for Chicago School believers to be ready with their solutions when everyone else was still asking questions and regaining their bearings.

A sort of revival meeting for those who embraced this worldview was held in that eventful winter of 1989; the location, fittingly, was the University of Chicago. The occasion was a speech by Francis Fukuyama titled "Are We Approaching the End of History?"[4] For Fukuyama, then a senior policy maker at the U.S. State Department, the strategy for advocates of unfettered capitalism was clear: don't debate with the third-way crowd; instead, preemptively declare victory. Fukuyama was convinced that there should be no abandonment of extremes, no best of both worlds, no splitting the difference. The collapse of Communism, he told his audience, was leading "not to an 'end of ideology' or a convergence between capitalism and socialism … but to an unabashed victory of economic and political liberalism." It was not ideology that had ended but "history as such."

The talk was sponsored by John M. Olin, longtime hinder of Milton Friedman's ideological crusade and bankroller of the boom in right-wing think tanks. The synergy was fitting since Fukuyama was essentially restating Friedman's claim that free markets and free people are part of an inseparable

4 The lecture formed the foundation for Fukuyama's book *The End of History and the Last Man*, published three years later.

project. Fukuyama took that thesis into bold new terrain, arguing that deregulated markets in the economic sphere, combined with liberal democracy in the political sphere, represented "the end point of mankind's ideological evolution and ... final form of human government." Democracy and radical capitalism were fused not only with each other but also with modernity, progress and reform. Those who objected to the merger were not just wrong but "still in history," as Fukuyama put it, the equivalent of being left behind after the Rapture, since everyone else had already transcended to a celestial "posthistorical" plane.

The argument was a magnificent example of the democracy avoidance honed by the Chicago School. Much as the IMF had sneaked privatization and "free trade" into Latin America and Africa under cover of emergency "stabilization" programs, Fukuyama was now trying to smuggle this same highly contested agenda into the pro-democracy wave rising up from Warsaw to Manila. It was true, as Fukuyama noted, that there was an emerging and irrepressible consensus that all people have the right to govern themselves democratically, but only in the State Department's most vivid fantasies was that desire for democracy accompanied by citizens' clamoring for an economic system that would strip away job protections and cause mass layoffs.

If there was a genuine consensus about anything, it was that for people escaping both left-wing and right-wing dictatorships, democracy meant finally having a say in all major decisions rather than having somebody else's ideology imposed unilaterally and with force. In other words, the universal principle that Fukuyama identified as "the sovereignty of the people" *included* the sovereignty of the people to choose how the wealth of their countries would be distributed, from the fate of state-owned companies to the level of funding for schools and hospitals. Around the world, citizens were ready to exercise their hard-won democratic powers to become the authors of their national destinies, at last.

In 1989, history was taking an exhilarating turn, entering a period of genuine openness and possibility. So it was no coincidence that Fukuyama, from his perch at the State Department, chose precisely that moment to attempt to slam the history book shut. Nor was it a coincidence that the World Bank and the IMF chose that same volatile year to unveil the Washington Consensus—a clear effort to halt all discussion and debate about any economic ideas outside the free-market lockbox, These were democracy-containment strategies, designed to undercut the kind of unscripted self-determination that was, and always had been, the greatest single threat to the Chicago School crusade.

The Shock of Tiananmen Square

One place where Fukuyama's bold pronouncement came in for early discrediting was China. Fukuyama's speech took place in February 1989; two months later, a pro-democracy movement exploded in Beijing, with mass protests and sit-ins in Tiananmen Square. Fukuyama had claimed that democratic and "free market reforms" were a twin process, impossible to pry apart. Yet in China, the government had done precisely that: it was pushing hard to deregulate wages and prices and expand the reach of the market—but it was fiercely determined to resist calls for elections and civil liberties. The demonstrators, on the other hand, demanded democracy, but many opposed the government's moves toward unregulated capitalism, a fact largely left out of the coverage of the movement in the Western press. In China, democracy and Chicago School economics were not proceeding hand in hand; they were on opposite sides of the barricades surrounding Tiananmen Square.

In the early 1980s, the Chinese government, then led by Deng Xiaoping, was obsessed with avoiding a repeat of what had just happened in Poland, where workers had been allowed to form an independent movement that challenged the party's monopoly hold on power. It was not that China's leaders were committed to protecting the state-owned factories and farm communes that formed the foundation of the Communist state. In fact, Deng was enthusiastically committed to converting to a corporate-based economy—so committed that, in 1980, his government invited Milton Friedman to come to China and tutor hundreds of top-level civil servants, professors and party economists in the fundamentals of free-market theory. "All were invited guests, who had to show a ticket of invitation to attend," Friedman recalled of his audiences in Beijing and Shanghai. His central message was "how much better ordinary people lived in capitalist than in communist countries." The example he held up was Hong Kong, a zone of pure capitalism that Friedman had long admired for its "dynamic, innovative character that has been produced by personal liberty, free trade, low taxes, and minimal government intervention." He claimed that Hong Kong, despite having no democracy, was freer than the United States, since its government participated less in the economy.

Friedman's definition of freedom, in which political freedoms were incidental, even unnecessary, compared with the freedom of unrestricted commerce, conformed nicely with the vision taking shape in the Chinese Politburo. The party wanted to open the economy to private ownership and consumerism while maintaining its own grip on power—a plan that ensured that once the assets of the state were auctioned off, party officials and their relatives would snap up the best deals and be first in line for the biggest profits. According to this version of "transition," the same people who controlled the state under Communism would control it under capitalism, while enjoying a substantial upgrade in lifestyle. The model the Chinese government intended to emulate was not the United States but something much closer to Chile under Pinochet: free markets combined with authoritarian political control, enforced by iron-fisted repression.

From the start, Deng clearly understood that repression would be crucial. Under Mao, the Chinese state had exerted brutal control over the people, dispensing with opponents and sending dissidents for reeducation. But Mao's repression took place in the name of the workers and against the bourgeoisie; now the party was going to launch its own counterrevolution and ask workers to give up many of their benefits and security so that a minority could collect huge profits. It was not going to be an easy task. So, in 1983, as Deng opened up the country to foreign investment and reduced protections for workers, he also ordered the creation of the 400,000-strong People's Armed Police, a new, roving riot squad charged with quashing all signs of "economic crimes" (i.e., strikes and protests). According to the China historian Maurice Meisner, "The People's Armed Police kept American helicopters and electric cattle prods in its arsenal." And "several units were sent to Poland for anti-riot training"—where they studied the tactics that had been used against Solidarity during Poland's period of martial law.

Many of Deng's reforms were successful and popular—farmers had more control over their lives, and commerce returned to the cities. But in the late eighties, Deng began introducing measures that were distinctly unpopular, particularly among workers in the cities—price controls were lifted, sending prices soaring; job security was eliminated, creating waves of unemployment; and deep inequalities were opening up between the winners and losers in the new China. By 1988, the party was confronting a powerful backlash and was forced to reverse some of its price deregulation. Outrage was also mounting in the face of the party's defiant corruption and nepotism. Many Chinese citizens wanted more freedom in the market, but "reform" increasingly looked like code for party officials turning into business tycoons, as many illegally took possession of the assets they had previously managed as bureaucrats.

With the free-market experiment in peril, Milton Friedman was once again invited to pay a visit to China—much as the Chicago Boys and the piranhas had enlisted his help in 1975, when their program had sparked an internal revolt in Chile. A high-profile visit from the world-famous guru of capitalism was just the boost China's "reformers" needed.

When Friedman and his wife, Rose, arrived in Shanghai in September 1988, they were dazzled by how quickly mainland China was beginning to look and feel like Hong Kong. Despite the rage simmering at the grass roots, everything they saw served to confirm "our faith in the power of free markets." Friedman described this moment as "the most hopeful period of the Chinese experiment."

In the presence of official state media, Friedman met for two hours with Zhao Ziyang, general secretary of the Communist Party, as well as with Jiang Zemin, then party secretary of the Shanghai Committee and the future Chinese president. Friedman's message to Jiang echoed the advice he had given to Pinochet when the Chilean project was on the skids: don't bow to the pressure and don't blink. "I emphasized the importance of privatization and free markets, and of liberalizing at one fell stroke," Friedman recalled. In a memo to the general secretary of the Communist Party, Friedman stressed that more, not less, shock therapy was needed. "China's initial steps of reform have been dramatically successful. China can make further dramatic progress by placing still further reliance on free private markets."

Shortly after his return to the U.S., Friedman, remembering the heat he had taken for advising Pinochet, wrote "out of sheer devilry" a letter to the editor of a student newspaper, denouncing his critics for their double standards. He explained that he had just spent twelve days in China, where "I was mostly the guest of governmental entities," and had met with Communist Party officials at the highest level. Yet these meetings had provoked no human rights outcry on American university campuses, Friedman pointed out. "Incidentally, I gave precisely the same advice to both Chile and China." He concluded by asking sarcastically, "Should I prepare myself for an avalanche of protests for having been willing to give advice to so evil a government?"

A few months later, that devilish letter took on sinister overtones, as the Chinese government began to emulate many of Pinochet's most infamous tactics.

Friedman's trip did not have the desired results. The pictures in the official papers of the professor offering his blessing to party bureaucrats did not succeed in bringing the public onside. In subsequent months, protests grew more determined and radical. The most visible symbols of the opposition were the demonstrations by student strikers in Tiananmen Square. These historic protests were almost universally portrayed in the international media as a clash between modern, idealistic students who wanted Western-style democratic freedoms and old-guard authoritarians who wanted to protect the Communist state. Recently, another analysis of the meaning of Tiananmen has emerged, one that challenges the mainstream version while putting Friedmanism at the heart of the story. This alternative narrative is being advanced by, among others, Wang Hui, one of the organizers of the 1989 protests, and now a leading Chinese intellectual of what is known as China's "New Left." In his 2003 book, *China's New Order*, Wang explains that the protesters spanned a huge range of Chinese society—not just elite university students but also factory workers, small entrepreneurs and teachers. What ignited the protests, he recalls, was popular discontent in the face of Deng's "revolutionary" economic changes, which were lowering wages, raising prices and causing "a crisis of layoffs and unemployment." According to Wang, "These changes were the catalyst for the 1989 social mobilization."

The demonstrations were not against economic reform per se; they were against the specific Friedmanite nature of the reforms—their speed, ruthlessness and the fact that the process was highly antidemocratic. Wang says that the protesters' call for elections and free speech were intimately connected to this economic dissent. What drove the demand for democracy was the fact that the party was pushing through changes that were revolutionary in scope, entirely without popular consent. There was, he writes, "a general request for democratic means to supervise the fairness of the reform process and the reorganization of social benefits."

These demands forced the Politburo to make a definite choice. The choice was not, as was so often claimed, between democracy and Communism, or "reform" versus the "old guard." It was a more complex calculation: Should the party bulldoze ahead with its free-market agenda, which it could do only by rolling over the bodies of the protesters? Or should it bow to the protesters' demands for democracy, cede its monopoly on power and risk a major setback to the economic project?

Some of the free-market reformers within the party, most notably General Secretary Zhao Ziyang, appeared willing to gamble on democracy, convinced that economic and political reform could still be compatible. More powerful elements in the party were not willing to take the risk. The verdict came down: the state would protect its economic "reform" program by crushing the demonstrators.

That was the clear message when, on May 20, 1989, the government of the People's Republic of China declared martial law. On June 3, the tanks of the People's Liberation Army rolled into the protests, shooting indiscriminately into the crowds. Soldiers stormed onto buses where student demonstrators were taking cover and beat them with sticks; more troops broke through the barricades protecting Tiananmen Square, where students had erected a Goddess of Democracy statue, and rounded up the organizers. Similar crackdowns took place simultaneously across the country.

There will never be reliable estimates for how many people were killed and injured in those days. The party admits to hundreds, and eyewitness reports at the time put the number of dead at between two thousand and seven thousand and the number of injured as high as thirty thousand. The protests were followed by a national witch hunt against all regime critics and opponents. Some forty thousand were arrested, thousands were jailed and many—possibly hundreds—were executed. As in Latin America, the government reserved its harshest repression for the factory workers, who represented the most direct threat to deregulated capitalism. "Most of those arrested, and virtually all who were executed, were workers. With the obvious aim of terrorizing the population, it became a well-publicized policy to systematically subject arrested individuals to beatings and torture," writes Maurice Meisner.

For the most part, the massacre was covered in the Western press as another example of Communist brutality: just as Mao had wiped out his opponents during the Cultural Revolution, now Deng, "the Butcher of Beijing," crushed his critics under the watchful eye of Mao's giant portrait. A *Wall Street Journal* headline claimed that "China's Harsh Actions Threaten to Set Back [the] 10-Year Reform Drive"—as if Deng was an enemy of those reforms and not their most committed defender, determined to take them into bold new territory.

Five days after the bloody crackdown, Deng addressed the nation and made it perfectly clear that it wasn't Communism he was protecting with his crackdown, but capitalism. After dismissing the protesters as "a large quantity of the dregs of society," China's president reaffirmed the party's commitment to economic shock therapy. "In a word, this was a test, and we passed," Deng said, adding, "Perhaps this bad thing will enable us to go ahead with reform and the open-door policy at a more steady, better, even a faster pace. ... We haven't been wrong. There's nothing wrong with the four cardinal principles [of economic reform]. If there is anything amiss, it's that these principles haven't been thoroughly implemented."[5]

Orville Schell, a China scholar and journalist, summarized Deng Xiaopings choice: "After the massacre of 1989, he in effect said we will not stop economic reform; we will in effect halt political reform."

For Deng and the rest of the Politburo, the free-market possibilities were now limitless. Just as Pinochet's terror had cleared the streets for revolutionary change, so Tiananmen paved the way for a radical transformation free from fear of rebellion. If life grew harder for peasants and workers, they would either have to accept it quietly or face the wrath of the army and the secret police. And so, with the public in a state of raw terror, Deng rammed through his most sweeping reforms yet.

Before Tiananmen, he had been forced to ease off some of the more painful measures; three months after the massacre, he brought them back, and he implemented several of Friedman's other recommendations, including price deregulation. For Wang Hui, there is an obvious reason why "market reforms that had failed to be implemented in the late 1980s just happened to have been completed in the post-1989 environment"; the reason, he writes, "is that the violence of 1989 served to check the social upheaval brought about by this process, and the new pricing system finally took shape." The shock of the massacre, in other words, made shock therapy possible.

In the three years immediately following the bloodbath, China was cracked open to foreign investment, with special export zones constructed throughout the country. As he announced these new initiatives, Deng reminded the country that "if necessary, every possible means will be adopted to eliminate any turmoil in the future as soon as it has appeared. Martial law, or even more severe methods, may be introduced."[6]

It was this wave of reforms that turned China into the sweatshop of the world, the preferred location for contract factories for virtually every multinational on the planet. No country offered more lucrative conditions than China: low taxes and tariffs, corruptible officials and, most of all, a plentiful low-wage workforce that, for many years, would be unwilling to risk demanding decent

5 Deng had some notable defenders. After the massacre, Henry Kissinger wrote an op-ed arguing that the party had no choice. "No government in the world would have tolerated having the main square of its capital occupied for eight weeks by tens of thousands of demonstrators. ... A crackdown was therefore inevitable."

6 As the New York University anthropologist David Harvey notes, it was only after Tiananmen, when Deng went on his famous "southern tour" of China, "that the full force of the central government was put behind the opening to foreign trade and foreign direct investment."

salaries or the most basic workplace protections for fear of the most violent reprisals.

For foreign investors and the party, it has been a win-win arrangement. According to a 2006 study, 90 percent of China's billionaires (calculated in Chinese yuan) are the children of Communist Party officials. Roughly twenty-nine hundred of these party scions—known as "the princelings"—control $260 billion. It is a mirror of the corporatist state first pioneered in Chile under Pinochet; a revolving door between corporate and political elites who combine their power to eliminate workers as an organized political force. Today, this collaborative arrangement can be seen in the way that foreign multinational media and technology companies help the Chinese state to spy on its citizens, and to make sure that when students do Web searches on phrases like "Tiananmen Square Massacre," or even "democracy," no documents turn up. "The creation of today's market society was not the result of a sequence of spontaneous events," writes Wang Hui, "but rather of state interference and violence."

One of the truths revealed by Tiananmen was the stark similarity between the tactics of authoritarian Communism and Chicago School capitalism—a shared willingness to disappear opponents, to blank the slate of all resistance and begin anew.

Despite the fact that the massacre happened just months after he had encouraged Chinese officials to push forward with painful and unpopular free-market policies, Friedman never did face "an avalanche of protests for having been willing to give advice to so evil a government." And as usual, he saw no connection between the advice he had given and the violence required to enforce it. While condemning China's use of repression, Friedman continued to hold it up as an example of "the efficacy of free-market arrangements in promoting both prosperity and freedom."

In a strange coincidence, the Tiananmen Square massacre took place on the same day as Solidarity's historic election sweep in Poland—June 4, 1989. They were, in a way, two very different studies in the shock doctrine. Both countries had needed to exploit shock and fear to push through a free-market transformation. In China, where the state used the gloves-off methods of terror, torture and assassination, the result was, from a market perspective, an unqualified success. In Poland, where only the shock of economic crisis and rapid change were harnessed—and there was no overt violence—the effects of the shock eventually wore off, and the results were far more ambiguous.

In Poland, shock therapy may have been imposed after elections, but it made a mockery of the democratic process since it directly conflicted with the wishes of the overwhelming majority of voters who had cast their ballots for Solidarity. As late as 1992, 60 percent of Poles still opposed privatization for heavy industry. Defending his unpopular actions, Sachs claimed he had no choice, likening his role to that of a surgeon in an emergency room. "When a guy comes into the emergency room and his heart's stopped, you just rip open the sternum and you don't worry about the scars that you leave," he said. "The idea is to get the guy's heart beating again. And you make a bloody mess. But you don't have any choice."

But once Poles recovered from the initial surgery, they had questions about both the doctor and the treatment. Shock therapy in Poland did not cause "momentary dislocations," as Sachs had predicted. It caused a full-blown depression: a 30 percent reduction in industrial production in the two years after the first round of reforms. With government cutbacks and cheap imports flooding in, unemployment skyrocketed, and in 1993 it reached 25 percent in some areas—a wrenching change in a country that, under Communism, for all its many abuses and hardships, had no open joblessness. Even when the economy began growing again, high unemployment remained chronic. According to the World Bank's most recent figures, Poland has an unemployment rate of 20 percent—the highest in the European Union. For those under twenty-four, the situation is far worse: 40 percent of young workers were unemployed in 2006, twice the EU average. Most dramatic are the number of people in poverty: in 1989, 15 percent of Poland's population was living below the poverty line; in 2003, 59 percent of Poles had fallen below the line. Shock therapy, which eroded job protection and made daily life far more expensive, was not the route to Poland's becoming one of Europe's "normal" countries (with their strong labor laws and generous social benefits) but to the same gaping disparities that have accompanied the counterrevolution everywhere it has triumphed, from Chile to China.

The fact that it was Solidarity, the party built by Poland's blue-collar workers, that oversaw the creation of this permanent underclass represented a bitter betrayal, one that bred a deep cynicism and anger in the country that has never fully lifted. Solidarity's leaders often play down the party's socialist roots, with Walesa now claiming that as far back as 1980 he knew they would "have to build capitalism." Karol Modzelewski, a Solidarity militant and intellectual who spent eight and a half years in Communist jails, retorts angrily, "I wouldn't have spent a week nor a month, let alone eight and a half years in jail for capitalism!"

For the first year and a half of Solidarity rule, workers believed their heroes when they were assured that the pain was temporary, a necessary stop on the way to bringing Poland into modern Europe. Even in the face of soaring unemployment, they staged only a smattering of strikes and waited patiently for the therapeutic part of their shock therapy to take effect. When the promised recovery didn't arrive, at least not in the form of jobs, Solidarity's members were simply confused: How could their own movement have delivered a standard of living worse than that under Communism? "[Solidarity] defended me in 1980 when I set up a union committee," one forty-one-year-old construction worker said. "But when I went to them for help this time, they told me that I have to suffer for the sake of reform."

About eighteen months into Poland's period of "extraordinary politics," Solidarity's base had had enough and demanded an end to the experiment. The extreme dissatisfaction was reflected in a marked increase in the number of strikes: in 1990, when workers were still giving Solidarity a free pass, there were only 250 strikes; by 1992 there were more than 6,000 such protests. Faced with this pressure from below, the government was forced to slow down its more ambitious privatization plans. By the end of 1993—a year that saw almost 7,500 strikes—62 percent of Poland's total industry was still public.

The fact that Polish workers managed to stop the wholesale privatization of their country means that as painful as the reforms were, they could have been far worse. The wave of strikes unquestionably saved hundreds of thousands of jobs that would otherwise have been lost if these supposedly inefficient firms had been allowed to close or be radically downsized and sold off. Interestingly, Poland's economy began growing quickly in this same period, proving, according to the prominent Polish economist and former Solidarity member Tadeusz Kowalik, that those who were ready to write off the state firms as inefficient and archaic were "obviously wrong."

Besides going on strike, Polish workers found another way to express their anger with their one-time allies in Solidarity: they used the democracy they had fought for to punish the party decisively at the polls, including their once-beloved leader Lech Walesa. The most dramatic trouncing came on September 19, 1993, when a coalition of left parties, including the former ruling Communists (rebranded Democratic Left Alliance), won 66 percent of the seats in parliament. Solidarity had, by this time, splintered into warring factions. The trade union faction won less than 5 percent, losing official party status in the parliament, and a new party led by Mazowiecki, the prime minister, won just 10.6 percent—a resounding rejection of shock therapy.

Yet somehow, in the years to come, as dozens of countries struggled with how to reform their economies, the inconvenient details—the strikes, the election defeats, the policy reversals—would be lost. Instead, Poland would be held up as a model, proof that radical free-market makeovers can take place democratically and peacefully.

Like so many stories about countries in transition, this one was mostly a myth. But it was better than the truth: in Poland, democracy was used as a weapon against "free markets" on the streets and at the polls. Meanwhile in China, where the drive for free-wheeling capitalism rolled over democracy in Tiananmen Square, shock and terror unleashed one of the most lucrative and sustained investor booms in modern history. Another miracle born of a massacre.

Engaging Social Change by Embracing Diversity

Resisting Homelessness

Learning to Listen

SO WHAT DO WE DO NOW?

ENGAGING SOCIAL CHANGE BY EMBRACING DIVERSITY

BY RASHAWN RAY

Individuals frequently say that race and ethnic relations is a depressing topic. Well unfortunately, the United States, like most parts of the world, has a sombering history with race. It is difficult to look at the history of the world and not acknowledge the pain our ugly relationship with race has caused. The important thing to remember is that although you may not discriminate against others or hold prejudice attitudes about certain race/ethnic groups, you still may be privileged, marginalized, or hindered by how race as a social structural force intersects with gender, class, education, crime, or employment to shape social interactions and life chances.

So the question that always remains is: What can we do about race and its consequences? The first thing is to acknowledge that race matters. Acknowledge how race privileges or constrains you. This is the same process that men should go through when acknowledging the privileges of maleness. Next, acknowledge how race infuses our language usage, media consumption, and interactions with others. After acknowledging the role of race in social life, you can then begin to learn more about how race functions on individual- and institutional-levels. Subsequently, you can start to hold others accountable for what they say and how they treat others. While it is difficult, we must hold our family members and friends accountable for what they say and do. Making simple statements such as, "That wasn't nice" or "I would appreciate it if you did not make statements like that around me" go a long way in changing the accepted culture about race and ethnic relations. For younger generations making statements such as, "That was so not cool" or "Stop stereotyping, it's not attractive or funny" work very well. Finally, you can take a more activist approach by getting involved in organizations and coalitions aimed to ameliorate systemic racial inequality.

One of the best ways to proceed on this journey is to engage diversity. As we have seen throughout this book, the racial/ethnic make-up of many countries around the world is changing. With these changes come more contact, group threat, and ethnic conflict. However, it is also a time for more harmonious interactions among individuals of diverse backgrounds. It is a time to learn, share, and practice tolerance by confronting the prejudices and biases that we have been socialized to accept.

Race still plays a profound role in determining who is considered what, who has access to opportunities, who can acquire or obtain desirable skills for upward mobility, and who can pass certain resources on to the next generation. As Cornel West's (1993) title asserts, *Race Matters*. However, things are changing. The election of Barack Obama as the 44th U.S. President is a testament to progress. Although many individuals around the world applauded, most countries have yet to elect racial/ethnic minorities in their own countries to high-ranking political positions. Altogether, race is no longer a Black/White issue. In this context, Du Bois' (1903) prophetic statement—"The problem of the 20th century is the problem of the color line"—may be more profound now than ever before.

Rashawn Ray, "Engaging Social Change by Embracing Diversity," *Race and Ethnic Relations in the 21st Century: History, Theory, Institutions & Policy*, ed. Rashawn Ray, pp. 383-389. Copyright © 2010 by Rashawn Ray.

This text has aimed to outline the conceptual meaning of race, ethnicity, and racism and discuss the main explanations regarding the socioeconomic divide among racial/ethnic groups. I hope it contributes to providing a baseline for incorporating a much needed positive, beneficial, and constructive discourse on race and ethnic relations in social life. Part IV of the anthology—Confronting the Pipeline: Social Policy Issues—focuses on ways to ameliorate racial-based inequalities through social policies and micro-level forms of social change including mentorship and social activism.

Katznelson's (2006) *When Affirmative Action was White: An Untold History of Racial Inequality in the Twentieth-Century America* provides a chilling historical account of the institutional biases ingrained in New Deal and Fair Deal policies such as Social Security and the GI Bill that privileged Whites while denying many Blacks the same access to resources and opportunities. In this anthology, I include an article highlighting many of the major findings and arguments from his book. Below I discuss some of the lingering consequences of the institutional biases of social policies, the triumphs of progress, and perceptions of these race-based policies.

Race-Based Social Policies: Consequences, Triumphs, and Perceptions

There are many misconceptions centering on social policies such as affirmative action and welfare. A personal story is fitting here. I have a very close friend who is a firefighter. A few years ago his station hired a Black fire chief. He called me stating that the new chief received the position due to affirmative action and that he did not deserve the promotion. He also remarked that some of his fellow colleagues were extremely disgruntled at his accusations and the accusations of others. I asked my friend what is his definition of affirmative action. He stated that affirmative action is allowing Blacks and other minorities to get positions they did not earn or have the credentials for. After explaining to him the actual definition of affirmative action (which I discuss below), I then asked him if he actually looked at his new chief's credentials and resume. My friend replied no. I asked him to do that. A week or so later my friend called and said he has so much respect for his new chief. He said that his credentials were so exceptional he wonders how the new chief did not get a promotion 10 years ago. We then had a very productive discussion about the persistent pipeline of institutional racism (as discussed in Part III of this anthology).

The reason I tell this story is not necessarily because it had a "happy ending" for affirmative action but to highlight the constructive conversation that my friend and I had as a White person and a Black person engaging in a healthy discussion about a contentious topic such as affirmative action. Unfortunately, most people do not engage in these types of discussions across racial/ethnic groups. Therefore, we make assumptions about what others think and why they think it without ever engaging in a healthy conversation. Asking a simple question can tell you so much.

So ask yourself, what is your personal stance on issues such as affirmative action and welfare? Do you know the actual meaning and stipulations of these policies? Do you know when or why these policies were devised? Since Katznelson (2006) goes into much detail about these policies, I will briefly underscore some key parts of his article.

Affirmative Action is defined as the policies and/or programs that seek to rectify past discrimination through active measures to ensure equal opportunity. According to Katznelson, "Affirmative action performs acts of corrective justice. Public policy is used to compensate members of a deprived group for prior losses and for gains unfairly achieved by others that resulted from prior government action." (2006: 556). Corrective justice "identifies interventions that remedy previously unjust decisions that made existing patterns of distribution even more unfair than they otherwise would have been." (Katznelson 2006: 556). Although we are talking about affirmative action in the context of race, affirmative action policies also extend to include gender, nationality, and mental and physical disabilities. Affirmative action is often reduced down to issues about race when it is much broader than that.

In the United States, affirmative action mostly occurs at life course transitional stages such as enrolling in school or applying for jobs. As has been discussed in this anthology, education (Lewis 2010), employment (Bertrand and Mullainathan

2004; Pager 2004), and mortgage loans (Sewell 2010) have all been susceptible to personal, legal, and institutional discrimination against minority groups. When implemented correctly, affirmative action is put in place to open doors that would normally be closed to minorities. To use Sewell's (2010) analogy, affirmative action allows for everyone to have the opportunity to eat *a la carte* and have similar life option menus. In short, affirmative action simply allows for qualified individuals to knock on the door and potentially sit at the table.

The 1960s is usually where scholars start the discussion regarding affirmative action. As we know, the early 1960s is when individuals, in and outside of the U.S., realized that Blacks were still experiencing blatant forms of discrimination including public lynchings and beatings. Following *Brown v. Board of Education* and the Voting Rights Act of 1965, America started aiming to function as if it was a race-neutral society. However, as Katznelson asserts, racial neutrality included historical and current forms of White privilege.

In 1961, President John F. Kennedy used affirmative action for the first time by instructing federal contractors to take "affirmative action to ensure that applicants are treated equally without regard to race, color, religion, sex, or national origin." Following President Kennedy's assassination in 1963, President Lyndon B. Johnson continued Kennedy's executive order by legislating the Civil Rights Act of 1964. The Civil Rights Act of 1964 was the landmark legislation that reversed Jim Crow laws by outlawing segregation in schools and public places. It was implemented to establish precedence that individuals should be treated like normal human beings.

President Johnson's Executive Order is as follows:

> "To enforce the constitutional right to vote, to confer jurisdiction upon the district courts of the United States to provide relief against discrimination in public accommodations, to authorize the Attorney General to institute suits to protect constitutional rights in public facilities and public education, to extend the Commission on Civil Rights, to prevent discrimination in federally assisted programs, to establish a Commission on Equal Employment Opportunity, and for other purposes."

Why Was Affirmative Action Needed?

As Katznelson argues, President Roosevelt's New Deal helped to create the White middle class we see today. Social Security is arguably the most influential and long-lasting social policy in American history. Likewise, the GI Bill is still one of the largest federal initiatives in U.S. history allocating over $95 billion to military soldiers from the early 1940s to the 1970s. While these legislations did not explicitly give privileges to Whites on the basis of race, they excluded Blacks and other minorities in specific strategic ways. For example, legislation that allocated Social Security, set minimum wages, regulated work hours, and established unions did not include professions that were highly represented by Blacks such as farm and domestic work. As a result, over 60 percent of the Black labor force in the 1930s and nearly 75 percent of the Black workers in the South were excluded from these legislations. Additionally, federal funds for assisting the poor and supporting veterans were controlled by local officials who frequently discriminated against Blacks. Consequently, funds were normally only provided to Whites to obtain well-paying jobs, establish economic security, ensure retirement, and build wealth. Katznelson (2006: 547) contends this created a form of "policy apartheid" that mainly benefited Whites.

Although Aid to Dependent Children (ADC), which is commonly known as welfare, was established for families that generally had one parent or caretaker, funds were still withheld from Black families who qualified (Edin and Lein 1997). In fact, about one-third of the Black children who qualified for ADC went without assistance. In the 1940s, Texas, Kentucky, and Mississippi did not participate at all, so children in these states did not receive assistance. Regarding assistance to the elderly, Blacks in the South, compared to the North, received only half of the assistance they qualified for. Concerning unemployment, it did not cover domestic and farm workers, left the funds in control of states, and required that individuals already be working to qualify.

The GI Bill (Servicemen's Readjustment Act of 1944) aimed to reintegrate veterans returning from war. The GI Bill impacted eight out of 10 men born during the 1920s; roughly 80 percent of men who were in their 30s with families in the 1950s. From these funds, millions of families were able to purchase homes, start business ventures, and send themselves and their children to college. For Black veterans, it was a different story. The GI Bill was distributed federally but controlled locally. As a result, Black veterans, particularly in the South, were not allocated GI Bill funds in the same way as Whites.

This brings up an interesting aside. Individuals wonder about the creation and sustainability of Historical Black Colleges and Universities (HBCUs). Of the Black veterans who did receive funds, 95 percent of them attended HBCUs because they were prohibited from attending Predominately White Institutions (PWIs). Although Blacks represented about 25 percent of the population in the South, only 15 percent of the schools were available to them. These schools were not large universities or smaller, elite colleges. Instead, these schools were very small with half enrolling less than 250 students and 90 percent enrolling less than 1,000 students. Furthermore, less than 5 percent of HBCUs were accredited and none of the schools offered a Ph.D. program. While some of the more prominent HBCUs such as Morehouse, Spelman, Xavier, Fisk, Hampton, and Howard are surviving, other HBCUs continue to falter. Some HBCUs, however, such as Tennessee State University and South Carolina State University have become state schools. At these universities, Whites qualify for minority scholarships.

The Employment of Affirmative Action

When President Johnson issued the executive order for job opportunities to be expanded to minorities, most of the favorable forms of affirmative action initiatives at the time included quota and point systems. However, these forms of affirmative action came under serious criticism. Although these forms are in limited use today, most individuals who oppose affirmative action do so because they believe Whites are being discriminated against due to minorities being allocated spots not accessible to Whites. The *Grutter v. Bollinger* (2003, also known as the University of Michigan Law School case) and the *Regents of the University of California v. Bakke* (1978) cases have received much publicity and played a profound role in shaping public opinion about affirmative action (see Brown 2004; Wilkenfeld 2004; Pollack 2005; Bankston 2006). While there is much to discuss in regards to the details of these important cases, two key components are noteworthy. First, the Supreme Court ruled that diversity is important and beneficial to the healthy development of individuals, companies, and social institutions such as schools. Second, in both cases (roughly 25 years apart) the majority judges stated that hopefully in twenty-five years discrimination will be a thing of the past and racial preferences will no longer be necessary.

What also should be noted is that discrimination cases based on unjust treatment due to the employment of race-based programs are just as likely to be won by Whites as they are by minorities (Katznelson 2006). It is also important to pay attention to the language used for affirmative action legislation. Although legislation places individuals into categories by race, gender, age, sexual orientation, or disability, court cases are generally on an individual basis. In turn, policies for the group can be upheld while making allowances for individuals. For example, Bakke was permitted to enter medical school in California although race could still be used as a factor in admission policies. Furthermore, while affirmative action is legislated federally, it is frequently institutionalized and enforced locally. Therefore, it is important to check the rules and bylaws for a specific school or company.

Perceptions of Race-Based Social Policies

Whites are normally more opposed to race-based policies than other racial groups (see Bobo 2001 in this anthology). Mazzocco and colleagues (2006) conducted a survey-based experiment with 958 Whites to determine the answer to one central question: "How much should you be paid to continue to live the rest of your life as a Black person?" Most respondents replied less than $10,000. In contrast, study participants stated that they would have to be paid about $1 million to give up T.V. This finding implies one of two propositions: 1) Whites think that being Black is not that big of a deal so why should anyone receive compensation for it; or 2) being Black is not worth much. Furthermore, Mahzarin Banaji, a co-investigator on the project, found that nine out of 10 Whites reject proposals for reparations. Mazzocco and colleagues assert that most Whites are not conscious of the persisting forms of racial discrimination and disparities that exist in America.

To test the propositions noted above, these researchers posed the central research question in a few different ways. First, after being told the income disparities between Blacks and Whites, White participants requested roughly $500,000 to be Black, compared to the less than $10,000 originally requested. Second, the study participants were asked to imagine a fictitious country called Atria where individuals were born either to the "majority" group or the "minority" group. Upon given a list of disadvantages of the minority group in Atria, White study participants requested an average of $1 million. What should be noted is that Atria is actually America. The majority group characteristics are current White characteristics, while the minority group characteristics are current Black characteristics. This survey-based experiment can be administered to students to help individuals objectively view the racial disparities that exist in America.

In regards to welfare, Edin and Lein (1997) conducted interviews with roughly 400 single mothers in four cities including Boston, Chicago, Charleston, and San Antonio. They wanted to know if single mothers fair better on or off welfare. Disproving a majority of the cultural theories about welfare mothers, Edin and Lein actually find that these women are more careful with the money they acquire. Although this study was not directly about race, it has huge racial implications based on the perceptions of welfare mothers as Black and lazy. Edin and Lein find that women of all races employ similar strategies for survival and that Black women are actually more frugal with their money. This means that social policies that allow welfare recipients to generate assets are desired among single mothers, despite perceptions to the contrary.

Solutions to Racial Inequality

So, where should solutions for racial inequality go from here? Aligning with President Johnson's and Supreme Court Justice Powell's perspective, Katznelson (2006) states that two conditions should be met to warrant affirmative action enactment. First, there must be a clear and concise connection between the affirmative action remedies and historical inequalities. Second, since a color-blind society is desirable, remedies that do not exclusively include race/ethnicity should be initially sought out. For example, universities such as UCLA are starting to view applicants in a holistic fashion by privileging the pluralism of their experiences and background beyond their GPA and test scores.

Oliver and Shapiro ([1995] 2006) assert that ending familial poverty begins by assisting individuals from the bottom up, and not just those who are perceived as the most upwardly mobile. They assert the government should focus on four essential programs including: 1) asset generation for welfare recipients to move from dependency to self-sufficiency; 2) start-up business grants; 3) nontaxable education asset accounts for four year institutions; and 4) renter and homeowner tax credits. Over the past couple of decades, government programs have focused on these issues.

In addition to these macro-level solutions to racial inequality, it is imperative that a discourse be established in the classroom and in social settings to discuss race and ethnic relations candidly. If we do not, similar to how gender is considered by some as a "women only problem" or sexuality is referred to as a "gay only problem," individuals will continue to view race as a "Black or minority only problem." On a trip to Chicago, I met a doctor who recently moved to an urban area on the East Coast. He remarked that he needed to increase his clientele so he decided to visit churches. Some of his fellow doctors were baffled by the target areas. Because certain markets were perceived to be saturated, this White doctor decided to visit Black churches. He stated that church members were very welcoming and many stated that a White person, nonetheless a physician, had never ventured into their sanctuary. The doctor remarked that he not only increased his clientele but has made several new friends that he has much in common with, engaged in more healthy conversations about race than he did in his previous 35 plus years of life, and had gotten many Blacks to schedule an appointment who had not been to the doctor in years due to previous forms of mistreatment in medical settings. As Jackman and Crane (1986) contend, the quality and quantity of contact across racial/ethnic groups assist in reducing stereotypes and prejudice attitudes. As Mauro and Robertson's (2010) chapter puts forth, everyone can do something to engage social change and embrace diversity, no matter how small or large. It starts with a simple conversation.

Supplemental Readings and Resources

Bankston, Carl. 2006. "*Grutter v. Bollinger*: Weak Foundations?" *Ohio State Law Journal* 67: 1–13.

Brown, Kevin D. 2004. "After *Grutter V. Bollinger*—Revisiting the Desegregation Era from the Perspective of the Post-Desegregation Era." *Constitutional Commentary* 21: 41.

Edin, Kathryn and Laura Lein. 1997. *Making Ends Meet: How Single Mothers Survive Welfare And Low-Wage Work*. New York: Russell Sage Foundation.

Jackman, Mary R. and Marie Crane. 1986. "Some of My Best Friends Are Black ... ": Interracial Friendships and Whites' Racial Attitudes." *The Public Opinion Quarterly* 50: 459–486.

Johnson, Jacqueline, Sharon Rush, and Joe Feagin. 2000. "Reducing Inequalities: Doing Anti-Racism: Toward an Egalitarian American Society." *Contemporary Sociology, Special Issue: Utopian Visions: Engaged Sociologies for the 21st Century* 9: 95–110.

Katznelson, Ira. 2006. *When Affirmative Action was White: An Untold History of Racial Inequality in the Twentieth-Century America*. New York. Norton.

Mazzocco, Philip J and et al. 2006. "The Cost of Being Black: White Americans Perceptions and the Question of Reparations." *Du Bois Review* 3: 261–297.

Pollak, Louis H. 2005. "Race, law & history: the Supreme Court from *Dred Scott* to *Grutter v. Bollinger*". *Dædalus* 134: 29–41.

Peffley, Mark, Jon Hurwitz, and Paul M. Sniderman. "Racial Stereotypes and Whites' Political Views of Blacks in the Context of Welfare and Crime." *American Journal of Political Science* 41: 30–60.

Thomas, Susan L. 1997. "Women, Welfare, Reform and the Preservation of a Myth." *The Social Science Journals* 34: 351–368.

Wilkenfeld, Joshua. 2004. "Newly Compelling: Reexamining Judicial Construction of Juries in the Aftermath of *Grutter v. Bollinger*." *Columbia Law Review* 104: 2291–2327.

RESISTING HOMELESSNESS

Global, National, and Local Solutions

BY J. TALMADGE WRIGHT

Introduction

The increase in numbers of people without homes both nationally and internationally reflects the deep neglect of basic human needs within modern capitalist society—a "social indicator" marking the decline of the welfare state and the rise of monetarist neoliberal economic strategies (Teeple 1995). Homelessness will end only with the widespread recognition that all societies have a responsibility to provide their citizens with decent and affordable housing, excellent health care, stable, meaningful, and well-paid employment, and freedom from arbitrary exercise of state and private authority—and when these are implemented. Ending homelessness is about creating a truly democratic human society beyond the barbarism of the current stock of social inequalities and economic and political violence.

First, I comment briefly on the increase in those living without homes both in the United States and internationally. Second, I examine how the prevalent ways of thinking have led to confusing effects with causes, and suggest other ways to think about the problem of homelessness. Third, I introduce a theoretical argument that attempts to integrate this apparent diversity of causes. Briefly, my argument asserts that the combination of rapid integration and monopolization of transnational corporations (TNCs) and the application of neoliberal economic policies of deregulation, privatization, and imposed financial austerity measures, privileges finance capital and accelerates the accumulation of capital at the expense of working families and the poor, locally (city), nationally, and internationally. These privileges, in turn, generate international, national, and local (city) extremes of social inequalities, putting populations at risk of losing their shelter. Fourth, I examine possible solutions. I have broken down these solutions into global, national, and local (city) levels, with the understanding that global solutions will be carried out at the national and local level, and across national boundaries. Given the limited scope of this essay, most of my solutions are designed for the United States.

Descriptive Trends

Since the 1980s, when people without homes first engaged the public consciousness, the poor have grown poorer and have included more women with children, and higher numbers of African Americans and Latinos. Without debating definitional problems of what homelessness is, I will simply note that most studies indicate that people without homes come predominantly from the bottom 20 percent of the population, from the ranks of the very poor. As Hopper and Milburn (1996) and Baker (1994) have observed, most of the urban homeless tend to be African American, Latino, and Native American, those segments of the population overrepresented among the poor. From the 1990 count of homeless persons conducted by the U.S. Bureau of

J. Talmadge Wright, "Resisting Homelessness: Global, National, and Local Solutions," *Contemporary Sociology*, vol. 29, no. 1, pp. 27-43. Copyright © 2000 by Sage Publications. Reprinted with permission.

the Census, African Americans make up close to half of families without homes (54%) and over one-third of individuals without homes living on the streets (Hopper and Milburn 1996:123). Given that people of color are disproportionately represented within the ranks of the poor and very poor, it is not surprising to find such a representation among those living without shelter. It is generally agreed that approximately one-quarter to one-third of people living on the street have some kind of serious mental disability, and a higher percentage suffer from substance abuse. Attributing these descriptors of disability to causes, however, is problematic (Snow, Baker, Anderson, and Martin 1986). While the figures vary depending upon which study one wishes to quote, it is generally acknowledged that approximately 60 to 70 percent of those without shelter are single males and approximately 30 percent are women with children. Of the latter group, children and youth comprise a growing category of the homeless population. While most of the shelter population is comprised of single women and children, most of those living on the streets are single males.

Studies conducted in the 1980s used widely inflated estimates, in the millions, to dramatize the nature and scope of people without shelter. However, the U.S. Bureau of Census, in a deeply flawed study, came up with a figure of about 200,000 unhoused people in 1990. Since counting the numbers of people who are actually homeless is a major methodological challenge, it is safer to use the estimates of increased shelter and food bank use as well as homeless episodes. Most people who experience a loss of housing do so occasionally, existing at or near the poverty level. This segment of the population moves in and out of homelessness depending upon the state of the economy and the availability of resources. From 1985 through 1990, over 5.7 million people reported having episodes of homelessness (Link, Susser, Sueve, and Phelan 1994:1907); 26 million people are estimated to have experienced times without shelter over their lifetime in the United States. Wolch and Dear (1993:32) estimated that between 840,000 and 1 million people experienced episodes of homelessness in 1991 alone. If we look at shelter requests, what is clear is the steady increase of demand for needed homeless services over the past two decades. In 1998, requests for emergency shelter increased by an average of 11 percent from 1997, in 72 percent of the 30 major cities surveyed by the U.S. Conference of Mayors (1999). Twenty-six percent of the requests for shelter were denied. Due to a lack of resources, 67 percent of the cities surveyed had to turn away families and individuals who had no shelter, at a time when the number of shelter beds in the surveyed cities remained constant and transitional housing units increased by only 11 percent. City officials identified lack of affordable housing as the lead cause of homelessness.

Declining incomes for the bottom 20 percent of the population, the decline in the absolute numbers of low-income housing relative to the need, and an impoverished community-based health care system define the immediate context of homelessness not only in the United States (Shinn and Gillespie 1994) but increasingly worldwide. According to the United Nations Center for Human Settlements, 40 million people were estimated to be without shelter globally during the 1980s (Bingham, Green, and White 1987). In 1996, the Habitat II conference held in Istanbul, Turkey, estimated that the numbers of people without homes had increased worldwide to 100 million, with over one billion people suffering from inadequate shelter. The fall of the Soviet Union and the rise of a market economy in Russia witnessed an increase in people living on the streets. In Germany families looking for shelter often live under bridges, in tents, and in squatter camps. Glasser (1994:89) estimated that in Cologne 45,000 people were living in emergency shelters. Mayer (1996:15) documented 15 housing encampments each containing about 300 people in and around Berlin. In Japan, single men without a fixed residence live in the tunnels of Tokyo, often suffering from some variation of mental illness or substance abuse. Even in a country with a very high social wage such as Sweden, social housing authorities have worked to exclude people rendered homeless by the open housing market when those people are perceived as costly, where "costs ... exceed the possible revenue from rents" (Sahlin 1997:151). While the Netherlands claims an unhoused population estimated at between 17,500 and 34,000, the causes have often been attributed to traditional forms of disaffiliation, such as substance abuse and loss of family supports. However, Deben and Greshof (1997) argue that the move toward increasing urban gentrification, the reduction of government subsidies for social housing, and the influx of immigrants without adequate income guarantees will expand the ranks of the homeless, converting a problem of disabilities into one of poverty. The numbers of people without shelter are even higher in developing countries, such as Brazil (Burns 1987) and Mexico, that have embraced "free" market economies.

The initial policy response by the United States and other countries to the expanding numbers of people losing their homes was to expand emergency services such as shelters and food banks. In the United States, the passage of the Stewart B. McKinney Homeless Assistance Act in 1987 guaranteed that federal support would be forthcoming for homeless services; fiscal support increased from $180 million in 1987 to almost $1.8 billion in 1994. When this did not reduce the numbers of people living without shelter, elite attitudes hardened. This has forced a more punitive response from local politicians and policy makers, criminalization (National Law Center on Homelessness and Poverty 1999; Barak 1992: 75–99; Stoner 1995; Fischer 1992), and containment. Discouraging loitering in public places, anti-camping and anti-panhandling ordinances, and arrests or detention for "quality of life" crimes are complemented by the attempt to contain homeless persons in institutional shelters and facilities—out of sight of the general public, especially the tourist trade. Shelters have implemented widespread regulations and sanctioning systems, not unlike TANF (Temporary Assistance for Needy Families) regulations. As more and more people living in the streets are arrested for violating local panhandling or camping ordinances or harassed into hiding in remote areas of a city, their disappearance from tourist areas and other public spaces creates the illusion that homelessness as a social problem is ending.

Harassment, arrest, and incarceration can be used, therefore, to back up city and state policies of removing people who lack shelter from public places when police sweeps fail. This points to a disturbing trend of using prisons and shelters as the housing of last resort for the very poor, but specifically poor people of color. With 1.63 million people incarcerated throughout the United States in 1996, a large increase from the 1980s, Western (1999:1031) argues that criminal justice policies have led to "a sizable, nonmarket reallocation of labor, overshadowing state intervention through social policy." Incarceration is most frequent for African-American men, who make up 51 percent of the prison population. Headley (1990–91) sees the increased incarceration of African-American men, homeless or otherwise, as a consequence of deindustrialization and job relocation by industries seeking to increase capital accumulation by moving to low-wage areas and non-union states.

Conceptualizing Causes: Individual, Social-Structural, Political-Economic

Developing solutions to shelter people depends upon our understanding of the causes of homelessness. Historically, discussion about the causes and effects of, and solutions to, homelessness has revolved around the differences between individual causes, normally attributed to deficits in individual character or ability, and social-structural causes, attributed to the lack of human services, affordable housing, and adequate income. A third, more productive route is to examine the interactions between individual "causes" and social-structural causes, and how those interactions fit within wider political-economic struggles for capital accumulation and racial privilege. The struggle to understand homelessness as more than an individual deficit or a lack of housing involves understanding the context of social, economic, and political power within which homelessness emerges. Therefore we must distinguish between proximate and ultimate causes (Wright, Rubin, and Devine 1998: 9).

Individual—Proximate Causes?

Koegel, Burnam, and Baumohl (1996) marked one set of explanatory "causes," those defined by a personal limitation—what we could define as proximate causes. Mental illness, substance abuse, inability to sustain relationships, and other individual factors make up this "cause" in explaining homelessness. While conservatives use a religious/moral framework to invite homeless people to repent of their sins, a liberal perspective built on these "causes" treats homeless people as victims in need of treatment, and therefore works to promote better rehabilitation programs and community care networks (Koegel, Burnam, and Baumohl 1996:25). Reducing the causes of homelessness to individual behavior or visible characteristics allows conservatives to claim that people without shelter choose to live on the streets because they lack the motivation and will to compete successfully, and thus end up at the bottom of the social ladder. Quick to distinguish between housed and homeless persons, conservatives react to homeless people as crazy, free-loading, or troubled and dangerous characters needing police action to contain their movements (Barak 1992:54). Such a traditional position is most closely related to the social perceptions of the "hobo," "tramp," or "bum" that accompanied the 1930s Depression Era.

The "liberal" position views the personal defects of homeless people as treatable—more a disease than a moral or personal failing. Adopting a "medical" model, those who embrace this position are motivated by assisting individual homeless people. This charity model typically is embraced by shelter and service providers. The expansion of shelter services and other medical services are thought to provide the solution to homelessness—getting individual people back on their feet. "Lack of proper services, that is, caused the problem, and only more and better services will solve it" (Wright, Rubin, and Devine 1998:11). While the first position sees the problem as one of moral choice, the second position sees it as a treatable disease. In the second explanation, critical political-economic causes are supplanted by individualized "languages of disability" (Snow, Anderson, and Koegel 1994) oriented toward client treatment, and a "politics of compassion" (Hoch and Slayton 1989) that privileges charity and the gift relationship. Adherence to the standards of the gift relationship can then be used to mark those people without shelter who are "deserving" (women with children) from those who are "undeserving" (single adult males).

For the first position, punitive solutions are necessary to shape moral behavior and discourage "bad" behavior. For the second position, compassionate solutions are important because people can end up homeless through no fault of their own, but rather through the progression of an addiction. Wright, Rubin, and Devine call these two theories "homeless by choice" versus "inadequate services." Both of these positions, embraced by Baum and Burnes (1993), are refuted by Wright, Rubin, and Devine because they ignore the role of social-structural factors. These factors—the creation of increased poverty, concentrated in inner-city areas, the loss of housing and jobs, and the abandonment of the social safety net—suggest that "defects and dislocations of social structure … create a population at risk of homelessness; defects of persons determine who within the at-risk population actually becomes homeless" (Wright, Rubin, and Devine 1998:9). A causal model of analysis that focuses on personal defects, therefore, misleads us into pursuing the wrong solutions. "Analyses that focus on personal deficits of the homeless mistake the characteristics of people who are homeless for the causes of the homeless" (Wright, Rubin, and Devine 1998:6). This confusion creates problems in so far as the application of treatments or "solutions" designed to correct or help personal defects fail because the basic issues of social structural poverty, housing, and income are not addressed. The overemphasis on treatment for mental illness or substance abuse does not consider the heterogeneous nature of the homeless population—the fact that while rates of mental illness and substance abuse appear higher in this population than in the housed population, it does not follow that treatment for these deficits is all that is required to take people off the street.

Academic researchers, foundations, and advocates for the homeless encouraged the fragmentation of the very poor as a constituency into separate categories defined by special needs (homeless teenagers, homeless families, homeless Veterans, homeless HIV drug users, and the like). This individuation of "deserving" people (Hopper and Baumohl 1994; Katz 1989) without homes, who were understood as having a variety of social and personal deficits, was supported by an institutional funding agenda. This agenda emerged from the medical field and was supported by the National Institute of Mental Health. As Blasi has pointed out in a search of the literature, which produced 539 entries including 354 articles on homelessness, two-thirds of the articles appeared in journals devoted to psychiatry, psychology, and medicine, with five percent in journals on political economy, economics, or housing (1994:580). "American social science is embedded in a broader culture in which virtually all social phenomena—particularly those related to poverty—are seen as reflecting personal characteristics, personal choice, and personal failings" (Blasi 1994:581).

Social-Structural—Proximate Causes?

The second explanation is that "homelessness was caused by structural forces" (Koegel, Burnam, and Baumohl 1996:25), usually defined as a lack of low-cost housing or lack of income. Wright, Rubin, and Devine, refusing the individual causal model of personal defects, assert that homelessness is a result of a wide "variety of complex social system dislocations" (1998:4) that render large numbers of people at risk of losing their shelter. The three social-structural "causes" most often quoted as contributing to a loss of shelter are inadequate income, declining welfare services, and loss of housing.

Increasing Income Inequality and Poverty

For over two decades, the United States has experienced a growing population in poverty, a deepening of poverty, an increase in the duration of episodes of poverty, and increased spatial and social isolation of the poor (Wright, Rubin, and Devine 1998). Contrary to what one might expect in a growing economy, the overall poverty rate—declining only a small amount in 1998 to 13.3 percent from 13.7 percent in 1996—has concealed the extent to which the number of those living in poverty has increased from 29.2 million in 1980 to 36.5 million in 1996, an increase of 7.3 percent. In addition, the bottom fifth of the population, which commanded 5.4 percent of the total national income in 1970, has experienced a decline in income to 4.2 percent of the total national income in 1996. The upper fifth, by contrast, experienced a massive increase in their share of the total national income. This increasing impoverishment of the bottom fifth conceals the degree to which those in extreme poverty, those making less than 50 percent of the poverty wage, have experienced even more dramatic declines in fortunes. The economic vulnerability produced by these declining incomes increases the risk of homelessness.

Using various time measurements and calculations of poverty rates, Devine and Wright (1993) concluded that indeed the bottom fifth of the United States population has experienced longer and longer episodes of poverty corresponding to the declining shares of national income. The increasing spatial and social isolation of the poor, noted by researchers in the 1980s and into the present, reveals that the vast majority of the poor reside in inner-city areas, isolated from job markets and subjected to higher crime rates and substance abuse patterns within their neighborhoods. These communities consist predominantly of people of color, a feature that also characterizes most homeless individuals in urban areas. What has produced this drop in income and the expansion of the poor population at risk of losing shelter?

Reducing Government Support for the Poor

The end of welfare, trumpeted as a way of taking the poor off of federal dependency, is improving the lives of some of the poor while increasing the impoverishment of others. Before the 1996 Personal Responsibility and Work Opportunity Reconciliation Act was passed, support levels of the prior program, Aid to Families with Dependent Children (AFDC), were steadily declining around the country relative to the increasing consumer price index. Not surprisingly, therefore, poor families with children have made up an increasing portion of those without shelter. Although the average earnings and overall incomes of low-income female-headed families with children increased between 1993 and 1995, with an expansion of the economy, the incomes of the poorest 20 percent of these (2 million families, 6 million people) fell an average of $580 per family from 1995 to 1997, as welfare reform took hold. These families have incomes below three-quarters of the poverty line. Cutbacks in government cash and food assistance can explain this decline. Between 1995 and 1997, the number of people living in poverty declined only 3 percent while those receiving food stamps declined 17 percent. In 1995 some 88 percent of poor children received food stamps; in 1998 only 70 percent received food stamps. From 1995 to 1997 the number of people on AFDC and then TANF (Temporary Aid to Needy Families) declined by 3 million or 22.2 percent. Had the safety net programs been as effective in 1997 as in 1995, there would have been 700,000 fewer poor children. Reductions in benefits thus exceeded new family earnings (Primus, Rawlings, Larin, and Porter 1999).

While some welfare mothers did find jobs and moved off of welfare, others have languished, trapped in low-paying jobs with few benefits, and still others are waiting for any type of job. It is most probable that while such families may barely hold on during this time of economic expansion, given the inevitable recession we can expect these families and other poor individuals to flood the ranks of the homeless. While it is true that some people are pulling out of poverty as a result of economic expansion and the elevation of the minimum wage, many are working longer hours at lower-paying jobs just to stay in place. Given an economic downturn, these segments of the working poor will join the extreme poor in increasing rates of homelessness. The result of welfare reform among poor families is mixed. For some, the reform has temporarily lowered the risk of homelessness. For many others, remaining in poverty with few benefits marks them as at risk for an episode of homelessness.

Decreasing Affordable Housing

In addition to declining incomes and reduced government support, the picture of low-income housing looks quite bleak, at least in the short term. As the pool of national and global poor populations expands, the availability of low-income housing is simultaneously shrinking, creating an "affordability gap" (Shinn and Gillespie 1994; Dolbeare 1996). For example, the number of poor renters in the United States making less than $10,000 a year increased from 7.3 million in 1970 to 9.6 million in 1989. The number of affordable housing units declined by 14 percent during the same time period, to 5.5 million housing units, generating a shortfall of 4.1 million units (Timmer, Eitzen, and Talley 1994:19). According to a recent U.S. Department of Housing and Urban Development study, *The Widening Gap*, 372,000 affordable units available to those at 30 percent of the area median income were lost between 1991 and 1997 alone. Rents are increasing at twice the rate of general inflation. In 1998, rents increased 3.4 percent while the CPI increased a mere 1.7 percent. Between 1995 and 1997 the number of Americans making less than 30 percent of the area median income increased 3.1 percent, expanding from 8.61 million to 8.87 million. This is one out of four households. As indicated above, the growth of the bottom 20 percent of income groupings, and the poor population as a whole accelerated in the 1990s, as has the decline of low-income housing units relative to the need. Too many poor are chasing too few units. Unless incomes are raised sufficiently and rents are lowered, or both, this gap between incomes and housing availability is expected to grow into the next millennium.

Housing discrimination continues to mark the housing choices for both poor and middle-income African Americans. In a tight housing market, such discrimination guarantees that African Americans will have few positive choices and a disadvantage in competing for what limited affordable housing is available. African Americans as a group are still locked in segregated neighborhoods within urban areas, and increasingly in suburban areas, even while some cities and suburban areas have managed to overcome these barriers to integration (Massey and Denton 1988, 1993).

Besides the escalating cost of housing and the declining incomes of the poor, housing often associated with low-income populations, such as single-room occupancy hotels (SROs), has declined rapidly through gentrification of urban areas and condominium conversions that favor upper-income home buyers. Homeless shelters have come to replace the housing often associated with the Skid Rows of the past. Federal attempts to grapple with this decline in affordable housing have been weak and inadequate. While it is true that budget allocations have increased to cover Section 8 housing vouchers, the Stewart B. McKinney Funds for homeless support, and various other housing programs targeted at the poor, the rates of increase have declined and the growth of the problem has expanded far faster than government planning can accommodate. The problem stems from both the decision by the federal government to remove itself from constructing and financing new housing for the poor, and a wholesale abandonment to the private market to provide needed housing.

Unfortunately, most explanations of homelessness in the literature have fallen between these twin poles of personal deficits and social-structural causes. The opposition between these two explanations is a false one. In fact, as Koegel, Burnam, and Baumohl point out, "lives of all people, homeless or not, are embedded in circumstances shaped as much by structural factors as personal and biographical ones" (1996:26). Both the personal defect and social-structural models fall short because they remain detached from a critical analysis that could explain why those conditions have emerged in the first place. They don't ask the deeper questions: Why has income dropped for the very poor relative to other income classes? And why have government benefits been reduced and affordable housing lost relative to need for the past 20 years? An answer requires a causal explanation that understands loss of housing, income, and welfare services as effects of a more profound restructuring of capitalism induced by political elites working for their self-interest within a market economy—a restructuring that allocates greater benefits to the wealthy and privileged than to the poor, working, and middle classes. If workers are rendered vulnerable because of downsizing, and then start drinking, having family problems, and ending up on the street, is it the problem of the worker or the problem of why the downsizing occurred in the first place? Who benefits from and who pays for this arrangement of social power? And how do these benefits and liabilities manifest themselves?

Political Economic—Ultimate Causes?

Individual and social-structural causes as explanations for the expansion of homelessness can be subsumed under political-economic explanations, which incorporate a historical perspective, the role of culture and ideology, and the role of markets in capital accumulation. Barak (1992:6) explains that "homelessness as characteristic of the new poverty that emerged in the 1980s is a product of the transition from an industrial-based capitalist economy to a postindustrial capitalist service economy within the context of internationally developing global relations." The decline in average real wages, the reduction in health care, and the inability to secure adequate housing are part of a "national crisis of profitability and productivity" that emerged in the 1970s (Barak 1992:53). U.S. corporate capitalists responded to this crisis in capital accumulation with extensive layoffs of blue-collar workers in the 1980s and white-collar workers in the 1990s, accompanied by outsourcing, an acceleration of technological innovation in communications and computers, and overseas expansion (Blau 1992:33–47). With wages driven down, families had to work harder and longer to stay ahead, increasing family stress and fraying fragile social networks.

Other countries, such as Japan and Germany, with more advanced levels of political struggles and higher social wages, resisted the "American model." They have attempted to regain their margins of profitability and productivity by innovating technologically, expanding markets, subsidizing industry and education, retaining skilled workers, and importing immigrant workers, even while carrying on a limited privatization of state assets. However, even for these countries the American model has beckoned as their financial situations deteriorated and as elites have moved toward a market model of allocative efficiency.

Historically, in the tradition of Keynesian liberal politics, government spending in the United States was understood as the most efficient vehicle for addressing and correcting social ills produced by the market. Raising money for needed social programs through increased taxes and expanding social services was an important part of this vision of creating civility. Federal enforcement of anti-segregation laws, combined with the Civil Rights Movement, was essential in ending legal racial segregation. In California, the struggle of the United Farmworkers Union to create decent working conditions for farmworkers would not have been successful without the establishment of the state Agricultural Relations Board to enforce the new policies. Social movements for justice went hand in hand with an increased government commitment to helping the poor and to curb racist and sexist policies. However, with the stagnation of the 1970s economy, the conservative backlash against the movements of the 1960s, and the questioning of democracy by national elites, concern about ending poverty shifted to concern about lowering deficits and ending stagflation. The solution adopted by policy elites was to embrace neoliberal market ideologies privileging supply-side economics, deficit reduction, privatization, and social conservatism. Public attitudes sympathetic to reduced government spending and rationalizations for those reductions by political elites moved beyond the marginal right-wing political groups of the 1970s into mass acceptance in the 1990s, partly because of the attractiveness of these simplistic antistatist metaphors and allegories (Block 1996). Liberal government's attempts to help the poor, not poverty itself, were now redefined as the problem.

This effectively rationalized the cutbacks in welfare payments as "tough love." By assuming that the market could do a better job of providing housing and with the desire to reduce government budgets, new federal housing construction was the natural victim for federal budget cutters.

The dominant cultural ideology now shared by both major political parties in the United States relies upon the assumptions that spending on social welfare increases dependency and that "excessive" government intervention in markets and state regulation makes it difficult for businesses to stay competitive in a global marketplace. This ideology, strengthened by the "no new taxes" rebellion of the 1980s, undercut attempts to use government for social good. The "no new taxes" rebellion started in California with the passage of Proposition 13 in 1978 (Schrag 1999), and spread to other states in the 1980s. Coupled with the twin ideological concepts of deficit reduction and privatization of public services, the reduction of government services increased the misery of the poor while advancing the economy for the benefit of upper middle-class professionals and wealthy investors. According to Block (1996:166), attempts to reform the market by countering investor ideology could be neutralized effectively by the reactions of bond traders. Integrated global financial markets, high rates of social inequality and incarceration, and the violence of poverty directed into nationalist ambitions, racist and sexist attacks, and anti-immigrant fervors appear to define the negative side of this neo-Gilded Age. The globalization of financial markets, the ease of capital movements, and endless currency speculation have produced widespread pleasure for the few at the expense of the many, the disintegration of local controls, and a fragmentation of civil society (Bauman 1998).

The limitations of the individual and social-structural explanations are apparent. Deepening poverty and homelessness, decreasing amounts of low-income housing, and a failing health policy are the surface effects of a deeper cause: the success of the neoliberal market model of capitalism in transferring wealth and power to an expanded and consolidated global and national elite at the expense of the majority of U.S. citizens (Blau 1999). I don't want to give the impression that individual factors are not important, only that they constitute "nested" causes within social-structural causes, which are in turn nested within political-economic causes. Following this argument, it makes sense to support service providers and increased funding for detox centers and mental health treatment, while also supporting better-paying jobs, more low-cost housing, and comprehensive health care. But this support is best served within a broader struggle for human rights and economic democracy that tackles the deepening social inequality, globally and nationally, that can put individuals at risk.

Simply put, my argument is as follows: At the level of appearance, homelessness is about poverty and ill health. However, these conditions are created by the normal capitalist production of low-wage jobs, high housing costs, coupled with a reduction in social welfare benefits from states attempting to compete with one another over the price of labor and the costs of benefits. In addition, such capital strategies have always depended upon differences in racial/ethnic and gender privilege to operate for the advantage of the privileged. Social conditions have worsened since the 1970s as the dual class compromise between labor and capital has dissolved and been replaced by neoliberal ideologies that subject all international and national policies to the criteria of market "efficiency," the privileging of allocative as opposed to coordination efficiency (Block 1996:56).

Globally, the neoliberal model depends on the strengthening of international bodies that will foster free trade as well as trade agreements that allow for the free circulation of capital and commodities. Nationally, neoliberalism depends on the "hollowed out state" (Jessop 1994; Hirsch 1991) where budget deficits are reined in through privatization, deregulation, and social wage cutbacks. According to Devine (see Barak 1992:58), who operationalized the links between political economy and homelessness, economic development under neoliberalist policies lowers elite interest in helping the poor. Locally, cities are invested with "entrepreneurial" functions acting as an independent player in private-public partnerships (Mayer 1994; Wright 1997). These policy shifts have increased the vulnerability of the poor, with the abolishment of the safety net, medicalization and criminalization of the homeless, and the shifting of funds from the civil welfare state to the corporate welfare state. Citizen rights and capital responsibility via progressive taxation and an expanded social wage have been reversed to capital rights and citizen responsibility via regressive taxation and a shrinking social wage. Hence, we have both increased numbers of people without shelter combined with a reduced commitment to solve the root causes.

The spread of neoliberal "free" market models is already under attack from both conservatives (Gray 1998) and progressives (Sassen 1998; Bauman 1998; Bourdieu 1998; Peck and Tickell 1994; Teeple 1995) who understand the manner in which economic chaos leads to political authoritarianism and the overall decline of capitalism. Even as these ideologies come under attack, they continue to spread through European welfare states threatening to generate new levels of homelessness.

Integrating Solutions: Global, National, Local

Given the above analysis, what can we put forward as positive solutions to end homelessness at the global, national, and local/city levels? Proposed solutions cannot be framed merely as a national problem or as a local problem, but must be thought of as a multidimensional problem with global, national, state, and local levels of intervention. Local actions without global commitments remain insular and weak. Global actions without local commitments remain elitist and disempowering. Any solution to end homelessness must consider how to curb the excesses of capitalism and promote the democratizing of every level of society, including the economic realm (Blau 1999).

Possible Global Initiatives

Contrary to the globalization thesis, which maintains that all nation-states have to adjust their economies to international market demands, states are not powerless (Weiss 1998). Governments can re-regulate capital flows and increase social investments, as we have seen in the withdrawal of Malaysia from the financial markets to curtail speculative investment during a crisis. While the pressure from corporate elites is intense, counterpressures can also be increased. States that have maintained a strong welfare state tradition are now doing better in both human and financial terms than those that have not, giving a lie to free market advocates. Contrary to free market polemics that criticize the extensive system of social benefits created by European countries, countries that have maintained their social wage have been able to reduce substantially their levels of poverty. This has also allowed for shaping more effective policies for ending homelessness.

While homelessness is increasing globally, it is increasing with more speed in countries that have adopted the neoliberal market model than in those that have attempted to defend their social wage while fighting homelessness. To be sure, pressures to readjust European economies have been great since the signing of the Maastricht Treaty encouraging the integration of European markets and since the creation of the World Trade Organization (WTO) to promote free trade. Limited privatization, wage reductions, and the cutback in some benefits have occurred in most European countries. But the degree of such free market impositions has been contested through popular protests. For now, well-organized labor unions and Left political parties have managed to hold off the Americanization of Europe. How long they can do so remains to be seen.

Promote Global Human Rights to Regulate Capital

Internationally, citizens can fight back; social problems such as homelessness and hunger can be addressed, financial markets regulated, and social investment increased. A new global vision of ending poverty and homelessness can become dominant through employing mass media techniques where possible and local, community-based organizing networked internationally. In 1966 the International Covenant on Economic, Social, and Cultural Rights provided one of the first attempts to globalize human rights. Since adopted by 135 countries, this covenant—along with ongoing pressure for the realization of political, social, and economic rights by member states of the United Nations, human rights groups, nonprofit development groups, ecology organizations, and Women's Rights groups—has helped shape the current debate on taming global markets. International social movements and global alliances of labor unions, women's organizations, homeless advocacy groups, and ecology groups can work to curb the power of international unregulated capital investments and the impoverishment of workers, and give priority to the construction and financing of low-income housing, jobs with decent wages, and decent health care for all. Accelerated capital mobility, the threat of investment withdrawal, can be blunted by international organizing depriving capital of its safe havens. Communication networks and computer programs that have helped free capital from national and local restraints can also be appropriated by activists and extended worldwide (Evans 2000).

Reform International Finance and Development

One step in ending homelessness globally is international financial reform (Block 1996:266), which would return control to national economies by restoring fixed exchange rates on currency to prevent speculative financial trading, which does nothing for local populations, and restricting the free movement of capital across national borders. According to Block, a transaction tax on international currency exchanges of around 1 percent would reduce the $1.2 trillion dollars a day traded on the global markets; only 5 percent of these transactions are for actual trade, investment, or travel (1996:267). Other controls on capital could be negotiated at a new Bretton Woods-style conference of nations; such controls would encourage legitimate business, but would return more capital to governments, enabling a more effective response to widespread social inequalities.

Reforming IMF policies of fiscal austerity, which enrich local elites at the expense of a nation's poorer citizens, would place greater emphasis on local community development and absolve poor nations of their debt to Western banks. Heavy debt loads impoverish local populations, restrict the overall rate of social development, and lead to loss of housing or inadequate shelter. World Bank policies of fiscal soundness are already being rethought and moved away from the dominant neoliberal market model to one of sustainable development with ecological considerations, and a fundamental respect for human, political, and economic rights. This requires a new model of development that places social capital, democratic rights, and public health above investor rights.

Develop Global Coalitions and Protect Social Housing

The conflation of what is "good" for global market investors with the general good conceals the reality that what is profitable for private real estate developers is not necessarily profitable for those who cannot afford to live in market-rate units. Gentrification of cities worldwide is forcing the poor (Smith 1996; Sassen 1998) to compete for limited housing. Resistance is possible, but homeless activists cannot resist alone. Developing strong coalitions that cross race, class, and gender boundaries, nationally and internationally, and exploring shared ideologies for a just and equitable world are essential. Activist organizations, such as the *Innen Stadt Aktion* (Inner City Action Group) and the *Anti-Racist Initiative* in Berlin, who oppose racial discrimination against immigrants and fight to stop gentrification, can find common cause with similar groups in the United States. The 1996 Habitat II agenda of a right to housing, sustainable development, and "enabling" partnerships can also provide an ideological framework to link activist groups. The right to shelter, common in most industrialized countries, could be extended to the United States in legislation through sustained advocacy.

Many European countries have resisted strict market ideology for years and have a diversity of housing stock that evolved out of the political struggles between business and labor informed by a much stronger Left tradition than in the United States. These large stocks of social housing, which are not part of the private housing market, provide one of the most effective ways to house the poor. From the subsidized housing units in Holland and Denmark to the social housing of Germany and Britain, various alternative housing arrangements not part of the private market are common, including co-housing arrangements and converted squatter buildings. The diversity of European housing stock provides many good examples of how housing policy could look in the United States. Defending social housing and enhancing its desirability is therefore one possible solution for global housing problems. But this will require a concerted and organized effort to resist the further implementation of market-driven policies for "reform" at the expense of working people and the poor. Similar to the national *Community Reinvestment Act* in the United States, which calls upon banks to justify their lending practices to poor communities before expanding their markets elsewhere, an *International Community Reinvestment Act* could be lobbied for. It would force transnational corporations (TNCs) to invest in the social capital of the host country before they would be permitted to engage in business. Those TNCs that showed the greatest ability and commitment to support the poor and develop local communities would be granted investment rights. Democratic assemblies responsible to regional and local populations within any given host country could guide the social capital investment offered by outside TNCs into productive channels.

National Initiatives

Organize Coalitions

Organizing a "coalition around common human needs" (Blau 1992:181) will link homeless advocacy to other social change groups. To achieve a more democratic political system responsive to the needs of the less privileged, labor would have to unite with community-based organizations and also work harder to organize the unorganized. In addition, the politics of identity would have to be refashioned with a new vision that can mobilize grassroots organizations around a populist democratic and progressive platform. This will mean moving from the ideology of individual empowerment to collective empowerment (Wright 1997:317) and direct action. It will mean placing more resources into the hands of the poor and homeless, offering collective mobility and collective resources to the homeless. Wagner comments (1993:180), "What if the dense social networks and cohesive subcultures that constitute the homeless community were utilized by advocates, social workers, and others?" One model of organizing that has proven effective in crossing race, class, and gender barriers, often cited in contrast to the Alinsky model, is that of the Piedmont Peace Project (Stout 1996). Providing social services is rejected in this model, because "we work to help people understand that they can bring about change if they are organized. They can get the services they need" (Stout 1996:106). However, people living without homes present a problem in that they have no home-based community that can be organized. Therefore, organizing will work best not in conjunction with formalized, institutionalized services, but rather with small actions, such as the serving of food that Food Not Bombs accomplishes, as vehicles for bringing people together for social change, or in the defensive civil rights struggles waged by the National Coalition on Homelessness, and its locals, against arbitrary police harassment of people living on the street. Bringing together the strategies of the Piedmont Project with those of Food Not Bombs and the Coalition on Homelessness could provide one way to bridge organizing gaps among people without shelter, homeless advocate groups, and housed social change groups.

Because we live in a media-saturated society, this will require establishing and using new media forms, co-opting corporate media outlets, and generating new networks to create the necessary cultural imperatives to push for change. Media campaigns can be shaped to hammer home the following agendas. However, for these kinds of political changes to occur, changes in campaign finance reform must be pursued at the national and state level. Blunting the power of large lobbyists affiliated with the real estate, health care, banking, and other business sectors is necessary, as is the true democratic opening of the political process. First I would like to discuss briefly the necessary political changes and then address specific policy issues such as health care, housing, jobs.

Reform Lobbying and Campaign Financing

It is clear that any progressive agenda to end homelessness must have a politics in place that is responsive to an alliance between the middle classes and the poor, not to the dollars of big business. The corruption of the democratic process is evident in the massive contributions given each year through lobbying in Washington, DC. To blunt the effect of big money, lobbying reform is essential. The recent replacement of the 1933 Glass-Steagall Act, which tightly regulated banking, finance, insurance, and real estate operations, by the 1999 Gramm-Leach Act, which lifts those regulations, came after a sustained lobbying campaign by the finance sector. In 1997–98 this sector spent $154.4 million dollars in soft money, PACs, and individual contributions to influence congressional sentiment, according to the *Center for Responsive Politics* in Washington, D.C. While this one example illustrates the power of banking and finance interests, the real estate lobby works hard to maintain mortgage interest deductions on homes, effectively cutting off other options for government housing investment. In addition, campaign finance reform is essential if candidates sympathetic to the needs of the poor and homeless are to have even a ghost of a chance of winning elections. To solve the problems that create homelessness will require electing officials who are not afraid to stand up to big business.

Change the Tax Code

The mantra of "no new taxes" is unsustainable in a civilized society. With corporate taxes at an all-time low (corporate taxes were 21 percent in 1962 and declined to 11.5 percent by 1997) and a disproportionate share of the wealth accumulated in the top 5 percent of the population, a vigorous progressive corporate and individual tax system should generate the required capital for social investments. Taxes on the assets and income of the wealthy have also declined over the past 20 years. Closing tax loopholes will be essential. The top 1 percent of wealthy families have managed to realize savings on average of $97,250 per family between 1977 and 1985, while the bottom 80 percent had an increase of only $221 per family (Blau 1999:196). Changing priorities to combat homelessness will require redistribution of income and wealth.

Change Research Funding Priorities and Develop Media Resources

Philanthropy- and foundation-sponsored think tanks have often led the way in new policy research and supportive services. Many progressive foundations have remained hampered, however, by their support of direct service, in the case of homelessness, and direct action of activist groups, and have not invested the funds necessary to build up a collection of progressive think tanks, as various conservative foundations have created their own. Funding new progressive research centers is just as essential as funding direct action groups, since direct action groups can benefit from the new knowledge generated by such policy organs. It is not a matter of either/or—both the development of new progressive think tanks and research centers and funding direct action groups are essential if political change is to occur. Changing priorities of fund raisers, an increase in private foundation commitment to progressive advocacy research, think tank development, and media/political resources to sustain a progressive vision are all important to help support grassroots efforts.

Push for a Single-Payer Health Care System

Raising the incomes of the very poor and redesigning a health care system that delivers decent health care for all, regardless of ability to pay, is also essential for ending homelessness. The current battles with managed-care HMOs reveal the inadequacies of a health care system built in conjunction with the insurance industry, whose primary motive is to secure greater returns on investments. A single-payer health care system is most effective in providing needed services and will ultimately prove less expensive than the current system of managed care. Providing increased health care services is essential to counteract the damage caused by homelessness, but not sufficient to stop the larger widespread impoverishment. Given the serious shortage of detox centers, mental health outreach clinics, and services for the disabled in general, ending homelessness will involve making the necessary investments in these services throughout the country. Specialized services (mental health and substance abuse treatment, shelters, transitional housing, job training), the most common benefits allocated for the poor, are important; but without more low-income housing, higher incomes for low-skilled work, and fast, accessible health care, those benefiting from such services will still find themselves exposed to intolerable living conditions.

Move Beyond Welfare Reform and Expand Child Care Support

While moving people off welfare and back to work may be a laudable goal in theory, accomplishing it through punitive sanctions and strict time limits is cruel and ineffective. Given that most people on welfare are there for only a short while, many people who have received jobs through TANF might have received them anyway. The poorest 20 percent of those recipients, however, have serious problems that are not being addressed by a forced work program. The lack of systematic and widespread funding of child care centers and the lack of good, well-paid jobs ensures that even those who are removed from the welfare rolls will be stuck in low-wage occupations. Since most women who have been on AFDC and are now on TANF work as mothers, subsidized child care is essential for any work base strategy to be successful. In fact, such a system is not unheard of. The Kellogg system of child care implemented during World War II provided subsidized federal day care, allowing many mothers to work in the defense industry.

Renew a Federal Commitment to Housing and Promote Social Housing

Following Habitat II, the United States should declare a national "right to housing" which calls for decent housing and a suitable living environment for all citizens. The United States needs to strengthen its social policy with renewed efforts to develop new low-income rental housing construction programs, programs that move beyond the voucher system or private-public systems for public housing. New public housing can easily compete with the private sector in developing low-cost and attractive alternatives, not the concrete megaliths of the 1950s. This is self-evident in the new attractive Gautraux scattered housing developments now being built in Chicago.

Since a major part of the problem, other than the lack of serious federal commitment, is the normal operations of the market, mechanisms must be found to curb the power of markets to distort housing affordability. For example, with the assistance of the federal government, a public capital-grant financing program could be implemented to support the development of the "social ownership" of housing (Stone 1993; Hopper and Baumohl 1994). This means removing permanently a portion of the housing stock from resale on the private market. After paying for the cost of producing or acquiring the housing stock, remaining costs would be reduced to capital improvements and operations. This expansion of the "social sector" of housing would increase the stock of affordable housing while allowing other market-rate units to service high-income persons. Ownership of housing can be assumed by many different entities from local nonprofit developers, housing agencies, churches, labor unions, and other community groups with federal assistance (Stone 1993:193).

End Housing Discrimination

State governments can put increased pressure on landlords to stop unfair evictions, rent gouging, and housing discrimination through vigorous enforcement of the Fair Housing laws and an expansion of housing litigation and testing procedures. Fair Housing Councils around the nation are hampered by insufficient budgets and lack of real commitment from both the business community and local cities in enforcing housing discrimination provisions. State governments also can discourage irresponsible redevelopment in local areas where such redevelopment threatens to gentrify an area at the expense of working and poor people, as is occurring in San Francisco, California. Housing and homeless activists can have a larger impact at the state level if there is a renewed federal commitment to working families and the poor.

Raise Wages and Rebuild the United States

At the most basic level of reform, increasing the minimum wage is essential to provide jobs with livable incomes. Already the small increase in minimum wages has generated more income for the bottom 20 percent of the population, decreasing the poverty level by a small amount over the past three years. While a step in the right direction, this is simply not enough to compensate for the widespread loss of union wage employment in the 1980s and the middle-management downsizing of the 1990s.

With the increase in temporary employment, many workers have to struggle just to break even every month. Two strategies that would help end homelessness would be a guaranteed annual income (Blau 1992:183) for everyone and a new federal "living" minimum wage indexed to the cost of living within a particular PMSA or rural area, enough to sustain a single person or family at or above the poverty level, where the poverty level is redefined according to a "market basket" approach for a particular region (being poor in San Francisco is very different from being poor in rural Mississippi). Similar to European plans, a guaranteed income plan would provide the bottom floor for sustaining a family and could replace welfare and many of the other social service programs that supported poor families who did not have sufficient income. This would also create incentives for business to pay their workers a decent salary; otherwise they would find themselves with serious shortages of labor. The second proposal would equalize wages among regions, discouraging businesses from moving into areas where land prices are high and encouraging moves into low-priced areas, therefore raising the livelihood of depressed economic zones.

To provide immediate help to the very poor and homeless, a public works program that expands opportunities for well-paid low-skilled labor and that addresses basic infrastructure repair integrated with community economic development could help raise people up off the streets. Long-term neglect of basic maintenance of bridges, roads, parks, and services calls for a solution. A National Marshall Plan to rebuild America could include social investments in new housing construction, city infrastructure repair, and national health care for all. The key is in providing not just make-work positions but ones that have a promise of a future and pay a livable wage. Job training in this context could directly link open positions in employment with needed jobs, promising continuity between low-skilled positions and ones calling for higher skills. Preferential treatment in hiring given to the poor and to people of color will also raise the income levels of the bottom 20 percent and to discourage the widening split between the primary and secondary labor markets.

The cost of such a plan would be expensive at first, but would be repaid many times over in the long run through lower costs in containing social problems, improving human happiness, and increasing productivity. After all, the time when government investment was at its highest, during the 1950s, was also the period of the highest growth rate in American history. We can easily afford larger government investments. United States government expenditures have risen only 5 percent between 1967 and 1994, to 33.5 percent of the GDP (Block 1996:87), far below that of European states. The problem is not that we spend too much, but that we spend so little. Spending has actually decreased on critical physical infrastructure, constituting only 1.9 percent of GDP in 1996 compared to 2.8 percent in 1976 (Block 1996:294). Japan spent 6 percent through the 1970s and 1980s, and former West Germany spent 4 to 6 percent of its GDP on infrastructure—substantially more than the United States. There is work to be done in the United States after these many years of neglect. Making decent well-paid jobs repairing the nation's infrastructure available to those with low and moderate skills will also provide an avenue for homeless people to get back on their feet. New housing will provide the places to live and a national health care system the necessary support services for those too disabled to work.

Local City Initiatives

Modest versions of all the national policies outlined above can be adopted at the state or local level. In fact, the creation of progressive coalition politics may be easier at the local than national level. Local minimum wage laws, child care initiatives, health care services, and social housing initiatives are all possible. As at the national level they will require the election of political leaders independent of local real estate growth coalition interests. Other initiatives are more fundamentally local.

Homelessness as a Community-based Human Rights Issue

Local homeless advocates, such as the Coalition on Homelessness in San Francisco and Chicago, are able to use the human rights perspective to educate the general public. This should not be viewed as counter to a proactive strategy (Shaw 1996:26), but rather as integral to developing a larger coalition based on human rights, social justice, and equity. Local struggles for human rights have an international dimension and, with modern technology, can easily link up with groups in other countries fighting similar battles. Activist groups in local neighborhoods in the United States may have more in common with working-class struggles in Berlin, London, Paris, Tokyo, and Mexico than with wealthy communities within their own city. Connecting these struggles using modern communications can help provide solidarity and work to globalize the local.

Responsible Redevelopment

The application of "quality of life" policing merely applies a cosmetic fix, moving social problems to less visible industrial areas. Cities can work to develop downtown areas with mixed-use housing, containing middle-class, working-class, and poor in the same areas, without robbing the poor, working class, or middle class of available units, services, or "quality of life." City redevelopment plans can be shaped as *responsible redevelopment* that recognizes the necessity to have all elements of the population represented in downtown core areas, not just the privileged—and represented in proportion to the actual composition of the employment base. This would include a renewed commitment to build more mixed-income single-room occupancy units in downtown core areas, as well as in suburban areas. These will become important not only for the very poor but also for those single working- and middle-class baby boomers who cannot afford to buy their own homes. Democratic downtown/suburban development can state publicly the types of new employment created by a particular project and its approximate pay scale to allow for planning a proper housing mix. Gentrification does not have to displace the poor and homeless segments of the community. A responsible gentrification can upgrade a community at a gradual pace, with safeguards to protect the less privileged. Vision statements and plans developed by local redevelopment agencies can be refashioned to represent all segments of the population, and can be assisted by grassroots advocate movements for the poor. This will require bringing homeless advocates, not just local business elites, into the very planning process of downtown areas and in suburban areas of outlying districts. The lack of federal funds makes it difficult for cities to reduce land costs that might attract affordable housing developers, and market models of housing only privilege the upper tier of citizens. However, the reliance upon tax increment financing (TIFs) and business improvement districts (BIDs) robs cities of necessary funds while giving developers unnecessary tax breaks. These can be reduced or reshaped to increase provisions for creating substantial amounts of low-income shelter.

Redevelopment agencies, in cooperation with state legislators, entrusted with applying 20 percent of their budgets to building affordable housing, should expand that percentage in line with the numbers of newly created low-income jobs within a city. The 20 percent figure can be amended by state legislators. However, cities can also increase their component of low-income housing construction by increasing the amount of redevelopment funds for low-income housing in proportion to the needs within their communities. For every new business (cafes, hotels, clothing shops) that services incoming clients, a host of low-income jobs will be created. City development plans can take this into account through their Environmental Impact Reports and push to build housing that can accommodate service workers near the site of new businesses, preferably within walking distance. Setting up Housing Trust Funds for low-income housing is one solution, but a better solution would be controlled development that balances the numbers of low-income housing units created with the number of jobs being proposed. An example of lopsided redevelopment are the plans for the Mission Bay development in San Francisco, which promises up to 31,000 jobs, but only 6,000 housing units in a city with an extremely low vacancy rate and the highest housing costs in the country. This will put even more pressure on the already squeezed housing market and certainly price the working poor out of San Francisco and make it impossible for people without shelters to get off the streets. A more rational redevelopment plan would allow for equal proportions of housing and jobs within a two-mile radius, to reduce transportation costs, in a mix proportional to the types and pay of jobs created.

Democratize and Support Shelters

While shelters are not the answer to homelessness, new shelters should be supported as an interim measure. Existing shelters can be encouraged to end restrictive shelter practices that treat homeless families and individuals in a degrading fashion, and can be supported to the extent that they have initiated democratic procedures of accountability for their patrons. In addition, such shelters can be maintained in downtown areas or in those areas where support services can be best organized, but not encouraged to relocate to degrading industrial areas or "refuse" spaces (Wright 1997: 101–11). Cities would be pressed to provide needed social services on a fair and equitable basis (Wolch and Dear 1993) with smaller shelters in all neighborhoods and a firm opposition to NIMBYism. There is always room for supportive services, like shelters, but we should not assume that they constitute solutions to homelessness.

Living Wage Ordinances

Cities can also enact "living wage" ordinances to improve the wages of city workers. In addition, preferences for minority-owned businesses can be built into city contracts for services to assist people of color, who make up the disproportionate number of poor in the inner cities. Given the advanced deterioration of infrastructure in most major cities, public investment in massive repairs employing both skilled and unskilled workers at a decent wage will allow the poor to accumulate the necessary income to provide for their families. With increased income, poor communities will be able to take care of many of their own. The decline of wages within minority communities and poor white communities over the past 30 years has meant a concurrent decline in the viability of social networks (Roschelle 1997), contrary to the earlier findings of Stack (1974). The increase of such wages will not only help the working poor, but also strengthen family networks.

Conclusions

While these proposals for global, national, and local solutions may seem utopian—read "unworkable"—I have drawn many of these examples from diverse social experiments already underway in various countries. This is a vision of where we might go, if not a finished plan. Any struggle to end homelessness will involve an open-ended process of conflict between competing political and economic interests, involving gender, racial/ethnic, and class conflict. These cannot be defined adequately ahead of time, but will emerge in the process of social change through collective empowerment. What is clear is that ending the bitter legacy of homelessness will require substantial changes in the strategies of capital accumulation, not just simple reform. To press these initiatives will take more than wishful thinking or even coalition building. It will take determined politics. A critically conscious political movement willing to take bold steps will have to emerge—a movement that calls into question the dominant strategies of neoliberalism and fights for the rights of working people and poor people everywhere, a movement connected deeply to grassroots activists who are mobilized to struggle globally and locally.

References

Baker, Susan Gonzalez. 1994. "Gender, Ethnicity, and Homelessness." *American Behavioral Scientist* 37:476–504.

Barak, Gregg. 1992. *Gimme Shelter: A Social History of Homelessness in Contemporary America*. Westport, CT: Praeger.

Baum, Alice C. and Donald W. Burnes. 1993. *A Nation in Denial: The Truths About Homelessness*. Boulder, CO: Westview Press.

Bauman, Zygmunt. 1998. *Globalization: The Human Consequences*. New York: Columbia University Press.

Bingham, R. D., R. E. Green, and S. B. White, eds. 1987. *The Homeless in Contemporary Society*. Newbury Park, CA: Sage.

Blasi, Gary. 1994. "And We Are Not Seen: Ideological and Political Barriers to Understanding Homelessness." *American Behavioral Scientist* 37: 563–83.

Blau, Joel. 1992. *The Visible Poor: Homelessness in the United States*. New York: Oxford University Press.

———. 1999. *Illusions of Prosperity: America's Working Families in an Age of Economic*

Insecurity. New York: Oxford University Press.

Block, Fred L. 1996. *The Vampire State and Other Myths and Fallacies about the U.S. Economy*. New York: New Press.

Bourdieu, Pierre. 1998. *Acts of Resistance: Against the Tyranny of the Market*. New York: New Press.

Burns, Leland S. 1987. "Third World Solutions to the Homelessness Problem." In *The Homeless in Contemporary Society*, edited by R. D. Bingham et al. Newbury Park, CA: Sage.

Deben, Leon and Dorine Greshoff. 1997. "Homelessness in the Netherlands: Facts and Perspectives." Pp. 31–40 in *International Critical Perspectives on Homelessness*, edited by Mary Jo Huth and Talmadge Wright. Westport, CT: Greenwood Press.

Devine, J. A. and J. D. Wright. 1993. *The Greatest of Evils: Urban Poverty and the American Underclass*. Hawthorne, NY: Aldine de Gruyter.

Dolbeare, C. N. 1996. "Housing Policy: A General Consideration." Pp. 34–45 in *Homelessness in America*, edited by Jim Baumohl. Phoenix, AZ: Oryx Press.

Evans, Peter. 2000. "Fighting Marginalization with Transnational Networks: Counter-Hegemonic Globalization." *Contemporary Sociology* 29:230–41.

Fischer, Pamela J. 1992. "The Criminalization of Homelessness." Pp. 57–66 in *Homelessness: A National Perspective*, edited by Marjorie J. Robertson and Milton Greenblatt. New York: Plenum Press.

Glasser, I. 1994. *Homelessness in Global Perspective*. New York: G. K. Hall.

Gray, John. 1998. *False Dawn: The Delusions of Global Capitalism*. NY: New Press.

Headley, Bernard D. 1990–91. "Race, Class and Powerlessness in World Economy." *The Black Scholar* 21: 14–21.

Hirsch, J. 1991. "From the Fordist to the Post-Fordist State." Pp. 67–81 in *The Politics of Flexibility*, edited by B. Jessop et al. Aldershot, UK: Edward Elgar.

Hoch, Charles and Robert. A. Slayton. 1989. *New Homeless and Old: Community and the Skid Row Hotel*. Philadelphia: Temple University Press.

Hopper, Kim and Jim Baumohl. 1994. "Held in Abeyance: Rethinking Homelessness and Advocacy." *American Behavioral Scientist* 37: 522–52.

Hopper, Kim and Norweeta G. Milburn. 1996. "Homelessness among African Americans: A Historical and Contemporary Perspective." Pp. 123–31 in *Homelessness in America*, edited by Jim Baumohl. Phoenix, AZ: Oryx Press.

Jessop, Bob. 1994. "Post-Fordism and the State." Pp. 251–79 in *Post-Fordism: A Reader*, edited by Ash Amin. Cambridge: Blackwell.

Katz, Michael B. 1989. *The Undeserving Poor: From the War on Poverty to the War on Welfare*. New York: Pantheon.

Koegel, Paul, Burnam, M. Audrey, and Baumohl, Jim. 1996. "The Causes of Homelessness." Pp. 24–33 in *Homelessness in America*, edited by Jim Baumohl. Phoenix, AZ: Oryx Press.

Link, B. G., E. Susser, A. Stueve, and J. Phelan. 1994. "Lifetime and Five-Year Prevalence of Homelessness in The United States." *American Journal of Public Health* 84: 1907–12.

Massey, Douglas S. and Nancy A. Denton. 1988. "Residential Segregation of Blacks, Hispanics, and Asians by Socioeconomic Status and Generation." *Social Science Quarterly* 69:797–817.

———. 1993. *American Apartheid: Segregation and the Making of the Underclass*. Cambridge, MA: Harvard University Press.

Mayer, M. 1996. "Assessing Urban Social Movements in the 1990s." Paper presented at the International Conference, Globalization and Collective Action: Strategies and Prospects for Oppositional Politics, of the Research Committee on Social movements and Social Classes, International Sociological Association, Santa Cruz, CA, May.

———. 1994. "Post-Fordist City Politics." Pp. 316–37 in *Post-Fordism: A Reader*, edited by Ash Amin. Cambridge: Blackwell.

National Law Center on Homelessness and Poverty. 1999. *Out of Sight-Out of Mind?* Report by the National Law Center on Homelessness and Poverty, 918 F. Street, NW, Suite 412, Washington, DC 20004.

Peck, Jamie and Adam Tickell. 1994. "Searching for a New Institutional Fix: The After-Fordist Crisis and the Global-Local Disorder." Pp.

280–315 in *Post-Fordism: A Reader*, edited by Ash Amin. Cambridge: Blackwell.

Primus, Wendell, Lynette Rawlings, Kathy Larin and Kathryn Porter. 1999. *The Initial Impacts of Welfare Reform on the Income of Single-Mother Families.* Report by the Center for Budget and Policy Priorities, 820 First St., NE, Suite 510, Washington, DC 20002. August.

Roschelle, Anne. 1997. *No More Kin: Exploring Race, Class and Gender in Family Networks.* Thousand Oaks, CA: Sage.

Sahlin, Ingrid. 1997. "Discipline and Border Control in Sweden: Strategies for Tenant Control and Housing Exclusion." Pp. 139–54 in *International Critical Perspectives on Homelessness*, edited by Mary Jo Huth and Talmadge Wright. Westport, CT: Greenwood Press.

Sassen, Saskia. 1998. *Globalization and Its Discontents: Essays on the New Mobility of People and Money*. New York: New Press.

Schrag, Peter. 1999. *Paradise Lost: California's Experience, America's Future*. Berkeley, CA: University of California Press.

Shaw, Randy. 1996. *The Activist's Handbook: A Primer for the 1990s and Beyond.* Berkeley: University of California Press.

Shinn, Mary B. and Colleen Gillespie. 1994. "The Roles of Housing and Poverty in the Origins of Homelessness." *American Behavioral Scientist* 37: 505–21.

Smith, Neil. 1996. *The New Urban Frontier: Gentrification and the Revanchist City*. New York: Routledge.

Snow, David A., Leon Anderson and Paul Koegel. 1994. "Distorting Tendencies in Research on the Homeless." *American Behavioral Scientist* 37: 461–75.

Snow, David A., Susan Baker, Leon Anderson, and Michael Martin. 1986. "The Myth of Pervasive Mental Illness among the Homeless." *Social Problems* 33: 407–23.

Stack, Carol. 1974. *All Our Kin: Strategies for Survival in a Black Community*. New York: Harper & Row.

Stone, Michael. 1993. *Shelter Poverty: New Ideas on Housing Affordability.* Philadelphia: Temple University Press.

Stoner, Madeline R. 1995. *The Civil Rights of Homeless People: Law, Social Policy, and Social Work Practice*. Hawthorne, NY: Aldine de Gruyter.

Stout, Linda. 1996. *Bridging the Class Divide: Grassroots Organizing*. Boston: Beacon Press.

Teeple, Gary. 1995. *Globalization and the Decline of Social Reform*. Toronto: Garamond Press.

Timmer, Doug A., D. Stanley Eitzen, and Kathryn D. Talley. 1994. *Paths to Homelessness: Extreme Poverty and the Urban Housing Crisis*. Boulder, CO: Westview Press.

U.S. Conference of Mayors. 1999. *A Status Report on Hunger and Homelessness in American Cities: 1998*. U.S. Conference of Mayors, 1620 Eye St. NW, Washington, DC 20006.

U.S. Department of Housing and Urban Development. 1999. *The Widening Gap: New Findings in Housing Affordability in America*. Washington, DC: U.S. Department of Housing and Urban Development.

Wagner, David. 1993. *Checkerboard Square: Culture and Resistance in a Homeless Community*. Boulder, CO: Westview Press.

Weiss, Linda. 1998. *The Myth of the Powerless State*. Ithaca, NY: Cornell University Press.

Western, Bruce. 1999. "How Unregulated is the U.S. Labor Market? The Penal System as a Labor Market Institution." *American Journal of Sociology* 104:1030–60.

Wolch, Jennifer and Michael Dear. 1993. *Malign Neglect: Homelessness in an American City*. San Francisco: Jossey-Bass.

Wright, James D., Beth A. Rubin, and Joel A. Devine. 1998. *Beside the Golden Door: Policy, Politics and the Homeless*. Hawthorne, NY: Aldine de Gruyter.

Wright, Talmadge. 1997. *Out of Place: Homeless Mobilizations, Subcities, and Contested Landscapes*. Albany: State University of New York Press.

LEARNING TO LISTEN

One Man's Work in the Anti-rape Movement

BY RICHARD S. ORTON

I believe that defensiveness and discomfort are inevitable for many men when we are challenged to acknowledge women's vulnerability to men's violence and the impact that it has on them.

PART I

MY TELEPHONE RANG AT MIDNIGHT. The rape hotline volunteer told me that a woman was waiting at the emergency room for a rape exam. The volunteer had been trying for an hour to locate someone to go and be with her. I was the only person available that night.

I had been on staff at the Austin Rape Crisis Center for over a year and knew that this moment might come. Even though my job focused on school and community education, I had been trained, like all staff and volunteers, to support rape survivors in crisis situations. I had done crisis counseling via the telephone, but I had never been face to face with a rape survivor shortly after the assault. My stomach tightened at the thought.

The most practical—and most difficult—part of rape crisis center training for me was the role playing, where trainees are put into unscripted scenarios similar to those they would encounter on the telephone, at the emergency room, or in other face-to-face encounters with rape survivors, their family members, or medical and law enforcement professionals. The crisis intervention skills that are taught in training get tested through role-playing. For me, it was like trying to walk through a minefield. I thought that if I failed to say the right thing, if I failed to anticipate correctly the needs of the survivor, I might set off emotional mines. No real harm was done in role-plays, but what was about to happen would not be a role-play.

I now understand that what most people need in such situations is to feel genuine concern and empathy from a helping person, to be listened to, to be allowed to express feelings (or remain silent), and to have their questions answered. But as I drove to the emergency room that night, I was only aware of how nervous I was. I went over in my mind all the do's and don'ts I had learned in training. And I had one additional concern: Having just been raped by a man, the woman I was about to meet might not want to deal with me, another man. Crisis center policy required that a female volunteer be provided in these situations, but none was available that night.

As I walked into the emergency room I saw a young woman I will call Sandy sitting on a bed dressed in a green hospital gown. A nurse stood behind her doing something to her hair. As I got closer I saw that the nurse was cleaning dried blood out of Sandy's hair and I saw a dozen or more stitches in her scalp.

I introduced myself, certain she could hear the pounding in my chest. I asked her how she was feeling. She smiled and said she was doing better now. She seemed calmer than I was.

Richard Orton, "Learning to Listen: One Man's Work in the Anti-rape Movement," *Transforming A Rape Culture* (Revised Edition), ed. Emilie Buchwald, Pamela R. Fletcher, and Martha Roth, pp. 233-248. Copyright © 2005 by Richard Orton. Reprinted with permission.

That afternoon a young man had approached her in a mall parking lot and asked for help. His car wouldn't start, he said, and he needed a ride to a friend's house a short distance away. Accustomed to helping people out in the farming community she had recently left, Sandy agreed to give him a ride. She ended up in a ditch outside of town, raped and beaten.

In addition to stitches in her scalp, Sandy needed to undergo a rape exam and get an X-ray of her skull. As we waited for these tasks to be completed, we talked about many of the things that come up in such situations. Why would someone do something like this? What was going to happen now? What would the police want to know? What would happen if they caught him? Was she going to be all right? What would this do to her life? How could she tell her family what had happened, and how were they going to react?

I was greatly relieved that Sandy accepted my presence. Like many people in her situation, she seemed to appreciate that a stranger would come to the hospital in the middle of the night to be with her—someone whose only purpose was to support her and advocate for her.

After spending four or five hours in the emergency room Sandy needed to decide where to go now that she was about to be released. She was new to Austin and had not made many friends yet, and her family was in another state. Her employer and his wife were the only people she knew well enough to call. She asked me to call her employer's wife, explain what had happened, and ask if she could stay with them that night. I made the call and we left the hospital.

We arrived at her employer's home around 5 or 6 a.m. Sandy went to bed right away, and I stayed a moment to talk with her friends. The sun was coming up as I left. I felt strange. Fatigue, I thought. I was numb from the previous six or seven hours. But about halfway home the numbness ended and I broke down. One moment I was fine, the next I was sobbing uncontrollably. I hadn't seen this coming, and I was unable to control it when it did. I was shocked and frightened at what was happening to me. I had never experienced anything like this before and now here I was, driving down the high way at daybreak, falling apart.

This was the first of several experiences I had in the late 1970s and early 1980s through my work with the Austin Rape Crisis Center that began to expose me to blank spaces in my awareness of the world. These blank spaces, which I attribute to growing up male, represented my lack of awareness of the world as women experience it, a world that in varying degrees creates in women a sense of being at risk simply because they are women. Though it took me years to fully assimilate the significance of these experiences, they ultimately had a profound impact on the way I view the world—as if I had entered a different dimension.

Being hired by the Austin Rape Crisis Center (ARCC) in 1978 was a lucky accident, though at the time I considered it only an interesting opportunity to do something different for a while. In the year or so that preceded my encounter with Sandy in the emergency room, I had learned a lot about rape from books, from the staff and volunteers at ARCC, and from several rape survivors who were volunteers. I had spoken frequently to school and community groups about rape awareness and prevention. I had helped train volunteers for ARCC.

Yet until that night, rape was only an idea to me. My connection to it was mostly intellectual. During the drive home at dawn, I felt it in my gut for the first time. Sandy's experience made it impossible for me to protect myself any longer from the emotional impact of sexual violation—something I had not allowed to touch me before. That experience put me on a different track and sent me into uncharted territory.

In August 1979, I attended the first conference of the National Coalition Against Sexual Assault (NCASA) in Lake Geneva, Wisconsin. Held at a rustic camp, the conference was attended by about two hundred people. I was one of six men. I knew that male involvement with rape crisis centers was a controversial topic for many, perhaps most, women doing the work, and that it was relatively rare at that time for centers to solicit male volunteers and practically unheard of to recruit male staff.

The Austin Rape Crisis Center had included a small number of male volunteers ever since its founding in 1974. Sylvia Callaway, who became executive director in 1977, embraced this policy wholeheartedly. She believed that the challenges male volunteers and staff might present were worth the effort. The long-term effect of meeting those challenges would be to educate a group of men about rape from a woman's perspective, and those men would then educate other men. The antirape movement's goal of ending rape could not be accomplished without male allies, and Sylvia was committed to creating male allies.

Lake Geneva was a different environment than anything I had experienced in Austin. I halfway expected to be challenged verbally, or worse. Nothing like that happened. What did happen was more subtle and indirect: I was mostly ignored. My clearest memory is of sitting in a workshop for an hour and a half, participating occasionally but not feeling part of the group. By the end of the session, I felt a combination of alienation and confusion, though I doubt I could have described my feelings so clearly then. I remember a frustrated conversation with Sylvia that evening, in which I tried unsuccessfully to understand the source of my feelings.

What was unfamiliar about that experience, as I began to understand later, was that I felt invisible. My presence was largely unacknowledged. The work shop proceeded without my influence. I might as well not have been there.

Many years after that first NCASA conference, I was at a conference for profeminist men. One of the keynote speakers, Harry Brod, was talking about his experiences with men who viewed feminism and feminists as antimale. His comments on where this attitude came from took me back to that Lake Geneva workshop. He said that what many men most misunderstand about feminism—a misunderstanding that leads them to view feminism as antimale—is that it is not about men at all. And this, he said, is what is so frightening about feminism to so many men.

What those women were doing in that workshop at Lake Geneva was not about me, and although I did not experience it as being against me, I did experience their way of being together without including me as something completely new, and I did not know what to make of it. It had not occurred to me before that gender might be part of what determines how a person is treated. I had not experienced the discriminatory behavior that females often do. This was largely invisible to me until the Lake Geneva conference, and it remained confusing and blurry in my consciousness for a long time afterward. To this day, I have to remind myself that women's experience in the world—women's reality—is not always the same as men's.

Another experience, this time at the second NCASA conference in Austin in 1980, exposed even more dramatically the blank spaces in my life as a man. One of the keynote speakers suggested that we show a new film on rape made by a group of Canadian feminists, and as an organizer of the conference I ordered the film and scheduled it for viewing. It arrived at the last minute and we did not have a chance to preview it.

As I recall, the film began with a didactic section, then shifted abruptly to a rape scenario. A woman walking down a sidewalk was grabbed by a man and thrown into a van, where she was terrorized and raped. It was highly realistic. The woman's terror permeated the viewing room. As the scenario progressed, women began to leave. Finally, someone stood up and demanded that the film be stopped. Many women in the room were survivors of rape or childhood sexual abuse. Several were outraged that they had not been warned about the content of the film. Some thought that such a film should not be shown at all. Others, while agreeing that the film was extremely difficult to watch, wanted to finish it, finding value in being able to confront it. After a brief but intense discussion, the women agreed that those who wanted to finish watching the film would do so, then join the others for a processing session.

I felt both responsible for what was happening and helpless to do anything about it. Many women were clearly in pain because of the film. Again, I felt myself sliding into unknown territory.

When the fifty or so women came together after the film, I remember what happened mostly as a succession of images as I might have seen them through a gauze screen, not as words in a narrative. Even more than in the hospital emergency room with Sandy, I felt completely unprepared for what I was experiencing. I was witness to an emotional outpouring that astonished me, frightened me, and left me dumbfounded. Nothing in my thirty-plus years had prepared me for the next hour or two.

The situation felt chaotic. Some of the women were angry that other women would watch the film. Others thought that seeing it allowed them to confront their own demons. Rape survivors did not have a consistent response. Some found it a test of their recovery, while for others it was a nightmare relived. Individuals made impassioned statements. Small groups came together for support. The film had ripped off the veneer of safety for many of them, and their vulnerability and outrage were on display in such a graphic way that I could not possibly intellectualize, rationalize, or compartmentalize my response. I was confronted by the reality of women's vulnerability in a way that made me feel helpless and completely unsure of myself, as if a very large person had picked me up by the shoulders, shaken me violently for a few seconds, then put me down and walked away. Nothing looked or felt the same.

I could not fully absorb the meaning and importance of these three experiences when they happened. I did not have the emotional awareness or vocabulary to talk about them, but they burned deeply into my consciousness.

Working at the rape crisis center, I was confronted daily by the world women experience, from petty injustices to fear to actual assault. I always had the option of filtering out what I was hearing, and I often did. But the cumulative effect, year after year, of exposure to this women's world gave me information about women's experience that men rarely acquire. I had information about what the fear of male violence, as well as the actual experience of it, does to their lives. Constant exposure to this information forced me, slow as I was, to open up to my own feelings—not my thoughts—about the fear and violence that many women live with simply because they are women.

Being bombarded with information from this parallel world could be tiresome and difficult, and I didn't always want to hear it. Sometimes the information was full of anger, and the anger might be directed at me because I was a man. Women's anger was a powerful force that pushed the movement for change forward. Indeed, one could argue that women's anger was the foundation upon which the antirape movement was built. But dealing with it was never easy. I often got defensive.

Defensiveness is, still, something I have to be conscious of when challenged by women. When women express their experiences and feelings honestly, it may be difficult to hear them. Their words, coming from this parallel world, may feel assaultive and hurtful. Denial and defensiveness can be reflexive responses in such situations.

I may hear a woman's truth as an accusation, not as an expression of her own experience. I may feel threatened by the new frame of reference she is challenging me to acknowledge: hers. The tacitly accepted values of the world I live in support my need to be right because I am a man. Defensiveness and denial are tools I can use to keep from having to confront my ignorance of and insensitivity to women's experience. And they can support my complicity in maintaining a man's right to define reality in a way that excludes or diminishes important experiences that women have.

The situation may be further complicated by the dual, sometimes contradictory, effect of anger. A rape survivor's anger may be the only piece of strength she has to assert herself in the immediate aftermath of being raped, the only way for her to say "I am a human being and I demand to be treated with respect!" Hearing and acknowledging the collective anger that many women feel about their at-risk status can reveal an important perspective on the world we all inhabit, a perspective largely ignored or otherwise discounted in male-defined reality because it is so uncomfortable to deal with and challenges so much in our culture.

On the other hand, anger alone does not create change. It can become destructive if one side or the other becomes stuck there, making it an end in itself. Overcoming this anger, in my view, requires a willingness to acknowledge the validity of its source instead of denying it, and to hear it as something more than personal accusation.

As challenging as it sometimes is for me to hear what women are saying, the effort has, over the years, made a more complete and caring human being out of me. Many women have been and continue to be a part of my educational process. None has had a greater impact on me than Sylvia Callaway, the woman who hired me in 1978. Sylvia's philosophy of "loving anger" bridges the opposing forces in antirape work. It allows her to condemn the act of rape and all that supports it in our culture while acknowledging the humanity of the rapist and the necessity of understanding how such a personality comes into being. For her, rape is a "rip in the spirit" for both the victim and the perpetrator. Her philosophy of antirape work acknowledges the needs of everyone in the community, including the perpetrator and his family.

From her, I learned that doing antirape work is mostly about teaching respect to counter the disrespect taught by sexism—a disrespect that, in its most extreme form, becomes gender-based violence. Rape is an ultimate act of disrespect, yet it is a common occurrence. It is vital that we understand why it is so common and the real extent of the damage it does to our society. The path toward a rape-free society will lead men, in particular, through unmapped areas in our consciousness and into some challenging personal encounters. This journey will take us very near, if not actually into, the world as women experience it—the world of women at risk.

PART II

I left a downtown building late one night many years ago. I had just spent several hours training new volunteers for the rape crisis center. I was in a hurry to get home and my car was parked in a lot across the street. As I left the building, I saw the traffic light turn green and I started to run toward the intersection, about thirty yards away. A woman walking ahead of me toward the same intersection suddenly turned and looked at me like an animal frozen in the headlights of an oncoming car. I stopped and for a brief instant we stared at each other. In her eyes, I saw a mixture of surprise and terror. She turned and hurried across the street. I didn't move until she was out of sight.

As I stood there, I felt foolish and hypocritical, as well as responsible for her distress. By then, I had spent several years talking about rape prevention to groups of all kinds, yet apparently I had not absorbed the full meaning of my own words. While I had talked about the distancing phrases we may use when thinking about rapists—"not normal," "not one of us"—I had not yet understood that a woman might view my normal behavior as threatening. Never mind that I had no intention of harming the woman on the street that night (or any other woman who might be distressed by my behavior, intentional or not). The lesson I learned that night, at that woman's expense, was that her feelings of vulnerability to sexual violence had been largely invisible to me, even though I might claim, with some justification, to be sensitive and enlightened.

I started talking about that incident in my presentations as a way of illustrating how easy it is for men to threaten women simply because we aren't paying attention, because we don't experience the world in the same way they do. Later, I used another illustration of the different ways men and women experience the world:

Imagine walking down a sidewalk in a part of town with which you are unfamiliar—not what's considered a bad part of town, just unfamiliar. At first you appear to be alone—no one else is around. Then, a block or two ahead, you see a person coming directly toward you on the same sidewalk, someone you do not know, someone of the opposite gender. The distance between you and the other person slowly decreases until you pass within a few inches of each other.

I have used this exercise around a hundred times, mostly with college and high school classes. After presenting the scenario, I ask individuals in the group what they would be thinking or feeling as they passed the stranger on the sidewalk. I invariably get the same responses. A woman always responds first, saying she would feel anything from mild discomfort to nervousness to outright fear. The majority of women say they would be on their guard; a few say they would employ avoidance tactics such as crossing to the other side of the street.

When I ask the men to respond, there is often a long silence. After I press the issue, a man usually volunteers that he would not be thinking or feeling anything in particular, implying that he doesn't see anything remarkable about the situation, that it is not anything he has really thought about. Occasionally a man will say that if he found the woman attractive he might try to start a conversation. This usually creates a negative reaction from several women, who say they would feel even more threatened if that happened. Once in while a man says he would feel a little nervous passing the woman because he would know she feels nervous. Some say they would consciously avoid eye contact or even cross the street to avoid making the woman uncomfortable.

I live in a relatively safe suburban environment. I would think nothing of taking a long walk in my neighborhood by myself in the middle of the night. Most of the women I know would not do that. Indeed, a woman who did and was assaulted would certainly be asked, "What were you doing walking by yourself in the middle of the night? Don't you know better?" Some people would blame her for what happened, while the actions of her nameless, faceless attacker would be taken for granted. Blame would not be placed where it belongs.

The classroom exercise I described above hardly constitutes a scientific study, but the consistency of responses it evokes shows that women as a group feel more vulnerable to harm than men as a group, even though men are victims of violence more often than women. Some men grow up in dangerous urban environments and fear walking to school or to the corner store. But the issue here is the threat of violence as women experience it and how that threat affects their lives.

For an instant on that night after volunteer training, I embodied that threat for the woman at the crosswalk. For me to argue that I did not intend to do harm would be true but irrelevant. The fact is, I did do harm.

I chose to acknowledge the experience instead of denying, ignoring, or forgetting it. It became an(other) important lesson, clarifying how invisible this women's reality can be, and challenging me again to learn to see the impact of the threat of rape on women's lives. Experiencing sexual violence is a debilitating experience, but so is living with the threat of it over a lifetime.

Becoming aware of these realities was like entering an uncharted sea without knowing that I was in a boat or on an ocean. Nothing had prepared me for the gut-level experiences, in an emergency room and at gatherings, that placed me on unfamiliar ground, in the blank spaces that came from experiences I never had or information I did not absorb because I grew up male.

Concern for my safety does not restrict my freedom now to the extent that it does for many women I know. The full impact of this threat on women is not something we talk about much—or at all—in public. Women's at-risk status is a given in our culture, something we tacitly accept as inevitable. I do not have to see or experience the world as women do. I can usually go through life with my blank spaces intact and suffer no negative consequences. If I am affected by women's vulnerability to sexual violence, it is usually because women I care about are hurt by it. A rape survivor is not the only person affected by the rape.

I learned to see the impact of the threat and experience of rape on women's lives by being willing to acknowledge and confront the blank spaces in my own. Doing this required humility and a willingness to listen to women in a way that was new to me. It required that I be willing to experience some of their vulnerability.

My blank spaces distanced me from the lives of the women I knew, allowing me, if I wanted it, the option of not thinking about their realities or doing anything about them. This distancing also allows me, if I want, to believe that the threat of sexual violence is not a serious problem, and that rape only happens to certain women and is perpetrated only by certain men—men who have nothing in common with me. It gives me deniability. I can stand on the sidelines of the issue and condemn rape without any understanding of how it looks or feels to those at greatest risk—without hearing their voices at all.

It has been hard to acknowledge that some important realities may have escaped me, or that I may have screened them out. Listening to women talk about the casual affronts and terrors they endure has challenged me. Sometimes I don't want to hear these stories because I feel helpless, or I choose to ignore them because I can, because I have no parallel experience.

A friend told me once about being stalked and harassed on the highway by a man in another vehicle while she was driving alone. He tailgated her, then got in the lane beside her and made obscene gestures. This continued for miles. Listening to her story, I felt outraged and uncomfortable. I empathized as best I could. At a certain point in our conversation I no longer knew what to say, so we just dropped the subject. I could escape back into my own relatively safe life, but she would take those feelings of terror with her forever.

The man who harassed my friend must have engaged in similar activities on other occasions, and he must have known that he would get away with it. His chances of being held accountable were remote. He had crossed a line, but it was surely not the first line he had crossed with women. His highway terrorism may have been preceded by more subtle or customary aggression, like making women uncomfortable by the way he looked at them, by commenting about their bodies, or by being physically aggressive. Perhaps he had already raped.

If we deal with this man at all, we call him a weirdo, a psycho, or a sociopath. We may not connect his extreme behaviors with the less extreme visual and verbal intrusions into women's lives that may have preceded the highway incident. And we might not want to acknowledge the acceptability of such behaviors—the fact that men are rarely confronted or held accountable when they engage in sexually harassing behaviors. In such a world, rapists find acceptance, if not for raping, then for the harassing behaviors that lead up to their rapes. This acceptance makes what they do hard to see for what it is, which is one reason they can get away with it.

The crowning sadness of this event is that my friend not only had no access to justice for herself, but also probably told no more than a handful of close friends what happened to her. Silence overwhelmed her story, as it does so many others. Surely this silence is related to the blank spaces in men's lives.

The silencing of women also allows us to avoid a fundamental reassessment of the relative power of women and men in our society. Such a reassessment could put at risk power arrangements we take for granted in a male-defined reality, power arrangements that help hold in place our blindness to—or disregard for—women's vulnerability to harm.

As I became more aware of the parallel world women often inhabit, I could no longer avoid responding to it. Instead of spending all my time in the familiar public world largely defined and controlled by men, I was in a rape crisis center, an environment defined and controlled by women that deals with tragedies largely hidden from view in the male-defined world. Because the women who worked there treated me well, I felt at ease from day to day. But over time, the issues we dealt with put me into a mental and emotional frame of reference that I could not control, and that compelled me to deal with issues in my own life. I had to confront my own sexism. I had to acknowledge that I was not always the model citizen I wanted to believe I was. I had to absorb the meaning of the term male entitlement. It was then that I began to be aware—vaguely—of the blank spaces.

Filling in these blank spaces made me defensive. Dealing with the consequences of male violence to women on a daily basis backed me into a corner. On some level, I felt guilty. My own past behavior was cast in a new light and I was uncomfortable.

I had to take another look at my own treatment of women. I've never been physically violent with anyone, man or woman, but male entitlement casts a broad shadow. I had to acknowledge that I had been verbally and emotionally insensitive or demeaning to women, though I would not have thought of my behavior in those terms at the time, and that I had felt entitled to behave that way. My behavior was unremarkable because it was common male behavior and therefore invisible to me. But I could no longer pretend not to see connections between different kinds of demeaning behavior, ranging from visual and verbal affronts to rape. The common denominator was lack of respect.

I came to understand how male entitlement legitimizes lack of respect in subtle ways. By giving primacy to male viewpoints and male needs, it creates unequal power between men and women, making it easier for men to ignore or belittle women's voices, particularly when they are confronting our behavior. Sexual harassment provides examples of this point. Women who are sexually harassed by men in the workplace may hesitate to make their feelings known. By objecting, they may directly oppose entrenched male power and risk ridicule and further harassment. Federal legislation and judicial rulings are forcing employers to be accountable for sexual harassment, but the real human cost is paid by individuals, mostly women, whose lives have been poisoned by the once invisible range of behaviors we now call sexual harassment. The vast majority of sexual harassment victims suffer in silence because they do not think they will be taken seriously, and so they choose not to risk making a complaint.

Finally, male entitlement has maintained the blank spaces in my life. It has supported me in the mistaken belief that my experience as a male is a complete view of the world. Male entitlement and the disregard of women's experience go hand in hand. If I participate in one, I participate in the other. This is not easy for me to acknowledge on a personal level, because it requires humility and an openness to my own imperfections, and those make me feel vulnerable. But unless I am willing to take this step, I limit my own development as a human being.

I believe that defensiveness and discomfort are inevitable for many men when we are challenged to acknowledge women's vulnerability to men's violence and the impact that it has on them. Most of us aren't accustomed to viewing ourselves in this light and would insist that we are not part of the problem. I have certainly done that. But whether we commit acts of disrespect against women, large or small, or simply fail to notice that others do, we are part of the problem. Some may hear this as an accusation. I have experienced it as an opportunity to learn and grow as a human being.

Men have some good (selfish) reasons to get beyond defensiveness. In my case, defensiveness has been a block to learning some important things about my relationships and myself. My ego becomes a barrier to my emotional and intellectual growth when I am defensive. I have come to view the discomfort I feel when confronted with the blank spaces in my life as part of the process of reintegration with the female side of my psyche, correcting a separation encouraged in me—as it is in most boys—from an early age. Part of what creates our defensiveness in the first place is the loss of control we experience when we can no longer so easily define reality in our customary way. The very idea that there might be another, female-defined, reality that parallels our own can be threatening. We are forced by that knowledge into a role reversal in which women's realities challenge our own, and this is unfamiliar ground for most men.

Defensiveness seems inevitable to me when men grow up with blank spaces in our awareness of women's vulnerability to men's violence and then are confronted with the need to respond to it. Whether we are rapists, saints, or something in between, we must account for gender-based violence that normally casts men as offenders and women and children as victims.

Fortunately, this dilemma pushed me in the direction of self-examination and self-discovery. Filling in the blank spaces has helped me become more empathetic. By dealing with my defensiveness, I became more willing to open my heart and accept as a part of my reality aspects of women's lives that I had not previously acknowledged. My defensiveness and discomfort eventually led me to an honest awareness of women's vulnerability to men's violence. Once that honest awareness was in place, it required a moral or ethical response in my behavior. It became a moral imperative for me to be proactive in helping to create a different world, a world in which women's lives are not seriously eroded simply because men choose not to pay attention to the power imbalances that cause women so much suffering. Altruism aside, this journey has benefited me emotionally and spiritually beyond measure.

CPSIA information can be obtained
at www.ICGtesting.com
Printed in the USA
LVHW09s0138040818
585770LV00008B/15/P